FRANCOPHONE
POST-COLONIAL CULTURES

After the Empire:
The Francophone World and
Postcolonial France

Series Editor

Valérie Orlando, Illinois Wesleyan University

This book series provides a forum for the publication of original works that explore the Francophone world through the lenses of art, politics, history, and culture. The series will also investigate and interrogate the relationship between the Francophone world and contemporary France.

FRANCOPHONE POST-COLONIAL CULTURES
Critical Essays

Edited by
Kamal Salhi

LEXINGTON BOOKS
Lanham • Boulder • New York • Oxford

LEXINGTON BOOKS

Published in the United States of America
by Lexington Books
A Member of the Rowman & Littlefield Publishing Group
4501 Forbes Boulevard, Suite 200, Lanham, Maryland 20706

PO Box 317
Oxford
OX2 9RU, UK

British Library Cataloguing in Publication Information Available

Library of Congress Cataloging-in-Publication Data

Francophone post-colonial cultures : critical essays / edited by Kamal Salhi.
    p. cm. — (After the empire)
  Includes bibliographical references and index.
  ISBN 0-7391-0567-1 (alk. paper) — ISBN 0-7391-0568-X (pbk. : alk. paper)
  1. French literature — French-speaking countries — History and criticism. 2. French-
speaking countries — Civilization. 3. Language and culture — French-speaking
countries. I. Salhi, Kamal. II. Series.
  PQ3897 .F73 2003
  840.9'917'541 — dc21   2002151169

Printed in the United States of America

♾™ The paper used in this publication meets the minimum requirements of
American National Standard for Information Sciences — Permanence of Paper for
Printed Library Materials, ANSI/NISO Z39.48–1992.

Contents

Acknowledgments

I AM DEEPLY INDEBTED TO MANY PEOPLE across various countries for helping to make the idea of this book a reality. I have been constantly challenged, stimulated and enlightened by those directly involved in the composition of this volume—the contributors. The aim of this long project was to examine Francophone and post-colonial cultures, and the chapters of this book were intended to develop my ideas into an overarching thesis. Ultimately, the cooperative work undertaken with my colleagues led to something much more complex than that. It was through the intense interaction between the contributors and myself that this book took on its final shape. Some of them presented papers and took part in fascinating discussions at the International Francophone Conference held in Leeds on September 9–10, 1999, though my queries and requests made their contributions to this volume vastly different from those that were presented at the conference. Other contributors who had not attended the conference found themselves involved in detailed, apparently endless discussions by e-mail. I am indebted not only to the authors of the following chapters; I am also highly aware of the special role played by the publisher's anonymous, external readers, who gave me much helpful advice, and the advisory board set up for the purpose of this project, whose members are:

Professor Alec Hargreaves (University of Loughborough)
Professor Rachel Killick (University of Leeds)
Professor Raija Koski (University of West Ontario)
Professor Valérie Orlando (University of Illinois Wesleyan)
Professor Eric Sellin (University of Tulane)

The publication support came from the Centre for Francophone Studies at the University of Leeds.

Introduction

Kamal Salhi

FRANCOPHONE POST-COLONIAL CULTURES is intended to combine a variety of approaches to twentieth-century Francophone and post-colonial forms of expression with a focus on the literatures and cultures of North and Sub-Saharan Africa, the Caribbean, the Pacific and Indian Oceans, Southeast Asia, North America, Europe and the Middle East. Although they cannot be exhaustive, it is hoped that these studies will provide a new critical introduction to this increasingly popular area within French studies. For some time there has been a need among academics and students for a book of this kind in English that deals with a wide range of subjects and a large geographical area in one volume and that can be used fruitfully for research and teaching purposes. There are, of course, a number of useful collections of essays and introductions to the field of Francophone studies. However, there are few with such wide coverage that provide a forum for new approaches to the textual and cultural analysis of Francophone material and combining genres and disciplines within post-colonial Francophone contexts. Despite their geographical differences, Francophone literatures tend to deal with a similar spread of issues. By dividing this book by the main geographical areas covered and making its span so ambitious, we are positioning the study of the Francophone world and its cultures as a comparative and relational project in which post-colonial Francophone countries and the specific alterity they embody inside and outside modern France, are "no less essential to the understanding of France than the history of French colonization is essential to the understanding of the French-speaking world."[1]

As we move into a new century the problems raised by mixed post-colonial identities are becoming more prominent in the consciousness of previously colonized peoples, whose cultures integrate diverse aspects of history and colonialism in different artistic and literary forms. This leads us to new understanding of Francophone discourse, post-colonial cultures and their relevance to identity formation. These approaches are not free of difficulties and have numerous implications, some of them welcome and some of them more problematic. In order to highlight these ambiguities, the introductory chapter discusses Francophone processes in relation to history and the concepts of space, geopolitics as it relates to notions of cultural identity, language, alienation and otherness. Further, having established a context set against a background of certain eurocentric approaches, chapters 2–16 discusses aspects of modernity and tradition in the light of global processes and local responses, drawing examples from Africa and the Caribbean.

They highlight the contributions of contemporary theorists and stresses the abstract and universal hegemony of colonialism as a determinant of local traditions and identity formations.

The chapters on Francophone Europe and North America provide illuminating insights into the literature, theater and linguistics of these culturally mixed regions, which have given rise to ever-changing hybrid forms but also breed obvious cultural antagonisms. For example, contemporary Quebec theater shows how the unsuccessful referendum on Quebec's independence in 1980 has become a symbolic border dividing two imaginary territories: "one characterized by the affirmation of a collective identity, the other intimate and creative, and bearing the imprint of the subject." Works from Acadia, France's first colony in North America, also explore notions of identity and power within the contemporary Acadian experience based on a shared heritage. Nevertheless, a dimension common to all the contributions to this volume is the attempt to reflect on how, within the sphere of criticism of French influence, colonialism and post-colonialism, we can contribute to the building of spaces for the representation of Francophone cultures and societies that are less dependent on rigidly defined differences and cultural particularism.

The rest of the chapters in this book examine the works of various Francophone writers from the areas mentioned above, considering the cultural hybridity of post-colonial national identities, a characteristic that is often misrepresented and subverted. The ethnic, racial and cultural differences that exist within the boundaries of the post-colonial nation-states are subordinated to notions of natural belonging and nationalism, and thus misrepresented within the assimilating logic of the concept of "a common culture." The Francophone, be it post-colonial or historically natural, is a set of cultures in which multiculturalism and cultural hybridity have been socially constructed through a series of historical inclusions and exclusions.

Our journey into post-colonial cultures has been a search to rediscover the potential for cultural transformation that has been inherent in Francophone forms of expression since the early years of French colonialism. This search has been motivated by an increasing sense that traditional approaches to literature and culture in French, viewed and read by passive readers and accepted by them as commodified literary exercises, will never engage post-colonial subjects at the level of cultural transformation. From the perspectives of the studies included in this volume, an emphasis on the innovative nature of such an understanding implies moving our interpretations of culture toward a dimension of cultural criticism that places subjects within fixed representations of cultural and political identities, which reproduce predictable contexts for ideological approaches. Our readings of Francophone cultures are attempts to distance ourselves from the framework of traditional conceptual approaches framed by long established, sometimes hegemonic, theories, some of which are highly complex and based, for example, on structuralist textural analyses and criticism of the limits of particular disciplines.

Our engagement in this area therefore includes the possibility of disseminating post-colonial claims and Francophone knowledge within increasingly widely defined cultural settings, since one of the things we need is detachment from the rigidity of representations of difference that reduce the world to binary opposites. Our thinking may be rhizomic in the sense that it is a means of imagining culture at the crossroads of multiple narratives. However, we are conscious of the fact that Francophone literature and post-colonial theory are not concepts that are particularly well understood either in France or in the Francophone countries themselves. This can be explained by the sometimes confused ideological debates that have raged about the Francophone world and by the fact that post-colonial theory is an idea that originated relatively recently in the English-speaking world and that has not yet had time to find a place in the academic scholarship of these countries. This book is intended to demonstrate that the application of post-colonial theory to the Francophone world can be highly fruitful, and that the results of such an application are not merely of relevance to students in America, Great Britain and other English-speaking countries. This leads us to insist on the need for a reform of the ways in which French culture is studied, as they are understood by mainstream French scholarship.

As a geographical term, *francophonie* refers to a highly diverse range of areas and regions, which are represented in the various chapters of this book, that are organized on the basis of linguistic and historical facts. Its first meaning is the totality of the regions in Africa, the Caribbean, and the Pacific and Indian Oceans where French is considered to play an undisputed social role, and the totality of the regions in Europe and North America where French is spoken as a first language. In the different countries under study here political and institutional aspects form the basis for linguistic situations that are much more complex than is generally recognized on account of the coexistence of various native and recently introduced languages, including English. In consequence, any attempt to present and criticize Francophone cultures and literatures as facts of nature runs the risk of misleading the reader and creating confusion about the real situation.

This confusion is a result of the distinction that has to be made between the Francophone world understood as a linguistic community and the Francophone world as a grouping with shared political and economic interests that is becoming increasingly important on the world stage. In consequence, in the perspective put forward by this volume, we sought from the beginning to approach the Francophone world as material constituting a corpus that has to be constructed and analyzed in accordance with pragmatic principles founded in post-colonial theory. The treatment of the Francophone subject in Africa is not the same as that found in Haiti or Guadeloupe; the concepts used in Europe are not elaborated in the same way as in Quebec. Ultimately, this volume is a very conscious attempt to reflect the reality created by new approaches without, for example, blurring the differences between the much studied features of the Negritude movement and the often isolated reactions found in recent Vietnamese trends or the latest work by the Kanak, Dewé Gorodé, and her associates. Finally, our project was intended to include recent developments in Francophone literature and cinema, such as the discussion of *Créolité* by Raphaël Confiant and Patrick Chamoiseau, and the aesthetics of Sembène Ousmane and Souleymane Cissé's political films.

We hope that this book will help researchers, students and teachers to find greater diversity of inspiration and methodology by setting out a space that is common to the various Francophone literatures and art forms. The studies in this volume examine their subjects by defining the relations between the texts and their social, cultural and historical environments. They concentrate on literary and artistic systems that the particular work articulates in the context in which it appears. They also pay attention to the cultural and theoretical plurality or singularity that characterizes the relationship between the text and its context, making it possible to identify and appreciate the qualities of Francophone and post-colonial culture.

The widest definition of post-colonial culture available in the context of this book includes all cultural production based in the historical fact of French colonialism or political presence and the diverse material effects to which this phenomenon has given rise. This definition, however, may not be of great use, especially as the concept suggests that these societies are in the process of recovering from their past misfortunes and working constantly to recover their own cultures. It encourages the interpretation of the themes and stories of a post-colonial work as an encounter between indigenous peoples and the French legacy. This is an accurate enough view of things, but it is also necessary to be aware of the danger that lies in looking no further for explanations of the social and personal turbulence found in these recently independent nations. As we know, problematic, oppressive structures have been put in place by many post-independence states, and any post-colonial approach to these cultures should not overlook the responsibility that post-independence regimes themselves have for the ongoing difficulties in these countries. Of course, such an oversight would reduce our understanding of the complexities of Francophone societies and peoples, thus undermining the aim of post-colonial theory, which is to make sense of the confusion found in post-colonial societies and cultures. This would make it impossible to identify the real roots of the very real problems faced and prevent us from finding solutions. Despite this, we hope that the message of this book is clear: The inclusion of a variety of themes seen from different perspectives, the discussion of works from many different places and the necessary adjustment of critical approaches to different contexts will open a dialogue between the different cultures that exist within the same world. Cultural development and growth represent our greatest hope for the post-colonial future.

Note

1. Kamal Salhi (ed.), *Francophone Studies: Discourse and Identity* (Exeter: Elm Bank, 2000), 3.

1

The Francophone World
Moves into the Twenty-First Century

Margaret Majumdar

A T THE BEGINNING OF THE NEW MILLENNIUM it is appropriate for students and scholars to take stock of the present state of the Francophone world and look forward to the twenty-first century, attempting to map out the likely shape and future prospects of this global entity.

This chapter proposes a four-track approach to this topic, dealing first with the Francophone relationship to history; second with the question of spatial and geopolitical relations; third with certain aspects of the relations between the different peoples that make up the French-speaking world (this third aspect will inevitably include the notions of cultural identity, alienation and otherness, as well as the ubiquitous question of language); and fourth with the embryonic development of a new political dimension and the relationship between politics and official forms of Francophone discourse.

To sum this up in more schematic terms, for the sake of argument, the intention is to address the three aspects of time, space and difference, which, it will be argued, can be loosely linked to three broad phases in the development of the Francophone world since the formal end of Empire, before concluding with a brief analysis of the latest, emerging fourth phase, which is linked to the new importance accorded to politics.

Time and *La Francophonie*

The first aspect of the topic is the notion of time, or history, which will be examined from the perspective of the founding discourse of the originators of the vision of *Francophonie* in the immediate post-colonial period. As is well known, this discourse was firmly rooted in the ideas of Enlightenment France and consequently took as its basis an axiomatic belief in the universalist values associated with the doctrine of the Rights of Man.

This chapter will not discuss at length the enthusiastic and often lyrical pleas made by figures like Léopold Senghor of Sénégal, Habib Bourguiba of Tunisia and the other founding fathers when they argued in favor of an idealistic community linked together by a common language (French), and a shared culture based on the republican ideals of liberty, equality and fraternity. Nor will it examine in any great detail the speeches made by French statesmen of this period, such as De Gaulle and Pompidou, who picked up and echoed these themes as a matter of expediency. Although language of this type has not entirely disappeared, it now inevitably strikes us as somewhat dated, given the subsequent development of discourses relating to the whole Francophone concept.

For the present purposes, it is necessary to pay attention not so much to the essence of what these key figures had to say, but more to what they did not say, particularly with regard to the role of history. For even in the first flush of enthusiasm for the brave new world of *Francophonie*, there was a significant silence about one of the key founding concepts of Enlightenment thinking, the role of history.

Although the modernizing project of the French Revolution depended first and foremost on the key notion of *progress*, this idea was largely absent from the early discourse of *La Francophonie*. Indeed, some of the more ecstatic prose of the Francophone elder statesmen would almost lead one to believe that the end of history had now come with decolonization, along with the establishment of a French-speaking paradise on earth.

The following examples are given as illustrations of the kind of discourse that developed in the 1960s and early 1970s.

Senghor, now considered as *le père de la Francophonie*, developed the working definition of *Francophonie* as "une communauté intellectuelle ou spirituelle dont la langue nationale, officielle ou de travail est le français."[1] However, he was also capable of lyrical flights concerning the mystical properties of *La Francophonie* as "Cet humanisme intégral qui se tisse autour de la planète, cette symbiose d'énergies dormantes s'élevant de tous les continents, de toutes les races qui s'éveillent à leur chaleur complémentaire."[2]

For Bourguiba, too, it was "la langue française [qui] constitue l'appoint à notre patrimoine culturel, enrichit notre pensée, exprime notre action, contribue à forger notre destin intellectuel et à faire de nous des hommes à part entière."[3]

In spite of a certain hesitancy, usually attributed to a reluctance to appear to be promoting an endeavor that some might see as a form of neo-colonialism, individual French leaders also had warm words for the Francophone project, which were trotted out as the occasion merited.

De Gaulle, for instance, had this to say on the universalism of the French language: "It is true that France has always ploughed the furrow of intelligence with passion and offered the entire earth a rich harvest; it is also true that she has given the world a language that is perfectly suited to express the universal character of thought."[4]

Pompidou asserted that "it was because of the French language that France stood out in the world and was not a country like any other."[5]

Numerous other examples could be cited. Yet, in all this rhetoric, the key element was not the *progressive* project of the French Revolution, as the universally valid prototype and foundation of political modernity, but the French language as a universal factor. Indeed, some of the standard quotes frequently cited to support this notion of the universality of the French language actually come from Antoine de Rivarol's *Discours sur l'universalité de la langue française*, which dates from 1784 and thus predates the French Revolution.

Cette universalité de la langue française . . . offre pourtant un grand problème: elle tient à des causes si délicates et si puissantes à la fois que, pour les démêler, il s'agit de montrer jusqu'à quel point la position de la France, sa constitution politique, l'influence de son climat, le génie de ses écrivains, le caractère de ses habitants et l'opinion qu'elle a su donner d'elle au reste du monde, jusqu'à quel point tant de causes diverses ont pu se combiner et s'unir pour faire à cette langue une fortune si prodigieuse.[6]

Yet, what is interesting is that, in the immediate aftermath of de-colonization, at the time when this discourse was being invoked most frequently, there was little doubt that the most pressing issue facing the newly de-colonized countries was their urgent need for the development and modernization that would enable them to take their place on an equal footing in the global political economy of the modern world. It may be argued that this is still the case at the beginning of the new millennium.

At this stage, two related factors might suggest themselves as aids to an understanding of the reasons why it was not possible for history to figure as part of Francophone discourse, which assumed a largely ahistorical form.

The first relates to the immediate origins of the Francophone project in the reality of the historical processes of colonization and de-colonization. In spite of the key role played by Quebec, and Canada as a whole, in the development of *La Francophonie*, particularly in connection with the establishment of AUPELF (Association des universités partiellement ou entièrement de langue française),[7] which was conceived in Montreal in 1961, and the development of links in the cultural and technological domain, the whole project received its main impetus from the ending of Empire. It is this history, the history of colonialism and the more or less peaceful transition to independence, that was signally incapable of providing a basis on which to ground the new type of utopian fraternal relations that were desired for the Francophone world.

The second factor is perhaps more fundamental from an ideological point of view and relates to the role played by the concept of historical progress in the rationalization of the colonial project itself. For the French colonial mission was not undertaken in the name of civilization alone, along the same lines as, say, the British imperial project. The particular character of Third Republic colonial ideology was the way it wrapped itself in the mantle of progress and modernization in terms that could be readily endorsed by the most advanced elements of the European left. Engels, for instance, applauded the capture of the Emir Abdelkadir, and Marx consistently stressed the progressive, as well as the negative, aspects of colonialism, particularly in his writing on India.[8]

This is not to say that there has been no debate about the significance of history in the former French colonies. However, as a result of this blanking out of history from the official discourse of *La Francophonie*, it is necessary to look elsewhere for the debates about the roles of tradition and modernity as well as for new approaches to the remoulding and reconceptualizing of the specific histories of the post-colonial countries, ways of restoring them to their full complexity and reestablishing a sometimes problematical continuity with the pre-colonial past. Many of these issues and debates will be reflected in other chapters of this publication.

The Spatial Dimension

The second aspect of the topic is broadly associated with space, another issue with which Habib Bourguiba was concerned. Referring to the Francophone community in its early days, the former Tunisian leader insisted on the fact that "this community is situated beyond politics or geography—its criteria are above all philosophical, involving the great ideals of 1789 and the aspirations of humanity to freedom, dialogue and mutual support."[9] This notion of a community "beyond politics or geography" is of course characterized by a highly abstract form of universality; indeed, one might almost say that its reality is more *virtual* than *concrete*. But it has not fared well in subsequent phases of the evolution of the Francophone concept. Indeed, unlike the continuing absence of history from Francophone discourse, geography has come to play an increasingly important role in its reformulation.

In its most obvious form, this is manifest in a continuing celebration of the presence of the French language and French culture "on all five continents," a mantra of official Francophone discourse. This spatial extension of the French language to "all five continents" reflects, of course, the continuing strategic presence and influence of France itself around the planet and its desire to maintain its role as a global power.

After an initial period of overt reticence with regard to the Francophone movement, its ideological value in this respect came to be regarded as an asset to French global strategy. Thus, the Francophone movement began a new second phase as the 1970s progressed, coming increasingly to be used as a vehicle for a discourse intended to defend French power against the hegemony of the "Anglo-Saxons" and articulated through a defense of the French language and French culture.

It eventually became apparent that changes were needed if this strategy were to be fully effective. In consequence, during the 1980s and early 1990s *Francophonie* underwent a transformation that allowed for the recognition of differential spaces within the French-speaking world. Increasingly, *Francophonie* was portrayed as the champion of pluralism, as against the overpowering pressure of monolithic American hegemony. While language was still the main unifying factor, it was recognized that difference was possible within the French-speaking world. Indeed; it was now portrayed as desirable.

This was, of course, also necessary in order to reflect the real geographical spread of *Francophonie* throughout the world and the very real differences between its different constituent parts: essentially the former French colonies, North America, European Francophone countries and France itself.

In concrete terms, this development was most visible in the creation of media vehicles, such as TV5 in 1984, specifically devoted to the articulation of the variety of the geographical and cultural spaces that make up the Francophone world. This extended to the recognition that the French language itself could not continue to maintain its status as a *homogeneous* world language, the universal norms of which were set by Paris. In a development that has run counter to the language policies still adhered to in metropolitan France, there was increasing acceptance of the fact that the different peoples of the Francophone world spoke and wrote French in their own particular ways, and that these needed to be accepted as valid. This has become apparent in the publication of textbooks specifically designed for Africa, for instance, and the recognition of the value of Francophone literatures that have their roots outside France. This is not, of course, to imply that the French purists' belief in the normalized standard language has disappeared, but merely to acknowledge that a space has now been created for Francophone literatures and cultures, albeit one usually demarcated from what constitutes "French" literature and culture. Similarly, the fact that subtitles are sometimes included to help viewers understand television programmes produced in nonstandard (i.e., non-French) French can also be adduced as evidence that the Académie Française is not about to shut up shop.

Clearly, the recognition of the importance of particular spatial ties was not delayed until this change of emphasis in official Francophone discourse, but was an important theme in the literatures of the national liberation period and after, in which the notions of dispossession and exile from the soil of the nation, as well as the reclamation of the nation's land, have played a major role.

However, what was significant about the shift in Francophone discourse was that the notion of differential space was defined almost entirely in *cultural* terms, rather than through any reference to real geographical territory, let alone to the major economic and political cleavages that effectively divide the Francophone world. It was a shift that was mainly related to a reassessment of the main dangers of American hegemony to Europe itself. These were no longer perceived to lie in the threat of economic, political and military domination, so much as the penetration of mass popular culture. The domination of the dollar economy, the NATO alliance, Polaris and Cruise missiles were replaced by a perception of Mickey Mouse and Ronald McDonald as major public enemies threatening to destroy European high culture and lower the cultural level to the lowest common denominator. This repudiation of American popular culture was well summed up in François Mitterrand's disdainful dismissal of Disneyland Resort Paris when it was first established as not quite his own "tasse de thé." However, the main argument against the domination of American mass culture did not relate so much to the perceived dangers of vulgarization and the downgrading of European "high culture," as to risks that the supposed "uniformity" of this American culture posed to French and, by extension, European culture in general.

What came to crystallize the shift to the cultural battlefield were the terms in which France fought the battle to defend French interests in the film, television and music industries against the power of Hollywood at the 1993 GATT negotiations, or, as expressed in the resolution put forward by France with the support of Senegal and Belgium at the Francophone summit held in Mauritius in October that year, in its fight against "Anglo-Saxon imperialism."[10] Rather than relying on economic arguments, the French defense rested on the principle of the *exception culturelle*, put forward as an inalienable right to defend particular identities and cultures from extinction. This concept of the *exception culturelle* is still, of course, very much on the agenda today in the current trade negotiations taking place in Seattle.

Yet, the arguments in favor of the *exception culturelle* could easily be turned against France itself, given the bombardment of French images and cultural artifacts to which indigenous cultures, particularly in Africa, have been subjected by the Francophone media.[11] As one African minister was heard to say at the time, the whole GATT controversy was a white man's quarrel. As far as he was concerned, there was little difference between CNN and Canal France Internationale; in either case, Africans were presented with a view of the world that was not their own.[12]

It was clear that France needed allies in this struggle against the USA. In consequence, it did not focus on the defense of the French language and French culture alone, but sought the support of other European countries by broadening its remit to the championing of Europe's right to defend the diversity of its own national languages and cultures through the preservation of its own cultural industries by means of mechanisms such as import quotas.

France also saw the role that the Francophone movement as a whole could play in this battle. Again, changes were needed to sustain the effectiveness of the discourse. Thus, by the time of the GATT debates, Francophone discourse had already begun its passage into a third phase, in which the concept of difference was extended beyond the French language and culture to incorporate a defense of other languages and cultures. Instead of the bipolar and sometimes rather crude opposition between French and English that France had used to rail against *Anglo-Saxon* hegemony and the domination of the English language, there was an increasing emphasis on eloquent pleas for multilingualism and multiculturalism in the world, and in defense of the need for diversity and pluralism.

As Jacques Toubon, speaking as French Minister of Culture and Francophonie just before the Mauritius summit, was to say in defense of the principle of "Unity in Diversity":

L'usage commun de français est un moyen offert à nos peuples de refuser l'uniformisation de la planète qui se dessine sur le mode anglo-saxon, sous couvert de libéralisme économique . . . . Il ne saurait y avoir de véritable liberté sans respect des identités culturelles et linguistiques, respect existant, lui, au sein de la francophonie. L'un des deux principes en honneur à Port-Louis sera d'ailleurs: *Unité dans la diversité.*[13]

Identity and Difference

It is now time to develop the third aspect of this topic that was raised in the introduction—the increasing role played by the concept of difference and its relation to the associated, but very different, concept of otherness during this third phase in the evolution of Francophone discourse. For the move toward a recognition of the need to acknowledge real differences within the Francophone world within the official discourse of *Francophonie* has now extended to an acknowledgment of the need to call into question the founding principle upon which its unity was initially posited, i.e., the French language itself.

Clearly, there has been a recognition of the diversity of practice within the language itself, reflecting varieties of syntax and lexis in different parts of the Francophone world. Or, as Margie Sudre, then *secrétaire d'Etat à la Francophonie*, put it in 1997: "nous découvrons progressivement que la langue française n'appartient plus aux seuls Français. D'autres peuples l'ont fécondée de leur génie propre, de leur civilisation et de leur culture. On peut parler d'une littérature francophone sans laquelle le français aujourd'hui serait moins riche, moins savoureux et ne saurait en tout cas prétendre à l'universalité."[14] However, this concept of linguistic difference should also include the different relationships that speakers of French have to the language itself, ranging from the minority who can truly be considered to be first-language, or more emotively, mother-tongue speakers, to the far greater numbers who have adopted French as a second or even a third language, and all the blurred categories of bilinguals and multilinguals in between.

Even within the two broad divisions of first and second-language speakers, there are further differentiations to be made. In the case of first-language speakers, there are those for whom the French language has been more than simply a "natural" or "organic" mother-tongue, to which they happened to be exposed in the first instance as a result of contingent personal, family and historical factors. This would apply to most of the first-language French speakers living within France itself, where the language has acquired, over the course of its history and through the practices of the state, a voluntaristic political role as a unifying national tool. The legal status of French as the "language of the Republic," together with the numerous statutes codifying the official language policy of the state, down to the very norms of the language itself, have combined with the state-inspired or state-directed policies and practices of educational and cultural institutions to constitute the French language as a highly politicized instrument of public policy that has acquired several layers of accretions. Its status as the national language of France owes its legitimacy to the constitution and not to any innate, organic link with the nation on the Herder model. This relationship to the language clearly does not exist in the same way for French-speaking Canadians, Swiss or Belgians.[15]

For those who have acquired French as a second language, the relationship may range from the extremes of viewing it as an imposition, as in certain colonial contexts, to that of a love-affair between consenting adults in which the language can be seen as a passport to freedom and the lover who ousts the mother associated with the speaker's mother-tongue. In both cases, the relationship to the language brings the relationship to the other into play in a particular way. This may be as a result of alienation produced by the imposition of a language identity, as in the case of Derrida, who expresses this alienation in a recent aphorism: "Je n'ai qu'une langue—ce n'est pas la mienne."[16] In a more positive sense, the relationship may be one in which the language is viewed as an object of desire, or in other words as a "significant other."

There is, however, a limited number of both first- and second-language French speakers in the world [17] and, given the limitations that have restricted the capacity of French to develop further as a world language through its appeal as a vehicle of communication and culture for elites, the expansion of the influence and effectiveness of *Francophonie* has now become dependent on its capacity to attract a new clientele of supporters. Indeed, many of the new members incorporated into the Francophone movement in recent years could only nominally or partially be described as French-speaking.

Increasingly, the credibility of *Francophonie* as a counter-force, and particularly as a counter-discourse, to globalizing American power has resided in its capacity to reinvent itself not simply as an alternative world language and culture that is universal in scope, nor even as the defender of Francophone cultural pluralism against homogenizing mass American culture and the domination of the English language, but through the championing of multilingualism. In this scenario the French language has acquired a new role, less essentialist and more instrumental, in which it has the function of linking together, and acting as a communicative vehicle between, the different spaces of particular concrete cultures—"un fil conducteur."[18] Thus, knowledge and/or use of the French language is not a qualification for membership of *Francophonie*; one becomes a member by participating in the summits and the Agence de la Francophonie (formerly ACCT).

La Francophonie politique

The move away from the sole reliance on the French language as a basis for the coherence of the Francophone community has coincided with belated attempts to provide a permanent political framework for the organizations of *La Francophonie*. This has happened under the aegis of the French President Jacques Chirac, who has continued François Mitterrand's efforts to provide it with an enhanced political role through the work carried out at the Francophone summits and other measures. Thus, over the last few years there has been a major shift in emphasis away from language and culture to a new stress on economics and politics.[19] The concrete result of this new tendency was the election of the Egyptian Boutros Boutros-Ghali to lead the new political institutions (again largely at the instigation, if not insistence, of France), reflecting the importance now given to countries marginal to the original Francophone project. At the same time, his experience as a former Secretary General of the United Nations was clearly considered appropriate for the new direction in which *Francophonie* is set to move in the first years of the twenty-first century and the importance now attributed to it.

Since Boutros Boutros-Ghali took up his post, *Francophonie* has moved into new areas of activity never considered before, a development that has coincided with a general reorganization and reconstitution of its institutions. Increasingly, *Francophonie* is coming to be seen, particularly by France, as an integrated vehicle for the pursuit of economic policies related to *coopération* and development, as well as more politically orientated policies—in addition to cultural and linguistic interests, which had previously provided the main focus of attention. This has had implications for the sphere of politics, as well as for the economic domain, although it is only slowly developing its new profile. The shift toward using *Francophonie* as a vehicle for economic development and cooperation appears to represent a move away from the bilateral relations that France has traditionally preferred. This seems to be the direction in which it has been evolving since the Hanoi summit of 1997 and as a result of the new policies particularly promoted by the government of Lionel Jospin.

With regard to its new-found political role, *Francophonie* has begun to take on what might previously have been considered some of the functions of the United Nations, sending observers to cover elections and organizing peace missions to countries suffering from internal conflicts and tensions, such as the Democratic Republic of Congo or Togo.[20] The 1999 Monckton Summit attempted to set a liberal/humanitarian political agenda, including in the final declaration a commitment to the protection of civilian populations, respect for the Geneva Conventions, a commitment to support the UN and NGO coalition's initiative to prevent children serving in armed forces, and a collective invitation to all members to ratify the treaty setting up the International Criminal Court. There will also be an international symposium at the beginning of 2000 on the practice of democracy, human rights and freedom in the Francophone world, and the establishment of a human rights observatory in close cooperation with the UN and NGO agencies.[21]

All of these developments have so far been characterized by an inclusive, non-confrontational approach. This has been the case as far as bilateral relations with the members of the Francophone community are concerned, in which persuasion, rather than threats, and a softly-softly approach to change and compliance have been the order of the day. It has also applied to relations with other bodies, in which a desire for cooperation and complementarity, rather than confrontation and rivalry, has so far predominated. This strategy implies working with other international bodies, including the UN, the Commonwealth and regional groupings, such as the Organization of African Unity, the League of Arab States, etc., as well as with national governments and NGOs. Increasingly, the representatives of these different bodies are attending each others' events: for instance, UN Secretary General Kofi Annan attended the Monckton Summit and Boutros Boutros-Ghali has been a guest at Commonwealth events.

To sum up these new developments, one might construe them as an attempt to constitute an alternative UN-style association of nations, which would outflank the United Nations on the left and offer a radical, utopian alternative to the US-dominated world institutions—perhaps developing into something akin to a latter-day version of the Non-Aligned Movement of the immediate post-colonial period. Something of the kind would clearly be attractive to countries that perceive a common interest in placing themselves under the umbrella of French economic and political power, as a viable alternative or addition to the other groupings on offer.

However, there are reservations about the new developments. Indeed, criticisms were heard at Monckton from some of the long-standing members of the Francophone club about the new UN-style of some of the Summit meetings. Clearly, if the new strategy is to succeed, it has to carry conviction.

There can therefore be no doubt about the importance of ideology and discourse in selling this new version of *Francophonie*. Always vital to the Francophone project, the ideological domain is now the crucial plane for the further development of *La Francophonie politique*. This importance has been illustrated by the issue of human rights, which was raised at both the Hanoi and the Monckton summits. Faced with the desire of the Canadian Prime Minister, Jean Chrétien, to institute a system of sanctions against countries that violate democratic norms and human rights, Jacques Chirac repeated his position that sanctions were not appropriate to *La Francophonie*. He was content to leave concrete political action of this kind to the United Nations; the Francophone way was to "persuade," rather than to force compliance.[22]

The final part of this chapter will suggest some of the difficulties that may beset the creation of a credible ideological framework intended to lend conviction and support to the recreation of *La Francophonie* as a global "political" entity at the beginning of the twenty-first century.

Politics and Ideology

There is clearly a perceived gulf between the idealism of the discourse and the political realities with which attempts are now being made to engage. As *Le Monde* put it in an editorial at the time of the Monckton Summit: "L'argumentation de la francophonie officielle n'est qu'apparemment réaliste. Depuis deux ans, celle-ci se cherche une dimension politique. Or une langue et une culture ne sont jamais, par héritage et pour l'éternité, les véhicules ou les réceptacles de l'universalité et de l'humanisme. C'est affaire de choix, de projet et de volontarisme politiques."[23]

At the same time, it has to be stated that, as has been seen, one of the strengths of Francophone discourse lies in its capacity to evolve and adapt, taking on new forms and reflecting a new content in line with changing circumstances. Jacques Chirac has referred to it as a "force tranquille" that makes progress one step at a time.[24]

It may, however, be argued that some of the most significant obstacles to the credibility of the Francophone discourse relate in one way or another to the problematic status of the other.

The first point refers back to the inadequacy of the original founding principles of the Francophone movement, which were, as discussed above, based on the same universalist Enlightenment tradition that, ironically, provided the rationalization of the French colonial project itself. Unfortunately, the ideological framework of the one and indivisible republic has traditionally provided no space for the theorization of political difference and, in particular, for the conceptualization of the other. Of late, this has been causing difficulties in France itself as far as the debates on parity of political representation for women are concerned, as well as the recognition of the status of minority, regional languages, among other issues.

As for the defense of colonialism in the name of the universality of French ideology, the contradictions were inherent from the outset, given the fusion of the particular national interests of the colonial power under the banner of universalism. Yet it is not surprising that this same ideology of freedom, equality and fraternity provided some of the very arms with which the nationalist struggles were to subvert the ideology that purported to justify colonial supremacy.

In fact, the *reality* of the relations between colonizers and colonized was lived on a different plane altogether, in which the representation of the other owed far more to an imaginary consciousness heavily influenced by ethnic and racial conceptions and far removed from the ethereal conceptualization of the universal rights of man. In the real world, the discourse of anthropology and the visual and literary representations of Orientalist art and culture expressed with a much greater degree of accuracy and transparency the nature of the relation to the other, the object of absolute difference.

On this plane too, the Empire has struck back with its powerful literary and artistic products, which have contributed to the subversion of the colonial gaze and the reconstitution of new relations to the other.

However, what was less predictable was the bizarre attempt by the official discourse of *Francophonie* to recast itself in the mantle of *subversion*. On the official French government Web page devoted to *Francophonie*, one finds the following formula, which was agreed by Boutros Boutros-Ghali, Nicephore Soglo and Jacques Chirac at the Cotonou Francophone Summit in 1995, and describes *Francophonie* in stirring terms: "La francophonie sera subversive et imaginative ou ne sera pas!"[25]

How far it will be possible for the modern version of *Francophonie* to achieve its subversive mission through the defense and celebration of difference remains to be seen. However, it is unlikely that its political institutions will provide the basis for a new Internationale of the twenty-first century.

On the level of organizational coherence alone, there are bound to be difficulties. The initial foundation of *Francophonie* on the shared French language and French culture, and its raison d'être as a homogenizing, totalizing project celebrated, and derived its rationale from, a notion of what the different participants had in common. However, the modern version of *Francophonie* takes *difference* to be its underlying principle, and this is necessarily a much less solid basis for the creation of a unifying ideological structure.

There is a further problem with the presentation of Francophone ideology as subversive of the monolith of American culture. Indeed, it is at its most unconvincing when it bases itself on the false premise of the uniformity of American culture. For, if Europe was the cradle of working-class ideologies of dissent in the nineteenth century, it is in the United States that the twentieth century has seen an explosion of dissident ideologies of difference, and a subversion of the liberal consensus by those groups, genders and races excluded from it, on both the political and cultural planes.

Thus, while the Francophone discourse may be appealing to French-speaking élites across the world, those who are marginalized and have no stake in the existing political status quo are likely to find the politicized American counterculture infinitely more appealing and, like their American counterparts, more subversive of American hegemony. The theme of the 1999 Monckton Summit, "la jeunesse," may be a sign that the weakness in this regard has been recognized, even though it was in fact eclipsed by human rights issues during the actual summit.

Finally, the new Francophone discourse has so far failed to overcome the central dichotomy that still persists with regard to the relationship between France and the Francophone world, in which *Francophonie* is still perceived in many respects as the other of France.[26]

Thus, Jacques Chirac has spoken eloquently of *Francophonie*'s mission to preserve cultural and linguistic diversity with an appeal for the "militants du multiculturalisme" to struggle against "l'étouffement, par une langue unique, des diverses cultures qui font la richesse et la dignité de l'humanité."[27] However, there has been a signal failure to translate this mission to France itself, where the old-style hegemonic model based on the "one and indivisible French Republic," and a homogeneous national language and culture has proved extremely resilient, and where anything resembling Anglo-Saxon "communitarianism" is still frowned upon. The principle of diversity, so in vogue on the global scale, is not normally extended to the heterogeneous population of metropolitan France. Thus the members of the post-colonial diaspora living in France find themselves in an ambiguous relationship with regard to *La Francophonie*: when identified by their origins, they are perceived as *francophones*, i.e., non-French; however, they are expected to conform to the norms applicable to French society and are not normally accorded the right to difference that now prevails in the Francophone world. This contradiction becomes even more acute, when it comes to the DOM-TOMs, which have no independent voice in the institutional framework of *La Francophonie*.

The whole issue of the relationship of France to *Francophonie* has now taken on a new shape, with France increasingly expressing a willingness, even a wish, to disengage from the leading role within the Francophone context and take a backseat. France's reluctance to continue to assume sole responsibility for military, economic and financial support results in it looking more and more to its partners within *Francophonie* to take a front seat, as well as seeking to involve its European partners in some of its traditional areas of influence.

This is not to deny the special relationships that exist between France and the Francophone world, particularly the Francophone African countries. However, it does seem to show a new realism. On the one hand, there seems to be a new capacity to face up to the reality of these relationships, including an acknowledgment of the historical and geographical importance of these ties.[28] On the other, there is a recognition of the need to persuade and convince people that this is not just France's show, but that the other countries have a real stake in the success of the Francophone movement.

At this point, it is necessary to stress again that what is at issue here is the ability of Francophone discourse to convince and influence. However, this seemingly anti-colonial stance on the part of France can also be interpreted as a lack of commitment to the Francophone concept.

This seems to be a case of France wearing different hats, or adopting different discourses, depending on the constituency that it is trying to court. France clearly has eggs in more than one basket, as a result of its role within the European Union, the particular bilateral ties that bind it to Africa, the close relationship between France and the Maghreb, and the even closer relationship with Algeria, and indeed the continuation of a strong French nation-state itself. The reluctance of France to commit itself fully to its own integration within *Francophonie*, rather than being both within and without, is a serious source of weakness and undermines the effectiveness of the new discourse. The new *Francophonie* could only really take shape if France were to become fully part of it and provide, in addition to its cultural prestige, the financial, economic, political and military clout to make it an effective alternative.

It is appropriate to conclude with a final quotation from Senghor, who already made this very point in the 1962 issue of *Esprit*, which did so much to launch the idea of *La Francophonie*:

> Au contact des réalités "coloniales," . . . l'humanisme français s'était enrichi, s'approfondissait en s'élargissant pour intégrer les valeurs de ces civilisations . . . . Au moment que, par totalisation et socialisation, se construit la Civilisation de l'Universel, il est question de nous servir de ce merveilleux outil, trouvé dans les décombres du régime colonial . . . . La Négritude, l'Arabisme, c'est aussi vous, Français de l'Hexagone![29]

Whether France will wish to respond fully to the challenge of making a greater commitment remains to be seen. What is clear is that *Francophonie* has embarked upon a new course for the twenty-first century that may radically alter its character, or may simply represent a further change in its discourse. The theme chosen for the next summit to be held in Beirut in 2001, "dialogue entre les cultures," suggests a continuing preoccupation with culture. It will be interesting to see whether further progress has been made by then on the construction of the political and economic dimensions as real pillars of the Francophone movement.

Notes

1. Léopold Senghor, quoted in Xavier Deniau, *La Francophonie* (Paris: Presses Universitaires de la France, "Que sais-je?", 1983)

2. Deniau, *La Francophonie*.

3. Habib Bourguiba speaking at the Assemblée nationale of Niger, December 1965, quoted in Deniau, *La Francophonie*.

4. Deniau, *La Francophonie*.

5. Deniau, *La Francophonie*.

6. Antoine de Rivarol, *Discours sur l'universalité de la langue française*, 1784, quoted on the official French government Web page devoted to *Francophonie*, www.france.diplomatie.fr/francophonie.

7. Later renamed AUPELF-UREF and expanded to include the Université des réseaux d'expression française, which was also founded in Quebec at the 1987 Summit and subsequently reconstituted as the Agence universitaire de la Francophonie. For the most up-to-date information on the institutions of *La Francophonie*, see www.france.diplomatie.fr/francophonie. See also Anne Judge, "Voices and Policies" in *Francophone Voices*, ed. Kamal Salhi (Exeter: Elm Bank Publications, 1999), 1–25; Dennis Ager, *Francophonie in the 1990's: Problems and Opportunities* (Clevedon, U.K.: Multilingual Matters, 1996).

8. Friedrich Engels, in *Northern Star* 11, (22 January 1848). See also Shlomo Avineri, ed., *Marx on Colonialism and Modernization* (New York: Doubleday, Anchor Books, 1969).

9. Habib Bourguiba, quoted in Deniau, *La Francophonie*.

10. See *Libération*, 16–17 October 1993.

11. "Précisément, dans le cadre des négociations du Gatt, les francophones veulent résister à l'invasion des productions américaines en arguant de la spécificité identitaire, à préserver, des *industries culturelles*" qui ne sont pas que des usines à films. Cet argument a cependant des effets boomerang, notamment en Afrique, envahie par des images qui viennent, presque toujours, d'ailleurs, et, souvent, de . . . France." Stephen Smith, *Libération*, 16–17 October 1993, 17.

12. *Libération*, 16–17 October 1993.

13. *Le Monde*, 15 October 1993.

14. Quoted in Judge, "Voices and Policies," 20. As Anne Judge has rightly pointed out, this leads to a new interpretation of the universality of French, which is dependent on its "expressing a maximum number of cultures." Going further, one might say that this new version of universality has much in common with the "concrete universalism" put forward by Aimé Césaire, who rejected an abstract universalism empty of real substance in favor of a universality that would be made up of all existing particularisms, but that would be more than the sum of its parts, since each would become further enriched by its coexistence with all the others. See Aimé Césaire, *Letter to Maurice Thorez* (Paris: Présence Africaine, 1957), 15.

15. The irrelevance of the mother-tongue concept to *La Francophonie* is clearly spelled out by Alain Peyrefitte: "La francophonie commence à l'école. C'est à l'école qu'elle apprend à se marier avec toutes les formes, les références, les valeurs, d'une humanité très ancienne. Il y a des écoles françaises au Chili ou en Bulgarie, comme il y en a dans nos banlieues difficiles et dans nos beaux quartiers. Sous toutes les latitudes, on y apprend à devenir plus: à entrer dans une histoire qui est le contraire d'une nostalgie, dans une communauté qui est le contraire d'un ghetto." *Le Figaro*, March 1996, quoted by www. france. diplomatie.fr/francophonie.

16. Jacques Derrida, *Le Monolinguisme de l'autre ou la prothèse d'origine* (Paris: Editions Galilée, 1996), 13 and passim.

17. Only in French-speaking parts of the European Francophone countries and in French-speaking parts of Canada is it genuinely a mother-tongue for a majority of the population. There are only three countries in which French is spoken by more than 50% of the total population—France itself (98%), Monaco (90%) and Luxembourg (80%). Indeed, the only territory that can claim 100% of its population to be French speakers is the French outpost off the Canadian coast known as Saint Pierre et Miquelon. There are problems, however, with the accurate determination of figures for first-language and second-language speakers of French. See Ager, *Francophonie*; Judge, "Voices and Policies."

18. Judge, "Voices and Policies," 19, quotes François Bayrou, writing in the preface of *La Francophonie: fresque et mosaïque*, as Minister of Education in 1996: "Le premier trésor du patrimoine d'un peuple, c'est sa langue . . . Toutes les langues ont leur noblesse, leur caractère, leur génie propre. C'est la raison pour laquelle il importe de développer le multilinguisme, seul moyen . . . de comprendre les autres peuples et échanger véritablement."

19. See *Le Monde*, 4 September 1999.

20. *Le Monde*, 4 September 1999.

21. *Le Monde*, 5 September 1999.

22. "Les sanctions ne sont pas dans la tradition de la francophonie; elles relèvent de la compétence de l'ONU. Ce que nous voulons, nous, c'est convaincre, pas contraindre." Jacques Chirac, quoted in *Le Monde*, 4 September 1999.

23. *Le Monde*, 5 September 1999.

24. "La francophonie est une force tranquille. A chaque sommet elle fait un pas dans la bonne direction." Jacques Chirac, quoted in *Le Monde*, 7 September 1999.

25. TV5, Cotonou, VIème Sommet francophone, 3 December 1995, quoted at www. france. diplomatie.fr/francophonie.

26. As Alec Hargreaves puts it: "While the champions of *francophonie* never tire of exalting the 'universal' vocation of the French language, their efforts are implicitly predicated on the affirmation of difference. Although the French language is an essential constituent of both, *francophonie* cannot be prop-

erly understood except in contradistinction to "Frenchness." "Francophonie and Globalisation: France at the Crossroads," in *Francophone Voices*, ed., Kamal Salhi, 49.

27. "La Francophonie a vocation à appeler toutes les autres langues du monde à se rassembler pour faire en sorte que la diversité culturelle, qui résulte de la diversité linguistique, que cette diversité soit sauvegardée. Au-delà du français, au-delà de la Francophonie, il nous faut être les militants du multiculturalisme dans le monde pour lutter contre l'étouffement, par une langue unique, des diverses cultures qui font la richesse et la dignité de l'humanité." Jacques Chirac, speaking in Hungary, 1997, quoted at www.france.diplomatie.fr/francophonie.

28. Cf. the interview with Charles Josselin, responsible for Co-operation at the Ministry of Foreign Affairs, carried out in 1997 and quoted by Judge, "Voices and Policies," 23: "La relation reste privilégiée et le restera longtemps car elle est inscrite dans l'histoire et la géographie. De plus, nos partenaires africains peuvent nous reprocher, dans la même phrase, d'être trop en Afrique et de ne pas y être assez. Il y a un point d'équilibre à trouver. Nous avons fait le choix d'une relation de partenariat et non de tutelle."

29. Léopold Senghor, *Esprit*, 1962, quoted at www.france.diplomatie.fr/francophonie.

I

NORTH AFRICA AND
THE MIDDLE EAST

2

Colonial Culture as Francophone?
The Case of Late Nineteenth-Century Algeria

Leonard R. Koos

WHILE THE DESIGNATION "FRANCOPHONE" literally means "French speaking" regardless of geographical location or cultural disposition, it is overwhelmingly applied to those postcolonial French-speaking societies that demonstrate significant cultural difference from their European counterparts. This chapter will examine French colonialist culture in North Africa in the late nineteenth century as an embryonic example of *francophonie*. The emergent culture of late-nineteenth-century French Algeria—arguably the most developed and significant colony in France's post-mercantilist empire—exhibits what Homi Bhabha has called "the conflictual economy of colonialist identity": the construction of hybrid identities whose selves were no longer metropolitan and not yet indigenous. As a result, a number of contemporary critics of colonialist culture have concentrated on the effects of colonialist discourse on the formation of indigenous identity and outlined how dominant discursive formations find their way into indigenous selfhood. This essay will use the same conception of cultural hybridity as way of understanding the colonialist self as it developed in ways that diverge from the cultural presuppositions of metropolitan discourses (in this respect, colonialist culture can be examined along with the "post-colonial" francophone cultures of nineteenth-century Canada and Louisiana). It is in the self-fashioning strategies of a number of writers living in the colony who began to publish their works in the 1890s in Ernest Mallebay's *Revue Algérienne Illustrée* (the colony's first significant journal primarily devoted to colonialist literature and culture) that the potentially francophone nature of French colonialist culture can be analysed. The discussion first considers Musette's tremendously popular *Cagayous* series and Stephen Chaseray's *Père Robin* letters in order to demonstrate how, both in terms of what they chose to represent and the language they used, colonialist writers in late nineteenth-century Algeria sought to create colonialist archetypes inscribed in stories representing the daily life of the *colon* communities that would be recognizable as such to a resident reading public. Next, lesser known writers will be considered, such as El Bah't, Yasmina, Bou-Yabès, Ali Ben El Messaï and Djabadouli, who, despite their obviously European origins, represent themselves textually in the pages of the *Revue* as narrative authorities on colonialist issues as well as indigenous knowledge, and who paratextually mimic the indigenous population by using ironic pseudonyms and by appearing in native dress in the photographs that illustrate their work, a travesty supported by editorial comments in the journal. Not to be confused with the assimilationist fantasies of the *mission civilisatrice* of nineteenth-century imperialism, which had been directed towards indigenous populations but were abandoned by the 1890s and replaced with the political theory of association, these rearticulations of formerly European selves suggest, in turn, the colonialist desire for a reconfiguation of the image of the indigenous into a less aleatory, post-exotic other that would more effectively conform to the discursive demands, however conflictual, of colonialist culture. It is in the rewriting of the colony by the colonialists themselves that a unique hybrid discursivity is articulated. Its linguistic, political, social and cultural ramifications create an authentic voice, which fulfils various demands in the historical constitution of what has come to be known as *francophonie*. "Le *nord-africanisme* en littérature ressort des faits et gestes des écrivains locaux. Les premières tentatives de décentralisation littéraire émanent de ceux qui les premiers se rapprochèrent pour fonder des publications d'art ou, de combat, échanger leurs idées et pour créer un milieu intellectuel et artistique dans une société par trop utilitaire."[1]

On the morning of 25 June 1830, a mere eleven days after the beginning of the French conquest of Algiers and just over a week before the capitulation of the *Dey* to the invading forces, a French military vessel laid anchor off the shore near Sidi Feredj to the west of Algiers. Aboard was a precious cargo, the necessary basis for a dimension of the conquest that had been hitherto overlooked during the military mission's detailed planning in the months preceding the invasion. Later that day, this final element of the invasion, along with other military necessities like gun carriages and sacks of flour, was transported to the shore. Five tradesman who had set sail with the brig in Marseille four days earlier worked feverishly throughout the day on the beach, assembling the various parts of the machine, a printing press, which, when operational, would replace the limited lithography equipment that had initially arrived with the troops. The next day, housed in two tents on the peninsula of the Régence, the printing press was inaugurated amid much fanfare, and cries of "Vive la France!" and "Vive le roi!" erupted from the assembled soldiers and sailors when the first copies of an army bulletin christened *L'Africaine* and detailing the recent landing and progress of the French troops in Algeria were distributed. As the director of this operation, Jean-Toussaint Merle, would sententiously recall in *Anecdotes historiques et politiques pouvant servir à l'histoire de le conquête d'Alger de 1830* (1831): "cette date signalera peut-être un des événements les plus influents de la civilisation sur la plus belle comme sur la plus florissante de nos colonies."[2]

While it remains to be seen whether Merle's imperial aspirations were in fact realized on the shores of North Africa, his comments underscore the conjunction and ultimate partnership between narrative and empire, between writing and colonization. The import of writing in the colony, and ultimately colonialist writing in Algeria, as a site for constructs of colonialist identity is the product of the complex evolution of the cultural politics that resulted from the unique status of this colony in the nineteenth-century French empire.

Algerian Impressions

"Comme les journaux parlaient beaucoup de l'Algérie et très peu de la Métropole, on avait l'impression que la France était loin, très loin."[3] The cultural dimensions of the conquest of Algeria in the nineteenth century depended to a great extent on the preeminent position the colony occupied in the metropolitan political and cultural imagination. As the first major acquisition following the dissolution of France's mercantilist empire in the seventeenth and eighteenth centuries, as well as the recent events of the Napoleonic wars and Waterloo, Algeria, particularly in the second half of the nineteenth century, not only evoked an image that nostalgically animated a discourse of regained power and glory, it also gave rise to the imperialist fantasy of "La Nouvelle France." As "La Nouvelle France," Algeria was differentiated from other French colonies with regard to the articulation of political, social, cultural and linguistic dimensions of the "mission civilisatrice" and assimilationist theories.[4] While the rhetoric of assimilation and the civilizing mission was rarely translated into real or effective colonial policy with respect to indigenous populations, it nonetheless accompanied the promotion in metropolitan politics and society of the permanent settling of the colony by Europeans with the ultimate desire of creating a France of "quatre-vingts à cent millions de Français, fortement établis sur les deux rives de la Méditerranée,"[5] a project reminiscent of ancient Greece and Rome It is germane to note other important ideological functions that this association of the French empire with ancient Greece and Rome accomplished. As is quite clear in the work of Prévost-Paradol and any number of other contemporary commentators, the ideological fervor with which an imperialist empire in the vicinity of the European continent was pursued and established came as direct response to the growth of Prussian militarism. More subtly perhaps, such an analogy, while propagating a "myth that legitimated colonisation as the recuperation of the Latin heritage,"[6] had the effect of rhetorically neutralizing Arab populations in the Maghreb. As Louis Bertrand, an important colonial novelist at the turn of the century and one of the major proponents of this myth, was to note later: "Nous sommes venus reprendre l'oeuvre de Rome en ce pays, que leur constitution géographique, leur voisinage et leur passé semblent placer naturellement sous l'hégémonie latine."[7] Of indigenous populations and culture, Bertrand valorized the Berbers, but considered the cultural legitimacy of the groups that had dominated Algeria since the arrival of Islam as "[d]u plaqué, du postiche, du rapporté, si vous voulez—mais c'est tout. Ici, le fond est latin, ou mieux helléno-latin, mais Oriental, jamais."[8] The "résumé de la latinité méditerranéenne"[9] of newly arriving immigrant groups were thus legitimated a priori as the inheritors of an interrupted tradition. By effectively marginalizing and excluding the Arabs from the representational landscape of the colony, colonial commentators and writers discursively paved the way for the shift in colonial policy from assimilation to association by the mid 1890s.

The "terre française" that Algeria came to represent provided writers and artists of nineteenth-century metropolitan France with a conveniently near destination where they could pursue or construct their Orientalist fantasies. While many of the writers and artists who produced for European audiences exoticist representations based on Algerian subjects—Eugène Delacroix, Eugène Fromentin, Théophile Gautier, Guy de Maupassant, to name but a few—had experienced the colony directly in the course of actual trips, their itineraries invariably proved to be tourist ones as they included return passage to the Metropole and familiar metropolitan values.[10] It was not until the final decade of the nineteenth century that a resident culture in the colony representing "l'Algérie travailleuse, inconnue des touristes, les centaines de villages crées, les milliers d'hectares défrichés, cultivés plantés en vigne, les villes poussant du jour au lendemain"[11] would effectively emerge.

Following the arrival of the first European printing press in 1830, printing and publishing developed quickly, yet were generally limited to the world of journalism. On 27 January 1832 the first issue of the weekly *Moniteur algérien* was published in Algiers and seven years later *L'Akhbar*, which was published until well into the twentieth century, began to appear. As the popular press proliferated in concert and complicity with the augmentation of immigrant colonial populations, and the expansion and consolidation of French control with its pacification of indigenous populations throughout the colony, the relative cultural isolation of French-speaking residents in Algeria was addressed as more specialized publications began to appear. The specialized reviews, like their journalistic counterparts in the colony, wholly participated in the ideological presuppositions of colonial life and therefore conceived of their role according to the desires and values of the colonial arena. For example, the *Revue africaine*, which began to appear monthly in September 1856, contended that its articles, which dealt mainly with the history and archaeology of Roman and Islamic North Africa, performed the same function as other cultural institutions, such as communal and military libraries, in that, particularly in remote locales of the colony, all would "empêcher la civilisation de rétrograder en contact avec de la barbarie et en absence de tout moyen d'étude."[12] Similarly, the short-lived *La Revue algérienne*, five numbers of which were published by the *Société des Beaux-Arts, des Sciences et des Lettres d'Alger*, beginning in 1877, sought, like the small museum the society had already founded, "à éveiller et à développer chez les Algériens le goût du vrai et du beau."[13] Such comments evince the recognition of the increasingly irrelevant legitimacy of metropolitan culture.

A major figure in the creation and promotion of resident culture in the arena of Algerian journalism during the late nineteenth century was Ernest Mallebay. Shortly after his arrival in the colony in 1880, Mallebay recognized that "[l]a presse d'Alger s'occupe de tout, excepté de pure littérature; du moins elle ne lui fait qu'une place ridiculement exiguë. Le poète qui frappe à la porte d'un quoditien quelconque est immanquablement éconduit. Le lettré, ciseleur de belles périodes, qui se préoccupe de l'harmonie des phrases plus que l'aigreur des polémiques, est toisé avec dédain."[14] In an effort to cultivate in the Algerian reading public a more refined appreciation of literature as well as give local writers the opportunity of publishing in a local review "où les violents ne pénétraient pas,"[15] apart from other influential reviews like *Le Turco*, on 15 April 1888 Mallebay founded *La Revue algérienne et tunisienne*, which was renamed *La Revue algérienne illustrée* in 1893. In this journal, Algeria's first weekly periodical with a certain amount of longevity devoted entirely to the cultural production of the colony, Mallebay self-consciously sought to extricate a colonial reading public from the hegemonic influence of metropolitan culture by publishing local writers whose knowledge and appreciation of the colony arose from residential experience, if not reality. As he would later remark about one of the first stories of Stephen Chaseray that he read: "C'était une nouvelle sur un thème algérien, avec des personnages et des paysages algériens, comme je recommendais à mes collaborateurs de m'en donner."[16]

The first recognisable and significant figure to emerge from, without being limited to, the pages of *La Revue algérienne illustrée* in the 1890s was *le Père Robin*, a character created by Stephen Chaseray. From 1893 on, in both the *Revue and Le Républicain de Constantine*, letters signed *le Père Robin* began to appear, comically chronicling the daily life of *Père* and *Mère Robin* in the fictive mixed village of *Oued Melouf* in the *département* of Constantine. The most significant of these letters written by Chaseray, who himself was a civil servant working in the colonial government in Constantine, appeared in the 20 May 1893 issue of the *Revue* and took the form of a response to a senatorial inquiry (meant in context to refer to the senatorial visit to the colony in 1891 led by Jules Ferry) on the "question algérienne" that asked about "la réforme de l'impôt arabe, les questions agricoles, l'instruction des Kabyles, l'assimilation des Arabes d'Algérie, la justice indigène, le transsaharien,"[17] among other subjects. What emerges in this letter, as in the many to follow, is a description of colonial life that often includes the theme of metropolitan misconceptions of the colony set against their correction by long-term residents who possess direct experience of the realities of daily life in the colony.

Among the best known and significant creations of popular literature in late nineteenth-century Algeria was the journalist Auguste Robinet's *Cagayous* series written between 1894 and 1908 and published under the pseudonym Musette. Perhaps more dramatically than the *Père Robin* letters, the *Cagayous* stories underscored the desire among readers and writers for representations of themselves that authenticated their experience as colonial residents. First appearing with illustrations in the *Revue* and *Le Turco*, then published separately in chapbook publications that reportedly sold thousands of copies, these stories depicted a band of working-class hooligans from Algiers's Bab el Oued neighborhood whose antics and adventures through the city with their leader Cagayous often ended in comical mishaps. Like Chaseray's *Père Robin*, the *Cagayous* series, while not always dealing with contemporary issues of import in colonial life, nonetheless provided the colonial reading public with a "vivante incarnation de la plèbe néo-francaise d'Algérie,"[18] no matter however fanciful it may have been. The *Cagayous* stories create a greater sense of colonial authenticity by participating in a linguistic reality that "reflects the disparate backgrounds and demographic characteristics of European settlers"[19] in Algeria. Cagayous's adventures are narrated in an urban dialect called "pataouète," which emerged in the final years of the nineteenth century and included words from French, Arabic, Spanish, Italian and regionalisms from the South of France. The creation and reception of *Cagayous* and *le Père Robin* in the 1890s, inasmuch as they develop a literature of colonialist types able to speak in their own idiom, signify the first cultural steps being taken during this decade toward the creation of a differentiated colonialist identity. As Cagayous himself puts it in *Cagayous à l'Exposition* (1900), when Parisian fairgoers at the *Exposition Universelle* hear Cagayous and his comrades speaking their strange dialect and ask whether they are French, he emphatically replies, "Algériens, nous sommes,"[20] which was to become a slogan, if not battle cry, for the emerging colonialist identity in Algeria.

Going Native?

"Mais il est bon de faire savoir au public, lorsqu'on a eu soi-même la chance de l'apprendre, qu'il existe partout des écrivains de talent, et que Paris n'est pas nécessairement la ville où sont installés leurs éditeurs."[21] Even the most casual of readers of *La Revue algérienne illustrée* of the 1890s cannot help but be struck by the large number of pseudonymously signed contributions. As with many documented examples of metropolitan journalism in *fin de siècle* France, particularly the more specialized literary and artistic journals, the profusion of pseudonyms in *La Revue* seems to have been motivated by the desire to create the illusion of a larger number of contributors than existed in reality. Playful, frivolous, and gently ironic pseudonyms, like Boule de Neige, Roumi, Pierre-qui-roule, Poil de tortue, Poil de truite, Le Saharien, Le Butineur, Le Liseur, Le Turco, Titi, Le Photographe, L'Homme masqué, Frivole, Don Juan, Candide and many others suggest a situational and perfunctory rather than a consistent and complete attempt to onomastically refashion the authorial self.

The reader of these pages is equally struck by the appearance of a number of authors whose names surprisingly suggest indigenous collaboration with *La Revue algérienne illustrée*. For example, a disparate number of short pieces describing local legend, history, and customs of both pre- and post-conquest Algeria are signed with the names El-Hamdouillah, Kheteb Mohammed, El Feriani, Alif., El Abrod, Dou-Bsiz and Djabadouli.[22] Moreover, beginning on 27 January 1900 and continuing weekly through until the 28 July 1900 issue of the *Revue*, readers were able to peruse a five-act play entitled *La Femme incendiée—drame algérien* signed with the name El Djeza-ïry. This play, fairly traditional in structure and melodramatic in plot, though set primarily in the colonial communities of Algeria, nonetheless implies an intimate knowledge of French theatrical traditions. In a postface to the as yet unproduced play, the author adds: "Si, de plus, quelque société d'amateurs algériens voulait monter ce drame algérien, je lui en serais reconnaissant et demanderais comme droit d'auteur, le compte rendu de l'effet qu'il produit à la scène."²³ Upon closer examination, the name "El Djezaïry" is a rough transcription of the Arabic for "the Algerian."²⁴ The nominal and adjectival "algérien" at the turn of the century, however, did not refer to native Algerian populations, who were overwhelmingly called "indigènes," but rather to the native and naturalized French, and the large European immigrant communities composed primarily of Spanish, Italian and Maltese immigrants.²⁵ These details, taken together, call into question the likelihood of indigenous collaboration with *La Revue algérienne illustrée* and invite an examination of the other authors who regularly appeared in its pages signing their stories and articles with seemingly authentic indigenous names.²⁶

From 1898 to 1901 twelve short pieces, for the most part autobiographical and lyrically descriptive of North African landscapes, appeared under the name Yasmina. However, after reading texts like "Pauvre Mingôh (souvenir d'enfance)," which is set in Auvergne, "Ma Première Heure en Afrique," which waxes nostalgic in typically Orientalist fashion as the narrator recalls her "amalgame de sentiments divers, une vague curiosité mélangée au vague effroi de l'inconnu qui vous attend à l'arrivée,"²⁷ and the wintertime story set in France "Flocons de neige," the reader surmises that a French-born woman author stands behind the indigenous moniker. In the journal's literary column of 3 March 1900, it was revealed that Yasmina, who had recently published a volume entitled *Croquis tunisiens*, was in fact, "la femme d'un de nos fonctionnaires algériens."²⁸ The column added the telling details that, while "le pseudonyme de Yasmina ne nous porterait pas à croire que notre écrivain est blanche et parfumée," the author elicits "l'admiration des femmes indigènes,"²⁹ and that she holds nothing but "affectueuse estime pour les Indigènes."³⁰ Although the actual name of Yasmina was never offered in the column, in 1897 the Algiers printer and publisher C. Zamith did publish a volume entitled *Croquis tunisiens* under the name Hélène Poncin.

Beginning in 1897, a large number of pieces appeared in *La Revue* signed with the name El Bah't. Some recounted local legends and historical events, others appeared regularly under the title "Proverbes indigènes," but all implied a knowledge of local culture and history that gave the impression that they had been written by an *indigène*. At the end of the piece published on 7 May 1898, "Le Canon des Beni Iffen," which recounted the story of an indigenous tribe during the insurrection of 1871, this illusion of indigenous identity was threatened by the parenthetical addendum of the initials "L. J."³¹ Paratextual suspicions about the origin of El Bah't are confirmed in the issue of 15 June 1901, in which a short article on the author, which repeated the initials but did not give a name, revealed to the public that the name El Bah't, in fact, "se dissimulait (oh! bien peu) un jeune magistrat qui a laissé à Oran le souvenir d'un homme du monde."³² This verbal portrait is accompanied by a reproduction of a photograph of El Bah't in native dress taken in a photographer's studio with an exotic backdrop.³³ Despite the photographic evidence that seeks to suggest an entirely different origin, and despite the fact that the literary column never fully names him, only referring to him as L. J. and Lucien J., El Bah't was the pseudonym of Lucien Jacquot, born in Metz in 1862.³⁴

Another writer whose name appeared frequently in the pages of *La Revue* throughout the 1890s, christened in an 1893 editorial note as "le roi des conteurs"³⁵ of Algeria, signed his stories on Kabyle culture and folklore with the decidedly strange, ultimately farcical pseudonym, Bou-Yabès. The same editorial note, directly addressing the author, remarks: "je ne sais si tu appartiens à cette étrange race kabyle dont tu as pénétré les mystères et que tu mets devant nous telle qu'elle est et telle qu'aucun Européen ne l'a connue."³⁶ The commentary on Bou-Yabès ends with the evocation of a mysterious, nearly occult figure who spends solitary, contemplative days "obscur dans quelque montagne de Kabylie."³⁷ In the issue of 10 April 1897, in a similarly laudatory tribute to the author, Ernest Mallebay claims that, through his stories, Bou-Yabès "nous présente l'âme kabyle; il l'a étudiée jusqu'en ses replis les plus ténébreux."[38] While the semantic shift between these two commentaries on Bou-Yabès from a potentially Kabyle author to one who has profoundly studied their cultural soul subtly problematizes the former, the accompanying portrait of Bou-Yabès in native dress disrupts such doubts.[39] Although the identity of this author was never revealed in the pages of the *Revue*, Bou-Yabès was, in fact, the pseudonym of Henri Dubouloz, who was born in the Savoy in 1857, arrived in the colony as an auxiliary draftsman for the colonial government in 1877 and worked in various mixed communities of the *département* of Oran until 1907.

The most baffling, mysterious, and ultimately problematic of the indigenous pseudonyms in the *Revue* during this period is connected with a serialized narrative in seventeen installments running from 28 April to 10 September 1894 entitled "Chez les Touareg" and signed with the name Ali ben el Messaï. By its very nature, the narrative suggests an indigenous author, as it recounts the disastrous *Mission Flatters* of 1881 in the first person. That military expedition, led by Lieutenant Colonel Paul Flatters, was part of the early push to bring the Sahara under complete French control and ultimately build a trans-Saharan railway. Composed of ten Frenchmen and 78 *indigènes*, the *Mission Flatters* ended in tragedy when, betrayed by their Chaamba guides, all but 21 members of the expedition were killed by Touareg horsemen. No Frenchman survived the massacre. As a result, the story of the Mission Flatters is recounted, to this day, "à la lumière des faits incomplets."[40]

A number of stylistic and thematic peculiarities in the text of "Chez les Touareg" deserve mention. In the opening installment the narrator enumerates by name the European members of the expedition and merely indicates by number its non-European members. Shortly before the massacre the narrator notes, using a conventional designation of colonial discourse: "Des *indigènes* venus de droite et de gauche circulent librement parmi nous. . . ."[41] After his captivity, without explanation regarding his captors' supposedly mistaken perception, the narrator contends that "[c]es gens doutaient certainement de ma religion et de ma nationalité, ils me prenaient pour un Européen. . . ."[42] After the narrator has been successful in convincing his captors of his indigenous identity, he adds that "ils n'avaient aucune notion de notre civilisation; ils apportaient une attention très grande à tout ce que je leur racontais ayant trait à l'Algérie et à ses habitants."[43] Later, Ali ben el Messaï says of the Touareg that "[l]eurs moeurs sont, à quelque chose près, comme celles de nos Arabes."[44] In these examples and many others, a pronominal ambiguity surfaces between the narrator's indigenous "je" and an equally present first-person plural expressed in references like "nos ennemis," "notre civilisation," "nos Arabes" and so forth, so that the location of Ali ben el Messaï's identity among the various groups living in colonial Algeria constantly shifts.

Two curious interruptions occur in the text during Ali ben el Messaï's narrative. In the instalment of "Chez les Touareg" published on 30 July 1894 the narrator recounts humorous details about the time he spent in the city of Aghir, which prompts an editorial note confirming that: "Ali bel Messaï était d'un comique abracadabrante en me racontant cela. . . ."[45] This unnamed editorial presence appears once again in the installment of 14 July 1894 when the narrator, recounting how he came to have a tattoo, states: "Ce taleb a dessiné sur mon bras le tatouage que tu y vois."[46] An editorial note confirms that "El Messaï me montra alors sur son bras un dessein fait dans la perfection."[47] The nearly invisible presence of an editorial interlocutor, combined with the pronominal and semantic variation that alternates between indigenous and colonial selves, raises serious questions about the narrative presence behind and around "Chez les Touareg." It is also notable that the name Ali ben el Messaï appears nowhere in the substantial documentation and commentary on the *Mission Flatters*.[48] Whether a fraudulent simulation, a translated interview, and/or something in between, it may never be possible to establish the truth beyond the certainty of a nearly invisible editorial presence negotiating this indigenous figure for a colonial reading public.[49]

A Place in the Sun

"Mais, une oeuvre intellectuelle n'est pas forcément une oeuvre révolutionnaire; elle n'est intéressante qu'en tant initiatrice; c'est le cas de notre tentative, qui vaut parce qu'elle fut faite à Alger, par des auteurs algériens, et imprimée à Alger, pour des lecteurs algériens."[50] The mock indigenous self-presentation and representation, coupled with editorial revelations of identity, in *La Revue algérienne illustrée* enact a kind of cultural striptease, the form and function of which appear as attempts to document a rite of passage from metropolitan to colonialist values. By easily appropriating and casting off indigenous selves, these authors establish a hybrid cultural rhetoric, the legitimacy of which no longer expresses itself in the terms of military conquest and "civilisation," but rather in its residential fiction of indigenous identity, which dramatically illustrates the ever present "conflictual economy of colonialist discourse."[51] In addition, these predatory authorial gestures of signature and self-fashioning lay the foundations for the reconfiguring of the indigenous other into a neutralizing, post-exotic superficiality that evinces "the increasingly problematic relationship between the discourses of exoticism and colonialism."[52] Although the writers of *La Revue algérienne illustrée* of the 1890s stand in the shadow of later, more widely recognized voices of colonialist literary culture in North Africa, such as Louis Bertrand, Robert Randau and Arthur Pellegrin, they nonetheless confirm the emergence of a colonialist literature, the spatial decentralization and cultural hybridity of which sufficiently distinguish it from metropolitan culture to qualify it, however embryonically, as "francophone."

Notes

1. Arthur Pellegrin, *La Litterature nord-africaine* (Tunis: Bibliothèque Nord-Africaine, 1920), 73.

2. Cited in Louis-Adrien Berbrugger, "Inauguration de la presse en Algérie," *Revue africaine* 1, no. 3, (1857): 216.

3. Ernest Mallebay, *Cinquante ans de journalisme* (Algiers: Fontana, 1937), 218.

4. One of most extravagant versions of "La Nouvelle France," published in 1847, proposed the renaming or founding in Algeria of cities and villages with the names of actual French communities. Evoking language as an essential feature of the civilizing mission and assimilation, the author contended that "il serait beau, en parcourant un jour l'Algérie, de marcher continuellement au milieu de villes, de villages, pourtant des noms nationaux au lieu de ces noms barbares qu'on a jusqu'à ce moment donnés au centres de populations, de rencontrer partout des noms français qui rappellent la patrie, la famille." B. S., "Réalisation du projet de fonder en Algérie une ville par chaque département français," *Revue algérienne et orientale* 3, no. 4 (1847): 147.

5. Lucien-Anatole Prévost-Paradol, *La Nouvelle France* (Paris: Michel Lévy, 1868), 418.

6. Azzedine Haddour, "Algeria and Its History: Colonial Myths and the Forging and Deconstructing of Identity in *Pied-Noir* Literature," in *French and Algerian Identities from Colonial Times to the Present: A Century of Interaction*, ed. Alec G. Hargreaves, Michael J. Heffernan (Lewiston: The Edwin Mellan Press, 1993), 80.

7. Louis Bertrand, *L'Afrique latine* (Rome: Reale Accademia d'Italia, 1938), 8.

8. Cited in Haddour, "Algeria and Its History," 80.

9. Louis Bertrand, *Sur les routes du Sud* (Paris: Fayard, 1938), 51.

10. Metropolitan culture did at times demonstrate a concern for more authentic representations of the colony. A number of Guy de Maupassant's entries in his series on Algeria in the metropolitan newspaper *Le Gaulois* in 1881 were signed "un Colon" and "un Officier." The first of these, which appeared in the issue of 20 July 1881, presented its author as "[u]n homme très considérable de l'Algérie, et qui l'habite depuis son enfance." Guy de Maupassant, *Lettres d'Afrique (Algérie—Tunisie)*, ed. Michèle Salinas (Paris: La Boîte à Documents, 1997), 55.

11. Claude Antoine, *Marthe Filmer, moeurs néo-algériennes* (Paris: Plon et Nourrit, 1895), 30–1.

12. Louis-Adrien Berbrugger, "Introduction" *Revue africaine* 1, no.1 (1856): 10.

13. Comité de Rédaction, "La Société des Beaux-Arts et *la Revue Algérienne*," *La Revue algérienne* 1, (1877): 1.

14. Mallebay, *Cinquante ans*, 278.

15. Mallebay, *Cinquante ans*, 278.

16. Mallebay, *Cinquante ans*, 404.

17. Stephen Chaseray, "Lettre du Père Robin," *La Revue algérienne illustrée* 15, no. 8 (1893): 227.

18. Gabriel Audisio, *Musette. Cagayous* (Paris: Balland, 1972), 11.

19. David Prochaska, *Making Algeria French: Colonialism in Bône 1870–1920* (Cambridge: Cambridge University Press, 1990), 224.

20. Cited in Audisio, *Musette*, 101.

21. Francis de Miomandre, *Figures d'hier et d'aujourd'hui* (Paris: Dorbon-Aîné, 1911), 188.

22. Although the identities of many of the pseudonymous authors of *La Revue algérienne illustrée* have been irrevocably lost with time, it is probable that the most frequently appearing name in this list, Djabadouli, who began writing a regular series of vignettes entitled "Les Veillées blidéennes" beginning in 1894, was Ernest Mallebay himself. After arriving in the colony in 1880, Mallebay lived in Blida until 1885 while he worked as a professor of history at the Collège de Blida. He also wrote in the *Revue* under the pseudonym Jean de Blida.

23. El Djezaïry, "Postface à la *Femme incendiée*," *La Revue algérienne illustrée* 40, no. 4 (1900): 124.

24. Even if regular readers of the *Revue* were not aware of the meaning of this transcription, they perhaps remembered Stephen Chaseray's story that appeared in installments from 20 February 1897 through until 20 March 1897, entitled "Djezaïra." In this story the main character receives a letter in Arabic from a mysterious unknown woman (who, incidentally, turns out to be European) signed "Djezaïra," which is translated in the text as "Algérienne."

25. As Prochaska, *Making Algeria*, 223, has perceptively noted in connection with the use of this designation, "Thus, at one blow the settlers proclaimed their hegemony in Algeria and at the same time obliterated the native Algerians in the very terms they used to describe them." Other common appellations in usage during this period that designated the European colonial populations in Algeria include "néo-français," "néo-algérien," "néo-latin" and "néo-africain."

26. Two additional pieces appeared in the Revue under the name El Djezaïry, "En pays de Cagayous" in the issue of 2 September 1899, and "Le Tableau" in the issue of 25 November 1899. By 1901, El Djezaïry's name, unlike Djabadouli's, does appear on the journal's front cover as one of the main contributors to the publication, suggesting that this pseudonym refers to someone other than the editor.

27. Yasmina, "Ma Première heure en Afrique," *La Revue algérienne illustrée* 36, no.11 (1898): 334. "Pauvre Mingôh (souvenir d'enfance)" appeared in the issue of 30 July 1893, and "Flocons de neige" was published in the issue of 2 March 1901.

28. Saint-Gemme, "Choses de la littérature," *La Revue algérienne illustrée* 39, no. 9 (1900): 282.

29. Saint-Gemme, "Choses de la littérature," 282.

30. Saint-Gemme, "Choses de la littérature," 283.

31. El Bah't (L. J.), "Le Canon des Beni Iffen," *La Revue algérienne illustrée* 35, no. 18 (1898): 567.

32. Parisette, "El Bah't," *La Revue algérienne illustrée* 40, no. 24 (1901): 752.

33. The idea of Europeans appropriating native dress while in the colony was by no means a novelty during the period. As the catalogue to the Musée-Galerie de la Seita's recent exhibition *Photographes en Algérie au XIXe siècle* (Paris: Musée-Galerie de la Seita, 1999) explains: "A l'époque des studios de photo, les photographes prêtaient des costumes aux touristes et les photographiaient dans un décor de style oriental, ce qui leur permettait de rapporter un souvenir exotique de leur séjour en Algérie" 95. While it is not known if El Bah't appeared like this in public, his donning of native dress in this photograph would seem to be a rare occurrence, particularly given his position in the colonial government. Beyond touristic culture, other colonial residents and travellers did appropriate native dress in a much more permanent way, a tendency that can be only partially explained by practicality. The members of the *Société des Pères Blancs* established by Monseigneur Charles Lavigerie in 1868, whose motto was "se faire arabe avec les Arabes, coucher sur la dure, manger la nourriture et parler la langue du pays" (cited in Jean-Charles Humbert, *La Découverte du Sahara en 1900* [Paris: L'Harmattan, 1996], 165, roamed the countryside and the desert as missionaries in indigenous clothing. During the second half of the nineteenth century explorers were often drawn and photographed for the popular press in native dress, the most famous example being Paul Nadar's 1882 photograph of Pierre Savorgnan de Brazza. Finally, mention should be made of the writer Isabelle Eberhardt, who frequently travelled in Tunisia and Algeria in male native dress between 1897 and 1904 and posed as a Tunisian Koranic student under the name Si Mahmoud Saadi. While the issue of practicality—a young woman travelling alone through indigenous North Africa—has been raised by a number of critics to explain Eberhardt's sartorial gesture, her cultural cross-dressing clearly enacts an anarchistic gendered political strategy that opposes itself to dominant European models of selfhood.

34. Lucien Jacquot also published in the *Revue* under his own name. Another of Jacquot's possible appropriations of indigenous identity concerns the regularly appearing sections of the *Revue* known as "Proverbes mozabites." In the issue of 4 June 1898 this section appears with the note: "Extraits de la *Grammaire mozabite* de MM. Nour et Moka (en collaboration avec M. Jacquot, substitut)" ("Proverbes mozabites," *La Revue algérienne illustrée* 35, no. 22 (1898): 682. The resemblance between Jacquot's own "Proverbes indigènes" and a number of these mozabite proverbs notwithstanding, the book in question, Ameur Nour ben si Lounis and Moka Messaoud ben Yahia's *Grammaire mozabite*, which was published in Algiers in 1897 by Baldachino-Laronde-Viguier, bears no indication of Jacquot's purported collaboration.

35. Francoeur, "Billet de la semaine," *La Revue algérienne illustrée* 15, no. 8 (1893): 224.

36. Francoeur, "Billet de la semaine," 224.

37. Francoeur, "Billet de la semaine," 224.

38. Ernest Mallebay, "Bou-Yabès," *La Revue algérienne illustrée* 28, no. 15 (1897): 458.

39. This ambiguity regarding the role of Bou-Yabès with respect to his literary work has its counterpart in the texts themselves, in which the narrator's cultural position is equally fluid. As Ouahmi Ould-Braham, the editor of the only contemporary edition of Bou-Yabès's stories, notes: "On ne sait trop parfois si l'auteur se place réellement dans cette 'communauté' ou s'il porte un regard extérieur mêlé de réactions critiques de volonté de comprendre ce peuple, son esprit et sa nature" (in Bou-Yabès, *Récits et légendes de la grand Kabylie* [Paris: La Boîte à Documents, 1993], 26. Ould-Braham, somewhat simplistically, contends that this authorial and narrative disposition heightens the effect of Bou-Yabès's stories by fusing a personal voice with a universal language.

40. Daniel Grévoz, *Sahara 1830–1881; les mirages français et la tragédie Flatters* (Paris: L'Harmattan, 1989), 10.

41. Ali ben el Messaï, "Chez les Touareg," *La Revue algérienne illustrée* 19, no. 5 (1894): 163, emphasis added.

42. ben el Messaï, "Chez les Touareg," 19, no. 10 (1894): 329.

43. ben el Messaï, "Chez les Touareg," 19, no. 11 (1894): 355.

44. ben el Messaï, "Chez les Touareg," 20, no. 2 (1894): 60.

45. ben el Messaï, "Chez les Touareg," 20, no. 1 (1894): 27.

46. ben el Messaï, "Chez les Touareg," 20, no. 3 (1894): 91.

47. ben el Messaï, "Chez les Touareg," 20, no. 3 (1894): 91.

48. It is interesting to note that, though it appears in *La Revue algérienne illustrée*'s tables of contents with the series title, the name Ali ben el Messaï frequently does not appear at the end of each installment, as is the case with the names of the journal's other contributors. In addition, Ali ben el Messaï's name never appears on the journal's front cover as a principal contributor. Finally, at the end of the last installment of "Chez les Touareg," the narrator concludes by stating: "En ce qui me concerne, j'étais né pour les pérégrinations lointaines, dangereuses et tourmentées, car à peine étais-je de retour du Soudan que je m'embarquai pour le Tonkin, d'où je suis, comme tu vois, revenu sain et sauf. Qu'Allah soit loué." (Ali ben el Messaï, "Chez les Touareg," *La Revue algérienne illustrée*, 20, no. 10: 310.) The parenthetical addendum "(à suivre)" suggests that the further adventures of the narrator in another colonial venue are to follow, but the name Ali ben el Messaï never again appears in the pages of *La Revue algérienne illustrée*.

49. In the wake of the *Mission Flatters* massacre, metropolitan and colonial rhetoric advocating the push for a trans-Saharan railroad waned until the mid-1890s, when calls were made for a renewed effort in order to bring the Touareg Hoggar under more complete French control. Renewed interest in the popular press in the *Mission Flatters* even spawned rumours, apparently attributable to a military interpreter, that Flatters and his fellow Frenchmen were in fact still alive as prisoners of the Touareg somewhere in the southern Sahara. It is, therefore, entirely possible that "Chez les Touareg" in *La Revue algérienne illustrée* is one of the products of the debate on the appropriate form for French expansionism of the late nineteenth century.

50. Robert Randau, "La Littérature dans l'Afrique du nord," *Les Belles lettres* 2 (1920): 365.

51. Homi Bhabha, *The Location of Culture* (London: Routledge, 1994), 85.

52. Leonard R. Koos, "Between Two Worlds: Constructing Colonialist Identity in Turn-of-the-Century Algeria," *French Literature Series* 26 (1999): 105.

3

The Closure and Opening of Domestic Space in *Ombre Sultane* by Assia Djebar

Philippe Barbé

Muslim sexuality is territorial: its regulatory mechanisms consist primarily in a strict allocation of space to each sex and an elaborate ritual for resolving the contradictions arising from the inevitable intersections of spaces. Apart from the ritualized trespasses of women into public spaces (which are, by definition, male spaces), there are no accepted patterns for interactions between unrelated men and women. Such interactions violate the spatial rules that are the pillars of the Muslim sexual order.[1]

The Gender Division of Islamic Social Space

IN HIS INFLUENTIAL ESSAY "Des espaces autres," Michel Foucault noted that, under the influence of structuralist theory, the nineteenth-century obsession with history has been partially transformed into a historical questioning of spatialization:

La grande hantise qui a obsédé le XIXième siècle a été, on le sait, l'histoire: thèmes du développement et de l'arrêt, thèmes de la crise et du cycle, thèmes de l'accumulation du passé, grande surcharge des morts, refroidissement menaçant du monde. C'est dans le second principe de thermodynamique que le XIXième siècle a trouvé l'essentiel de ses ressources mythologiques. L'époque actuelle serait peut-être plutôt l'époque de l'espace. Nous sommes à l'époque de la simultanéité, nous sommes à l'époque de la juxtaposition, à l'époque du proche et du lointain, du côte à côte, du dispersé.[2]

This reassertion of space continues to shape the major trends in contemporary thought. From the French renewal of Marxism initiated by Lefebvre and Althusser to the most recent postmodern and post-colonial theories, discourses of critical social theory rely increasingly on an expanding web of interconnected sociospatial figures and concepts.[3] Questions of "center versus margins," "social and cognitive mapping" or "politics of location and subject positioning" cross many disciplinary boundaries and are radically reshaping the contemporary intellectual landscape. Strongly influenced by this renewed Marxist and postmodern interest in human geography, the most recent feminist and post-colonial theories have also benefited greatly from this theoretical turn to space. As emphasized by Kathleen M. Kirby in her book *Indifferent*

Boundaries, this new emphasis on the geographical imagination allows feminist thinkers and writers to deconstruct and ultimately subvert the traditional hierarchy that submits private and feminine spaces to the penetrating force of public and masculine spaces.[4]

As Fatima Mernissi explains in her work *Beyond the Veil*, it is impossible to understand the sociality of the Muslim world without first taking into consideration its roots within a strict spatialisation of sexuality. Largely inspired by the comprehensive sociology of Max Weber, F. Mernissi deconstructs the imaginary, social structures of the Muslim world through a spatial and sexual dichotomy. According to Mernissi the masculine universe corresponds to the public sphere, the *Umma*. The principles that regulate this masculine domain are equality, reciprocity, confidence and unity in the aggregation of individuals. In clear opposition to this public *Umma*, one finds the private, feminine sphere. In this domestic space to which women find themselves confined, the principal social rules correspond to an inverted model of the *Umma*. Thus, the private sphere is regulated by the principles of inequality, segregation, subordination and mistrust.

Mernissi is inspired by Max Weber and his *Theory of Social and Economic Organization* above all because the Weberian sociology was one of the first to show that societies were built as much around a harmonious principle of social contract (i.e., *Gemeinschaft*) as around a conflictual principle of social tension (i.e., *Gesellschaft*). As Raymond Aron recalls in his work *Les Étapes de la Pensée Sociologique*, "les sociétés ne sont pas, comme certains sociologues sont enclins à le croire, un ensemble harmonieux. Auguste Comte insistait sur l'idée de consensus et disait que les sociétés sont composées d'autant de morts que de vivants. Pour Max Weber, les sociétés sont faites autant de luttes que d'accords. Le combat est un rapport social fondamental."[5] In order to preserve this strict separation between the public and the private spheres, women historically found themselves sequestered behind the high walls of the harem. If the Western imagination most often describes the harem in terms of polygamy, Fatima Mernissi demonstrates that, in fact, the *raison d'être* of the harem is the confinement of women. At the heart of Muslim social order, the first function of the harem is therefore to preserve the integrity of the sexual hierarchy that structures the totality of the Muslim social space.

As Fatima Mernissi explains in the introduction to her work *Dreams of Trespass*, the cohesion of Muslim societies around the harem is embedded in the very foundations of Islamic thought. One of the cornerstones of Muslim social organization is the notion of *hudud*, in other words the "sacred frontier" that separates both men and women as well as Christians and Muslims. The first mission of a Muslim is to respect and, especially, to protect this sacred frontier, the only guarantee of social harmony. Thus, the Muslim order can be negatively defined in relation to two potential enemies who have the power to transgress these sacred boundaries of Islam. These two enemies are women and Westerners. Due to their expansionism, Westerners represent, in the eyes of Muslims, a threat because they have historically sought to conquer this sacred Islamic space. On the other hand, the desire of Muslim women to leave the closed, private space of the harem represents a potential challenge to the same Muslim social order. Deeply rooted in Islamic culture, this belief in the absolute authority of the *hudud* is potentially dangerous because it creates an enemy at the very heart of the Muslim community. By identifying the feminine with the foreign threat in this way, Muslim fundamentalism can only reject all feminine aspirations to contest this sociospatial order. Such a transgression of the clear boundary separating the public space of the street and the private space of the harem would represent one of the most serious crimes against the social cohesion of the Islamic world: "When Allah created the earth, said Father, he separated men from women, and put a sea between Muslims and Christians for a reason. Harmony exists when each group respects the prescribed limits of the other; trespassing leads only to sorrow and unhappiness."[6] An analysis of Djebar's novel *Ombre sultane* shows that her depiction of feminine, domestic spaces allows the reader to identify most of the characteristics revealed by Fatima Mernissi in her sociological reading of the harem.

Ombre sultane is a central work because Djebar is not content to illustrate and to denounce the captivity of Muslim women. Rather, the novel demonstrates a series of tactics that can be used by captive women in their quest for emancipation. Following Hajila's path, this study will examine the different phases that captive women might go through as they move toward emancipation.

Topo-Political Reading of the Closure of the Feminine Space in *Ombre sultane* by Assia Djebar

In her earlier works,[7] Assia Djebar places great emphasis on the denunciation of the harem as a morbid site of imprisonment of female bodies and spirits. Two years later, in *Ombre Sultane*, Assia Djebar describes the sociocultural impact of this confinement on contemporary Algerian women. While the narrative in *L'Amour, la fantasia* is constructed primarily around the story of "trois jeunes filles cloîtrées," *Ombre sultane* introduces two new female characters, Isma and Hajila, who both live in contrasting relationships to the Algerian social space. Although they share the same husband, their existences are nonetheless diametrically opposed. Isma, the narrator, is a free woman She is not subject to the authority of her husband and therefore has the freedom to wander in the city outside the conjugal domicile. Conversely, the character of Hajila, as described by the emancipated Isma, is a passive, imprisoned and voiceless woman. Although everything seems to separate these two spouses, Isma secretly dreams of a shared childhood spent in the company of this other wife who could have been her rival. Hajila ultimately becomes an imaginary sister in the eyes of Isma.

As in the majority of her novels, Djebar begins *Ombre sultane* by situating a character in a key space that will remain central to the rest of the novel. The first character described is Hajila and "le lieu du mélodrame" is the kitchen.[8] Enclosed in her house, Hajila comes and goes. She sadly circulates from room to room. Like a butterfly attracted to the external light, finally alone in her fortress, Hajila is irresistibly attracted to the closed shutter. However, this movement toward the outside is stopped when her hand "cogne à la vitre."[9] Isolated in her room, the smallest room in the home, her only contact with the outside world is imaginary. Unable to leave this closed space, she more or less succeeds in mobilizing her senses. She manages to hear and feel what passes outside her apartment. In order to better emphasize Hajila's sequestration, Djebar alternates descriptions of Hajila, the recluse, and Isma, the emancipated woman. Isma represents all that Hajila cannot be, in other words, a woman with freedom of movement. By contrast with Hajila, who lives closed up in her apartment, Isma is a free woman. As in all of Djebar's texts, this liberty is materialized by the freedom to drift, the freedom to stroll in a large, unknown city.[10]

While Hajila's apartment is closed in on itself, Isma introduces her own place of residence by insisting on its openness and its proximity to the external world, which literally comes to penetrate the private space: "La porte demeure ouverte."[11] In this home without curtains, space penetrates the room shared by the married couple and metamorphoses the bodies nestled under the light. "Traversant la vitre nue, la lumière nous inonde de ses nappes inépuisables."[12] The most closed places, like a bedroom, a hallway, or a closet, open onto an infinite space: "L'espace se courbe."[13] Just like the entwined bodies, the walls of the bedroom vibrate from this contact with the torments outside: "Le vent isole notre chambre. Les murs s'allongent."[14] To paraphrase the title of another work by Djebar, one could say that the woman is in prison, but that this prison is ultimately "vast." Consequently, Isma's marital home displays all of the qualities that Hajila can only imagine in the forbidden outside space. In order to show the openness that characterizes Isma's domestic space, Djebar speaks of "la ruelle du lit."[15] The apartment strangely becomes an infinite place of wandering, a place that Isma and her partner will never completely succeed in mastering.

While Hajila still has to fight to gain access to the outside world that she secretly desires, Isma lives with all her senses in perfect harmony with her surroundings. This polysensoriality enables her to connect with the body of the masculine other on a closed and private territory that then becomes a place of love and intense sensuality. While the sequestered Hajila still has to conquer this forbidden outside space and slowly learn to map it, the emancipated Isma embarks on an inner search for the body of the other, as well as for its cartography. Isma literally travels through the body of her lover as she would going on a voyage of discovery to an unknown territory:

Chaque nuit, j'affine la connaissance de l'autre par degrés imperceptibles—éprouver le creux de son cou, la confiance de ses épaules, tâter d'un doigt qui prend son temps toutes ses côtes, percevoir les battements de son coeur tout en levant les paupières vers son visage; retrouver sous ma paume, qui glisse contre son aine, puis son ventre, le rapport connu des jambes avec les hanches; retracer la forme du crâne, le considérer d'un oeil scientifique avec des mains d'archéologue. Mes caresses deviennent gestes d'arpenteur.[16]

Polysensoriality and Hajila's Mental Projection Outside Her Domestic Space

Ombre sultane is a central text in Djebar's work because it offers more than a predictable denunciation of women's entrapment in the harem. As revealed by Hajila's trajectory, it is possible for a secluded woman to escape her imprisonment. It is indeed when Hajila's confinement is most restrictive that she develops a series of tactics of resistance or compensation. Trapped in her marital home, Hajila first gains mental access to the forbidden outside world dominated by men. Like a blind person who is forced to rely on her other senses, Hajila secretly develops her polysensoriality without leaving the walls of the harem. Despite her husband's desire to totally close her domestic space, Hajila develops skills that help her to stay in touch with the outside world. Even if she does not manage to physically leave the harem, she can partially compensate for her isolation by developing her five senses. Hajila's sensory opening to her surroundings corresponds with the dialectics of penetration between the inside and the outside as described by Bachelard in his work *La Poétique de l'espace*. Hajila's marital home is indeed a closed space that can nonetheless be partially decompartmentalised. Of the five senses, sight plays a dominant role in her sensory emancipation. Before asserting herself as a "femme-voix," , Hajila must become a "femme-regard."[17] To fully understand the importance of the gaze, one must remember that the original function of the harem is to isolate women by making them both blind and invisible. By discovering the power of sight, the female recluse enacts a first symbolic exit from the harem.

As early as 1980, with the publication of *Femmes d'Alger dans leur appartement*, Djebar accorded the gaze a central role in the feminine transgression of the boundary arbitrarily separating the inside from the outside. In effect, it is in the pages designed to describe the most rigid closing of the harem that Djebar gives her readers the richest description of the outside world.

Even if the women cannot exit from the harem, the odors and noises of the city, and especially the natural light still penetrate inside their homes. Opposing first the luminous and bellicose virility of the outside to the obscure and silent passivity of the inside, Djebar attempts to understand why the famous painting by Delacroix remains one of the few attempts to challenge this strict dichotomy between the feminine inside and the masculine outside. Due to the precision of his brushstrokes and the striking luminosity of his colors, Delacroix exposed the feminine side of the Orient under the natural light of day for the first time. Although the women remain silent and resigned, the penetrating rays of the sun facilitate their reconnection to the very site of their entrapment: "Tout le sens du tableau se joue dans le rapport qu'entretiennent celles-ci avec leur corps, ainsi qu'avec le lieu de leur enfermement. Prisonnières résignées d'un lieu clos qui s'éclaire d'une sorte de lumière de rêve venue de nulle part—lumière de serre ou d'aquarium—le génie de Delacroix nous les rend à la fois présentes et lointaines, énigmatiques au plus haut point."[18]

The power to capture the exterior light also plays a fundamental role in *Ombre sultane*. The character of Isma recounts a story that took place within her own family more than twenty years previously. When one of the uncles controlling the house made the decision to cover the patio with a large glass roof, the women of the harem united for the first time in order to jointly oppose the project. This helps Isma to understand that for these recluses the construction of such a roof would have deprived them of the little blue sky that they could still see: "Deux décennies plus tard, l'amertume de ces femmes m'atteint enfin. Est-ce dans cette clairière que, retrouvant gestes et paix séculaires, elles se quêtent désespérément? Le lieu n'est pas tout à fait clos, le patio ruisselle de lumière."[19] To emphasize the topology of feminine resistance revealed in this patio episode, this essay will borrow from Michel Foucault's definition of heterotopia in "Des Espaces Autres."[20] Foucault establishes a central distinction between utopia and heterotopia. While utopia is a place without any real location, heterotopia is a real site that functions like a counter-location, a place in which "tous les autres emplacements réels sont à la fois représentés, contestés et inversés."[21]

The patio described by Djebar in chapter XII of *Ombre sultane* shares the same function as Foucault's heterotopia. If the patio functioned for Isma's ancestors as a counter-location that enabled them to compensate for their imprisonment, the uncles who controlled the household only saw in this interior court a space void of all social life, a simple extension of the harem and its rules. In his essay "Espaces humides féminins dans la ville," Traki Bouchrara Zannad describes the same discrepancy in the way that men and women perceive the patio. The men who live on the perimeter of the central court only see it as a zone of transit that strongly resembles the non-place described by Marc Augé in his book *Non-Lieux: introduction à une anthropologie de la surmodernité*. By contrast, the women transform this empty space into a lively, social site:

> Les pièces sont toutes orientées vers le patio, seul point de lumière et d'aération. L'espace de ces pièces est l'espace de l'homme: il s'y restaure, il y dort, procrée, prie ou veille, puis se retire. Le *west eddar* constitue pour lui "exclusivement" un lieu de passage. Ainsi, l'espace périphérique est un espace masculin, extérieur au territoire de la femme. Et le west eddar, vide, disponible, est appréhendé par la femme comme son espace propre et, paradoxalement, le plus intime.
>
> Les activités périphériques situées au niveau de ces pièces se trouvent incluses dans l'espace et le volume du périmètre qui entourent west eddar: sommeil, sexualité, relâchement et détente. Ainsi, les pratiques centripètes se déroulent dans l'humidité et sont actives, alors que les pratiques périphériques se déroulent dans le sec, et sont de repos. Il en résulte une relation dialectique entre les pratiques féminines à caractère centripète et les pratiques masculines à caractère périphérique: entre le sec et l'humide, entre la ligne droite et la ligne courbe.[22]

In her account of the patio of her childhood, Isma remembers the liveliness and sociability of this central feminine space. "Patios de mon enfance! Me hante le trajet de connivences dont ces lieux de rassemblement quotidien étaient le coeur."[23] This house, where many generations of women remained imprisoned, is paradoxically perceived by the young Isma as a vast and open territory, "comme si la maison devenait la ville entière."[24]

Despite its importance, this sensory emancipation only offers the recluses a mental decompartmentalisation. In order to gain total freedom, they must also succeed in physically projecting themselves outside of the harem. Such a passage is made partially possible when the secluded women appropriate a series of border locations inside the household, such as a portal, a garden or a balcony that enable them to come dangerously close to the forbidden outside.

The character of Hajila is indisputably one of the most symbolic figures of feminine resistance to imprisonment in Djebar's works. Indeed, Hajila's story reveals that captivity is never absolute. It is possible to isolate two episodes in which Hajila physically accesses two of these heterotopic places that help her to approach the outside world without openly challenging the social order that regulates her captivity. These two locations are the balcony and the car.

The first episode describes a visit, in the company of her mother, to an apartment which she is about to move into with her husband and his children. Because the apartment is situated on the 7th floor, Hajila is first struck by its brightness and the majestic view overlooking the city. Conditioned by their common history as recluses, at first Hajila and her mother "Touma la vieille" do not dare to approach any of the windows: "Devant, Touma la vieille prend l'initiative de l'inspection et toi, Hajila, tu suis docilement. Ni l'une ni l'autre, vous ne vous êtes approchées des fenêtres."[25] After some hesitation, Hajila succumbs to the irresistible call of the exterior. She courageously moves away from her mother, leaves the center of the kitchen and ventures out, prudently at first, onto the balcony. It is with immense emotion that she discovers the spectacle of an open city, a city that seems for the first time to offer itself without resistance. Hajila has learned to develop her auditory skills in the harem, and her presence on the balcony now allows her to sharpen her visual acuteness:

> Durant cette première visite et après avoir toutes deux tourné au centre de la cuisine, tu t'étais aventurée sur le balcon. Le panorama te laissa émerveillée, par ses contrastes de lumière, surtout par l'exubérance des couleurs, comme sur le point pourtant de s'évaporer sous le ciel immuable: sur le côté, un lambeau de mer presque violette, puis une étendue zébrée de taches de verdure sombre séparant les terrasses des maisonnettes blanchies de neuf; au fond, un minaret aux briques roses rutilait d'ampoules multicolores.
>
> Derrière, Touma poursuivait ses commentaires. Le concierge, revenu, actionnait pour la deuxième fois la cloison de verre. Toi, tu fixais toujours le paysage, les yeux aveuglés par cet éclat du jour inaltéré. Pour la première fois dominer la ville, ne plus se sentir un grain de poussière dans un des cachots du monde.[26]

A few days after this episode on the balcony, Hajila has the opportunity for a second escape, a "seconde échappée."[27] This time her husband drives her to her family home in a slum located on the outskirts of the city. Like the scene on the balcony, this journey by car plays a key role in Hajila's future decision to transgress the law of the *hudud* and to venture out into the forbidden streets. Once again, this partial contact with the exterior world, which runs past before her eyes, is a spectacle of such sensory intensity that Hajila nearly collapses and has to close her eyes: "Tu regardes. Tu tournes la tête vers la vitre du fond. Les paysages—immeubles blancs, terrasses découvertes sur des tranches d'azur métallique—reculent inexorablement. Cela te donne une sorte de vertige. Tu fermes les yeux."[28] When she finally reopens her eyes, Hajila catches a glimpse of a Muslim mother playing with her child in the town square. With envy, Hajila repeats to herself: "sans voiles, dehors, en train d'aimer son enfant!"[29] Back in her apartment, Hajila is unable to return quietly to her everyday routines. While she continues with her domestic tasks, she cannot erase the journeys through the city from her memory. She finally falls asleep promising to go outside again on her own the following day: "L'esprit envahi par le souvenir du square, tu te découvres une certitude: "Demain, une seconde fois!"[30]

In summary, Hajila begins on the road to emancipation after two major steps. Firstly, she has developed her sensorial skills, projecting herself mentally outside the confinement of her home. Secondly, she has had the opportunity to access a number of border zones, and this has allowed her to get physically closer to the outside. Nonetheless, developing her sensorial acuteness and gaining access to compensatory micro-places are not sufficient. To be truly emancipated, Hajila must be able to freely leave her apartment. She has to find her way out.

Hajila's Final Emancipation through Total Physical Access to the Outside World

After adjusting her senses to her place of captivity and then having traveled in her husband's car after going onto the balcony of her future apartment, Hajila makes the courageous decision to go out on her own. She has never developed her sense of direction and feels totally lost in the spacious city during her first outings. Unable to find her way back home, at the end of the day she is forced to ask passersby to guide her. Nevertheless, Hajila slowly compensates for her disorientation by learning to walk and position her awkward body in the surrounding city. Like an explorer conquering a new world, Hajila creates her own cognitive map of the city: "Chaque jour donc, tu t'échappes. Tu apprends à connaître les squares, les places de ce quartier. Pour te diriger, tu te rappelles la veille, l'avant-veille, ainsi de suite. . . . Dehors, tu ne te lasses pas de marcher; tu apprends à découvrir. Choses et personnes se diluent en taches à peine colorées. Un vide se creuse où ton corps peut passer, sans rien déranger."[31]

At first, her encounter with the lively streets is unbearable. Overwhelmed by the intensity of the city, Hajila shuts herself off from these sensorial delights, which she had only been able to imagine during her captivity. The urban noises physically hurt her, the odors envelop and assail her body. "L'exubérance des parfums t'agresse. . . . Une profusion de senteurs, douces ou acides, t'enveloppe, te retient."[32] After only a week of exploring the outside world, Hajila's senses adapt to this new environment, allowing her to become more receptive to her surroundings. "Dehors, les sons en particulier commencent à t'atteindre."[33] Her daily adventures start to shape her new existence. Hajila no longer considers herself as a recluse, but rather as a *woman who goes out.* "Après une semaine ou davantage, te voici devenue 'une femme qui sort.' Quand tu rentres, chaque fin d'après-midi, une sensation de durée s'étire en toi."[34] The spatialisation and movement of her body help her to gain full consciousness of her emancipated self. Hajila patiently constructs a new identity. In the plenitude of her senses, she discovers an image of herself and awakens as a Subject. Walking freely in the city gives Hajila the intimate intuition that she truly exists and has a story, a history. "Le soir, les jambes lourdes, le coeur submergé par la rumeur extérieure, tu te dis que tu as une histoire."[35]

> Tu mets le *haïk* sous le bras: tu avances. Tu t'étonnes de te voir marcher d'emblée d'un pas délié sur la scène du monde![36]
>
> Tu te vois marcher sous le regard de la fille voilée.[37]
>
> Dehors, tu es; ne le savent-ils pas? Le souvenir de la femme qui riait te revient. Tu pourrais t'entendre, à ton tour t'exclamer, ou chanter, pourquoi pas. . . .[38]

Each excursion into the open, forbidden city renders more painful her return to the apartment. In order to ease her suffering, Hajila tries to preserve the sensations of the outside world for as long as possible in the confinement of her house: "Tu rentres le soir; tu constates que le soleil est tombé derrière la baie du salon restée ouverte. *Tu reviens sonore.*"[39] Her nostalgia for the city is so strong that she spends most of her days trying to recreate the outside world that she unwillingly leaves behind her. In the privacy of her bathroom, facing the reflection of her naked body, Hajila reconnects with the lost city and its anonymous crowd: "Les autres continuent à défiler là-bas; tu les ressuscites dans l'eau du miroir pour qu'ils fassent cortège à la femme vraiment nue, à Hajila nouvelle qui froidement te dévisage."[40] Hajila miserably wanders from room to room like a caged animal waiting for her next outing. Her desire for the outside world is so powerful that she wonders if she could make the rooms seem larger by removing the furniture: "Si l'on enlevait les meubles, l'espace s'agrandirait";[41] "Les murs semblent trop proches, les meubles encombrent. Un désir incoercible te prend d'effacer le contour des choses."[42] The very thought that she will no longer be able to escape terrorizes Hajila: "Si le jour ne revenait plus, si, plus jamais, tu ne te retrouvais au-dehors, si tu ne devais plus jamais marcher en pleine lumière, si. . . ."[43] Contaminated by the vivid images of the city, Hajila struggles to return to her daily chores. Each domestic gesture is erased by a pervasive memory of the outside. Her whole domestic life is directed toward a single moment: when she completes her morning duties and waits for her husband to leave, the sign that she can finally escape. Before her daily outings, Hajila had liked to spend hours indoors listening to the radio or standing by the window. Now, these activities are unbearable. The memory of life on the street is so overwhelming that Hajila meticulously avoids the windows of her apartment, which will only make her all-consuming passion for the outside flare up:

> De la blancheur du matin, alors que les quatre personnes de la maison commencent à s'épier, tu t'extraies: vite, que le début du jour meure, vite qu'arrive, après le déjeuner, le moment où tu pourras sortir! Jusque-là, tu évites les fenêtres.[44]
>
> Auparavant tu restais allongée dans la chambre des enfants. Le poste de radio déversait de la musique folklorique arabe ou berbère selon les jours. Ces derniers temps, tu ne l'allumes plus. Quand tu ne sors pas, tu préfères laisser parvenir jusqu'à toi la rumeur du dehors.[45]

Hajila becomes increasingly resistant to the reprimands of her husband and the needs of her children. Next, Djebar describes a scene in which Hajila is raped by her husband. The brutal penetration of her body only exacerbates her latent desire for the outside world. While her husband soils her womb, images of crowded streets unfold in her mind:

> Rappelle-toi les rues, elles s'allongent en toi dans un soleil qui a dissous les nuées; les murs s'ouvrent: arbres et haies glissent. Tu revois l'espace au-dehors où chaque jour tu navigues. Quand le phallus de l'homme te déchire, épée rapide, tu hurles dans le silence, dans ton silence: 'non! . . . non!' Tu te bats, il te fouaille, tu tentes de revenir à la surface. 'Laisse-toi faire!' susurre la voix à ta tempe. La déchirure s'étend, les rues déroulées en toi défilent, les ombres des passants reviennent et te dévisagent, chaînes d'inconnus aux yeux globuleux. . . . Dehors est un autre pays.[46]

If Hajila has managed to trespass the sacred frontier that separates her domestic space from the public sphere, it is primarily because she uses a veil. Unfortunately perceived in the West as a pure symbol of women's alienation under the Islamic order, the veil can be diverted from its official function by a woman seeking emancipation. The tactical complexity of the veil, *hijab* in Arabic, can be partially explained by its polysemy. In *Le Harem politique*, F. Mernissi notes that the concept of *hijab* is three-dimensional.[47] The first meaning is dominated by a strong visual dimension. The word *hijab* is in fact derived from the verb *hajaba*, which means "to hide." The veil's function is therefore to conceal women from the masculine gaze. The second dimension is more strictly spatial: As discussed above in relation to the *hudud*, the "sacred frontier," the veil imposes a boundary that separates men from women. Finally, the third and last dimension is more strictly ethical. The veil signals what is supposed to remain forbidden and inaccessible. If the meaning of the *hijab* is three-dimensional, it is also necessary to understand its function through history. As revealed by its etymology, the use of the *hijab* has varied according to its historical context. In Arabic, *hijab* means both "curtain" and "veil." As F. Mernissi recalls, the first *hijab* mentioned in the Koran was in fact a curtain. It is only later that, under the pressure of fundamentalism, the notion of the veil became dominant in Islamic culture. It is therefore important to keep in mind that the original function of the *hijab* was not to isolate women from the outside world. On the contrary, it served to protect the couple's intimacy from the gaze of other men. It was indeed to preserve the private life of the married couple that the prophet Muhammad used the curtain for the first time. After he had just married the young Zaynab, Muhammad could not stand the presence of his faithful disciples in his residence. Wishing to maintain the intimacy of his wedding night without having to ask his guests to leave, the prophet adopted a compromise solution: he pulled down the curtain in the entrance of his nuptial chamber. The curtain therefore went down, not to put a barrier between men and women, but rather to separate a married man from his brothers: "Réduire ou assimiler ce concept à un morceau de chiffon que les hommes ont imposé aux femmes pour se voiler lorsqu'elles marchent dans la rue, c'est vraiment appauvrir ce terme, pour ne pas dire le vider de son sens, surtout lorsqu'on sait que le Hijab, d'après le verset du Qoran et l'explication de Tabari donnée ci-dessus, est 'descendu' du ciel pour séparer deux hommes."[48] While the *hijab* evolved against the will of the prophet into a means of controlling Muslim women, it is important to note that the veil is now sometimes used by women as a practical tool of emancipation. If the veil has been historically used and abused to control Muslim women, the very same veil may help them to escape from their submission.

As noticed by Assia Djebar in *Femmes d'Alger dans leur appartement*, the only free women in the modern city are in fact the veiled cleaning ladies who leave their homes early in the morning to go to work. As a symbol of submission and captivity, the veil can be transformed into an emancipatory object once it is worn outside: "les femmes voilées sont d'abord des femmes libres de circuler, plus avantagées donc que des femmes entièrement recluses, celles-ci général les épouses des plus riches."[49]

This elaborate tactical use of the veil plays a particularly important role in Hajila's emancipation. Conceived first as a way to extend her captivity into the outside world, the texture of the veil (its lightness, its fluidity, its volatility) allows Hajila to leave her apartment without openly challenging her membership of the domestic space of the harem. Paradoxically, the imposition of the veil liberates Hajila by permitting her to cross the threshold of her home: "Tu vas 'sortir' pour la première fois, Hajila. Tu portes tes babouches de vieille, la laine pèse sur ta tête; dans ton visage entièrement masqué, un seul oeil est découvert, la trouée juste nécessaire pour que ce regard d'ensevelie puisse te guider. Tu entres dans l'ascenseur, tu vas déboucher en pleine rue, le corps empêtré dans les plis du voile lourd. Seule, au-dehors, tu marcheras."[50] The veil also allows Hajila to go out without being recognized. Since she conceals her face behind the veil, Hajila cannot be seen and will therefore remain unidentified. If the veil enables her to be anonymous, the slit at eye level permits her to watch the outside world with complete impunity. The more comfortable Hajila feels during her daily outings, the more likely her hand is to release its pressure, thereby letting go of the veil: "Le coeur se met à battre sous le tissu de laine, la main soudain mollit, serre moins nerveusement le voile sous le menton. Pouvoir lâcher le bord du drap, regarder, le visage à découvert, et même renverser la tête vers le ciel, comme à dix ans!"[51]

Hajila is well aware that her husband might beat her if he discovered that she ventured out freely into the city. Nonetheless, she finds comfort in the idea that he cannot take away the excitement she gains from the outside world. "L'homme ne peut rien! Surtout pas te dépouiller des frémissements du dehors, des moissons de ton errance."[52] After several months of secret outings, her worst fears come true. On her way back from one of her daily strolls, she finds her husband on the steps of their apartment. When he questions her, Hajila confesses that she has enjoyed walking through the city streets "naked," in other words, unveiled. The word "naked" enrages Hajila's husband, who threatens to blind her with a piece of broken bottle: "je t'aveuglerai pour que tu ne voies pas! pour qu'on ne te voie pas!"[53] This assault is the last one Hajila has to endure. Courageously, she now decides to leave her husband's house for ever. Hajila's fate proves that captivity is neither absolute nor permanent. Though she can finally go out unveiled, her newly gained freedom also obliges her to face the next challenge in her life. This is therefore the beginning of a long and uncertain journey for Hajila, who aimlessly strolls on one final excursion without any possibility of return:

> Tu t'es élancée trop avidement, personne ne t'a mise en garde contre le soleil. Il aurait été si facile d'esquisser une parade. Un retrait rapide, un retour temporaire au harem. Dehors, tu te découvres tatouée. Tu ne peux pleurer; tu regrettes le douceâtre relâchement des larmes. Mais le désir du monde t'éperonnant soudain, tu t'arraches à la chambre, tu sors. Tandis que tu marches au hasard, hésitante, enfin les yeux libres, tu regardes.[54]

Notes

1. Fatima Mernissi, *Beyond the Veil: Male-Female Dynamics in Modern Muslim Society* (Bloomington/ Indianapolis: Indiana University Press, 1987), 137.

2. Michel Foucault, "Des espaces autres" in *Dits et écrits—tome 4* (Paris: Gallimard, 1994), 752.

3. In his book *Postmodern Geographies* Edward Soja analyzes the various pivotal moments in this "reassertion of space in critical theory." While Marxist thought originally conveyed what Soja describes as "a deep tradition of anti-spatialism," the theoretical turn to space initiated by Henri Lefebvre in the 1960s opened the door to new fields (or *terrains*) of social inquiry largely based upon geographical and spatial imaginations. The impact of this spatial problematic goes beyond a single influence on Western Marxism and Marxist geography. As Edward Soja demonstrates, this spatial inquiry creates a series of epistemological passages between Marxist, poststructuralist, postmodern and, more recently, post-colonial theories. The current research led by Fredric Jameson, David Harvey or Derek Gregory are very good examples of the importance of spatial metaphors as a common ground for various and interdisciplinary cultural studies.

4. Kathleen M. Kirby, *Indifferent Boundaries: Spatial Concepts of Human Subjectivity* (New York and London: The Guilford Press, 1996), 9; Alison Blunt and Gillian Rose, *Writing Women and Space: Colonial and Postcolonial Geographies* (New York and London: The Guilford Press, 1994), 1–25; Chandra Talpade Mohanty, "Cartographies of Struggle: Third World Women and the Politics of Feminism," in *Third World Women and the Politics of Feminism,* ed. Chandra Talpade Mohanty (Bloomington: Indiana University Press, 1991), 1–47; Chandra Talpade Mohanty, "Feminist Encounters: Locating the Politics of Experience," in *Copyright* 1, (1987): 30–44; Adrienne Rich, *"Notes toward a Politics of Location,"* in *Blood, Bread, and Poetry: Selected Prose 1979–1985* (New York: Norton, 1986), 210–31.

5. Raymond Aron, *Les Etapes de la pensée sociologique* (Paris: Gallimard, 1967), 552.

6. Mernissi, *Dreams of Trespass, Tales of a Harem Girlhood* (Reading: Perseus Books, 1994), 1.

7. *Femmes d'Alger dans leur appartement* (1980), *L'Amour, la fantasia* (1985).

8. Assia Djebar, *Ombre sultane* (Paris: J. C. Lattès, 1987), 15.

9. Djebar, *Ombre*, 16.

10. Djebar, *Ombre*, 19.

11. Djebar, *Ombre*, 30.

12. Djebar, *Ombre*, 32.

13. Djebar, *Ombre*, 31.

14. Djebar, *Ombre*, 34.

15. Djebar, *Ombre*, 33.

16. Djebar, *Ombre*, 57.

17. Djebar, *Ombre*, 61.

18. Djebar, *Femmes d'Alger*, 148.

19. Djebar, *Ombre*, 88.

20. First published in 1984.

21. Michel Foucault, "Des espaces autres" in *Dits et écrit -tome 4* (Paris: Gallimard, 1994), 755.

22. Traki Bouchrara Zannad, "Espaces humides féminins dans la ville," in *Espaces Maghrébins; pratiques et enjeux. Actes du colloque de Taghit, 23–26 novembre 1987*, ed. Nadir Marouf (Oran: URASC/ENAG Éditions, 1989), 234–35.

23. Djebar, *Ombre*, 85.

24. Djebar, *Ombre*, 86.

25. Djebar, *Ombre*, 21.

26. Djebar, *Ombre*, 23.

27. Djebar, *Ombre*, 35.

28. Djebar, *Ombre*, 35.

29. Djebar, *Ombre*, 36.

30. Djebar, *Ombre*, 37.

31. Djebar, *Ombre*, 49.

32. Djebar, *Ombre*, 40.

33. Djebar, *Ombre*, 50.

34. Djebar, *Ombre*, 51.

35. Djebar, *Ombre*, 49.

36. Djebar, *Ombre*, 40.

37. Djebar, *Ombre*, 41.

38. Djebar, *Ombre*, 50.

39. Djebar, *Ombre*, 64.

40. Djebar, *Ombre*, 43.

41. Djebar, *Ombre*, 48.

42. Djebar, *Ombre*, 51.

43. Djebar, *Ombre*, 65.

44. Djebar, *Ombre*, 63.

45. Djebar, *Ombre*, 64.

46. Djebar, *Ombre*, 67.

47. Fatima Mernissi, *Le Harem politique: le prophète et les femmes* (Paris: Albin Michel, 1987), 119.

48. Mernissi, *Le Harem*, 122.

49. Djebar, *Femmes d'Alger*, 165.

50. Djebar, *Ombre*, 27.

51. Djebar, *Ombre*, 27.

52. Djebar, *Ombre*, 94.

53. Djebar, *Ombre*, 96.

54. Djebar, *Ombre*, 99.

4

The Interruptive Dynamics of History and Autobiography in *L'amour, la fantasia*

Dominique Licops

THE DUALISTIC MODEL OF MUCH POST-COLONIAL THEORY, literature and criticism, which opposes colonizer to colonized, has been questioned by many critics. Françoise Lionnet, for example, has argued that the analyses of the colonial situation by such thinkers as Aimé Césaire, Frantz Fanon and Albert Memmi "remained dependent upon a Hegelian view of the master-slave dialectic."[1] In the rest of her book, *Postcolonial Representations*, she analyses how post-colonial women writers undo the dichotomies on which this view is based and function within what she has called an economy of *métissage*. In particular, she argues that their writings promote the view that neither the dominated nor the dominant culture is a self-contained and homogenous entity, but that cultures are interdependent and have porous boundaries.[2]

Michel De Certeau, for his part, thinks of these two different views of culture in terms of either having a territory or not, and differentiates between the kinds of action available on this basis: if the person can capitalize on a territory of his or her own, he or she can resort to strategies, but if he or she can't, he or she will deploy other tactics.[3] De Certeau's distinction between strategy and tactic is worth explaining in further detail, since the parallels between Assia Djebar's writing as fantasia in her novel *L'Amour, la fantasia* and Gayatri Spivak's notion of intervention are clarified if they are thought of as "tactics." For De Certeau, a strategy is "le calcul des rapports de force qui devient possible à partir du moment où un sujet de vouloir et de pouvoir est *isolable d'un 'environement*,'" whereas he defines a tactic as "un calcul qui ne peut pas compter sur un propre, ni donc sur une frontière qui distingue l'autre comme une totalité visible. *La tactique n'a pour lieu que celui de l'autre*."[4] Strategies, then, imply the existence of well-defined boundaries, which go hand in hand with a model of resistance that partakes of the Hegelian model refuted by Françoise Lionnet. Tactics, on the other hand, are a type of action that takes place when no such boundaries exist, and implies a porosity that undermines the clear dichotomies on which the dualistic view of post-colonial cultures rests.

This chapter examines a theoretical critique by Spivak and a narrative critique by Djebar of the Manichean vision of colonialism that Fanon denounced but partly reproduced and that, according to Mireille Rosello, "empoisonne . . . souvent la grammaire de la représentation ainsi que la grille d'interprétation que nous apposons aux textes."[5] In a series of essays, Gayatri Spivak develops the notion of interventionist or interruptive practice in order to make clear how, even though post-colonial female subjects are, as she puts it, "imprisoned"[6] in dominant social texts such as capitalism, patriarchy, and neocolonialism, they can "rewrite the social text [of a tradition, a contemporary or historical situation of exploitation or unequal power relations] in an interventionist way."[7] The post-colonial female subject, to use De Certeau's terms, does not have a territory of her own: her actions are circumscribed within the territories of capitalism, patriarchy and neo-colonialism, but they are tactics that produce multiple small breaks and transformations of the laws of these dominant systems.[8] Spivak's notion of intervention thus offers an example of a theoretical critique of the Manichean model of (post)colonial cultures that is characteristic of earlier thinkers of de-colonization.

Assia Djebar also questions this model of culture and, more specifically, exposes the dualistic logic of colonialist and nationalist representations of history in her fifth novel *L'amour, la fantasia* (1985).[9] A brief overview of her oeuvre will introduce the problematic relationship of history and autobiography that dominates this novel. Between 1957 and 1967 Djebar wrote four novels, the first two focused on individualist themes, whereas the perspective of the latter two expanded into a social fresco.[10] Then came a silence of ten years. As she explains in her interview with Marguerite Le Clezio, she stopped when her writing came too close to autobiography, because she felt that such a writing in "the language of the enemy" was a dangerous enterprise.[11] Her cinematic experience played a crucial role in her return to writing. In an interview with Clarisse Zimra she commented on her film *La Nouba des femmes du Mont Chenoua* (1976–1977) and the importance of "the lengthy, unending, private conversations with the women of [her] own tribe."[12] Her second full-length feature, *Zerda*, taught her "that the new novel would have to encompass a double experience," that of the past and the present, that of the world of men and of women. *Nouba* helped her figure out how she could navigate between these two worlds: "I suddenly found my answer: I thought of the interwoven polyphony of all the women's voices in *Nouba*. They formed a chorus—a choir into which I wanted to plunge myself, but without completely dissolving, losing my own sense of self. I wanted to remain myself, yet become one of their voices. At that precise moment I discovered how to write my quartet: I had to reenter my own autobiography."[13] The narrator of *L'amour, la fantasia* dwells in and traverses at least two territories that are not her own: the language and history of the colonizer, on the one hand, and the world of the harem, on the other. Autobiography thus becomes a tactic that interrupts and rewrites the colonial history that erased the presence of the native and exoticized the native woman, and the national history of de-colonization that relegated the *mujahida* to the harem.

In Djebar's work historical rewriting is a complex process of interruption that avoids the replacement of one history by another. Her polyphonic interweaving of history and autobiography not only reveals the violence of colonialist and nationalist manipulations of history. It also highlights how histories, as well as personal and communal identities, are produced in relation to one another. Through an analysis of the structure of *L'amour, la fantasia* and the metaphors deployed to articulate the rapport between autobiography and multiple histories, this essay attempts to show how such a rewriting, in figuring the complex relations between the narrative subject and different histories, different spaces and different communities, offers a narrative performance of what Spivak calls an "interventionist practice." In this case, patriarchal colonial and nationalist histories appear as the territories in which the narrator is circumscribed. However, Djebar's rewriting interrupts them, and in so doing, exposes their laws and seeks to transform them.

Intervention: A Theoretical Critique of History as Counter-Narrative

In the history of Algeria colonialist and nationalist rhetoric resorted to a Manichean view of history and identity that violently negated a more complex reality in order to implement and justify certain power structures. The colonial subject defined itself against an other that it constructed as the negative image of itself (i.e., as inhuman or simply absent). For instance, Djebar's comment on archival cinematic images emphasizes how the colonizer's gaze negated the reality of the colonized population: "Reconstituer sur un écran quelques décennies d'un peuple colonisé, c'était faire sentir combien le réel, à chaque image, était *en marge*, comment tout, autrefois, à peine vu, *se vidait* de son sens. . . . En somme, ces images *cachaient* le passé, en proposant une sorte d'écran déformateur, illusoire. . . ."[14] Djebar's emphasis on the process of emptying and deformation foregrounds how the erasure of the native culture justified colonization. Benjamin Stora and Clarisse Zimra have shown how the revolutionary movement that threw off French domination in 1962 used a similar process of erasure and replacement in order to produce a common identity and so form a nation. Stora argues that the revolutionaries erased the traditions inherited from the French presence and resorted to Islam,[15] which, according to Zimra, "represented the fastest road to a common identity, a powerful counterweight against the Westernised modernisation imposed by the coloniser."[16] Before analyzing how Djebar's intertwinement of history and autobiography confronts the dualistic and sexist logic of colonialist and nationalist interpretations of history in *L'Amour*,[17] it is necessary to delineate two similarities between Spivak's notion of intervention and Djebar's rewriting of the histories that have shaped her position.

Spivak differentiates between a dualistic historical approach that "assigns a new subject-position to the subaltern" in a counter-narrative and a literary approach that seeks to "unrave[l] the text to make visible the assignment of subject-positions."[18] Spivak's concept of intervention is based on the Derridian conception of the world as text and a Marxist notion of group identity. In this view of the world as text, the subaltern, best described as subject-effect, is always produced relationally, that is, as different from something else. Spivak's model of subaltern identity derives from Marx's notion of class. The working class is not a positive identity, but a subject-effect produced by the play of economic and political interests. Spivak considers that a Derridian approach is the best way to read this reality, since it focuses on the erasures and silences of the text, that is, the suppressions and erasures that have made the constitution of a certain order possible.

More specifically, Spivak describes the text within which the subaltern is inscribed as a narrative of imprisonment that she can nevertheless interrupt. Although the notion of absolute alterity suggests a position that the dominant logic cannot comprehend, the instances of interruptive practice she discusses always stage a subaltern who is caught within a dominant logic, but can nevertheless produce fragmentary instances "against the inherent logic which animate[s] the development of the narrative [of imprisonment] and disarticulates it in a way that seems perverse."[19] For Spivak, then, the production of historical counter-narratives gives way to an interventionist practice intent on reading these fragmentary instances of interruption.

A first similarity is between Djebar's exposure of the erasure of the native population by the colonizer, and Spivak's argument that absolute alterity is occluded by the colonizer's production of a self-consolidating other. Djebar's description of how French painters and writers elide the presence of the native population to produce Algeria as a penetrable land and an interpretable text reveals that it was an act of epistemic violence that followed upon the literal massacre of rebellious tribes by *enfumades* (smoking out of the caves in which they were hiding). She makes this obvious by pointing out that Fromentin's perception of the Sahel as a land of emptiness and absence depends on its having been *vidée* by "une génération d'affrontements sanglants."[20] This description resonates with Spivak's critique of how the production of a self-consolidating other occludes absolute alterity, which she glosses as a "blank space circumscribed by an interpretable text." Djebar juxtaposes these literal and epistemic acts of colonial violence to the patriarchal violence of Algerian society described in terms of women's *enfouissement, ensevelissement* and asphyxia, by linking the space of the cave to that of the harem.[21] By focusing on moments and practices that Spivak would describe as disarticulating the dominant logic, Djebar's text interrupts dominant histories in that she orchestrates historical narratives in such a way as to sound the voices that have been silenced by them. Her own voice can therefore rise as apart from, yet be a part of, this choir of feminine voices.

A second similarity between Spivak's interventionist reading practice and Djebar's rewriting of history is the autobiographical dimension of their reading of history through the recognition of the role played by the imagination of the historian, writer or critic. This recognition leads Spivak to contest the strict opposition between history and fiction, on the basis that the representation of the subaltern is real in the former and imagined in the latter. Instead, she suggests that "it is a bit of both in both cases. The writer acknowledges this by claiming to do research (my fiction is also historical). The historian might acknowledge this by looking at the mechanics of representation (my history is also fictive)."[22] This insight entails a certain amount of autobiographical self-reflection in Spivak's critical writing, whereas Djebar recognizes that re-entering her autobiography was necessary if she was "to move back and forth between the past and the present."[23] As a historian and writer of fiction, she incorporates this double dimension in her fiction[24] by rereading written, oral, and personal histories that she momentarily interrupts in order to imagine them differently: "Je m'imagine, moi. . . ."[25] The complex, dynamic interplay between autobiography and multiple histories in Djebar's novel exemplifies how Manichean representations of history occlude the reality of certain communities, and serve colonial and nationalist power structures. Instead, its complex structure and multiple metaphors suggest how history (events and discourses) assigns a certain subject-position to the "I" of autobiography, who nevertheless intervenes in these discourses that constitute her position.

L'Amour, la fantasia: *A Narrative Performance of Intervention*[26]
A Structure of Interruption: *é-cri-tu-re* as Fantasia

The novel is structured in three parts: the chapters of the first two parts, "*La Prise de la Ville* ou l'amour s'écrit" and "*Les Cris de la Fantasia*," alternate between the narrator's reading of French documents on the conquest of Algeria and her childhood memories, establishing a binary structure opposing history to autobiography that is undermined at several levels.[27] The third part, "*Les Voix Ensevelies*," is symphonic: there are five movements, which all have a double tripartite structure, except for the fifth movement, which is composed of two chapters, and a three-chapter finale. Each movement combines autobiographical episodes, transcriptions of Algerian women's stories about the War of Independence, and the narrator's meditations about the dialogues she has had with these women.

The opposition between the historical and autobiographical sections in Part One and Two is undone in the play of language, in the cross-reference from one title to the other and in the breaking-up of the dual pattern for a symphonic organization in Part Three. The title of the first part—"*La Prise de la Ville* ou l'amour s'écrit"—seems to set the sections concerned with historical rereading in opposition to the autobiographical episodes, as the first half of the title applies to the former and the second half to the latter. However, the opposition between autobiography and history is undone by the fact that the alternance between numbered sections referring to the conquest and titled sections relating to personal memories in Part One is inverted in Part Two, where the numbered sections depict autobiographical episodes and titled sections are about the conquest.

Furthermore, the homonymy of the titles—"L'amour s'écrit" becomes "L'amour, ses cris,"[28] and by extension "*Les Cris de la Fantasia*" refers to "L'écrit de la fantasia"—suggests that, in the same way that French representations of the fantasia fictionalized the *cris* of the marginalized Algerian reality, the French language now fictionalizes her autobiography: "L'autobiographie pratiquée dans la langue adverse se tisse comme fiction, du moins tant que l'oubli des morts charriés par l'écriture n'opère pas son anesthésie."[29] Just as Djebar's writing attempts to interrupt French texts in order to sound the hidden reality of the ancestors,[30] so the lyrical sections in italics articulate the narrator's language of desire, for a moment tearing the veil of the French language. The interruptive dynamic of history and autobiography suggests that Djebar's *écriture* is both *é-cri-ture*, that is, a constant imaginative effort to chart the marginal moments when the French colonizers were able to hear and listen to the cries and voices of the people they conquered, as well as *écri-tu-re*, a writing practice that is either dialogically produced within the reading of other texts or results from the dialogues that the narrator has with her maternal relatives.[31]

However, the *cris* are not more primal or primary than the *écriture*; they are not representative of an authentic identity. Like the *écriture*, they are fundamentally ambiguous, as her epigraph to the finale of the book, *Tzarl-rit*, makes clear. In an interview she says, "Je rappelle rapidement que les oreilles étrangères ne vont pas comprendre si ces cris sont cris de joie *ou* cris de deuil. En réalité, il s'agit des deux."[32] The "or" of the first part's title, then, as in this quote, is not the sign of a strict opposition; rather, it shows that the opposites are caught in a game where each is interconnected with the other, suggesting that writing and cries are always already infiltrated by one another[33] and are, in fact, constitutive of each other. The written (l'écrit) is always already inhabited and interrupted by the oral (les cris); joy is always already haunted by sorrow.[34]

The double dimension of her writing as both *é-cri-ture* and *écri-tu-re*, as a listening for the silenced, buried, cries and a dialogue, takes on a new quality in Part Three, "Les voix ensevelies": Its structure is culturally double in the sense that it refers both to Beethoven's sonata and to the North African war tactic, the fantasia. The layout of the table of contents—which is "en escalier"[35]—suggests what Djebar has said in both her novel and in an interview, namely that the undermined dual structure of Parts One and Two gives way to a form of writing that mimics the movement of the fantasia and appropriates the strategy of the "rebato."

The culturally double concepts of fantasia and rebato share another doubleness: they both relate to musical forms and war tactics. Djebar uses them in the two following passages to express two different aspects of her writing, her relation to the French language, on the one hand, and to "the women of her own tribe,"[36] on the other.

Bien avant le débarquement français de 1830, . . . la guerre entre indigènes résistants et occupants souvent bloqués se faisait selon la tactique du "rebato": point isolé d'où l'on attaquait, où l'on se repliait avant que, dans les trêves intermédiaires, le lieu devienne zone de cultures, ou de ravitaillement. . . .

Après plus d'un siècle d'occupation française—qui finit, il y a peu, par un écharnement—un territoire de langue subsiste entre deux peuples, entre deux mémoires; la langue française, corps et voix, s'installe en moi comme un orgueilleux préside, tandis que la langue maternelle, toute en oralité, en hardes dépenaillées, résiste et attaque, entre deux essoufflements. Le rythme du "rebato" en moi s'éperonnant, je suis à la fois l'assiégé étranger et l'autochtone partant à la mort par bravade, illusoire effervescence du dire et de l'écrit.[37]

In this first excerpt, the comparison of her relationship to French culture and its language and history to the tactic of the "rebato" is remarkable for its very ambiguity: the "contact zone" (between the opponents in the war as well as between her and French) is both the point of attack and a "zone de cultures, ou de ravitaillement," suggesting that the two conflicting traditions eventually constitute a social and cultural space occupied by the narrator. The second quote suggests that the fantasia also renders the relation between her writing and her matrilineal relatives:

> Qu'est-ce que c'est que la fantasia? Ce sont des cavaliers qui s'initient à la guerre par le jeu de la guerre. . . . Dans la fantasia, vous avez un premier galop de cavaliers qui courent, courent, courent; à un certain moment ils tirent en même temps. Une fois qu'ils sont partis, le deuxième galop va se faire plus rapide, et ainsi de suite. Alors, pour moi, mes romans sont un peu comme des galops. Lorsque les cavaliers tirent, c'est le moment où lécriture [*sic*] devient une écriture en italique, où il y a volontairement, mais brièvement une écriture lyrique.
> . . . Cette structure "en fantasia" me permettait d'entrelacer ma propre voix avec les voix des autres femmes. Cela m'a donné un peu de courage pour parler de moi, intimement.[38]

Here, Djebar uses the fantasia to convey the ambiguity of her relationship to her maternal relatives: they are the silenced women who allow her to speak. On the one hand, the tradition these Algerian women represent is what holds her back and, on the other, their voices and the long dialogues with them encourage her to write. The cultural doubleness of the fantasia and the rebato, then, not only connotes her at least double cultural heritage—Western and "Algerian." It also conveys the different kind of relation she entertains with these two traditions.

"L'écriture en fantasia" thus appears as a suitable model for a post-colonial writer from Algeria as it encompasses cultural doubleness, without erasing the complex relations to and between the two conflicting cultures—the relation to either culture is not simply one of endorsement or rejection. This metaphor also suggests that Djebar's narrative staging of polyphony is much less a politically ineffectual dream than a potentially effective tactic, since she stresses that the fantasia is both a game of initiation to war and a form of warfare. The fantasia is a valuable concept because it helps visualize the narrator's *va-et-vient* between several territories, none of which she unequivocally or naturally belongs to. It therefore emphasizes the constant need to negotiate her position within a complex sociohistorical text. Djebar's "chant solitaire" can only begin if she can hear her ancestors' laments as they interrupt, but are nevertheless mediated through, the French texts and the women's voices, which assure "l'orchestration nécessaire."[39] Djebar can be figured as the *cavalier* who advances forward, leaving the group. The fantasia and rebato as war tactic and musical form thus provide the structure of the novel and symbolize the interventionist quality of her reading and writing practice.

Writing (Outside) the Cave and the Harem Speleology, Volcanic Eruptions, and Veiling

The fantasia, however, is not the only practice that Djebar presents in *L'amour, la fantasia* as a metaphor of the complex relationship between her writing and various histories, between personal memories and conflicting historical and communal traditions. The images of silence and voice, which are current in post-colonial and feminist criticism and perpetuate the Manichean structure of earlier views of (post)colonial cultures, are complicated by the specific cultural and historical context in which they can take on different and conflictual significations. Algerian history and culture provide Djebar with two sets of related images: first, those of speleology, geology and the volcano, which are related to the historical episode of the *enfumades* in the caves of Dahra; secondly, the notions linked to the veil and the harem. Djebar's speleological reading of the French texts in the first two parts gives way to the volcanic explosion of her voice in the third part. However, her autobiography in French, she realizes, is not a *dévoilement*, but just another *voile*.[40]

Post-colonial and feminist literature and criticism frequently use the tropes of silence and (coming) to voice to describe the accession of (formerly) oppressed people to writing.[41] Christopher Miller rightly observes that "the rhetoric of speech and silence . . . dominates this field" and that "[t]here is no question that . . . silence is the most powerful metaphor for exclusion from the literary mode of production."[42] Nevertheless, he qualifies the adequacy of such metaphors: "The metaphors of speech and silence in feminist literary criticism on Africa, . . . perhaps blur a certain historical and sociological specificity."[43] He warns that "[w]hat may be lost is the specificity of a particular literacy like French interacting with a particular local culture." He stresses the importance of contextualization and urges critics to neither overlook "the global and continental patterns of oppression" nor the cultural specificity of concepts: "Terms such as "speech," "silence," and even "man" and "woman" cannot be assumed to be identical from culture to culture: each is a social construction demanding precise analysis."[44] By staging the complex net of relations between the narrating "I" and the written voices of the French soldiers and writers who conquered Algeria in the 1830s, and the spoken voices of the women who took part in the Algerian revolution, Djebar conveys how complex the interaction between "the specificity of a particular literacy like French [and] a particular local culture" can be, especially when the gendered aspect of each culture (the French and the local)[45] is not given full attention.

Djebar's novel renders the neat distinction between silence and invisibility on the one hand and voice and visibility on the other dysfunctional when she describes the culturally specific experiences of Algerian women.[46] Voice and visibility do not necessarily go together, as the following passage suggests: "Chaîne de souvenirs: n'est-elle pas justement 'chaîne' qui entrave autant qu'elle enracine? Pour chaque passant, la *parleuse* stationne debout, *dissimulée derrière le seuil. Il n'est pas séant de soulever le rideau et de s'exposer au soleil. Toute parole, trop éclairée, devient voix de forfanterie, et l'aphonie, résistance inentamée . . .*"[47] This disjunction of voice and visibility—what is heard, or who speaks, is not seen—helps to undermine the neat opposition between silence and voice in which the first connotes powerlessness and oppression, and the second is seen as empowerment. This disjunction manifests itself in various episodes of *L'Amour, la fantasia*. In fact, the binary opposition between silence and voice gives way to a staging of various in-between states of feminine discourse, such as whispers and murmurs, and bodily movements and states, such as dancing and trances.

The opposition between silence and voice is further complicated by the, at least, bilingual situation, since expression in the colonizer's language inevitably enforces the absence and silencing of the other language. Furthermore, the interplay between French, Arabic and Berber and their specific significance in the narrator's life cannot be grasped by this simple opposition. As learning French preserves her from having to take the veil, the young narrator believes that the fact that "elle lit" makes her pubescent body "invisible": it functions as a "veil" that protects her from having to wear the veil. In the episode in which she discovers that she is not invisible,[48] she reflects on her own "aphasie amoureuse"[49] and the strange phenomenon by which the word of the would-be lover is neutralized, silenced, because it is spoken in French. In this case, there is a complete reversal of the traditional opposition between silence and voice, since, as she puts it: "Seule éloquence possible, seule arme qui pouvait m'atteindre: le silence . . ."[50] The narrator sees this *étanchéité* as inherited, as a *reprise de voile symbolique*, since her foremothers felt that *l'homme tabou* is blind, that his gaze cannot touch them. The narrator situates the source of her aphasia in the episode where the daughter of the "gendarme français" makes a spectacle of her love.[51] Nevertheless, she already foresees that this aphasia will lead to an explosion: "Un jour ou l'autre, parce que cet état autistique ferait chape à mes élans de femme, surviendrait à rebours quelque soudaine explosion."[52]

The anticipated release takes place at the beginning of the third part, which opens with the volcanic explosion of her voice. This long passage is worth quoting in full because it brings together both the images related to the volcano and the ones related to the veil and the harem:

> L'espace est nu, la rue longue et déserte m'appartient, ma démarche libre laisse monter le rythme mien, sous le regard des pierres.
>
> . . . soudain la voix explose. Libère en flux toutes les scories du passé. Quelle voix, est-ce ma voix, je la reconnais à peine.
>
> Comme un magma, un tourteau sonore, un poussier m'encombra d'abord le palais, puis s'écoule en fleuve rêche, hors de ma bouche et, pour ainsi dire, me devance.
>
> Un long, un unique et interminable pleur informe, un précipité agglutiné dans le corps même de ma voix d'autrefois, de mon organe gelé: cette coulée s'exhale, glu anonyme, traînée de décombres non identifiés. . . . Je perçois, en témoin quasi indifférent cette écharpe écoeurante de sons: mélasse de râles morts, guano de hoquets et de suffocations, senteurs d'azote de quel cadavre asphyxié en moi et pourrissant. La voix, ma voix, (ou plutôt ce qui sort de ma bouche ouverte, bâillant comme pour vomir ou chanter quelque opéra funèbre) ne peut s'interrompre. Peut-être faut-il lever le bras, mettre la main devant la face, suspendre ainsi la perte de ce sang invisible?
>
> Amoindrir au moins l'intensité! Les étrangers, derriere leurs murs, se recueillent et je ne suis, moi, qu'une exilée errante, échappée d'autres rivages où les femmes se meuvent fantômes blancs, formes ensevelies à la verticale, justement pour ne pas faire ce que je fais là maintenant, pour ne pas hurler aini continûment: son de barbare, son de sauvage, résidu macabre d'un autre siècle! [. . .] Atténuer quelque peu ce râle, le scander en mélopée inopportune. Incantation dans l'exil qui s'étire.
>
> La rue Richelieu se déroule longue, étroite, désertée. Parvenir au bout et arrêter mon pas; du même coup cette voix de l'étrange, ce lamento qui m'appartient malgré moi.[53]

This passage reveals the inadequacy of the attempt made to distinguish different sets of images, since Djebar's writing weaves them all into an inextricable net. Nevertheless, the juxtaposition of multiple metaphors produces a specifically feminine signature of a cultural and mythical imagination as marked by a specific history.[54] The juxtaposition of the space of the cave with that of the harem, through the notion of asphyxia, inscribes the volcanic eruption of the voice within the multiple layers of oppression.

As a historian, Djebar practices a "speleological" reading that consists of tracing and deciphering the petrified debris of earlier eruptions or *enfumades* within the very texts of those who gave the orders to carry out such horrors. As she herself puts it: "je m'exerce à une spéléologie bien particulière, puisque je m'agrippe aux arêtes des mots français—rapports, narration, témoignages du passé."[55] Her writing exhumes buried (*enfouis, ensevelis*) episodes of colonialist history—the *enfumades*—and then uses the specificity of the ancestors' experience to figure her own experience of *enfouissement*,[56] as well as women's historical and contemporary *ensevelissement*. It is no coincidence if the explosion of the voice is included in the opening chapter of Part Three, "Les voix ensevelies," in which she mingles her own voice with those of the forgotten participants in the Algerian war.[57]

The volcanic metaphor brilliantly figures the accumulation of oppressions, and the explosion that "libère en flux toutes les scories de passé."[58] The fragments of lava left over from of previous explosions can be seen as an image that summarizes the status of the discrete stories, for example that of "La mariée nue de Mazouna," the stories of Fromentin, etc., that float in the flux of "ce lamento qui m'appartient malgré moi."[59] Her writing appears as a confluence of various, discrete voices that are like the unidentified debris floating on and fusing with the river of lava, which is Djebar's voice, her writing.

Djebar also uses the experience of asphyxia, specific to that historical trauma, in conjunction with the idea of haunting, to configure her ambivalent position in relation to both the French "intercessors" and the women she interviews. She wonders "quel cadavre asphyxié en moi et pourrissant."[60] It could be that the suffocated corpse that inhabits her is the phantom of what she would have been, had her father not sent her to the French school. However, this image also suggests that she is haunted by other, more ancient corpses, those of the smoked-out caves, and that this is where she begins.[61] Moreover, she is also haunted by "l'émoi même des tueurs" (which can also be read as "le moi-même des tueurs"[62]), whose texts she in turns haunts as she insinuates herself into them. Finally, she questions the legitimacy of her project of resurrecting the voices of the women who participated in the war of independence, in the same terms: "Vingt ans après, puis-je prétendre habiter ces voix d'asphyxie?"[63]

Indeed, the *enfumade* projects the writer to another kind of asphyxia: that of her veiled female relatives, and the space of the grotto is juxtaposed with that of the harem. Because the women are not allowed to be fully outside, they can only become ghostly, suffocated, blind dwellers of the inside. The veil becomes the wound the woman and the writer has to deal with.[64] Thus Djebar asks: "Comment trouver la force de m'arracher le voile, sinon parce qu'il me faut en couvrir la *plaie* inguérissable, suant les mots tout à côté?"[65] The veil here is both the French language that has enveloped her like a "tunique de Nessus,"[66] and the veil of her grandmothers, cousins, and aunts. The wound is one more polyvalent image, since the historian has to confront the unhealed wounds of the historical and geographical landscape of her country: "Lors j'interviens, la mémoire nomade et la voix coupée. Inlassablement, j'ai erré aux quatre coins de ma région natale—entre la Ville prise et les ruines de Césarée, elle s'étend au pied du mont Chenoua, à l'ombre du pic de la Mouzaïa, plaine alanguie mais aux *plaies* encore ouvertes."[67] These diverse images[68] are all linked to the two juxtaposed enclosed spaces of the cave and the harem. Pelissier's act of taking the corpses out of the smoked-out caves uncannily prefigures Djebar's father's "intercessory" act of taking her to the French school and so liberating her from the harem. In consequence, Djebar can circulate in the outside world, but also between two worlds: she presents herself as nomadic, and in the episode in which her voice explodes, the flux of her voice matches the rhythm of her step. In fact, ever since the day she took the path to the French school, the I-narrator has dwelt in border zones. Djebar's explanation that the harem is the *interdit* suggests that the opposition between the interior and exterior is only one of degree. It is nevertheless within this *inter-dit*, that women's muffled, whispered or screamed defiance (her grandmother's trance, for instance)[69] emerges, that a feminine tradition, described elsewhere by Djebar as "[surnageant] en pointillé,"[70] survives, expressing itself between the lines imposed by patriarchy. Her voice is both rooted (*enracinée*) in the interstices of this world and simultaneously hindered (*entravée*) by them.[71] Her creativity is grounded in this space of exclusion, from which she is excluded, since she has been expulsed from it by her education. However, it is because she is an exile who errs within other linguistic, historical, and physical territories that she can write. The sources of her writing are thus multiple and contradictory.

The complex web of images is a metaphor for the narrator's (coming to) writing, her relationship to different oral and written historical accounts, as well as to her own memories, suggest that Manichean counter-narratives cannot render the complex nature of the negotiations a French-educated Algerian woman writer has to carry out in order to rewrite and sound history. Her novel makes it obvious that the articulation of suppressed voices and histories is never a simple matter of retrieval and replacement, thereby exposing the nationalist move to erase "la tradition héritée de la présence française" and replace it with an Islamic, Arabic identity.[72] Indeed, she shows that the dominant history itself is always already infiltrated by the culture and reality of those the powerful seek to oppress and reduce to being their opposite, uncivilized "other." She acknowledges this by presenting herself in a strange filial relationship with Fromentin, whom she describes as "seconde silhouette paternelle."[73] Thus, her writing does not participate in the logic of absolute opposition or dualism that Dine sees as characteristic of *Algérie française*[74] (and which is generally seen as characteristic of colonization and its supporting discourses), but concentrates on showing the complex layering of all situations of oppression, and focuses especially on moments of collusion and mediation, encounters, betrayal and complicity. This strategy is set out in the first part of the novel, in which she suggests that the original confrontation between Algiers and the French navy is a moment of reciprocal fascination. Other episodes that are symptomatic of this approach are the one in which she shows how one woman is excluded for having shouted too loudly, thus revealing the others' collusion in their own oppression, as well as the episode of les "voyeuses" in the chapter of the same title. All these moments are important because the victim is not presented as such, and the emphasis is on his or her agency. Djebar focuses on these possibilities of "échappées," suggesting how they intervene in and interrupt the dominant logic of colonialism and patriarchy.

The narrator does not, however, gather these moments in order to make a coherent counter-narrative. Rather, she exposes the discontinuities within the dominant histories. The autobiographical voice does not attempt to mask the episodic nature of the novel or its heterogeneity in order to make her own narrative coherent. Rather, she shows that these discrete images and episodes are part of multiple and conflicting heritages, which she has to negotiate. Throughout the novel, the writing is moderated by the presence of the "I" who explicitly stages herself as mediating her, at least, triple inheritance, which is French, Arabic and Berber.[75] As she elaborates these historical moments of interruption to create metaphors for her own writing practice, these episodes in-form the dynamics of her struggle with the autobiographical form that has to intervene in multiple spaces and interrupt various historical texts.

Notes

1. Françoise Lionnet, *Postcolonial Representations: Women, Literature, Identity* (Ithaca and London: Cornell UP, 1995), 14–15.

2. Lionnet, *Postcolonial*, 6–19.

3. This concept has been instrumental in Mireille Rosello's analysis of Caribbean literature and women's writing. In the first context, she develops the notion of opposition as distinct from that of resistance, and in the second, the concept of infiltration, in order to suggest how people without a territory of their own momentarily play with and escape the laws of oppressive orders. *Littérature et identité créole aux Antilles* (Paris: Karthala, 1992), 35–37 and *Infiltrating culture* (Manchester and New York: Manchester UP, 1996), 9–15.

4. De Certeau, *L'invention du quotidien* (Paris: Gallimard, 1990, first published 1980).

5. Rosello, *Littérature et identité*, 171.

6. Gayatri Spivak, "Teaching for the Times," in *Dangerous Liaisons. Gender, Nation, and Postcolonial Perspectives*, ed. Anne McClintock, Aamir Mufti, and Ella Shohat (Minneapolis and London: University of Minnesota Press, 1997), 482–83.

7. Gayatri Spivak, "Can the Subaltern Speak?" in *Colonial Discourse and Post-Colonial Theory*, ed. Patrick Williams and Laura Chrisman (London: Harvester Wheatsheaf, 1993), 103.

8. As De Certeau puts it: "les usagers 'bricolent' avec et dans l'économie culturelle dominante les in-nombrables et infinitésimales métamorphoses de sa loi en celle de leurs intérêts et de leurs règles propres." *L'invention*, xxxix.

9. Assia Djebar, *L'amour, la fantasia* (Paris: Albin Michel, 1995: 1st published Lattès, 1985). Reference is made to the Albin Michel edition.

10. Summarized from: Marguerite Le Clezio/Assia Djebar, "Assia Djebar: Écrire dans la langue ad-verse," *Contemporary French Civilization* 9, no. 2 (1985): 230–31.

11. Djebar/Le Clezio, "Assia Djebar: Écrire," 238

12. Djebar/Zimra: "'When the Past Answers Our Present': Assia Djebar Talks about *Loin de Médine*," *Callaloo* 16, no.1 (1993): 124.

13. Djebar/Zimra, "When the Past," 124–25.

14. Assia Djebar, "Ecrire dans la langue de l'autre: pour une quête d'identité," in *Identité, culture et changement social*, ed. M. Lavallée, F. Ouellet, F. Larose (Paris: L'Harmattan, 1991), 27.

15. Stora suggests that one of the reasons for the nationalist "tabula rasa" was to erase the confronta-tions within the Algerian political past, as well as the origins of the resistance movement within the cir-cles of immigrants in France. Cf. "La dissimulation des origines" and "Le procès du passé," in *La Gangrène et l'oubli* (Paris: La Découverte, 1991), 121–26, 231–34.

16. Djebar/Zimra, "When the Past," 119.

17. The Manichean logic of both colonialism and nationalism in Algeria inscribed the native female body in their rhetoric. See Djebar's analysis of this in "Regard interdit, son coupé," in *Femmes d'Alger dans leur appartement* (Paris: des femmes, 1980).

18. Spivak, "A Literary Representation of the Subaltern: A Woman's Text From the Third World," in *In Other Worlds* (New York and London: Routledge, 1987), 241.

19. See her discussion of Rokeya Sakhawat Hossain's *Abarodh-bashini* in "Teaching for the Times," in *Dangerous Liaisons: Gender, Nation, and Postcolonial Perspectives*, ed. Anne McClintock, Aamir Mufti, and Ella Shohat (Minneapolis and London: University of Minnesota Press, 1997), 482–83.

20. Djebar, L'Amour, 252–53.

21. See the third section of this chapter.

22. Spivak, "A Literary Representation," 244–45.

23. Djebar/Zimra, "When the Past," 124.

24. Indeed, she both fictionalizes historical documents and explains that, as she writes in French, the autobiographical episodes inevitably take on a fictional quality. Cf. Clarisse Zimra, "Sounding Off the Ab-sent Body: Intertextual Resonances in 'La femme qui pleure' and 'La femme en morceaux,'" *Research in African Literature* 30, no. 3 (1999): 108–24.

25. Djebar, *L'Amour*, 16.

26. Mireille Rosello has analysed how Djebar's novel goes beyond the Manichean framework of his-torical narratives by showing how "Djebar changes the whole matrix of stereotypical historical narra-tives." She argues that in *L'Amour*, "History remains a palimpsest and is not treated like a repossessed ob-ject. Djebar allows layers of writing to accumulate rather than proposing an alternative genealogy that would be constructed on the same model as the one she wishes to contest." Mireille Rosello, *Declining the Stereotype* (Hanover and London: University Press of New England, 1998), 159.

27. Anne Donadey has also analysed how Djebar's work goes beyond the Manichean framework of re-sistance literature and has suggested that Djebar's novel, *L'amour, la fantasia*, "establish[es] a pattern of dichotomization which she immediately subverts at several levels" and uses Irigaray's notion of mimicry as opposed to Harlow's notion of resistance literature to convey how the Djebarian text "moves away from oppositional discourse to subversive reappropriation" as it subverts these master texts by "mocking the bi-nary structure" and "undoing the dichotomy between inside and outside." Anne Donadey, "Assia Djebar's Poetics of Subversion," *L'Esprit créateur* 33, no. 2 (1993), 107, 112.

28. Djebar, *L'Amour*, 240.

29. Djebar, *L'Amour*, 243.

30. For an insightful analysis of the impact of Djebar's refusal to use the possessive adjective, see Rosello, 1998, *Declining*, and note 26.

31. The dialogic dimension as interaction between the narrative "je" and a "tu" in the text also forms the basis of the narrative structure of Djebar's *Ombres Sultanes*.

32. Mildred Mortimer, "Entretien avec Assia Djebar, écrivain algérienne," *Research in African Literature* 19, no. 2 (Summer 1988): 203. My emphasis.

33. For an elaboration of the concept of infiltration, cf. Rosello, 1996, *Declining*,

34. That the relation between these two strands, the history of the conquest and autobiographical events, is not dualistic is further suggested by the fact that the vocabulary used to describe the autobiographical episodes is also the one used to describe the history of conquest. For example, Djebar uses the word "explosion" to refer both to the inner experience of the I-narrator and the war of conquest. This is made evident as it is the last word of the chapter entitled "La fille du gendarme français" and the first word of the next chapter numbered III (*L'Amour*, 38–39). This is a device that is repeated in other chapters. Thus, "aube" connects the chapter entitled "Fillette arabe allant pour la première fois à l'école" and the chapter numbered I; "combat" connects the chapter entitled "Trois jeunes filles cloîtrées" and the chapter numbered II; "ouverte(ment)" connects the chapter entitled "Mon père écrit à ma mère" and the chapter numbered IV. Another striking method Djebar uses to suggest that these seemingly separate historical episodes—the autobiographical ones and the ones relating to the conquest—are in fact haunted by each other is her interweaving of struggle and sexuality in both.

35. Djebar, *L'Amour*, 257–58.

36. Djebar/Zimra, "When the Past," 124.

37. Djebar, *L'Amour*, 241.

38. Mildred Mortimer, "Entretien avec Assia Djebar," 202–3.

39. See the following passage: "Avant d'entendre ma propre voix, je perçois les râles, les gémissements des emmurés du Dahra, des prisonniers de Sainte-Marguerite; ils assurent l'orchestration nécessaire. Ils m'interpellent, ils me soutiennent pour qu'au signal donné, mon chant solitaire démarre." Djebar, *L'Amour*, 243.

40. Djebar, *L'Amour*, 243.

41. See, for example, Carole Boyce Davies, and Elaine Savory Fido, "Introduction: Women and Literature in the Caribbean: An Overview," in *Out of the Kumbla. Caribbean Women and Literature* (Trenton, N.J.: Africa World Press, 1990). Novels also explore these images. See, for example: J. M. Coetzee, *Foe*; Keri Hulme, *The Bone People*; Marina Warner, *Indigo*; Michelle Cliff, *No Telephone to Heaven*.

42. Christopher L. Miller, "Senegalese Women Writers, Silence, and Letters: Before the Canon's Roar," in *Theories of Africans. Francophone Literature and Anthropology in Africa* (Chicago and London: Chicago University Press, 1990), 250.

43. Miller, "Senegalese Women," 252.

44. Miller, "Senegalese Women," 251.

45. This very distinction seems somewhat spurious, considering that French has to a certain extent become "local."

46. This collective itself hides specific groups, which become visible in Djebar's fiction, as she interacts with the *citadines*, the *bourgeoises*, the peasants, the Berbers, etc.

47. Djebar, *L'Amour*, 201, my emphasis. The notion of *forfanterie* is related to that of French as the language which "s'installe en [elle] comme un orgueilleux préside" (*L'Amour*, 241).

48. Djebar, *L'Amour*, 143–45.

49. Djebar, *L'Amour*, 145.

50. Djebar, *L'Amour*, 144–45.

51. Djebar, *L'Amour*, 38.

52. Djebar, *L'Amour*, 38.

53. Djebar, *L'Amour*, 131–32.

54. For the notion of an image as the signature of a culture, see Mireille Rosello, "De la révulsion à l'éruption—les métaphores de la révolte," in *Littérature et identité créole aux Antilles* (Paris: Karthala, 1992), 113–43 and in particular, 139.

55. Djebar, *L'Amour*, 91–92.

56. Djebar, *L'Amour*, 132.

57. However, this *ensevelissement* is not a limited comment on the betrayal of women by the FLN. It is a more general comment on how a patriarchal culture has (ab)used religion in order to perpetuate a patriarchy that is, as Djebar would have it, "loin de Médine."

58. Djebar, *L'Amour*, 131. It is noteworthy that other post-colonial writers have used the image of the volcano, in different ways and very different contexts. A famous example is the work of Aimé Césaire, and his notion of Pelean poetry. Bessie Head's *Question of Power* (Oxford, Portsmouth and Ibadan: Heinemann, 1974) is also very interesting, since, like Djebar's novel, it combines the image of the volcano with that of haunting to express the madness and alienation experienced as a result of being born colored into a white South African family.

59. Djebar, *L'Amour*.

60. Djebar, *L'Amour*, 131.

61. As she writes: "Une constatation étrange s'impose: je suis née en *dix-huit cent quarante-deux*, lorsque le commandant de Saint-Arnaud vient détruire la zaouia des Beni Ménacer, ma tribu d'origine. . . ." Djebar, *L'amour*, 243.

62. Djebar, *L'Amour*, 69. Thanks are due to Scott Durham for suggesting this reading.

63. Djebar, *L'Amour*, 227.

64. Katherine Gracki suggests that Djebar can be seen as a healer in "Writing Violence and the Violence of Writing in Assia Djebar's Algerian Quartet," *World Literature Today* 70, no. 4 (Autumn 1995): 835–43.

65. Djebar, *L'Amour*, 245.

66. Djebar, *L'Amour*, 243. The "tunique de Nessus" adequately renders the double-edged quality of the liberation afforded by her father's taking her to the French school: once it is worn it becomes smaller and smaller: it is at once a gift that liberates her from the harem, but at the same time alienates her from her relatives. Moreover, it confines her to having to express herself in what she has called the language of the enemy.

67. Djebar, *L'Amour*, 255, my emphasis.

68. A few of which are analyzed here (the volcano, the veil, asphyxia, the wound).

69. There are links here with *Ombre Sultane* and the daughter's condemnation of her mother for too readily obeying her father in the chapter "L'adolescente en colère," 140–45, as well as the *aïeule's* delirious accusations about her cousins' letters being smuggled in and out of the harem (Djebar, *L'Amour*, 18).

70. Djebar, *Femmes d'Alger dans leur apartement*, 185.

71. Djebar, *L'Amour*, 201.

72. Stora, *La Gangrène*, 233.

73. Djebar, *L'Amour*, 255.

74. Philip Dine, "Le Même et l'autre: Imaging the Algerians," in *Images of the Algerian War: French Fiction and Film, 1954–1992* (Oxford: Clarendon Press, 1994), 5.

75. The most heavily erased voice is that of her mother, and in the third novel of the quartet, *Vaste est la prison*, Djebar explores her Berber inheritance.

5

Collective Memory and
Representation in Tunisian Literature

Mohammed-Salah Omri

FAWZI MELLAH (BORN 1947) HAS PUBLISHED two plays, two novels and one essay.[1] Despite this, he has received little critical attention.[2] It is not possible to treat all the facets of his work, nor indeed all of his writings, within the constraints of this chapter, which will be limited to Mellah's novels, as these constitute a tightly linked narrative project. They show a simultaneous questioning and reconstruction of memory as a form of communal and personal meaning in a modern Tunisia intent on the erasure of the past.[3] The novels, *Le Conclave des pleureuses* and *Elissa, la reine vagabonde*, differ in their time frame, narrative structure and narrative focus. Yet, a close comparative reading reveals that *Elissa* is embedded in *Le Conclave*. Numerous references to Elissa, the Phoenician founder of Carthage, prepare the reader for a full treatment of her story. Allusions to Western misrepresentations of this local foundational legend create the need for the story to be rewritten from a local perspective. Monsieur, a character in *Le Conclave*, enters into an argument with a person who goes by the name of Virgil, "auquel il reprochait de défigurer la reine Elissa en l'appelant Didon et en lui prêtant des amours ridicules avec un marin grec: 'Il faut appeler les reines par leur nom et s'abstenir de les vieillir de trois siècles!' répétait-il. Qui est cet Énée, sinon un vagabond indigne de notre Elissa qui, elle, savait d'où elle venait."[4]

There is a hint that significant issues in Elissa's life have been neglected in existing biographies. Mellah writes: "Il [Monsieur] relut cent fois l'histoire d'Elissa en pensant y déceler les traces d'un inceste qui aurait fait fuire la grande reine phénicienne, érigeant la mer comme un barrage entre elle et son frère Pygmalion."[5] She is portrayed as worthy of a better representation: "On ne dénature pas l'histoire d'une bâtisseuse d'empire, on l'accompagne dans sa glorieuse épopée."[6] *Elissa* can be seen as this attempt to accompany the queen during her epic journey by 'translating' her own account of the perilous flight from Tyre and the legendary creation of Carthage.[7] By giving her a voice, the novel extends *Le Conclave* in a significant direction. It provides immediate and extensive access to a myth, which persists in the collective memory of Elissa's modern heirs. As narrative, *Elissa* is, for the most part, a letter addressed by the Queen to her brother Pygmalion before she throws herself onto the sacrificial pyre. She recounts her journey and questions the possibility of representing her own motivation and ideas. *Le Conclave*, on the other hand, focuses on contemporary life in Tunisia (without ever mentioning the country by name); it involves a larger number of characters and points of view and discusses the interface between journalism and literature. The following reading of the two novels focuses primarily on personal and collective memory in *Le Conclave* and analyses representation in *Elissa*. A comparative approach highlights the common thread running through both works. Other interpretative possibilities and directions for further research are suggested in the course of this chapter.

Memory and Space

Le Conclave is divided into five chapters ("Biographie d'un saint," "l'Oeil-de-Moscou," "La Montagne Rouge," "Les Pleureuses," "Les deux Statues"). Although the narrative does not follow a clear plot line, a fabula can be gleaned from the text.[8] A journalist is sent to investigate alleged rapes in a city. The family suspected of masterminding the rapes is run by a matriarch, Aïcha-Dinar, and includes six brothers and one sister. Members of the family occupy odd, mostly underground, functions and represent various characteristics reflected in their nicknames. Aïcha-Dinar manages the family's finances and occasionally works as a mourner. Le saint-de-la-parole is the central figure and the spokesperson for the community. Tawfik-Grain-de-Sel is famous for his capacity to melt away into the neighborhood like salt at the sight of a uniform. Hamma-le-Rouge is the red-headed brother who maintains German connections and runs an underground trafficking operation. Moha-le-Fou claims prophetic faculties while Ali-Doigts-d'Argent specializes in robbery. Mustafa-Canari is a bird trainer with links to the police. The city itself is never named. But those who are familiar with the Tunisian capital will easily recognize the desolate neighborhood of La Montagne Rouge (*al-Jabal al-Ahmar*) and the two statues representing the former President Habib Bourguiba and the historian Ibn Khaldun that stood in the city's main boulevard until the early 1990s. Numerous references to other places, events, and people point to the writer's home country.

As the journalist's investigation (*enquête*) progresses and more witnesses and informants are introduced, versions of events and people proliferate. Interwoven with the investigation is the journalist's personal quest (*quête*), which yields some sketchy autobiographical detail. He had personal knowledge of Le saint-de-la-parole and his family twenty years before the investigation and the matriarch had expelled him from the saint's shrine for being too old to mix with women.[9] Aïcha-Dinar appears to be responsible for what the journalist calls his "exile masculin." He says: "C'est, peut-être, ce désir de remonter aux origines de la grande séparation (et des viols?) qui m'a propulsé au numéro sept de l'impasse de la Patience."[10] The saint himself is unable to help since he is not versed in the world of men. Yet he is able to predict the course of the narrative. The saint warns the journalist: "Ton enquête sur les viols va se rétrécir tandis que ta propre quête va s'élargir."[11] The saint understands and foretells the narrative as a whole. *Le Conclave* is as much a personal quest as it is an inquiry into events of public interest. The parallel line of personal narrative continues throughout. While the journalist's role forces him to allow the others to speak, his own voice gradually emerges and becomes stronger. By the end of the book the investigation and the personal story have become one and the same. When the journalist meets his nemesis, Aïcha-Dinar, he finds her diminished. He says: "Cette femme qui présidait aux oracles et qui prédisait les miracles n'est plus aujourd'hui que citoyenne hasardeuse d'une république de rumeurs! La cité l'a-t-elle vomie? Par crainte ou par mépris?"[12] And although he finds that he is still unable to express his personal grudge (except when he smokes *kif* and loses all his inhibitions),[13] a personal victory is achieved. He says: "J'ai tué la rumeur intérieure; c'est ma modeste, mon humble victoire."[14] The public rumor remains, however, unvanquished.

Acting upon instructions from the chief editor, referred to only by the derisory name L'Oeil-de-Moscou, the journalist focuses his investigation on the saint's family, who used to live at 7 Impasse of Patience in the Phoenician quarter and who were forced to relocate to the Montagne Rouge.[15] The family, however, prompts him to look elsewhere for clues, namely in the "quartier nouveau" where government employees and the new rich have taken up residence. He gradually discovers that the rapes are indicative of a deeper conflict in the community. The saint's sister, Fatma-la-Lampe, a former singer and beauty reduced to the position of housekeeper in the new quarter, accuses her employers, known only as Monsieur and Madame, who are the central figures in this part of the story. When Madame's father dies, mourners are hired; and it is in their conclave (hence the title of the book) that the rift comes to the open. There is a split between the proponents of memory, whose emblem is Le saint-de-la-parole, and those who support progress, whose mouthpiece is the chief editor of the newspaper. They represent opposite sides in the conflict between what the journalist calls "historians" and "geographers." The investigation is designed as part of the attack mounted by the "geographers" against the proponents of history. Yet the journalist's personal tale links him closely to the latter. He decides not to take part in the attack, opting instead for voluntary exile. The opposition between history and geography is among the most telling themes in the book. The two statues erected in the main avenue of the city express the relationship between historians and geographers and serve as an aesthetic condensation of their conflicting worldviews.[16]

Conceptions of the community, hopes for its future and political allegiances can be detected in the way the two statues are perceived and accessed. The journalist, the chief editor, and the crowd all have different views on Ibn Khaldun and Bourguiba, and see them from different spaces. The journalist examines them from the newspaper's office, overlooking the main avenue of the city.[17] They face each other and seem to approach one another. But the leader (Bourguiba), who is riding a horse and waving his right hand, appears more confident and more dominant than the historian, who is portrayed walking and holding an open book. The journalist observes: "La statue du chef est plus au fond; elle tourne le dos à la mer et fait face à celle de l'historien. Le chef regarde à l'ouest, le savant à l'est."[18] The chief editor, who is a historian by training, is expected to side with Ibn Khaldun. He has even been fired from a job for criticizing the sculptor for failing to represent the historian on horseback.[19] Yet he expresses his kinship to Ibn Khaldun only insofar as the latter can be considered a fellow journalist. He notes that "Le pouvoir et l'histoire sont fait pour s'ignorer, s'essoufler ou se détruire."[20] The crowd has no direct access to the statues, since they are not visible from the Montagne Rouge. But, when confrontation breaks out in the city, the statues appear to polarize the allegiances of the crowd. People are undecided, like a woman who cannot choose between her husband and her lover. Mellah says: "L'époux lui offre les certitudes de la nation, l'amant les aventures du récit: comment opter sans craindre d'être orphelin?"[21]

The statues represent what the book refers to as the geographer and the historian and relate to one another in the way space relates to history, amnesia to memory, statement to narrative, fact to myth and legend. "La république," the new quarter and L'Oeil-de-Moscou belong to the world of geography, which rules the day and dominates the proponents of history. The saint, the inhabitants of La Montagne Rouge, and the mourners all own time, history, and legend.[22] The art of the city, commissioned by the new state, reflects the divide and reveals the differing status of the community's memory and its future. The relationship between the statues reflects the advancing power of the statesman and the receding authority of the historian. During the riots, the statesman seems to go forward confidently while the historian appears to seek refuge for his book in the old city.[23]

Another focal point of the community's history and personal perceptions of that history is provided by the figure called Le saint-de-la-parole. There are four versions of his life, which reveal a number of appropriations of his story. The book opens with the saint's autobiographical narrative. According to him, he was born in a place where the river meets the sea to a saint father and a mother who was a mourner. He was then immersed in the well of Sarah and Agar, where he learned a special language, a mixture of Arabic and Yiddish.[24] At the age of fifteen he was circumcised and his family began what he calls "commerce mystique."[25] Women flocked to see him, but when he flew across the ceiling out of fear, the family decided to put him in chains. Once he had been chained, women began to touch him and tear off his clothes.[26] His mother decided to expose him naked to visitors but prevented them from touching him. At this stage he entered a phase he calls the "abstract saint," during which he developed the look as his means of communication.[27] It was his mother's job to interpret his look and set the appropriate charges. He says: "D'étape en étape, de prédisposition en apprentissage, je suis devenu, à quarante ans, le saint parfait."[28] Not long after that, the saint lost his sight, and the family's business collapsed. The saint claims that, because the community is of Phoenician descent, it is cursed and doomed for mocking the gods. Only a select few keep the memory: "Nous ne sommes plus que quelques-uns à remonter aux sources brûlantes de l'amnésie: des historiens silencieux, quelques pleureuses sincères (lorsqu'elles exigent un conclave) et certains saints en exil."[29]

The saint's mother and sister give two different versions of events. The mother calls her account an authentic and beautiful story.[30] She claims that her son was neither blind nor dumb; he simply liked the company of women. When it was time for his circumcision he took refuge in a well. His father shunned him but was punished and died of hiccups. The mother was advised by a Jewish physician either to restrain the boy or to declare him a saint.[31] Theologians and healers gave her permission to claim sainthood for her son: "Ils m'autorisèrent à déclarer mon fils voyant, à condition toutefois qu'ils fût circoncis."[32] At the age of twenty she forced him to be circumcised and moved the family to a different neighborhood. The mother became aware of her son's healing powers and chained him up in order to prevent violence. In her story, she shows an awareness that her son possesses a gift, which goes beyond the power to heal. He plays a key social role. She says: "Mon fils faisait la communauté car il aidait à transformer la douleur qui se pensait unique en destinée commune."[33] The sister, Fatma-la-Lampe, gives a version she describes as the simple and innocent story of her brother and his solitude.[34] According to her, he was a voracious reader and a solitary man. In particular, he read about Elissa ("Il lisait beaucoup de livres sur Elissa la fondatrice de Carthage et sur les guerres puniques").[35] Girls liked his company because he knew Phoenician songs, but boys did not accept this. They even pushed him into a well where he caught pneumonia and suffered a speech impediment. As a result, he gave up any hope of becoming a history teacher. As more and more women sought his answers to various queries and concerns, his mother feared trouble, forced him to have a vasectomy and chained him up.

The chief editor has, as might be expected, a completely unrelated version of the story. He appears to have had direct experience with the saint during the colonial period. He claims that the saint wrote Punic poetry and dedicated it to Elissa, refusing to call her Dido.[36] The saint refused to collaborate with the chief editor during protests against the burial of Christians in cemeteries reserved for Moslems.[37] Their ways parted, and the editor became convinced that the saint had since lost any claim to history. He says: "Mais il se voulait historien; et il n'était que conteur."[38]

The saint sees himself as the repository of the community's memory. For the mother, he embodies the sense of social bonding in a country where the community is breaking up and individualism is gaining dominance. The sister, on the other hand, perceives him as a poet and the custodian of a collective foundational myth. The editor-in-chief, however, denies the saint any ties with history and sees him as a storyteller. Yet the notion of history that emerges from the book does not support that of the chief editor. It defines the historian as the figure who bonds the community together by offering a narrative that preserves memory and propagates legend. The community finds an anchor and voice in its founding myths, living memory and continuous story.

The depth of the rift between the two halves of the community, which manifests itself in an exchange of charges of rape, is reflected in the way both sides relate to their collective memory and how it touches the very basis of their identity. There is a clear and unbridgeable divide between the new quarter of the city and La Montagne Rouge, the saint and the chief editor, Aïcha-Dinar and Madame. Their identities stem from different origins and represent themselves in different ways. Aïcha-Dinar sees her identity engraved on her body in the form of tattoos. She rejects the identity card and all other means of identification adopted by the new state to classify its citizens. She says: "A l'époque du miel et de la confiance nous n'avions pas besoin de cartes d'identité; le nom du père et les tatouages suffisaient. On peut falsifier une carte d'identité, on ne peut pas déformer un tatouage."[39] When the journalist points out that the citizens of the republic need to be identified in a different way, she replies: "Ta ville et ta république ne sont que par hasard . . . elles cherchent leurs racines et leurs origines. Pour nous, elles sont ici: inscrites sur nos peaux."[40] She perceives such inscriptions as permanent, personal, and limited only by death. The state's inscription, however, is ephemeral, impersonal and transitory.

The Pitfalls of Memory and the Limits of Representation

Even so, while the writer of necessity sides with historians, preservers of memory and creators of narrative, memory itself is often questioned through narrative technique. The juxtaposition of several versions of the same story results, inevitably, in a slippage of meaning. The saint's biography becomes uncertain as each new version introduces elements of doubt. The variations between the versions can of course be attributed to the subjectivity and selectivity of human memory. Yet it is possible to argue that, in addition to biographies or representations of the saint by other characters, Le Conclave also includes his autobiography, since the saint dictates his story to the narrator.[41] The saint's own account of events is, however, marred by uncertainties and doubt. He describes his first miracle—flying across the ceiling—in the following terms: "Ce fut mon premier miracle; ou, du moins, c'est ainsi qu'aujourd'hui je me présente mon premier miracle. A moins que ce soit une pure vision, l'un de ces multiples pièges que nous tend la mémoire et que nous nous entêtons à nommer souvenir."[42] It gradually becomes apparent that memory is unreliable in Le Conclave. It plays tricks by blurring the distinction between visions and memory. In Elissa, the possibility of self-representation is explored in a broader way.

The novel is set in Phoenician times and retells the story of Carthage through a translation of Punic inscriptions. These have presumably been found in the ruins of the city and are alleged to be a letter by Elissa herself. The letter reconstructs the queen's journey in detail, explains her ideas on leadership and government, and dwells on her musings about her motives and dreams. The narrative of the journey combines vivid descriptions of events and places with reflections and ideas. Elissa sets out from Tyre with one hundred men, including senators, priests, soldiers and rowers. The dynamics within the fleet change constantly as these individuals gradually co-alesce into a small community. Elissa uses her skill to keep the community together, allotting responsibilities and practicing the art of government. The group's first stop is Cyprus, where they are not allowed to stay but are given twenty-seven virgins. The second stop is Sabratha in Libya, a city without music that performs curious religious practices. Elissa makes special note of a cathartic communal evening at which gods are erected, pleaded to and abused, and then destroyed and buried. Sabratha is completely devoted to agriculture. An exchange of expertise takes place, navigation skills being traded for agricultural knowledge. Of Elissa's community, two women who have become pregnant, one priest, and two soldiers remain behind in Sabratha. The following stop is Hadrumet, where Elissa is accused of barbarously sacrificing children. Phoenicians already living in the city are expelled and join her convoy. The fleet then heads for Utica, but, due to a navigation error, ends up at the foot of a "perfumed hill." The group likes the place, purchases it by tricking Hiarbas, the African king of the region, and builds Carthage. Hiarbas is keen to assimilate foreigners and asks Elissa for marriage. She accepts in public, but decides privately not to consummate the union out of respect for her dead husband. Accepting this offer of marriage is part of her strategy to protect and preserve her community by creating a matrimonial alliance with the African inhabitants of the area. The architecture, the deity and the communal relations of the new city state are debated and considered at length.

Just as in *Le Conclave*, and running parallel to the main narrative, there is a story of personal anguish and an attempt to disentangle intimate motivations from a desire to serve the public interest. Elissa's personal narrative runs through the whole text. It seems that, in addition to the political circumstances, there is at the root of her flight a dream, in which she finds herself in a relationship of complicity with, and forbidden desire for, her brother, Pygmalion. In the dream she participates in the murder of her husband and uncle, Acherbas. Elissa also recalls how she and her brother played at dressing in each other's clothes, and reflects on her desire for him. Throughout the letter the distinction between the two motives becomes blurred, since the jour-ney is portrayed as a flight for secret personal reasons just as much as it is an escape from the brother's tyrannical rule.

Elissa is a complex, multilayered narrative open to diverse interpretations from a number of theoretical angles. An allegorical reading of the book is conceivable. It is easy to draw parallels between this story and events that are chronologically closer to us. One might think of the Arab conquest, during which the Qur'an supplanted the religious narrative indigenous to seventh-century Tunisia, or even the French colonial conquest of a country believed to be essentially il-literate and oral. The establishment of the contemporary nation-state offers another direction for interpretation. Elissa's letter can also be seen as a sort of "mirror for princes" addressed to modern-day rulers. The book engages with a number of issues, including the interface between history and myth, national community and self, and femininity and masculinity. Most relevant here, however, is the reading of *Elissa* as a rewriting of Western representations of Dido, in par-ticular in the Roman epic poem *The Aeneid*.[43]

The story of the founder of Carthage is included by Virgil (70–19 B.C.) among the en-counters of Aeneas as he sets out from Troy to fulfil his destiny, which is to build Rome. The story of Dido, who is also referred to as Sidonian Dido or Queen Dido, starts in Book I: "Carthage this realm, Agenor's Tyrian town/But Libyans bound it, tribes intractable/Here reigns, from Tyre and from her brother fled/Queen Dido. Long her sorrows, long and dark;/But I will tread the surface of the tale." In the epic she falls in love with Aeneas and adopts Roman culture and Roman religion. Her role in the epic, however, has more to do with Rome than with Carthage or even with history altogether. In *Innovations of Antiquity* Ralph

Hexter argues that Carthaginian history is made to fit the overall Roman view of the world. Dido in Virgil's poem is not Sidonian (historically speaking) but is part of the Roman imagination. Her myth is "buried" in the overall foundational myth of the Roman Empire. For instance, gods are seen in Roman terms: Baal Hammon is taken to be Saturn, while Tanit is considered to be Juno.[44] Even Dido herself is portrayed as trying to incorporate Roman history and culture into her own city. Hexter concludes: "Sidonian Dido is the one Dido that Virgil's foundation epic does not present."[45] Mellah's attempt to extricate Elissa from Dido is an effort to re-present her from the perspective of a descendant. It proposes the reconstruction of a history that does not fit into a Roman view of the world, one that predates, ignores and challenges any such presumed tie. He is convinced that: "Dido can hardly be considered worthy of Elissa."[46] The queen reflects on the treatment of her own name: "There will even be poets who will distort it so that it sounds quite ridiculous."[47] In Mellah's book Elissa's story is foundational in its own right: it founds a civilization and originates a myth. Roman civilization and mythology are seen as conquering, alien. In Mellah's version Tanit is the creation of Elissa alone; and it is the African Hierbas who devises a fitting symbol for the goddess. The original title Mellah gave his book captures and transforms the Roman meaning of the name. *Elissa, la reine vagabonde* keeps the meaning of Dido, "wanderer," but calls the queen by her name, Elissa (Elisha in Phoenician) and title (Queen).

Yet Mellah's post-colonial aim of reclaiming his history and mythology through rewriting is not as straightforward as it seems. The style of representation makes reclaiming the myth a complex affair. The novel plays on the historical ambiguity surrounding the legendary founder of Carthage in order to create a narrative that operates through processes of doubt and uncertainty. In fact, doubt is embedded in the frame of the story and spreads within Elissa's self-narrative.

In what resembles a prologue, called "By Way of Introduction," the narrator describes the origin of the story and the process of translating it. About 2200 stelae, believed to contain a letter addressed by Elissa to her brother Pygmalion, were discovered in 1874 by an amateur archaeologist, M. de Sainte-Marie, but were lost at sea. Fortunately, the narrator's grandfather happened to own 250 stelae. The grandfather was translating them into Arabic when he died. He urged his grandson to complete the task: "Continue the work. Decipher these stelae. Classify them. Give them a voice. Do not give up. . . . Promise me. . . ."[48] It is this promise that the narrator claims to have kept.[49] The narrator undermines his own translation by confessing to extensive interventions in the original text. He explains (notice his verbs): "Here and there, I have had to fill a gap, to imagine a continuation, invent a transition, correct a turn of phrase, emphasize a point, tone down an epithet, qualify a verb, delete a sentence."[50] Once the translation/recreation is finished, the narrator is left with incomplete fragments. His dilemma is described in the following terms: "As you can imagine, Dido's royal lack of concern threw yours truly into the deepest depression, and gave him his most sleepless nights."[51] He decides to classify the fragments according to his state of mind and his imagination "on a particular day or night."[52]

However, the most striking feature of the book is not so much this irreconcilable distance between the narrator's version and the original letter, but the gulf between Elissa's description and the object of her description. The process of description of her fiancé is as follows: "Thin, slight, young, vigorous, beardless, courteous, gentle: seven adjectives intended to give an account of what Hiarbas is."[53] She realizes that "Hiarbas is not these adjectives."[54] The description does not coincide with the described. It misses him. She explains: "Inevitably so, for every description misses its object, the object is always either more or less than the words which have served to describe it."[55] The sign does not represent the referent. Elissa says: "Writing and description are only approximations, ruses and reductions."[56] Convinced of the futility of her attempt, she gives up all description of Hiarbas. She does not want to kill him by describing him.[57] Elissa is aware of the limits of language. Yet she writes and she attempts to represent.

Moreover, confusion due to representation is linked closely with the origins of the city Elissa is credited with founding. The alphabet mastered, if not invented, by the Phoenicians, and completely unknown to the African king Hiarbas, serves Dido's trick well.[58] When she shows him the written document, which represents the borders of the plot on which Carthage is to be built, he reacts with disbelief and suspicion. Elissa writes: "Between the real object and the written term that signified it, Hierbas discerned a great deformation, a diabolical transformation which prefigured, perhaps, the day when the world would be drowned beneath a flood of fossilized words."[59] For Hiarbas, writing bears no relation to what he understands and perceives through his senses. He may accept a pictographic representation of reality, but never the alphabet. Hiarbas gives in to writing and Carthage is born—an unreal city. The founding of Carthage signifies the victory of the written over the oral, of the sign over the referent, of Phoenicia over Africa. As the name indicates, *Qart Hadasht* is a combination of city (*qart*) and new (*hadasht*). Elissa writes in this regard: "The city being nothing but a series of signs, novelty will be our sign, our illusion and our paradoxical memory."[60] *Qart Hadasht* would therefore be no more than a dream of newness, a name that is crumbling, deconstructing.

Mellah replaces the question, "What do we know about Elissa?" with the more postmodern question, "What can we know about Elissa?"[61] She is heterogeneous, contradictory and unstable. Throughout the book, she continually changes places (she travels from port to port), gender appearance ("The oldest of the priests cut my hair; it was the first time I had worn it short"), and identity (she is queen, city, nation, lover, and myth). Mellah's novel does not reveal hitherto hidden knowledge about Elissa, but analyses the very ontology of knowledge.[62] To capture the diversity of Elissa's myth would be an attempt to "represent the unrepresentable."[63] To search for truth in the various historical versions of Dido and document the foundation of Carthage in a translation of fragments attributed to Elissa betrays a naïve belief that one fiction is better or more truthful than another. In *Elissa*, description points the reader to writing or the signifier.[64] Narration draws attention to its own ways of functioning as narrative.

Conclusion: A Tale of Two Cities

Mellah maintains throughout *Le conclave* and *Elissa* an attempt to construct a narrative of the loss of memory in a modern city, Tunis, and the redemptive power of memory in its ancient ancestor, Carthage. *Elissa* is the book of Carthage. It retraces the climactic journey of its founder. *Le Conclave* is a narrative about contemporary Tunis. It investigates its anticlimatic existence. Carthage and Tunis reflect their founders and their times. Carthage is mysterious, labyrinthine, secretive, perfumed and anchored in water. It is an image of its founder, the "Queen of the Seas," who perfumes herself and guards her secrets (her incestuous desire, her planned suicide, her dreams).[65] Elissa defends her dreams and her secrets to her death, offering her body to fire rather than to Hiarbas.[66] Carthage is protective of its purity, its ideal and its statues. Baal Hammon and Tanit, a god and a goddess, constitute the focal point of the city and the focus of its community of residents. The city's fortifications suggest openness. Yet its structure forbids conquest. Its conquerors will have to fight their way from house to house and body to body (*corps-à-corps*).[67]

Its modern counterpart could not be more different. Tunis is nameless, severed from the sea, open to the invader, flat and odorless. It is a bastard construction, with no anchor or roots. It segregates its citizens by means of an anonymous line (Route X), as if its geographers feared the meanings of history and memory, and took refuge in meaningless abstract mathematics. And when it names its streets and neighborhoods, it fails miserably to link memory to name. Its statues polarize loyalties and disfigure history. Tunis is a masculine city, devoid of mystery, temptation and dreams. It is plain, aggressive and practical. Like its arrogant and calculating leader, the city turns its back on the sea, and faces West. It forces its historians to hide in the old city and banishes its citizens to the outskirts (Montagne Rouge), severing their ties with history.[68] The movement from past to present seems a passage from legendary fame to anonymity, from memory to amnesia and from dream to a short-sighted vision. While Carthage protects its memory and claims it like a treasured child or a cherished dream, Tunis disowns its history and shuns it, like an unwanted child or a disturbing nightmare. While the letter in *Elissa* reconstructs a legendary chastity and a foundational vision, the journalist's investigation in *Le conclave* pieces together shattered dreams. The condemnation is complete: Tunis is a disappointment, a disfigured image of its ancestral past. Mellah attempts a double critique: a rehabilitation of Elissa from reductive and alienating Western representations, and a parallel project to rescue her legend from the short-sighted contemporary history dominating the country that bears her legacy.

Notes

1. These are the plays *Néron ou les oiseaux de passage* (1974) and *Le palais du non-retour* (1976); the essay, *De l'Unité arabe* (1985), and the novels, *Le Conclave des pleureuses* (1987) and *Elissa, la reine vagabonde,*(1988). The latter has been translated into English as *Elissa* by Howard Curtis (London: Quartet Books, 1990). In this essay all references are to the English version.

2. Mellah only features in introductory essays or studies that treat him along with other writers. See, for instance, A. Maazaoui, "Eroticism and the Sacred: The Novels of Tahar Ben Jalloun, Assia Djebar and Fawzi Mellah," *Romance Notes* 38, no. 2 (1998): 149–56; Pierrette Renard, "Le miroir d'Elissa ou les lectures contemporaines de Carthage," *Recherches et travaux* 54 (1998): 249–59; and Mansour M'henni, "Fawzi Mellah," in *La littérature maghrébine de langue française*, ed. Charles Bonn, Naget Khadda and Abdallah Mdarhri-Alaoui (Paris: EDICEF-AUPELG, 1996).

3. Tunisia is not an exception in this respect. Henri LeFebvre associates this erasure of memory with the "brutal liquidation of history and the past in an even manner" perpetrated by the modern world. See *The Production of Space*, trans. Donald Nicholson-Smith (Oxford: Blackwell, 1991), 121.

4. Fawzi Mellah, *Le Conclave des pleureuses* (Paris: Seuil, 1987), 154.

5. Mellah, *Le Conclave*, 175.

6. Mellah, *Le Conclave*, 176.

7. Fawzi Mellah, *Elissa, la reine vagabonde* (Paris: Seuil, 1988) has been translated into English as *Elissa* by Howard Curtis (London: Quartet Books, 1990). In the present essay, all references are to the English version.

8. *Fabula* is defined as by Gerald Prince as "The set of narrated situations and events in their chronological sequence; the basic story material." *A Dictionary of Narratology* (Lincoln: University of Nebraska Press, 1987), 30.

9. Mellah, *Le Conclave*, 40.

10. Mellah, *Le Conclave*, 42.

11. Mellah, *Le Conclave*, 44.

12. Mellah, *Le Conclave*, 80.

13. Mellah, *Le Conclave*, 124–25.

14. Mellah, *Le Conclave*, 198.

15. This address is a thinly veiled allusion to the family's connection with popular memory and mythology. The number seven, Phoenicia and fruitless patience (Impasse de la Patience) refer to the beliefs and the plight of the poor, and set them against the rootless rich who live in the nameless streets of the "New Quarter."

16. There are other issues, which cannot be treated here. The journalist's personal narrative is dominated by gender identity and male/female relations. Writing itself, in particular the differences and parallels between journalistic reporting and the writing of fiction, is discussed many times. There is a continuous and progressive uncertainty about events as well as about the saint's biography.

17. Mellah, *Le Conclave*, 55.

18. Mellah, *Le Conclave*, 69.

19. Mellah, *Le Conclave*, 62.

20. Mellah, *Le Conclave*, 69.

21. Mellah, *Le Conclave*, 185.

22. Mellah, *Le Conclave*, 97.

23. Mellah expresses a concern shared by other compatriots. In "A Hymn to the Six Days" the poet Muhammad al-Saghayyir Awlad Ahmad writes:

Dear Ibn Khaldun! The city is too narrow for your stride.
   How often I passed by your cloak of steel . . . and loathed my time!
Shed the new idol!
And write to the opposite idol what he is worth.
Say what you please:
"Your horse has stopped while your hand continues to welcome the stranger"
Say what you please.
For we are destined to last
And he is doomed to rust.
A Hymn to the Six Days (Tunis: Dimitir, 1988), 40.

The government that took over from Bourguiba in November 1987, a date that coincides curiously with the publication of *Le Conclave des pleureuses*, removed Bourguiba's statue and replaced it with a giant clock. The poet Awlad Ahmad foretells the change in a satirical poem written three years before the event.

"My country is precise, like a clock / A country where each person is an arm / And where the individual elects the group," 35. See Mellah, *Le Conclave*, 185.

24. Mellah, *Le Conclave*, 14.

25. Mellah, *Le Conclave*, 16.

26. Mellah, *Le Conclave*, 36.

27. Mellah, *Le Conclave*, 26.

28. Mellah, *Le Conclave*, 30.

29. Mellah, *Le Conclave*, 47.

30. Mellah, *Le Conclave*, 86.

31. Mellah, *Le Conclave*, 85.

32. Mellah, *Le Conclave*, 86.

33. Mellah, *Le Conclave*, 86.

34. Mellah, *Le Conclave*, 119.

35. Mellah, *Le Conclave*, 118.

36. Mellah, *Le Conclave*, 172.

37. A reference to popular resistance to French plans to convert Tunisians into French citizens. Protests included actions to prevent the burial of those who took up French citizenship in Islamic cemeteries, especially in 1932–1933. See Muhammad al-Hadi al-Sharif, *Tarikh Tunis* (*A History of Tunisia*) (Tunis: CERES, 1985), 119.

38. Mellah, *Le Conclave*, 173.

39. Mellah, *Le Conclave*, 78.

40. Mellah, *Le Conclave*, 78.

41. Philippe Lejeune defines autobiography as "Récit retrospectif en prose qu'une personne réelle fait de sa propre existence, lorsqu'elle met l'accent sur sa vie individuelle, en particulier sur l'histoire de sa personnalité." *Le pacte autobiographique* (Paris: Seuil, 1975), 14. He adds that autobiographies seek not verisimilitude but resemblance to reality, 36. Peter Abbot thinks that the audience for the novel is creative; it takes part in the book, while that for the autobiography is analytical. See Peter Abbott, "Autobiography, Autography, Fiction: Ground work for a Taxonomy of Textual Categories," *New Literary History* 19, no. 3 (1988): 608. On the fictional autobiography, see Alain Robbe-Grillet's work, especially *Le Miroir qui revient* (Paris: Minuit, 1985) and *Angélique ou l'enchantement* (Paris: Minuit, 1988).

42. In Robbe-Grillet's *Le Miroir qui revient*, one character expresses a similar stance. He says: "Qu'on me comprenne bien: il s'agit seulement ici de dire, d'essayer de dire, comment je voyais les choses autour de moi; ou même, de façon plus objective encore, comment je m'imagine aujourd'hui que je voyais alors les choses" (*Miroir*, 47). The relationship between Mellah's work and the Nouveau Roman is quite strong and requires further research. For more on the theory of the New Novel, see Alain Robbe-Grillet, *Pour un nouveau roman* (Paris: Minuit, 1963). Mellah, *Le Conclave*, 17.

43. Virgil, *Aeneid*, trans. Charles J. Billson (New York: Dover, 1995). For an analysis of the treatment of Elissa's story by Virgil, see Ralph Hexter, "Sidonian Dido," in *Innovations of Antiquity*, ed. Ralph Hexter and Daniel Selden (London: Routledge, 1992).

44. Hexter, "Sidonian Dido," 347.

45. Hexter, "Sidonian Dido," 357.

46. Hexter, "Sidonian Dido," 160.

47. Hexter, "Sidonian Dido," 160.

48. Hexter, "Sidonian Dido," 3.

49. The grandfather's intention was to translate the Punic inscriptions into Arabic. His grandson completed the transfer into French. The mediation of Arabic is at the heart of the project from the point of view of language. The relationship between what might be called Mellah's de-Romanisation of Elissa at the narrative level and his attempt to rewrite her story in a romance language, French, is simply too complex to pursue here. To point to what appears to be a contradiction is to ignore the fact that part of Mellah's implied audience is well versed in the Virgilian tradition. Otherwise, the argument that Mellah rewrites Virgil would lose its potency. A narrative analysis of the novel as a message to Western readers is given in Emma Kafalenos's unpublished conference paper, "Mythmaking as Dialogue: Fawzi Mellah's Elissa (Re)Tells the Founding of Carthage." Mellah, unlike, for instance, his compatriot Abdelwahad Meddeb, does not dwell on the language of his writing in any explicit way.

50. Hexter, "Sidonian Dido," 3.

51. Hexter, "Sidonian Dido," 4.

52. Hexter, "Sidonian Dido," 5.

53. Hexter, "Sidonian Dido," 110.

54. Hexter, "Sidonian Dido," 110.

55. Hexter, "Sidonian Dido," 110.

56. Hexter, "Sidonian Dido," 111.

57. Hexter, "Sidonian Dido," 111.

58. According to legend, Carthage was built thanks to a trick. Local chiefs allowed Elissa to buy a piece of land the size of an ox's hide. She accepted and then cut up the hide into small pieces, which were used to cover the Byrsa hill on which Carthage was to be built. See David Soren et al., *Carthage* (New York: Simon and Shuster, 1990). See *Elissa*, 104–5, for Mellah's version of the ruse.

59. Hexter, "Sidonian Dido," 105.

60. Hexter, "Sidonian Dido," 124.

61. Of Elissa Soren writes: "Of course we can never be really sure if she ever lived at all, so romanticized and distorted her story has become over the centuries" (*Carthage*, 17).

62. According to McHale the postmodern novel is characterized by the change from the epistemological dominant to the ontological dominant. See David Harvey, *The Condition of Postmodernity* (Cambridge: Blackwell, 1990), 41. The interest is no longer in how to convey and handle the meaning of a com-

plex situation (the project of the modernist novel) but instead in how radically different realities can co-exist, mingle and interact. The subject is no longer treated as stable or fixed but as a moving and ambiguous construction.

63. Harvey, *The Condition*, 25.

64. Postmodern literary creation is a mere play of signifiers, says Harvey, 53. On postmodern representation, see Linda Hutcheon, *The Politics of Postmodernism* (London: Routledge, 1989), and Frederic Jameson, *Postmodernism, or the Cultural Logic of Late Capitalism* (Durham: Duke University Press, 1990).

65. There is a significant feminist perspective in the book that needs to be treated at a length not possible here. Elissa identifies with Carthage and perceives it as a woman's achievement. She says: "My history is totally as one with my veneration for the community and my founding of Qart Hadasht" (160). And adds: "At any rate, it was thus that I imagined the new state. It was thus and not otherwise that I wished to dream Qart Hadasht before men built it and spoiled it" (132). Here again, Mellah is in tune with his compatriots writing in Arabic. Jamila al-Majiri celebrates Elissa's role as a woman in Tunisian history in the poem "Mistress of the Seas." She writes:

> The sea color turns more beautiful / whenever the Mistress of the Seas / passes by and throws a greeting. / And history acquires a scent/ When it is built by the dreams of women.

See Jamila al-Majiri, *Diwan al-Nisa* (*The Women's Diwan*) (Tunis: SOTEPA, 1997), 92.

66. Mellah, *Le Conclave*, 139.

67. Elissa describes the aim behind the layout of the city: "And if, by some misfortune, an enemy were to climb them [the walls], he would then quickly lose himself in the narrow, tortuous alleys, and have to ransack the very houses to find the inhabitants; he would need to burn the city to the ground in order to conquer and subjugate it" (131). This is exactly what the Romans were forced to do in order to subdue Carthage in 146 B.C. (*History of Tunisia*, 22).

68. The saint's family is relocated from the Phoenician Quarter to Montagne Rouge across Route X.

6

Francophone Literature of the Middle East by Women: Breaking the Walls of Silence

Mary-Angela Willis

WOMEN WROTE PROFUSELY DURING the Lebanese Civil War. However, women had struggled unsuccessfully to find their voice, particularly in poetry, a literary form steeped in tradition and dominated by men. The novel, on the other hand, provided a new form of expression open to innovation and experimentation. Seizing the opportunity, women novelists not only followed in the footsteps of earlier writers, but also actively influenced and contributed to the development of the novel along unconventional lines. The oppression of women within a male-dominated society, an issue that had not hitherto been addressed, was not merely exposed, but vehemently rejected. Of course, such outspokenness met with objections and scandal. The story of oppressed Arab women was finally being told.

For the first time, women were speaking out against their forced enslavement and shedding light on harsh customs such as "enforced virginity, arranged marriages, production of male children on demand, and, finally, prolonged isolation from men and from the outside world during adulthood."[1] Through their writing, they publicly denounced the conditions that they were subjected to in the name of custom and tradition.

Some of the women writers who wrote during the Civil War in Lebanon became known as the Beirut Decentrists. Through their novels they were able to comment on a society that they were a part of and yet purposely excluded from. This group includes Ghada al-Samman, Hanan al-Sheikh, Emily Nasrallah, Laila Usairan, Daisy al-Amir, Claire Gebeyli and Venus Khoury-Ghata (who write in French), and Etel Adnan and Evelyne Accad (who both write in French and English). Miriam Cooke defines the Beirut Decentrists as:

> a group of women writers who have shared Beirut as their home and the war as their experience. They have been decentred in a double sense: physically, they were scattered all over a self-destructive city; intellectually, they moved in separate spheres. They wrote alone and for themselves. They would not conceive of their writings as related to those of others, yet their marginal perspective, which gave insight into the holistic aspect of the war, united them and allowed them discursively to undermine and restructure society around the image of the new center.[2]

What bound these female authors together was the fact that they shared a common perspective as individuals struggling to survive a war as observers, a role reserved for the women, children and the elderly, rather than as active participants. According to Cooke, this exclusion from participating in violence allowed them to introduce a unique critical perspective on Lebanese society and its political, military and religious leaders as well as to create a voice that would influence the process of social reconstruction once the war was over. The term "marginal" used by Cooke refers to the exclusion of women from the male-dominated roles of authority in social, political, familial, literary and religious spheres. In these domains controlled by men, a woman is only a partial participant and is thus stripped of a voice and of rights. Deemed of lesser value, she exists on the margins of society, where she is kept quietly at a safe distance from events. She is an observer looking in from the outside at the center, where power and authority dictate the laws that she is subjected to. Women therefore write from the margins of the society and the literary tradition that are their inheritance since they are not accepted within the established literary canon.

Breaking the Code of Silence

When civil war broke out in Lebanon, female authors seized the opportunity to look ahead and discuss reform. Walls and lines of demarcation were used to symbolize the barriers erected to limit the freedom and maintain the silence of voices that are excluded from the circles of power. Although war stands for everything that is vile within a society, it also serves as the catalyst for change and helps destroy the very foundations that have brought about the country's downfall. The war in Lebanon was therefore the result of an oppressive, patriarchal tradition, which had spread inequality between men and women, and subjected women to the domination of men, in both the private and public domains. However, the war was a necessary part of the equation. War represents a society as it crumbles and provides an opportunity for women to speak out against oppression. It allows them to take advantage of the chaos and strife caused by the war in order to ensure that all voices are heard during the healing and restructuring period after the war ends.

In *Sitt Marie Rose*[3] and *Coquelicot du massacre*,[4] Adnan and Accad demonstrate the effect that patriarchy has had on society and the divisions that it has created among its people. Patriarchy has successfully erected walls between men and women, confining women within a domestic space while restricting their participation as subjects in society. That same system of exclusion and oppression is the cause of society's self-destruction, which is embodied in the war. The war itself is a symptom of an oppressive society that has taken a path that will culminate in its own destruction. The result is a society in need of rebuilding, a situation in which previously silenced voices are able to contribute to the restructuring process. Adnan and Accad portray women's stifled voices through heroines who resist society's overpowering hold on them. Through Marie Rose the teacher, Nour the mother, Najmé the student, and Hayat the writer Adnan and Accad forge new a space where women fight against oppression and create roles based on their newfound identity.[5]

Sitt Marie Rose is based on an actual event: the execution by Christian militiamen of a Christian woman, Marie Rose, who had organized social services in the Palestinian camps and ran a school for deaf-mute children. The novel is divided into two sections entitled "Temps I" and "Temps II." A female Christian scriptwriter who is invited to collaborate with a male Christian filmmaker, Mounir, narrates the first section, which is set in the pre-war era. Mounir wishes to make a movie narrating Lebanon's return to a pre-colonial state based on outdated traditions.

Mounir and his friends show a video clip of their hunting trip in the Syrian desert to the women who, according to Madeline Cassidy, "are fulfilling the traditional role, kept within the family circle, watching, admiring, supporting, reflecting the exploits and performance of the men, the doers, the hunters."[6] Madeline Cassidy alludes to this scene as an illustration of a society in which "the distinctly masculine sphere of hunting, war, commerce and power is traditionally separated from the distinctly feminine sphere of nurturing, domestic work, the family and sub-servience."[7] Adnan is clearly portraying the men's mentality as "competitive, destructive, mind-lessly exploitive"[8] and contrasting it to the women's silent observation of their men's exploits. The scenario illustrates the divisions between the traditional roles of men and women. Men embody roles of power that emphasize performance, destruction and exploitation, whereas women adhere to the role of the supporter and observer. This dichotomy only emphasizes the tension that underlies the semblance of calm before the onset of the war.

In the second section Marie Rose is taken hostage at her school, where she is interrogated by Christian militiamen and a member of the Christian clergy. Until her execution, Marie Rose verbally engages her captors, critiquing the oppressive lifestyle imposed on women by a ruth-less patriarchal society. She blames this system for the war and the disintegration of society. As Marie Rose's words grow stronger and more logical, her captors' arguments ring increasingly hollow. According to Cassidy, Marie Rose occupies a space that exists very much on the bound-ary, both literally and intellectually."[9] Marie Rose not only crosses the external boundaries sep-arating the Christian community from the Palestinian camps, she also rejects her role as a sub-servient wife and chooses a life that defies the restrictions imposed upon her by society. According to her Christian executioners, she has "passée à l'ennemi . . . [une] femme impu-dente, . . . et se mêlant d'événements politiques, leur chasse gardée d'habitude."[10] In other words, she dares to interfere in politics, which is traditionally the men's personal hunting ground. The men proceed to execute her on these grounds and, as Cassidy states, "the dehu-manization that allows these young men to justify the kidnapping, torture, and execution of Marie Rose can be seen as a reflection of their hierarchical world view."[11] Marie Rose's death is due to her refusal to adopt the role dictated to her by an oppressive social system.

Marie Rose blatantly defies the traditional role of a woman. She is accused of betraying not only her husband but also her country and her religion: "Toute action feminine même béné-fique et apparemment non politisée est considérée comme une rebellion dans un monde où la femme est asservie depuis des siècles. Marie Rose provoquait donc la risée et la haine bien avant le jour fatidique de son arrestation."[12]

Her defiance incites "la risée et la haine," yet she refuses to be swayed by differences in reli-gion or held back by restrictive patriarchal beliefs. Her actions in embracing people of a differ-ent nationality and religion alarm and even scare the soldiers and clergyman. The narrator re-veals the men's reaction to her: "Marie Rose leur fait peur. Ils ont tous les moyens du monde pour l'écraser en une seconde. . . . Mais ils ont su dès le premier moment qu'ils n'allaient vain-cre ni son cœur ni son esprit."[13] They have the power and authority to kill her, but they cannot erase the truth in her words. She is therefore a threat to their positions. The solution is to elim-inate this source of rebellion, as the narrator explains: "Mais une femme qui se tient debout et les regarde dans les yeux est un arbre à abattre et ils l'abattent. . . . C'est la peur, non l'amour, qui est ici la grande génératrice de toutes les actions."[14] Marie Rose accepts difference, and in doing so, she herself is considered different by society. As someone who is highly educated and independent, Marie Rose does not embody the traditions and conventions of her society, and is therefore executed. However, Marie Rose's words reveal the oppression to which women are subjected. By voicing these conditions, she demands an explanation from her listeners, the men who capture her. She also articulates her refusal to accept her situation, and according to Adnan, this is where hope lies. Adnan chooses to focus on the "healing violence of the words spoken by Marie Rose to her captors [rather] than in the final violence of her death."[15] One must at all costs avoid silence, which is the ultimate failure. Once the silence is broken, there is hope for the future. Furthermore, once Marie Rose's voice is joined by the voices of others, they will no longer be ignored. She dies, accused of loving a foreigner, and abandoning a morality that condemns difference and perpetuates silence. She is victorious in the sense that she succeeds in piercing the walls of silence with her words.

Piercing the Walls of Oppression

In *Coquelicot du massacre* Evelyne Accad picks up where Adnan left off. Whereas the defiant act of refusing to submit to oppression is accomplished through words in *Sitt Marie Rose*, Evelyne Accad's heroines break with tradition through movement, and their acts pierce the walls of silence and cross the line of demarcation. Among the vivid images of the destruction inflicted upon Lebanon and its people are images of walls: barriers that separate one side from another and restrict an area within a confined space, and images of the line of demarcation that separated the city of Beirut into the Christian Sector and the Muslim Sector during the Civil War. Accad uses this imagery as representative of the war's destruction and the pollution of society.

In *Coquelicot du massacre*, Accad uses the line of demarcation created by the war as an image that also represents the barrier between men and women, the oppressor and the oppressed, war and peace. In order for Nour to transport her son, Raja, to safety, she must cross the line of demarcation. She believes that on the other side of the line of demarcation "c'était plus calme . . . il n'y avait pas de combats . . . on pouvait marcher dans les rues, que chrétiens, musulmans et druzes se côtoyaient comme par le passé."[16] The other side provides a way out of the current hazardous situation: "Il fallait traverser la ville, essayer de rejoindre son frère pour que l'enfant cesse de trembler, et qu'ils puissent de nouveau respirer, bouger, vivre."[17] She is searching for a place where people of different genders and religions live together in peace, and where her son will be safe. However, in order to reach her safe haven, she must first brave the dangers of crossing the line of demarcation "qui coupe la ville en deux, le no-man's land, empire de la terreur, de la destruction et de la mort."[18] Another character describes it as "le pont de la mort, [. . .] le point de rencontre de la ville brisée."[19] The line of demarcation is infested with snipers who shoot at innocent victims attempting to cross the line. It therefore serves as an obstacle to freedom as well as a division that separates violence from peace. It is the point of utmost danger as well as the only possible escape route, since by crossing the line and reaching the other side she will come to a place of peace and freedom.

Walls are another prominent image used by Accad to represent the silence imposed upon women throughout history. They stand for women's exclusion from the public governance of their society. Built to separate the oppressors from the oppressed, walls invade Nour's nightmares:

Dans ses cauchemars, la femme cherche à atteindre une mer paisible et transparente. Elle court dans une plaine de canons et d'obus. . . . Elle arrive dans un village étrange—maisons grises, fenêtres vertes et bleues—comme si la mer avait pénétré la desolation. Des monstres—animaux aux corps longs et visqueux, portés par mille pattes—sortes des lézardes. Des insects noirs et velus surgissent de chaque trou des murs percés par les balles. Une vie grouillante et fiévreuse semble naître des cendres, jaillir d'un monde souterrain.[20]

Nour's dream of walls symbolizes her hazardous trek across the city. The tranquil sea represents the peaceful destination that she seeks by crossing to the other side. First, she must cross an area that is being shelled by artillery and mortar fire. She reaches an abandoned village where the walls of the houses act as a barrier to the peaceful sea that "la femme cherche à atteindre."[21] The windows of the houses reflect the sea in the distance, giving the illusion that the sea is reaching out to her in her state of desperation. But first, she must break through the walls erected by patriarchal oppression, which is represented here by "[des] animaux aux corps longs et visqueux" and "[des] insectes noirs et velus" hiding inside the walls. This creates a surreal view of the city of Beirut, from which Nour has to escape by crossing the barriers put in her way by the infested walls.

Nour's success in reaching the other side is therefore dependent on her being able to safely cross the line, as she admits: "Si tu parviens à franchir le pont de la mort, alors l'espoir peut renaître."[22] Hope lies in demolishing the walls and crossing the boundaries that separate tradition from freedom. It lies in uniting the two sides. Nour endeavors to break through the confinement of the walls by defying tradition and bravely speaking out against the authority that has erected the walls. According to Nour: "Si je n'essaie pas de franchir ce mur de mutisme, d'absence, et de désolation, qui le fera?"[23] Nour represents women who are now ready to confront the danger entailed by breaking through the barriers and speaking out in opposition to oppression. It is the only way to provide a safe future for their children, who also represent the future of the country. The woman's courage is expressed when she states: "je ne peux pas rester. La mort est partout. Je préfère l'affronter."[24] Accad warns against the danger of complacency and failures to seize the opportunity for change. Complacency and the inability to act will only lead to death. The solution is to confront Lebanon's problems in order to vanquish them. The narrator alludes to the danger involved: "C'est un risque de traverser la ligne de demarcation, rupture de la ville, centre de violents combats, et d'affrontements meurtriers, siège de vendettas, des confrontations des zaïmes, et des askaris, déferlement de la haine."[25] This description places the center of violence at the line of demarcation. The actual front line shifted from day to day, as different factions entered and withdrew from the fighting. The line of demarcation, on the other hand, saw continuous fighting over seventeen years of civil war. The battles there were not necessarily organized violence perpetrated by the army or militia factions, but were often the result of actions by individuals who felt an urge to kill or who had a personal agenda. It was a place where murderers carried out their vendettas and where bloody confrontations took place. The line of demarcation is littered with images of destruction, such as ruined houses and collapsing buildings, and with weapons of war such as canons and soldiers. The line itself is denoted by barbed wire.

The walls are tainted with signs of violence: "Le mur est couvert de larges taches de sang auréolés de noir."[26] The pain and suffering inflicted by the war are encapsulated in a cry that resounds throughout the neighborhood, echoing between the walls: "Soudain, un long cri lugubre retentit et glace l'atmosphère, renvoyé de mur en mur, de pierre en pierre. La femme hurle sa douleur et son malheur. Rien n'arrêtera ce cri d'écorchée vive."[27] Women are choosing to remain silent no longer. It is a cry of refusal and a rejection of silence. Once the walls crumble, they can no longer serve as barriers: "Tout le quartier est empli de la mélodie qui traverse murs écroulés."[28] The words within the song refer to the breaking down of the walls:

> J'aimerais tellement percer le mur
> retrouver mon rêve
> marcher dans le sable des plages de mon pays refleuri
> courir à l'infini vers la mer
> Dans un horizon dégagé des voiles de haine et de violence[29]

The walls are obstacles that prevent the central character from realizing her dream and finding peace, obstacles that are incorporated into the image of the sea, a refuge free of hate and violence. However, silence and surrender to the status quo are greater dangers. As Nour crosses the city, she encounters a friend who speaks words of courage: "Continue ta quête. Reprends ta marche. Tu trouveras d'autres réponses. En les plaçant les unes à côté des autres, elles formeront peut-être le fil de vérité que nous cherchons, le nœud brisant la rupture—ligne de démarcation—réunissant les différences, tissant la toile sur laquelle une nouvelle société surgira."[30] According to Nour's friend, Nour must overcome her fear and face the danger in order to reach beyond the other side of the line to a place without walls. This place that she seeks is free of oppression and violence. It is an ideal that can only be made into a reality by rejecting the status quo and embracing difference and freedom. The answers that she will find along her journey and once she reaches the other side will not be those fabricated and dictated by men to maintain their domination over women. They will be new truths based on equality between the genders and celebration of their difference. Hayat defines this new place: "c'est le pluralisme, l'acceptation des différences, dans la tolérance . . . c'est le soleil de demain."[31]

Crumbling Walls

The walls erected by patriarchy to separate the oppressor from the oppressed, men from women, also serve to separate enforced silence from freedom of expression. In essence, these walls forbid the flow of communication between men and women. According to Accad, the walls of silence will disappear once the division between men and women fades and women become equal participants in society. In *Coquelicot du massacre*, a tender moment is shared between Hayat, a writer, and Adnan, her partner. The man succeeds in breaking through the wall that separates him from the woman and embraces her. Encouraged to bridge the distance between them, she in turn utters words of love kept hidden until now. The power of her words proves overwhelming, and he retreats back into the role of the rational, level-headed male: "Il a pris un ton de professeur. Il dissèque des idées qu'il retourne dans sa tête sans la regarder, sans l'écouter."[32] The line of communication is abruptly interrupted, followed by the physical separation of their bodies: "Ils marchent dans l'herbe, pas séparés, mur qui vient de se dresser, silence qu'elle ne peut plus briser, transie qu'elle est par l'impossible communication."[33] The walls come between them, interrupting all communication and separating them once again. Accad draws parallels between the effects of war, which culminate in the destruction of the walls, and the disintegration of barriers by verbal expression. In other words, the power of words is in some ways equivalent to the power of bombs: "Les mots éclatent comme une bombe. Le silence est insoutenable."[34] Only by breaking down the walls separating men and women can the silence be broken. This direct comparison then points to a correlation between the breakdown of society as a result of the war and the breakdown of silence as a consequence of the war waged by women to end their oppression.

The Faces of War

Etel Adnan uses Marie Rose to depict the battle fought by women, and gives names and faces to the oppressor in the form of three soldiers and a clergyman. In order to illustrate the violent mentality imposed by patriarchy, she describes a scene that compares men on a hunting trip to soldiers on the battlefield: "les chasseurs ressemblent aux soldats. . . . Les chasseurs braquent leurs fusils en direction du ciel comme des lance-fusées. Ils rient. Ils montrent leurs dents, leur santé, et leur plaisir."[35] Before the war, men romanticized the role of soldier and the glory associated with it. However, after the outbreak of the war, the soldier adopts a sense of omnipotence. His enthusiasm for hunting animals is transformed during the war into an enthusiasm for killing people. Fouad, a fanatical militiaman, declares: "Une milice, c'est un gouvernement sans gouvernés. Une milice a toujours raison . . . je suis l'ordre absolu. Je suis le pouvoir absolu. Je suis l'efficacité absolue. J'ai réduit toutes les vérités à la notion de vie et de mort."[36] Fouad represents the ideal image of the domination of the all-powerful and the enslavement of the weak. His world is composed of order, power and efficiency, all of which are controlled by the militia. Everything is reduced to life and death. Such absolutism goes hand in hand with fanaticism. Through Fouad, Adnan reveals the dangers of this mentality, its extremism and its obsession with power. Even Mounir, a fellow militiaman with a somewhat less fanatical nature, falls into the same trap when he declares: "C'est la violence qui accélère le progrès des peuples."[37] The war perpetuates the idea that violence is irrevocably linked with power to the point that, once it has destroyed everything in its path, there is nothing and no one left to violate or dominate.

Mounir represents the more moderate view of a man who is forced to take up the role of soldier, but who is aware of the futility of war and begins to question its significance: "Il se battait. C'est tout. Pourquoi? Pour préserver. Préserver quoi? Le pouvoir de son groupe. Qu'allait-t-il faire avec ce groupe et ce pouvoir? Refaire le pays. Quel pays? Là, tout devenait vague. Il perdait pied. Car dans ce pays il y avait toutes sortes de factions, de courants d'idées, de cas précis et individuels qu'aucune théorie ne pouvait contenir."[38] It is no longer clear why and for whom the war is being fought. Mounir becomes aware of the numerous political, religious and cultural faces of Lebanon, each with its own agenda and ideas that cannot be embodied within one single force. At the heart of these differences, patriarchy takes hold and excludes women's voices. Power lies in the hands of the factional leaders, and the authority of central government soon fades as these different factions gain strength. The issues that originally drove them to fight the war become irrelevant. Their battles are now purely a fight for power.

In *Coquelicot du massacre* Adnan, Hayat's lover, a man with no military affiliations, also talks of the futility of the war: "Cette guerre est tellement absurde. Toute cette jeunesse qu'on a armée et entraînée au combat ne sait plus faire autre chose maintenant. On lui a bourré le crâne de slogans et d'idéologies politiques et religieuses dont elle ne saisit pas la portée. Elle meurt pour rien, absolument rien."[39] Adnan discusses the absurdity of war and young people who have only ever known life during wartime. He even attacks religion, with its false ideologies and simple slogans. The desperation associated with the young people of Lebanon is represented in Najmé, who fights her own war against the oppression imposed on women. She dons a soldier's uniform: "Le placard est bourré de vêtements à la dernière mode. Elle s'attarde devant plusieurs toilettes et, finalement, choisit son ensemble guerilla: veste avec pantalons bouffants gris-verts, striés de lignes brunes et oranges."[40] She chooses to adopt the role of a fighter instead of being a woman dressed in the latest fashions. She is thus refusing to conform to the ideals imposed upon her of how a young woman ought to present herself, striking her own blows in the war against oppression.

Images of the war intensify the sense of the desperation and destruction inflicted upon Lebanon and its people: "de nombreuses maisons, des pans de murs sont écroulés, des vitres éclatées. Les femmes sont vêtues de noir. Les balcons des immeubles sont enveloppés d'un drap blanc en signe de deuil."[41] Even the characters compare themselves to dust, as if they too are disintegrating: "Au loin, la bataille fait rage, alors je me suis réduite en poussière, pour qu'on ne m'aperçoive pas."[42] The young university student, Najmé, represents the younger generation in Lebanon. Furthermore, Accad uses her to show women's imprisonment upon reaching adulthood. As the narrator says: "Tout le drame de la crise et la jeunesse de son pays est incarné dans cette belle jeune fille devenue épave."[43] She is a wreck, broken down by the destructive forces of patriarchy and war. A singer echoes her sentiments:

> Je veux vivre pour effacer la peur
> Je veux vivre pour effacer la haine
> Pour apprendre à ma sœur à relever la tête
> Etoile renaissante de la cendre des ruines[44]
> Il n'y a plus de soleil
> . . .
> Mon pays de poussière
> Est passé sous la mer. . . .[45]

Although reduced to ashes, she sees herself as rising again, like a phoenix, from the ruins, reborn, free from fear and hatred. According to Accad, hope lies in the ability to reconstruct after the destruction.

Lebanon's landscape is not spared either. Described as a "paysage apocalyptique,"[46] the city disintegrates as its patriarchal foundations collapse: "Vis-à-vis, un pan de la maison est écroulé. Les fenêtres sont noires, ce qui reste des murs est criblé de balles."[47] From the very start Accad describes a city that is being transformed into ash and dust: "Cendres, poussière et brindilles s'éparpillent au vent."[48] Accad evokes a horrific, surreal view of Beirut ravaged by war. The city is lifeless. Nothing moves. The streets are littered with decaying bodies and collapsed buildings. Yet Nour traces her way through the rubble, braving the danger in her search for safety: "Elle avance frôlant les murs, tirée par une force invisible, guidée par le besoin de survie."[49] She is accompanied by the power of the song, which inspires her with hope and courage, as she reveals to her friend: "J'aimerai que ton chant m'accompagne jusqu'au pont et au-delà de la ligne de démarcation. . . . Si ton chant marche avec moi, j'aurai la force d'aller jusqu'au bout."[50]

The Triumph of Song

Adnan and Accad weave different forms of narration that deviate from traditionally accepted techniques into their texts. For example, they adopt a non-linear narrative and use multiple narrators. Song is also integrated as a dominant feature of *Coquelicot du massacre*. In a song, the meaning of words is enhanced by their musical setting, which makes it possible for them to fill a space where words fail to express meaning. A song therefore makes it possible to utter the forbidden. The use of song for expressive purposes has been a typical feature of women's lives that can be traced back to the Middle Ages. Excluded from actively participating in the established literary heritage, women have nonetheless left their mark in the oral tradition. Women's singing of odes guaranteed their survival within the literary tradition over the centuries. By the constant repetition of others' words, they echoed the creative, and therefore superior, voices of men. As in the myth of Echo, women were unable to form and articulate their own verse, and so resorted to reciting the poetry of others. Still faced with opposition and resistance, women writers, such as Evelyne Accad, have turned to the heritage of their past as a source of creativity and expression. Their words, whether spoken, written or sung, now echo their resistance to oppression and the power of their own creativity. Song is therefore a common device adopted by those who have been oppressed. It serves to convey hope, as illustrated by an excerpt from the last song in the novel:

> Il suffirait d'écrire peut-être
> Une mélodie ou un refrain
> Pour que les cris deviennent chant
> Pour que l'enfant devienne oiseau
> Pour que l'homme apprenne à aimer[51]

Accad links the act of writing with the act of composing songs. According to her, a song has the power to stifle cries and communicate love. It is also a device that supplements the traditional literary text. Danielle Marx-Scouras explains that song is an "alternative form of discourse" that is used to replace "the progressive breakdown of linear narrative and character identity, [and] the paralysis of events."[52] Accad and Adnan both shift from a specific, protagonist-centerd narrative to multiple narratives woven around the situation in Lebanon and the war. As a result, they provide a forum where a multitude of voices can be heard, all accorded equal importance.

In *Sitt Marie Rose*, the novel represents the crisis of war by displacing the first-person narrator and transforming itself into a series of monologues by seven different characters. Each represents different opinions typical of their respective places in society: Marie Rose, Mounir and two of his militia fighters, a friar, the deaf-mute children who always speak together as one voice and, finally, the narrator. Each speaker appears three times, a structure that offers a range of perspectives. This method allows the reader to trace the development (or lack of development) of each character. As Cassidy puts it, "the important distinction among them lies in the point of view of each of the storytellers as each reveals an internal response to traditionally held concepts of identity, gender, and society."[53] Accad, by contrast, weaves together a multitude of voices throughout the novel, but, unlike Adnan, once the silence is broken and the path of courage is chosen by Nour to reach a safe haven, she also intersperses her text with songs that express pain and destruction as well as compassion and hope. A new space becomes possible, a space that refuses to be subjected to the violence created by war, a space where old forms of expression, such as the repetition of songs, and new forms of expression, such as multivocal, non-linear narratives, can be heard.

Conclusion

Etel Adnan and Evelyne Accad portray a society that is disintegrating on two levels: physically, as the war destroys the country, its buildings and infrastructure, cripples the economy and annihilates a vast proportion of its population; and morally, as a long, oppressive tradition that enforces the enslavement of women while upholding the power and authority of a patriarchal system of values crumbles. In Adnan and Accad's novels female protagonists speak out, and their newfound voices resound and break through the walls that have prevented them from participating in society. As female authors, Adnan and Accad themselves have defied whole literary tradition by breaking the silence imposed on women throughout Lebanese literary history.

Adnan and Accad succeed in creating a new space beyond the center of the literary tradition by articulating resistance to oppression and creating a reality with fewer barriers and restrictions. By writing in French, they reject the traditional literature of Lebanon, which embodies archaic and exclusionary practices dating back thousands of years. This use of the French language distances them from this tradition and allows them to articulate forbidden themes relating to women's oppression and marginalization. New forms of expression are adopted, intertwining the novel with songs and poems, making use of fragmented, multivocal forms of narration. In doing so, they seek to escape conformity and welcome change and difference in a space where all voices are given the chance to be heard. To write is to elicit a response, to mould and influence the reader. Since words create new realities that are communicated to the reader, they describe alternative ways of resisting injustice and oppression. Adnan and Accad also create new models that will help guide the reconstruction of a society that will need the participation of all of its citizens, especially its women, to survive and flourish.

Notes

1. Evelyne Accad and Rose Ghurayyib, eds., *Contemporary Arab Women Writers and Poets* (Beirut: Institute for Women's Studies in the Arab World, 1985), 30.

2. Miriam Cooke, *War's Other Voices: Women Writers on the Lebanese Civil War* (Cambridge: Cambridge University Press, 1988), 3.

3. Etel Adnan, *Sitt Marie Rose* (Paris: Editions des Femmes, 1978).

4. Evelyne Accad, *Coquelicot du massacre* (Paris: L'Harmattan, 1988).

5. In *The Location of Culture* Homi Bhabha gives a detailed analysis of peripheral existence and the ways in which people in this situation reinvent their space: "These 'in-between' spaces provide the terrain for elaborating strategies of selfhood . . . that initiate new signs of identity, and innovative sites of collaboration, in the act of defining the idea of society itself" (1–2).

6. Madeline Cassidy, "Love Is a Supreme Violence," *Violence, Silence, and Anger: Women's Writing As Transgression*, ed. Deirdre Lashgari (Charlottesville: University Press of Virginia, 1995), 283.

7. Cassidy, "Love Is a Supreme Violence," 283.

8. Cassidy, "Love Is a Supreme Violence," 283.

9. Cassidy, "Love Is a Supreme Violence," 284.

10. Adnan, *Sitt Marie Rose*, 110–11.

11. Cassidy, 285.

12. Adnan, *Sitt Marie Rose*, 112–12.

13. Adnan, *Sitt Marie Rose*, 76.

14. Adnan, *Sitt Marie Rose*, 75.

15. Cassidy, *Sitt Marie Rose*, 289.

16. Accad, *Coquelicot*, 23.

17. Accad, *Coquelicot*, 24.

18. Accad, *Coquelicot*, 25.

19. Accad, *Coquelicot*, 46.

20. Accad, *Coquelicot*, 30–31.

21. Accad, *Coquelicot*, 30.

22. Accad, *Coquelicot*, 47.

23. Accad, *Coquelicot*, 47.

24. Accad, *Coquelicot*, 63.

25. Accad, *Coquelicot*, 129.

26. Accad, *Coquelicot*, 67.

27. Accad, *Coquelicot*, 66.

28. Accad, *Coquelicot*, 72.

29. Accad, *Coquelicot*, 107.

30. Accad, *Coquelicot*, 93–94.

31. Accad, *Coquelicot*, 154.

32. Accad, *Coquelicot*, 5.
33. Accad, *Coquelicot*, 7.
34. Accad, *Coquelicot*, 29.
35. Adnan, *Sitt Marie Rose*, 8.
36. Adnan, *Sitt Marie Rose*, 45.
37. Adnan, *Sitt Marie Rose*, 63.
38. Adnan, *Sitt Marie Rose*, 83.
39. Accad, *Coquelicot*, 57.
40. Accad, *Coquelicot*, 34.
41. Accad, *Coquelicot*, 64.
42. Accad, *Coquelicot*, 106.
43. Accad, *Coquelicot*, 77.
44. Accad, *Coquelicot*, 71.
45. Accad, *Coquelicot*, 142.
46. Accad, *Coquelicot*, 130.
47. Accad, *Coquelicot*, 23.
48. Accad, *Coquelicot*, 5.
49. Accad, *Coquelicot*, 24.
50. Accad, *Coquelicot*, 72.
51. Accad, *Coquelicot*, 155.
52. Danielle Marx-Scouras, "Muffled Screams/Stifled Voices," *Yale French Studies* 82 (1993). 179.
53. Cassidy, "Love Is a Supreme Violence," 14.

II
SUB-SAHARAN AFRICA

7

The Negotiation of Identity in the Francophone African Novel

Jonathan Carr-West

FOR CENTURIES THE EUROPEAN MIND HAS imag(in)ed Africa as a locus of radical alterity. Standing as a symbolic counterweight to Europe, it is figured as a site of exoticism and power, of extreme opulence and appalling poverty, a continent of primal, elemental forces. It is unknowable. It is the heart of darkness that beats beneath the light of European civilization. Onto this dark continent, this blank space on the map, many discourses have been inscribed. But Africa is not empty and, unlike a blank page, it speaks back.

By examining the forms of cultural and personal identity articulated in the contemporary francophone African novel, this chapter represents an attempt to listen to some of these African voices. However, it is also a study of how different discourses interact, and how they can be read together to create something new. It begins with a diversion to the Caribbean, where a number of theories of cultural identity have been proposed based on a historical experience of displacement. Returning to Africa, it will be shown that colonialism created an internalized version of this displacement that cannot simply be erased by the rhetoric of independent nationalism; so the modern African novel must develop forms of identity more akin to those developed in the Caribbean, which rely upon the interplay of different discursive traditions. Having established this, it becomes apparent that reading in this way not only allows a mode of identity that transcends rigid cultural distinctions between Africa and Europe, but also makes it possible to read different types of discourse in positive interaction.

Theories of Identity in the Caribbean

For the purposes of this study, the modern material relationship between Europe and Sub-Saharan Africa can be separated into two phases: the Atlantic slave trade and the political colonialism that followed it. Both these projects had far-reaching consequences. While the economic and political ramifications of the slave trade are well known, its cultural effects are perhaps less familiar. Through the politics of displacement and the diasporic communities it engendered, the slave trade gave rise to a different mode of cultural identity. Unable to rely on the historical/geographical contingencies of time and place within which to locate identity, the victims of the slave trade were forced to confront the possibility of identity as a non-racinated process.

In the Caribbean, thinkers such as Glissant, Chamoiseau and Confiant have replaced the essentialisms of the négritude movement with a view of identity as hybrid or Creole. Despite significant differences in detail, all these writers would agree with Chamoiseau that such a culture results from "La mise en contact brutale . . . de populations culturellement différentes."[1] Its strength, however, lies in the transformation of this enforced culture clash into "l'agrégat interactionnel ou transactionnel"[2] of different cultural elements. So Creolization is the process by which diverse cultural elements interact to produce an entirely new, composite culture.

For Glissant, this is more than a simple hybridization or *métissage*, as its results cannot easily be predicted: "la créolisation est imprévisible alors que l'on pourrait calculer les effets d'un métissage."[3] The enforced migrations of the slave trade triggered precisely this sort of process in the Caribbean: "Ce qui se passe dans la Caraïbe pendant trois siècles est littéralement ceci: une rencontre d'éléments culturels venus d'horizons absolument divers et qui réellement se créolisent . . . pour donner quelque chose d'absolument imprévisibles, d'absolument nouveau et qui est la réalité créole.[4] The essential feature of this sort of culture is that its identity is generated not by a myth of origin, or legitimating historical genesis, but by its relational interaction with other cultures. Borrowing an image from Deleuze and Guattari's *Mille plateaux*,[5] Glissant defines this distinction in terms of the difference between two root systems, the "racine unique" and the "rhizome," explaining that, "la racine unique est celle qui tue autour d'elle alors que la rhizome est la racine qui s'étend à la rencontre d'autres racines."[6] In other words, identity that is rhizomatic is based on interaction with, and acceptance of, a variety of cultural forms, not on a single imagined point of origin.

Expanding on this distinction, Glissant identifies two types of culture: "cultures ataviques," "qui part du principe d'une Genèse," and "cultures composites," "dont la créolisation se fait pratiquement sous nos yeux."[7] Furthermore, each type of culture is characterized by a certain type of literature. Atavistic cultures are based upon "Mythes fondateurs," which tend toward "cet accomplissement d'absolu que deviendront l'écriture, les écritures."[8] In other words, writing performs a functional role, supplying a racinated foundation for the culture in question, an ontologically absolute account of cultural genesis that is legitimized through its concrete incarnation in the written word. *L'histoire* (story) becomes *l'Histoire* (history) with a capital H. By contrast, composite cultures "commencent directement par le conte qui par paradoxe, est déja une pratique du détour. Ce que le conte ainsi détourne, c'est la propension à se rattacher à une genèse."[9] The story, thus conceived, is an open ended, mobile structure that resists the hermeneutic closure of genesis. Even when the oral tale becomes a written form, it remains "une autre configuration de l'écrit, d'où l'absolu ontologique sera evacué."[10]

It is clear, then, that Glissant derives a sophisticated cultural and literary model from his reading of Caribbean history, what he terms his "vision prophétique du passé."[11] Central to this vision is the literal geographic relocation generated by the slave trade.

Alienation and Displacement in Colonial Africa

On the other side of the Atlantic, in Africa, no such spatial displacement occurred. It can be argued, however, that political colonialism lead to a form of interior displacement that offered an equally radical challenge to the politics of identity. Despite its various detrimental effects, the slave trade had in many areas left the organizational structures of African life largely untouched. Colonialism, by contrast, established a dramatically new way of life. This was particularly true in those areas controlled by the French, who applied direct rule via colonial officials, rather than indirect rule through existing power structures favored by the British. The French also applied a different conception of the colonial project to their European neighbors. In theory, if not in practice, Africans living in the French colonies were to become citizens of the indivisible Republic. Through a system of education and cultural promotion, the lucky few were to be elevated above the savagery of their primitive origins to share in the benefits of advanced European civilization. The term used to describe these educated Africans carries a chilling echo of the racial Darwinism so often invoked to justify the Colonial project; they were *évolués*—evolved, changed, different.

The result of the erosion of traditional culture and its partial replacement with European outlooks and structures was a sense of profound cultural uncertainty. In the texts of the 1950s and early 1960s this alienation is expressed in terms of a rupture or discontinuity of identity. This anxiety is articulated in two early "classics" of francophone African fiction, Camara Laye's *L'Enfant noir*[12] and Cheikh Hamidou Kane's *L'Aventure ambiguë*.[13] Laye's novel achieved resounding success on its publication in 1954, winning the Charles Veillon prize that year. Christopher L. Miller has claimed that, since that date, "*L'Enfant noir* has probably been taught, read, and analyzed more than any other francophone African novel."[14] The majority of this work has tended either to praise or to criticize *L'Enfant noir* as a pastoral idealization of an African childhood, which many African critics have considered too politically quiescent.[15] However, the novel also tackles issues of cultural identity. These are immediately signaled by a confusion over the author's name. On the book's cover and in nearly all bibliographical references this is given as Camara Laye, but as several critics have pointed out—as is made clear in the text of the novel—that the author's name is actually Laye Camara.[16] So, for Camara/Laye entry into the Western publishing system immediately involves a misnaming, a distortion of identity.[17] While there is probably nothing malicious in this error, it does seem to symbolize the fact that for Laye the ability to represent himself in literary terms is predicated on the adoption of an identity that is not his own. This theme is addressed explicitly throughout the novel.

When Laye describes the row of fetishes in his father's hut he writes of "chaque liquide, chaque gri-gri a sa propriété particulière; mais quel le vertu précise? Je l'ignore; *j'ai quitté mon père trop tôt*."[18] As Laye's French education progresses, taking him from the village school to technical college in Conkary and ultimately to France, he becomes increasingly distanced from the cultural practices and beliefs of his Mande background. This is epitomized by an incident toward the end of the novel. When his sick friend Check is visited by the local medicine men, Laye remarks: "Je ne sais pas si Check avait trop grande confiance dans les guérisseurs, je croirais plutôt qu'il en avait pas; nous avions maintenant passé trop d'années à l'école, pour avoir encore en eux une confiance excessive."[19] As it happens, neither traditional nor western medicine can save Check, but the comment is indicative of Laye's growing estrangement from his cultural origins. The adult Laye, narrating the story, shows himself aware of this process of change within him. Explaining his mother's totemic identification with the crocodile, he notes that "le monde bouge, le monde change . . . à telle enseigne que mon propre totem—j'ai mon totem aussi—m'est inconnu."[20] Yet if the process of education has led Laye to lose touch with his culture, the existence of this memoir, with its detailed and loving depictions of Mande life, demonstrates a desire to identify with these roots. The paradox here is that the educational process that has enabled him to produce this text is also the process that distances him from his subject.

Similar concerns are foregrounded in *L'Aventure ambiguë*. Kane's novel recounts the education of Samba, a young member of the Diallobé of Senegal. The question of whether to send their children to colonial schools is seen by the elders as a vital political decision. Here too is an expression of the idea that learning the ways of another culture means forgetting the ways of your own. This is made explicit by the chief of the Diallobé, who asks, "Ce qu'ils apprendront vaut-il ce qu'ils oublieront? . . . peut-on apprendre ceci sans oublier cela, et ce qu'on apprend vaut-il ce qu'on oublie?"[21] Eventually, Samba is sent to French schools, initially in Africa and then in Paris. This education forms the ambiguous adventure of the novel's title, a cultural transformation that Samba analyses in the following terms: "Il nous apparaît soudain que, tout au long de notre cheminement, nous n'avons pas cessé de nous métamorphoser, et que nous voilà devenus autres. Quelquefois la métamorphose ne s'achève pas, elle nous installe dans l'hybride et nous y laisse. Alors nous nous cachons, remplis de honte."[22] He has not become European, but nor is he any longer African in the way that he once was. Unable fully to identify with either culture, he becomes stranded in an indeterminate area of non-belonging from which there is no obvious escape. The impossibility of this position is emphasized by Samba's murder at the end of the novel. As he dies he hears a voice saying, "Tu entres où n'est pas l'ambiguïté."[23] Death, it is implied, is the only way for Samba to evade his dilemma. So the crisis of identity produced in the colonial subject by the process of becoming *évolué* can only be resolved by the complete destruction of that subject.

What Kane and Laye share, then, along with so many authors of the period, is an internalization of difference, a sense of already being other to oneself. This is no accident. The ability to speak in literate Western terms is purchased at the price of this difference, which is thus a precondition of the text's existence. One can expect, then, to find these characteristics, not only in the two texts analysed above, but also in other texts produced in the same conditions.

African Literature and the Quest for Authenticity

In the light of this it comes as no surprise that in the aftermath of political independence (and probably as a conceptual prerequisite for its attainment), African writing attempts to heal this rupture through the promulgation of an authentically African identity.

One aspect of this is the appeal to an essentialized, pre-colonial African culture. More significant, perhaps, is the adoption of a realist aesthetic to produce politically engaged novels concerned with the establishment and status of the nation-state.[24] Both approaches are characterized by a movement from hybridity to unity, from composite to atavistic—a trajectory that is antithetical to that of the Creolization Glissant advocates.

Although this schematization misrepresents the complexities of the novels concerned, it is certainly how many critics, both African and European, have read the literature of post-colonial Africa. Thus Mohamadou Kane can claim that, "c'est dans le roman africain que trouve sa plus grande légitimité l'assertion de L. Goldmann lorsqu'il écrit que le roman se caracterise comme l'histoire d'une recherche de *valeurs authentique*."[25] Richard Bjornson can assert that, "the print culture of the Cameroons has been *largely responsible* for creating the universe of discourse that enables people to conceptualize a national identity."[26] While Bernard Mouralis agrees that "la littérature négro-africaine s'est consacrée très largement . . . à l'expression des revindications sociales, politiques, culturelles qui allaient être resomés dans le mot d'ordre d'indépendance."[27] Even though many of these novels are explicitly critical of the post-colonial African state, they still contribute to a national culture. As Christopher L. Miller argues, "What any writer says about the nation matters less than the fact that he or she is addressing the question of the nation in the first place and thereby contributing to a national discourse."[28]

This alignment of cultural praxis and national identity requires the adoption of what Glissant calls a "principe d'une filiation, dans le but de rechercher une légitimité sur une terre qui à partir de ce moment devient territoire."[29] Identity becomes equated with geohistorical gene-sis; the *racine unique* is reconstituted and reinforced.

The Hybridity of Post-Colonial Literature

The assertion of an independent African identity appears to be, and indeed is, a positive move. It may be, however, that the cultural racination it entails is ultimately untenable. The hy-bridization effected by colonialism is not simply reversible. As Helen Tiffin puts it: "post colo-nial states are inevitably hybridized, involving a dialectical relationship between European on-tology and epistemology and the impulse to create or recreate an independent local identity."[30]

Furthermore, the totalising narrative of demotic nationalism—"You are Senegalese. I am Cameroonian"—is itself unable to fully describe the lived experience of personal identity, which is an infinitely mobile, unfixable phenomenon. Benedict Anderson famously described the nation as an "imagined community,"[31] but he is also quick to point out that such imagin-ing is strictly delimited. This delimitation describes the boundaries of the nation—who is in, who is out—but in doing so it also signals a limitation of what the nation as imagined com-munity can contain. So the nation operates through a process of exclusion, not only of those who are outside it, but also of those aspects of its members that cannot readily be encompassed by description in terms of national identity. Anderson's definition of the nation is always vul-nerable to Partha Chatterjee's question, "Whose imagined community?"[32] Homi Bhabha quotes the Afro-American artist Renée Greene, "Who's saying what, who's representing who? What is a community anyway?"[33] The nation state does provide one way of representing identity, but it is constantly threatened by the competing claims of other ontological sites, such as ethnicity, gender, class or religion. One need only look to the ethnic violence recurrent in a number of African states to see the most extreme and disturbing example of how nationality can fail to ac count for all aspects of identity. Even when identity is constructed in terms of a pan-continental "Africanness," the same difficulties are met with.

This is important because it indicates that even where it is possible to make a claim for historical/geographical racination, the sorts of identity that arise in displaced communities may still be a more satisfactory form of engagement with the world. So despite a rhetoric of national coher-ence, the modern African state is significantly more hybrid, more Creole than it appears. It may therefore still be necessary to negotiate a mode of subjectivity that is sufficiently mobile to evade the monolithic prescriptions of totalizing discourse—Black/White, African/European. The chief contention of this paper is that literature provides a privileged locus for this activity.

Why should this be so? Why literature? Why, more specifically, the fictional prose narrative? To grasp this point it is necessary to consider in greater detail the theoretical grounding of the notion of personal identity. Of course there are dangers in applying a Western theoretical dis-course to a non-Western object. This risks becoming a form of intellectual colonialism. For the moment, however, this difficulty may be tolerated, as the case studies that follow will show that the theory is no more than a way of highlighting certain features that derive naturally from a close reading of the texts. Moreover, the form of identity negotiated by the modern African novel is such as to break down the rigid distinction between Western and African thought that creates this problem.

It is not necessary here to closely examine the philosophical history of thinking about per-sonal identity, but it should be noted that this thinking consistently displays all the characteris-tics of the "metaphysics of presence" that Derrida claims has dominated Western thought.[34] As human beings, we are subject over the course of our lives to a variety of perceptions, emotions and other experiences. We are apt to posit some object that collects and orders these experiences. The existence of this object has traditionally been seen as either an empirical truth (e.g., Locke[35]) or an *a priori* truth (e.g., Descartes,[36]) according to philosophical persuasion. Furthermore, it is common to ascribe certain properties, pertaining over time, to this posited object. This, despite the fact that such an object can only be experienced, if at all, sequentially. This enduring, property-bearing object is what is termed personal identity. There is a general belief that each individual is constituted by such an object, which they experience, as it were, from the inside, as subject. This idea that if there are things that happen, there must be a thing to which they happen is, though not necessarily false, an archetypal example of the "metaphysics of presence." However, the predominance of such thinking has begun to be displaced.

If there is any unifying trope within which modern theorizing about the self can be located, it must surely lie, as Foucault suggests, in the shift from an imagined ontology, the fiction of being as essentialized totality, to an attitude that is at once epistemological and creative.[37] Identity is seen, not as an enduring, property-bearing entity, but as a mobile iterative phenomenon. It becomes a discursive relation between different points of experience the knowledge of which is created rather than discovered. This paradigmatic shift is discernible not only in the French intellectual tradition, but also in the works of English philosophers, such as Derek Parfitt.[38]

One way of theorizing identity in these terms may be loosely drawn from the psychoanalytic thinking of Lacan.[39] For Lacan meaning is generated through a process of identification and differentiation. The formulation of subjectivity (the meaning of the self) is equally subordinate to this principal. The unified self the infant sees in the mirror is illusory; the reality of subjectivity is a fragmented dialectic of identification and differentiation with otherness. The subject is thus endlessly displaced and recreated by a process of signification within the symbolic order. So, if the subject is not a stable entity, but the product of a signifying process, then the subject can exist only in as far as it is able to signify/articulate itself as subject and to differentiate itself from other objects. Subjectivity is thus inseparable from a demand for recognition addressed to the other.

There is a danger here, as pointed out by feminist critiques of Lacan, of being forced back into the politics of binarism—Self/Other. Within such a binary system one term will inevitably be privileged over another. This is a danger recognized in the post-colonial context by Frantz Fanon, who says, "On me démontrait que ma demande n'était qu'un terme dans la dialectique."[40] However, this danger can be avoided by reference to two related points. Firstly, the demand for recognition is a contradictory moment. The desire for the other to recognize one as a differentiated entity is also a moment of institutionalization. The assertion that "I exist/I am different from you," can only be met by a reductive gesture that identifies the self in that difference. The "self" can only exist as subject through the recognition of that subjectivity by another, but that very recognition objectifies the self, transforming it into what is nothing but a thing that is different. To be recognized by the other is then, as Fanon shows, to be fixed by that gaze into a specific ontological space. So, the process Lacan describes is kept in perpetual motion by the impossibility of its own successful completion.

The second factor that allows Lacan's schema to escape simple binarism resides in the nature of signification itself. The subject exists via its ability to articulate itself as such, but the signs it uses to do this are inherently unstable. Lacan's idea that the subject is endlessly displaced and recreated through the process of signification can be elucidated in the light of the Derridean notion of *différance*.[41] If the sign has no static meaning, but bears within it the traces of a plethora of other meanings, then it can be seen how whatever "sign position" the Lacanian subject adopts from which to articulate his differentiation will already be in retreat. Each and every ontological site the subject chooses, exceeds and unmakes itself by virtue of its articulation. There is no one meaning that can be ascribed to the subject. It is already contaminated by a host of other meanings, between which it describes an endlessly mobile trajectory. In other words, whichever sign an individual may use to denote himself or herself—white, male, European, even cheerful or gloomy—is already overdetermined and undermined by the play of signification. So the ontological fixing of the self is permanently deferred. Any attempt to talk meaningfully about subjectivity must, therefore, acknowledge that the idea of a unified self is a narrative, a fictional totality, the uncertain foundations of which are the endlessly shifting sands of the signifying process.

Reading Lacan's thinking in this way means moving away from his Hegelian sternness to a schema that is more dialogic than dialectical. Lacan's Western theorizations of individual psychology thus come to seem quite similar to the Creole theories of culture discussed earlier. In both cases, identity is located, not in historical genesis, but in the interstices of a number of discursive locations. The restless movement of the subject/sign away from a final determination, imagined by Deleuze and Guattari as "lignes de fuite," or "déterritorialisation,"[42] allows a re-configuration of identity as a locus of infinite diversity and possibility.

This convergence between Lacanian and Glissantian thought makes it possible to draw a link between Western and non-Western theoretical discourses and between the ways in which individual and collective/cultural identities are structured. The old slogan "The personal is the political" holds true here for a variety of reasons. As Said, Bhabha and other critics have argued, "nations are narratives,"[43] so the discursive processes by which a corporate identity is constructed will be structurally analogous to those that operate on the level of individual psychology. At the same time, however, the discursive epistemes of the wider culture will also determine the forms of discourse that are available for individual subject formation. Furthermore, the awareness of individuals that their identity is not a prescribed, monolithic entity has a political dimension. As Homi Bhabha puts it: "Political empowerment and the enlargement of the multiculturalist cause, come from posing questions of solidarity and community from the interstitial perspective. Social differences are not simply given to experience through an already authenticated cultural tradition: they are the signs of the emergence of community envisaged as project."[44]

It becomes clear why conceiving of identity in the terms outlined above might be politically and ethically significant. It is also clear why the literary text should provide so suitable a forum for the exploration of this type of identity. If the self is, as has been claimed, a form of narrative, it seems likely that it will share some of the characteristics of the narrative text. Consider the following points: a text demands to be read, it exists to be read and to some degree it exists only insofar as it is read. Like the self, the text is dependent upon its own articulation. Moreover, the text also works through the ascription of meaning to inherently volatile signs, both on the level of individual signs and in the creation of a narrative that will ascribe meaning to the totality of those signs. The text also possesses, however, the ability to manipulate and exploit this very volatility for its own ends. It is clear then, that there are deep structural similarities between the process of textual production and the processes by which self-identity is produced. What is interesting is the way in which some texts exploit these similarities to explore the possibilities that identity has to offer. Such texts use the unstable, polyphonic nature of signification to inhabit a multiplicity of ontological sites, to create new discursive spaces, to interrogate culture from below, outside and in between its normative parameters. Using their awareness of the lacunae and aporiae that exist within the process of representation, these dissident texts are able to articulate and explore ways of being and feeling that evade the normalizing discourse of social *doxae*. They enter into the negotiation of modulations of identity that play off the demands of totalizing ontological topoi to emerge as something new and creatively vibrant. Put more elegantly in the words of the Congolese poet and novelist Sony Labou Tansi, "L'art c'est la force de faire dire à la réalité ce qu'elle n'aurait pu dire par ses propres moyens ou, en tout cas, ce qu'elle risquait de passer volontairement sous silence."[45]

Creole Readings: Sony Labou Tansi, Calixthe Beyala and Werewere Liking

It has been seen how African writers like Kane and Laye are keenly aware of the problems arising from the attempt to inhabit multiple discursive paradigms. Within this context it would seem natural for novelists to experiment with hybrid discourses in the attempt to reformulate a more flexible mode of identity. Indeed, Labou Tansi's own novels are fine examples of this process. In his work and that of other modern writers such as Mariâma Bâ, Calixthe Beyala, Ken Bugul, and Werewere Liking, there is a concern with a unitary cultural identity has been replaced by a more pluralistic stance, which works through the incorporation and celebration of difference rather than through its exclusion. This is particularly notable in their treatment of collective/national and personal identity.

Crucially, Labou Tansi locates collective identity as a function of discourse. The assembly of multiple individual subjects into a collective group must be regulated by language/discourse, both as a prerequisite for intersubjective communication and because the formulation of subjectivity, be it collective or individual, can occur only through the essentially discursive processes of identification and differentiation. Furthermore, the ascription of properties to a posited object is itself a discursive procedure, a naming device. The identity of a group, a nation, a tribe or a family is thus largely a matter of the stories its members tell about themselves. Stories are the ties that bind, but they are also the forum in which positive characteristics are ascribed to the group. Labou Tansi's novels are both depictions and examples of this practice. Throughout his work there is an emphasis on the centrality of discourse to social experience, a conviction that both contemporary identity and cultural history are constituted by discursive practices. As the character Estina Bronzario says in *Les sept solitudes de Lorsa Lopez*, "l'homme n'a que les mots pour dire même ce que les mots ne savent dire.... Que les mots pour exister."[46] and Labou Tansi himself claims that "Il n'y a que la fable qui nous permets d'approcher les choses."[47] There is an echo here of the Foucauldian insistence that discourse forms the basis of all cultural praxis, but there is also an awareness of the dangers inherent in this discourse. Like Foucault, Labou Tansi knows that if discourse is power, then this power can be manipulated and abused; as a kikongo proverb has it, *ludimi i kima kiamba*[48]—language is a dangerous thing. Conversely, however, the amelioration and elucidation of social relations must also be discursively mediated.

The struggle to control discourse is a consistent concern in Labou Tansi's novels, and authority over the social/collective subject is equated with the ability to command the terms of its representation. In *La Vie et demie*[49] control of the post-colonial state of Katamalanasie is contested between the followers of the rebel leader Martial and the despotic "Guides providentiels." This struggle is, at least in part, a discursive one. The sanctioned discourse of the Guides portrays them as the paternalistic leaders of a unified nation-state, benevolently directed through a "communautarisme tropical."[50] Any deviance from this party line is brutally repressed. The followers of Martial challenge this hegemony with a proliferating discourse of defiance: "Au paravent ideologique que le guide avait enfourché Martial avait opposé une seule phrase: 'Qu'on me prouve que la dictature est communautaire', et les gens de Martial paraphrasait Martial en disant 'Qu'on me prouve que l'inhumanité est communautaire.'"[51] These aphorisms are inscribed everywhere, in books, on walls, even on people. Martial's discourse is open, allowing for paraphrase and transformation, whereas the discourse of the Guides is closed, adhering to a fixed pattern from which no transgression is permitted.

Control of the collective subject can only be exercised if social discourse is (falsely) represented as a containable, monologic phenomenon. That is, as something that can be entirely defined by a combination of one or more fixed discursive sites (e.g., nation, race, class, gender). Such sites are portrayed as ontologically real, as being *genuine* properties that are in themselves sufficient to represent the individual or collective subject. Discursively, they function through a process of static differentiation; one can be outside or inside, but not both. Labou Tansi refuses to be constrained by the apparent authority of such a *doxa*. He repositions collective identity within a dialogic, overdetermined discourse that operates outside and between the circumscriptive parameters of these monologic, discursive topoi and their ontological corollaries. He is thus able to articulate a vision of collective identity and of cultural history that revels in fluidity and openness, not stasis and closure. Such an identity allows a positive interaction between apparently different subjects or cultures, who can no longer define themselves simply in terms of this difference.

This is the case in novels such as *Les Sept Solitudes de Lorsa Lopez*, in which the people of the coastal province of Valancia combine a sense of place ("On n'est jamais de nulle part. La terre nous marque.")[52] and of history ("Nous avons derrière nous vingt-sept siècles d'histoire dans la dignité.")[53] with a conception of collective identity that is defiantly nonexclusive, as witnessed by the fact that many of their key representatives are actually incomers from other regions. Tradition is seen not as a totalizing point of origin, but as the foundation for innovation. A similar emphasis is to be found in Labou Tansi's last novel *La Commencement des douleurs*.[54] There is the same concern with *terroir*, "Les géographies sont coupables de l'histoire qu'elles sécrètent,"[55] but also a need to configure an identity that transcends it. Throughout, the novel expresses an urge to reconcile respect for tradition ("Arrête donc de mettre ton doigt dans les yeux de la coutume.")[56] with the awareness that "le monde a changé de fesses."[57] The idea that tradition should form the basis of further development is also something Labou Tansi ascribed to in the context of literary production, claiming that "il faut inventer une tradition."[58]

These examples involve the construction of a hybrid cultural identity based on a mediation between localization and universality, between tradition and modernity, which could well be described in terms of a Creolization. Similar themes are played out on a more personal level in the works of women writers such as Bâ, Beyala, Bugul. In their novels, gender politics are privileged over those of the nation. This too, it might be argued, is a form of Creolization, valorizing cultural ties between women above those of geohistorical genesis. A good example of this is Beyala's novel *Tu t'appelleras Tanga*.[59] This text tells the story of an encounter in a Cameroonian prison cell between Anna-Claude, a middle-aged white French woman, and Tanga, a young black girl who is slowly dying. As Tanga tells Anna-Claude the story of her life, a remarkable fusion occurs between the two women. By telling her story Tanga hands on her identity to Anne-Claude: "désormais tu seras moi. Tu auras dix-sept saisons, tu seras noire, tu t'appelleras Tanga."[60] Through a narrative act, the telling of a story, a new, hybrid identity is created, a new cultural space is opened up.

There is a danger, of course, that the emphasis on connections between women could merely replace one form of essentialized identity with another. It seems to me, however, that in their formulation and exploration of cultural and personal identity, the protagonists of all these novels do not make simple choices between cultural paradigms. Instead, they experiment with combinations of different cultural practices and values in an attempt to find the mode of life best suited to them and the discourses that best express the complex reality of their subjectivity. Often this takes the form of an amalgamation of African and European culture. If, for some characters, the attempt to reconcile them ends in failure, as it does for the protagonist of Bugul's *Le Baobab fou*,[61] for others like M'am in Beyala's *Le Petit Prince de Belleville*[62] and *Maman a un amant*[63] it is broadly successful. She manages to retain those aspects of her African heritage she values—an emphasis on family and "l'esprit du tribu"[64] in the wider African community—while simultaneously liberating herself from domestic drudgery and becoming financially and intellectually independent.

These sorts of cultural choices are only possible, however, if one possesses a language in which to articulate them; a conceptual discourse in which to think them. This is why the creation of discursive plurality and openness is a consistent concern.

Of course the novels themselves represent such a pluralist discourse. As noted above, the African novel is in many ways a culturally hybrid form from the outset. For writers of an earlier generation this issue may have been politically troubling. Indeed many critics have seen this as the central problem of the African novel. As Jean-Michel Dévesa puts it, "comment dire l'authenticité du terroir, dans la langue et les catégories des autres?"[65]

The contention of this paper, however, is that the texts examined here, which are not concerned with the "authenticité du terroir" as such, are happy to embrace and enhance this hybrid status. Thus a novelist like Labou Tansi, though he writes novels in French, draws heavily on the images and refrains of kikongo mythology and even inserts vocabulary and grammatical structures from the kikongo language into his work. The presentation to the reader of unfamiliar grammatical structures, new words and contradictory phrases, necessarily brings about a recognition of the opacity of language. The very terms in which Labou Tansi's discourse is articulated, its linguistic characteristics, force the reader to recognise its open, heteroglossic nature, its irreducibility to a closed system of interpretation. In this way Labou Tansi reinscribes the French language as the articulation of an identity that cannot be contained within a totalized ontology, creating a text that is literally a cultural *métissage*. Perhaps the best example of this generic experimentation is Werewere Liking's *Orphée Dafric*.[66] Half novel, half poem, this text reworks the Orpheus myth in an African context, charting Orphée's descent into the underworld through a series of tests based on the initiation rituals of the Bassa people. Although the text explicitly concerns itself with the clash of tradition and modernity, its most striking feature is the way it complements this thematic concern with an audacious interworking of European and African literary traditions.

Conclusion

What all these texts have in common, then, is that identity is constructed in the interstices of a variety of ontological loci (nationality, gender, race, etc.) and not by any single one of them. Identification replaces differentiation as the primary determinant of subjectivity. It is also clear how, in all these examples, the texts display hybrid characteristics that could easily be described in terms of Glissant's theory of Creolization. New identities are derived from the interaction of a variety of discourses, what Glissant describes as "une poétique de la Relation,"[67] rather than by historical determinacy. This has radical implications for the ways in which we think about both identity and its representation in art. These revisions have political and ethical conse-quences that are far-reaching and significant, connecting the analysis of literary texts to a broader cultural debate.

This type of reading is becoming increasingly familiar. But the very popularity of "hybridity" as a mode of cultural or literary analysis gives rise to two related objections. The first is that these consciously anti-dogmatic readings risk becoming dogma themselves, reproducing in their opposition of singularity and plurality the type of binary hierarchies they sought to re-place. As Christopher L. Miller puts it, "this body of thought that abhors borders and limita-tions can itself be limiting."[68] "It makes little sense to be either 'for' or 'against' either national-ism or hybridity in a systematic and absolute way since both are *real*."[69] This is a serious objection and it is aligned with the anxiety expressed above about the use of theory. Both ques-tions are essentially about respect for the specificity of the text. Does not an insistence on read-ing texts through fashionable theoretical paradigms risk ignoring what the text says, in favor of what the reader or theorist wants them to say? Furthermore, if these texts are, as has been claimed, actually about issues of cultural hybridization, it is not immediately clear why it is nec-essary or helpful to apply theory to them at all. Should the text not be allowed get on with its own purposes, without having theoretical preoccupations imposed onto it?

In many ways these issues are reformulations of the perennially agonistic relation between theory and literature. In this case, however, when dealing so specifically with the imposition and negotiation of discursive power, these questions have a particular resonance. In terms of the African novel, it might also be argued that reading it purely in terms of a universal theory of cultural Creolization denies it a distinct identity of its own. Moreover, the emphasis on hybrid-ity may undermine the characteristics of a specific environment, which are, as Miller points out, particular and real.

These are certainly serious objections, but they can be resisted. As discussed above, the texts we have examined do concern themselves explicitly with cultural interaction and the negotia-tion between different modes of discourse. Given this, it does not seem inappropriate to place these texts in dialogue with other discourses. In this case, the juxtaposition of literary and the-oretical texts makes it possible develop a deeper understanding of both. This reading might it-self be described as "hybrid," pertaining as it does to both literary and theoretical concerns. To read in this way does not demand that the specificities of the literary text are ignored, nor does a theory of Creolization require the realities of the African milieu to be passed over. Glissant points out that "la Relation vraie n'est pas du particulier à l'universel, mais du Lieu à la totalité-monde."[70] It is not always easy to grasp, however, how this relationship between location and a globalized system of creolized or rhizomatic cultural relations is to be maintained, at least not without reverting to the sort of racination it is necessary to avoid. Yet the texts examined show precisely this sort of process in operation. In Labou Tansi or Liking's novels do show respect for "le Lieu" coexisting with an openness that can be described as creole. The novels provide con-crete examples of how Creolization might actually work, both in their depiction of such iden-tities and in their own créolised nature as cultural artifacts deriving from variety of traditions. So theorizing runs into trouble, but the novels, by their very existence, demonstrate the possi-bility of Creole thought. They perform what theory struggles to describe. Glissant, himself a novelist, encourages this perspective, arguing that, "c'est dans les oeuvres littéraires, et non dans la tentatives théoriques que l'approche de la totalité-monde se dessine d'abord."[71]

This chapter has discussed the colonization of text by theory, but it may be more helpful to reverse the terms of this argument. It is not necessary to claim that Creolization or any other cultural theory is needed in order to understand the African novel. If this analysis has shown anything, however, it is that these novels may provide a way of understanding the theory; that reading the two together makes it possible to find something new and unexpected in each of them.

Notes

1. Patrick Chamoiseau, Raphaël Confiant, Jean Bernarbé, *Éloge de la créolité* (Paris: Gallimard, 1993), 30.
2. Chamoiseau, Confiant and Bernarbé, *Éloge*, 26.
3. Édouard Glissant, *Introduction à une poétique du divers* (Paris: Gallimard, 1996), 19.
4. Glissant, *Introduction*, 15.
5. Gilles Deleuze, Félix Guattari, *Mille plateaux* (Paris: Editions de Minuit, 1980).
6. Glissant, *Introduction*, 59.
7. Glissant, *Introduction*, 22.
8. Glissant, *Introduction*, 63.
9. Glissant, *Introduction*, 63.
10. Glissant, *Introduction*, 63.
11. Glissant, *Introduction*, 86.
12. Camara Laye, *L'Enfant noir* (Paris: Presses Pocket, n.d. [first published Plon, 1953]).
13. Cheikh Hamidou Kane, *L'Aventure ambiguë* (Paris: 10/18, n.d. [first published Juillard, 1962]).
14. Christopher L. Miller, *Theories of Africans: Francophone Literature and Anthropology in Africa* (Chicago and London: Chicago University Press, 1990), 125.
15. See for example, A. B. (Mongo Beti), "Afrique noire, littérature rose," *Présence Africaine*, nos. 1–2 (April–July 1955): 133.
16. See Miller, *Theories of Africans*, 116, or Eric Sellin, "Alienation in the Novels of Camara Laye," *Pan-African Journal 4*, no. 4 (Fall 1971): 471.
17. Henceforth in this article I shall follow convention and refer to Camara as Laye.
18. Laye, *L'Enfant noir*, 11. Emphasis added.
19. Laye, *L'Enfant noir*, 205.
20. Laye, *L'Enfant noir*, 80.
21. Kane, *L'Aventure ambiguë*, 44.
22. Kane, *L'Aventure ambiguë*, 125.
23. Kane, *L'Aventure ambiguë*, 190.
24. Senghor is probably the best known exponent of the first of these tendencies, while Ousmane Sembène, Mongo Beti and Ferdinand Oyono might all be seen as examples of the latter.
25. Mohamadou Kane, *Roman africain et traditions* (Dakar: Les nouvelles éditions africaines, 1982), 27. Emphasis added.
26. Richard Bjornson, *The African Quest for Freedom and Identity: Cameroonian Writing and the National Experience* (Bloomington & Indianapolis: Indiana University Press, 1991), 459. Emphasis added.
27. Bernard Mouralis, *Littérature et développement* (Paris: Éditions Silex, 1984), 145.
28. Christopher L. Miller, *Nationalisms and Nomads: Essays on Francophone African Literature and Culture* (Chicago: University of Chicago Press, 1998), 147.
29. Glissant, *Introduction*, 59.
30. Helen Tiffin, "Post-colonial Literatures and Counter-discourse," in *The Post-colonial Studies Reader*, ed. Ashcroft, Griffiths and Helen Tiffin (London: Routledge, 1995), 95.
31. Benedict Anderson, *Imagined Communities: Reflections on the Origins and Spread of Nationalism* (London: Verso, 1983).
32. Partha Chatterjee, "Whose Imagined Community?" in *Mapping the Nation*, ed. Gopal Batakrishna (London: Verso, 1996), 214.
33. Homi K. Bhabha, *The Location of Culture* (London: Routledge, 1994), 3.

34. See Jacques Derrida, *L'Écriture et la différence* (Paris: Éditions de Seuil, 1967).

35. See John Locke, *An Essay concerning Human Understanding*, ed. Peter H. Nidditch (Oxford: Clarendon Press, 1975).

36. See René Descartes, "Meditations on First Philosophy," in *Descartes: Selected Philosophical Writings*, ed. Cottingham, Stroothoff, Murdoch (Cambridge: Cambridge University Press, 1988), 73–159.

37. See Michel Foucault, *Les Mots et les choses: une archéologie des sciences humaines* (Paris: Gallimard, 1966).

38. See Derek Parfitt, "Personal Identity," *The Philosophical Review* 80 (January 1971): 3–27.

39. See Jacques Lacan, *Écrits vol. ii* (Paris: Seuil, 1966–1971).

40. Frantz Fanon, *Peau noire, masques blancs* (Paris: Seuil Points, 1952), 107.

41. See Jacques Derrida, *Marges de la philosophie* (Paris: Éditions de minuit, 1972), 1–29.

42. See Deleuze and Guattari, *Mille plateaux*, 9–37.

43. See Edward Said, *Orientalism* (London: Penguin, n.d. [first published Pantheon Books, 1978]) and Homi K. Bhabha (ed.), *Nation and Narration*, (London: Routledge, 1990).

44. Bhabha, *The Location of Culture*, 3.

45. Sony Labou Tansi, *Les Sept Solitudes de Lorsa Lopez* (Paris: Seuil Points, n.d. [first published Éditions du Seuil, 1985]), foreword.

46. Labou Tansi, *Les Sept*, 148.

47. Sony Labou Tansi, "Entretien avec Bernard Magnier," cited by Jean-Michel Devésa, *Sony Labou Tansi: écrivain de la honte et des rives magiques du Kongo* (Paris: L'Harmattan, 1996), 53.

48. Cited by Devésa, *Sony Labou*, 47.

49. Sony Labou Tansi, *La Vie et demie* (Paris: Seuil Points, n.d. [first published Éditions du Seuil, 1979])

50. Labou Tansi, *La Vie*, 64.

51. Labou Tansi, *La Vie*, 64.

52. Sony Labou Tansi, *Les Sept Solitudes de Lorsa Lopez*, 109.

53. Labou Tansi, *Les Sept*, 21.

54. Sony Labou Tansi, *Le Commencement des douleurs*, (Paris: Éditions de Seuil, 1995).

55. Labou Tansi, *Le Commencement*, 16.

56. Labou Tansi, *Le Commencement*, 33.

57. Labou Tansi, *Le Commencement*, 56.

58. Sony Labou Tansi, "Rencontre écrivain public," *Écrire de l'école à université* (numéro spécial "Lettres francophone," Nice: 1990), 73; cited by Devésa, *Sony Labou*, 125.

59. Calixthe Beyala, *Tu t'appelleras Tanga* (Paris: Éditions J'ai Lu, n.d. [first published Éditions Stock, 1988]).

60. Beyala, *Tu t'appelleras*, 14.

61. Ken Bugul, *Le baobab fou* (Dakar: les nouvelles éditions africaines, 1984).

62. Calixthe Beyala, *Le Petit Prince de Belleville* (Paris: Éditions J'ai Lu, n.d. [first published Éditions Albin Michel, 1992]).

63. Calixthe Beyala, *Maman a un amant* (Paris: Éditions J'ai Lu, n.d. [first published Éditions Albin Michel, 1993]).

64. Beyala, *Maman a un amant*, 246.

65. Dévesa, *Sony Labou*, 112.

66. Werewere Liking, *Orphée Dafric* (Paris: L'Harmattan, 1981).

67. Glissant, *Introduction*, 24.

68. Miller, *Nationalisms and Nomads*, 6.

69. Miller, *Nationalisms and Nomads*, 7.

70. Glissant, *Introduction*, 105.

71. Glissant, *Introduction*, 104.

8

The Myth of the Garden of Eden and the Symbolism of the Baobab Tree in West African Literature

Chantal P. Thompson

A s THE "ROMAN DE MOEURS" BECAME the most popular form for Senegalese literature in the 1970o, 1980o and 1990ε, women writers came to the fore, and, in this respect, Senegal stands again as a pioneer in women's literature in Francophone Africa. Nafissatou Diallo was the first African woman to publish an autobiography in 1975 (*De Tilène au Plateau*) and Aminata Sow Fall published the first francophone novel by an African woman in 1976 (*Le Revenant*), followed by *La Grève des bàttu* (1979), in which she exposed the ills of tradition as well as those of modernity. That same year (1979), Mariama Bâ took the daring step of speaking out, as a woman, about the problems of polygamy in *Une si longue lettre*. This opened the door for other women to find their voices. Of these writers, Ken Bugul has been the most outspoken, drawing much attention particularly with *Le Baobab fou* (1982), the story of her own descent into hellish degradation, and *Riiwan* (1999), which describes her return to inner peace as she became the twenty-eighth wife of a "marabout." Aminata Sow Fall's most recent novels (*L'Appel des arènes*, 1982; *L'Ex-Père de la nation*, 1987; *Le Jujubier du patriarche*, 1993; *Douceurs du bercail*, 1998) temper social criticism with a message of hope for Africa.

In sharp contrast with the moderate realism of the "romans de moeurs," the "romans du chaos" written by authors such as Boubabacar Boris Diop (*Le Temps de Tamago*, 1981; *Les Tambours de la mémoire*, 1990; *Les Traces de la meute*, 1993; *Le Cavalier et son ombre*, 1997) are novels of social, political and literary deconstruction, reflecting the chaos of African societies at the threshold of the twenty-first century. The search for the lost paradise in the midst of chaos may be a matter of sheer survival.

This chapter analyses the similarities between the myth of the Garden of Eden and the itinerary of Ken Bugul and Aminata Sow Fall's characters through the journey of life. Symbolically, this journey is also that of Africa. First, there is life in the garden of innocence; then, the tree of Western knowledge offers its tempting fruit, bringing about the fall. Amidst the thorns and thistles of alienation and acculturation, the dream of returning to the lost paradise remains alive— is it possible to make it come true?

Ken Bugul's life, as portrayed in *Le Baobab fou*, begins in the warmth and light of a West African village, at the foot of a "faithful baobab" where dreams and reality are indistinguishable. The baobab tree, however, stops growing when the railroad and the "industrial shoe," symbols of the Western world, invade the warm garden. Stubbornly believing that it is possible to wear high heels in the hot sand, Ken boards the train of europeanization, only to find solitude and cold in a world of stone and glass. Displaced and torn between two cultures, Ken descends into the hellish degradation of literal prostitution, which leads to her figurative death. Only when she returns to the abandoned baobab of her African village can dawn and light reappear. All is not lost.

In *L'Appel des arènes* by Aminata Sow Fall, another woman abandons the tree of her homeland for what she calls a paradise of individuality and modernity. However, when Diattou rejects her roots, her own community rejects her in return. Trained as a midwife to bring life into the world, Diattou becomes an angel of death. Her only son, Nalla, also rejects her and sets out on "a quest to recover the paradise lost." The wrestling ring, a symbol of tradition, becomes this paradise, filled as it is with legends and myths, but also with the charms of a simple life, which can be found at the foot of a "sacred baobab," the roots of which draw nourishment from the ancestral soil. Whereas the Westernized mother falls from the tree and finds herself in a hell of her own making, the son rediscovers the tree of life in the garden of tradition. This same garden is the paradise of *Douceurs du Bercail*, Aminata Sow Fall's latest novel (1998), in which the protagonist, Asta, fails to fit into the Western world and is deported back to Senegal, where she buys a plot of land and lays out a garden. She does not plough over the land completely, but chooses to weed out some plants while keeping others. As a result, she discovers a rare herb in the garden that promises personal fulfilment as well as financial survival. Similarly, the rare herb of hope can be found growing in the garden of Africa. The challenge is to cultivate it and make the return to the lost paradise a reality.

The myth of the Garden of Eden is a familiar one in Judeo-Christian and Muslim societies. In the midst of the Garden stood two special trees, the Tree of Life, bearing the fruit of immortality, and the Tree of Knowledge of Good and Evil, bearing the fruit of knowledge, which brings about the Fall. As it says in the Book of Genesis, "The Lord God commanded the man, saying, Of every tree of the garden thou mayest freely eat: But of the tree of the knowledge of good and evil, thou shalt not eat of it: for in the day that thou eatest thereof thou shalt surely die." Adam and Eve lived in a state of innocence and bliss in this garden of lush abundance, until the day that Eve, under the influence of the serpent, "saw that the [forbidden] tree was good for food, and that it was pleasant to the eyes, and a tree to make one wise, [and so] she took of the fruit thereof, and did eat, and gave also unto her husband with her; and he did eat." This led to the Fall, which brought with it the prospect of sorrow and death. However, before Adam and Eve were driven out of the garden, the Lord God "placed at the east of the garden of Eden Cherubims, and a flaming sword to keep the way of the tree of life, lest man put forth his hand, and take also of the tree of life, and eat, and live forever" in his fallen state. From this point on, the ground was cursed to bring forth "thorns and thistles," forcing man to "eat bread" by "the sweat of his face."[1] But the memory of the garden must have lingered, for the dream of returning to the lost paradise has haunted man ever since, and the Tree of Life has become a symbol of endless regeneration. As Charles Hirsch and Marie Madeleine Davy point out, "L'Arbre de Vie est la source de la vie inépuisable, le vivant par excellence, incluant toutes choses dans une dynamique créatrice qui est le fondement du monde cosmique. Car, à l'image de l'arbre, le cosmos se régénère sans cesse. L'arbre symbolise ainsi la vie et l'univers lui-même."[2]

This harmony with life and the universe is at the heart of the protagonists' search for happiness in *Le Baobab fou* by Ken Bugul, and in *L'Appel des arènes* and *Douceurs du bercail* by Aminata Sow Fall. All three novels portray the village as a garden of Eden, a place of innocence and dreaming. The Fall occurs when the protagonists partake of the fruit of Western knowledge and move to the city, where the thorns and thistles of alienation infest the soul. For some, alienation leads to damnation and death. For others, the road through Hell stops under the shade of a baobab tree, reminiscent of the Tree of Life, which speaks of traditions and values, identity and peace. Armed with hope, these travelers then attempt to return to their lost paradise, by regaining or recreating the village. These three novels and their descriptions of life in the garden, the Fall and the return to paradise will be examined in this chapter, drawing out their implications for Africa in general.

The Garden of Eden

Ken Bugul's life, as portrayed in *Le Baobab fou,* begins in the warmth and light of a West African village where "everyone was happy": "Tout le monde y était heureux, car tout le monde partageait tout. La naissance, la vie et la mort. Les douleurs et les peines, les bonheurs et les joies. Dans ce village, les gens étaient ensemble. Les vieux vieillissaient et les naissances étaient accueillies comme l'immortalité. Le nouveau-né était toujours une réincarnation."[3] The sun was always shining, giving a mystical aura to people and things: "les cases étaient jaunes, les hautes herbes jaunes, le sable jaune, les animaux jaunes, les êtres humains jaunes." The only green note in this symphony of yellow was provided by a majestic baobab tree, "le baobab fidèle à l'ombre duquel la réalité se substituait au rêve et devenait rêve."[4] This tree was truly a Tree of Life, for it sustained all aspects of life.

> Il donnait les meilleurs fruits. On en faisait du jus pour arroser la bouillie de mil; on soignait la rougeole en le faisant boire au malade et en lui en faisant tomber des gouttes dans les yeux; il traitait la diarrhée. Ses feuilles séchées servaient à préparer la poudre qui engluait le couscous lui donnant une saveur de lait frais; malaxées fraîches, elles étaient le meilleur remède contre la fatigue. Son écorce servait à tisser les hamacs célèbres du pays du soleil. Le pays du baobab.[5]

The village is thus described as a paradise where "life is pure," a land of "poetry and rites" where "everyone is integrated, concerned, surrounded,"[6] and where the original ancestor, "le père," dispenses wisdom in a godly manner. "Je suis le plus ancien, le plus savant de tous. Je connais tout. Je détiens tous les secrets de ce village; j'avais une famille ici, il y a plus de cinq siècles. . . . J'ai toujours vécu, et croyez-moi, je suis immortel. Dans mille ans, je serai encore là. . . . J'espère que le soleil vous chauffera longtemps. Si vous voulez l'immortalité; pour me trouver, je suis sous les arbres toujours."[7] All the elements of the Garden of Eden seem to be present in the village: the innocence, the bliss, the tree of life, the omniscient father, light and immortality. For Ken Bugul—and for Africa—the village embodies security and cultural identity, a "protective womb"[8] that provides feelings of safety.

It is this same haven of safety and harmony that is found in the villages of *L'Appel des arènes* by Aminata Sow Fall. The first village is the place where Nalla, the young boy who is the main character in the novel, spends part of his childhood with his grandmother, Mame Fari. Nalla loved to hear his grandmother talk about her past. "A travers les nombreuses histoires qu'elle lui racontait, Nalla avait pu reconstituer le portrait d'une jeune fille auréolée de la beauté des jardins de l'Eden."[9] He recalls "l'univers paradisiaque" where he had lived a simple life, free of artificial devices and constraints; where he could run barefoot and shirtless with the other children, playing hide-and-seek in the lush vegetation; where Mame Fari would fill the evening hours with beautiful stories and legends, introducing him to "l'univers éthéré du merveilleux"; where he could pick wild cherries at will and understand the language of animals; where the griot Mapaté, dressed in a white boubou trimmed in red, would make the ancestors live again and again as he told their stories under the big flame tree in bloom.[10]

The second village is that of André, the wrestler who becomes Nalla's friend. He describes his native Saalum in paradisaical terms.

> Là-bas, il y fait bon vivre. Des champs s'étendent à perte de vue. Il y a des arbres toujours verts. Des arbres de toutes sortes: des tamariniers aux branches géantes et touffues procurent une ombre aussi vivifiante que le jus du tamarin qui nous désaltère. . . . D'innombrables manguiers peuplent tout le pays; à l'heure de la maturation, ils sont lourds de fruits dorés à la chair tendre; les enfants en cueillent à volonté. . . . Là-bas, s'étire le fleuve miroitant comme une lame d'argent, qui coule, coule, coule, et qui nous bénit à l'aube, et qui nous dorlote la nuit. Un fleuve généreux, grouillant de poissons.[11]

It is a garden where man and beast live in harmony, even the serpent with whom man has made a pact and who actually protects man.[12] The descriptions André gives are so vivid that Nalla often imagines himself in this paradise of abundance and bliss. "Il 'voyait' des enfants gambader et aider aux travaux champêtres. . . . Sans transition, les champs se couvraient de verdure, les épis de mil pointaient vers le ciel, et le maïs se parait de sa chevelure dorée. Les paysans, vigoureux et gais, s'extasiaient devant les montagnes de mil, d'arachides et de maïs."[13] The evidence of the reality of this paradise is the "conkom," a drink made from the sap of palm trees, that André has brought back from the Saalum and that he gives to Nalla every day from an old tin cup. To Nalla this drink is like the sap of the tree of life, giving joy to the soul and making dreams bloom.

The third garden in *L'Appel des arènes* is the one where Malaw, another wrestler, takes Nalla after André has died. There, the two friends kneel at the foot of a "sacred baobab," which Malaw identifies as "a symbol of life."[14] Then they make offerings to Malaw's ancestors, who long ago founded the village of Diaminar, a retreat from the ills of the world, a paradise, a mythical stage for the dawn of life.

> Au-dessus d'eux, les pains verts de baobab se balancent au vent, sous le bleu dégradé du ciel. La rosée peu à peu se dissipe et les joyaux de cristaux qui tout à l'heure ornaient les feuilles pleuvent dans l'herbe grasse. Celle-ci se pare à son tour de boucles perlées. Des 'ramatous,' oiseaux dits *du Paradis* à la gorge chatoyante de reflets phosphorescents, gazouillent joyeusement en menant une ronde orchestrée par le roucoulement des pigeons sauvages et par le chuchotement cadencé des palmiers qui s'entrelacent.[15]

It is interesting to note that the three gardens in *L'Appel des arènes* are all filled with light. As Suzanne Crosta points out, "Ce qui distingue nettement l'univers de cette communauté culturelle, c'est la présence de la lumière, que ce soit le soleil, les étoiles ou les lampes. André, Malaw et Mame Fari sont plus souvent évoqués le matin[16] et l'auteure fait souvent référence à la présence du soleil—ardent, de plomb.[17] S'il est question de la nuit, on fait mention de la lune,[18] des étoiles,[19] ou de la lueur de la lampe à petrole."[20] Light, abundance, bliss, the tree of life—the distinguishing features of the Garden of Eden are indeed present in Aminata Sow Fall's villages. In *Douceurs du bercail*, the author adds an idyllic social dimension to the village: it is a place where there are no beggars; "everyone works, even the handicapped who haven't lost the use of their arms," and when calamities strike, people take care of one another. "Et la vie continue sans gloire pour les uns, sans honte pour les autres. Ceux qui ont reçu savent au fond d'eux-mêmes qu'ils devront un jour ou l'autre être du côté des bienfaiteurs. Afin que l'honneur soit sauf . . . [Dans les villages,] la fierté n'était pas l'apanage des riches, la pauvreté n'était pas considérée comme une tare. Tout le monde en était conscient et cela créait un certain équilibre que chacun se devait de sauvegarder scrupuleusement."[21] When personal and social harmony cease, however, "society is destroyed and the individuals are lost."[22] The garden is left behind, paradise is lost.

The Fall

In the myth of the Garden of Eden, the Fall comes about when Adam and Eve partake of the fruit of knowledge of good and evil. Innocence in the Garden had brought changeless contentment beyond the boundaries of time. Knowledge, on the other hand, brings sorrow and is bound to time. As Anthony Mountain puts it, "time and knowledge have much the same character, for both are the recognition of difference, of separation."[23] In the context of colonial Africa, the difference was black and white—pun intended—and the separation was a cultural one as Western values were pitted against African traditions.

In *Le Baobab fou*, the Fall is announced by the "piercing cry" of two-year-old Ken as she finds an amber bead in the sand and forces it into her ear. "The bead becomes one of the novel's primary symbols, representing the moment at which the young Bugul first becomes estranged from the world."[24] The bead foreshadows the Western world that is about to come into Ken Bugul's life, causing a loss of personal balance, shattering the harmony in which she has lived so far. From this point on, Ken's life is a series of separations or falls. First, her mother leaves on a train, a symbol of the Western world that tears all security apart. Although Ken does see her mother again, the umbilical cord with the mother has been cut for good, creating feelings of bereavement that obsess her. Why did her mother have to leave? She says she had to take care of a grandchild and did not want to deprive Ken of the opportunity to go to school. Her simple answer, "Mais tu allais à l'école, c'est pour cela que je ne t'ai pas emmenée avec moi," prompts Ken to reflect on that school: "L'école française qui allait bouleverser mille mondes et mille croyances qui se cachaient derrière les baobabs médusés en prenant des formes humaines."[25] The tree of life has definitely been supplanted—by foreign "human forms," causing yet another kind of separation. As Ken discovers "her ancestors, the Gauls," she becomes estranged from her own roots, a foreigner or "toubab," among her own people.

> Dans le village de la mère, je ne parlais qu'en français avec les jeunes gens et jeunes filles qui fréquentaient l'école française. Je croyais avoir trouvé un moyen de me rassurer en me faisant "toubab." Toujours les revues de mode de Paris qu'on pouvait acheter de seconde main au marché, toujours faire un tour dans le village pour me montrer, chaussant des chaussures à talons aiguille qui me donnaient si chaud et m'empêchaient de marcher gracieusement. Les décrépages permanents des cheveux, l'imitation des coiffures occidentales qui donnaient des visages déstructurés, le vernis rouge comme du sang qui me coulait des doigts. Ah, Dieu! Que j'étais épuisée de vouloir plus que "ressembler," me déformer.[26]

Seeking an elusive identity, Ken eventually ends up in Belgium, which she sees as a "promised land."[27] What she finds, however, is a "cold and lonely" world where "everyone walks too fast," "as if pursued by some monster."[28] Like Samba Diallo in *L'Aventure ambiguë*, she quickly becomes "un être hybride en détresse de n'être pas deux."[29] She is barely able to recognize herself in the mirror: "Comment ce visage pouvait-il m'appartenir? Oui, j'étais une Noire, une étrangère. Je me touchais le menton, la joue pour mieux me rendre compte que cette couleur était à moi."[30] In an attempt to ignore the emptiness and rejection she feels, she abandons her studies and seeks acceptance in all the wrong places. Her descent into Hell starts with an abortion, at which time she realizes how alienated she has become and yearns for the security of the baobab tree, "before the amber bead." As she falls further into the abyss of drugs, alcohol and prostitution, visions of the baobab tree and the village come back to haunt her.[31] Yet, there seems to be no way out for Ken: "Je virevoltais dans le tourbillon chutant. Je n'avais pas trouvé mes ancêtres les Gaulois et rien à la place."[32] She reaches the point where she contemplates suicide. Having partaken of the fruit of knowledge of good and evil, she has undertaken what Elisabeth Mudimbe-Boyi calls "an underground journey, in both the literal and metaphorical senses,"[33] a journey that leads to a symbolic death. In the case of Ken Bugul, the fall is thus complete and extreme, but because the baobab has continued to haunt her, the return to the lost paradise remains a possibility.

In the case of Diattou, in *L'Appel des arènes* by Aminata Sow Fall, the tree is consciously rejected. Diattou is Nalla's mother, educated in Europe, determined to look and act like Europeans do.

> Elle avait parié qu'elle se coulerait dans un nouveau moule conforme à l'idée qu'elle se faisait du modernisme. Travail de longue haleine qu'elle commença en se détachant de l'arbre aux multiples ramifications que constitue le village. Tantes, oncles, cousins, neveux, grands-oncles, trêve de parenté tentaculaire! "Peut-on s'encombrer, à l'âge où nous vivons, de tant de sollicitations! . . . Peut-on se comporter, à l'âge où nous vivons, comme au Moyen-Age!" Et Diattou, attisée par les vents d'Ouest, est tombée de l'arbre.[34]

She claims she has found a new paradise, the paradise of individualism: "Chacun pour soi et Dieu pour tous."[35] She has taken the greatest care to achieve what she calls her metamorphosis; she has "tamed and polished" her vocal cords, trying to copy the West in every aspect of her demeanor, yet the Western lifestyle remains awkward on her.

> A son retour d'Occident, lorsqu'elle était [allée récupérer Nalla dans son village,] elle avait débarqué en mini-jupe. Son accoutrement et ses cheveux coupés ras avaient scandalisé les villageois. La stupeur n'était pas encore passée qu'elle osa se promener en pantalon, cigarette au coin des lèvres. Les villageois, en observant ses fesses en forme de calebasses moulées dans le pantalon et en les voyant rebondir lorsqu'elle marchait, avaient pensé que Diattou leur jouait une scène de dérision.[36]

When her mother and some of the villagers try to reason with her, Diattou instructs them to mind their own business, for she answers to no one. "Except the devil," the village elder wants to add. Diattou thinks of her fellow Senegalese as "barbaric and dirty" and forbids her son to play with the boys in the neighborhood. As a result, she is ostracized by the whole community, blamed for the mysterious illness and death of one of the neighbor's little boys, and she and her family are eventually forced to move. Her reputation as "sorcière anthropophage" and "mangeuse d'âme"[37] follows her to the clinic where she works as a midwife. Blamed again for a stillbirth there, she quickly loses her clientele and finds herself confronted with a tragic vacuum. "Diattou's alienation is all the more dramatic and ironic since she is a midwife, and by definition, is supposed to be the person who gives life."[38] Instead, Diattou is sterile: her maternity ward is deserted and her own womb is empty. In spite of her intense desire to have more children, her only son rejects her, and even her husband, Ndiogou, who once lived by the same Western ideals, begins to turn away from her. As Aminata Sow Fall describes Diattou's world, the open spaces filled with light that had characterized the village give way to closed spaces filled with obscurity, silence and solitude. As Crosta points out, "Le rétrécissement physique et psychologique de l'espace de Diattou correspond à son aliénation culturelle croissante dans le texte. Au fur et à mesure du récit, on atteste la détérioration et la destruction progressive de la personnalité de Diattou. Le silence,[39] la solitude[40] et l'immobilité[41] suggèrent sa mort inéluctable."[42]

At the end of the novel, she is described as a shapeless form bundled under a blanket, cold and lifeless. On the last page, she crosses the room with rings under her eyes, her face limp, her back bent, her lipstick smeared, her clothes wrinkled—she says she is going to work, but it is only six thirty in the morning, and the maternity clinic is closed. She seems to have lost her mind. Diattou's linear path of individualism has led her to self-destruction. Through Diattou's tragic fate, Aminata Sow Fall raises the issue of the tragic alienation and loss of identity that so-called "emancipated" African women are imposing on themselves as they reject African traditions.[43]

This same alienation is found in *Douceurs du bercail*, in which the protagonist, Asta, is torn between two worlds. Most of the novel takes places in an airport depot where she is awaiting her eventual deportation back to Senegal. "The depot is a symbolic location where she is neither in France nor in Senegal. She belongs neither in the Western culture nor in the African culture, and is therefore without an identity."[44] She sees herself as an educated pseudo-European, yet when she is stopped by customs officials and thrown into the depot like an animal, she realizes that she is nothing in the Western world. A call by her French friend to her place of employment in Dakar confirms that there too she is "unimportant"—she does not even have a secretary! Although the circumstances of Asta's psychological and cultural fall are not given in the novel, the result is very clear: a depot described as "un espace rectangulaire surpeuplé," "un calvaire," "un chemin de croix," "un enfer."[45] The description of Asta in this enclosed space is reminiscent of Diattou's: "Yeux hagards, tresses dans tous les sens, orteils enflés débordant des bas troués. L'air d'en avoir marre de vivre."[46]

Such are the consequences of the Fall. M. Niang, the wiseman of *L'Appel des arènes*, sums that matter up as follows: "L'aliénation est assurément la plus grande mutilation que puisse subir un homme. Le désordre qui bouleverse le monde a pour cause l'aliénation collective. Chacun refuse d'être soi-même et se perd dans l'illusion qu'il peut se tailler un manteau selon sa propre fantaisie. . . . Personne ne sait plus à quoi s'accrocher. L'homme perd ses racines et l'homme sans racines est pareil à un arbre sans racines: il se dessèche et meurt."[47] What happens to Ken, Diattou and Asta is what happens to many Africans as they leave their village in search of another paradise in the big city, where they partake of the fruit of different values. Malaw's father, the other wiseman in *L'Appel des arènes*, explains this to his son. He has seen Diaminar, the ancestral village, lose most of its sons and daughters to the big city, and he has seen them lose their souls in the big city. His own daughter died in prison at the age of eighteen after killing her illegitimate baby—a victim of city life. His predictions are prophetic:

L'euphorie passera. . . . La solitude les frappera tous, comme elle a déjà frappé ceux qui, à la ville, étaient partis au loin et qui sont revenus en emportant dans le coeur la froideur des brumes du Nord. La grande ville sera malade de ses habitants: il y aura d'un côté ceux qui sont enflés de l'orgueil d'avoir trouvé une autre vérité, et de l'autre ceux que la fumée et le vrombissement continu des machines auront abrutis. Il y aura aussi ceux que le désoeuvrement aura disloqués s'il ne les a réduits à tendre perpétuellement une main quémandeuse. Ils formeront un peuple désintégré et se livreront un combat sans merci pour survivre aux tourments qu'ils se seront créés. Ils ne sauront plus sentir, ni chanter, ni rêver. Ils seront au bord du précipice. Il faudra les sauver avant qu'ils ne s'y engouffrent.[48]

Return to Paradise Lost

Is it possible to "save them"? In the myth of the Garden of Eden, before Adam and Eve were driven out of the garden, the Lord God "placed at the east of the garden of Eden Cherubims, and a flaming sword to keep the way of the tree of life, lest man put forth his hand, and take also of the tree of life, and eat, and live forever" in his fallen state. In other words, the Kens, Diattous and Astas of today's Africa do not have to stay forever in their fallen state, if they choose not to. There *is* a way to return to the lost paradise.

For Ken Bugul, this realization comes in the night of her greatest despair. She has fallen as low as a human being can fall, her soul "has been dead for a long time,"[49] but she is able to cling to memories—real or imagined—of the primeval garden. "Je me fabriquais des souvenirs et ils étaient intenses. Je suis née dans le Ndoucoumane. Le soleil a bercé ma première vie, les baobabs hauts et gros s'élançant vers les cieux en applaudissements effrénés m'ont apporté le souffle profond de la racine, le sable des matins froids et des nuits ensorcelantes m'avait aiguisé les sens, les flots de ses atmosphères m'avaient emportée dans la hauteur du rêve."[50] In the night of despair, she is still able to hear "le tam tam lointain [qui] faisait frémir l'ancêtre [somnolant] sous le baobab,"[51] and it is this that will save her. "Le voulant ou non, la vie m'attendait juste derrière la porte. La conscience de tout ce qui m'était arrivé si loin du village où je suis née, me faisait prier Dieu de me faire renaître."[52] She decides, "in time," to go back to the village, where she is greeted by the baobab that had witnessed the first signs of the Fall, when the amber bead and the piercing cry of separation had "shattered the harmony" of her life. The baobab is now dead, but Ken Bugul has come full circle, and the morning of the reunion is a dawn of redemption, full of light and hope. "Le matin où je suis arrivée au village, tous les autres baobabs s'étaient cachés derrière leurs troncs, en repliant leurs branches en un feuillage touffu. Le soleil veillait le défunt qui était tout en lumière. Les petits papillons blancs et jaunes sillonnaient l'air de leurs ailes lumineuses et tremblantes. . . . [C'était] le premier matin d'une aube sans crépuscule."[53]

The dead baobab can be seen as a symbol of Ken Bugul's life up to that point. As she pronounces her eulogy to the baobab, she is saying farewell to her life of alienation and welcoming a new and better life back in the village.[54] "The peace of the ending in front of the baobab suggests that the narrator has exorcised herself of the European influence."[55] She has recovered from the "cultural amnesia that had led her to embrace a false ancestry," and she re-discovers Africa, which becomes her new reference point, putting an end to her life of exile and errancy.[56] By returning to the life-giving tree of her own ancestry, Ken Bugul has regained her paradise lost.

In *L'Appel des arènes* the "moving quest to reintegrate paradise lost"[57] is best exemplified by the young boy Nalla. His mother has done everything in her power to make him forget his own ancestry; she has tried to sever all ties with the village, but the boy "feels that his life with his Europeanized parents is cold and sterile, lacking all mystery, all symbolic richness. He emotionally rejects that life and gives himself up to the magic world of the wrestling arena."[58] The wrestling arena represents African tradition. By contrast with the linearity of individualism, the arena is a circular space of communal togetherness. Crosta elaborates on this contrast:

> Les chemins linéaires de Diattou et de Ndiogou débouchent sur la dépersonnalisation et sur la destruction inéluctable de ceux qui les suivent ou les traversent. Par contre, les chemins tracés par Mame Fari et les lutteurs aboutissent à la circularité. *L'Appel des arènes* souligne de façon symbolique le désir de Nalla de quitter la linéarité de la pensée européenne de Diattou pour s'inscrire dans la circularité de la pensée africaine des lutteurs. . . . La forme circulaire évoquée par les arènes, les danses, les demi-cercles que forment les lutteurs,[59] le cercle des voisines qui entourent Diattou, Ndiogou et Nalla,[60] l'encerclement du village Diaminar,[61] [tout ceci] suggère l'intégration de l'individu à un ensemble.[62]

The wrestling arena is a recreation of the village within the city. The mission that Malaw's father gives to his son, the wrestler, is clear. "Sauve-les, mon fils. Va à Louga [la ville]. Ouvre des arènes et remue-les. Fais-y bouillonner le tam-tam comme une mer en furie. . . . Il faut que le tam-tam aux arènes gronde! Ils l'entendront, et ceux qui ne sont pas les damnés éternels finiront par venir parce qu'ils ne pourront pas résister à l'appel de la terre."[63]

Malaw goes to the city, and the call of the tom-tom is heard: by Nalla, but also, eventually, by his father, and a whole crowd of the most unexpected people, whom Aminata Sow Fall takes great pleasure in describing: Saer, a renowned physician who has spent twenty-five years in Europe; Fara, a state inspector who was believed to have no heart; Anthiou, the prosecutor whose fame fills the country's courts of law; Gartinet, the racist "toubab," etc. They have all heard "l'appel des arènes," the call of tradition, the call to return to the lost paradise. In the arena the wrestlers do not fight each other, they fight together for a common cause, the resurrection of Africa. This resurrection does not exclude the knowledge acquired in or through the Western world. "Knowledge is a good thing," says the wrestler André to Nalla[64]—as long as one does not forget the village. Nalla's tutor M. Niang provides the best example of synthesis as he uses the wrestling tales and songs to teach Nalla French grammar.[65] Tradition and modernity are not incompatible, provided that one remembers the arena, the village and the garden.

This garden is what saves Asta and her friends in *Douceurs du bercail*. It is a literal garden, a plot of land that Asta has purchased after being deported back to Africa. She does not have much money and she realizes that it will take time to develop this piece of ground, but she says she has "faith, ideas, willpower and hope."[66] The local farmers are quite sceptical at first, but after a few months of observing the city "toubabs," who work with their bare hands and just a few tools, even they agree: "Ils ne connaissent rien de la terre, mais ils l'aiment. Il n'y a pas de raison qu'elle ne le leur rende pas."[67] Asta and her friends call their garden Naatangué, which means happiness, abundance, peace. It is described as "un endroit vierge comme le jour de la Création" and the power of the woman to make it prosper is defined by Mapenda the griot in edenic terms: "la force est en la femme; les hommes n'en ont jamais douté depuis le jour où Eve a fait manger la pomme à Adam!"[68] Asta explains that she plans to proceed slowly and methodically with the help of her friends, who need above all to feel their worth as human beings by making themselves useful. The first thing she has to do is "convince them that Paradise is not necessarily elsewhere."[69] The second task is to sort out the plants that grow in the African soil: the weeds must be pulled out, the good plants "regenerated," and new crops can be brought in—"new species to enrich the site."[70] The symbolism is transparent: some existing traditions will fall in the weed category, but most traditions will be regenerated, and new techniques and new seeds will complete the modern picture, enriching the soil. Who knows? With hard work and faith, one might find a gold mine in that soil! And that is exactly what happens to Asta and her friends. In a corner of the garden they discover a rare strain of a precious herb called "guewê," which is used to make incense. The steps that follow the discovery carry a significant message for Africa: first, Asta and her friends "work hard to make the most of their treasure,"[71] then they involve the villagers around them in their labors, and as they increase production and revenue, they are able to buy new equipment and pay for major land improvements, such as the construction of a canal to bring water from the river. They consult an agronomist and various books to find out which parts of the land are best suited to which crops, and they plant new species along with the more traditional ones.

> L'aventure était lancée à Naatangué, et bien lancée, avec au fil des ans, les bonheurs, les angoisses, les jours de grisaille et les matins de soleil; avec les joies, les difficultés et le combat quotidien, comme dans toute oeuvre humaine. Et la prospérité, avec le temps, avait pointé le bout du nez. Elle s'était

consolidée grâce à l'imagination, le dynamisme et l'enthousiasme fou des promoteurs. Ils avaient brûlé des étapes à une vitesse vertigineuse, portés par leur foi et l'espérance. Du guewê aux cultures de rente, du coton filé et tissé sur place par des tisserands du coin, à la teinture et à la vannerie, sans oublier la poterie, le maraîchage, l'élevage de poulets et la cueillette d'herbes bienfaisantes, les conquêtes avaient été vécues avec satisfaction mais aussi avec l'ambition d'aller plus loin sur la route du succès qui leur semblait désormais ouverte. Mais leur grand bonheur avait été de s'identifier à un label: DOUCEURS DU BERCAIL.[72]

If this is not a recipe for re-creating the lost paradise, what is? It is interesting to note that Asta and her friends also plant *a circle* of trees in the garden, and in the middle of that circle of trees, a baobab, the tree of life.[73]

Conclusion

This chapter has examined the myth of the Garden of Eden as it is reflected in three novels: Life in the Garden was one of innocence and bliss, sheltered by the life-giving baobab tree and the security of the ancestral village; the tree of Western knowledge, growing nearby, seemed very tempting; the villagers did not suspect that partaking of its fruit would bring trouble on them; but the Fall came, with its thorns and thistles, its alienation and acculturation. Some, such as Diattou, died as a result of the Fall, because they cut themselves off from their roots and did not know how to "assimilate or adapt" the European model.[74] Others, such as Ken, remembered enough of the lost paradise to just make it back home. Nalla, Asta and their friends went further: they recreated the garden and proved that their paradise was not necessarily lost.

And so it is with Africa. Life in the pre-colonial village was one of innocence, if not bliss. The pace of progress was limited, perhaps, but the tree of tradition provided security and identity. Colonization brought the Fall, as the villagers partook of the fruit of different values. Torn between two worlds, colonized Africa was "forced to become what it was not."[75] As Ken Bugul puts it, "L'arrivée des Blancs avait sapé des fondements sacrés, les avait disloqués pour faire du colonisé un angoisse à perpétuité."[76] Some thought Africa was dead. "Diaminar n'existe plus!" Nalla cries in *L'Appel des arènes*. Diaminar, the African village, symbol of African tradition, was indeed losing all its sons and daughters to the dehumanized world of the big city, but if Africa could recreate the village within the city, as Malaw did with the wrestling arena, redemption would follow the Fall. "Diaminar est en exil mais il existe! Diaminar n'est pas mort!" replies Malaw at the end of the wrestling match.[77] Aminata Sow Fall's message of hope and determination is even stronger in *Douceurs du bercail*, in which Asta replants the garden against all the odds.

L'eldorado n'est pas au bout de l'exode mais dans les entrailles de notre terre. . . . L'argent est roi en notre siècle. Or nous sommes pauvres—matériellement pauvres. . . . Pauvres d'argent. . . . Riches tout de même de notre coeur et de nos rêves. . . . Le plus dur aujourd'hui est que l'espoir s'en va. Malgré tout je continuerai à prêcher: aimons notre terre; nous l'arroserons de notre sueur et la creuserons de toutes nos forces, avec courage. La lumière de notre espérance nous guidera, nous récolterons et bâtirons. Alors seulement nous pourrons emprunter les routes du ciel, de la terre et de l'eau sans êtres chassés comme des parias. Nous ne serons plus des voyageurs sans bagages. Nos mains calleuses en rencontreront d'autres en de chaudes poignées de respect et de dignité partagée. . . .[78]

As Ken Bugul and Aminata Sow Fall demonstrate, redemption is within reach for Africa. The tree of life may have seemed dead in Africa, but its roots are very much alive—it is a matter of finding them and revitalizing them with a proper balance of modernity and tradition.

Notes

1. *Genesis*, Chapters 2 and 3 (King James Bible).

2. Charles Hirsch and Marie Madeleine Davy, *L'Arbre, les symboles* (Paris: Éditions du Félin, 1997), 16.

3. Ken Bugul, *Le Baobab fou* (Dakar: Les Nouvelles Éditions Africaines, 1982), 18.

4. Bugul, *Le Baobab*, 15, 19.

5. Bugul, *Le Baobab*, 23.

6. Bugul, *Le Baobab*, 121, 143, 87.

7. Bugul, *Le Baobab*, 21.

8. Susan Stringer, *The Senegalese Novel by Women* (New York: Peter Lang Publishing, 1996), 133.

9. Aminata Sow Fall, *L'Appel des arènes* (Dakar: Les Nouvelles Éditions Africaines, 1982), 61.

10. Sow Fall, *L'Appel*, 62, 63, 75, 85, 113.

11. Sow Fall, *L'Appel*, 32–33.

12. Sow Fall, *L'Appel*, 42.

13. Sow Fall, *L'Appel*, 53.

14. Sow Fall, *L'Appel*, 74.

15. Sow Fall, *L'Appel*, 79, emphasis added.

16. Sow Fall, *L'Appel*, 32, 39, 58, 78, 111, 123, 137.

17. Sow Fall, *L'Appel*, 27, 49, 51, 83.

18. Sow Fall, *L'Appel*, 32.

19. Sow Fall, *L'Appel*, 38.

20. Suzanne Crosta, "Les structures spatiales dans *L'Appel des arènes* d'Aminata Sow Fall," *Revue francophone de Louisiane* 3, no. 1 (1988): 60.

21. Aminata Sow Fall, *Douceurs du bercail* (Abidjan: Nouvelles Éditions Ivoiriennes, 1998), 155–56.

22. Sow Fall, *Douceurs*, 157.

23. Anthony Mountain, "Eden, a Modern Myth," *The Dalhousie Review* 52, no. 2 (1972): 268.

24. Susan Stringer, "Innovation in Ken Bugul's *Le Baobab fou*," *Cincinnati Romance Review* 10 (1991): 202.

25. Bugul, *Le Baobab*, 114, 115.

26. Bugul, *Le Baobab*, 138–39.

27. Bugul, *Le Baobab*, 33.

28. Bugul, *Le Baobab*, 47.

29. Cheikh Hamidou Kane, *L'Aventure ambiguë* (Paris: René Julliard, 1961), 164

30. Bugul, *Le Baobab*, 50.

31. Bugul, *Le Baobab*, 64, 87, 102, 160–61.

32. Bugul, *Le Baobab*, 88.

33. Elisabeth Mudimbe-Boyi, "The Poetics of Exile and Errancy: Ken Bugul's *Le Baobab fou* and Simone Schwarz-Bart's *Ti Jean L'Horizon*," *Yale French Studies* 83, no. 2 (1993): 203.

34. Sow Fall, *L'Appel*, 94–95.

35. Sow Fall, *L'Appel*, 95.

36. Sow Fall, *L'Appel*, 131.

37. Sow Fall, *L'Appel*, 67, 96.

38. Odile Cazenave, "Gender, Age and Reeducation: A Changing Emphasis in Recent African Novels in French, as exemplified in *L'Appel des arènes* by Aminata Sow Fall," *Africa Today* (3rd Quarter 1991): 56.

39. Sow Fall, *L'Appel*, 100–108.

40. Sow Fall, *L'Appel*, 100.

41. Sow Fall, *L'Appel*, 133–134.

42. Crosta, "Les structures," 59.

43. See Cazenave, "Gender, Age," 58.

44. Bethany Kolbaba, "The Healer's Touch: The Role of Women in Healing Africa's Woes," unpublished Honors' Thesis (Brigham: Young University, 1999), 38.

45. Sow Fall, *Douceurs*, 39, 40, 41, 131.

46. Sow Fall, *Douceurs*, 43.
47. Sow Fall, *L'Appel*, 72.
48. Sow Fall, *L'Appel*, 138–39.
49. Bugul, *Le Baobab*, 180.
50. Bugul, *Le Baobab*, 159–60.
51. Bugul, *Le Baobab*, 161.
52. Bugul, *Le Baobab*, 180.
53. Bugul, *Le Baobab*, 181–82.
54. See Stringer, *Senegalese Novel*, 133.
55. Stringer, *Senegalese Novel*, 136.
56. See Mudimbe-Boyi, "The Poetics of Exile," 205.
57. Sow Fall, *L' Appel*, 63.
58. Susan Stringer, "Cultural Conflict in the Novels of Two African Writers, Mariama Bâ and Aminata Sow Fall," *Sage: A Scholarly Journal on Black Women, Student Supplement 1988*, 37–38.
59. Sow Fall, *L'Appel*, 33.
60. Sow Fall, *L'Appel*, 63.
61. Sow Fall, *L'Appel*, 73.
62. Crosta, "Les structures," 61.
63. Sow Fall, *L' Appel*, 139.
64. Sow Fall, *L' Appel*, 36.
65. Sow Fall, *L' Appel*, 91.
66. Sow Fall, *Douceurs*, 188.
67. Sow Fall, *Douceurs*, 205.
68. Sow Fall, *Douceurs*, 195–96.
69. Sow Fall, *Douceurs*, 201.
70. Sow Fall, *Douceurs*, 205.
71. Sow Fall, *Douceurs*, 215.
72. Sow Fall, *Douceurs*, 216–17.
73. Sow Fall, *Douceurs*, 221.
74. Sow Fall, *L' Appel*, 65.
75. Aminata Sow Fall, personal interview with Chantal Thompson, July 1999.
76. Bugul, *Le Baobab*, 102.
77. Sow Fall, *Appel*, 141.
78. Sow Fall, *Douceurs*, 87–88.

9

Revisiting the "Roman de la Désillusion": A Semiotic and Cultural Reading of Ousmane Sembène's *Xala*

Gloria Nne Onyeoziri

A LTHOUGH THE EARLIEST WRITTEN LITERATURE produced in Senegal, dating from the nineteenth century, was created by French colonial administrators and travelers, the first writing by a black Senegalese author dates from 1916, when Ahmadou Magaté Diagne, an educator, wrote his *Trois volontés de Malic*, a short fictional text (referred to by Dorothy Blair as "the first Senegalese, indeed the first African, novel in French"[1]). This text was to influence in a decisive way the next generation of Senegalese intellectuals, including Birago Diop, whose *Contes d'Amadou Koumba* in turn inspired Léopold Sédar Senghor, arguably Senegal's best known writer to date. In 1926 Bakary Diallo, a previously uneducated *tirailleur sénégalais* who had learned French in the army, wrote his autobiographical *Force Bonté*, naively praising the authority and generosity of the French colonizer.

By the 1930s, the Négritude movement, a cultural awakening that was to affect writing by Africans, especially by Senegalese authors, for decades, was born among black students in Paris, including Aimé Césaire (from Martinique), Léon Damas (from Guyana), and the Senegalese Senghor, Birago Diop and Ousmane Socé. Most of these intellectuals either wrote poetry, translated folklore into French, or produced autobiographical narrative. Subsequently, many, especially in the 1950s, continued to express their opposition to colonialism, through the ironic portrayal of either the colonizer or the ambiguous situation of partially assimilated African intellectuals, and call for the cultural and political self-affirmation of African peoples. Among these figures, the Senegalese authors included Cheikh Hamidou Kane (*Aventure ambiguë*, 1961) and Ousmane Sembène, an autodidact who was to become a key figure in Senegalese literary production (working in the novel, short story and film) throughout the second half of the twentieth century. His first novel, *Le Docker noir*, was published in 1956.

No works by Senegalese women writers were published during the entire colonial period, but women forced their way into the world of published writing in the 1970s. Like the men, many began with autobiography, spontaneously bringing their experiences as women into Senegalese literature. The best known of the autobiographical or semi-autobiographical novels by Senegalese women are Nafissatou Diallo's *De Tilène au Plateau: une enfance dakaroise* (1975), Mariama Bâ's *Une si longue lettre* (1979) and Ken Bugul's *Le Baobab fou* (1982). Aminata Sow Fall, one of the most prolific Senegalese women writers (with six novels published to date), deals not only with the experiences of women, but also with manifold cultural and social problems, such as polygamy, government waste, conspicuous consumption, corruption, begging and cultural alienation.

By the 1960s Ousmane Sembène, who was to become decisively involved in cinema, had already proved himself "the most prolific and versatile of Senegal's writers."[2] His first novel, *Le Docker noir*, was written in the tradition of social realism of Ousmane Socé and Abdoulaye Sadji. *O pays mon beau peuple* followed in 1957 as a representation of anti-colonial struggle characteristic of African novels of the 1950s. But it is Sembène's third novel, *Les Bouts de bois de Dieu* (1960), a great classic of African literature published at the moment when independence came to most African states, that truly foregrounds Sembène's literary vocation to represent the lives, daily reality and political potential of both the men and women of Senegal. In this novel, despite the many tragic events connected with the historic railway workers' strike of 1947 it relates, space is a symbolic affirmation of the significance and efficacy of collective consciousness. *Xala*, published in 1973 after the early optimism of the Independence era had given way to the disillusionment and disappointment of the 1970s, reflects the general impression characteristic of this period that the newly empowered Dakar (and implicitly African) bourgeoisie was essentially a self-serving, unfruitful minority opposed to progress.

Narrative Structure and the Discourse of Disillusionment

What better place to appreciate the artistic dimensions and qualities of Ousmane Sembène's work than in the play of language? And yet, the implicit presence in the text of this play allows the reader to attach value to the political and revolutionary timeliness of this author and his determined pursuit of progress, development and justice. It is important to bear in mind that social injustice and moral crises have always been targets for literary satire throughout the world. Secondly, the period between 1968 and the early 1990s was a time of global crisis that each region lived out in a specific way. The play of language in *Xala* helps the reader to grasp one of the specific ways that these years of crisis were experienced in Africa.

This disillusionment may be seen as part of what Eric Hobsbawm in his book *Age of Extremes* refers to as a global crisis of the late twentieth century: "Even more obvious than the uncertainties of world economics and world politics, was the social and moral crisis reflecting the post-1950 upheavals in human life, which also found widespread if confused expression in these crisis decades. It was a crisis of the beliefs and assumptions on which modern society had been founded since the Moderns won their famous battle against the Ancients in the early-eighteenth century."[3] These assumptions, some of which Rivkin and Ryan discuss in their introduction to Marxist literary theory,[4] were about liberal capitalism and enterprise, about the control of private and public space. In *Xala*, a narrative of both personal and social history, a handful of unscrupulous upstarts try to exercise such control—disinheriting, exploiting and alienating the rest of their people. The play of language helps the reader to follow the utopian reversals of power relations Ousmane Sembene's narrative proposes in response to this crisis.

Hobsbawm adds: "However, the moral crisis was not only one of the assumptions of modern civilization, but also one of the historic structures of human relations which modern society inherited from a pre-industrial and pre-capitalist past. . . ."[5] What is exposed in the "roman de la désillusion" is how the confidence in both the capitalist and socialist (Communist) systems was shaken in Africa because it was neither well founded nor authentic. In the case of Africa, this confidence was that, with what Hobsbawm calls the "Golden Age" (from the 1950s to the 1970s—characterized by expansion of the world economy, technological advancement, general improvement in social conditions), the newly "independent" African states would conveniently develop into democratic, progressive, well-balanced states.

There has been considerable interest in the relationship between the sociopolitical and structural aspects of Ousmane Sembène's writing. Ronnie Scharfman's 1983 study, for example, discusses the possible symbolic significance of certain characters or groups of characters in *Les Bouts de bois de Dieu*, the importance of the fates they meet and the ideological values associated with them.[6] Both Françoise Pfaff's[7] and Bernth Linfors's articles, the one feminist and gynocritical, the other a "phallocentric exegesis," are important contributions to the reading of *Xala*, in spite of their rather excessive conflation of the female characters with opposite tendencies.[8] Linfors reiterates what constitutes the sociopolitical point of departure for most critics of this strategic novel of the period of disillusion in African literary production: "El Hadji Abdou Kader Beye's sexual impairment operates metonymically to signify a much larger systemic malfunction in a political economy of post-colonial Africa. That is, a part . . . represents the wholesale public emasculation of Africa's petite bourgeoisie who are seen as a sterile class of corrupt, parasitic entrepreneurs, incapable of engaging in productive activities."[9] However, in order to focus as much as possible on the formal aspects of Sembène's *Xala*, it is advisable to openly recognize and emphasize its narrational properties so that any interpretations proposed will help develop an understanding of the context and co-text of the *énonciation*[10] (process of utterance) and the individual utterances (*énoncés*). This makes it possible to avoid "lévy-bruhlien" assessments (i.e., seeing all "primitive" thinking as metonymical)[11] of the thoughts and linguistic competence of the characters. The narrative utterance is a key tool of the interpreter in his or her effort to reconstitute textual meaning in the face of considerable linguistic complexity. According to Frederick Ivor Case, writing on Ousmane Sembène and Assia Djebar: "C'est le domaine précis de l'énonciation qui nous révèle les dimensions diverses de l'esthétique africaine. La polysémie des mots et des concepts, le sémantisme engendré par l'enjeu d'au moins deux langues différentes et la sémiotique née de l'imposition d'une structure culturelle sur une autre se cristallise en une production littéraire caractérisée par une préoccupation primordiale avec la condition humaine."[12] S. Ade Ojo, whose study most closely examines the signification of the word *xala* as a sign, adds that *Xala* is "le roman symboliste par excellence" and sees the word *xala* itself as a recurring polyvalent symbol of "impuissance" at all levels.[13] Ojo bases his reading of *Xala* on Senghor's theory of the sign in African literary art as functioning simultaneously as sign and sense, and approaches the interpretation of the sign *xala* from the point of view of the assimilation of the signifier to the signified: "Comme il est permis d'assimiler le signifiant au signifié, on peut aussi assimiler la force génératrice à ce qu'elle déclenche. Nous pouvons assimiler le 'xala' à l'impuissance."[14]

A structural study taking account of narrativity, in the sense of A. J. Greimas, for example, might set out valid meanings at the supra-segmental level in a way that would articulate the literary *engagement* and the political significance of Sembène's writing, particularly in *Les Bouts de bois de Dieu* and *Xala*, two works that are quite complementary in their representation of oppression, but that are fundamentally different in their narrative structures.

The De-Collectivization of Space in *Xala*

The collective space represented in *Les Bouts de bois de Dieu* is founded on a consciousness of sociocultural belonging preceded by a consciousness of political community. In *Xala* it deteriorates and becomes an individualistic space, both crushing and unstable, characterized by binary oppositions: tradition/modernity, us/me, external greatness/internal emptiness, to suggest some examples. The only short-lived meeting point between the two novels is seen in the fact that the Chamber of Commerce and Industry in *Xala* seems to be the later equivalent or continuation of the collective social space represented in *Les Bouts de bois de Dieu*. This apparent similarity is a result of the emphasis placed on the victory that comes when an African is at long last named as president of this organization. This victory suggests that these "libérationnistes-nationalistes," including El Hadji Abdou Kader Bèye, had established a solid foundation and had indeed penetrated ever higher social spheres. But in examining the narrative modes in *Xala*, one discovers that this "rise to power," like El Hadji's own co-textual and contextual "rise to power," is ultimately illusory, if not a source of ridicule. The white man is displaced and the black man who replaces him assumes the right to dispossess his fellow Africans of their land, to control the revenues of the State and to spread satellites of his "material power" throughout the space represented: "ils avaient énuméré les branches clef de l'économie nationale qui leur revenaient de droit: le commerce de gros, les entreprises de travaux publics, les pharmacies, les cliniques privées, les boulangeries, les ateliers de confection, les librairies, les salles de cinéma, etc."[15] Thus the organizing narrative principles become those of the problematic foundation of a desired new society and the founding of social status for self-serving individuals within that society. Pharmacies and public clinics suggest the private exploitation of a public, purportedly "socialist" state function. The bakeries imply the ability to manipulate values directly affecting the daily life of the people. The manufacturing industries ironically allude to precisely what this new bourgeoisie is not able to control. The bookshops and cinemas are connected with cultural politics, and the desire to control knowledge and human creativity.

The vertical and horizontal movements of the protagonist El Hadji proceed from his initial to his final co-textual position, and from his position as a member of the elite to that of a condemned or rejected member of society.[16] The manifest oppositions resulting from an association of the categories of expression and content (that is the figural aspect of the text) are shown. The homologation that opposes, for example, categories of geometrical movement to values of solidity is also brought out. In particular, the free triangular movement represented by El Hadji's movements between the villas of his wives is to the immobility of his final state as lightness is to heaviness, once again touching on mobility versus stasis, expansiveness versus isolation. Moreover, in both the production and the reception of these significations, language, a semiotic form of organization of the first order, plays a prominent role.

The function of the modalities of *pouvoir-faire* and *devoir-faire* are examined in the light of this order of homologation in the distribution of actantial roles. The more El Hadji's commercial empire expands, the further he, as an initial actantial subject, commits himself to an exaggerated show of wealth. The same homologation helps to explain the actantial roles that transform another initial *individual* actant (the role played by the beggar as an apparently isolated character) into a final *collective* actant who gathers together the energies of many fellow victims of oppression. Ultimately, the transformations affecting El Hadji and the beggar translate into a chiasmic figure—impotent power and powerful impotence.

An account of the action of the novel will show that space (represented and implied) breaks up into places of meeting and confrontation. This is all quite subtle, except perhaps in the final scene in which judgment is pronounced by the subject/sender (whom the reader ultimately perceives to be the beggar himself). The following semiotic model applies in *Les Bouts de bois de Dieu*: "[C]e sont les acteurs qui créent les lieux par leurs actions et leurs interactions. Ils les détruisent en les abandonnant. À ceci près, l'espace semble garder en mémoire les performances accomplies. En d'autres termes, certaines parcelles de l'espace disponible sont investies de sens;

sémantisées par le faire des acteurs."[17] In *Xala*, the actors are not the ones who create the places by their actions and interactions. The subject's identity is attached to the formation of a particular place. These spaces appear as "projections lisibles de l'être des sujets, de leur compétence et de leur incompétence."[18] For example, the space surrounding the third wife (N'goné) leads directly to the appearance of the Badyan (Yay Bineta). The Badyan plays the role of N'goné's guard dog and alter ego. Thus, the place occupied by the third wife is given its semantic value neither by the hero's actions nor by those of the Badyan, but by the complementary relationship that, in this situation, is established between the two women. Together, they plan to take from the hero while he has "nothing" to offer (being impotent), so that they can later refuse him when he comes to offer a potency that by that time will have become superfluous.[19]

From the point of view of narrative grammar, the syntactic component pushes toward the final 'scene' of the spectacle, which apparently constitutes the interpretation of all the implicit sites of the narrative, the parody of modern material success. In the processes of prolepsis and analepsis that alternately initiate the narrative, the protagonist is designated not only as a part of a whole in relation to economic power (the collectivity of the newly enriched social stratum), but also as an individual who has distinguished himself in his political and economic activities.

The textual space of the narrative is divided, ironically, into two unequal parts: 153 pages in the original Présence africaine edition devoted to the impotent individual subject and 12 pages at the end devoted to the collective impotent-but-empowered subject. The narrative programme, which corresponds to the object of El Hadji's search or desired object—the improvement of his socioeconomic status—is interrupted a quarter of the way through the first part of the story by his growing realization of a paradoxical situation involving the loss or the lack of what was already empty. Reflection on the title and the theme of the *xala* reveals linguistic aspects that call for precise interpretation. Firstly, at the level of linguistic connotation, the signifier *Xala*,[20] as a title and as a Wolof cultural signifier, removes the cultural "ground" or space, from beneath the feet of the novel as a *French* cultural artifact or "African novel of French expression." According to Alioune Tine, with the publication of *Xala*, "l'essentiel des mots wolofs est transcrit correctement à l'aide d'un alphabet qui consacre la reterritorialisation graphique du wolof et *le passage d'un vouloir-écrire à un pouvoir-écrire wolof*."[21]

Sexual Impotence and the Ironical Language of Disillusionment

The title given to the work designates a cultural and traditional phenomenon that is difficult for readers unfamiliar with the implications of "giving sexual impotence to someone" to understand; the reader will remain excluded from the full meaning of the text unless he or she possesses the necessary background cultural knowledge. Moreover, *xala*, a curse or evil fate, pulls away the ground from under El Hadji's feet, so that he feels "disoriented" and destroyed, and his heart and body are tormented with anguish. He feels like an exile on his own soil and even in his own body. A homologation is thus established between the two levels of interpretation: the linguistic status of the text and the social status of the protagonist. But one wonders then what El Hadji lacks—his masculine identity, his masculine virility (tautology intended) or his illusion, which could be either his phallus or his dysfunctional economic empire. The beggar tells him: "Tu n'as plus rien! Rien de rien, que ton *xala*."[22] Given that the phallus, as a symbol of power, represents something imaginary, the *xala* remains doubly imaginary since the signifier *xala* represents the absence of an absence, the cancelling of what was already an illusion.

The logical consequence of these reflections is that the imaginary phallic ground is a part, has to be a part, of the space of the concrete foundation. Before the *xala* episode, the sexual potency of El Hadji, his masculine power, which, in a phallocentric culture, is tied to his socioeconomic power, was considered to be a given. Thus the three villas, metonymically associated with the wives and their children, represent satellites of his socioeconomic power, which is in turn metonymically associated (as effect for cause) with his sexual potency. The other symbols of this power are, for example, his business office, a luxurious chauffeur-driven car, servants and other employees.

With this *xala*, which, at the logico-semantic level, represents the absence of masculine identity, his socioeconomic power also disappears because his business is neglected, the *xala* itself having become his principal, if not his sole, preoccupation: "Insensiblement son magasin périclitait. Il devait maintenir son grand train de vie, son standing: trois villas, le parc automobile, ses femmes, enfants, domestiques et les employés. Habitué à tout régler par chèques, il en usait pour éponger d'anciennes dettes et pour l'économie domestique. Il dépensait; son passif avait grevé son actif."[23] The system of signification represents El Hadji's situation as one in which heaviness overpowers lightness, constraining his freedom of movement: debts restrict his lucrative activities, and his liabilities outweigh his credit.

The beggar's revelation of the corruption (exploitation and expropriation) that constituted the concrete basis of El Hadji's wealth thus reveals that his socioeconomic power was in fact illusory, an absent power. His last wife opts for divorce because their marriage has not been consummated due to sexual impotence; the second leaves because of the evaporation of his socioeconomic power. The one who stays is his first wife, whom he married before he was carried away by the current of economic corruption and social injustice. Finally, in reconstituting the text, the reader discovers the true absence, i.e., the lack of a solid foundation in sociocultural space.

As a result, the vertical and horizontal movement of the story changes along with the action of the principal actor. The remaining three quarters of the first part of the textual space are devoted to the self-conscious and bitter experience of reality, the totality of which continues to elude him due to the inadequacy of his self-examination. Three implicit questions (the wrong questions, since they fail to provoke any fundamental self-questioning) constantly come back to him: Will he ever regain his potency? Who is responsible for his state of impotence? How can he get even with this person?

The first two preoccupations generate the narration, while punctuating it with insinuations and question marks signalled to readers in relation to the place he occupies, his true "home," in the milieu in which he finds himself. From the moment when he realizes his lack and his powerlessness in relation to the *xala*, with every passing minute El Hadji becomes more conscious of the instability, if not the vacuum, that lies literally before his feet: he does not even have a home of his own in which to live at this moment of crisis. There are three richly furnished villas, and yet their owner is out of place. Each of the three villas becomes a place of torment, confrontation and even insult for him. He would have liked to take refuge in a more welcoming environment, but there is none for him. His "office" at work, the center of his power, no longer offers him any peace; in addition, the beggar's voice irritates him to no end, ironically enough, without his considering this character among his possible adversaries.

El Hadji's situation at this juncture suggests a view of the self, as a spatial category under the relation container/contained.[24] The container, in this case the self, is afflicted with the permanent torment of the negation of his identity: "Que dirait-on de lui qui n'était plus un homme"; "si tu m'obéis tu seras un homme comme nous" the beggar tells him;[25] "alourdi, il perdit sa souplesse"; "affreusement déprimé . . . [il] contemplait sans rien voir."[26] The other container is the space that encompasses the little corner he called his "bureau." This space is described in such a way that it reflects the state of the protagonist's mind: full of cockroaches, flies, mildew—signs of decay. Like his containing self, the space of his contained self is also dysphoric; thus he closes his window in an unsuccessful attempt to cut off the relationship between his contained self and the street from which the beggar's song originates. The irony of El Hadji's fate is such that the description constantly interrupts the narration, so that the symbolic aesthetics of the story and the narration function in concert. For example, the narration points out that El Hadji's professional activities no longer interest him. He sees himself *brought down* from the heights he has scaled and reduced in social standing. The linguistic context of the comparison of El Hadji to a silk-cotton tree evocatively suggests his final fate: "Soleil après soleil, nuit après nuit, son tourment permanent corrodait ses activités professionnelles. Comme un fromager imbibé d'eau sur la rivière, il s'enfonçait dans la vase. Souffrant, il s'éloignait du cercle de ses paires où se nouaient, se scellaient les transactions."[27] The figurative language employed to signify El Hadji's tragic fall through the image of a silk-cotton tree stuck in the mud constitutes a double of his sorry state in the last scene, in which he is placed on a mock throne and metaphorically surrounded by "les déchets humains." By means of a discursive discrepancy between the *énonciation* and the *énoncé* (underscoring the ironic intention), El Hadji is at one and the same time elevated (as he himself would have liked to be) by the comparison with the silk-cotton tree, a cultural symbol of majesty and strength, and isolated and denounced, since the silk-cotton tree is stuck in the mire ("vase"), which connotes stagnation and putrefaction, not to mention that a tree trunk sinking into soft mud might suggest a flagging erection. This figurative representation of the socioeconomic upstart emphasizes the unstable foundations of his world, the corrupt collectivity he thinks he belongs to and the decay, deficiency and stagnation that characterize his economic empire.

The narrative technique of prolepsis, which links the discursive description of El Hadji's metaphorical state with his final diegetic state, is certainly not exclusive to *Xala*. Narration in Sembène's novels is strongly marked by complex processes of analepsis and prolepsis, both homodiegetic and heterodiegetic, internal and external, as one observes especially in *Le Dernier de l'empire* (1981) and *L'Harmattan* (1964). The sarcastic irony of *Xala* is found in the analogy between El Hadji's situation in the story and the symbolic situation (thus a popular and collective representation) of the silk-cotton tree. This symbol is filtered *first* through the prolepsis to evoke the last "scene." Inversely, in the last scene it is through analepsis that the reader is presented with a parody of the elevation and coronation in caricature of the narrative subject El Hadji-a satire on the high social and political rank he desires as well as his last extravagant, yet phoney marriage.[28] Through the parodic representation of these two concurrent stages, which marked the height of El Hadji's success and his "rise" in terms of his economic and social status, the beggar (implicitly representing both the narrative voice and mode) unmasks the corruption and injustice upon which El Hadji's status is built: the forceful expropriation of the land of his own kinsfolk and the imprisonment of those who dare to protest, including the beggar himself. In very powerful ways, through practical and invented metaphors and "dramatized" episodes, the *énonciateur*, who is responsible for the social and political satire, directs the reader to reconceptualize social space during this period of global moral crisis brought about by past assumptions. Thus, the importance and the impact of the scene in which El Hadji is humiliated in a confrontation with the "underclass" cannot be overemphasized: at his "great height" the space under and around him designates and symbolizes the foundation of his commercial and conjugal empire as an inauthentic, unstable and uncertain process. Only at this final moment can the reader understand and reconstitute the full analogy between El Hadji's situation and that of the silk-cotton tree.

As the narrative unfolds, due to the conundrum of the *xala*, El Hadji is forced out of his neo-colonial urban cocoon and pushed into marginalized semi-urban spaces, which he neither *knows* nor *controls*. In order to extricate himself from the "mud" he is stuck in, he is reduced to accepting exploitation by various marabouts (seers/healers). In his desperate efforts to find them and obtain their assistance, he comes into contact, perhaps for the first time, with the reality of his macrocosmic *entourage*, understanding the outlying neighborhoods where some of the marabouts live, collections of dusty little streets leading to villages in the forests, with real silk-cotton trees, places that are all inaccessible to his Mercedes, a clear indication of his cultural alienation and lack of authenticity. Until now, he has never been exposed to such public places because of his reliance on cars (the ultimate symbol of mobile private space), exclusive private parties and *in camera* boardrooms. Moreover, he once had the right to see all, to know all and to sanction all in the places where his power was recognized. At the homes of the marabouts he is alienated and is not *permitted* to see all, because there the other has authority over him, contrary to his own illusion of authority.

The marabouts give him a mixed bag of truth and untruth. His own blind spot is his notion of those who make up his "entourage" and his forgetfulness of the traditional African meaning, or at least implications, of the term "entourage."[29] This misunderstanding throws him off track and for a while distances him from reality. He suspects all the members of his immediate, "modern" entourage, thus creating a new dynamic of tension between them and himself. Yet, the words of one of the seers he consults about healing his *xala* ("c'est quelqu'un de ton en-tourage"[30]) and the beggar's voice seem to join together in forming an overall picture, a signi-fying code, the meaning of which completely escapes him in his present condition. Neverthe-less, these words pursue him, invading his heart and his ears, without its ever occurring to him to put them together. As a result of a complex irony the reader is drawn into a smile of com-plicity at El Hadji's expense: El Hadji sees himself as powerless ("impotent"), and indeed he is powerless in the face of both voices; and he can neither decode the one nor smother the other as he desires:

> À l'angle de la même rue, à droite—une rue passante, animée—le mendiant, sur sa peau de mou-ton usée, les jambes croisées en tailleur, psalmodiait. Sa voix perçante dominait par instant le tinta-marre. . . . Modu goûtait avec raffinement les passages vocalisés. Le chant montait en spirale,[31] s'él-evait, puis se rabattait au ras du talus comme pour accompagner les pieds des marcheurs. Le mendiant *faisait partie du décor* comme les murs sales, les vieux camions transportant de la marchandise. Le mendiant était très connu à ce carrefour. Le seul qui le trouvait agaçant était El Hadji. El Hadji, maintes fois, l'avait fait rafler par la police. Des semaines après il revenait reprendre sa place. Un coin qu'il semblait affectionner.[32]

The narrator also adopts a modality of innocence by stating that the beggar "seemed" to have a special preference for the place he occupied. This suggests a discrete avowal by the narrator of his complicity with the beggar, the true *destinateur* (sender) of his imminent revelation.

The Beggar as Sociocultural "Sender"

Modu the chauffeur only plays the role of focal point briefly, but it is the dominated class (rep-resented by the boy employed to wash the car for Modu, i.e., a servant to a servant), the people who have been dispossessed of their land, who are heard through the narrator's insistence on El Hadji's attitude toward the beggar. This is comparable to Mour's attitude toward the beggars in Aminata Sow Fall's *La Grève des bàttu*. By saying that the beggar is a part of the backdrop, and by connecting him with the walls and trucks, the narrator (and in this case the *énonciateur* or implicit, ironical voice of the author) underscores the reification, accepted as normal by society in general, of such marginalized persons. Since the beggar himself rejects this norm by the force of his voice alone, he puts into question the authority of those who, like El Hadji, consider themselves to be the masters of the place. El Hadji's train of thought, even at this moment of crisis, is continually interrupted by the voice of the beggar's song: "Dans son "bureau" El Hadji Kader Bèye tempêtait contre le mendiant, ce gueux."[33] The term *gueux* (vagabond) signals the *énonciateur*'s ironic attitude toward to El Hadji. The reader will tend, at least initially, to accept the term as referentially true of the beggar. It is also worth noting how the narrator distances himself from the concept of the *"bureau"* (using quotation marks in the original) in the context of El Hadji's business; the irony here will be echoed in the revelation to be made by the beggar at the end of the novel. The beggar's voice has haunted him everywhere like a gnawing claim to justice: "Le chant du mendiant comme s'il était dans la pièce, s'éleva d'un [*sic*] octave."[34] El Hadji's unconscious functions in relation to the beggar's voice, which destabilizes his whole being in this context, although none of the three villas of his three wives offers him the comfort and peace he so much needs either. He fails to hide his exasperation: "Ces mendiants il faut les tous boucler pour le restant de leur vie."[35]

The *énonciateur* insinuates that, if El Hadji feels torn, it is because the synthesis of the two cultures in him is not complete. In spite of himself, he believes in the message of his people's seers, but he is unable to go back to his ancestors to look for the mode of signification of African discourse as it presents itself in this context. Todorov's idea (based on Saussure) about the relationship between the diachronic and the synchronic in the figurative domain is not borne out, in this case, in the decoding of the sembenian sign.[36] The "questioning of origins" does not always proceed from "an a-historic thinking." Sembène is perfectly aware of the history, and the translinguistic and transcultural changes involved in his use of "entourage," a word that, while polysemic, is morphologically motivated, and the meaning of which remains enigmatic to his main character. The "ahistoric" thinking of El Hadji prevents him from "seeing" the one who is doubly present in his "entourage"—that is the beggar.

Situated in time and space outside El Hadji's "modern" world, the beggar, who is very close to him on both levels, is nothing but a nuisance in the eyes of El Hadji. The latter cannot really conceive of the beggar as a potential threat. The beggar's physical proximity and his voice (in his songs), which seem to echo some past event, mean nothing to El Hadji.

Granted that the beggar himself is (as he claims) the sender of the *xala* (and the narration encourages the reader to disregard all other possible explanations), his locus, both near and distant, constitutes a site of confrontation and justice that will be revealed with the completion of El Hadji's fate. In the meantime, while the meaning of the signifier *entourage* escapes him (along with the significance of the beggar's voice), and while El Hadji intensifies his "witch hunt" in order to shake off his *xala* and re-establish the dignity of his masculine identity, his world (consisting of his modern entourage) falls apart, and his financial success evaporates. Instead of dominating the air, sea and land via which he imports the commodities he sells, instead of continuing to spread himself out over the spaces symbolized by the countries he trades with, he isolates himself, neglects his affairs and finds himself excluded from his milieu: "Le magasin d'import-export-qu'il nommait son 'bureau'—se situait au centre de la cité commerciale. . . . Aux heures de son apogée il regorgeait de sacs de riz (en provenance du Siam, du Cambodge, de la Caroline du Sud, du Brésil), de produits de ménages, de denrées alimentaires (importées de France, de Hollande, de Belgique, d'Italie, du Luxembourg, d'Angleterre, du Maroc . . .)."[37] Ironically, in spite of his re-valorization of his way of life and his actions, the only thing he wants to get rid of at all costs is also the only personal thing he has left: his *xala*. What he thought was his place of esteem and dignity, his union with his third wife, becomes the ultimate site of disgrace and loss. The office (shared with his fellow businessmen) he thought was a source of economic support and collective solidarity is revealed to be nothing more than a place of manipulation and individualism. Finally, El Hadji is excluded once his *vouloir-pouvoir-faire* is transformed into a *devoir-faire* (in the two senses of responsibility and obeying an order) because of the vengeful curse that has stricken him.

Thus, the sender of the curse, the beggar, is found to be on the side of the *pouvoir-vouloir-faire* modality, conceding to El Hadji his former actantial role of *devoir-faire* (as an oppressed and marginalized member of society). The narrative places El Hadji in a state of disjunction in relation to his dynamism, and his comfortable social and economic status. Ironically, one of the key operators of the disjunction, the association of businessmen, excludes him precisely because his own failure (and the lucidity that failure produces) reveals publicly the lack of substance to their collective existence as a new social stratum. Responding to his colleagues' accusations, El Hadji says to them: "Et nous? . . . Culs-terreux, commissionnaires, sous-traitants, par fatuité nous nous disons 'Hommes d'affaires.' Des affairistes sans fonds."[38]

While El Hadji is transformed in the last part of the novel from a state of social conjunction to one of disjunction, the beggar only passes from disjunction to conjunction in the sense that it is he who now possesses, at least in a utopian sense, the *vouloir-pouvoir-faire*, the power to free El Hadji of his *xala*. Subjection to the deontic modality (*devoir-faire*) passes from the beggar to El Hadji: "Je ne lui demanderais pas de l'argent, c'est vrai. Mais j'exigerais qu'il m'obéisse," says the beggar to Modu concerning the latter's employer.[39] El Hadji, stripped of illusions as to his real power, has no choice but to obey. On the other hand, the narrative programme of privation that used the beggar as its focal point begins outside the narrative, remains an indeterminate signifier up to the final scene and ends only at the moment of El Hadji's final fall. This implies the possibility (albeit ambiguous in the light of the novel's last sentence) of a future euphoric space for the beggar and his people.[40]

Conclusion

In conclusion, it is by the negation of a negation that the narrator of *Xala* puts into question the foundation of a social stratum. The importance of this foundation appears, at the end of the analysis, in the implicit relationship between the very notion of *xala* as the absence of an absence and the possession and dispossession of land. This analysis is not limited to a series of ideological associations of characters and values, but also involves a juxtaposition and intertwining of contrasting actantial and modal transformations. These transformations, however, do not depend on the actions of the characters as much as on spatial configurations heavily charged with historical connotations and cultural figures. The work that the narrator seems to invite the reader to share therefore consists of reconstructing and designating the conceptual and real problems implicit in the literary discourse of the age of disappointment in post-Independence Africa.

The comparison between *Les Bouts du bois de Dieu* and *Xala* reveals that the paradigm shift the two novels represent is not only the expression of political disappointment, but also a change in the quality of social space as it functions in the poetic imagination of African fiction. It is not just that the post-Independence African regimes have tended to be (to the disillusionment of their peoples, including writers) undemocratic, and even repressive in many cases, and anti-progressive socially and economically, not having fared as well as the people had perhaps hoped they would, but that the "roman de la désillusion" represents a reconceptualization of social space. This reconceptualization has more constructive elements than might be realised, to the extent that recent works in the 1980s and 1990s may in fact owe a debt to the "roman de la désillusion."

Notes

1. Dorothy Blair, *Senegalese Literature: A Critical History* (Boston: Twayne, 1984), 40.

2. Blair, *Senegalese Literature*, 80.

3. Eric Hobsbawm, *Age of Extremes: The Short Twentieth Century 1914–1991* (London: Abacus, 1995), 11.

4. Julie Rivkin and Michael Ryan, *Literary Theory: An Anthology* (Oxford: Blackwell, 1998), 231.

5. Rivkin and Ryan, *Literary Theory*.

6. Ronnie Scharfman, "Fonction romanesque féminine: rencontre de la culture et de la structure dans *Les Bouts de bois de Dieu*," *Éthiopiques* 1, nos. 3–4 (1983): 134–44.

7. Françoise Pfaff, *The Cinema of Ousmane Sembène, a Pioneer of African Film* (Westport, Conn.: Greenwood Press, 1984), 160–61. M. I. Ijere extends Ousmane Sembène's idea of social progress to the recognition of women: "toute institution qui relègue constamment les femmes au second plan doit être abolie. . . . Dans ses romans, Sembène Ousmane montre que le femmes africaines peuvent former une force que les hommes sont obligés de reconnaître." "La Condition féminine dans Xala de Sembène Ousmane," *L'Afrique littéraire* 85, (1989): 32.

8. Bernth Linfors, "Penetrating *Xala*," *The International Fiction Review* 24 (1997): 65–66.

9. Linfors, "Penetrating *Xala*," 65.

10. According to C. Kerbrat-Orecchioni, "each unit of content, explicit or implicit, is directly or indirectly anchored in the text, which is based on certain supporting signifiers that were needed for it to come about." These supporting signifiers are either co-textual (from the surrounding words in the text), paratextual (in the prosody or in accompanying gestures) or contextual (based on the presence of the referent). Catherine Kerbrat-Orecchioni, *L'Implicite* (Paris: Armand Colin, 1986), 16.

11. See Tzvetan Todorov, *Théories du symbole* (Paris: Seuil, 1977), 262–63.

12. Frederick Ivor Case, "Esthétique et discours idéologique dans l'œuvre d'Ousmane Sembène et d'Assia Djebar," in *Littérature et cinéma en Afrique francophone*, ed. Sada Niang (Paris: L'Harmattan, 1996), 35.

13. S. Ade Ojo, "Le Xala" dans *Xala* de Sembène Ousmane," *Éthiopiques* 5, nos. 1–2 (1988): 203.

14. Ade Ojo, "Le Xala," 202.

15. Ousmane Sembène, *Xala* (Paris: Présence Africaine, 1973), 7–8.

16. Linfors, "Penetrating *Xala*," 67–68, stresses the dimension of physical mobility and locomotion, of privilege and access to space, a situation of power relations that is reversed by the effect of the *xala*, not only putting brakes on his motion, but actually rendering him motionless. He becomes like a mannequin, one might add, as the *disabled* and disenfranchised people of the final scene settle their account with him.

17. Jean-Claude Coquet, "École de Paris," in *Sémiotique: l'École de Paris*, ed. Jean-Claude Coquet et al. (Paris: Hachette, 1982), 46.

18. Coquet, "École de Paris,"

19. After N'goné corroborates the Badyan's claim that N'goné is unavailable because of her period, the narrator comments on El Hadji's behalf (addressing the reader directly): "Si N'Goné avait pu, à toutes les occasions, lui glisser entre les mains, c'est qu'elle, tapie dans l'ombre, était la conseillère." Sembène, *Xala*, 117.

20. Ade Ojo, "Le Xala," 186–87, discusses at length the role of this title as "titre-image" and "mot-image."

21. Alioune Tine, "La Diglossie linguistique et la disglossie littéraire et leurs effets dans la pratique esthétique d'Ousmane Sembène," in *Littérature et cinéma en Afrique francophone*, ed. Sada Niang (Paris: L'Harmattan, 1996), 89.

22. Sembène, *Xala*, 165.

23. Sembène, *Xala*, 81.

24. This analysis draws on François Rastier, who, in his analysis of Mallarmé's poetry, says: "Pour l'englobant, sa manifestation la plus évidente est le Moi. Nous ne pouvons, comme le fait Mallarmé, mêler le vocabulaire du sensible et celui de la métaphysique, aussi nous considérerons le Moi comme un lieu de l'espace." François Rastier, *Essais de sémiotique discursive* (Tours: Mame, 1973), 34.

25. Rastier, *Essais de*, 170.

26. Rastier, *Essais de*, 81.

27. Rastier, *Essais de*.

28. Of this marriage the narrator caustically notes: "Cette troisième union le hissait au rang de la notabilité traditionnelle. En même temps, c'était une promotion" Sembène, *Xala*, 12.

29. The beggar is a part of El Hadji's entourage in at least two traditional senses: as a fellow human being begging at the rich man's door and as a dispossessed, though conveniently forgotten, member of El Hadji's family clan. The question of the exact contextual meaning of the word *entourage* could also be extended to one of the most burning questions of the disillusionment period (and even today) in African societies, one that creates tension and conflict within families, countries and ethnic groups: who is one of *us* and who is not?

30. Sembène, *Xala* , 85.

31. "Spiral" symbolises force and rebirth in contrast to the symbolic weakening and death with which El Hadji is faced.

32. Sembène, *Xala*, 48–49.

33. Sembène, *Xala*, 50.

34. Sembène, *Xala*, 52.

35. Sembène, *Xala*.

36. See Todorov, *Théories*, 275.

37. Todorov, *Théories*, 94.

38. Todorov, *Théories*, 139.

39. Todorov, *Théories*, 151.

40. The last sentence casts a definite shadow on the seemingly positive outcome of the kind of revolution the beggars' actions imply: "Dehors, les forces de l'ordre manipulaient leurs armes en position de tir. . . ."

10

Challenging the Colonization of Space: Exteriors and Interiors in the Films of Ousmane Sembène and Souleymane Cissé

Rachael Langford

THE IMPACT OF COLONIALISM AND NEO-COLONIALISM WAS, and is, particularly perceptible in the spatial realm, for colonialism reconfigured the space of Africa on the ground and in the imagination of both colonizers and colonized. This chapter will seek to explore some of the ways in which Ousmane Sembène and Souleymane Cissé use space in their films to challenge colonial and neo-colonial horizons of understanding of Africa and Africans.

An essential part of the colonial project consisted in the exploration and conquest of land in order to demarcate and annex territories. These explorations and conquests were underpinned by conceptual frameworks that disassociated center and periphery, and self and other. Neo-colonial discourses largely share these colonial frameworks. They either disguise the hierarchy of the First, Second and Third Worlds behind the spatial rhetoric of economic and cultural "globalization" and the expansion of "world" markets; or they more blatantly impose an absolute "otherness" on the "underdeveloped" world, an otherness that is posited as the cause of its problems, but also renders these problems incomprehensible to, and incapable of resolution by, the West.[1]

It therefore seems likely that when politically committed filmmakers such as Ousmane Sembène and Souleymane Cissé manipulate space in their works, they do so against the spaces of colonialism and neo-colonialism. Ousmane Sembène's own words on the subject lend weight to this hypothesis. When asked about European audiences' inability to understand his films, he polemically inverted colonialism's hierarchy of center and periphery with his reply: "L'Europe n'est pas mon centre. L'Europe est une périphérie de l'Afrique. Si vous prenez la carte de l'Afrique, géographiquement vous pouvez y mettre l'Europe et l'Amérique et il nous restera encore de la place. Pourquoi voulez-vous ce tropisme? Pourquoi voulez-vous que je sois comme le tournesol qui tourne autour du soleil? Je suis moi-même le soleil."[2] And Souleymane Cissé, questioned about the reception of his most recent film *Waati* (1995), emphasized the artificiality of colonialism's legacy to Africa of nation-state borders, with his statement that film goes beyond borders: "Je me sens profondément concerné par tous les bouleversements non seulement en Afrique du sud mais un peu partout dans le monde. Par conséquent, je voulais sortir des frontières du Mali. Certains m'en ont fait le reproche. Mais c'est tout simplement parce que je pense que le cinéma n'a pas de frontières."[3] Such remarks suggest that, to comprehend the significance of the use of space in films by directors such as Sembène and Cissé who contest the

West's categories of understanding for Africa, we need to be able to recognize the historically dominant representations of African space that their films rework or reject.

Colonialism and Space

In his study of the culture of colonialism, Nicholas Thomas argues that the discourses and practices that are collectively referred to as colonialism have often been falsely homogenized by those analyzing them, and he notes the pervasiveness of this approach in the work of even the most prominent figures in postcolonial criticism. [4]

The variability and discontinuity of the colonialist project as emphasized by Thomas should be kept in mind when considering the spatial configurations that (re)produced the power relations characteristic of colonialism. As Thomas also points out, "colonial discourse" as a homogenous entity is an invention. What actually existed was a plurality of discourses generated from different positions within the colonial project, and aimed at different groups engaged with the colonial project, both at home in the imperial nation and abroad in the colonies.[5] This is not to say that no elements of these differing discourses were held in common, but rather (as Thomas suggests) that colonialism is best understood in a para-Bourdieusian sense as a field. Inside this field a variety of discursive positions was available to the agents of colonialism, who actualized the positions they took up in word and deed in the furtherance of one or other element of the colonial project.

Where space is concerned, this means that the spatial discourses of, for example, the missionary, the secular philanthropist, the colonial administrator, the adventurer, the scientific explorer and the ethnologist all differed in certain ways; and that these discourses also differed among themselves according to the class, gender and national-cultural determinations (the *habitus*, so to speak) of those who used them. At the same time, however, these multiple discourses articulated the objective ideologies that legitimated Europe's interventions in non-European lands. It is this shared ideological ground that has allowed the circumscription of an object of study called "colonial discourse" and that makes it possible to concentrate on what can be identified as the "characteristic" features of French colonialism's spatial discourses on its African possessions. Thus, while the examples of colonial discourse quoted in what follows each emanate from an individual *habitus* inflected, for example, by gender and national-cultural determinations, such examples are used here to illustrate some of the common *topoi*, or "commonplaces," of colonial discourses on space.

Mapping African Space

From the late nineteenth century onwards, much of the agitation in favor of French colonial expansion came from the French geographical societies. As early as 1943, Donald McKay argued that the significance of the sudden rise of these geographical societies had lain precisely in their ability to propagate and legitimize, in the name of scientific discovery, the territorial ambitions of France.[6] The depiction of Africa in French maps of this period reflects this colonial orientation of geography. Historical atlases are particularly revealing, for they attempted to chart the expansion or withering of political power (in the form of empires, monarchies and dynasties) across landmasses, and were frequently accompanied by texts that reveal the ideology behind the cartography.

Jeremy Black points out that the maps in late nineteenth-century atlases provided concrete images of power and the opportunity to "meditate on or exult in the purposes of power."[7] They were, moreover, intensely nationalistic and placed a strongly didactic emphasis on the importance of imperialism and territorial control, expressing the nation-state's political agenda through "a cartographic style that stressed undifferentiated blocs of territory . . . separated by clear linear frontiers."[8]

Where non-European landmasses were concerned, natural features, cities, states and regions were identified with European names, and native boundaries were passed over in favor of borders created by European imperialism. European empires were presented as at once the high point and the conclusion of a historical process in which the forces of civilization succeeded in repelling the forces of barbarism. In this way the succession of maps in historical atlases presented a teleology according to which centers of civilization (ancient Rome followed by France, or more generally Europe, in French atlases) spread their influence across the world from their central position in the map projections employed.[9] In such mappings "there was little sense of interaction . . . and the principal reverse thrust was that of the barbarian invasions. These were presented as destructive and incoherent: the assault of barbarian peoples in the shape of colored arrows on the territorial bloc of the Roman Empire."[10]

The obsession with frontiers and homogenous territorial blocs in European imperialist mappings of the world is a revealing one, for it emphasizes the extent to which political and economic rapports de force were prized over any inquiry into social or cultural formations in the mapping of knowledge about the colonial possessions of the imperial powers. And yet atlases of the late nineteenth and early twentieth centuries maintained an ambivalent attitude to the importance of frontiers and territorial homogeneity, asserting their absolute necessity at the same time as they denied their importance. This technique allowed the boundaries of metropolitan France and the colonial partition of Africa to be represented as natural phenomena. The introduction to Vast and Malterre's turn-of-the-century *Atlas historique. Formation des états européens* provides a good example of this, for it maintains that: "Les frontières naturelles, entre lesquelles les peuples naissants se sont cantonnés, ont été la garantie de leur indépendance: c'est grâce à leur protection qu'ils ont pu grandir. . . . Les grands Empires n'ont, en effet, réussi à se fonder que sur des pays bien soudés entre eux, où la terre et la race s'accordaient dans un ensemble harmonieux et homogène. Les États qui ont englobé des pays sans affinités naturelles n'ont eu qu'une existence difficile et une durée éphémère."[11] Such assertions would seem to invalidate France's colonial extension into the rest of the world, but no contradiction is felt here by the writer, for he goes on to explain that: "Les expéditions lointaines, les aventures de colonisation sont devenues les facteurs indispensables de l'existence des nations riches. Elles donnent un aliment aux intelligences sans emploi, aux forces inoccupées, et, d'autre part, elles répandent, dans le monde, le génie de la race et de sa civilisation."

This is a striking example of Eurocentrism. The space of the colonies becomes an adventure-playground area facilitating the *rayonnement* of Europeans. The colonized space is not presented as populated, and the atlases of the period concur with this conceit of Africa as a vast "virgin territory" of commercial riches waiting to be exploited by Europeans. In Britain during the same period, J. G. Edgar proposed the establishment of a colonial museum where colonized space would be represented through multiple mappings that would demonstrate the resources available to the colonizing nation, but which make no mention of any population already living among and husbanding these resources. The space of the colonies is envisioned in thoroughly objectified terms, as unmodified by human intervention, as transparently knowable, and as consumable, both as knowledge and as material resource.[12] Almost forty years later in

France, the anarchist geographer Elisée Reclus was moved by a similar vision to suggest that a huge model of the globe be displayed at the *Exposition Universelle* of 1900.[13]

It thus becomes clear that one of the spatial discourses characteristic of the high colonial period was a utilitarian representation of space: the physical elements making up the space of the colonies are seen only as objects for consumption, in the form of portions of knowledge or resources for commercial exploitation. This representation codifies a thoroughgoing commodification of space, and grasps three-dimensional *space* as a two-dimensional *surface* without any established social significance.

The space of the colonies thus codified in colonial discourse shares significant features of what Henri Lefebvre terms "abstract space," the spatial understanding underpinning capitalism. Lefebvre sees abstract space functioning "objectally, as a set of things/signs and their formal relationships" that erase distinctions deriving from nature, from history and from the body. As the dominant form of space, "it seeks, often by violent means, to reduce the obstacles and resistance it encounters. . . . Lived experience is crushed, vanquished by what is conceived of. . . . Affectivity . . . along with the sensory/sensual realm, cannot accede to abstract space and so informs no symbolism. . . . Abstract space tends toward homogeneity, toward the elimination of existing differences or peculiarities."[14] The emphasis in the spatial discourses of colonialism on territorial homogeneity, and on the colonies as a *tabula rasa* unincorporated into any human's social practice, betrays the extent to which there lies embedded within colonialism's discourse this violent ideology of space as abstract space. The diverse spaces of the colonized lands are mapped as unitary in offering to the colonizer human and natural resources for exploitation, and unitary in their lack of any preexisting ties to society and culture.

Viewing African Space

This discursive emphasis on the surface or exterior is also apparent in written and filmed representations of African space from the colonial era. Early ethnographic films made in colonized lands exemplify this. Such films include the *chronophotographie* film-stills made by the Parisian doctor and ethnographer Félix-Louis Regnault in pursuit of a racial taxonomy of human movement, and those in the *Archives de la planète* established in 1909 by the French financier and patron of the sciences, Albert Kahn. These latter films were collected in the interests of "taxidermy," to use Fatima Tobing Rony's categories: they were not intended for viewing by the general public, but were destined to preserve "vanishing" ways of life for the scrutiny of the intellectual.[15] The material of Kahn's ethnographical films is of a stereotypical nature, closely conforming to the travelogue genre much in vogue in commercial cinema of the time. Thus the films, made not only in France's colonies in Africa but also in Europe, Asia and the Middle East, repeatedly show dances and religious rituals, market scenes and street scenes; and almost invariably include panoramic sweeps of the landscape from the point of view of the arriving outsider.[16]

Regnault's ethnographic films are of a different kind, being time-and-motion studies of indigenous people's movements, in which the body is captured by the camera as a side-on silhouette. Tobing Rony points out that, aside from the visible outline of clothes which denote the exotic otherness of the photographed bodies (the *boubou*, for example), individuating features are suppressed in these films in favor of a distillation of movement. The objective was to record each micro-movement composing an essential "native walk," "native jump" or "native run." and thus constitute an index of the way that races, not individuals, revealed themselves in movement.[17]

What is striking in the images of people in Kahn and Regnault's archives, and in the landscape scenes in Kahn's archive, is the way in which the subjectivity of the native is conceived. Land and native are filmed not by the eye that scans them for marks of similarity to itself, nor by the eye that has incorporated them into a web of personal memories and emotions. Thus the native is not recognized as a subject, but is an object that is all surface. Further, this surface caught on film is taken to constitute a portion of knowledge susceptible of being placed in an archive, such as the *Archives de la planète.*

In the same way that mapping the native's land renders it reducible and graspable, showing the landscape panorama from the point of view of the "self-effaced, noninterventionalist eye"[18] empties it of social significance and presents it, too, as pure surface. So while the European nationalisms contemporary with colonialism were promoting "land" as a binding social, emotional and even spiritual attachment; and while in the European academy the new discipline of human geography was investigating the development of man and the landscape in tandem,[19] no affective tie or historical impact on the landscape was imagined for the human objects occupying the colonized lands before the arrival of the colonizers.

Portrayals of land and portrayals of the native's body in colonial discourse thus mirror each other. Where the land is presented as pure surface void of social significance, the native himself or herself is presented as pure exterior without subjectivity. Such representations legitimized the conquest and possession of overseas territory, and the extraction of forced labor from native people—for those at home. But they did not generally succeed in repressing the anxiety of colonial administrators on the ground that African space and Africans might be rather less transparent and rather more impenetrable than this.

Imagining African Space in the Face of Reality

However forcefully colonial discourse (re)produced Africa and Africans as administrable plane surfaces, the practicalities of imperial rule meant using individuals indigenous to the colonized space in the furtherance of the colonial project. Administrators relied not only on native cooks and cleaners, but also on native secretarial and interpreting staff, so that one of the objects of colonial administration—the native—became enmeshed in the administration at a fundamental level as an acting subject. Thus while the colonial imagination continued to see the African subject as a pure object, the documents of colonialism show administrators recognizing the weakness of Europeans when confronted with the inscrutability of "something like a million fairly intelligent, slightly civilised negroes,"[20] or with the transgressive agency of the Dahomian who had "established a court in which he regulates all matters before admitting them to the administrator. . . . [He] has said that the white man will believe anything he says."[21]

Confronted with such realities, the colonial imagination faced an impasse. Its promotion of the lands to be colonized as unoccupied, traversable surfaces, and its promotion of indigenous people as transparently knowable objects encouraged majority acceptance of colonialism in Europe. This acceptance shored up a set of social and economic structures fundamental to the (re)production of European society. To call these commonplaces of the colonial imagination into question would therefore have been to loosen the bolts in the ideological scaffolding surrounding the expansion of capitalism into the world via the colonial project. And yet, not to prescribe a role in the colonial imagination for the agency of the native, or for the occupied three-dimensionality of the land, would have left these realities available for appropriation by the colonized as oppositional forms. Incorporated into colonial discourse as tamed and contained commonplaces, they would not be so threatening.

It is no coincidence, then, that the colonial imagination was greatly preoccupied with journeys into the "interior" of Africa, into the continent's infamous "heart of darkness." What is particularly significant about these explorations, both real and imaginary, is that they formed written and filmed narratives through which the imagination of African spaces was mapped onto the body of the African. Fear of the "uncivilized" lands of the interior was mediated through a hypostatization of Africa, while the African stood as a metonym of the continent. Fear of the "interior" lands therefore carried within it fear of the uncivilized interior of the native left to his or her own devices. A subjectivity for the native and an ungraspable depth to the land were posited through narratives of exploration and discovery, but contact with such interiors, human or geographical, was strongly marked with tropes of fear and rejection.

So, was the land of the colonies empty virgin territory or impenetrable jungle peopled with unfathomable natives? Were these natives inert inferior beings with no interior life? Or were they disturbingly able to think and act for themselves in ways escaping European comprehension? Both sides of this dichotomy were upheld in colonial discourse, so that the utopian vision of empty lands and docile bodies found its counterpart in a paranoid fear of what might lie beyond the visible exterior.

Challenging the Colonization of Space: Sembène and Cissé's Films

The films of Sembène and Cissé date from the post-Independence period, and seem predominantly to deal with contact and contrasts between age-old patterns of social interaction and the dynamics of contemporary, post-Independence Africa. One might therefore wonder how relevant an understanding of colonial discourse is for the interpretation of Sembène and Cissé's films. In answer to this, it should be noted that the strength of colonial discourse lay not in the internal coherence of the beliefs that it promoted, but in the affective strength of the images it generated. David Spurr's study of the rhetoric of colonialism demonstrates the extent to which rhetorical strategies over a century old still persist in popular and official discourse on the "Third World" today, and still frame Europe's understanding of its former colonies in the post-colonial world.[22] This continuing circulation of colonialism's images obfuscates the dynamics of neo-colonialism as actualized in the rapacious economics of globalization. For neo-colonialism denies subjectivity to non-Western peoples in a far more extreme fashion than did colonialism: despite the crimes perpetrated in its name, the *mission civilisatrice* was not wholly cynical, and the subjectivity of the native formed at least a concern in colonial discourse. It is of *no account* to neo-colonialism. Accordingly, for Sub-Saharan filmmakers to treat space and subjectivity is inescapably for them to engage with the West's determination of Africa in both the past and in the present.

In his examination of space in francophone African cinema, André Gardies makes the point that the first film to be made in Africa by an African, Sembène Ousmane's *Borrom Sarret* (1962), sets a pattern for much black African cinema to come in its desire to re-conquer African space in order to assert identity.[23] And yet colonialism did not deprive colonized peoples of identity; indeed, supplying identity, in the sense of defining and labeling, was a vital part of colonial discourse. In many cases colonialism worked hard to give the colonized firm and inescapable identities that they had never had before, such as "heathen," "native," "black," or "uncivilized." These supplied identities, which grasped the colonized from the outside as the negative image of Western values, were designed precisely to deny subjectivity and agency. Thus, while challenges to colonialism's division of African space are mounted through counter-discursive portrayals of space and place in the films by Cissé and Sembène that are considered below,[24] a more complete challenge to colonialism's spatial discourses is mounted by the films' challenging of the fundamental *effects* of this portrayal of space on subjectivity. I will therefore argue that it is not so much a re-conquest of identity, as a re-conquest of subjectivity, which is portrayed through the use of space in Sembène and Cissé's films.

Sembène Ousmane's most recent feature film is *Guelwaar* (1992). The narrative of the film deals with the search to recover a lost body, that of the political activist Guelwaar. At several points in the film, Guelwaar is shown in flashback making rousing speeches that reject Western food aid as a neo-colonial means of subjugating the African. Guelwaar's body is figured as a present "absence" throughout the film, denoted, for instance, by the presence of his empty coffin at the funeral reception, and the bitter comments about their life together his wife addresses to his burial clothes set out on their bed. Furthermore, it is strongly suggested that Guelwaar has been disposed of on account of his political activities. His body thus embodies a whole-hearted commitment of himself to politics as both exterior (body) and interior (mind). But Guelwaar's absent body also figures as an exemplum of his political beliefs, for he has argued that food aid is wiping out the African, and his disappearance quite literally embodies this destruction. Moreover, although Guelwaar does not have a corporeal existence in the narrative present of the film, so that his exterior is always absent, his beliefs and words are depicted as continuing to inform actions in the narrative present right up to the very end of the film. They therefore rehearse the longevity of Guelwaar's agency and subjectivity in contrast to his relatively short existence as body.

The sequences of the film following the recovery of Guelwaar's body translate his beliefs into spatial terms. After the young people have broken into the sacks of food aid and strewn it all over the ground, the carts of the funeral party are seen driving over the food aid, and then moving out toward the upper edge of the screen. The recovery of Guelwaar's body thus presages the people's crossing over the barriers to progress presented by Western aid, and food aid no longer dictates to them from above, having been symbolically thrown down and trampled underfoot. In this way the film rejects the administration and regulation of the African's body by outside interests at the same time as it emphasizes the possibilities for the African subject's agency.

Yet *Guelwaar* does not present the struggle to be free from the reduction to mere object only in terms of success. If Guelwaar's body and mind seem to combine to spur on others, his daughter Sophie is seen to embody a point of failure of his thought. Her character articulates this struggle for subjectivity through issues of gender. Indeed, it is Guelwaar's wife who points out to him that, despite all his talk of self-sufficiency, he has not been able to provide adequately for his own family, since his daughter subsidizes the family with her earnings as a prostitute in Dakar. Guelwaar's daughter's body thus bears witness to the local failure of his project, while her social situation and that of her prostitute friend Hélène Sène attest to the particular difficulty for (African) women of gaining the freedom to be self-determining subjects rather than objects for purchase and exchange between men. In this way, Sembène succeeds not only in describing an ideal, in which Africans are full subjects, but also in presenting barriers to the attainment of this ideal.

It is no coincidence that Guelwaar's youngest son in the film, Aloys, is disabled as a result of falling out of a tree. At one time his mother's bright hope for the future, she now sees him as a "useless cripple" who will be unable to support her in her old age. Aloys's infirmity provides another example of the film's use of embodiment to depict the weakening of Africa, and particularly of Africa's youth. The bodies of Guelwaar's youngest children in the film can be seen to symbolize the extent to which the body of young, independent Africa and the bodies of post-Independence Africans are always already determined by outside forces, to the detriment of agency. Moreover, the throwing down of the food sacks in the final sequences can be read as depicting an ideal, the symbolic reversal of Aloys's disabling fall from a height and of the disabling of African youth by the West. Hence, it is the youths who climb up onto the aid truck, and the food sacks from the West that are cast down and trampled.

The situation of Guelwaar's highly Europeanized, Paris-dwelling, eldest son, Barthélmy, is depicted somewhat differently. He shows continual signs of bodily discomfort now he is back in Africa, repeatedly mopping his brow, brushing the dust from his clothes, being "caught short" while traveling out in the countryside and ostentatiously wiping his hands with a handkerchief once he has relieved himself. This physical discomfort signals to the viewer the inner discomfort that Barthélmy feels (and is made to feel) as both "faux nègre" and "faux blanc"[25] returnee to the country of his birth. Yet these repeated signs of discomfort abate as Barthélmy becomes committed to Africa toward the end of the film. Thus his inability to feel physically comfortable with his situation is shown as spurring him to commit himself to different values. It also stands as the physical expression of his mental struggle to reconcile his previous value system with the reality confronting him. Consequently, body and mind are not shown as separated; but rather, with strong echoes of Fanon, Barthélmy's bodily experience of discomfort is shown to lead to a reconceptualization of the place of that body in the scheme of things, and thence to a commitment to values other than those of Europe and (neo-)colonialism. As a result, Barthélmy's body, in contrast to the bodies of Sophie and Aloys, is presented not as the object that he is reduced to, but as integral to his subjectivity. And indeed, the physical change in him portrayed over the course of the film accompanies a fundamental change in his dichotomous understanding of the world. By the end of the film, the opposition that Barthélmy maintained between Europe and Africa at the beginning of the film, and which is present as a metonym in the relationship between his body and mind, has been replaced with a dialectical understanding of the relationship between the African and the European. These two are now conceived as held in tension rather than in opposition or hierarchy.

Guelwaar's portrayal of narrative space echoes this depiction of the triumph of dialectical relations over dichotomies as an essential move in the struggle to win back subjectivity. The dramatic conflict in the film arises because of sharp divisions of space: the body of the Christian Guelwaar has been buried by mistake in a Muslim village's cemetery and occupies space that is Muslim. Neither side believes that Muslim and Christian bodies are simply interchangeable, and the film uses differences of gesture, language and dress to emphasize the distinctions between the two sides. Furthermore, the two communities involved live at a distance from each other, separated by an uninhabited "middle space" that Barthélmy and the police sergeant traverse in order to negotiate. And when the communities march on each other in anger, they do so from opposite sides of the camera frame, highlighting spatially their counter-position to one another. It is therefore highly significant that Guelwaar is referred to in the film as having entered the Muslim village long before his death and occupied Muslim space dressed as an old woman, in order to have sexual relations with the village chief's wife. For it is Guelwaar who, though flawed, is shown to rise most frequently above the reduction to mere object by the film's emphasis on his strong agency. Guelwaar's transgression of spatial, social and gender boundaries during his life explodes the myth of discrete or hermetic social and physical spaces defined by their opposition to one another that is the cause of the film's central conflict. It reveals that his dead body only repeats the penetration of out-of-bounds spaces already carried out by his living body. Guelwaar's refusal to be spatially bound serves to critique colonialism. Colonialism's legacy is most evident in spatial terms in the presence on the ground of post-Independence Africa of the frontier-bound nation-state,[26] and Guelwaar's movements replace a dichotomous understanding of space with one in which different spaces are seen as mutually constitutive and dialectically related. The fact that these are the actions of the character whose agency and subjecthood are most strongly stated in the film means that the critique of divisions of space is accompanied by a forceful depiction of African agency.

Thus *Guelwaar's* portrayal of the African body and of African space rejects the determination of space and the denial of subjectivity perpetrated by colonialism and perpetuated by neo-colonialism. Souleymane Cissé's films *Den Muso* (1975), *Baara* (1978) and *Finye* (1982), have similar preoccupations.

Ténin, the female protagonist of *Den Muso* (1975), is mute. She is raped by Sékou, her father's former employee who resigned over pay and conditions. Cissé has said that Ténin's muteness symbolizes the voicelessness of women African society,[27] and it is clear that when the women in the film transgress the order of the male-dominated society in which they live, they have no right of reply. They are chastised with violent words that call into question the integrity of their bodies, and violent actions that force them to embody their transgressiveness and their subjugated position. Yet it is not just gender in Cissé's films that causes the body to be squarely in the frame, for Sékou's rape of Ténin can be read as the re-enactment of, and revenge for, the exploitation of his own body in the factory run by Ténin's father. It thus comments on class-relations in post-Independence times.

In *Finye* (1982) the bodies of women and young people are assaulted and called into question to such an extent that they are often reduced to mere things. In contrast, the bodies of older men, those who have power over families and communities, remain inviolable so that their power appears disembodied and therefore hard to challenge because unlocated.[28] The eventual political commitment in both body *and* mind of the young protagonists of *Finye* contrasts both with the mental absence and physical dispossession of the film's drug-taking students, who disengage from society, and also with those in power, who are disembodied and therefore appear as all (violent) mind.

In Cissé's films, the individuals who are subjugated but resistant cross backwards and forwards over social boundaries. In *Den Muso* and *Finye*, for example, poor men have congress with the daughters of the rich élite; in *Baara* the porter Balla eats at the home of his wealthier *homonyme*, while one of the factory managers sleeps with the factory owner's wife in the factory owner's home. Those who cross these sociospatial boundaries travel on foot, on scooter or even, in *Den Muso*, in a rowing boat. By contrast, figures with power institute and maintain social and spatial boundaries, and travel hermetically sealed in their motor cars. Thus, the military governor of *Finye* is seen inside his office, in his home, in the interrogation center and in his garden, traveling between all these in chauffeured cars. His daughter Batrou, however, and his youngest, troublesome, wife, are seen in other people's rooms and homes, and in the city streets, travelling between these spaces mainly on foot.

Cissé's films thus show corrupt power creating and enforcing boundaries and hierarchies, while those contesting the legitimacy of corrupt power disregard such divisions. Cissé also shows corrupt power attempting to reduce those who resist to mere objects through extremes of corporal punishment that deny the resistors all agency and subjectivity. The overt critique is of abuses of power by the post-Independence African élites, but behind this lies a causal chain that can be understood to implicate colonialism and neo-colonialism. From whom did the post-independence élites take the baton of power, and from whom were the anti-democratic structures inherited and the mind-sets learned, if not from the European colonizers? Who has maintained corrupt regimes in power, allowing abuses where these suit their own interests, if not the former colonizing nations and their allies?

The link is particularly clear in Cissé's film *Baara*, where it is emphasized by the cinematography. The film includes a considerable number of close-ups of the faces of the porters and factory workers during which there is no dialogue or action. During these shots the camera rests entirely on the surface or exterior of its subject, and no clue is given to the thoughts or emotions passing beneath the body surfaces shown. The camera thus mimics the stance of the colonizer. This is a striking approach in the context of post-Independence Africa, and it makes a strong visual connection between the denial of subjectivity to workers in the present of post-Independence African society—a society that is to a significant extent configured by the neo-colonialism of global capitalism—and the denial of subjectivity to all Africans in the past of European colonialism.

Such an approach is radical because the repetition of an element of colonial discourse at a historical distance puts the economic back into the question of African subjectivity in a way that fundamentally undermines colonial and neo-colonial discourse. Both these discourses strenuously deny that their interventions in Africa are for the economic betterment of the West and allude instead to the "civilizing mission" or to the "development" of "underdeveloped" countries. Cissé's films demonstrate a concern to show class and gender conflicts among Africans, and this emphasis challenges the colonial and neo-colonial refusal to differentiate Africans at the same time as it gives the lie to the idea of Africans as administrable, unresisting, docile bodies.

The final sequences of Sembène's film *Xala* (1975) show physical conflict between the rich élite and the dispossessed of Senegal. The beggars who invade El Hadji's home have him strip naked and spit on him in front of his first wife and daughter. Two things are particularly striking about these scenes. First, much as in *Guelwaar*, this ending to the film inverts the hierarchy of power so that agency is restored to the subjugated. Second, this restoration of agency takes place through embodiment. El Hadji has already embodied his immorality unwittingly through the initial curse of impotence, but his nudity in these scenes forces him to occupy the place of the outcast, at the same time as he is forced to embody his immorality, this time knowingly, through being spat on. The agency of the dispossessed is thus depicted at the same time as the body is brought into question, and there seems to be hope for El Hadji precisely because he is willing to recognize his wrongness in body and in mind.

These scenes take place within an interior, the home of El Hadji and his first wife. In *Xala*, therefore, the interior serves as a prime site of conflict and the resolution of that conflict. This use of the interior can be read simply as working against the colonial denial of interiority to Africans, but it also depicts the interior as a site for the resolution of moral problems by Africans. Moreover, in figuring the interior as a space of conflict and tension, it can also be seen alluding to the colonizers' contradictory acknowledgment and denial of Africans' interiority, as well as to their fear of the obscure interior of the African continent.

One of the starkest demonstrations of this use of the interior comes in Sembène's *La Noire de* . . . (1966). The white family employing "la noire" of the title, Diouanna, treat her as no more than a household appliance. Diouanna's rejection of this subjugated identity culminates in an ultimate act on her part, for she commits suicide by slitting her wrists lying in the white family's bath. Since the bathroom is the most intimate room in a house and the one room dedicated to the care of the body, Diouanna's death is a highly didactic act that challenges colonial discourse in several ways. The whites' most intimate room is invaded by Diouanna's proof of her own agency, her act of suicide, and this forces them to the recognition that she can "disposer d'elle-même." By deciding to die naked in the bath, Diouanna also forces recognition of herself as both subject (agency) and object (body) in life, and as an unadministrable body in death. Furthermore, throughout the film the audience has access to Diouanna's interior thoughts as a voice-over in the sound-track, so that she appears as the character who, more than any other, integrates existence as subject and object in the film, while in contrast the whites appear as mere martinets of colonial discourse.

In *La Noire de . . .* full use is made of the cinematographic possibilities afforded by black and white film stock for symbolic juxtapositions of dark and light. Thus the black and white striped and checked floors of the white family's home are highlighted, and give a visual image of black and white set against each other in opposition. Against this, the scene of Diouanna dead in the bath depicts an invasion or conquest of white by black, for the white bath is shown full to the brim with water turned dark by Diouanna's blood, in which her own dark body lies. Diouanna's act affirms her being as more than mere object through the narrative of the film, while the visual depiction of the place of her suicide inscribes the struggle for African agency right into the heart of the white home. At a metaphorical level the point is thus made that for the home of the whites (the West), the African is a more or less useful object; and that resistance consists in the struggle to assert subjectivity and lay claim to space.

Conclusion

By creating images of this kind, the films by Ousmane Sembène and Souleymane Cissé can be seen to challenge the ideological legacy of colonialism by attacking elements of colonial and neo-colonial discourses of space. In particular, the works discussed here can be seen to represent a concerted engagement with notions of *boundary*. A key characteristic of colonialism's spatial discourses lay in its translation of cartographic concerns relating to the insertion of clear boundaries in the physical space of Africa into abstract boundaries that then formed the frontiers of colonial and neo-colonial engagement with African people. In the films of Cissé and Sembène discussed here the maintenance of hermetic divisions between mind and body, self and other, and interior and exterior are figured as throwbacks to the colonial past, and as barriers to progress in the present. The protagonists of Cissé and Sembène's films negotiate their way past these boundaries with increasing success. It is striking that in Cissé's most recent film *Waati*, the central character Nandi traverses huge geographical, cultural, political and linguistic boundaries, and studies to receive her doctorate in African Civilization. In *Waati*, creativity and an ability to negotiate boundaries between past, present and future are seen as the key to the future. At a key point in the film, Nandi asks her teacher, "Maître! Où est notre espoir?" and receives a prophetic answer: "Notre espoir est en nous-mêmes, en l'humanité. . . . Pour un seul homme, tout prend fin à sa mort. Mais pour un peuple, l'avenir est *illimité*" [my emphasis]. Thus Cissé's most recent work does not deny the existence of boundaries, but affirms that the future of Africa and Africans will not be limited by them.

Notes

1. Representations of this kind figure Africans as the passive objects of "natural disasters" or "tribalism" No cause for such problems is ever be uncovered, and so they become naturalized as the defining characteristics of Africa and Africans. See David Spurr, *The Rhetoric of Empire: Colonial Discourse in Jour-*

nalism, Travel Writing and Imperial Administration (Durham and London: Duke University Press, third edition, 1996), 46–48.

2. Interviewed by Férid Boughedir in the documentary *Caméra d'Afrique*, 1983.

3. "Waati, une œuvre politique et culturelle," *Ecrans d'Afrique/Screen Africa* 11 (1st quarter 1995): 46–47.

4. Nicholas Thomas, *Colonialism's Culture: Anthropology, Travel and Government* (Cambridge: Polity Press, 1994).

5. Thomas, *Colonialism's Culture*, 57.

6. Donald Vernon Mckay, "Colonialism in the French Geographical Movement 1871–1881," *The Geographical Review* 33 (April 1934): 214–32.

7. Jeremy Black, *Maps and History: Constructing Images of the Past* (New Haven and London: Yale University Press, 1997), 63.

8. Black, *Maps and History*, 68.

9. On the implications of the widespread use of the Mercator projection in European maps of the period, see Jeremy Black, *Maps and Politics* (London: Reaktion books, 1997), 29–42.

10. Black, *Maps and History*, 58. Black's comments here refer specifically to British atlases of the period, but similar observations can be made about French historical atlases such as Vast and Malterre's *Atlas historique. Formation des états européens* (Paris: 1900).

11. Quoted in Black, *Maps and History*, 86.

12. J. G. Edgar, "The Colonial Museum," *Kingston Annual for Boys* (London, 1863), 249–52. In *Imperialism and Orientalism: A Documentary Sourcebook*, ed. Barbara Harlow and Mia Carter, 337–39.

13. M. Bell, R. Butlin, M. Hefferman, eds., *Geography and Imperialism 1820–1940* (Manchester: Manchester University Press, 1995), 5.

14. Henri Lefebvre, *The Production of Space*, trans. Donald Nicholson-Smith (Oxford: Blackwell, 1991), 49–52.

15. Fatima Tobing Rony, *The Third Eye: Race, Cinema and Ethnographic Spectacle* (Durham and London: Duke University Press, 1996).

16. Tobing Rony, *The Third Eye*, 80–83.

17. Tobing Rony, *The Third Eye*, 45–62.

18. Mary Louise Pratt, "Scratches on the Face of the Country, or what Mr. Barrow saw in the land of the Bushmen" in *"Race," Writing and Difference*, ed. Henry Gates Jr. (Chicago: University of Chicago Press, 1985), 143. Quoted in Rony, 82.

19. See, for example, *Le Tableau Géographique de la France*, ed. Paul Vidal de la Blache (Paris: 1903 [Paris: La Table ronde, 1994]), Part 1, Chapter 1, 20; Conclusion, section 2, 547.

20. Quoted in John Iliffe, *Africans, the History of a Continent* (Cambridge: Cambridge University Press, 1995), 196.

21. Iliffe, *Africans*, 199.

22. Spurr, *The Rhetoric of Empire*.

23. Gardies, *Cinéma d'Afrique*, 17–19.

24. As Gardies partially argues, *Cinéma d'Afrique*, 19–20.

25. Werewere Liking, *Elle sera de jaspe et de corail* (Paris: L'Harmattan, 1983) 15, 16.

26. For more on the way in which the Western concept of the nation-state has affected the understanding of African identity, see Black, *Maps and History*, 86–192.

27. The quotation is from the cover sleeve of the Médiathèque des Trois Mondes video of Den Muso.

28. A partial exception to this is Kansaye, whose body and mind are fully involved in his consultation with the spirits. However, Kansaye is not himself attacked or harmed, and though told by the spirits that he must act on his own initiative, he passes the torch of resistance on to the youths.

11

The Other I:
Questions of Identity in *Une Vie de Boy*

Kristin Swenson Musselman

POST-COLONIAL LITERATURES HAVE SEEN SIGNIFICANT transformations over the past half century. The colonial subject's conquest of the right to speak, be heard, exploit language and develop a counter-discourse in the face of political, social and psychological oppression has given rise to diverse literary forms. These have ranged from colonialist propaganda (pre-Independence) to patriotic nationalistic impulses (post-independence); from historical rewritings to realist "testimonial" novels that have been compared formally to the novels of nineteenth-century Europe. Within the last thirty-five years, post-colonial literatures have supported an explosion of linguistic innovation and exploration in an attempt by former colonial subjects to reappropriate European languages rather than borrow them intact. In Francophone West Africa, this has been called an "africanisation" of the French language, introduced and expertly manipulated by writers such as Ahmadou Kourouma. Creative thematic and stylistic innovations invoking oral traditions, the surreal and the magical have been incorporated into the work of writers such as Yambo Ouologuem and Hampâté Bâ.

Ferdinand Oyono's novel *Une vie de boy* recounts the story of a young boy, Toundi, who becomes sensitive to the inconsistencies and hypocrisies within the workings of both the colonial culture and his own culture in colonial Cameroon. He has to come to terms with the inconsistencies around him as he searches for a place to belong between two radically opposed societies that share the same space, but little else. Oyono's novel, today considered as part of the "canon" of African literature, could be placed in the category of early postcolonial literatures that rewrite history from the perspective of the colonial subject. *Une vie de boy*, however, takes the unusual critical position of scrutinizing both black and white societies at once, avoiding simplistic binaries of black/white, victim/oppressor in favor of a nuanced approach, personalized by the intimate form of the novel. Oyono's work is framed by the discovery of the hero's dying body and his diary. The novel invites readers to join the discoverers, in the tradition of the oral history, and listen as the boy's private journal discloses the profound psychological schisms he developed under the strain of forced dissimulation. The novel hinges on scenes in which blacks imitate white and whites imitate blacks, in the first case disguising disdain and mockery, and in the second cruelly exposing it. The following study focuses on these scenes, and the ways in which Homi Bhabha's theory of mimicry and the threat that mimicry conceals in colonial dynamics can provide a forum for the evaluation of the novel's protagonist's death.

Bhabha's Theory and Its Implications for Oyono's Novel

"[J]e bute, et l'autre, par gestes, attitudes, regards, me fixe, dans le sens où l'on fixe une prépa-
ration par un colorant. Je m'emportai, exigeai une explication. . . . Rien n'y fit. J'explosai. Voici
les menus morceaux par un autre moi réunis."[1]

Une vie de boy is one of the most forthright denunciations of French colonial domination
in modern African fiction. Oyono conveys a defiant and ultimately destructive opposition
of self and other on both sides of the barricades in colonial Cameroon. As Toundi, the protagonist, becomes aware of his political and social surroundings, he is caught in the cross-
fire between cultures, and through his words a picture emerges of the complex social mechanics of his threatened community. Toundi looks for allegiance and guidance to both of
the elusive factions—that of the powerful French colonials and that of his impotent fellow
countrymen—that have been built up around him. In the course of the novel both European and African communities begin to collapse, ultimately losing cohesion and dignity in
a desperate struggle for survival and dominance.

Although the tension created by this friction is most readily apparent in Toundi, it pervades
the entire community. Toundi's sense of his own cultural identity is problematic from a young
age, beginning with his rejection of his family's home in favor of life in the service of a French
missionary. Through Toundi's journal entries, the reader is privy to events and conversations
around him that elaborate his own crisis. This greater malaise manifests itself in both the traditional representatives of political and religious power in Dangan, and in the colonial community as they discover the implications of their hypocrisy.

This chapter is an investigation of how mimicry is essential to the destructive play of differences in the novel. Repeated scenes at pivotal moments in the text can be noted for their insistence on mimicry as a mode of oppression, a mask for survival, a tool for assimilation, and a
method of social ostracism. In "Of Mimicry and Man," Homi Bhabha defines a "metonymy of
presence"[2] in colonial dynamics in which the narcissistic imposition of mimesis on the colonial
subject creates partial representation. Bhabha describes this situation as the "almost but not
quite/almost but not white" problematic. Mimicry is often, through inappropriate and partial
resemblance, a menacing phenomenon. Bhabha elaborates on his theory: "[Mimicry] problematizes the signs of racial and cultural priority, so that the 'national' is no longer naturaliz-
able. That which emerges between mimesis and mimicry is a *writing*, a mode of representation,
that marginalizes the monumentality of history, quite simply mocks its power to be a model,
that power which supposedly makes it imitable. Mimicry repeats rather than *re-presents*."[3]
Mimicry inevitably gives way to hollow and disjointed mockery that subverts the colonial intention by calling into question the values, social institutions and forms of oppression it had
hoped thereby to maintain. The colonial subject's desire to become "authentic" through repetition is "the final irony of partial representation."[4] The result is a fissure in perceptions of reality; in other words, a situation in which the extent to which subjects embrace aspects of mimicked acquiescence or simply feign assimilation in order to survive is unknowable.

Mimicry involves assimilation and transformation, but it is also a disguise for what lies behind
the mask of repetition. This is most immediately evident in the novel through Toundi's lived and
related experiences, during which dangerous rifts develop in his conscience through which he
must navigate in order to survive. While the concept of mimicry is useful in the context of colonial cultural and political domination, it is also an appropriate theoretical tool with which to examine the transformations of a character in the process of coming of age. The following reading
of *Une vie de boy* explores Toundi's attempts and failures to identify with the reflections he sees

in a vitiated mirror of cultural disunity. He faces psychological obstacles and physical danger as he seeks to conceptualize a recognizable self-image in the face of conflicting authorities in colonial Cameroon. Furthermore, this reading will introduce the concept of reverse mimicry, a process similar to what Bhabha describes, but in which the threatened colonials react to the instability around them by miming various aspects of the subjected culture, thereby only amplifying the capacity for corruption within the ranks of the oppressed.

Mimicry and the Public Sphere

As a young boy, Toundi goes to live in the service of Father Gilbert, a Catholic missionary. Father Gilbert is represented as generally inoffensive, but he is certainly infected with the desire to promote assimilation through religious conversion. He initially attracts children and parishioners not with convincing rhetoric or the promise of eternal life, but with bribes and a gentle, disarming comportment. Children rally around him as he throws cubes of sugar to them. They scramble and fight for the unfamiliar, tempting sweets. Toundi recalls his first encounters with the priest with nascent cynicism: "J'allais connaître la ville et les Blancs, et vivre comme eux. Je me surpris à me comparer à ces perroquets sauvages que nous attirions au village avec des grains de maïs et qui restaient prisonniers de leur gourmandise."[5] It is not for religious reasons that Toundi leaves home. Rather, he wants to escape from his abusive father and he is mesmerized by the thought of what sugar cubes and other treasures await him in the city. He is aware that Father Gilbert believes that it is the Holy Spirit that brought Toundi to him, but even at the beginning of his apprenticeship with Father Gilbert, Toundi characterizes him as "l'homme blanc aux cheveux semblables à la barbe de maïs, habillé d'une robe de femme, qui donnait de bons petits cubes sucrés aux petits Noirs."[6] Father Gilbert, for all his supposed magnanimity as he seeks to save Toundi's soul, treats Toundi more like "un petit animal familier"[7] than a cherished convert.

At the beginning of the novel Toundi is preparing himself to enter into a new world, one in which he sees a future vision of himself transformed. He predicts the kinds of cultural contortionism that will take place in his new life, in which he will learn all he can by rote. He will respond to his new Christian name, Joseph, and repeat his scriptural lessons in exchange for his dinner and the chance to remain in favor among the whites. For Toundi, mimicry of European language, dress, religion and mannerisms represents not only an escape from a difficult family situation, but a chance to enjoy a change in status and significant material gain. To emulate certain aspects of the whites' lives in order to access these benefits is Toundi's strategic choice, although, as a young child, he does not yet understand the consequences of his decision. Nor does he realize what he risks in this process. He is given new European clothes at the mission: "une culotte kaki et un tricot rouge qui firent l'admiration de tous les gamins de Fia qui vinrent demander au prêtre de les emmener avec lui."[8] This uniform represents a physical distinction for Toundi, as he is now presumably quite different in appearance from his peers. It is at this point that Toundi begins the transformation to what he will later describe as the "chien du roi [qui] est le roi des chiens."[9] In an article examining narrative form in *Une vie de boy*, O. Ogunsanwo perceptively evaluates Toundi's relationship with Father Gilbert in terms of the mockery that Bhabha has articulated: "[B]oth of them are pretenders; but ironically, Toundi is the better pretender as he calmly makes Father Gilbert underrate his intelligent awareness of their relationship. . . . [Oyono's satiric style succeeds in] making the mockery urbane and double-edged. For it subtly reveals both Father Gilbert's pretentious charity and the narrator's own backward background."[10] Toundi's position is ambiguous, but the "backward background" Ogunsanwo refers to can be interpreted as the lack of stability in his young life. His childhood and his development into a young man are characterized by transitory fluctuation between filial and fraternal loyalty to family and kinsmen, his self-motivated expatriation before he could be submitted to the traditional rites of initiation that awaited him and his insatiable curiosity about foreign ways. His non-induction into his own culture, and the limited but perceptive gaze with which he regards the white community at the mission make it possible for Toundi, at an early age, to reconcile evident contradictions in the competing cultures quite easily. Both are others in relation to Toundi, but he is not yet engaged in internal moral conflict with either one of them. From this peculiar outpost, he is still only an observer. His earliest journal entries offer descriptions of Africans and Europeans written with apparently artless curiosity.

Father Gilbert baptizes Toundi and instructs him to participate in distribution during communion. The pleasure Toundi derives from this participation in the sacrament comes from an unexpected blurring of the boundaries that have been drawn for him: "J'aime surtout la distribution de la communion le dimanche. . . . Tous les fidèles se présentent à la Sainte Table, yeux fermés, bouche ouverte, langue tendue, comme s'ils faisaient une grimace. . . . Ils n'ont pas de belles dents. J'aime surtout caresser les jeunes filles blanches sous le menton avec la patène que je leur présente lorsque le prêtre leur introduit l'hostie dans la bouche. . . . C'est par ce moyen que nous pouvons les caresser."[11] Here, Toundi mechanically follows through with the motions of intimate participation in what the Europeans purport to be the act of communion with their God; it represents a holy and serious occasion. While Toundi outwardly creates the impression that he has converted to Catholicism and is a devout and practicing member of the congregation, his inward motivations suggest a corruption of the sanctity of this repeated mimed act of conciliation. He violates the colonial intention by observing his oppressors in a vulnerable and ungainly position. In a kind of metonymy of faith, he violates the boundaries of contact between blacks and whites. It is at these moments, when the threat behind partial representation comes boiling to the surface, that *Une vie de boy* reveals the nature of its narrative. Toundi takes advantage of this occasion to caress the young white girls—certainly a sign of the inappropriate in the colonial state—while maintaining perfect accord with the external requirements of the colonial mandate.

Toundi does, for a time, show signs of ritualistic adhesion to Catholicism. But with the death of Father Gilbert comes the death of whatever limited faith he had assumed through repetition. Father Gilbert acquires the alias "le martyr" after his death. Toundi believes this is "sans doute parce qu'il est mort en Afrique."[12] He has begun to see his world through the lens of the white missionaries. Henceforth, Toundi becomes the "boy" of the Commandant of Dangan, M. Decazy, in whose service he suffers more than he had ever imagined under the auspices of Father Gilbert. In his new position, Toundi comes into contact with new arenas in which to collect information about the relationship between blacks and whites in Dangan, and to draw conclusions from what he observes.

The students in a village the Commandant visits with Toundi are brought out to perform for him, and their display is an awkward illustration of the ineffectiveness of assimilationist educational policies: "Le moniteur cria encore 'Fisk!' Les enfants semblaient complètement affolés. Ils se serraient comme des poussins apercevant l'ombre d'un charognard. Le moniteur donna le ton, puis battit la mesure. Les élèves chantèrent d'une seule traite dans une langue qui n'était ni le français, ni la leur. C'était un étrange baragouin que les villageois prenaient pour du français et les Français prenaient pour la langue indigène. Tous applaudirent."[13] The colonialist design was one that permitted indigenous men, educated in the French tradition, to become

translators, teachers and scribes. They were meant to satisfy the need for subordinate administrators who were to work for the state, thus becoming servants of the system.[14] The products of
this system promote partial representation, and in the articulated desire of the colonial administration, they will only mimic their "superiors" up to certain well-defined limits. The slippage
that occurs, and the real and imagined differences between colonials and subjects in this case
allow the whites to continually justify their control, pointing to these visible, but artificially constructed differences as indicators of a natural racial order. This zone comprised of predetermined
differences inevitably manifests itself visibly in the schools, in the streets, in the church, and in
domestic servants, like Toundi, who are employed in colonial households. In this way, "mimicry
emerges as the representation of a difference that is in itself a process of disavowal."[15]

Private Affairs and Domesticity: Critical Revelations

Toundi, from his unique vantage point as the Commandant's boy, has a particularly revealing
window on the private affairs of the Commandant and his wife, along with considerable
amounts of incriminating information about the lives of others in the European community in
Dangan. Domestic servants in this position were naturally privy to quite intimate details of
their employers' lives. They were expected to operate according to European norms of behavior, and to function in denial of their personal beliefs and traditions. At the same time, they
were prevailed upon to stay well within the carefully defined and separate spaces created for
them by their employers, remembering their position relative to the whites.[16] From this position, Toundi quietly scrutinizes his oppressors. He re-evaluates his former appraisals of the Europeans, with Madame Decazy and the Commandant at the forefront of his investigations. His
early journal entries full of admiration for the strength of the Commandant and tender effu-
sions on his first contact with Madame give way to more critical observation. Open sarcasm,
and a detailed inventory of Madame's infidelities and her cruelty toward Toundi characterize
the latter part of the novel.

   Crucial turning points in Toundi's conceptions of the Commandant and his wife occur when
he observes both of them in physically vulnerable positions. He sees the Commandant naked,
discovers that he is uncircumcised, and is suddenly no longer afraid of him. With similar results, he happens upon some condoms under Madame's bed after her lover has come to call,
and he learns what they are used for. The washman and the cook explain to him: "Paraît que
c'est pour faire bien. . . . Ils mettent ça comme ils mettent le casque ou les gants. . . . C'est un
petit vêtement pour ça."[17] Toundi's surveillance, in both of the above instances, and during the
countless betrayals, bribes, inconsistencies and infidelities he witnesses, allows him to stockpile
evidence drawn from private aspects of the colonials' lives that challenge the moral and intellectual supremacy they pretend to intrinsically possess. He discovers that the space between the
whites and blacks in Dangan is imagined territory.

   Whites in the novel are primarily shown not as public figures, but in their private weaknesses
and inconsistencies. It is the fear inspired by Toundi's dangerous custody of these vulnerable
moments in their lives that finally motivates the prison director, the agricultural officer and
Madame Decazy to take the actions that bring about Toundi's torture and eventual death.[18] The
dynamics of colonial mimicry and particularly the intense gaze of the colonial subject directed
at the colonizers comprise what Bhabha describes as: "the process of the *fixation* of the colonial
as a form of cross-classificatory, discriminatory knowledge in the defiles of an interdictory discourse [which questions] the *authorization* of colonial representations. A question of authority

that goes beyond the subject's lack of priority (castration) to a historical crisis in the conceptuality of colonial man as an object of regulatory power, as the subject of racial, cultural, national representation."[19] This knowledge forms the basis of an immanent threat to colonial representations of power. The colonials' knowledge of this knowledge constitutes the point at which Toundi's subject position is transformed. It is at this moment that his mask falls away, revealing the real threat that had been disguised by partial assimilation.

Toundi keeps a watchful eye on *le quartier indigène* as well. He finds no more promise for a model of morality or dignity there than he does in his scrutiny of the Europeans. In accounts of his conversations with the washman, the cook, and Sophie (the agricultural engineer's girlfriend) and in observations of an informal community meeting centered on the arrival of Madame Decazy, Toundi registers the same disappointments that he habitually records in his journal about the white community in Dangan. The severity of his judgment is tempered with some filial loyalty. However, a simple assessment of the kinds of exchanges he records clearly reveals his conclusions. Despite the cultural vacuum in which Toundi finds himself in relation to his portraits of both black and white communities, there remains a fundamental difference for him in relation to the former, which he carefully articulates: "Bien que Dangan soit divisée en quartier européen et en quartier indigène, tout ce qui se passe du côté des maisons au toit de tôle est connu dans le moindre détail dans les cases en poto-poto. Les Blancs sont autant percés à nu par les gens du quartier indigène qu'ils sont aveugles sur tout ce qui se passe. Nul n'ignore que la femme du commandant trompe son mari. . . ."[20] Therein lies the larger threat to the colonial community of which Toundi is emblematic. Toundi is perceived as posing a threat to the established order in Dangan because of the things that he knows. Toundi becomes the object of fear and resentment, as the Decazys and others come to understand the scope of the information he possesses. He has not only registered innumerable affronts directed at him and the larger black community, he has also been witness to infidelities and betrayals among the whites that could damage not only solidarity within the white community, but could also break up families and create new alliances.

While Toundi is the obvious target for reactions to this fear in the white community, the colonials remain unaware of the arsenal of knowledge in the rest of the black community generated by a steady collective gaze fixed on the white faction in Dangan. This more powerful, collective other is fully conscious of the infidelities and weaknesses displayed by the whites, despite the apparent distance that separates them. Toundi and the entire community actively participate in a demystification of the whites, bridging the fictional space between them. The colonial mandate requiring a kind of mimicry that is founded on a fabricated desire inspires, through constant repetition, "pseudo-scientific theories, superstition, spurious authorities, and classification [that] can be seen as the desperate effort to 'normalize' *formally* the disturbance of a discourse of splitting which overturns the intentions of its authors."[21] Faith in this desire keeps the whites from seeing the deconstruction of the social and political myths they have created in the intense collective gaze of the others. It is the black community at large that poses the real threat to the colonizers, but Toundi bears the brunt of their escalating paranoia. The whites predetermine his insurrection.

Toundi has become estranged from his own community. He has been rejected by the European culture he had hoped, early on, to assimilate into. The connections he still maintains with the indigenous community of Dangan make it impossible for him to wholeheartedly embrace either group. He can no longer justify an image of himself reflected in either of the inadequate ideological, social and familial models available to him. Both cultures continue to represent others for him, but now they are social structures from which he must distance himself. He must keep himself distinct from them. He is a hybrid of his own making whose limitations have serious implications for his own survival. He can neither continue to exist at the crossroads of two cultures, nor can he create his own satisfactory amalgamation of cultural realities and ideologies in Dangan.

Seduction, Repulsion and Sexual Immobility

When Toundi is charged with protecting Sophie, the black mistress of the agricultural engineer, overnight during an official visit to a village some distance form Dangan, the engineer severely admonishes Toundi not to touch Sophie, threatening to clinically verify whether anything transpires between them. He warns: "J'enverrai Sophie à l'hôpital. . . . Je saurai te retrouver."[22] Sophie, a black woman, is seen as a desired sexual object by both black and white men in the novel. She is an object only, and the mistress of a white officer who refers to her in public as his *cuisinière-boy* and warns her not to address him in front of other people, especially in the company of white women. An impersonal exchange takes place in the space where love could have happened. The engineer wants sexual pleasure from Sophie; he wants private love with no public consequences. Sophie, in turn, recognizing that she will never be allowed to show love for, or receive love from, her white engineer, schemes to steal his money. These are the truths that lie beneath their mimicry of love, the repetition of meaningless acts that eventually threatens the controlling element of the relationship. The engineer is duped in the end as a result of the performance he imposes on Sophie, the artificial space between them that she will not accept as natural. In public, she must represent a submissive domestic servant. She must remain under control, she must be malleable and show no emotional inconsistencies. In private, she must force herself into the semblance of a love that could have been real beyond the parameters of the colonial encounter.

These masks shield characters from any true exchange with one another in the novel. Sophie asks in desperation after her lover submits her to a particularly hurtful public denial: "Mais qu'est-ce qu'elles ont et que je n'ai pas? . . . Les bonnes manières des Blancs, si c'est seulement pour entre eux, merde alors! Mon derrière est aussi fragile que celui de leurs femmes qu'ils font monter dans la cabine."[23] Sophie knows only too well that she is no different from a white woman. She is an example of what Bhabha terms "almost the same but not white."[24]

Toundi desires Madame Decazy both before she arrives and in their first few encounters, admiring her whiteness and what he describes as her elegance. In public, he follows orders, behaves according to the Commandant's wishes, dresses as he is required to and answers submissively to the name Joseph. Underneath his subordinate exterior, however, he dreams of the Commandant's wife in tender and familiar terms. This transferred desire never escalates to a stage where he would entertain thoughts of possessing her, in what Fanon has dramatized as the subjugated black man's wish to "marry white culture, white beauty, white whiteness . . . [t]o grasp white civilization and dignity and make them mine."[25] Toundi's immediate seduction fades and is replaced with disappointment, and later repulsion, toward Madame Decazy. In fact, though Toundi matures physically into a young man during the course of the novel, he never expresses sexual desire for another person, black or white. The difficulties he faces when grappling with questions of identity, fraternity and loyalty seem to translate into an inability to mature sexually, the charged moment that normally signals a coming of age. The humorous verses he records in Madame Decazy's honor, however, express a chaste abstraction of love. He writes in his journal: "[Son regard] vous inonde de sa lumière qui vous embrasse jusqu'au plus profond du cœur. J'ai peur … j'ai peur de moi-même."[26] He is afraid of his first laudatory impulses toward the wife of his employer. His adoration quickly fades as Madame's initial fascination with the foreignness around her disappears, and is replaced with bitterness and antagonism. She adopts a violent attitude toward the black men in her employ, flying into a rage at the slightest provocation. In this transition she makes from celebratory to hostile attitudes toward the *indigènes* and their customs and traditions, she engages, as do other whites in the novel, in a kind of reverse mimicry that represents another source of friction contributing to the breakdown of established measures of control and oppression in Dangan.

Reverse Mimicry

Bhabha's theory is concerned with a kind of mimicry in which colonial subjects mime certain aspects of the colonials' culture in order to secure employment or financial gain, in response to an anticipated desire (real or imagined) to emulate certain parts of the dominating culture, or simply in order to survive in that ambiguous and dangerous space within which the colonial subject exists. Furthermore, Bhabha's argument continues, the mimicry itself comes to mask what actually happens beneath the surface in the colonial subject's psyche, symbolizing a potential threat to Dangan's sociopolitical order. In *Une vie de boy* particular attention is directed at scenes in which *colonials imitate subjects* in a curious reversal of what Bhabha articulates. These instances represent the same kind of mimetic phenomenon contributing equally to the breakdown of colonial imperatives in the novel. These scenes reinforce what can be interpreted as the consequences of colonial domination in Cameroon as witnessed through the progressive portrayals of reverse mimicry recorded in Toundi's journal throughout the novel. The results are represented finally in Toundi's psychological implosion, his flight and finally his death.

Reverse mimicry manifests itself in two ways in the novel. In the first, it appears as ignorance or arrogance in white characters who adopt a more or less neutral attitude toward the subjected culture. In the second instance, reverse mimicry is overtly threatening, based on anger and fear of revolt. Both imply disconnections between competing cultures brought face to face with one another. Close examination of several of these scenes will illuminate these observations.

Toundi's position relative to Catholicism and his religious instruction at the hands of Father Gilbert fluctuates in the novel in tandem with the motives behind the mimicry he performs. Father Gilbert himself unknowingly performs reverse mimicry of the first order, not in response to a force to which he must defer, but in an apparently sincere effort to appear gentle and unintrusive as he attempts to encourage conversion among the indigenous peoples of the region. He insists on proselytizing in a garbled, inconsistent Ndjem, one of the regional languages spoken around Dangan. This places him and other Catholic officials who attempt to use this language in an unexpected and precarious position *vis à vis* their local auditors. Their attempts at conciliatory and persuasive communication become nothing more than ridiculous monologues that are amusing to local listeners.

Several passages in the novel highlight these failed attempts by the clergy to reach the population. In one passage depicting a typical mass in a local church, Toundi describes the effect produced by Father Vandermayer, who, "dans son mauvais Ndjem, commençait à truffer son serment d'obscénités."[27] The clergy's purposeful and repeated efforts to communicate with their new congregation do not promote ideological conviction in their prospective converts. Conversely, their actions mire them in ridicule, as their audience is entertained by the spectacle of a man on a throne wearing a dress and shouting obscenities. This implicitly threatens the religious

leaders' proclaimed intentions. Their tenets are echoed in the church with the sounds of muffled laughter, misinterpreted by the priests as the sounds of zealous celebration erupting from
new Christian followers who are just beginning to see the Catholic light.

Madame Decazy, too, performs this kind of reverse mimicry on several occasions. She is easily seduced during her first days in the colony by the open market and by what she perceives in
a positivist light as the friendly manner of the *indigènes*. She soon senses the danger, however,
in approaching too openly a difference that she learns must continually expose itself, must continually *be* exposed in its difference in order to be contained. Her early enchantment with local
activity and community lead her to be wholly demystified in local eyes and she quickly becomes
fair game for lewd commentary in the marketplace. Toundi refuses to translate their insults for
her, preferring instead to let her imagine that they are praising her beauty. Her experiences in
the market, although they presuppose a representation of the way indigenous women travel and
buy food, make her difference from them all the more glaringly apparent.

Beyond the obvious othering signs of skin and dress, Madame Decazy is set apart from the
people in the market by her ignorance of their language and her misinterpretation of their
comments about her. Her attempted representation of the women in the marketplace is never
fully complete. She comes to the market with Toudi, a servile guide, and her financial status
gives her purchases a different respective value from those of the indigenous women who shop
there. She is the object of their collective attention, which is also a collective scrutiny. This gaze,
which she now finds charming and seductive, contains the same hidden threat that will later
cause her to feel the fear and repulsion that characterizes the oppositional relations in most of
the white and black interchanges that take place in the novel.

Later instances of reverse mimicry occur as whites begin to perceive the menace beneath the
mask of partial representation in their employees, in the rising ranks of educated locals and in
the community at large. Reactive mimicry that is clearly meant to taunt and persecute blacks
can be interpreted as stemming from a realization of the ways in which differences between
blacks and whites are constructed and artificial. The culmination of fear and mistrust complicated by mimetic performances on either side finally forces Toundi to collapse just as colonial
and traditional structures around him begin to collapse.

Toundi's Dilemma and the Politics of Language

Toundi is effectively trapped at the margins of two cultures and cannot finally identify with either
one. In the process, he becomes not only noncommittal, but asexual and immobilized. He has not
found satisfaction in either the colonial community or the activities of his countrymen. His cultural development stagnates, and he fails to become emotionally attached to others. He is never able
to establish himself as a sexual being. Both black and white men and women speak directly and
openly to him about sexual desire, yet Toundi remains frozen and numb to both advances and
speculation. He is incapable of sexual desire. During the night discussed above when he and Sophie
sleep under the same roof, Toundi does not so much as hint the slightest desire for a sexual liaison
with her. Sophie is surprised, and perhaps disappointed. She calls him "un drôle d'homme"[28] and
reflects on his inaction, saying: "Tu es enfermé dans une case la nuit avec une femme . . . et tu dis
que ta bouche est fatiguée! Quand je raconterai cela, personne ne me croira. On me dira: c'est peut-
être parce que son coupe-coupe n'est pas tranchant qu'il a préféré le garder dans son fourreau."[29]

Toundi lives in a self-imposed exile. He is in a dark cave by himself. He writes down his
thoughts and reflections in a journal, written to himself and for himself. He is isolated, without

family or a confidant. He is unable to love, just as he is unable to take decisive action until, near death, he is forced to flee from Dangan to Spanish Guinea. Just as both the white and black communities begin to fold in on themselves, unable and unwilling to assimilate or accommodate cultural difference out of fear or repulsion, or both, so for Toundi no peaceful harmonization with the others around him is possible. Both black and white characters in the novel stagnate, steeped in their fear, anger, and growing hatred. Toundi too, is wrapped tightly inside himself, unable to move freely, make alliances, love or revolt.

Toundi cannot conceive of having a family. Madame Decazy asks him why he does not think of starting one of his own, pointing out that he earns enough money to purchase a wife. In his sarcastic reply Toundi unexpectedly reveals both the revulsion that is quickly rising in him for the whites' domination and his inability to justify his own place in either culture. His telling answer reads: "Peut-être, Madame, mais ni ma femme ni mes enfants ne pourront jamais manger ni s'habiller comme Madame ou comme les petits Blancs."[30]

Une vie de boy is written in the form of a journal (in itself a mimicked form of expression that Toundi borrows from Father Gilbert). In the case of the journal, the evident slippage separating it from its Western model lies in the language used. Toundi writes in Ewondo, limiting the kinds of people who would have access to what he writes. By appropriating certain structures borrowed from the journal and then using Ewondo to transform the medium for his own purposes, Toundi practices the kind of partial representation that may constitute a threat to existing power structures. His words are not available to the colonials, but they are eventually available to Toundi's countrymen when he dies in a foreign land. His words are then magically delivered to readers everywhere via Oyono. The journal is finally shared aloud with presumably sympathetic compatriots and refugees. Toundi's experiences are given new life even as he dies, and in this way, Toundi seems to make the connection with his own community that he was unable to sustain in life. This last gesture suggests a solidarity that succeeds Toundi.[31]

In many respects, Toundi's journal is written in the tradition of the ethnocentric ethnographer's account. Toundi's version is neither Euro-centric nor Afro-centric. His space is an isolated one; it is an ideological outpost. Toundi repeatedly describes the colonials as animal-like and barbaric, participating in strange rituals and exhibiting unsavory behavior. Here, the Western form of the journal reverses the colonial ambition by subjecting colonials to an essentializing interpretive framework that often portrays whites as one-dimensional and contributes to value-based binarisms that, in this case, do not favor the whites.

The priests' butchery of Ndjem represents one way in which language enters into a discourse of colonial mimicry as reverse mimicry. French too, used by characters both black and white in the novel, becomes a locus for mimesis that subverts the original assimilationist project envisioned by early colonials. Madame mimics the cook, only to display her immaturity and portray herself as a cruel and undignified figure: "Elle imitait avec une drôle de grimace tout en allongeant sa lèvre inférieure et en balançant sa tête à droite et à gauche."[32] Gosier d'Oiseau and others regale one another with their own interpretations of the way *indigènes* speak French: "Mon z'ami, . . . nous pas buveurs indigènes!"[33] The traditional leaders and African politicians in Dangan make alliances with the colonial administration, not understanding anything that is said to them, but agreeing to anything with an enthusiastic *oui* in exchange for protection, medals or other gifts. Fanon describes the ways in which a colonial language imposed on a culture can destroy its pride and sense of identity: "Every colonized people—in other words, every people in whose soul an inferiority complex has been created by the death and burial of its local cultural originality—finds itself face to face with the language of the civilizing nation; that is, with the culture of the mother country. The colonized is elevated above his jungle status in proportion to his adoption of the mother country's cultural standard. He becomes whiter as he renounces his blackness, his jungle."[34] These partial presences of language, and the imposed colonial desire for affirmation and elevation of status in the structure of white/black relations help to bring about the dissolution of Toundi's sense of personhood and destroy his identification with either culture. Language is also a tool for cruel mockery and a constant reminder of sociopolitical domination. Finally, language can become a threat, as colonial subjects emerge not only as servants of the system in the assimilationist educational model, but eventually as writers and exposers of colonialist injustices, like Fanon and Oyono, brought by mimicry and an imposed linguistic assimilation to rise up and challenge the oppressors in their own language. They are not perhaps on equal ground, but at least they are on common ground. In this case, French becomes the colonial subject's weapon.

Toundi never escapes his unfortunate dilemma. Only his journal survives. He is immobilized in his lack of affiliation with subject or empire. The demystification of white domination and his disengagement with the black community leave Toundi with no place to assume, no hero to champion, no patrimony to defend, no ground to stand on. As he lies dying in a hospital bed before his final journey he writes:

> J'étais au faite du fromager . . . A mes pieds s'étendait le monde, un océan de lépreux, de pianiques, de femmes enceintes, éventrées, visqueux où des millions de Gosier-d'Oiseau, juchés sur des tertres à termitières, faisaient l'ordre à coups d'hippopotames. . . . Je pris mon élan sur ma branche et fonçai, tête baissée, faisant un plongeon de mille kilomètres sur ce monde où ma tête éclata comme une bombe. Oui, je n'étais plus qu'une nuée de lucioles, une poussière de lucioles qu'emporta le vent . . . et ce fut le noir.[35]

C. P. Sarvan explains Toundi's failure to escape by asking whether "having known electricity, can one return to the lamp?"[36] Ogunsanwo claims that it can only be attributed to delusion and masochistic madness created by the overwhelming circumstances surrounding him.[37] Another explanation for Toundi's inability to escape is the final stasis he achieves in the novel following the deconstruction of black and white social and cultural myths in his community. Geographically, emotionally and ideologically, he has nowhere to go. Key passages in the novel suggest that mimicry, reverse mimicry and knowledge of what lies beneath these false partial forms of representation lead to this stasis, in which Toundi cannot find an ideological foothold. The ambiguous *noir* at the end of the quoted passage above may refer to the disjointed subject, uprooted and subjugated, explosive and stripped of weight, and no longer certain where its substance might lie.

Notes

1. Frantz Fanon, *Peau noire, masques blancs* (1952; Paris: Éditions du Seuil, 1995), 88.
2. Homi Bhabha, "Of Mimicry and Man," in *The Location of Culture* (London: Routledge, 1994), 87–88.
3. Bhabha, "Of Mimicry and Man," 89.
4. Bhabha, "Of Mimicry and Man,"88.
5. Ferdinand Oyono, *Une vie de boy* (Paris, Julliard, 1956), 22.
6. Oyono, *Une vie*, 16.
7. Oyono, *Une vie*, 24.
8. Oyono, *Une vie*, 22.

9. Oyono, *Une vie*, 32.

10. Olatubosun Ogunsanwo, "The Narrative Voice in Two Novels of Ferdinand Oyono," *English Studies in Africa* 29, no. 2 (1986): 113.

11. Oyono, *Une vie*, 23.

12. Oyono, *Une vie*, 52.

13. Oyono, Oyono, *Une vie*, 63

14. Abdou Moumouni, *Education in Africa* (New York: Praeger, 1968), 37.

15. Bhabha, "Of Mimicry and Man," 86.

16. Anne Menke, "Boy!: The Hinge of Colonial Double-Talk," *Studies in Twentieth Century Literature* 15, no. 1 (1991): 12.

17. Oyono, *Une vie*, 134.

18. Ogunsanwo, "The Narrative Voice," 122.

19. Bhabha, "Of Mimicry and Man," 90.

20. Oyono, *Une vie*, 106.

21. Bhabha, "Of Mimicry and Man," 91.

22. Oyono, *Une vie*, 67.

23. Oyono, *Une vie*, 60.

24. Bhabha, "Of Mimicry and Man," 89.

25. Fanon, *Peau noire*, 63.

26. Oyono, *Une vie*, 74.

27. Oyono, *Une vie*, 55

28. Oyono, *Une vie*, 68.

29. Oyono, *Une vie*, 68.

30. Oyono, *Une vie*, 88.

31. Menke, "Boy!" 17.

32. Oyono, *Une vie*, 112.

33. Oyono, *Une vie*, 77.

34. Fanon, *Peau noires*, 18.

35. Oyono, *Une vie*, 182.

36. Sarvan, 336.

37. Ogunsanwo, "The Narrative Voice," 118.

III
THE CARIBBEAN

12

Landscaping Identity in Contemporary Caribbean Literature

Eric Prieto

IT HAS BECOME A COMMONPLACE ASSERTION of post-colonial cultural theory that the landscape and geography of colonized or formerly colonized territories have provided an especially potent source of symbols for the cultural identity and nationalist (or proto-nationalist) aspirations of the people who inhabit those territories. Edward W. Said, for example, has written of the "primacy of the geographical" in anti-imperialist literatures, and explains this geographical focus as a response to the territorial aggression of colonizers: "For the native, the history of his or her colonial servitude is inaugurated by the loss to an outsider of the local place, whose concrete geographical identity must thereafter be searched for and somehow restored."[1] Homi K. Bhabha has also noted the importance of the landscape and local environment as symbols of national identity, emphasizing above all the rhetorical utility of this type of environmental discourse, which he sees as providing a way "to naturalize the rhetoric of national affiliation and its forms of collective expression."[2] But the very efficacy of landscape imagery as a means for "naturalizing" expressions of power, value and cultural identity suggests the importance of questioning such images in terms of their motives. For Bhabha, this type of suspicion is necessary and implies a corrective appeal to narrative and history: "there is . . . always the distracting presence of another temporality that disturbs the contemporaneity of the national present" that is inscribed into images of the landscape.[3]

This tension between the temporality of history and the ahistorical permanence of national identity implied by the use of landscape imagery has special significance in the cultural context of the French West Indies. From the earliest Creole (i.e., native-born) poets, to the writers grouped around Aimé Césaire and the journal *Tropiques*, to the generation of Edouard Glissant, to the more recent *Groupe de la Créolité*, the landscape and natural environment of the islands have played a key role in the struggle to articulate the contours of a specifically Caribbean cultural identity. But the particularities of the Caribbean context make it necessary to revise Said's territorial explanation of the nation-building role of the geographical imagination. Simply put, there is no one in the French Antilles who can claim the kind of originary bond to the land described by Said. Apart from the original Arawak and Carib inhabitants of the islands—who have been almost completely decimated—no one can claim to have any privileged link to the land. Thus, as Edouard Glissant has repeatedly pointed out, Caribbean nationalists must deal with a built-in legitimation crisis. It has been all but impossible to found a sense of Caribbean identity on the type of ancestral, historical and filial bonds of originary kinship and rightful ownership invoked in more traditional societies.[4]

This absence of an originary bond—aggravated by the injustices of colonial history and the absurdities of its ideology—seems to have instilled in West Indian writers a particularly acute sensitivity to the landscape's power as a symbol of regional identity, but also to the unstable, ideological nature of all such symbols. Well before Homi Bhabha, West Indians understood the need to think of the landscape in relation to the narrative temporality of history and the processes of national becoming.[5] Thus, each successive generation has used the landscape in its own way, by modifying or even rejecting outright the nature imagery of its predecessors. These revisions, which are often framed as a reaction to the purportedly facile exoticism of preceding generations, tend to focus on the need to institute new conventions for the representation of the local environment.[6] But despite this emphasis on change and reform, these writers seem to agree on one important point: the determinant role played by the landscape in shaping the character and identity of the populace.

One of the most interesting consequences of this "identitarian" attitude toward the environment has been the recurrent tendency to depict the landscape as an active agent in the drama of the region's history. Some, like Daniel Maximin, have gone so far as to suggest that the natural environment of the islands should be understood, not as mere setting, but as "a character in our history."

> Every time that you forget to describe tropical nature as a character in our history and not as its setting, a character with its own revolts and cowardice, every time you find yourself giving too many flowers to the gardeners and too many beaches to the clipper ships, then you will remember that lands where the weather is too beautiful are like maternal wombs hostile to rebirth. [7]

If, as Maximin suggests, tropical nature is to be understood as "a character in our history," then it functions as more than just a symbol of regional identity, it is understood to have played an active role in shaping that identity. To the reader coming to Caribbean literature from the outside, this treatment of the landscape compels interest. What is the significance of this tendency to depict tropical nature as an active agent of Caribbean history? How has this quasi-anthropomorphic treatment of the environment evolved, and what does that evolution reveal about the development of the culture of the French West Indies? And why insist on this specifically narrative treatment of the environment, an entity that is usually considered to exert its influence in a more static, diffuse manner? The present chapter attempts to answer such questions through a comparative reading of three novels that mobilize the landscape in the overtly anthropomorphic, ideologically charged manner described by Maximin: Edouard Glissant's *La Lézarde*, Patrick Chamoiseau's *Texaco* and Maryse Condé's *Traversée de la Mangrove*.

Each of these novels emphasizes a different element of the Caribbean environment. Glissant allegorizes the course of the Lézarde river, Chamoiseau studies the "urban mangrove" of shantytowns around Fort-de-France and Condé describes life in a small village hidden in the mangrove swamps of Guadeloupe. But each of them attributes such an unusual amount of active agency to the landscape that they might well be called "landscape narratives." Moreover, these authors share, whether implicitly or explicitly, a similar evolutionary understanding of West Indian culture. Reasoning from the biological to the anthropological, from the agricultural to the sociocultural, Glissant, Chamoiseau and Condé study the myriad ways in which the current cultural mix of the islands has resulted from the adaptive transformations of its components. In this, their work is representative of the latest phases of the cultural theory of the French Antilles, which has shown a gradual historical movement away from the divisive race-based arguments inherited from the colonial period and a growing desire to embrace a less conflictual model of cultural change.

Aimé Césaire had already begun to explore Antillean identity in specifically environmental terms as early as the 1940's. The *Cahier d'un retour au pays natal* is loaded with references to the tropical environment of the Antilles, and it is arguably his awareness of the specificity of Caribbean culture that kept Césaire from adopting the more strongly essentialist vision of Negritude promoted by Senghor. Nevertheless, Césaire's approach differs in significant ways from those studied here. Presiding over Césaire's environmental imagery are two central figures: the tree and the volcano. The tree, roots plunging into the soil and branches aspiring to the sky, is usually taken to symbolize the ancestral link with the African past. The volcano, on the other hand, is a revolutionary image and reflects Césaire's Marxist view of history and cultural change. The volcanic imagery of the *Cahier*—along with the various other plagues and natural disasters that punctuate the poem—symbolizes Césaire's desire to sweep away the injustices of the past in a cataclysmic moment of renewal. Intent upon bringing about sudden change, Césaire shows little interest in the more gradual, long-term changes that occur in populations from generation to generation. It is on this point that Edouard Glissant will break with Césaire.

Glissant: "Car c'est d'un pays qu'il s'agit là, et non pas d'hommes"[8]

The two terms with which Edouard Glissant's thought is most closely associated—*antillanité* and *métissage*—emphasize, respectively, his devotion to the Antilles as an autonomous cultural domain and his interest in the hybridization or cross-fertilization of cultures. The second term, which is also a botanical term, is of particular relevance for the subject of this essay. Like Césaire, Glissant works for a renewal of Caribbean society, but the term *métissage* implies an evolutionary, as opposed to revolutionary, model for change. This is the model at work in *La Lézarde*.

As the title of Glissant's novel suggests, *La Lézarde* is as much about the Lézarde River and the island as a whole as about the group of political activists at the center of the novel's plot. Michael Dash, in his helpful introduction to the English translation of *La Lézarde*, emphasizes the allegorical use that Glissant makes of the landscape: "It is the story of the familiar tensions between the values of the plain and those of the hills, between the slave who revolted and the one who remained in bondage."[9] But in order to fully understand what makes this mode of environmental symbolism more than just a decorative, and ultimately superfluous, poetic trope it is necessary to go beyond Dash's historical rationale (where the maroons are identified with their historical home in the hills and the city with the plains). Specifically, we must understand that Glissant's approach to culture, and to the elaboration of a specifically Caribbean identity, is predicated upon the same type of considerations that motivate environmentalists in their defense of the globe's natural resources: Glissant emphasizes man's place *within* nature, rejecting any view that would present humans as having risen above nature and, by virtue of their intelligence and industry, mastered it.

At the most basic allegorical level, the Lézarde River symbolizes the historical trajectory of the island. Flowing from its source up in the mystical shade of the mountains, the river drops down to the plain, where it cradles the town Lambrianne before flowing into the swampy delta that obscures its path to the sea. The river is explicitly personified and its path compared to the history and destiny of the people of Martinique.

> puis soudain elle bondit, c'est comme un peuple qui se lève . . . la Lézarde, croupe élargie, ventre de feu sur les froides profondeurs de son lit, comblée, s'attarde et se repaît dans le cri de midi . . . aux abords de la ville, la Lézarde s'humanise . . . la Lézarde continue vers le soir et la mer noire, ainsi accomplissant sa mort et sa science . . . ce flot sans retour mène au delta de nos magies, qui est l'aube de la vraie et douloureuse science. . . .[10]

Not coincidentally, the central narrative strand of the story precisely doubles the path of the river to the sea. Thus Thaël, a mountain dweller entering into the political life of the town for the first time, has been assigned an important mission: to assassinate a political enemy named Garin. Garin has committed two unpardonable crimes: collaborating with profiteering capitalists who want to skew the outcome of upcoming elections, and building a house around the source of the Lézarde. In trying to control the source of the river, Garin's goal is to enrich himself by controlling access to a crucial natural resource of the island; by collaborating with the enemies of Martinican democracy, he helps them control the island's political resources, keeping them out of the hands of the people. The first crime is political, the second ecological, but for Glissant they are simply the two opposing faces of a single crime. In both cases, the premise is the same: control the source and you control the country.

Glissant has Thaël assassinate Garin in a way that reflects the double nature of Garin's crime. Rather than simply killing Garin outright, which he has ample opportunity to do, Thaël seeks him out in his house at the source of the river. The two then travel together, in full knowledge of the other's intentions, and follow the river down to the sea. Finally, in a mode of murder that is much more symbolically satisfying than, say, a simple push off a cliff or a knife in the back, Thaël takes Garin out to the sand bar at the mouth of the river and drowns him at the precise point where the Lézarde empties into the ocean.

So far, this equation between the human and the natural seems conventional enough. It might call to mind Balzac's habit of reinforcing his plot lines with allegorical descriptions designed to make explicit the larger implications of the action. But for Glissant, the relation between the human plot line and the environmental allegory is more than explanatory, it is also causal. The genius of his characters, that which makes them heroes, is to have understood the nature of their link with the land. This sets them above the rest of the population, which fails to understand that the town in which they live is not so much an assemblage of people and buildings as a particular manifestation of general laws determined by the natural environment. As Thaël puts it:

> [La ville] pousse dans la terre, comme une fleur. C'est plein de gens, et ils croient qu'ils sont quelque chose d'à part, une catégorie à part, parce qu'ils ont des salons, des services, qu'ils vont se promener le dimanche après-midi. Mais ce n'est pas vrai! Au fond d'eux il y a toute la terre d'alentour . . . cette ville c'est un produit de la terre, ce n'est pas séparé, il n'y a aucun mur, c'est un passage, un rassemblement . . . elle continue la terre . . . Il n'y a pas de ville, il n'y a que la terre qui a fait des maisons, voilà.[11]

Whether they are aware of it or not, these people live in a town that is itself a "product" or "continuation" of the land, growing out of the ground like a flower. But because they have not sufficiently acknowledged the symbiotic relationship between town and country, the townsfolk are easily controlled. Like the town itself, they suffer from being subjected too strictly to the rationality of an urban model that has no link with the local environment. Dominated by asphalt, Cartesian rationality, European colonizers and their mulatto imitators, the town lacks life. This lack is particularly apparent when contrasted with the life of the river: the town's main road, for example, is presented as a kind of rationalized imitation of the river, "un autre fleuve mais infécond."[12] Repeatedly in his descriptions of the town Glissant uses words like "inflexible,, "flat," "banal," and "monotonous" to oppose the town to the supple curves and resplendent proliferation of the natural landscape. The river, on the other hand, seems intent on protecting, reassuring and helping people ("cerner un peu d'humanité, pour rassurer les hommes, les aider") in their struggle against the inhumanly linear inflexibility of the town's streets.[13]

This opposition between the "humanity" of the river and the alienated rationality of the town governs the other central plot strand of the novel, which is the relationship between Mathieu and Thaël. Mathieu represents the ethos of the city, Thaël the mountains. Thus Thaël describes Mathieu in the following way: "Il ne comprend pas, il a l'esprit tout en formes, il est comme une machine, il sépare tout, à gauche le jour, à droite la nuit, mais tout ça, la ville, la terre, les gens, la mer, les poissons et les ignames, tout ça c'est le jour et c'est la nuit, la droite et la gauche."[14] Mathieu has not yet understood the interdependence of town and earth; it will be up to Thaël to teach it to him. Conversely, Thaël has lived too reclusively. Exposed only to the legends and folk wisdom of the mountains, he will remain unable to act efficaciously without the initiation into the political realities of the city that Mathieu can offer him. The two enter into a reciprocal pact of mutual aid that will allow them to supplement the shortcomings of the other. This will entail a loss for Thaël ("désormais une force étrangère intervenait entre lui et la terre des hauts"), but also a crucial gain ("Il était distinct, il avait dénombré. Il était sorti de la force obscure, entré dans une force plus évidente, plus calculée").[15]

Following the lead of his characters, the narrator of *La Lézarde* comes to understand that his historical task will be to develop a new aesthetic mode capable of synthesizing these two complementary forces, addressing the political realities of the city without losing contact with the obscure natural forces embodied by the legends of peasant mythology and the mountain landscape. It is interesting to note, incidentally, that this opposition between town and country echoes a similar opposition developed in Césaire's *Cahier d'un retour au pays natal*. But whereas Césaire symbolically destroys the town, allowing a re-emergence of pristine nature, Glissant seeks a reconciliation, a symbolic mating (*métissage*) of the two cultures. The Thaël/Mathieu couple embodies this reconciliation, and Glissant's narrator takes on the task of disseminating it, because, as Thaël puts it, "il n'est de richesse . . . que pour un pays qui a librement choisi l'ordre de ses richesses, par telle ou telle organisation qui convient à sa nature."[16]

It is important to emphasize that, for Glissant, this reconciliation of mountain and plain— nature and city, myth and realism, mysticism and pragmatism—remains to be accomplished. As Glissant was to put it in a later novel: "Les lecteurs d'ici sont futurs." In this sense, Glissant's work still has a certain Césairean dimension: it too is a call for renewal, albeit one that works through an evolutionary, rather than revolutionary, process.

Chamoiseau's Urban Mangrove

The contrast with Chamoiseau's approach is revealing. Like Glissant, Chamoiseau emphasizes mankind's place within nature: culture is simply a particular expression of the more general laws of nature, not its incommensurable other. And like Glissant, Chamoiseau sets out in search of an authentically Caribbean culture, one that respects the conditions in which it has developed. But whereas Glissant sees this authentic culture as an ideal to be achieved with the help of visionary leaders, Chamoiseau sees it all around him, in the Creole culture and folk traditions of the islands. To be sure, Chamoiseau understands as well as Glissant the problems that plague Caribbean society—poverty, alienation, a color-bound social hierarchy, economic and political dependence on the French *métropole*, the threat of being assimilated into a homogenized global culture and so forth—but Chamoiseau explains the genesis of such problems in a different way. The real problem as Chamoiseau sees it is not that an authentic Caribbean culture has not yet evolved, but that Caribbean intellectuals have either not known where to look for it (in the popular culture of the islands) or have not been able to understand its vitality. He accuses the intellectual elite of the islands of an unwillingness to acknowledge Creole culture because it appears to them as rustic and uncouth, as at best a proto-culture. Chamoiseau's hope for establishing a coherent Caribbean identity does not lie in some future avant-garde hybrid of mountain and plain *à la* Glissant, but in the Creole traditions of the islands. Thus Chamoiseau turns to the local folk culture for inspiration, embracing not only its stock of legends, but also its manners, idioms, style, and history, warts and all.

Texaco offers what is no doubt the most complete novelistic realization of the theory of Creolity, as presented in such texts as the *Éloge de la Créolité* (written with Raphaël Confiant and Jean Bernabé) and *Lettres Créoles* (written with Confiant). In *Texaco* the shantytown that lends its name to the novel serves as an emblem of Creole culture as a whole. The novel revolves around the stories of Marie-Sophie Laborieux, who recounts the histories of the Creole *quartiers* that she has known personally or through the stories passed on to her by her father Esternome. These stories focus on the contentious relations between the Creole *quartiers* and the city (or *"en-ville"*) around which they have formed and upon which they depend for their economic survival.

The environmental component of the novel appears most explicitly in the notes of the *Urbaniste*, or urban planner. A representative of the city government, the urban planner comes to Texaco in order to prepare for its demolition. Like the other city bureaucrats, he initially sees Texaco as nothing more than a menace to the public health. But, having been convinced by a well-aimed rock to spend a few days in Texaco, he has time, while recuperating, to hear Marie-Sophie Laborieux's account of the place's history. She is able to convince him not only that Texaco provides an important repository for the history and culture of the island, but also that it plays a key role in the continued survival of Fort-de-France itself. Without places like Texaco, he finally concludes, the city would die of its own order and rationality. "Au coeur ancien: un ordre clair, régenté, normalisé. Autour: une couronne bouillonnante, indéchiffrable, impossible, masquée par la misère et les charges obscurcies de l'Histoire. Si la ville créole ne disposait que de l'ordre de son centre, elle serait morte. Il lui faut le chaos de ses franges."[17]

The urban planner repeatedly describes Texaco as a cross between town and country. And one might notice here that this relationship between city and nature, center and periphery bears a strong resemblance to the type of relationship that Glissant set up between the plain and the mountain. But there is a crucial difference: Texaco has grown up spontaneously. This point must be emphasized, because for Chamoiseau it is the spontaneous nature of Creole culture that guarantees its authenticity. Chamoiseau sees Creole culture as a fully constituted, coherent response to the challenges posed by the environment and history of the Caribbean. Significantly, his justification of this view makes an implicit appeal to an evolutionary argument. For Chamoiseau, the very fact that Creole culture has managed to survive in the crucible of West-Indian history—an ordeal comparable to Darwin's process of natural selection—proves its viability and worthiness. Creole culture is, in other words, an eminently *adaptive* response to its environment. For this reason, it is possible to say that Chamoiseau is in a very real sense an environmental determinist: the mark of authenticity of Creole culture is the fact that it has evolved autonomously, without conscious design, in response to pressures beyond the control of individuals and governmental agencies.

In his authorial postface to *Texaco*, Chamoiseau cites Glissant on the necessity of striving for "la vivacité féconde d'une dialectique réamorcée entre nature et culture antillaises."[18] This is a goal that appears to resemble the one found in *La Lézarde*. But, for Chamoiseau, Glissant's mystical union between nature and culture is somewhat of an anachronism, because, by the time he writes, the city has already more or less overrun the natural landscape. Indeed, as paradoxical as it may sound, Texaco *is* nature; or, to put it more accurately, places like Texaco represent what nature has become in an island increasingly devoid of unspoiled terrain. Even as the *en-ville* continues to encroach upon whatever greenery remains around the city, spawning ever more *quartiers* like Texaco, those *quartiers* themselves help to compensate by integrating environmental imperatives into their structure. Impromptu developments like Texaco do not destroy nature, as the bulldozers of the *en-ville* would, because the Creole culture that reigns there encourages them to maintain an organic, symbiotic relationship with nature. Thus, as Marie-Sophie's father Esternome liked to put it, "Quartier créole est comme fleur de l'endroit."[19] The *quartiers* obey the same laws as the island's flora and fauna. Creole gardens, construction techniques, folklore and folk remedies are all based on customs that prove again and again to be of vital importance for their survival.

The citified inhabitants of the *en-ville*, in their desire to imitate European ways, attempt to subjugate the Martinican environment by force; the *quartiers*, on the other hand, represent the wisdom of the oppressed, those who know to bend before breaking. The *quartier* is an intermediary, hybrid form of urbanism, a transitional zone: "Texaco se souvient du jeu de forces entre la case et la Grand-case, entre l'habitation et le bourg, entre le bourg rural et la ville."[20] Halfway between plantation and village, rural life and urban, "Texaco était ce que la ville conservait de l'humanité de la campagne."[21] It is this transitional status that explains why the urban planner calls it an urban mangrove. "Texaco n'était pas ce que les Occidentaux appellent un bidonville, mais une mangrove, *une mangrove urbaine. . . .* Texaco n'est ni de la ville ni de la campagne. Pourtant, la ville se renforce en puisant dans la mangrove urbaine de Texaco, comme dans celle des autres quartiers, exactement comme la mer se repeuple par cette langue vitale qui la relie aux chimies des mangroves."[22] If the mangrove swamp is a place of transition and exchange, where ocean and dry land meet and replenish each other, then the urban mangrove is where exchange between city and country takes place. It provides two crucial services for the city: it acts as a repository for the *disjecta* of the *en-ville*—the poor, tired, old, and weak—but it also fosters the kind of cultural ferment that will help to replenish the city and keep it from losing touch with the source of its vitality.

Condé's *Crossing the Mangrove*

Given the type of link between landscape and cultural identity examined so far, along with the suggestive title of Maryse Condé's *Traversée de la Mangrove*, it seems reasonable to expect to find in this novel yet another study of the environmental determinants of Caribbean identity. This is, in a sense, what *Traversée de la Mangrove* offers, but anyone who has followed Maryse Condé's career knows not to expect the type of monolithic cultural program that Césaire, Glissant and Chamoiseau have produced. Condé does not share their desire to promote a normative vision of what is authentically Caribbean. Nor does she believe that West Indian literature should seek its identity within the confines of the cultural and natural environment of the islands. On the contrary, Condé has published strongly worded articles condemning this obsession with local color and calling for a stop to what she sees as authoritarian attempts to regulate West Indian society by using localness as a test for cultural authenticity.[23] This critical stance reflects the path she has taken in her creative work, much of which is set outside the Caribbean. Her refusal to submit to the dictates of the theorists of authenticity has not, however, kept her from writing novels that explore the culture of her native Guadeloupe. *Traversée de la Mangrove* offers what may be the most notable example of this aspect of her work.

How, then, does Condé use the landscape in *Traversée de la Mangrove*? Like Chamoiseau and Glissant, she links her characters, the inhabitants of an isolated village named Rivière au Sel, with the local landscape. For example: Mira claims the Gully (Condé capitalizes the word, suggesting allegorical possibilities) outside town as a kind of refuge; her brother Aristide is a self-proclaimed man of the mountains who spends his time seeking out the Edenic, pre-colonial landscape about which his father told him. Then there is Xantippe, who, one of the most shadowy figures in the novel, is also the one most closely identified with the landscape. Indeed, Xantippe goes so far as to claim to have personally named the elements of the landscape in a primal, Adamic gesture: "En un mot, j'ai nommé ce pays. Il est sorti de mes reins dans une giclée de foutre."[24] But the central figure of the novel is Francis Sancher, and his link to the land is not so clear.

Traversée de la Mangrove is structured around the wake of Francis Sancher (a.k.a. Francisco Sanchez). Although he lived among the villagers for several years, he died as a stranger to them, and each of the inhabitants of the village spends the duration of the wake trying to pierce the secret of his identity.[25] Who was Sancher? The only thing that can be said with certainty is that his presence among them has irrevocably upset the life of the village, disrupting the balance of power and changing the lives of its inhabitants forever. What the net result of this change will be, whether positive or negative, cannot yet be said. This mystery of identity extends to cover the novel as a whole. Condé writes in such a way as to avoid imposing any univocal meaning on the town, its inhabitants, its natural surroundings, or on Guadeloupian identity in general. Each of the characters in the novel examines the same limited set of facts, but draws different conclusions about their meaning. The landscape around Rivière au Sel, in particular, is subject to this kind of contradictory scrutiny. The village is seen as a prison by some, a refuge for others, and for yet others it is simply the only place they have ever known. The same uncertainty hovers over Mira's Gully. She goes there to find solitude and escape from her claustrophobic home life, but Sancher goes there to await his destiny; for others, gullies simply represent lurking danger (rape), while for yet others the Gully's waters embody an active threat to the town (flooding). Other features of the landscape (mountains, springs, beaches, the Soufrière volcano, etc.) receive the same range of divergent interpretations. All judgments in the novel are inconclusive because based on dubious information or coupled with other, contradictory interpretations. And even where the reader has no information explicitly contradicting a given judgment, he is often led to question its pertinence. Carmélien, for example, has spent his life searching for a spring, not because he has any special affinity for them, but because he has read Jacques Roumain's *Maîtres de la rosée* and is determined to have his own mystical back-to-nature experience.

How, then, does this novel relate the local landscape to the question of Guadeloupian cultural identity? At first reading, it is extremely difficult to tell, because Condé so consistently puts individual variation before theoretical generalization. The indeterminacy described above makes it difficult for the critic to forward any univocal statements about the meaning of the novel without falling back on clichés of the "la bêtise est de vouloir conclure" sort. One might be tempted to conclude, then, that Condé simply has no opinion on the subject, or that her novel is about other, perhaps equally important, things. But then, upon closer inspection, it becomes clear that she is deeply concerned with this question, and that if her novel seems to offer no clear-cut responses to the type of identity questions posed by Césaire, Glissant, and Chamoiseau, it is precisely because it is written in response to their grand cultural theories, as a kind of point-by-point rebuttal. For each stereotypically "classic" Caribbean figure, Condé offers her own problematic counter-figure, one who, without exactly undermining its right to enter into the Caribbean pantheon, flies in the face of received conventions. Thus there is the classic figure of the *mento* or *homme fort*, to whom she opposes Xantippe (who, if his neighbors are to be believed, is simply a half-deranged old hermit); to the figure of the supportive daughter and/or wife she opposes the fiercely independent Vilma and Mira; to the figure of the cruelly assimilationist schoolteacher she opposes Léocadie Timothée (whose cruelty stems from her difficulty relating to men, not her difficulties relating to her native culture); to the politically committed writer, she opposes "the writer," Lucien Evariste, who is committed, but for all the wrong reasons (and who never manages to get any writing done); to the historian, she opposes Emile Etienne, who, instead of writing History with a capital H, has his own, more humble, documentary project, called "Parlons de Petit Bourg"; to the masterful storyteller, she opposes Cyrille, a *conteur* who gets outtalked by Sancher and then seems to have lost all vestiges of eloquence at Sancher's wake. And so on.[26] Finally, there is Francis Sancher himself, who, despite his heroic stints abroad and his ambition to write a novel called "Traversée de la Mangrove," is no Césairian prophet, but just an ageing man with a history, haunted equally by his personal demons, a sense of historical guilt (his ancestors may or may not have been involved in a slave massacre) and a bad case of writer's block.

What links all of these characters is Condé's careful attention to situating them within the dialectic of imprisonment and exile. Some wonder why a man such as Sancher—who has fought with Castro and seen the world—would choose to settle in a backwoods village like Rivière au Sel. Interestingly, one of the refrains of the novel—used by Mira, Aristide, and others—is "partir." Readers of Césaire's *Cahier* will recognize an important motif of that text, but whereas the Césairian departure prepares a more complete and satisfying return to the native land, this is by no means assured in Condé's text. The few glimpses that one gets of locals who have actually left the island reveal pale and depressed, if relatively affluent, exiles who miss their home, but cannot return without giving up the standard of living and freedoms to which they have become accustomed. This, Condé seems to be saying, is the dilemma facing all those who have grown up in a small island community: life at home offers only limited opportunities, but life away from home is exile. Lucien Évariste's thoughts upon returning to Rivière au Sel after his studies in Paris are typical of Condé's approach to this theme: "Lucien était heureux d'être revenu au pays, sitôt terminée sa maîtrise. Plus souvent qu'à son tour, c'est vrai, un poignant regret le prenait de la torpeur de cette terre stérile qui ne parvenait pas à accoucher de sa Révolution."[27] Lucien bemoans the lack of revolutionary spirit of the people, while others hate the insularity, xenophobia, or lack of economic opportunities of Rivière au Sel. But all share this kind of love-hate relationship with the village and with Guadeloupe in general. It is what they know, it is home, and it feels comfortable, but it is not enough.

Given all of this, *Traversée de la Mangrove* is perhaps best understood as a response to the type of monolithic ideological message characteristic of Césaire, Glissant and the Créolistes. Condé remains warmly sympathetic to Creole culture, and acknowledges its role in shaping the identities of Guadeloupians, but she insists repeatedly on her ambivalence about the ultimate value of relying on creolity, localness and a tropical sensibility as defining criteria for determining the authenticity of any given expression of Guadeloupian culture. Instead, her message seems to be that there is no single Guadeloupian or Caribbean or Creole identity. The lesson she has drawn from the Caribbean environment involves not the deterministic pressures of natural selection, but rather the irrepressible diversity of nature.

Condé's novel is, in this sense, a call for writers to resist imposing their ideological programs onto the landscape. If so, then Sancher does in the end turn out to be a personification of Guadeloupe, but one whose purpose is not to promote a certain vision of what the island is or should be, but rather to force the reader to question the nature of the relationship between the island and its inhabitants, and, in so doing, to understand the risks inherent in trying to impose a univocal view of what it means to be Guadeloupian. Condé's novel suggests that Caribbean writers must work as empiricists, telling the story of the private side of Guadeloupe in its multiplicity, without imposing an authoritarian interpretive schema on it. For Condé, then, "Parlons de Petit Bourg" is potentially a more important book than Sancher's *Traversée de la Mangrove*, Glissant's *Discours Antillais*, or the *Éloge de la Créolité*.

Mangrove—Swamp—Delta

If it were necessary to choose an emblem for the type of landscape writing studied here, a likely candidate would be the mangrove swamp. The mangrove, a geographical feature that has considerable ecological significance for tropical islands like Martinique and Guadeloupe, also provides a useful symbol for comparing the cultural theories of these three writers. Each of them uses the imagery of the coastal flood plain in significant ways. The mangrove swamp supplies both the title and the setting for Condé's novel and, taken as a metaphor for Creole urbanism, it provides the guiding model for Chamoiseau's urban planner and the central metaphor of *Texaco*. Glissant, it is true, does not introduce a mangrove swamp into the imagery of *La Lézarde*, but he focuses on a closely related feature of the coastline: the swampy delta at the mouth of the Lézarde river.[28]

Asked to name the place where land and sea meet, the tourist would no doubt think first of the beach. But for one who understands island ecology, the swampy terrain of the mangrove and delta are of far greater significance: resistant to human exploitation, they provide the refuges necessary to guarantee the health and diversity of the local flora and fauna. To be sure, only certain species, adapted to both land and water, can survive there, but it may be precisely this dual nature of the mangrove-swamp complex—fertility and delicacy, land and sea—that explains its interest for Glissant, Chamoiseau and Condé.

Nevertheless, each of these writers draws a different lesson from the image. For Glissant, the delta marks the point where men must finally intervene in order to aid the river in its descent to the city. Only with the help of men building dykes and canals can the Lézarde be made "claire devant la mer. Comme un peuple assuré vient au-devant des autres peuples."[29] For Chamoiseau, the urban mangrove acts as a kind of lifeline for the city: it is there that the city can plunge its rhizomatic roots into the nourishing muck, discharge accumulated sediment, and replenish itself, "exactement comme la mer se repeuple par cette langue vitale qui la relie aux chimies des mangroves."[30] Finally, Condé emphasizes the dense, fiercely impenetrable vegetation of the mangrove, which symbolizes the writer's limited ability to penetrate the secrets of a community. (Upon discovering that Francis Sancher is writing a novel called "Traversée de la Mangrove," Vilma objects: "On ne traverse pas la mangrove. On s'empale sur les racines des palétuviers. On s'enterre et on étouffe dans la boue saumâtre.")[31]

In a sense, then, one might argue that these three related images only confirm what was already known: that Glissant, the theorist of *métissage* and *antillanité*, has a heroic conception of the Caribbean, which will be led to its destiny by visionaries who have maintained both a vital link to the land and the will to build cultural dykes and canals; that Chamoiseau, the *Créoliste*, sees Creole culture as a vital resource, necessary for the continued development of Caribbean society; and that Condé, the aggressively dissenting female voice, questions the legitimacy of making such grandiose claims about what Caribbean culture is and is not, should or should not be. But by testing these images against the logic of environmental determinism and the environmentalist's view of culture as a subset of nature, it is possible to perceive some of the patterns at work in these texts that might otherwise have gone unnoticed. This kind of analysis helps to confirm, for example, the profound adequation of form and content in these works, explaining why these writers have chosen to illustrate their views in terms of images borrowed from nature. Far from being an idly conventional poetic trope, the landscape imagery in these novels brings to the surface deeply felt convictions about the ontology of culture and the genesis of identities, both individual and collective. It is, moreover, precisely this type of thought on the relationship between cultural identity and its determinants that has made these writers so important, both in and beyond the Caribbean. Their shared preoccupation with the relationship between nature and culture, place and personality, local and global cultures, puts them at the forefront of contemporary debates about the identitarian dilemmas of the post-colonial era.

Notes

1. Edward Said, "Yeats and Decolonization," in *Nationalism, Colonialism and Literature* (Minneapolis: University of Minnesota Press, 1988), 77.

2. Homi Bhabha, "DissemiNation," in *Nation and Narration* (New York: Routledge, 1990), 295. W. J. T. Mitchell makes a related point about landscape painting, which has been used by colonial powers to "naturalize" colonial power by inscribing ideologically determined messages into images of nature. (W. J. T. Mitchell, "Imperial Landscape," in *Landscape and Power* (Chicago: University of Chicago Press, 1994), 5.

3. Bhabha, "DissemiNation," 295.

4. This is a recurrent theme of *Le discours antillais* and *Poétique de la relation*.

5. Derek Walcott provided an early articulation of this problem in his now classic essay on "The Muse of History." Walcott considers the landscape in relation to historical discourse and decides that the latter can only lead to endless cycles of recrimination and guilt about the islands' colonial past. For Walcott, the best response to the traumatic pressures of the past is not to attempt a symbolic "repossession" of the landscape (as for Said), but to concentrate on the future and the "elemental privilege of naming the new world" (Walcott, "The Muse of History," in *Is Massa Day Dead?* ed. Orde Coombs (New York: Anchor, 1974), 5.

6. For an example of the vehement insistence on the need to overcome the exotic, see Suzanne Césaire's "Misère d'une poésie" in *Tropiques* 4 (January 1942): 48–50. (Reprint: Paris: Jean-Michel Place, 1978). Her argument is picked up later by the *Créolistes* in *Éloge de la Créolité* and *Lettres Créoles*.

7. Daniel Maximin, *Lone Sun* (Charlottesville: University Press of Virginia, 1989), 10.

8. Edouard Glissant, *La Lézarde* (Paris: Gallimard, 1997), 20.

9. Michael Dash, "Introduction," in *La Lézarde*, trans. Michael Dash (Portsmouth: Heinemann, 1985), 9.

10. Glissant, *La Lézarde*, 33–35.

11. Glissant, *La Lézarde*, 128–30.

12. Glissant, *La Lézarde*, 126.

13. Glissant, *La Lézarde*, 34.

14. Glissant, *La Lézarde*, 129.

15. Glissant, *La Lézarde*, 249.

16. Glissant, *La Lézarde*, 184.

17. Chamoiseau, *Texaco*, 204.

18. Chamoiseau, *Texaco*, 421.

19. Chamoiseau, *Texaco*, 150.

20. Chamoiseau, *Texaco*, 344.

21. Chamoiseau, *Texaco*, 309.

22. Chamoiseau, *Texaco*, 289.

23. See, in particular, Maryse Condé, "Order, Disorder, Freedom, and the West Indian Writer," *Yale French Studies* 83 (1993): 121–35.

24. Maryse Condé, *Traversée de la Mangrove* (Paris: Laffont, 1989), 236.

25. In this, *Traversée de la Mangrove* calls to mind Chamoiseau's *Solibo Magnifique*, which also centers on a wake. But whereas Chamoiseau's novel memorializes a way of life (Solibo is taken to represent the last of the great Martinican *Conteurs*), Condé's novel offers no such evaluation of Sancher's cultural role.

26. Each of these figures appears over and over in West Indian literature, not only in Césaire, Glissant, and Chamoiseau, but also in Roumain, Zobel, Confiant, Schwarz-Bart, etc.

27. Condé, *Traversée*, 229.

28. Like mangroves, deltas demarcate a zone that is neither land nor sea, but a point of exchange between the two. Subject to saline tides from the ocean and sedimentation from the land, both deltas and are related to the swamp in that they support both marine and terrestrial vegetation.

29. Glissant, *La Lézarde*, 85.

30. Chamoiseau, *Texaco*, 289.

31. Condé, *Traversée*, 202.

13

Breaking the Metronome:
Community and Song in Maryse Condé's
Moi, Tituba Sorcière . . . Noire de Salem

Holly Woodson Waddell

PAIN, LOSS AND SUFFERING CHARACTERIZE the fictive autobiographical narratives within Maryse Condé's text *Moi, Tituba sorcière . . . Noire de Salem* (1985). While the most obvious approach may be to seek to draw sharp distinctions between the characters' various tribulations, in fact, Condé's narrative represents a synthesis of disparate painful experiences. Using rape as both a lived experience of physical violation and a metaphor for the oppressor's cruelty, Condé links the degradation and humiliation suffered by women, Jews, Indians, and slaves through storytelling.[1] Condé does not erase the historical and physical differences that inform the subject positions of the Jew, the Slave, the Indian and the Woman; rather, she emphasizes the common experience of suffering in order to highlight the oppressor's invariable act of degradation. By identifying the oppressor as a "rapist," Condé reveals his lack of generative humanity; the rapist/oppressor implements his cruelty with horrific predictability across racial, gender and religious lines. Paradoxically, however, through the exchange of narratives, the victims can potentially destabilize the oppressor's power by forming a community with political agency.

Condé represents the oppressor of the unstable New England society as a Puritan and, using the white zealot as the figure of evil, Condé creates a structure that deviates significantly from the pervasive Western delineation between good and evil, black and white.[2] Rather than following the European tradition, positing Satan as the "Black Man," Condé instead insists on the figure of Satan as a white Puritan, thereby changing the correlation of white-as-good to white-as-evil.[3] By emphasizing the Puritan's fixation on the evils of the flesh, moreover, Condé reveals that the "black" sin forever plaguing him invokes the impossibility of achieving white morality. As a result, Condé's text reveals the fundamental division that defines the Puritan and yet also reveals how this division ultimately prevents him from uncovering his own identity.

Franz Fanon's dialectic of black skin/white masks goes far to explain Maryse Condé's representation of the Puritan. In *Peau noire, masques blancs* (1952), Fanon specifically treats the effect of the dialectic on black identity formation. Fanon argues that European culture is directly responsible for the black's existential crisis, for his identity is always already infiltrated by the white's metaphysical notion of the color black: "Le Noir évolué, esclave du mythe nègre, spontané, cosmique, sent à un moment donné que sa race ne le comprend plus. . . . Ou qu'il ne la comprend pas."[4] Fanon argues that as the black must find his identity within a social system of confusion and disharmony he cannot escape the hegemonic culture of the oppressor. Maryse

Condé also addresses the ontological implications of the black/white dialectic in her book *Moi, Tituba*, but rather than finding that only the black is caught in the flux of his ambiguous identity, she reveals that the Puritan suffers from a profoundly split consciousness—his crippling and even fatal mentality prevents both humane actions and the creation of a generative community.

As the Puritan/oppressor enacts his crisis, it is important to note that he embodies a significantly different problem of identity formation. Unable to escape the monotonous ambiguity of his own divided identity, he asserts his sadistic will to punish and torture those around him. Thus, the Puritan possesses an "essentialized," static identity based on his very adherence to the concept of the innate duplicity in human nature. Ironically, his need to preserve an unchanging divided identity points to a further duplicity, or the disavowal of change among the circumscribed group of Puritans.[5] The Puritan's refusal to define himself in terms of new experiences leaves him in a state of constant reduction—he is unable to embrace any identity outside his group.

Fanon and Condé: *peau blanche, masques noirs*

Franz Fanon's text provides a valuable analytical basis for the critical examination of *Moi, Tituba*. Fanon defines the blacks' formation of identity by opposing it to that of another oppressed group, the Jews, a juxtaposition that not surprisingly reveals irreconcilable differences: "Bien entendu, les Juifs sont brimés, que dis-je, ils sont pourchassés, exterminés, enfournés, mais ce sont là petites histoires familiales. Le Juif n'est pas aimé à partir du moment où il est dépisté. Mais avec moi tout prend un visage nouveau. Aucune chance ne m'est permise. Je suis sur-déterminé de l'extérieur. Je ne suis pas l'esclave de 'l'idée' que les autres ont de moi, mais de mon apparaître."[6]

For Fanon, the Jew, despite his persecuted religion, retains the right to choose his moral actions and thus has some agency within the system of his oppression. The Jew suffers from a specifically internalized moral crisis imposed by Catholic European culture. The black, on the other hand, undergoes an exteriorized rupture over which he has no control; his color is permanently fixed in both his eyes and those of the oppressor. As a result, the black is fundamentally divided—at each moral instant, he confronts his self-image as he tries to rid himself of the "dark part" of his conscience and retain only what is white and "clear."[7] Because of the European vilification of blackness, skin color becomes integral to the black's identity formation—it causes both self-alienation and alienation from his race. Consequently, the black is forever caught in a dialectic imposed by European culture, which opposes his black skin to an idealized "white" morality.

Condé's representation of identity formation in *Moi, Tituba*, however, contains significant differences and important reversals when compared to Fanon's conception. Although an intertextual connection with *Peau noir, masques blancs* has not been widely identified, Fanon's theories of color and identity inform Condé's novel at many levels. Condé herself suggests the link to Fanon through pointedly anachronistic references to his work. For example, John Indian instructs Tituba to interact with her peers, warning her, "Ils diront que ta peau est noire mais que par dessus tu portes masque blanc."[8] Yet, Condé resists the sharp distinction between the black and the Jew, preferring to focus instead on the shared biographical narratives of the Slave, the Woman, the Indian and the Jew. Significantly, in constructing the white oppressor as Puritan, she maintains Fanon's black skin/white masks dialectic, even though she has reversed Fanon's application by representing the Puritan as divided by his white flesh and his black deeds.

For Condé, it is the Puritan, and not the black, who is afflicted with a debilitating existential crisis. In fact, many of the Puritans Condé describes do suffer from severe mental illnesses.[9] As the Puritan repeatedly confesses his sins, he internalizes a deep disgust for his own white skin. The Puritan's revulsion at the mere sight of white flesh is so strong that he can no longer participate in intimate physical activities without disgust. Elizabeth, the wife of Samuel, reveals the extent of her husband's prudery to Tituba: "Si tu savais! Il me prend sans ôter ni mes vêtements, ni les siens, pressé d'en finir avec cet acte odieux. . . . Sexe, c'est l'héritage de Satan en nous."[10] As the Jew for Fanon, the Puritan also internalizes a metaphysical condemnation of his immoral behavior. Yet, as a result of the constant fixation on sin, he wears a metaphorical black mask. Thus, the Puritan is divided along exactly the lines of Fanon's oppressed, for he condemns and confronts his "black" behavior and "white" skin. Hence, Condé represents the Puritan as undergoing an identity crisis that mirrors Fanon's analysis of what is experienced by blacks. Contrary to the black, who cannot change the color of his skin, however, the Puritan's crisis is self-inflicted. Perversely, the Puritan ideology privileges the reversal of the black skin/white mask dialectic, thereby encouraging the self-imposition of a crisis of consciousness.

In Fanon's work, as a result of the "peau noire/masques blancs" opposition, blacks are subject to both self-alienation and alienation from their race. In Condé's text, however, the Puritan suffers from a much more debilitating and harmful malaise: the relentless confrontation of black morality and the mortification of white flesh results in nearly clinical paranoia. Mme. Parris describes the fear of witches and the ensuing witch trials in Salem as a crippling malady that first attacked the unimportant parts of the town's metaphorical body and then destroys its vital organs: "Je ne peux comparer cela qu'à une maladie que l'on croit d'abord bénigne parce qu'elle affecte des parties du corps sans importance . . . puis qui graduellement s'attaque à des membres et à des organes vitaux."[11] The public succumbs to the irrational fear of witchcraft to such a degree that it supports accusations against even the most godly of its citizens. Consequently, the Puritan group is fundamentally divided by the fear of being watched and the act of detecting others' black deeds. For Condé, then, the Puritan creates evil because he sees it everywhere.[12]

Ultimately, the Puritan's ruptured consciousness leads to the complete breakdown of his social system. Rather than exemplifying the purity of a privileged utopia, Condé's New England is a veritable hell on Earth. Condé epitomizes the ironic corruption of Salem, as the spinster Sarah Hutchinson cries: "Un jour, la vengeance de Dieu va s'abattre sur les habitants de Salem comme celle de Dieu sur les habitants de Sodome—et comme à Sodome, il ne se trouvera pas dix justes pour épargner la ville le chatiment suprême. Voleurs, caverne de voleurs!"[13] When Sarah Hutchinson identifies her village as a cavern of thieves, she exposes the debilitating fear of evil that haunts her society. Furthermore, Condé suggests that a fixation on evil results in social chaos, emphasizing the failure of a Puritan society replete with matricides, parricides, rapes, thefts and murders. Tituba describes her experience in the Salem jail: "Incrustée dans mes narines, l'odeur de tant de crimes: matricides, parricides, viols et vols, homicides et meurtres et surtout, l'odeur de tant de souffrances."[14] As Michael Warner argues, Puritan society, defined so fundamentally by its comparison with other "Places and Societies," loses its own rationale more completely than any other society if it turns out to be like them. And sodomy, of all practices, most conjures the image of the other societies that this one has willed itself not to be.[15]

Warner highlights two crucial aspects of Puritan society; the first is its connection to the city of Sodom, and the second is its dependence on the human will. Warner argues that the biblical city of Sodom supposedly defines that which Salem is not, thereby indirectly addressing the significance of dialectical reasoning within the Puritan ideology. Hence, rather than accepting difference within their community, the Puritans strictly oppose themselves to all other groups, focusing instead on others' negative characteristics, which they loathe to possess.

In Condé's text, however, the Puritan village of Salem paradoxically resembles, rather than differs from, Sodom. As the Salem jail overflows with criminals, the people's paranoiac fears are realized; the town itself creates evil because it "sees" it everywhere. Moreover, according to Warner, the Puritans' social system directly reflects the privileged strength of the human will. Yet, while will power is considered a crowning virtue, ideally enabling the Puritan to resist the temptations of his (white) flesh, Condé exposes the way that severe detachment from one's own body actually makes inhumane cruelty possible. Thus, it is with the aid of his perversely strong will that the Puritan becomes capable of torturing the bodies of others.

Condé identifies the Puritans' will power not as the facilitator of moral restraint, but rather as the evil force behind the Puritans' inhumanity: the society that has willed itself into being is profoundly corrupt. Furthermore, the character with the strongest will power, Samuel Parris, is capable of the most heinous crimes. Dressed all in black, and thereby actually wearing the "black mask," he physically dominates his victims, forcing them to submit to his iron will. Condé compares Parris and his accomplices to birds of prey as their perverse will power enables them to commit acts of torture and rape. Their perversion culminates in the attack on Tituba, during which the white men render her helpless and sodomise her with a pointed stick: "Pareils à trois grands oiseaux de proie, les hommes pénètrèrent dans ma chambre. Ils avaient enfilé des cagoules de couleur noire, percées seulement de trous pour les yeux et la buée de leurs bouches traversait le tissu."[16] The Puritans lose all generative humanity and physically embody the "black" morality. By donning black hoods, the men hide their white flesh and literalize the dialectic of white skin/black masks.[17] The visual representation of binary opposites further complicates Fanon's analysis. Whereas Fanon writes, "Tous les oiseaux de proie sont noirs," Condé presents the bird of prey as white.[18] Condé thus reinvents the symbolic lexicon of black/white, associating that which is white with evil and the Devil.

For Condé, then, white is the repulsive and frightening color that betokens moral depravity. Condé carefully distinguishes the white skin of the Puritans as "la peau la couleur du lait suri," and "le teint d'un blanc crayeux."[19] This chalk-white, sour-milk skin terrifies Tituba, even as it conjures up for her the threatening black mask of morality.[20] When Tituba meets Susanna Endicott, her new husband's mistress, she admits, "Car je ne saurais expliquer l'effet que cette femme produisait sur moi. Elle me paralysait. Elle me terrifiait."[21] With the appearance of her new master, Samuel Parris, Tituba once again experiences terror and paralysis:

> Grand, très grand, vêtu de noir de la tête aux pieds, le teint d'un blanc crayeux. . . . Mais là! Imaginez des prunelles verdâtres et froides, astucieuses et retorses, créant le mal parce qu'elles le voyaient partout. C'était comme si on se trouvait en face d'un serpent ou de quelque reptile méchant, malfaisant. J'en fus tout de suite convaincu, le Malin dont on nous rébattait les oreilles ne devait pas dévisager autrement les individus qu'il désirait égarer puis perdre.[22]

Condé attacks the Christian metaphysical symbolism of black/white at its core; by representing the Serpent, or Satan, as a white Puritan, Condé effectively reverses this age-old European symbolism.

Indeed, rather than condemning Tituba as a witch, Benjamin, Tituba's new owner, dismisses the Puritans' accusations: "Il la mettait au compte de cette foncière cruauté, qui lui semblait caractériser ceux qu'ils appelaient les Gentils."[23] Benjamin's recognition of the Puritans' cruelty suggests that the white race, and not the black one, is fundamentally linked to Satan and Hell.[24] By exposing their corruption and hypocrisy, Condé constructs the Puritans as victims of their own black/white dialectic. Even as they inflict pain upon the Slave, the Jew, the Indian and the

Woman, they contribute to the ultimate breakdown of their own society. As discussed above, Condé describes Puritan society as diseased; as the narrator suggests, it is like the plague, the ailment that first attacks the "unimportant" parts of the body, then gradually destroys "the vital organs."[25] Metaphorically, as Puritan society degenerates, the black-masked morality infects even the most trusted leaders, thereby slowly and inevitably crippling the entire social system.

Puritan "Rape" and Its Effect on the Victims

When the oppressor/Puritan tortures the Slave, the Woman, the Indian and the Jew, his brutal actions deny the victim's human subjectivity: yet when the victims share their intimate histories of pain, they both establish and reinforce their own subjective realities. Although rape serves to physically degrade and torture the other, Condé makes it explicitly clear that it nevertheless provides a founding experience around which a victim's identity is constructed. As a result, the victims' narratives develop their individual empathetic relations with other victims, a process that creates the possibility of establishing a diverse, if diminished, community of human survivors.

Rape is both a lived experience of physical violation and a metaphor for the oppressor's gaze and general cruelty. From the opening sentence of the novel, in which Tituba reveals how her mother was violated on the slave ship, rape becomes an important signifier denoting the suffering caused by the oppressor: "Abena, ma mère, un marin anglais la viola sur le pont du *Christ the King*, un jour de 16 . . . alors que le navire faisait voile vers la Barbade. C'est de cette aggression que je suis née. De cet acte de haine et de mépris."[26] Significantly, the physical act of aggression and disregard that serves to conceive Tituba also metaphorically gives birth to the colonized territory. As Hortence Spillers argues, "The New World was a scene of actual mutilation, dismemberment and exile, where the seared, divided, ripped-apartness of the flesh serves as primary narrative."[27] Thus rape is not only a corporeal reality in Condé's novel, but also represents the horrific founding experience of the colonized lands. As the oppressor forcefully enters the "virgin" territory, he irreparably mutilates its natural purity and disinherits its non-European, non-Christian inhabitants. The Native Americans, as well as the imported Africans, are left with no claims on what are now for them dismembered, mutilated lands. For example, after living in Salem, Tituba describes her homecoming and her first impressions of her island in an implicit reference to Aimé Césaire: "Qu'elle était laide, ma ville! Petite. Mesquine. Un poste colonial sans envergure, tout empuanti de l'odeur du lucre et de la souffrance."[28] Condé's anachronistic play on words, "un poste colonial" (a center for colonial activity and a neologism designating the study of "former" colonies) emphasizes the bareness, the long history of suffering, and the unrealized potential of her violated, colonized city even as it points to the troubles that still plague post-colonial countries.[29] The mere physical appearance of the city, like a wound, recalls the history of violation and oppression upon which it was founded. Thus, for the colonized territory, the feminized, raped "mother-land" embodies an ambivalent pathos; she is at once the humiliated and powerless woman and the life-giving, nurturing maternal figure.

Condé repeatedly represents the violated mother as a locus of suffering in the novel and as a specific victim of the oppressor's gaze: Tituba's mother, Abena, and Iphigène's mother conceive their children as a result of rapes.[30] Condé's insistence on the raped slave mother has both historical and thematic significance. Firstly, the slave woman was a frequent victim of rape in the colonized lands; the white man violated her frequently to satisfy his sexual aggression and to produce more slaves.[31] Secondly, in *Moi, Tituba* the act of rape is accompanied by the voyeuristic gaze, a form of moral surveillance, that depends upon the other's self-exposure:

> At the heart of Christian penitence there is the confessional, and so the admission of guilt, the examination of conscience, and arising from that the production of a whole body of knowledge and a discourse on sex which engendered a range of effects on both theory . . . and practice. . . . In the same way I have described the way in which different instances and stages in the transmission of power were caught up in the very pleasure of their exercise. There is something in surveillance, which is no stranger to the pleasure of surveillance, the pleasure of the surveillance of pleasure.[32]

Thus, much like the exercise of religious control, the Puritan's colonial project depends on an extreme form of surveillance that Laura Mulvey regards as voyeurism; voyeurism "has associations with sadism: pleasure lies in ascertaining guilt . . . asserting control and subjugating the guilty person through punishment or forgiveness."[33] Voyeurism, as opposed to fetishistic objectification, imputes subjectivity to the victim; "sadism demands a story, depends on making something happen, forcing a change in another person, a battle of will and strength, victory/defeat."[34] Although voyeurism places the subject in linear time, valorizing subjectivity through the discourse of guilt and blame, it represents only one element in the colonial system of representation.[35] Yet for the Puritan, whose religious identity depends upon the definition of morality along the axis of guilt and blame, voyeurism is privileged above the fetishistic and the imaginary. Hence, the Puritan must investigate and demystify the slave just as he investigates and demystifies his fellow Puritan; his insistence on voyeurism thereby disrupts his colonial authority, which is already weakened by the instability of skin as a signifier of morality. Thus voyeuristic sadism frustrates the Puritan's colonial prerogative to alienate and dominate the other; moreover, because sadism fixes the victim's subjectivity in narrative, the Puritan cannot entirely contain him/her in the gaze. Consequently, voyeuristic sadism disrupts the smooth circulation of colonial power. As a result, the presence of the colonial other causes the Puritan an exaggerated anxiety, for in order to preserve his colonial fantasy, the Puritan must disavow congruity between his religious and colonial projects.

Thus, for Condé, rape on the slave ship represents both a lived experience of physical violation for the slave woman and an important example of the significance of the spectacle in the Puritan's aggressive oppression. In *Moi, Tituba,* the oppressor's gaze either accompanies the scene of physical rape, or it metonymically takes the place of rape as an independent act of violation. Voyeurism plays a central role in each rape described in the novel. For example, during Abena's violation a circle of sailors gathers around the slave woman, looking on as one of them tortures and degrades her body. Tituba's light skin reminds her mother of the rapist and the group of sailors who watched: "Je ne cessais pas de lui remettre en l'esprit le Blanc qui l'avait possédée sur le pont du Christ the King au milieu d'un cercle de marins, voyeurs obscènes. Je lui rappelais à tout instant sa douleur et son humiliation."[36] Rape encompasses not only the act of physical aggression, but also the obscene voyeurism of the oppressor—a violating gaze that further degrades and humiliates the victim. When, on the deck of a boat, the *Blessing,* Tituba and John Indian are forcibly married, the scene recalls Abena's earlier rape. Like her mother, humiliated by the onlookers, Tituba too is surrounded by a new circle of sailors; the white men watch her subjugation with perverse curiosity as she and John Indian helplessly submit to the Puritan's will. In the culmination of a series of voyeuristic rapes, Tituba again suffers from the violent aggression of the Puritan who demands confession; this time, two pastors look on as Parris sodomises her with a pointed stick, crying, "Prends, prends, c'est la bite de John Indian."[37] The three pastors represent to an extreme degree voyeuristic sadism toward the colonial other.

The inter-textual dialogue created by Hester's appearance in Condé's novel also suggests a rape that metonymically takes the form of the gaze. In Nathaniel Hawthorne's novel *The Scarlet Letter* (1850) Hester is convicted of adultery and forced by a group of Puritan men to wear a red letter "A" on her breast, thereby relentlessly exposing her guilt. The whole town participates in moral surveillance as they focus on the red letter she wears: "It was not an age of delicacy; and [Hester's] position, although she understood it well and was in little danger of forgetting it, was often brought before her vivid self-perception, like a new anguish, by the rudest touch on the tenderest spot."[38] The imagery of rape emphasizes the moral and physical effect of the voyeuristic gaze on the victim. Similar to the sharpened stick that violated Tituba, entering "la partie la plus sensible de son corps," the scarlet letter inflicts pain as "the rudest touch on the tenderest spot." Like the sodomized body, then, the mark that focuses the oppressor's gaze is a site of pain—its throbbing insistence keeps the experience of rape constantly present to the victim. It follows that the inescapable gaze of the oppressor, humiliating and violating, produces much the same type of suffering for the victim of the scarlet letter as for the victim of rape.

In fact, the scarlet letter, like the color black, is symptomatic of a larger characteristic of Puritanical oppression—visual marking. If the other is not already marked, by his "red" or "black" skin, for example, the Puritan marks him, as with Hester, thereby inflicting a forced display of visual distinction, a form of exposure that imputes guilt to the object of the gaze.[39] Thus, while the mark serves to delineate the pure from the impure, it also becomes the object of the Puritan's voyeuristic sadism. Yet Condé's Hester refuses to submit to the power of the Puritan's gaze. Indeed, although the reader is always already aware of the significance of the red letter "A" through his/her knowledge of Hawthorne's story, in *Moi, Tituba* Hester does not even wear the scarlet letter; instead she is visually marked by her defiance of the Puritan dress-code and her extraordinary physical beauty. Not only does Hester not resemble a victim, she also espouses a modern feminist agenda. However, while her educated rejection of the patriarchal society subverts the Puritanical system, it clearly opposes Tituba's own philosophy: "Tu aimes trop l'amour, Tituba! Je ne ferai jamais de toi une féministe!"[40] Indeed Hester's complete rejection of men aligns with the feminist project that Condé defines as "l'écho tapageur de revendications féministes et de la haine du mâle perçu comme dominant."[41] Tituba, on the other hand, accepts men as fellow sufferers and comes much closer to Condé's own understanding of social relations.[42]

Thus. *Moi, Tituba* explicitly inter-relates men's and women's histories of violation—Hester, Tituba, Benjamin, John Indian and Iphigène all suffer figurative or literal rape at the hands of the sadistic Puritans. As a victim of physical or metaphorical rape, the oppressed is forced into a crucial moment of introspection; the experience of violation causes him/her to question the connections between his/her body and soul, and to find that these relations are socially constructed. By subjugating the body, however, the oppressor proves (if only figuratively) his greater physical strength. If, in the ethics of subjugation, physical inferiority is directly linked to moral inferiority (to a weakness of spirit that is described in traditional misogynistic interpretations of the Bible), then the violated subject is seen as doubly inferior. Ironically, as a result of his own logical construction, by violating the other, the oppressor successfully reinforces his system. For the victim, however, the ideological system is still open to interpretation. Having suffered violation, the victim must ask himself/herself if the oppressive social construct is reasonable and/or worthy of respect. His/her response, like that of Tituba, is clearly negative. So, instead of aborting his/her ability to reason, rape actually reinforces it—thereby enabling the violated subject to forge his/her identity around a horrific experience of pain and suffering.

Community in *Moi, Tituba*

While the rejection of the oppressor's system and the individual's reintegration of his/her body and soul is the first step in healing, it is followed by another that proves even more important: the creation of a community.[43] The formation of a diminished community of victims provides not only a possibility for healing through shared empathetic relations, but also a potential source of power that could ultimately topple the oppressor's social system. In *Moi, Tituba* the community is primarily created through shared autobiographical narratives. Thus, the telling and hearing of one's own "song" and the "songs" of others becomes vitally important for the generation of social strength.

Condé therefore raises many issues that belong to a current discussion of political and social options for diverse marginal populations, none more so than those concerning the interrelatedness of oppressed subjectivities. The author undoubtedly faces the social realities of disintegration plaguing today's marginal communities and depriving them of political agency. In her novel, rather than harking back to a nostalgic ideal family as the defining institution of community, Condé emphasizes that these and similar options were never viable in creating a strong, connected group of marginal peoples. As an alternative way of constructing community, *Moi, Tituba* offers storytelling, a form of mutuality in community that embraces diverse subjectivities.

Defining the Goal: Constructing a Community of Resistance

In "The Spaces that Difference Makes" Edward Soja and Barbara Hooper explore the concept of the "Other" in terms of the recent theoretical turn away from strictly historical conceptions toward geographically based identity politics. Starting with the spatially conceptualized binary of center/margin, Soja and Hooper combine a number of theoretical mappings of otherness to arrive at a call for what they term as "postmodern geographies." In Soja and Hooper's view, the postmodern geographies embrace the fragmented reality of multiple subjectivities and create "strategic alliances among all those who are peripheralised, marginalised and subordinated by the social construction of difference (especially in its binary forms)."[44] However, rather than merely critiquing the modernist tendency to avoid ambiguous spaces and to privilege ordered opposition, Soja and Hooper suggest that the innovative spatialization of postmodern geographies will serve to create a practical political space of resistance. They quote Bell Hook's "combinatorial rather than competitively fragmented and separated" concept of communities of resistance: "The politics of location necessarily calls those of us who would participate in the formation of counter-hegemonic cultural practice to identify the spaces where we begin the process of re-vision. . . . For me this space of radical openness is a margin—a profound edge. Locating oneself there is difficult yet necessary. It is not a 'safe' place. One is always at risk. One needs a community of resistance."[45] Hook's process of re-visioning the margin deconstructs the confirmed binary of center/margin by choosing the edge as a place of opportunity. According to Soja and Hooper, the radical displacement of the central hegemony also initializes a third space, a space open to a pluralist community of others—or the space that difference makes.

The third space is important not only because it disrupts the essentializing modernist binaries of subject/object, man/woman, white/black, etc., but also because it permits the creation of new communities of resistance. These heterogeneous communities are formed by the recognition of individuality and the risky choice to join with other marginal subjectivities. The choice to enter this third space offers both a liberatory alternative to "assimilation, imitation or assuming the role of rebellious exotic" and gives political agency and legitimization to the marginal subject in a realm formerly defined only by the oppressor.[46] Furthermore, as an act of resistance, this choice represents an opportunity to reclaim subjectivity and to make it visible. Consequently, the active association of multiple subjectivities configures a marginal community with political as well as social agency in the "third-space" of Condé's novel.

What can be referred to as the "third-space-community" intersects provocatively with George Revill's analysis of the value of community as a confrontation between self and locality. While Revill acknowledges that the concept of community is charged with both the notions of repressed individuality and romanticized nostalgia, he too seeks to redefine the community as a vibrant space in which the marginal subject can explore his/her individual identity. For Revill, as for Soja and Hooper, the community is more than a caring organic society of shared consciousness—it is a space that privileges diverse modes of living and thinking about a specific locality that are "fluid, permeable and conflictual."[47] Thus Revill's analysis similarly defines a place of openness and individual agency, while, at the same time, offering a configuration of space or settlement that, like the edge, is specific to the marginal community.

The process of defining the "common grounds" or a "third-space-community" differs radically from delineating the limited marginal space created by the repressive central hegemony. In fact, the "third-space community," representing the marginal subject's radical choice to occupy the edge, is not easily opposable to the generic central space of the oppressor. Rather than defining the space of the new community in the terms dependent on the center-margin-edge, one could propose that the third-space-community exists in a "deep space" contrary to the static plane dominated by the oppressive, hegemonic community. As such, the "deep space" requires the marginal subject to step off the "flat space" of the edge and enter an uncharted realm. With this step, the subject chooses a space that is simultaneously dangerous and unfamiliar, and full of opportunity and generative links to other subjects. Moreover, by rejecting the edge, he/she now occupies a community that is not rigidly structured by the linear constraints of time and space. The "marginal" subject is thus free to explore the space surrounding him/her and to simultaneously "live in" his/her past, present and future.

Storytelling as Bridging—Creating the Links between Marginal Subjects

While Revill, like Soja and Hooper, acknowledges the importance of choice in the formation of the community, he also insists on storytelling as the crucial element that serves to negotiate multiple subjective identities. In Revill's analysis, the individual defines himself/herself through language and the construction of texts; the story is a "psychological, social and spatial entity."[48] Using the concept of storytelling as bridging that Michael de Certeau develops in his work *The Practice of Everyday Life* (1984), Revill emphasizes how these stories or bridges not only create a shared sense of space, but also open new voids to be crossed, thereby re-invigorating the communal space and allowing for its fluidity. Storytelling, then, is a creative process that can both produce links between disparate subjects and charter new, unterritorialized space: "[S]tories build bridges between self and locality, certainty comes from possessing the means to describe oneself, and security comes from doing this in a way that is shared by the group and unavailable to outsiders. . . . [S]tories are spacious and . . . community is about creating a sense of space, rooted in the worldliness of locality and its everyday life."[49] As a means of expressing the imagination, stories allow marginal subjects to represent their experiences and ideas within a communal space. It is perhaps in this sense that Soja and Hooper's "third-space-communities" can best be understood as "real, imagined and more."[50] Because they are "real, imagined and more," these "third-space-communities" require the autobiographical expression of subjects who have not only made the choice to step out of their marginal positions, but also to actively participate in bridging the gaps dividing them from other subjects. Hence, autobiographical narratives or stories in the context of the "third-space-community" may be regarded as important and even political tools that ultimately link fragmented subjectivities.

Tituba as a Source of Community

Tituba, who dreams of hearing her song shared by her people, is the figure in whom the potential for a generative community centers in Condé's novel. Throughout the work Tituba is the prime example of the healing and reintegrating power found in telling and hearing autobiographical narratives. As she both reveals and accepts frank admissions of pain, she finds that the process provides more comfort than even intimate physical relations. She tells of the bond formed between herself and Benjamin through the exchange of autobiographical stories of suffering: "je dérivais tout aussi bien sur la mer de délices. Les moments les plus doux étaient cependant ceux où nous parlions. De nous. Seulement de nous."[51]

In the novel, speaking of oneself, openly revealing one's experiences of suffering and violation, and listening to the stories of others are fundamental aspects that define the bonds formed between sufferers. As Tituba talks with John Indian, Hester, Iphigène, Elizabeth Parris and Deodatus, she breaks a restrictive silence and admits her pain, suffering and imperfection. While the shared narratives might seem to leave the victim weak and vulnerable, in fact, Condé emphasizes that they form the foundation for strong communal bonds. In a voluntary and intimate relationship—so different from the forced Puritanical confession—the victim reintegrates himself/herself and joins a chorus of once-silent victims.[52] While, for Condé, the victims' voices are still soft and disharmonious, in her epilogue, she represents the solidarity of a united community of victims and its potential for enacting real change.

Notes

1. Maryse Condé's use of the word "Indian" to designate the Native American will be followed throughout this chapter.

2. Throughout this chapter, the masculine singular subject pronoun will be used for the Puritan/oppressor, because in Condé's work, he is typically male. Similarly, the masculine singular will refer to the black man, as in Fanon's work the black subject is most often male. Frantz Fanon, *Peau noire, masques blancs* (Paris: *Editions de Seuil*, 1952).

3. Condé's narrator describes Tituba's trial: "En effet, les accusées ne cessaient de mentionner un 'homme noir' qui les forçait à écrire dans son Livre." Maryse Condé, *Moi, Tituba* (Paris: Mercure de France, 1988), 170.

4. Fanon, *Peau noire*, 11.

5. John McCumber defines "essential identity" as "an inconsistency: while it has no other legitimacy than that of being derived from certain chaotic experiences, this is the very legitimacy that it now denies to the new characteristics which have emerged from the new experiences of the group." John McCumber, "Dialectic Identity in a 'Post-Critical' Era: A Hegelian Reading" in *The South Atlantic Quarterly* 94 (Fall, 1995): 1154. Tituba, and the group of 'others' who unite at the end of Condé's novel, possess what McCumber positively refers to as a "dialectic identity": the identity of the group is no longer a static set of

essential determinations, but something that transforms itself over time—changing to meet new challenges. What belonging to the group means is not a matter of having a certain set of characteristics, but of fitting oneself into a certain story, taking a particular identity and helping to transform it over time. McCumber, "Dialectic Identity," 1155.

6. Fanon, *Peau noire*, 93.

7. Fanon, *Peau noire*, 156. As Fanon argues, "[les Noirs sont] enfermés dans cette objectivité écrasante." Fanon, *Peau noire*, 88.

8. Condé, *Moi*, 56.

9. One such case of mental illness among the Puritans is Samuel Parris's son.

10. Condé, *Moi*, 70. Tituba emphasizes the Puritan's repugnance toward their own flesh: "Ces gens-là ne supportaient pas la nudité, même d'un enfant." Condé, *Moi*, 128.

11. Condé, *Moi*, 169.

12. Condé, *Moi*, 58.

13. Condé, *Moi*, 136.

14. Condé, *Moi*, 162.

15. Michael Warner, "New English Sodom," in *American Literature* 64, no. 1 (1993): 25.

16. Condé, *Moi*, 143.

17. This scene throws up interesting analogies with the masks of the Ku Klux Klan.

18. Condé, *Moi*, 143. Condé highlights the "bird of prey" symbolism, referring to "les oiseaux de proie" five times in chapter one of Part Two. Consequently, the bird of prey, which earlier epitomized an extremely negative connotation of "blackness," now ironically represents the white Puritan.

19. Condé, *Moi*, 43.

20. Fanon shows how the mere sight of black skin can cause irrational terror among whites, quoting a young white boy: "Maman, regarde le nègre, j'ai peur!" Fanon, *Peau noire*, 90.

21. Condé, *Moi*, 46. Tituba describes the especial fear that Susanna's blue eyes cause. Fanon writes, "Et nous qui sommes Antillais, nous ne le savons que trop: le nègre craint les yeux bleus, répète-t-on là-bas." Fanon, *Peau noire*, 34.

22. Condé, *Moi*, 58.

23. Condé, *Moi*, 193. The understated word-play in Condé's text, as in the sentence, "Il la mettait au compte de cette foncière cruauté, qui lui semblait caractériser ceux qu'ils appelaient *les Gentils*," repeatedly emphasizes her often ironic tone.

24. When she learns of the murder of Gilles Corey, Tituba asks in a similar vein, "Où était Satan? Ne se cachait-il pas dans les plis des manteaux des juges? Ne parlait-il pas par la voix des juristes et des hommes d'Église?" Condé, *Moi*, 182.

25. Condé, *Moi*, 169.

26. Condé, *Moi*, 13.

27. Hortence J. Spillers, "Mama's Baby, Papa's Maybe: An American Grammar Book," in *Diacritics*, (Summer, 1997): 67.

28. Condé, *Moi*, 219. Aimé Césaire writes, "Au bout du petit matin bourgeonnant d'anses frêles les Antilles qui ont faim, les Antilles grêlées de petite vérole, les Antilles dynamitées d'alcool, échouées dans la boue de cette baie, dans la poussière de cette ville sinistrement échoués." Aimé Césaire, *Cahier d'un retour au pays natal* (Paris: Présence Africaine, 1994), 8.

29. Anne McClintock rejects the term "post-colonial," emphasizing, among other things, its complicity with the myth of progress, its denial of multiplicity and difference, and its neglect of the specific role of women. Anne McClintock, "The Angel of Progress: Pitfalls of the Term "Post-Colonialism," in *Social Text* 31, no.2 (1992): 84–98.

30. Tituba (like many slaves) is actually of mixed race, having a white father and an African mother.

31. Edouard Glissant describes the white man's physical violence on the slave ship: "Dans l'univers absolument fou du bateau négrier, là où les hommes déportés sont annihilés physiquement, la femme africaine subit la plus totale des agressions qui est le viol quotidien et répété d'un équipage de marins rendus démentes par l'exercice de leur métier; après quoi, au débarquement sur la terre nouvelle, la femme

a sur l'homme un inappréciable avantage; elle connaît déjà le maître." His powerful narrative illuminates Tituba's experience as a slave. Edouard Glissant, *Caribbean Discourse: Selected Essays*, trans. J. Michael Dash (Charlottesville: University Press of Virginia, 1989).

32. Michel Foucault, "The History of Sexuality," in *Power/Knowledge: Selected Interviews and Other Writings*, ed. Colin Gordon (New York: Pantheon Books, 1980), 186.

33. Laura Mulvey, *Visual and Other Pleasures* (Bloomington: Indiana University Press, 1983), 22.

34. Mulvey, *Visual and Other*, 22.

35. Homi K. Bhabha, *The Location of Culture* (London: Routledge, 1994), 79. Homi Bhabha identifies fetishism, scopophilia, and the Imaginary as the primary regimes of visibility and discursivity within the circulation of colonial power. Bhabha defines the role of the fetish in the colonial fantasy as: "What Fanon calls the epidermal schema—it is not, like the sexual fetish, a secret. Skin, as the key signifier of cultural and racial difference in the stereotype is the most visible of fetishes . . . it is a fixated form of the colonial subject which facilitates colonial relations, and sets up a discursive form of racial and cultural opposition in terms of which colonial power is exercised." Bhabha, *The Location*, 78. According to Bhabha, the tropes of the fetish within the colonial fantasy's system of representation are metaphor and metonymy. Bhabha defines the scopic drive as: "The drive that represents the pleasure in 'seeing.' Which has the look as its object of desire, is related both to the myth of origins, the primal scene, and to the problematic of fetishism and locates the surveyed object within the 'imaginary' relation. Like voyeurism, surveillance must depend for its effectiveness on the 'active consent' which is its real or mythical correlate (but always real as myth) and establishes in the scopic space the illusion of the object relation." Bhabha, *The Location*, 78. Finally, Bhabha defines the imaginary as a realm containing two forms of identification—narcissism and aggressivity. Although the argument is not developed here, the voyeurism that Mulvey describes as sadistic is slightly different from Bhabha's definition of the scopic drive, thereby suggesting another possible element within the colonial regimes of visibility and discursivity.

36. Condé, *Moi*, 18.

37. Condé, *Moi*, 144.

38. Nathaniel Hawthorne, *The Scarlet Letter* (New York: New American Library, 1959), 88.

39. The Puritan's insistence on spectacle is revealed as the crowd of Puritans gathers to watch the slaves being sold at the market: "Toute la bonne société de Bridgetown s'assemblait pour regarder, afin d'en railler en choeur la démarche, les traits et la posture . . . des esclaves qui descendaient par fournées entières." Thus, in addition to suffering physical mutilation, the slave is further tortured as he is subjected to the degrading and violating gaze of the oppressor. Condé, *Moi*, 45. As well as the black and the Indian, already marked by their inescapable skin colors, the Puritan marks the Jew—visually dividing him from that which is pure and white. Condé not only points to the historical suffering of the Jewish race, she also specifically emphasizes that the Jew does not escape the voyeuristic puritanical oppression: "Cela commença quand la mézuzah, placée au-dessus de la porte d'entrée de la maison de Benjamin Cohen d'Azevedo comme de celle des deux autres familles juives, fut arrachée et remplacée par un dessin obscène à la peinture noire." Condé, *Moi*, 205. Even as the Puritans violate and destroy the sanctity of the Jewish homes, they inflict their familiar brand of rape on the inhabitants of the houses. Once the house is violated, the door—the entryway to the home—becomes a locus of pain, forever recalling the humiliating gaze of the oppressor and degrading the one private space the Jews are allowed. Moreover, by relegating the Jew to the private, "feminine" sphere and then degrading that space, the Puritan makes gendered as well as religious attacks on the Jew, who is figured both as a woman and an infidel.

40. Condé, *Moi*, 160.

41. Condé, *Moi*, 39.

42. Condé writes: "[Pour des écrivains femmes des Antilles] s'agit beaucoup plus d'une dénonciation subtile de la condition des rapports homme/femme, d'une réflexion sur leurs difficultés ou leur dégradation. L'homme est présenté comme une victime dont le sort se joue en d'autres sphères et dont les fautes peuvent être expliquées." Condé's text, *La Parole des femmes*, is theoretically linked to her novel, *Moi, Tituba*. Maryse Condé, *La Parole des femmes* (Paris: Editions l'Harmattan, 1993), 39.

43. Patrick ffrench's article, "Community in Maryse Condé's *La Traversée de la Mangrove*," emphasizes that "the literature of the Antilles, in which the community, rather than the individual hero or heroine, is

valorized and recognized as constructed out of relations to the other, relations of ethnic, sexual or generation differences, provides a concrete and vital focus for . . . debate . . . involving the recognition of a non-unified, relational community." His important article focuses on the dead stranger as an absent central figure that brings together a multiplicity of interrelating voices. In *Moi, Tituba*, Tituba similarly unites a group of voices, each with his/her own interrelated song, in a life pattern that continues after her death. Patrick ffrench, "Community in Maryse Condé's: *Traversée de la Mangrove*," *French Forum* 22 (1997): 94.

44. Edward Soja and Barbara Hooper, "The Spaces that Difference Makes," in *Place and the Politics of Identity*, ed. Michael Keith and Steve Pile (London: Routledge, 1993), 187.

45. Bell Hooks, 145–49.

46. Edward and Hooper, "The Spaces that," 190.

47. George Revill, "Reading *Rosehill*: Community, Identity, and Inner-city Derby," in *Place and the Politics of Identity*, 121.

48. Revill, "Reading *Rosehill*," 130.

49. Revill, "Reading *Rosehill*," 137.

50. Edward and Hooper, "The Spaces that," 192.

51. Condé, *Moi*, 198.

52. McCumber defines a group of people such as the community of sufferers that Condé represents in *Moi, Tituba* as possessing a "dialectic identity." He describes the importance of the discrete story/history within a larger group of universal humanity: "For to be a "Jew" (or anything else) is not to have a unique set of properties, but to have a history in the course of which various properties are added and subtracted at various times. And while this history may be unique and 'particular' to a group's identity, it is also always in constant interplay with a larger history, ultimately that of unrealized humanity." McCumber, "Dialectic Identity," 157.

14

Literature in Guiana: The D'Chimbo Narratives

Florence Martin

I NTRODUCING FRENCH GUIANA'S LITERATURE is a deceptively simple matter: simple because it is relatively new and unknown;[1] deceptive because its very identity seems as elusive and diverse as *guyanité* (the identity of French Guiana).

The debate around the notion of a distinctive Guianese identity—or *guyanité*—is at once complex and acute. According to Ndagano,[2] the terms *négritude, créolité* and *antillanité* (Glissant) do not apply to French Guiana. *Guyanité* is shared by a number of various ethnic groups settled in a mosaic-like space: the large Creole community (from Martinique, Guadeloupe and Guiana), various Amerindian communities, the Bushinenge (of African descent), an Arabic community (since the late nineteenth century), an Asian community (the Hmong since 1977, the Chinese), a South American community (particularly Brazilian), a group of Haïtian refugees and the "métropolitains" (from France). Hence a large part of *guyanité* seems to reside in its historical, ethnic, and linguistic multiplicity, expressed in the multilingual tales, songs and carnival performances of its rich oral literature.

Most of Guiana's written literature in French was produced during the twentieth century against the backdrop of *guyanité's* oral literature and culture. At the risk of oversimplifying, it follows two basic directions: Creole and Francophone.[3] This overarching duality in Guianese literature reflects some of the tensions between the ex-centric territory of Guiana and the French seat of power and discourse, as its authors negotiate a distinct Guianese identity and tradition, "differing" in the Derridian sense of the term (*différant* in space, time, and obviously meaning) from the identity and tradition of France. In this sense, the D'Chimbo narratives constitute an exemplar of Guianese literary production. Each narrative deconstructs the discourse of power from within the ruler's linguistic code and rhetoric, and can be read as a textbook Foucauldian case study.[4] Each narrative adopts the rhetorical tricks of the ruling discourse to better subvert it and replace it with its own discourse.

The Black Code

The repressive discourse to be deconstructed can be traced back to the 1685 *Code Noir*, the King's "legal" document regulating the situation of black slaves. As such, it represents the subtext or prehistory of the first D'Chimbo narrative by Frenchman Frédéric Bouyer, with which the latter engages in intertextual play.

According to Louis Sala-Molins, the *Black Code* rested on a colossal paradox: "la monarchie française fonde en droit le non-droit à l'État de droit des esclaves noirs, dont l'inexistence juridique constitue la seule et unique définition légale."[5] Under the guise of legislating masters' behaviors toward their slaves (and perhaps, limiting various forms of abuse), this code bridged two distinct spaces: the European space of France, where slavery was prohibited, and the French king's distant colonies, where it was thriving. In France, the slave did not exist. But in the colonies, he/she did, and legally so, when he/she disobeyed the master or the king. Such a code was possible in Catholic France because of a peculiar reading of a particular episode in the Bible: Ham, who disrespected his father by gazing at his nudity, provoked the wrath of Noah and, above him, God (the ultimate Father). As a result, his son, Canaan, and all his descendants were cursed. The whole dynasty was therefore punished and reduced to slavery, in order to expiate the original sin of their ancestor Ham. An absurd parallel is then drawn, allowing this divine punishment to become a justification for trading in black slaves, "obviously" all descendants of the accursed Ham, and exploiting them on the colony's plantations. A dizzying syllogism led to the emergence of an eerie existential equation between skin tone and social rank or economic function: to be black = to be a slave.

This equation was so well understood by the beneficiaries of the triangular market that the precise term "black slave"—as opposed to, simply, "slave"—only appeared in Black Code B (appended to the Black Code in 1724). Throughout the 1685 *Code Noir* "esclave" and "nègre" are interchangeable terms that denote the same entity. The code strips African slaves of their identity and humanity, and reduces them to working bodies, tools. The slave thus becomes a body-being, codified and mute, who must be taught work and Catholicism. Slaves are not subjects of the kingdom: they are its property. The code effectively places them in a double locus: a no man's land with respect to civil rights and the Catholic Church[6].

Although slavery was first abolished in 1794, when, in the *élan* of Revolutionary ideals, the slaves became citizens, the colonists were quick to organize resistance, and, less than a decade later, reinstated slavery. Various updated codes sprang up in the colonies, including Victor Hughes's Ruling Decree of April 1803 in Guiana: "le but du rétablissement de l'esclavage est de faire prospérer cette colonie dont le sol avide de culture . . . n'attend que des bras, de bonnes lois et la protection du gouvernement."[7]

Hence the slaves, once again subjected to the Black Code (only repealed for good in 1848), once again non-citizens, were now reduced to the status of "hands" whose purpose was to cultivate a "hungry land." The slave was perceived as a controlled, lucrative bodily machine intended to help produce cotton, cocoa or coffee; he or she was a useful body in the Foucauldian sense of the term,[8] socially located somewhere between nature (the soil to be tilled) and a certain form of anonymity (no access to property or titles). The French code defined the black negatively through a series of absences, and by erasing his or her very being from his or her social identity. But how did this representation change in post-slavery times?

D'Chimbo: An Unlikely Guianese Character

It is perhaps one of the lesser ironies of French Guiana's history that one of its most celebrated figures, D'Chimbo, was not Guianese, and yet has become an icon for *guyanité* at various points in history. It is also in keeping with the nineteenth-century colonial culture of the place: like many other residents, D'Chimbo was born elsewhere and later brought to the colony, where he died.[9]

His name started to appear repeatedly in the news section of the local newspaper in 1860 and 1861 in connection with alleged thefts, murders and rapes, which were described in sensational journalistic terms, and the seemingly vain attempts of the colonial police to arrest him. Although his story took place over a decade after the second (and final) abolition of slavery, D'Chimbo's portrayal by the newspapers and colonial authorities presents striking similarities to the image of the (disobedient) slaves of former times, or more exactly to the "Nègres marrons," i.e., the dreaded "slaves who escaped into the forested interiors, and were called 'Maroons' or 'wild cattle' after the Spanish term 'cimarrón', . . . established independent communities, and . . . became a feared fighting force."[10] D'Chimbo is perceived as a dangerous outcast escaping into the forest (nature) from society's order (civilization). Viewed through the prism of the old Black Code, he is further dehumanized as a monstrous criminal. Such a conflation of representations crystallized into the figure of the "Nègre sauvage" dreaded by the European and Creole colonists.[11] His story spilled out beyond the reductive frame of the *Feuille de la Guyane Française*: over the following century and a half, the name reappears in various tales, oral and written, in French and Creole. The oral tales fashioned a legendary character endowed with magical powers (thanks to which he kept the police at bay for two years), whose "exemplary" death was inhumane (after he was beheaded, the authorities preserved his head in a jar and buried his body), whose voice was the voice of the people (he spoke Creole). The written narratives, though nurtured by the oral tales, have a more political orientation: they deconstruct the first French story written about D'Chimbo and recreate a new symbolic character with his own code.

Frédéric Bouyer's *Notes et souvenirs*

The first fully fledged D'Chimbo narrative (*Le brigand D'Chimbo, dit le Rongou. Ses crimes, son arrestation, sa mort*) was published in 1867 as an account within Frédéric Bouyer's travel book (*La Guyane Française. Notes et souvenirs d'un voyage effectué en 1862–1863*), which he wrote shortly after his return from Guiana.[12] One of its most striking features is that, almost twenty years after the abolition of slavery, it shares a troubling semantic code with the larger narrative of slavery in the French colonies as it appears in the Black Code.

In his historical account, Bouyer hints at the reason why the African D'Chimbo found himself in Guiana in the 1850s. In 1848 the former slaves' strike led desperate white settlers to recruit workers from outside Guiana, and the new "hiring" procedure of "engagés" (hired immigrants) or "captifs" was devised:

> Les futurs travailleurs immigrés sont amenés sur les côtes africaines sous le statut de "captifs." Après la visite médicale, les captifs sélectionnés (en fonction de leur état de santé et de leur âge) prennent connaissance, par l'intermédiaire d'un interprète, du contrat qui leur est proposé: il y est question de liberté, de salaire et d'un éventuel rapatriement à l'issue des années d'engagement.[13]

Bouyer's chronicle presents "un immigrant africain nommé D'Chimbo, plus généralement connu sous le nom de Rongou. Les Rongous sont une tribu de nègres qui habitent la rivière du Gabon, sur la côte occidentale d'Afrique."[14] At this early point, the individual disappears in the collective tribal name, Rongou, before being reduced to a monstrous body in the classical sense of the term, a body that evades any strictly human classification and combines elements from the human, the vegetal and the animal. "Il est nu jusqu'à la ceinture. Son torse noir et athlétique exhibe de nombreuses cicatrices et d'étranges tatouages. Les épines de la forêt et les balles ont déchiqueté cet épiderme sombre. . . . Il ressemble au djina, à ce gorille colossal, dont il est le compatriote, et dont il a en partagé la force redoutable et les appétits sensuels." This polymorphous racist image is then finished off with a good pinch of sexism: "Les bras musculeux de cet hercule africain se terminent par des mains d'enfant. Ses jambes, pareilles à des piliers, reposent sur des pieds qui feraient l'envie et l'orgueil d'une jeune fille. Ces mains s'attachent par des poignets, ces pieds par des chevilles d'une finesses extrême." [15]

Some monster indeed! The comparison with the child is a common racist cliché, but the mention of his delicate feminine joints is troubling. D'Chimbo's idiosyncratic brand of monstrosity assembles mismatched elements: virile muscles, the sexuality of a gorilla, a dark skin tattooed by the forest (an enduring, indeed bullet-proof bark), *and* charming, feminine features. This body is disorienting, both fearsome and eerily attractive, never seen in its entirety: the epidermis, an ankle, an arm, a "bull's neck," the text keeps adding to the list. The entire body is carefully deconstructed (fetishized?) to then be reassembled as the monster-body of Nature. D'Chimbo has trespassed the permissible limits of Hughes's ruling text: from a "hand" intended to till the land, he has become an unruly, threatening "bricolage" (man, beast, woman, child) erring in the woods, beyond the reach of the colonial order.

Bouyer often compares D'Chimbo to a wild animal; his shelter becomes "l'antre de la bête fauve." [16] Even his speech attests to his monstrosity in two separate ways: first, he does not speak the language of civilization and requires Bouyer to be his "interpreter" for the (civilized) reader ("D'Chimbo s'exprime en langue créole que je traduis en français pour l'intelligence du lecteur" [17]); secondly, he cannot control his verbal outbursts after he has kidnapped and raped one of his victims, Julienne Cabassou. "Dans les intervalles de ses lubriques désirs et ses jactances cruelles, entre ses cyniques élans et ses menaces de mort, sa nature sauvage se répand en impressions naïves et en puérilités. S'il a la passion de la bête il a les étonnements et les admirations de l'enfant." [18] He embodies a total lack of self-control: like a child, he acts on impulse and cannot rein in his desires, instincts or chatter. He knows no social rules, no constraint.

Yet this wild monster evades the police for two years and is soon believed to have magical powers that allow him to make himself invisible and invincible, as well as appearing in two different places at the same time. [19] In the end, he is caught not by the police but by a fellow Rongou, brought in to Cayenne in front of a gaping crowd, tried and executed. Only at his trial is he given access to direct speech, and, when asked how his tribe punishes a killer, replies: "on le tue." [20] Bouyer's conclusion reads him as a terrifying criminal only: "Le nom du Rongou restera toujours à la Guyane comme un sinistre épouvantail. Amplifiée par l'imagination populaire, son histoire sera le sujet de terribles récits. . . ." [21]

Serge Patient's "Chronique Coloniale"

Guiana's twentieth-century (re)creations of the narrative play with Bouyer's image of the *Nègre* D'Chimbo attribute other qualities and values to the protagonist's body and language, and sometimes situate the story in a different time frame altogether.

Serge Patient's *Le Nègre du Gouverneur* (1972) dates the legend a little earlier in history: the protagonist is a slave who ends up working for Victor Hughes, then governor. The novel, ironically subtitled "Chronique coloniale," introduces semantic ambiguity even before the first page: will the narrative be written from the standpoint of the colonist or the colonized? The narrative voice remains at an ironic distance throughout the tale. It is ruthless in its evaluation of the small, stuffy world of the colonists, while maintaining the same ironical play with the character of D'Chimbo.

The narrative starts by describing how D'Chimbo was brought from Africa to Guiana against his will. A first inner monologue gives the reader an insight into the hero's new identity:

> Avant même de la comprendre, il prêtait à la langue des blancs mille prestiges et mille sortilèges. N'était-ce pas là qu'il fallait chercher le secret de leur puissance? Ainsi, quand ils le regardaient tout droit dans les yeux, et prononçaient distinctement ce mot: nègre, il ne pouvait douter que "nègre" fût désormais à la fois son prénom et son patronyme. Il sentait D'Chimbo menacé par quelque mort initiatique, et, cessant d'être D'Chimbo, il devenait nègre.[22]

The name—and very being—of D'Chimbo has been erased by the master's language. This language, still unknown to him at this point, exerts a formidable fascination over the vanquished man. It seems to have the power of making and undoing people's identities, just as it threatens him with "ritualistic death" and reduces him to a black body. D'Chimbo realizes that if he wants to be free again he will have to "master" this language in all the senses of the word: learn and know its every subtlety; command it, and no longer be commanded by it, no longer have his own identity at the mercy of the foreign tongue.

At the slave market where he is put on display he is perceived first and foremost as a body. At the time of the narrative, the slave trade is about to become illegal, and the only way for the planters to ensure a free available work force in the future is to have their own slaves reproduce. Hence the auctioneer's speech on the value of D'Chimbo:

> D'où la valeur exceptionnelle d'un étalon tel que D'Chimbo.
>   Comme pour étayer sa démonstration le commissaire-priseur, d'un doigt preste et habile, défit le noeud qui retenait le pagne autour des hanches de l'esclave. . . .
>   Mesdames, voilez-vous la face; messieurs les habitants, voici le sexe de l'étalon.[23]

The body is by now no longer a mere productive tool ("hand"), but a showpiece that is "spectacular" in more ways than one and prized for its other function: a body to reproduce other tool-bodies. Once demoted to the status of silent stud, the unwitting D'Chimbo nonetheless notes the term that signals his second difference to the viewers of his body: "Un mot l'avait frappé: sexe. Le commissaire, en le prononçant, faisait curieusement claquer sa langue et pointait sa baguette de bambou sur un détail d'anatomie que même les bêtes ont coutume de dérober à la curiosité des foules. Si bien que D'Chimbo, comprenant à la longue ce qui, chez lui, était le sexe: 'voilà mon vocabulaire enrichi,' pensa-t-il."[24] Bestiality has been displaced here: it is now located in the eyes of the voyeurs, the beholding authorities and the indiscreet crowd, and no longer inscribed on D'Chimbo's body. The authorities, by revealing the most intimate part of his body to the public, have refused him a courtesy even granted to animals. Patient has inverted the code of Bouyer's narrative: D'Chimbo is no longer a rapist, but the victim of a symbolic rape (the gaze of the crowd on his nudity). Here, D'Chimbo is no longer a monster endowed with animal and feminine traits, but rather, the titillating hyperbolic representation of virility. However, it is thanks to this hypnotic organ of his that he will hoist himself out of slavery. For, once he realizes that this part of his body heightens his commercial value, he learns to play the whites' game to his own advantage. He exchanges lessons in French for sexual favours with Lady Stanley (which rhymes with Chatterley). By means of this barter he comes to share in the master's language and power, even reverses the master/slave relationship with Lady Stanley (one of several ironic dialectical moves in the novel).

This first Guianese rewriting of the legend subverts the values of the initial narrative from within, as if D'Chimbo were the Guianese equivalent of the African-American trickster figure. This African-American folklore hero was at first a powerless yet cunning slave who tricked his oppressor through his own manipulation of the master's discourse and system—a rhetorical strategy called "signifying." The latter, originating in Western Africa, was transmitted through the oral tradition tales featuring the Lion (the powerful) and the Monkey (the apparently weaker yet shrewd one).[25] The Monkey mimics the Lion and tells him tall tales replete with rhetorical figures that the Lion interprets literally. The Lion then finds himself trapped, isolated outside the Monkey's discourse, unable to understand the double voice of the Monkey, who is playing on two discursive registers simultaneously.

Similarly, D'Chimbo acquires two languages and plays on two registers. His barter with Lady Stanley soon disrupts the initial meaning of "mistress": "M. Stanley était son maître; milady pouvait bien être sa maîtresse."[26] He has a double identity: he is both the African slave and the one who has mastered the master's codes and can play with them for his own benefit. He ends up achieving a relatively high level of power by "playing white": Victor Hughes hires him as a black sergeant to chase Maroon slaves and he falls in love with white Virginie, whom he hopes to marry. His story is one of social success—he is no longer a slave, but a man—but also alienates him from the black population and assimilates him to the white. Here the trickster not only survives but regains his lost status as a man.

The subsequent readings of D'Chimbo tend to highlight a different double vision in which he is both a victim and a resistant. The identification of D'Chimbo as an ambiguous Maroon becomes more and more frequent.

Elie Stephenson's "théâtre bilingue"

Elie Stephenson's two plays, *La Nouvelle Légende de D'Chimbo* (1984) and *Massak* (1986) both invite D'Chimbo to speak on stage, and achieve a double makeover of the legendary character. Both plays turn D'Chimbo into an identity-grounding political and cultural figure. Interestingly enough, both plays are published in one book under the general title *La Nouvelle Légende de D'Chimbo suivi de Massak: Théâtre bilingue* (in the *"Paroles"* series of Ibis Rouge Éditions). Here, D'Chimbo definitely speaks out.

The first play presents D'Chimbo as the victim of a triple illusion: the promise of full integration into Creole life through the making of money (he is a gold digger but is exploited by his boss); the hope for love (but no Guianese woman wants a "nègre gros-sirop"—a man as dark as cane syrup); and the expected recognition of his identity via a form of négritude (but he comes directly from Africa, not Guiana, and is not forgiven for his origins). His disappointment is so bitter that D'Chimbo becomes an outlaw, a rapist and a murderer. The play seems to illustrate that, to parody de Beauvoir's formula, one is not born a monstrous criminal, one becomes so.

When D'Chimbo appears on the stage of the *Nouvelle Légende*, he introduces himself thus: "Ils me traquent tous les jours. . . . Ils veulent ma peau, disent-ils, ils veulent m'attraper, m'emprisonner et me guillotiner! Mais moi, D'Chimbo aucune chaîne ne peut me retenir, je brise toutes les chaînes."[27] Refusing to be a victim, he proclaims himself invincible. Of the supernatural qualities alluded to by Bouyer, he has kept an ancestral (African) knowledge of the plants that protect him. But, in a state of drunkenness, he reveals his secret to Elena[28] (a reincarnation of Julienne Cabassou), who subsequently betrays him. He is then arrested, tried and executed. The last image of D'Chimbo in *La Nouvelle Légende* offers a counterpoint to the ones found in the texts by Bouyer and Patient. The picture of the mute slave offered to the gaze of an indiscreet crowd now gives way to one of a man watching the crowd and talking back. D'Chimbo has moved from being an object (of a gaze or a sentence) to a subject and orator: "Vous savez, si les Blancs n'avaient pas amené nos ancêtres ici, si les Blancs ne m'avaient pas fait quitter mon village Roungoun, si nous-mêmes Nègres nous ne laissions pas les Blancs nous mener comme des enfants, peut-être tout ceci ne serait pas arrivé, peut-être je ne serais pas aujourd'hui D'Chimbo, le criminel."[29] D'Chimbo incriminates everyone in his speech: the white raiders, himself, his ancestors, the onlookers. Everyone has a role to play in his story. He is no longer the monstrous outcast of the first legend, but the result and victim of all the stories that have preceded him and led to his own. He is not the *Nègre du Gouverneur* who wants to master the French language and European know-how. Although the quotation above is in French, it comes from a translation printed opposite the original text: the play was produced in Creole, then published in a bilingual edition.

The second play, *Massak*, a rewriting of Patient's novel, *Le Nègre du gouverneur*, features Kalimbo (as a new version of the governor's "Negro"), whose vision of freedom as negotiable stands in sharp contrast to the warring, uncompromising ideas of Pompée, the Maroon leader. *Massak*, with its ambiguous title,[30] presents Kalimbo (alias D'Chimbo) after his initiation into French, white culture, working within the colonial system (he is employed by Hughes). Pompée, who has found refuge in the woods with his fellow rebels to fight against the white system, only sees Kalimbo as a "Nègre Blanc," i.e., a black dedicated to mimicking the whites. Kalimbo, however, claims that he too is a fighter: "Et c'est là ma force, je prends la langue du Blanc, je vole sa culture, je vole ses connaissances et je deviens aussi capable que lui. Il m'apprend, il m'apprend des choses, le Blanc, il m'apprend ses manières, ses méthodes et il s'amuse de mes imitations. Mais il ne sait pas qu'il me nourrit, qu'il me donne des forces, ses forces pour le vaincre."[31] Here, Kalimbo hesitates between the signifying trickster figure and an eagerly acquiescing figure who seems to embrace the whites' methods, knowledge and way of life. This reading of the *Nègre du gouverneur* is intended to highlight the valor of the resisting hero, Pompée, who refuses compromise and defines himself as "un homme en guerre pour la liberté," as opposed to Kalimbo, whom he deems "un homme de génuflection."[32] In the end Kalimbo is betrayed by the Governor, whom he believed to be honest, but who cannot forgive him the color of his skin and his achievement in regaining his status as a man (Kalimbo was seen kissing Virginie).

Yet, Kalimbo and Pompée can be seen as the two faces of a Janus-like interpretation of the original D'Chimbo figure: Pompée the Maroon in the woods, is believed to have magical powers (Victor Hugues: "Ne dit-on pas maintenant que les balles ne peuvent l'atteindre!"[33]) while Kalimbo disobeys the governor in the end, refusing to lead him and his troops to massacre the Maroons, thus becoming a Maroon himself. In the last scene both characters are merged in an eerie vocal call-and-response: the jailed Kalimbo listens to Pompée's voice off stage: "Ils te trahiront, ils saliront ta mémoire. Ils feront de toi un être sans foi ni loi. Un violeur de Blanches qu'on a dû assassiner pour le bien de la société."[34] Here the narrative has come full circle: Stephenson alludes directly to the first legend written by Bouyer. Kalimbo knows "les mensonges des livres"[35] in this last scene, but still hopes that future generations will distinguish between the white written legend and the black oral story. Just before the curtain falls, he starts singing Pompée's song, showing that it is through performance that the authentic narrative of Kalimbo/D'Chimbo and Pompée and the Maroons will be handed down from generation to generation.

This final scene is perhaps the most enlightening of all the rewritings of the D'Chimbo story because it sheds light on two questions: access to speech, and cultural transmission.

D'Chimbo: A Liberated Guianese Character

In these various narratives D'Chimbo gradually speaks out against the one who had turned him into a tongue-less body. Bouyer's D'Chimbo only acquires access to direct speech at the end of the text, when he pronounces his own death sentence, translated by the French author from Creole into French. The language of power is still out of D'Chimbo's reach.

In Patient's novel D'Chimbo appropriates French and even outgrows his mistress's knowledge. "Le temps vint où sa soif insatiable de savoir excéda les modestes connaissances de son institutrice anglaise."[36] He can therefore talk to Lady Stanley on equal terms in his "carbet" (his dwelling in the woods) and insists that she use the formal mode of address with him, as opposed to the denigrating "tu" which has hitherto marked their social difference linguistically: "Ici, dans mon carbet, je ne suis l'esclave de personne. Dites-moi vous, je l'exige."[37] Once he has mastered the language of power, he can define the code of Lady Stanley's behavior on his own terms.

In Stephenson's *Massak* Kalimbo uses his linguistic skills to affirm his superiority over Victor Hughes: "J'avais ma langue. Elle est aussi riche, aussi complète que la vôtre. Je peux tout exprimer dans ma langue. D'ailleurs, j'ai appris votre langue, je l'utilise, alors que vous ne connaissez même pas la mienne. N'est-ce pas que je suis plus intelligent que vous!"[38] This time, the other is Victor Hughes, who is in the dark, so to speak. Kalimbo may be about to die, but he has achieved a formidable role reversal: the master is now the ignorant one.

In *La nouvelle légende* speaking out is given two meanings: the character expresses himself directly on stage; furthermore, the play was written in Creole and published alongside its French translation. This distance from the French language can be seen as a political and ontological gesture toward (re)defining a Guianese *Être-au-monde*: "J'écris en créole pour le lecteur créolophone dont la relation avec cette langue a quelque chose d'indéfinissable. J'écris ou je fais traduire en français pour partager avec d'autres mon appartenance à ce monde. C'est ma façon à moi de me réconcilier avec moi-même."[39] The choice of two languages may also reflect the author's desire to express the reality of polyglossia in Guiana. The audience watches the performance of a play that, written from within the Guianese author's own bilingualism, (re)claims its linguistic plurality, and unites the oral and written traditions of Guiana. D'Chimbo's tale can now be both performed in Creole and read in French.

This enterprise does not follow the diktats of the French hegemonic discourse on "francophonie." In some ways, Patient and Stephenson are engaged in a literary form of "marronnage," writing in the language of the fugitive, the man who escapes from the official French language and reality. Writing from the periphery, the authors are themselves D'Chimbos of a kind, liberating their own writing from the strictures of the remote French center.

This literary "marronnage" contaminates the core of the narrative, transforming the story of a serial killer into an empowering tale of liberation. In Bouyer's version, D'Chimbo breaks free of his condition of "engagé" in the woods, but, once away from "civilization," he turns into a brutal criminal. His freedom is interpreted as a regression to the chaos of "nature." In the hands of Guianese authors his tale becomes a liberation narrative meant to inspire the people of Guiana. Addressing a twentieth-century audience, Patient's chronicle then becomes a political interrogation of the benefits and drawbacks of assimilation, while Stephenson's plays read D'Chimbo and Pompée/Kalimbo as figures of political "engagement." In the last scene of *Massak* the imprisoned Kalimbo sees his own sacrifice as a victory over the temptation to assimilate.[40]

D'Chimbo can thus be read as a significant thread running through the history of Guiana's dynamic recent literature: each D'Chimbo narrative reflects a moment of political consciousness and another step in the home-grown, organic construction of *guyanité*. Yet the written litera-ture in French and/or Creole is only the tip of the iceberg: numerous oral D'Chimbo narratives contribute significant variations on the theme. In fact, the legend of D'Chimbo as a founding text is still in the making, for the character offers endless opportunities for improvisation, like a jazz standard waiting to be picked up at the next jam session.

Notes

1. Books on the francophone literature of the region mention only Guiana briefly—if at all. Corzani's *La littérature des Antilles-Guyane françaises* (Fort-de-France: Désormeaux, 1978) devotes a few pages of its six volumes to Guianese authors. Colette Maximin's comparative work *Littératures caribéennes com-parées* (Pointe-à-Pitre and Paris: Éditions Jasor-Karthala, 1996) studies carnavalesque literature and a Guianese brand of magical realism only in relation to the "other" two "Guyanes" (Surinam and Guyana). Finally Patrick Chamoiseau and Raphaël Confiant's study *Lettres créoles. Tracées antillaises et continentales de la littérature, 1635–1975* (Paris: Hatier, 1971) uses the historical differences between the Antilles and Guiana to discuss Guiana only briefly.

2. Biringanine Ndagano, "La Guyanité ou la question de l'avenir Guyanais," in *La Guyane entre mots et maux. Une lecture de l'œuvre d'Elie Stephenson* (Paris: L'Harmattan, 1994), 17–39.

3. The first Guianese novel, published in 1885 by Alfred Parépou (whose real identity remains un-known to this day), was written in Creole. The playwrights Constantin Verderosa (1889–1970) and Elie Stephenson (1944–) followed in Parépou's footsteps. Verderosa's plays show a diverse, harmonious Cre-ole society in which assimilation is a smooth process, which Stephenson's oppose. Parallel to this Creole writing, the better-known francophone literary tradition includes authors of international reknown such as René Maran (1887–1960), a precursor of the *négritude* movement,whose novel *Batouala* received the *Prix Goncourt* in 1921, and Léon-Gontran Damas (1912–1978), possibly the most famous Guianese poet, a member of the *négritude* trio (with Césaire and Senghor). Their politically engaged successors are Bertène Juminer (1927–), whose work constitutes an appeal to political action, and the poet and novelist Serge Patient (1934–).

4. See Michel Foucault, *L'archéologie du savoir* (Paris: Gallimard, 1969), and the introduction to *La volonté de savoir* (*Histoire de la sexualité, Tome 1*) (Paris: Gallimard, 1976), 9–22.

5. Louis Sala-Molins, *Le Code Noir ou le calvaire de Canaan* (Paris: PUF, 1987), 24.

6. The very first article of the Black Code is quite clear on its religious mission (and land-owning greed): "Enjoignons à tous nos officiers de chasser hors de nos îles tous les Juifs qui y ont établi leur rési-dence, auxquels, comme aux ennemis déclarés du nom chrétien, nous commandons d'en sortir dans trois mois à compter du jour de la publication des présentes, à peine de confiscation de corps et de biens," 92.

7. Jacques Adelaide-Merlande, *Histoire Générale des Antilles et des Guyanes* (Paris: Éditions Caribéennes and L'Harmattan, 1994), 172.

Victor Hugues, a man of apparent contradictions, although he had implemented the 1794 Emancipa-tion Decree in Guadeloupe, was the author of the decree which reinstated slavery.

8. "Le corps ne devient force utile que s'il est à la fois corps productif et corps assujetti." Michel Fou-cault, *Surveiller et punir: Naissance de la prison* (Paris: Gallimard, 1975), 30–31.

9. "Once Guiana had been turned into a penal colony, it became an anti-chamber of death—either civil or literal: its new immigrants, who were taken there to expiate their crimes, stood no chance of es-caping alive. Although D'Chimbo was not a criminal at first, he became one, and his fate followed a pat-tern comparable to those of the French convicts."

10. Louis James, *Caribbean Literature in English* (London and New York: Longman, 1999), 22.

11. "Pendant longtemps, [le Créole de Guyane] distingua le monde 'civilisé' produit par la 'Mère Pa-trie' (la France) auquel il appartenait et celui des 'sauvages' où il classait les Africains fraîchement débar-qués comme D'Chimbo, les Bonis du Maroni et les Amérindiens. D'Chimbo faisait peur non seulement

parce qu'il était étranger à la société créole, originaire de cette Afrique qui, dans la représentation créole de la seconde moitié du 19e siècle, passait encore pour la terre des 'sauvages.'" Serge Mam Lam Fouck, *D'Chimbo du criminel au héros. Une incursion dans l'imaginaire Guianais* (Cayenne: Ibis Rouge Editions, 1997), 23.

12. D'Chimbo inspired a first fictitious written text by Frédéric Bouyer, published in the Parisian daily newspaper *L'Événement* in July and August 1866. The resulting exotic serial novella *L'Amour d'un Monstre: Scènes de la vie créole* describes a romance between the (white) Frenchman Maurice and the beautiful, innocent Julienne (a very pale octoroon). The tale takes an abrupt tragic turn when a (very dark) African immigrant from the Congo, D'Chimbo, appears on the scene. D'Chimbo, described as a savage outlaw, has taken refuge in the woods, from where he pounces on women, robs them, rapes them and occasionally kills them. Although this is the first literary text about D'Chimbo, this chapter focuses on Frédéric Bouyer's other narrative, published a year later in his book *La Guyane Française. Notes et souvenirs d'un voyage effectué en 1862–1863* (Paris: Librairie Hachette, 1867; reprinted Cayenne: Guy Delabergerie, 1990; 11–133) in which D'Chimbo is the main protagonist, and not an accessory to a maudlin love-story set in the exotic landscape of the colonies.

13. Fouck, *D'Chimbo du criminel au héros* (Cayenne, Ibis Rouge Editions, 1997), 16.

14. Frédéric Bouyer, "Le brigand D'Chimbo, dit le Rongou. Ses crimes, son arrestation, sa mort," *La Guyane Française. Notes et souvenirs d'un voyage effectué en 1862–1863* (Cayenne: Guy Delabergerie, 1990), 115.

15. Bouyer, "Le brigand D'Chimbo," 120.

16. Bouyer, "Le brigand D'Chimbo," 126.

17. Bouyer, "Le brigand D'Chimbo," 125.

18. Bouyer, "Le brigand D'Chimbo," 126.

19. "Le bonheur avec lequel D'Chimbo se dérobait aux agents de la force publique, sa présence presque simultanée sur plusieurs points de la colonie, ajoutaient quelque chose de surnaturel et de mystérieux à l'effroi bien justifié qu'il inspirait déjà." Bouyer, "Le brigand D'Chimbo, " 118–19.

20. Bouyer, "Le brigand D'Chimbo," 132.

21. Bouyer, "Le brigand D'Chimbo," 133.

22. Serge Patient, *Le Nègre du gouverneur* (Honfleur: Pierre Jean Oswald, 1972), 20.

23. Patient, *Le Nègre*, 21.

24. Patient, *Le Nègre*, 22.

25. "Motivated Signifyin(g) is the sort in which the Monkey delights; it functions to redress an imbalance of power, to clear a space, rhetorically. To achieve occupancy of the desired space, the Monkey rewrites the received order by exploiting the Lions' hubris and his inability to read the figurative other than the literal." Henry Louis Gates Jr, *The Signifying Monkey: Theory of African-American Literary Criticism* (New York and Oxford: Oxford University Press, 1988), 124.

26. Patient, *Le Nègre*, 25.

27. Elie Stephenson, *La Nouvelle Légende de D'Chimbo* (Cayenne: Ibis Rouge Éditions, 1996), 65.

28. ELENA: Je veux savoir pourquoi ni fusil ni sabre ne te font rien.

D'CHIMBO (a un petit rire entendu): Il faut les laver avec de l'eau de coeur de maripa.

ELENA (ravie): D'Chimbo, ah chéri, je t'aime beaucoup, mon homme. Mais dis-moi, doudou . . . pourquoi les chaînes ne peuvent-elles t'attacher?

D'CHIMBO: Parce que ce ne sont pas des lianes de patates!

Stephenson, *La Nouvelle Légende*, 104.

29. Stephenson, *La Nouvelle Légende*, 105.

30. "Massak, Kam" is the ritual formula used to start an evening of "dolos" (guessing games or riddles). "*Massak*, le titre de la pièce, est un terme créole faisant référence aux 'dolos', c'est-à-dire énigmes créoles. Le tire est déjà une énigme, même pour un créolophone. Il pourrait d'ailleurs se lire comme l'écriture créole de massacre." Biringanine Ndagano, *La Guyane entre maux et mots* (Paris: L'Harmattan, 1994), 159–60.

31. Ndagano, *La Guyane entre maux et mots*, 138.

32. Ndagano, *La Guyane entre maux et mots*, 141.

33. Ndagano, *La Guyane entre maux et mots*, 123.

34. Ndagano, *La Guyane entre maux et mots*, 158.

35. Ndagano, *La Guyane entre maux et mots*.

36. Patient, *Le Nègre*, 27.

37. Patient, *Le Nègre*, 28.

38. Patient, *Massak*, 154.

39. Stephenson, *La Nouvelle Légende*, 20.

40. "Mais je suis tout de même victorieux. Je pars avec la joie d'avoir retrouvé le sens du combat et de la fierté." Stephenson, *Massak*, 157.

15

Guadeloupean Literature:
Multiple Versions of *Créolité*

Pascale de Souza

GUADELOUPEAN, GUYANESE AND MARTINICAN WRITERS have explored, and continue to explore, the processes of *métissage* and assimilation in the French Caribbean. From Fanon's *Peau Noire, masques blancs*[1] to his *Les Damnés de la terre*,[2] from Léon-Gontran Damas's *Pigments*[3] to Aimé Césaire's *Cahier d'un retour au pays natal*[4] and *Discours sur le colonialisme*,[5] from Edouard Glissant's *Discours Antillais*[6] to his novels, from the Creolists' *Éloge de la créolité*[7] to their numerous literary publications in Creole and French, French Caribbean writers have attracted attention and garnered literary awards well beyond the shores of the Caribbean. Fanonism, and the *Négritude*, *Antillanité* and *Créolité* movements that Césaire, Glissant and the Creolists (Jean Bernabé, Raphaël Confiant and Patrick Chamoiseau) spearheaded continue to influence critical approaches in the post-colonial world at large.

However, with the exception of Damas, who is of Guyanese ancestry, all the authors mentioned above are from Martinique. Though several precursors to the Négritude movement were active in Guadeloupe, and Guadeloupean writers have long enjoyed both literary success and critical acclaim, Guadeloupe's contribution to post-colonial studies has been less prominent. Many Guadeloupean writers are engaged in a personal exploration of "multiple versions of créolité,"[8] which may explain a reluctance to draft or follow any prescriptive model.

One of the foremost characteristics of Guadeloupean literature is the large number of women writers from the island and the tendency identified by critics for its male writers to adopt feminine approaches to literature or claim this to be their practice. The long list of female writers from Guadeloupe would include (in alphabetical order) Dany Bébel-Gisler, Maryse Condé, Suzanne Lacascade, Michèle Lacrosil, Jacqueline Manicom, Gisèle Pineau, Simone Schwarz-Bart and Myriam Warner-Vieyra, while Daniel Maximin's exploration of verbal imagery and adoption of complex female characters has been seen as indicative of a generally feminine approach to writing, and Ernest Pépin argues that, in *Le Tango de la haine*, Maximin has written a feminist novel.[9] Several hypotheses may help explain the emergence of so many feminine voices. Strong female writers, such as Simone Schwarz-Bart, who wrote in the 1970s, have served to inspire a younger generation of writers, not so much as models to emulate but as breakers of new ground. The literary situation for women in Martinique was far less propitious, as the influence exerted by Fanon's views of colored women's responsibility in the loss of Caribbean identity as a result of lactification[10] and the domination of

"Papa" Césaire contributed to the silencing of several Martinican women writers, such as Mayotte Capécia and Suzanne Césaire.

The distance between the two islands, both in geographical and historical terms, may also have facilitated the development of women's writing. The greater accessibility of its low-lying shores, its fertile land and its mild climate have helped to foster closer ties between Martinique and metropolitan France. Notwithstanding the higher proportion of people of European descent in Martinique, France's phallocentric traditions have left their mark in the shape of various monuments and a more masculine literary lineage. If the plaque at the Matouba comes readily to mind in connection with Guadeloupe, Joséphine de Beauharnais's statue in Fort-de-France dominates the image of Martinican statuary.[11] Martinique's closer ties with France may also help to explain metropolitan interest in a literature that better meets its liberal-minded expectations than Guadeloupe's multifaceted explorations of *créolité*. The awarding of several French literary prizes to Chamoiseau (Prix Kléber Haedens, Grand prix de la littérature de la jeunesse Prix Goncourt) and Confiant (Prix Antigone, Prix Novembre, Prix Jet Tours) attest to this interest.[12]

While the preeminence of women writers from the island that Maryse Condé refers to as "l'île aux femmes" cannot be denied, another salient characteristic of Guadeloupean literature, in keeping with the reluctance to follow prescriptive (male) models, is an interest in an all-inclusive approach to *créolité*, one that encompasses Guadeloupean identity within the diaspora. It may be argued that the most prestigious precursor in this respect is none other than Saint-John Perse. While his first text, *Éloges*, "unambiguously celebrate[s] the natural and cultural environment of the Caribbean,"[13] his later poetry is "no less marked by the poet's colonial origins . . . Indeed, in so far as it is marked throughout by an atavistic belief in the creative potential of the renewal born of ruptures such as those of exile or migration, all of Saint-John Perse's writing could be seen to spring from a problematic closely related to that of Creole identity."[14] Despite the way his poetry is infused with Caribbean imagery and that he grapples with such fundamentally Caribbean issues as exile and migration, the Guadeloupe-born poet was long considered to be French rather than Caribbean on account of his descent from a plantocratic family and the fact that he left Guadeloupe at the age of 12 and never returned. More recently, however, Saint-John Perse has gained recognition as a Guadeloupean poet in his own right. The inclusion of this diasporic voice in Guadeloupean literature illustrates critical approaches that underline Guadeloupean authors' interest in challenging (mis)interpretations, shattering (mis)conceptions, and seeking identities beyond their own shores. Leah Hewitt's comment on Maryse Condé, "[Condé] shakes up complacent thinking about what a black Antillean woman writer is supposed to think and with whom she might identify,"[15] is indeed applicable to several authors from Guadeloupe.

Guadeloupean Contributions to Negritude
and a Definition of French Caribbean Literature

After outlining Guadeloupean contributions to the negritude movement and a definition of French Caribbean literature, this chapter will focus on *Pluie et vent sur Télumée Miracle*[16] by Simone Schwarz-Bart and *Traversée de la Mangrove*[17] by Maryse Condé to show how these novels, which are often perceived as the most Guadeloupe-centered fictional works by these authors, actually inscribe Guadeloupe within an African sociohistorical framework and encompass recent diasporic trends.

In the early twentieth century, Oruno-Lara, a descendant of slaves, was one of the first writers to wonder about his Caribbean identity, to valorize his "négritude" and to claim the right to his difference. As he asserts, "how can we impose ourselves, assert our personality . . . how in the process of being assimilated into French civilization, do we preserve our own identity?"[18] This early formulation of the Caribbean quest for identity underlined the dangers of assimilation even before the *départementalisation* of Guadeloupe, Guyane and Martinique, and reveals an awareness of wider issues facing post-colonial societies. In 1924 another Guadeloupean writer, Suzanne Lacascade, published her only novel, *Claire-Solange, ame africaine*,[19] which Maryse Condé has lauded as the first novel featuring a colored female protagonist who prides herself on her African ancestry. Though Claire-Solange claims descent from African kings and queens rather than the commoners who were more often deported to the Americas, her refusal to focus solely on her white ancestry and seek assimilation into the metropolitan branch of her family emerges early on as an expression of pride in her difference. Though he only published one volume of poems and one of texts, Guy Tirolien also contributed to this early exploration of Afro-Caribbean identity in poems such as "Prière d'un petit enfant nègre," while Paul Niger drew recognition for his poems, fiction and political militancy as a leader of the *Front antillo-guyanais*.

More recently, authors such as Bébel-Gisler, Condé, Maximin, Pépin and Pineau have enriched critical studies with their articles and longer essays. A variety of book-length studies have been published on such topics as *La Civilisation du Bossale, La Parole des femmes, Le Roman antillais* and *La Poésie antillaise*[20] by Condé, and *La Langue créole: Force jugulée*[21] by Bébel-Gisler. Critical essays by Condé, Maximin, Pépin and Pineau have also explored such themes as "Order, Disorder, Freedom and the Caribbean Writer"[22] and "The Role of the Writer" (Condé),[23] the "Antillean Journey" (Maximin),[24] "The Stakes of Créolité" (Pépin),[25] and "Ecrire en tant que noire" (Pineau).[26]

As several critics have argued, *Négritude* was intended to beget other movements from the very moment of its inception. Indeed, whereas authors such as the Martinican Madeleine Carbet viewed it with mild benevolence, Guadeloupean writers such as Manicom, Lacrosil and Condé gave black men, as well as white, their "share of moral responsibility" for the islands' caste system.[27] The *Antillanité* proclaimed by Glissant was a second step toward an exploration of fragmented Caribbean identities more focused on the "native-natale" complex. In *In Praise of Creoleness*, the Creolists put forward their theory of a Caribbean-centered literature that should depict island life, its linguistic specificity and its "small people," and yet eventually reach out to encompass a French Creole-centered linguistic sphere. While Glissant aimed to write complex novels that reflected what he perceived as the opacity of Caribbean history, the Creolists focused on the "small people" of Martinique, whether in rural settings, as in *Eau de Café*[28] and *Le Meurtre du Samedi-Gloria*[29] by Raphaël Confiant, or poor urban areas, as in *Solibo magnifique*[30] and *Texaco*[31] by Patrick Chamoiseau. In a critical review of Condé's *Traversée de la Mangrove*, Chamoiseau argues that Creoleness has no normative goals: "It is therefore not a question of enlisting anyone, nor of prescribing a way of writing, painting, or performing,"[32] but nonetheless praises Condé for the numerous Creole expressions she uses and decries her use of non-local terms such as "île" or "village." Chamoiseau also condemns Condé for including explicatory notes aimed at a non-Caribbean audience. As a result of this approach to authenticity, which is based on his own (limited) views of Creoleness, Chamoiseau fails to take into consideration that Caribbean identity is a fluctuating concept bound neither by historical constructs nor geographical limits and that, as Maryse Condé recently argued in "Créolité without Creole Language," being Creole or speaking Creole may no longer be a requirement for someone claiming a Caribbean identity. This leads to a consideration of Guadeloupean contributions to the ongoing debate on Caribbean identity.

In "The Role of the Writer," Condé sets out her own critical discourse on Caribbean literature. She states her belief in "a West Indian identity, regardless of colonial language and political status"[33] and argues that it is necessary to look beyond the confines of each island and its "petit peuple" in order to find a vanishing West Indian identity. In keeping with these conclusions, several Guadeloupean writers have sought inspiration beyond the shores of the Caribbean and its "petit peuple."

Beyond the Caribbean "Petit Peuple"

As early as 1960, Michèle Lacrosil's *Sapotille et le serin d'argile*[34] explored the complexities faced by someone schooled in an educational system dominated by ethnically and socially biased beliefs as seen through the memories of a migrant Guadeloupean. Her second novel, *Cajou*,[35] delved further into the effects of racial prejudice on a talented Guadeloupean researcher who cannot shake the yoke of an oppressive past or "assimilate" into the Parisian world. Similar challenges face an Indo-Guadeloupean woman in *Mon Examen de blanc*[36] by Jacqueline Manicom when she tries to integrate into life in a hospital and gain recognition on the basis of her credentials. Of Simone Schwarz-Bart's three novels, one also focuses more on the middle classes than the peasantry, while two explore settings away from Guadeloupe. Her collaborative work with her husband, *Un plat de Porc aux bananes vertes*,[37] is set in an retirement home in Paris and follows the struggles of an educated, well travelled elderly Guadeloupean woman as she tries to survive cut off from her island of birth and its traditions, while *Ti-Jean l'horizon*[38] wanders between Africa and Guadeloupe on the wings of magical realism. Only *Pluie et vent sur Télumée-Miracle* may be said to be exclusively focused on life in Guadeloupe and Guadeloupean characters, with the exception of Xango, who comes from Dominica. However, Schwarz-Bart's use of magical realism in the latter two novels recalls similar experiments in Latin American literature.

Most of Maryse Condé's literary production, even her so-called "Caribbean novels," likewise explore the complexities of being Caribbean in a world that extends well beyond the shores of the island and its "petit peuple." While her first two novels, *Heremakhonon*[39] and *Une Saison à Rihata*[40] are based on her own experience in Africa, *Moi, Tituba, Sorcière . . . Noire de Salem*,[41] *La Vie scélérate*,[42] and *Traversée de la Mangrove* are regarded as the novels of her real and literary return to Guadeloupe. Yet, none of them are set exclusively in the Caribbean. Quite the contrary, it seems that, unlike her first novels, which focus on a French Caribbean female protagonist and her wandering/wondering views on her own destiny, the later novels either wander themselves between various countries and/or feature protagonists of diverse origins, social classes and life experiences. While *Moi, Tituba* follows the travels of a poor rural Bajan woman from her island home to New England and back in the eighteenth century, *La Vie scélérate* presents the rise of a Guadeloupean family into the middle classes and is set in Panama, France, Guadeloupe and Cuba. It may seem a paradoxical conclusion to argue that *Traversée de la Mangrove* is not entirely focused on the Caribbean, since the whole novel takes place during a wake in the small village of Rivière au Sel. Yet a closer look at the villagers reveals that Rivière au Sel reflects globalizing trends insofar as several of the characters come from elsewhere or have experienced life overseas. It seems that Condé returned to Guadeloupe only to discover that the insular world of her island-home is but a microcosm of the planet. Her later novels *Le Dernier*

Roi-Mage,[43] *La Colonie du nouveau monde,*[44] *La Migration des coeurs*[45] and *Désirada,*[46] which were written while she spent most of her year teaching at Columbia University, likewise explore Caribbean identities on a global basis. *Le Dernier Roi-Mage* takes place in the southern United States and focuses on the rifts and disjunctions in the relationship between a man of Guadeloupean origin and an African-American woman. *La Colonie du nouveau monde* is set in Central America and features protagonists from places as far apart as Germany and Haiti. *Désirada* takes place in France, the United States, La Désirade and Guadeloupe, and Haitians born in Cuba, one of whom works in Guinea, a Russian woman and a music group composed of Antilleans born in Cape Verde are among its multitude of diverse, globetrotting characters. Indeed, in the last chapter Condé mentions students from Iran and Africa doing their research on various francophone writers under the guidance of their Guadeloupean professor, their fate being a reflection of the journeys that dominate the novel. *La Migration des coeurs*, published two years later, is a rereading of *Wuthering Heights* by Charlotte Brontë set in Cuba, Guadeloupe, Marie-Galante and Dominica, while her latest novel *Célanire cou-coupé*[47] follows its female protagonist from Guadeloupe to the Ivory Coast and Peru. Indeed, it seems that one dominant characteristic of Condé's prolific literary production is her refusal to be limited to the Guadeloupean context.

Though less worldly, authors such as Myriam Warner-Vieyra, Daniel Maximin and Gisèle Pineau likewise write about protagonists who have experienced migration either to France or Africa. In *Le Quimboiseur l'avait dit*, Warner-Vieyra, a Guadeloupe-born writer resident in Senegal, explores the slow descent into alienation of a young girl whose dreams of studying in France are thwarted by her own misunderstanding of the challenges ahead, and her mother and stepfather's ill intentions. In *Juletane* Warner-Viyera follows the similar descent into alienation of a young Guadeloupean woman whose dreams of finding family among her in-laws founder on the reality of polygamy and differing social customs. *L'Isolé soleil*[48] by Maximin is the first part of a trilogy that explores the fragmented past and volcanic present of the Caribbean. The novel follows the protagonist's recreation of the past through an exchange of letters between Guadeloupe and France. However, it is Pineau who emerges as the writer most focused on the French Caribbean diasporic experience in France. In *Un Papillon dans la cité*[49] and *L'Exil selon Julia*[50] this Guadeloupe-based writer draws upon her childhood in France to explore the challenges facing a young Guadeloupean girl as she seeks to recreate "un pays pas natal" in France.[51] Both novels are set in France and Guadeloupe or Martinique, and examine the effects of migration on the maintenance of Caribbean traditions.

Anancy in *Pluie et Vent sur Télumée Miracle*

Following this brief review of Guadeloupean literature, this chapter will focus on two novels, *Pluie et vent sur Télumée-Miracle* by Simone Schwarz-Bart and *Traversée de la Mangrove* by Maryse Condé. Both apparently focus on life in rural Guadeloupe. *Pluie et vent* takes place in various small villages and hamlets, while *Traversée* is entirely set in a single house in Rivière au Sel. A closer study of the novels, however, reveals the extent to which both reach beyond Guadeloupe to encompass wider diasporic trends.

Though Schwarz-Bart sets her novel in Guadeloupe, she makes Télumée a spiderwoman who owes much to the Anancy folklore found throughout West Africa and the Americas. From Nova Scotia to Brazil, from the Carolinas to the Caribbean, Anancy the spider, the quintessential hero of traditional folklore, provides "a tolerated margin of mess."[52] His liminality manifests itself in his geographical location and functions, as well as in his appearance and language. Anancy dwells at crossroads, an inhabitant of nooks and crannies as in "Anancy and Brother Tiger" (Jamaica), or "Bone for a Stump" (Jamaica). This *hero-scamp*, as Roger Abrahams calls him,[53] may be a villain and dupe at the same time, as in "How Spider Read the Sky God's Thoughts" (Ghana) or "Tiger in Well" (San Andrés Island, Colombia). Perceived as a villain by those whose taboos he has broken, whose property he has infringed upon, Anancy remains a hero for the downtrodden, those who need to develop strategies of coping. As Leonard Barret argues, "Regardless of his treachery and cunning, Ananci has those components which make him a folk-hero par excellence, for elusive and nimble of spirit and witty of tongue, he is representative of techniques of survival at their best."[54] Anancy's appeal among slaves and Caribbean peoples whose fate is vulnerable to the vagaries of international trade lies in his being the epitome of survival, a figure who holds out the hope that anyone can transcend the limitations of his condition.

In several New World tales Anancy is either human or spider, or both. In one Uncle Remus story Anancy is a half-woman, half-spider creature called Aunt Nancy. In the Bahamas, Bánansi is a trickster and hero, either boy, man or monkey. Anancy does not content himself with his hybrid identity, but adopts various temporary disguises to reach his objectives as in "Pig and Long-Mout" (Jamaica), "Nancy Gives a Bath" (Nevis), "Bird Cherry Island" (Jamaica, Grenada and Cape Verde Islands) and "Bone for a Stump" (Antigua). However important they may be, his geographical liminality, role playing and multiplicity of incarnations are but superficial manifestations of a deeper liminality that is grounded in language. In *The Signifying Monkey*[55] Gates draws both on the standard definition of signifying—carrying meaning to the surface— and on the African-American usage of the term "Signifyin(g)"—testing the ability of a word to bear its conventional meanings—to posit a discourse of trickery. Through his constant use of Signifyin(g), Anancy dupes other animals to ridicule them or bring about their demise, as in "Anancy and the Yam Hills" (Jamaica).

In *Pluie et vent sur Télumée Miracle* several characters display Anancyan characteristics that anchor them firmly within an African tradition. All the female members of the community contribute their thread to the creation of a web, either by constant movement back and forth (suggestive of the spinner's shuttle) or through language. Indeed, various characters discover the importance of this network when they stop spinning their own thread. Télumée's grandmother (Toussine) and her husband, Jérémie, cut themselves off from the communal web when they isolate themselves on the periphery of L'Abandonnée. It is only when local people start coming and going between the couple's home on the hill and the neighboring village that they are finally rewoven into the community. Likewise, Télumée is able to survive various threats to her existence and sanity because she remains within reach of the web. When she loses her grip on reality as a result of her companion's betrayal, her shack appears to become detached from the rest of the village: "Je voyais maintenant qu'aucun fil ne reliat plus ma case aux autres cases."[56] Being aware that Télumée has fallen too far to reintegrate into the social web without their help, the villagers of Fond-Zombi, like those of L'Abandonnée, start spinning toward her: "A quelques jours de la fête, les gens se mirent à passer et à repasser devant ma case, sans mot dire, afin de me prouver tout simplement qu'il ne pouvait y avoir de coupure dans la trame."[57] However, to spin a strong-enough yarn, language must be used: "De temps en temps, une femme s'échappait d'un groupe, levait au ciel des bras suppliants et en modulait d'une voix aiguë . . . naissez, naissez pour changer nos destins . . . et l'entendant j'avais le sentiment étrange qu'elle me lançait un fil dans l'air, un fil très léger en direction de ma case. . . ."[58]

Several women eventually gather in front of her home and continue talking loudly, exchanging stories about her to remind her that her thread has not been permanently severed. As Télumée's grandmother tells her, "Tu le vois, les cases ne sont rien sans les fils qui les relient les unes aux autres, et ce que tu perçois l'après-midi sous ton arbre n'est rien d'autre qu'un fil, celui que tisse le village et qu'il lance jusqu'à toi, ta case."[59] Like this epitomic village in Guadeloupe, the whole African diaspora is nothing but a web that owes its existence to all yarns spun literally by its members as they go back and forth and metaphorically as they talk. Anancy's interwoven strands are a Signifyin(g) web "suspended between, and drawing together, separate worlds."[60]

Pluie et vent sur Télumée Miracle has often been interpreted as a celebration of the resilience of West Indian women. However, this hopeful interpretation fails to take account of the fact that a web is first and foremost a trap. The web that binds the black inhabitants together is also intended to imprison them and expose them to a predatory community. As Schwarz-Bart notes, "La vie à Fond-Zombi se déroulait portes et fenêtres ouvertes, la nuit avait des yeux, le vent de longues oreilles, et nul jamais ne se rassasiait d'autrui."[61] Toussine and Télumée are both made aware of this when they try to escape from a community married to its own fateful defeatism. And when Toussine and Jérémie announce their intention to marry, the spider refuses to let them escape its deadly embrace: "Cependant que se préparaient les noces, c'était toujours la même platitude à L'Abandonnée, le même acharnement des humains à faire descendre d'un cran le niveau de la terre, le même poids de méchanceté accroché aux oreillettes de leur cœur."[62] Télumée shares Toussine's fate insofar as her attempt to find happiness with Elie also elicits jealousy and ends in despair. The novel draws to a close on the image of Télumée contentedly tending her garden. However, this apparently happy ending needs Signifyin(g), as such contentment exacts a terrible price: one's right to search for and find ways to escape the fateful web.

Télumée has to resort to her Anancyan powers in order to escape the webs spun by the inhabitants of Fond-Zombi and become a miracle woman. These powers are manifest in her geographical marginality, her performance of various roles, her capacity to change her appearance, if only metaphorically, and her ability to spin a Signifyin(g) discourse. Most of the Lougandor women display a tendency to live on the edges of society. Toussine, Télumée's grandmother, first settles in a shack outside the village of L'Abandonnée, then moves into an abandoned Great House away from the villagers' gaze and finally lives in the last shack abutting the mountain in Fond-Zombi. Victoire, Télumée's mother, raises her daughters just beyond the limits of the village. When she goes to work for the Desaragnes, Télumée is relegated to an outhouse next to the stables. She spends the rest of her life living in various locations—a shack in the woods, an isolated settlement called La Folie, villages called Bel Navire, Bois Rouge, la Roncière and even Pointe-à-Pitre—before settling in La Ramée, a village whose name evokes the tree branches where spiders often anchor their webs. As the English title of the novel suggests, Télumée is a dweller of the in-between places, an inhabitant of the "bridge of beyond."

Like Anancy, Télumée escapes most attempts to stop her Signifyin(g) but also falls into a trap another character has set for her. Though Elie had forewarned her that she is but a young goat tethered to his whim,[63] Télumée takes him as her companion. When Elie is no longer able to make a living as a carpenter, he turns his anger against her. Having been duped by her love for him, Télumée endures his blows silently until forced to leave their home. In spite of her trials, however, she can still draw upon her Anancy powers to weave this particularly traumatic episode into the fabric of her life and emerge as a heroine.

Both her grandmother, Toussine, and Man Cia, the obeah woman, teach Télumée that she lives in a world where the barriers between the human and the animal kingdoms are permeable and where, as a true Anancy, she can survive through the adoption of various disguises. Man Cia, who can turn herself into a black dog, offers to teach her about metamorphosis. Télumée never summons enough courage to learn this art, but instead becomes deft at practicing it metaphorically in her dreams and her thoughts. Toussine tells Télumée the story of the bird who could only rely on his song to escape the hunter[64] and warns her that "si les petits poissons les [les mauvaises langues du village] écoutent, sais-tu? ils perdront leurs nageoires."[65] Télumée conjures up both images to protect herself while in the Great House: "Je partais moi aussi en songe, m'envolais, me prenais pour l'oiseau qu'aucune balle ne pouvait atteindre, car il conjurait la vie par son chant. . . ."[66] She always keeps a watchful eye, "me tenant sur le qui-vive, toute prête à esquiver, à me faufiler à travers les mailles de la nasse."[67] These various animal images enable Télumée to maintain her links with her teachers, Man Cia and Toussine, and through them to her diasporic heritage.

Two objects play a similar role in the novel: the stone and the drum. Télumée compares herself to a little stone[68] and a drum,[69] which both preserve their underside from life's turmoil. The two-sidedness of both stone and drum alerts the reader to Télumée's dual nature, as the side kept whole enables her to Signify her way through life. The choice of the drum is particularly pertinent on two other accounts. Firstly, as Abena Busia recalls, the drum binds Télumée to her African Caribbean heritage as it was "the sacred and primary instrument of *within*-group social communication in African heritage communities."[70] Secondly, it was used to convey messages Signifyin(g) the masters' attempt to subdue slaves in the New World in the form of calls for uprisings.

The web spun by the villagers owes its existence in part to discourse. Man Cia, Toussine and Télumée are all aware that language can shape, deform and reshape the world around them. From the point when Télumée crosses the bridge of beyond, she enters into a magical realm where women Signify the discourse of the other. Their Signifyin(g) takes on various forms: singing, gesturing and repetition. Toussine teaches Télumée not to fall prey to the hunter by telling her the story of the singing bird and not to listen to the perfidious song of the washer women by humming "quelque biguine des temps anciens qu'elle modulait de façon très particulière, avec une sorte d'ironie voilée."[71] Thanks to Toussine, Télumée learns to preserve her identity through drumming and singing: "Je battais en mon coeur un tambour d'exception, je dansais, je chantais toutes les voix, tous les appels."[72]

Télumée's conversations with Mrs. Desaragne, the mistress of the plantation house where she works, illustrate her mastery of verbal trickery. On a superficial level, Mrs. Desaragne seems to be in full control of the verbal exchanges. A Signifyin(g) reading, however, reveals otherwise. Part of the first dialogue reads as follows:

—C'est une place que vous cherchez?
— Je cherche à me louer.
—Qu'est-ce que vous savez faire, par exemple?
—Je sais tout faire.
—Vous connaissez cuisiner?
—Oui.
—Je veux dire, cuisiner, pas lâcher un morceau de fruit à pain dans une chaudière d'eau salée.
—Oui, je sais.
—Bon, c'est bien, mais qui vous a appris?
—La mère de ma grand-mère s'était louée, dans le temps, chez les Labardine.[73]

Several Signifying processes are at play here. First Télumée limits herself to laconic answers, compelling Mrs. Desaragne to abandon her standard French in favor of creolized expressions. She then shares some personal information,[74] a move aimed at asserting her place within a female continuum.

Télumée finally reveals the full extent of her mastery over language when she uses her talents as a spying spider to weave a story out of her life at Galba. Spinning animal metaphors, singing, reversals of the Master's trope, she constantly reiterates her belonging to the world beyond the bridge, to the world of the Anancy women who Signify the other's discourse and ultimately her belonging to the world of the African diaspora.

A Diffracted Créolité in *Traversée de la Mangrove*

At the end of the novel, Télumée has discovered that her centering enables her to find contentment in her small garden; yet, electricity pylons loom in the distance, harbingers of new threats to the villagers' ability to retain Afro-Caribbean traditions. In many ways, *Traversée de la Mangrove* presents their situation some forty years later. The villagers of Rivière au Sel have kept some of their traditions, such as the wake during which the novel takes place, but have also had to adapt to life in a globalized world. In her novel Condé underlines how villages are both predatory and protective webs, showing how African traditions and socio-ethnic divisions from the times of slavery have endured, but also how open to the world Guadeloupe has become. She finally points to the difficulties facing Guadeloupeans in their quest for identity, as most of the villagers choose to remain in Rivière au Sel, but several seek another path.

As Condé says, "Even the most superficial study of literature from the West Indies demonstrates that every writer keeps to his or her island."[75] Condé both abides by that model and challenges it in *Traversée de la Mangrove,* her only novel set entirely in Guadeloupe. By contrast with the villagers of Fond-Zombi, the inhabitants of Rivière au Sel come from different places (Saint-Martin, Dominica, Haiti, Colombia, Cuba) and therefore contribute to the spinning of a web that transcends linguistic and political barriers. Several villagers have also spent time overseas. Dinah lived in Holland with an Indonesian partner, Carmélien studied in Bordeaux and Cyrille travelled to Africa, while Désinor dreams of going to North America when he reads his brothers' letters. All these experiences intermingle to shape Rivière au Sel, a village that becomes emblematic of the whole Caribbean archipelago and its diaspora.

While the island becomes a haven for Ti-Jean in *Ti-Jean l'horizon* or Télumée in *Pluie et vent sur Télumée Miracle*, it only represents a temporary anchorage for several characters in *Traversée de la Mangrove.* Carmélien and Cyrille are both compelled to return home, one after giving up medical school in France, the other after being kicked out of Africa, as Cyrille explains: "Je serais bien resté, là, moi, en Afrique. Mais les Africains m'ont donné un grand coup de pied au cul en hurlant: 'Retourne chez toi!'"[76] Though Désinor l'Haïtien has been able to find a job in Guadeloupe, he does not find a home in Rivière au Sel, where he and his fellow Haitians are ostracized. In this way Condé underlines that neither France nor Africa can offer Guadeloupeans a "chez soi," while Guadeloupe would rather see Haitians remain "chez eux." The United States emerges as Désinor's ultimate dream, but, as he is well aware, answering the call inscribed on the pedestal of the Statue of Liberty would hardly offer an opportunity to find a "chez soi" for a colored migrant. Sancher, the descendant of a planter's family who comes to Guadeloupe to seek out his ancestry in Rivière au Sel, also remains "sans chez"[77] until his death enables the villagers to renew their ties with Africa by means of the wake.

One could quote the famous words of the prologue of *Éloge de la créolité* in which Bernabé, Chamoiseau and Confiant assert, "Ni Européens, ni Africains, ni Asiatiques, nous nous proclamons Créoles."[78] However, these words would not serve to underline the existence of a Caribbean identity, but rather that Carmélien, Cyrille and Francis return to their Creole environment because they have no other home. This is very far removed from the situation of the contented figure of Télumée standing in her small garden.

In her novel, Condé also refutes two prevailing Caribbean myths. On the one hand, she underlines the rifts and disjunctions that characterize social interactions, in direct opposition to the Creolists' views on *métissage*. On the other, she refuses to focus solely on the tensions inherited from the ethnosocial division of power between planters and slaves to be found in various Martinican and Guadeloupean novels, such as *Pluie et vent sur Télumée Miracle, Eau de café, Rue cases-nègres,*[79] *Texaco* and *Demain Jab-Herma.* In *Traversée de la Mangrove* the diversity of ethnic origins encompasses not only descendants of African slaves and European planters, but Asian, Haitian and recent European migrants. Moïse's mother is Chinese, the Ramsarans of Indian descent, Désinor Haitian, and Léocadie mentions "métros, toutes qualités de blancs venus du Canada ou de l'Italie, des Vietnamiens."[80] As Marie-Agnès Sourieau underlines, "si pour les auteurs d'*Éloge de la créolité*, 'la créolité, c'est le monde diffracté mais recomposé' (Eloge, 27), dans le roman de Condé, la créolité, c'est le monde diffracté mais décomposé."[81] Moïse is ostracized because of his Chinese origins and the Haitians relegated to a ghetto, while Loulou Lameaulnes and Sylvestre Ramsaran pride themselves respectively on their white and Indian ancestry, which sets them apart from the descendants of slaves. The light-skinned Mira Lameaulnes rejects any suitor whose skin is not as light as hers, while, by (ab)using the Haitian labour force at his nursery, Ramsaran perpetuates the plantocratic regime. Far from transcending their ethnic differences, the villagers use them to comfort their prejudices. As Munley argues, "Deeply rooted prejudice against anyone 'different,' 'from the outside,' or from a different ethnic or racial background smothers at least half of the characters in *Traversée de la Mangrove.*"[82]

If poverty was the common lot of colored people in *Pluie et vent sur Télumée Miracle,* in Rivière au Sel, wealth introduces further rifts among the villagers. Poverty as depicted in French Caribbean novels is most often the heir and reflection of times of slavery, planters and their descendants enjoying the privileges of wealth while slaves and their descendants eke out a meagre living. In *Traversée de la Mangrove,* Condé presents a more complex picture of contemporary Guadeloupe. The mulatto Loulou Lameaulnes runs a flourishing crayfish business, while Sylvestre Ramsaran, who is of Indian descent, owns a large nursery. Both dream of a return to former times when the master's rule was unchallenged, without being aware they themselves would then have been slaves or indentured servants.

The world presented in Condé's novel has more in common with so-called "developed societies" than the colonial world. Rifts no longer occur along historical lines but along the divisions created by economic privilege, "car dans la Guadeloupe d'aujourd'hui, ce qui comptait, ce n'était plus la couleur de la peau, enfin plus seulement, ni l'instruction. . . . Non, ce qui comptait, c'était l'argent."[83] To quote Françoise Lionnet, "la Guadeloupe, loin d'être ce pays marginal, est en fait un microcosme du globe."[84]

By the end of the novel several women characters have decided to seek their fortune elsewhere. Their rejection of life in Rivière au Sel stands in stark contrast to the choices made by Télumée in *Pluie et vent sur Télumée Miracle.* Mira, Vilma and Dinah first try to connect to the outside world through their relationships with Francis Sancher "parce qu'il venait d'Ailleurs. D'Ailleurs,"[85] but soon realize that this path is a dead end. As Dinah concludes, "Maintenant que je connais la suite de cette histoire, mon histoire, . . . je ne comprends plus pourquoi j'avais placé tous mes espoirs sur cet-homme-là que je ne connaissais ni en blanc, ni en noir."[86] In the end it is only his death that empowers them to choose a different path: "Ma vraie vie commence avec sa mort,"[87] as Dinah asserts when she leaves.

The Guadeloupe presented in Condé's novel is multifaceted and fluid. Not only do characters come from various countries or have experience of living overseas, they also claim complex, mixed ancestries and belong to various social classes. Condé's decision to focus on Caribbean characters of various nationalities, origins and social classes, and create an open-ended novel underlines the challenges awaiting Guadeloupeans today. If some villagers choose to return to their former lives at the end of Sancher's wake, others opt for a new path. But where will it lead them?

Concluding Remarks

In an essay published in 1994 entitled "Regard d'un écrivain antillais," Ernest Pépin argued that French Caribbean people are "emportés par la déferlante d'une mondialisation sans précédent, europeanisés, gavés et anesthésiés par la consommation,"[88] that "Légitimus et Souques[89] ont disparu du paysage. Saint-John Perse et Guy Tirolien se sont tus. Depuis, l'horizon est bien vide."[90] Since 1994 several Guadeloupean authors have made attempts to fill the "empty horizon" with novels and essays that explore the new complexities of Caribbean identity. The horizon is not empty, but limitless, as restrictive definitions of *créolité* give way to an expanding Caribbeanness no longer constrained by historical constructs or geographical boundaries. The literature of Guadeloupe thus reflects a time when local, national and regional classifications of literature are increasingly being challenged by diasporic trends. As Condé argues, "I believe that we are faced with a need for redefinitions. What is a Caribbean person, and consequently, what is a Caribbean writer? Are they always creole? Where are they born and where do they live?"[91] These questions will continue to enrich Guadeloupean literature as new voices from the diaspora, such as Daniel Picouly, who was born and raised in Guadeloupe but now lives in France, emerge to explore *Le Champ de personne*.[92]

Notes

1. Frantz Fanon, *Peau noire, masques blancs* (Paris: Seuil, 1952) English translation: *Black Skin, White Masks* (New York: Grove Press, 1967).

2. Frantz Fanon, *Les Damnés de la terre* (Paris: Gallimard, 1991) English translation: *The Wretched of the Earth* (London: Penguin, 1990).

3. Léon-Gontran Damas, *Pigments* (Paris: GLM, 1937).

4. Aimé Césaire, *Cahier d'un retour au pays natal* (Paris: PUF, 1993) Several English translations.

5. English translation: *Discourse on Colonialism* (New York: MR, 1972).

6. Edouard Glissant, *Discours Antillais* (Paris: Gallimard, 1997) English translation: *Caribbean Discourse* (Charlottesville: University Press of Virginia, 1992).

7. Jean Bernabé, Raphaël Confiant and Patrick Chamoiseau, *Eloge de la Créolité* (Paris: Gallimard, 1993), bilingual edition.

8. Maryse Condé, "Créolité without Creole Language?" in *Caribbean Creolization*, ed. Kathleen Balutantsky and Marie-Agnès Sourieau (Gainesville: University Press of Florida, 1998), 101–09.

9. Ernest Pépin, *Le Tango de la haine* (Paris: Gallimard, 1999).

10. The choice of a light-skinned partner to ensure that one's children have as fair a skin as possible.

11. It should be noted that the statue of the beautiful Creole who married Napoleon and pressured him to reinstate slavery has been beheaded.

12. Chamoiseau and Confiant were also each given the Grand Prix Carbet de la Caraïbe, and Confiant received the Prix Casa de Las Americas. The Guadeloupean writer Maryse Condé has received the Prix Littéraire de la Femme for *Moi, Tituba* and the Prix de l'Académie française for *La vie scélérate*.

13. Mary Gallagher, "Seminal Praise: The Poetry of Saint-John Perse," in *An Introduction to Caribbean Francophone Writing*, ed. Sam Haigh (Oxford: Berg, 1999), 17–33. It is interesting to note that Gallagher's essay is the first one in this volume, preceding essays on Césaire and Fanon, and that Haigh presents Saint-John Perse as a major influence on contemporary Antillean writers.

14. Gallagher, "Seminal Praise."

15. Leah Hewitt, "Inventing Antillean Narrative: Maryse Condé and Literary Tradition," in *Studies in Twentieth Century Literature* 17, no. 1 (1993), 79–96, 81.

16. Simone Schwarz-Bart, *Pluie et vent sur Télumée Miracle* (Paris: Seuil, 1972). English translation: *The Bridge of Beyond* (New York: Atheneum, 1994).

17. Maryse Condé, *Traversée de la Mangrove* (Paris: Mercure de France, 1992). English translation: *Crossing the Mangrove* (New York: Anchor Books, 1995).

18. Cited in Michael Dash, "The World and the Word: French Caribbean Writing in the Twentieth Century," *Callaloo* 11, no. 1 (Winter 1988), 112–30, 118.

19. Lacascade Suzanne, *Claire-Solange ame africaine*. No references to this publication could be found.

20. Maryse Condé, *Le Roman Antillais* (Paris: Nathan, 1977); *La Poésie Antillaise* (Paris: Nathan, 1977); *La Civilisation du Bossale* (Paris: L'Harmattan, 1978); *La Parole des femmes* (Paris: L'Harmattan, 1979).

21. Dany Bébel-Gisler, *La Langue créole, force jugulée* (Paris: L'Harmattan, 1976).

22. Maryse Condé, "Order, Disorder, Freedom and the Caribbean Writer," *Yale French Studies* 83, (1993): 121–35.

23. Maryse Condé, "The Role of the Writer," *World Literature Today* 67, no. 4 (Fall 1993), 697–99.

24. Daniel Maximin, "Antillean Journey," in *Caribbean Creolization*, ed. Kathleen Balutansky and Marie-Agnès Sourieau, 13–19.

25. Ernest Pépin and Raphaël Confiant, "The Stakes of Créolité," in *Caribbean Creolization*, ed. Kathleen Balutansky and Marie-Agnès Sourieau, 96–100.

26. Gisèle Pineau. "Ecrire en tant que noire," in *Penser la créolité*, ed. Maryse Condé and Madeleine Cottenet-Hage (Paris: Karthala, 1995), 289–95.

27. Clarisse Zimra, "Negritude in the Feminine Mode: the Cases of Guadeloupe and Martinique," *The Journal of Ethnic Studies* 12, no.1: 53–77, 64.

28. Raphaël Confiant, *Eau de café* (Paris: Grasset, 1991).

29. Raphaël Confiant, *Le Meurtre du Samedi-Gloria* (Paris: Mercure de France, 1999).

30. Patrick Chamoiseau, *Solibo Magnifique* (Paris: Gallimard, 1988).

31. Patrick Chamoiseau, *Texaco* (Paris: Gallimard, 1992).

32. Patrick Chamoiseau, "Reflections on Maryse Condé's *Traversée de la Mangrove*," *Callaloo* 14, no. 2 (1991): 389–95, 390.

33. Maryse Condé, "The Role of the Writer," 698.

34. Michèle Lacrosil, *Sapotille et le serin d'argile* (Paris: Gallimard, 1960).

35. Michèle Lacrosil, *Cajou* (Paris: Gallimard, 1961). Lacrosil also wrote a novel set on a Guadeloupean plantation that features characters from France and Guadeloupe: *Demain Jab-Herma* (Paris: Gallimard, 1967).

36. Jacqueline Manicom, *Mon examen de blanc* (Paris: Sarrazin, 1972). Manicom also wrote *La Graine*, a semi-autobiographical diary-novel set on a French maternity ward that denounced the dangers and indignities facing poor immigrant women during childbirth.

37. André and Simone Schwarz-Bart, *Un Plat de porc aux bananes vertes* (Paris: Seuil, 1967).

38. Simone Schwarz-Bart, *Ti-Jean l'Horizon* (Paris: Seuil, 1979).

39. Maryse Condé, *Heremakhonon* (Paris: Union Générale d'Editions, 1976). English translation: *Heremakhonon* (Boulder: Lynne Rienner Publications, 2000).

40. Maryse Condé, *Une Saison à Rihata* (Paris: Laffont, 1981). English translation: *A Season in Rihata*, (London: Heinemann, 1988).

41. Maryse Condé, *Moi, Tituba, Sorcière . . . Noire de Salem* (Paris: Mercure de France, 1986). English translation: *I, Tituba, Black Witch of Salem* (Charlottesville: University Press of Virginia, 1992).

42. Maryse Condé, *La Vie scélérate* (Paris: Seghers, 1987). English translation: *Tree of Life* (New York: Ballantine Books, 1994).

43. Maryse Condé, *Le Dernier roi mage* (Paris: Mercure de France, 1992). English translation: *The Last of the African Kings* (Lincoln: University of Nebraska Press, 1997).

44. Maryse Condé, *La Colonie du nouveau monde* (Paris: Laffont, 1993).

45. Maryse Condé, *La Migration des coeurs* (Paris: Laffont, 1995). English translation: *Windward Heights* (New York: Soho, 1998).

46. Maryse Condé, *Désirada* (Paris: Laffont, 1997). English translation: *Desirada* (New York: Soho Press, 2000).

47. Maryse Condé, *Célanire cou-coupe* (Paris: Laffont, 2000).

48. Daniel Maximin, *L'Isolé soleil* (Paris: Seuil, 1981). English translation: *Lone Sun* (Charlottesville: University Press of Virginia, 1989). The other novels in the trilogy are *Soufrières* (Paris: Seuil, 1995) and *L'Île et une nuit* (Paris: Seuil, 1995).

49. Gisèle Pineau, *Un Papillon dans la cité* (Paris: Sépia, 1993). This novel has been classified by some as children's literature.

50. Gisèle Pineau, *L'Exil selon Julia* (Paris: Stock, 1996).

51. Sylvie Durmelat, "Récit d'un 'retour au pays pas natal': Jardins et migrations dans *L'Exil selon Julia* de Gisèle Pineau," *Journal of Caribbean Literatures* 3, no. 3.

52. Barbara A. Babcock. "A Tolerated Margin of Mess": The Trickster and His Tales Reconsidered, *Journal of the Folklore Institute* 2, (1975): 147–86.

53. Roger Abrahams, *The Man of Words in the West Indies: Performance and Emergence of Creole Culture* (Baltimore, Md.: Johns Hopkins University Press, 1983).

54. Leonard Barrett, *The Sun and the Drum* (Kingston, Jamaica: Sangster Book Stores, 1976), 35.

55. Henry Louis Gates, Jr., *The Signifying Monkey* (Oxford: Oxford University Press, 1998).

56. Simone Schwarz-Bart, *Pluie et vent sur Télumée Miracle*, 153.

57. Schwarz-Bart, *Pluie et vent*, 160.

58. Schwarz-Bart, *Pluie et vent*, 161

59. Schwarz-Bart, *Pluie et vent*, 127.

60. Joyce Jonas, *Anancy in the Great House* (New York: Greenwood Press, 1990), 2.

61. Simone Schwarz-Bart, *Pluie et vent sur Télumée Miracle*, 53

62. Schwarz-Bart, *Pluie et vent*, 18.

63. Schwarz-Bart, *Pluie et vent*, 85.

64. Schwarz-Bart, *Pluie et vent*, 75

65. Schwarz-Bart, *Pluie et vent*, 50.

66. Schwarz-Bart, *Pluie et vent*, 75.

67. Schwarz-Bart, *Pluie et vent*, 93.

68. Schwarz-Bart, *Pluie et vent*, 92.

69. Schwarz-Bart, *Pluie et vent*, 94.

70. Abena P. A. Busia, "This Gift of Metaphor. Symbolic Strategies and the Triumph of Survival in Simone Schwarz-Bart's *The Bridge of Beyond*," in *Out of the Kumbla: Caribbean Women and Literature*, ed. Carole Boyce Davies and Elaine Fido (Trenton: Africa World Press, 1990), 289–301, 296.

71. Simone Schwarz-Bart, *Pluie et vent sur Télumée Miracle*, 51

72. Schwarz-Bart, *Pluie et vent*, 97.

73. Schwarz-Bart, *Pluie et vent*, 90.

74. It must be noted that Télumée spins a Signifyin(g) discourse in that her answers are not aimed at imparting information. Toussine's earlier visit to the Desaragnes would have provided them with all the information they needed regarding Télumée's qualifications.

75. Maryse Condé, "The Role of the Writer," 698.

76. Maryse Condé, *Traversée de la Mangrove*, 154.

77. René Larrier, "A Roving 'I': 'Errance' and Identity in Maryse Condé's *Traversée de la Mangrove*," *L'Esprit Créateur* 38, no. 3 (1998): 84–94, 88.

78. Jean Bernabé, Raphaël Confiant and Patrick Chamoiseau, *Éloge de la créolité*, 13.

79. Joseph Zobel, *Rue Cases Nègres* (Paris: Présence Africaine, 1974). English translation: *Black Shack Alley* (Washington, D.C.: Three Continents, 1980).

80. Condé, *Traversée*, 139.

81. Marie-Agnès Sourieau, "*Traversée de la Mangrove*: Un champ de pulsions communes," *Francofonia* 13.24 (1993), 109–22: 112.

82. Ellen Munley, "Mapping the Mangrove: Empathy and Survival in *Traversée de la Mangrove*," *Callaloo* 15.1 (1992), 156–66: 163.

83. Condé, *Traversée*, 135.

84. Françoise Lionnet, "*Traversée de la Mangrove* de Maryse Condé: Vers un nouvel humanisme antillais?" *The French Review* 66, no. 3 (1993), 475–86, 479.

85. Condé, *Traversée*, 63.

86. Condé, *Traversée*, 63.

87. Condé, *Traversée*, 231.

88. Ernest Pépin, "Regard d'un écrivain antillais," 225.

89. For further information, see Henriette Levillain, *La Guadeloupe 1875–1914. Série Mémoires* no. 28 (Paris: Autrement, 1994).

90. Ernest Pépin, "Regard d'un écrivain antillais," 225.

91. Maryse Condé, "Créolité without Creole Language?" 109.

92. Daniel Picouly, *Le Champ de personne* (Paris: Flammarion, 1995).

16

History and Cultural Identity in Haitian Writings

Suzanne Crosta

THE HISTORY OF HAITIAN LITERATURE IS TIED to the island's distinctive political status as the first Caribbean nation to win its freedom from French colonial rule. It took more than thirteen years of militant resistance and tactical warfare to defeat Napoleon's expeditionary force and proclaim its national independence on 1 January 1804. Names of militant resisters like Makandal, Daniel Boukman, Toussaint L'Ouverture, Jean-Jacques Dessalines, and Henri Christophe are etched in the national collective consciousness and figure prominently in Haitian cultural expressions.[1] Once the "pearl of the French Antilles," now the third poorest nation of the planet, Haiti continues to struggle for its freedom and its dignity. January 1, 2004, will mark Haiti's bicentennial, and it appears fitting to revisit Haiti's past which fueled and yielded a rich literary legacy. This chapter[2] focuses on the wealth and breadth of literary writings and discourses that have shaped, influenced and enriched Caribbean narratives within a continuum of tradition and innovation.[3] It begins with a view of the literary history, then examines contemporary texts of four Haitian writers.[4] In all these texts, social or literary conventions are the basis for subversion, transformation and innovation, and their narrative and discursive strategies are manifest in the way they negotiate between past and present, between freedom and constraints, between the same and the diverse.

Two Centuries of Haitian Writings

The status of French and Creole are inscribed in uneven power dynamics. Consequently, the status of a national literature in one of these two languages has fueled debate about the social and political implications and significance of these two bodies of literature. Some literary critics have proposed a literature *within* and *outside* of Haiti; others have included it within transnational, transcultural and translinguistic frameworks (Francophone Literatures, New World Literatures, Post-Colonial Literatures, etc.). Haitian writers in exile or based abroad have also seen their works integrated in the national literatures of their adopted country, or the country where they wrote or published their writings. Whereas before one could sketch out a literature written in French and another written in Haitian Creole, we now find Haitian writers opting for other languages. As linguistic boundaries are being crossed, so abound questions on a weakened Haitian state, the impact of transnational communities, globalization of markets and the future of Haitian literature, as both a symbolic commodity, to borrow Pierre Bourdieu's term, and a work of art.

It is, therefore, difficult to fix a definite point of departure to any overview of Haitian literature. Whereas the tenants of the Créolité Movement trace "Creole Letters" as far back as 1635, Haitian literary historians and critics tend to choose the date of its independence, 1804, as the beginning of Haitian literature. As Léon-François Hoffmann and Maximilien Laroche concur, writings published during the colonial period are scarce, given the economic imperatives of the plantocracy. January 1, 1804, represented not only a turning point in French literary production but also an epistemological break with French literary history. In his seminal essay, *L'Avènement de la littérature haïtienne*, Maximilien Laroche argues that this epistemological break did not occur in Creole writings. He notes that this body of literature, relegated to the margins until 1944, continued to evolve out of necessity and effort, and its development depended on the talents, sensibilities and contributions of its writers from the colonial period to the present day.[5] Indeed Haitian Creole writers like Oswald Durand, Georges Sylvain, Georges Castera, Félix-Morisseau-Leroy, and Frankétienne have sought, each in his own way, to use Creole as a vehicle to renew and revitalize Haitian aesthetic expression while addressing contemporary social issues. This continuity of commitment informs the ethical and aesthetic concerns of these writers for whom Creole is not only the repository of popular cultural traditions and wisdom but also the site of Creole subjectivity and identity.

Alongside literary activities in Haitian Creole is a prolific literary production in French by the Haitian elite. The French language occupied a privileged position for it remained the foundation of education, daily communication among the elite and the language of administration. For many Haitians, the use of French in their literary works was not only a logical consequence of their schooling but also a medium to widen their audience and gain recognition in European or North American literary circles and institutions. It is therefore not surprising that the most abundant corpus of Haitian literature is in French.

Historically, poetry was the favored genre, and the poetic works of Edmond Laforest, Damoclès Vieux and Etzer Vilaire rivaled those of the French literary establishment of the period. The generation of poets (1888–1915) which collaborated to the review *La Ronde* asserted an ideology of opposition that had a profound influence on the poets of the Indigenist movement (1928–1956).[6] It propelled the latter to envisage and create an autonomous literature. However the political conjuncture of the indigenous movement, that is the American Occupation (1915–1934), would give birth to a fairly bleak nationalist vision. Jean Price Mars' groundbreaking essay, *Ainsi parla l'oncle* (1928), rekindled critical reflection on Haitian nationalism and unity. In response to the cultural alienation suffered by his compatriots during the American occupation, Price Mars advocated a return to indigenous values and encouraged Haitian intellectuals and writers to cultivate a form of moral and intellectual resistance against Western domination. Reflecting on the problem of what he called the "bovarysme collectif" (cultural alienation), due in large part to intellectual subjugation of Haitians, Price-Mars encouraged artists and writers to reject the vocabulary and the logic of colonial cultures and revisit their African heritage in order to renegotiate their multiple cultural legacies and review critically the foundations of their Haitian identity (political and social commitment, celebration of its popular religion, vodou, and inscription of its national language, Creole). Poets such as Carl Brouard, Philippe Toby Marcellin, Émile Roumer, Normil Sylvain and Antonio Vieux, who collaborated to the *Revue Indigène*, gave eloquent expressions to this trend.

The most renowned militant poet of his generation would have to be René Depestre, with his *Un arc-en-ciel pour l'Occident chrétien* (1967) (*Rainbow for a Christian West*). Opting for Haitian cultural forms and expressions, he advocated a form of protest literature against Western military conquests and moral superiority while extolling the virtues of a renewed humanism, of a creative and heterogeneous future. The vitality of Haitian poetry continues to flourish and Christophe Charles will identify three major trends in Haitian poetry since 1960:

> Je distingue trois vagues au sein de cette nouvelle génération de poètes qui a émergé en Haïti vers 1960:
> 1) celle des années 60 avec les groupes et collections littéraires Régénération du Nord-Ouest d'Haïti (1960), Haïti littéraire (1961), Houguénikon (1963), les théories du merdisme (1964) et du spiralisme (1968),
> 2) celle des années 70 avec la génération de vertige (1968–1971), le pluréalisme (1972–1973) de Gérard Dougé, le Cénacle de la revue des écoliers (1974–1979) et le mulâtrisme culturel (1977),
> 3) celle des années 80 qui a amené, entre autres, les poètes des éditions Choucoune et deux de l'école Surpluréaliste à travers les éditions Damour et les éditions Kauss.[7]

As its continuity in Haitian literature bears witness, Haitian poetry remains a dynamic field of reflection, inquiry, innovation, solidarity and openness to a multiplicity of relations.

If poetry is the heart and soul of Haitian literary production, the novel is the privileged site for exploring historical and contemporary issues in all its complexities. According to Hoffmann and Laroche, the first chronicled Haitian novel, *Stella* (1859) by Eméric Bergeaud, focuses on Haiti's struggles for independence.[8] In addition to Frédéric Marcelin's realistic novels *Thémistocle-Epaminondas Labasterre* (1901), *La Vengeance de Mama* (1902) and *Marilisse* (1903), Justin L'Hérisson's *Famille des Pitite-Caille* (1905), *Zoune chez sa nainnainne* (1906) and Fernand Hibbert's *Séna* (1905), *Les Thazar* (1907) and *Romulus* (1908) are satiric if not ironic yarns about Haiti's military governments in the first century of its independence. Political and social critiques become less veiled during the Indigenist movement that contributed to a new genre: the peasant or rural novel. Jacques Roumain's *Gouverneurs de la rosée* (*Masters of the Dew*), first published in 1944, is the most representative of its type and one of the most internationally acclaimed Haitian novels.[9] It is interesting to note that Roumain's novel will give a new countenance to the novel tradition in Haiti. Its emphasis on contemporary issues and, more specifically, on the plight, views and expressions of ordinary people, point to a new class-consciousness, and a political ideal of Marxism. The inscriptions of Haitian Creole, of vodou rituals, of popular traditions are but a few of the characteristics from which future writers will draw their literary inspiration and imagination. Jacques Stéphen Alexis' avant-garde theories on the *réalisme merveilleux* (magical realism) will add another dimension to the Haitian novel by mixing political, social, cultural realism with the magical, mysterious layers of reality.[10] As this new trend moves from its experimental phases to become a political and an aesthetic imperative, it forges interesting ties and dialogues with its Caribbean (Cuba, Dominican Republic, Puerto Rico) and Latin American (Argentina, Brazil, Columbia . . .) counterparts. Alexis's novels, *Compère général soleil* (1955), *Les Arbres musiciens* (1957), *L'Espace d'un cillement* (1959), and *Romancero aux étoiles* (1960) are more than peasant novels for these narratives intersect race, class and culture politics within the nation-state of Haiti.

However, the tyranny of the Duvalier's regime seriously undermined individual rights and freedoms and the novel tradition responded in kind. Most notably, within Haiti, Frankétienne, Jean-Claude Fignolé and René Philoctète created the Spiralist Movement whose main goals were to fight against political hegemonic discourses and practices, encourage creativity and a renewal of language, and engage the reader in the process of meaning and signification of their narratives. Outside Haiti, those in forced or voluntary exile felt an urgency to address the contemporary problems of Haiti and were much more virulent and strident in their criticism of the Duvalierist dynasty,[11] whether based in Canada (Gérard Étienne, Dany Laferrière, Émile Ollivier, Anthony Phelps), in France (René Depestre, Jean Métellus, Jean Claude Charles) in Senegal (Jean F. Brierre, Roger Dorsinville, Félix Morisseau-Leroy) or in the United States (Georges Castera, Paul Laraque, Marie Vieux).

With the advent of globalization and the powerful presence of American ideology and global networks, Haitian literary productions in French are competing with those written in other languages, the most influential of which is English. This last decade, in particular, has seen Haitian writers choose English, garnering prizes and attaining international recognition. Such is the case of Edwidge Danticat, who appeared on Oprah's book list and who has figured in very prestigious reviews. For those who do not write directly in English, many opt for translation of their works to widen their audience. Whereas, in the past, only a handful of Haitian writings were translated (Jacques Stephen Alexis, Marie Chauvet, Jacques Roumain . . .), there is now a growing trend among the new generation of writers to have their works translated within a relatively short amount of time. There is also growing interest in British and North American literary circles in post-colonial theories and understanding literary and cultural diversity. This has increased sharply the growing criticism in English on Haitian literature. Alongside these writings, we are also witnessing a rise in political tracts, literary works and criticism in Haitian Creole. Michel-Rolph Trouillot's *Ti difé sou istwa Ayiti* (1977), George Castera's *Konbèlann* (1976), and Maximilien Laroche's *Teke* (2000) provide exemplary cases of the continuity of production in Creole. There are also a number of websites in which coordinators and collaborators operate solely in Haitian Creole. Clearly, Haitian literary production is a vibrant and dynamic site for theorizing on Haiti's legacy of political resistance, cultural diversity and cross-cultural connections.

Songe d'une photo d'enfance: Oppositional Discourse to Authoritative Politics

As this brief historical and literary incursion has attempted to demonstrate, struggles for independence and the consequent seizures of power by successive political leaders, some totalitarian, others democratic, are common themes in Haitian historiography and literary writings. In keeping with the tradition of political commitment of Haitian writers such as Jacques Stephen Alexis, René Depestre and Jean-Claude Fignolé, Louis-Philippe Dalembert's *Le Songe d'une photo d'enfance* (Dream of a baby picture) also constitute an innovative response to closed political authoritative discourse. In his collection of short stories, opposition to Duvalierist discourse takes place at the level of form and verbal manipulation. Dalembert blends traditional realism with magical realism, uses wordplay and repetition to create a certain rhythm within his narrative. Contrary to Roumain's optimistic view of Haiti's future in *Master of the Dew*, Dalembert's *Songe d'une photo d'enfance* offers a somber portrayal of Haiti. There is no Manuel extolling political virtues, no happy ending to the characters' quest for affection, love or happiness, no illusion of better times ahead.

From the very first short story of the collection entitled "Frontières interdites" (Forbidden Borders) to his last "Caraïblues," the reader is introduced to characters who fall prey to senseless violence ("Frontières interdites"), to aggressive judgmental attitudes ("L'Authentique histoire de Tikita-Fou-Doux," "La Dernière Bataille du général Pont-d'Avignon," "Délices port-aux-crassiennes"), to arbitrary arrest and imprisonment ("Macaronade"), to political repression involving suffering and death ("Le Songe d'une photo d'enfance" and "Caraïblues"). Replete with historical references to persons, places and events with imagined material, Dalembert's text revisits Haitian history with emphasis on the Duvalier period in light of its traumatic effects on the poor, the resisters, and those living on the margins of society. In "Frontières interdites," Ti-Noir, a blue-collar factory worker, frequents the mysterious underworld of Port-aux-Crasses (a play on Port-au-Prince, the capital of Haiti). He represents the plight of the working class, toiling long hours for meager wages. He rarely sees daylight, frequents the neighboring brothel once every three months. Not surprisingly, his relationships are reduced to a series of instant conquests; his dreams of a better life are as elusive as the stars he contemplates hours on end. However, his life is inexorably transformed when he falls for *Número Uno's* female companion. If, for a brief moment, Ti-Noir's life shows some glimmer of hope, in the cross-cultural encounter and romance between Ti-Noir and his beloved, his senseless murder in plain view is a reminder of the violent hierarchies that determine human destinies. As in all his short stories, Dalembert's characters remain impenetrable and distant, if not mysterious. In their respective lives, the barriers of reality tend to disappear and each one tries to forge a hybrid space where individual expression and fulfillment are valued. For the star-crossed lovers, this hybrid space is found in their fantasies and their expressions of love through music and sensual contact as they dance:

> De l'intérieur lui venant, par flots intermittents, les notes languissantes de la voix féminine.
> *Te quiero como nadie te ha querido*
> *Te quiero como nadie te querrá . . .*
> Le rythme lent des hanches qui se cherchent, s'arc-boutent. Les bas-ventres se touchent, libérant une ondée de rêves à la fois lubriques et tendres dans sa tête. Ti-Noir jubilait d'impatience.[12]

This glimpse into Ti-Noir's fleeting happiness is also evident at the level of structure: The juxtaposition of a childhood sequence in which he reaches for a mango with episodes of his adult years in which he reaches to the woman he loves; both result in his fall. Although he is able to survive his first fall from a tree, he dies mercilessly from the second with neither cries of dismay nor legend of the fall to consecrate Ti-Noir's life and death.

As in "Frontières interdites," every short story revisits the past in order to address contemporary issues but the gaps and the manipulation of history point not only to the constructed nature of history and identity but how it is wielded by those in power and those divested of power. In "L'authentique histoire de Tikita-Fou-Doux," the narrator offers bits and pieces of Tikita-Fou-Doux's life history through polyphonic interactions of multiple characters sharing various points of view on Tikita's multi-faceted character. Tikita-Fou-Doux's identity remains as enigmatic as the testimonies about him, and the reader becomes acutely aware of how context, actions and interactions, exclusion and inclusion affect individual identity and destiny. In "La Dernière Bataille du général Pont-d'Avignon," "Délices port-aux-crassiennes" and "Macaron," individual and collective struggles for freedom are expressed in the form of marvelous tales, such as the epic battles waged by Pont d'Avignon against the onslaught of giant ants. However, the parody of authoritative figures and the paradoxical reverence and debasement of Haitian resisters underscore a critical examination of the unequal but competing power relations along political, cultural and gender lines.

The last two short stories, "Songe d'une photo d'enfance" and "Caraïblues," concentrate more on political justice and respect for basic human rights than on demystification and subversion of Duvalierist discourse. The short story that bears the name of the collection depicts a Haitian child in search of a picture of his own childhood. He pleads repeatedly to his father who, unable to fulfill his son's requests, suffers from silence, frustration and despair. As the story unfolds, the child's past remains out of his reach while his present is weighted with propaganda and mystifying discourses. As political indoctrination and appropriation of belief systems take on the form of a new catechism for pupils to recite and to commit to memory, the child's tenacious search for his own image is fraught with risks. At a symbolic level, the Venerable's conquest of young pupils' mind parallels Duvalier's assault on Haitian imagination and culture during his political dynasty.[13] In the story, tensions heighten as political repression bears down on the community. Cold political tactics such as outlawing beggary in response to mass starvation borders on the absurd. The narrative subverts the dictator's discourse through parody and naturalist imagery. The figure of the Venerable as omnipotent, omniscient and ubiquitous is undermined by ironic and sarcastic comments highlighting his human weaknesses. Inversely, the fragility of the child's identity is strengthened by his relationship with the natural world. Although denied of an image of himself, the child finds glimpses of his reflection in the river he frequents. In fact, the river plays a role that is at the same time symbolic and intrinsic to the development of the story. It is there that the child forges new relationships with the surrounding fauna and it is there that the child is apprised of his country's prophetic vision of the past, as is clearly evident in this passage: "Je ne suis qu'une pauvre rivière de province, me répond l'eau calme et claire. Je n'ai jamais vu la capitale; et puis, je ne crois pas avoir tellement envie de la voir. Si j'allais là-bas, je me changerais en une mer furieuse qui gronderait, bondirait, mugirait, piafferait; je balaierais tout sur mon passage. . . . Tout, jusqu'au dernier grain de poussière! Ce serait le nouveau déluge de l'histoire de l'humanité."[14]

There is a deliberate attempt in presenting the natural voice of the river in much the same way as the voice of the people from the quarter of Salbounda. This passage highlights the complementary and meaningful role occupied by nature in this short story: the words of the river are intrinsic to the story, but its activation in the context transforms them in such a way that they represent inflammatory indictments. However, the narrator also points to the community's propensity to present itself rather than reflect on itself and this may explain the tearful despair of the child after hearing the river's apocalyptic assertions. Moreover, images of meteorological catastrophes (hurricanes, torrential rains, flash snowstorms . . .) infused with political references to Duvalier's dictatorship converge to signal an absence of balance and harmony both in the cultural and natural worlds. After the Venerable's expulsion, the child, now a man, takes on the task of revisiting critically his country's history. The author's voice figures among those of his characters and this presence reinforces his ideas that everyone should have an active role in documenting Haiti's history. However, the narrator doesn't advocate blind or blanket endorsements. The narrator underlines such fundamental questions as: "Quoi écrire et comment le dire?"[15] Indeed, for those who have never known freedom, the opportunity to express what one really wants to say can be a painful experience, as the narrator asserts: "Est-ce que l'histoire de cette île caraïbe devait continuer à être un long récit de cauchemars, où il est toujours question de croque-mitaine, de fourmi-à-z'ailes, de zombies et de la quête interminable du sel de la vraie vie?"[16] It is difficult to redress a historical vision that already exists with all the stereotypes and the injustices, with the historical vision that should exist.

The last short story starts where "Le Songe d'une photo d'enfance" finishes. It is overtly political in its content with implicit and explicit sexual connotations. "Caraïblues" comes full circle, for it also documents a tragic love story, this time between a professor of Latin-American literature and one of her students called Solé. Under close surveillance for her subversive ideas, Madame L. is wanted for questioning by political authorities. Fearing for her life, she has gone underground. In her secret meetings and discussions with Solé, she expounds and professes her political affiliation with communism while criticizing the regime responsible for imposing censorship on its citizens. Alternating with sexually and politically charged dialogue between lovers are the vivid descriptions of an anonymous tortured body whose cries of pain and despair are said to be "inhuman." As in "Frontières interdites," the lovers in "Caraïblues" also speak through songs and the lyrics are fraught with political overtones. "Et nous nous surprenions toujours à fredonner les mêmes strophes de la *Canción por la unidad latinoamericana* du compositeur cubain Pablo Milanes. Ou bien à déclamer les vers du Nicolás Guillén de la *Elegía a un soldado vivo*."[17] Music is no longer just a theme of the narrative but its underlying structure. In their defiance of political and cultural boundaries, the lovers speak a new language. This is also manifest at the level of form where the composition of the "Twelve Bar Blues" is reproduced in the twelve sections of the short story. The thirteenth section, a turnaround in blues composition, reverts and reinforces the theme of liberation implicit at the beginning of the short story. Meshed in the narrative are episodes of suffering and joy, in much the same way the blues creates pauses in between verses to heighten tension or emotion. As in the first short story, "Frontières interdites," alternating voices and perspectives are carefully woven as they intensify themes and emotions. The narrative structure in "Caraïblues" oscillates between two opposing scenes: the love scene between Madame L. and Solé alternates with the descriptive sequence of a mysterious body in agony. Dalembert's narrative has an opaque quality to it and the reader plays an important role in identifying the tortured body and deciphering the plot. The story remains fragmented: we still do not know the full name of Madame L., how she died, how the body of Solé was transported and why it is confined in a cold cell. The absence of an authoritative voice invites an active participation from the reader in the construction of meaning and signification.[18] "Caraïblues" also plays on the visible graphics of the written word. The use of italics and parentheses emphasize the effects of political repression and censorship on individual expression. Although the narrative ends without answering the questions it raises (the most important of which is how to combat a nameless, faceless, omnipotent and ubiquitous enemy) it remains a strong indictment against the tyranny of oppression which determines human destinies and congeals human needs such as love and affection.

Dalembert's collection can be viewed as a post-colonial literary kaleidoscope, for it combines tradition with innovation, political realism with magical realism, direct and indirect discourses, and polyphonic interaction through multiple points of view in a complex and inflammatory vision of the history of Haiti. The intent is to provoke reflection on social transformations at both local and global levels. While it is true that the tone oscillates between sadness and melancholy, that the language evokes ambiguity and veiled subversive meanings, there is a positive awareness based on solidarity and justice for the poor and the oppressed. This vision also shapes the literary form of Dalembert's text through references to different disciplines (history, politics, and music), the frequent use of parody, irony and hyperbole, as well as the play on various perspectives. The active role assigned to readers in the process of ascribing meaning to Haiti's woes opens a space for cross-cultural dialogues not only on the extent of human suffering in Haiti but on a transnational consciousness of the struggle of the poor for basic sustenance and human dignity.

La Discorde aux cent voix: Reflections on Language and National Identity

La Discorde aux cent voix is an exemplary novel to study the problem of communication and isolation in Haiti. René Depestre in *Alléluia pour une femme-jardin* and Louis-Philippe Dalembert in

Le Songe d'une photo d'enfance have among many others included in their narratives the constructed nature of identity by popular discourses, especially the impact of rumors, gossip and other forms of popular discourses on the lives of ordinary men and women. For Ollivier, speech is a vehicle of communication with a capacity for compromise: As his narrator asserts: "Par le biais de la parole, on finit par établir un compromis avec la réalité."[19] There is an underlying awareness that the spoken word or spoken conversations are effective weapons of power and control but also of change and transformation. As *La Discorde aux cent voix* reveals, the daunting challenge lies in the negotiation of these weapons and their consequences on the lives of Haitians.

In the novel, the source of rumors remains for the most part enigmatic but its profound effects are no less devastating for the inhabitants of Cailles. As Ollivier states, rumors can exude a thousand flavors; in other words, they circulate in much the same way as the quality of air we breathe. Rumor's capacity to mobilize individuals and groups appears endless as the refrain in Ollivier novel's suggests: "Et vogue la rumeur."[20] In *La Discorde aux cent voix*, truth remains as elusive as its spokespersons. Rumors circulate in most public spaces: the café La Glacière, funeral parlors and especially Leclerc's grocery store: "C'était là que se distillaient les mille saveurs de la vie des Cailles: confidences amoureuses, discussions esotériques, questions politiques, problèmes de santé . . . tout passait par la tonnelle de l'épicerie Leclerc."[21] These are not mere idle chatterings but provide insights into the unequal social and power dynamics of Haitian society where ordinary people wield unknowingly or naively their own brand of justice and power. We see here allusions to Duvalierism's legacy of what Laënnec Hurbon has called "total confusion between reality and its representation."[22] In Ollivier's novel, Duvalierist dictatorship is not only an assault on Haitian imagination and culture but also on Haitian language and popular discourse as they traverse different media.

The anonymous inflammatory note addressed to Max Masquini is a case in point. Through a series of assertions based on assumptions, hearsay, false allegations or attributions based on circumstantial evidence, bandwagon appeals and ad hominem attacks, the author(s) of the letter seeks to undermine and destroy Denys, who in their view poses a national threat. The letter attempts to mobilize Masquini's attention to the widow and her son Denys, who in their view have brought shame on their family and their community. The reader is never apprised of the reference points or the facts. In the final analysis, there is no measure of truth and the appearance of impropriety is more important than the act of impropriety itself. Ollivier explains this problem in light of the community's trauma by political oppression: "Que les faits rapportés soient exacts, démésurément grossis ou tout bonnement inventés, peu importe au fond. Dans les sociétés humaines et surtout en période de crise, les dénonciations fleurissent et se multiplient."[23] As a result of this letter, Denys is brutally condemned by his community. His exile will end in death on a foreign battlefield and he will return home in a casket. The effects of the anonymous letter addressed to an authority figure like Max Masquini, who pays attention to all disseminated information and who has the ability to suppress even the alphabet, are given ample treatment in the novel.[24] The misfortune of Denys and his mother, Madame Anselme, whose heartaches precipitate her death, reveal to what extent rumors constitute a barometer of tensions in the community, between the state and its citizens. These tensions resulting from the language of pure force become so unbearable that the novel alludes to mass migration toward Cuba, the Dominican Republic and Miami.

In Ollivier's novel, there is great concern for the potential dangers of rumor on the poor, on women, on the marginalized members of the community. The narrator focuses on the tortured or dysfunctional bodies of its victims. In spite of Monsignor Lenet's warnings of the perilous effects of rumor and its potential to exploit the vulnerability of the poor and the illiterate, the community is unable to refrain from participating in it. This is also dealt with at a mystical level when rumors abound that the statue of Mary sheds real tears or that of the Christ figure trickles blood. Its effects on the faith community take on fantastic proportions when couples complain of sexual dysfunction or when women commit suicide from despair.

Everyone participates in circulating rumor but no one escapes its grasp or its stranglehold on individual destinies. This is also exacerbated by the proximity of individuals living in insular communities. Diogène Artheau's legendary arguments with his neighbor are symptomatic of his feelings of entrapment. A semi-recluse individual, Diogène Artheau has on different occasions played different roles in circulating rumors that have allowed him to survive but not to thrive. Rumors in Ollivier's novel are more than predictors of behavior, they more often than not determine the thoughts and actions of ordinary people caught in the web of political repression. In this way, Ollivier provides an intimate portrait of its effects and points to the culture of fear and suspicion that erodes human relationships and impedes progress or any other positive initiative.

Le Chant des sirènes: Demythification of the American Dream

Le Chant des sirènes (The Song of the Sirens) is also concerned with the impoverishment of Haiti as a result of the political dictatorship of the Duvaliers but its emphasis is on the internalized image of the United States as paradise among Haitians. Colimon-Hall addresses this issue in her collection of short stories and urges Haitians to reject the alienating ideologies which permeate Haitians' visions of themselves and the ultimate tragedies that mark their lives. It becomes apparent that the United States and to a lesser extent France continue to play a significant role in the political, economic and social realities of life in Haiti and this troubled relationship informs Colimon-Hall's writing at the level of content and form.

Le Chant des sirènes by Marie-Thérèse Colimon-Hall unites six short stories on the theme of exile. The author underlines the erosion of a national identity due to political and economic instability and the short- and long-term effects of American ideologies on the future of Haiti. The collection establishes a correlation between emigration and the "culture of misery"(to borrow Lyonel Trouillot's expression) that afflicts Haitians. *Le Chant des sirènes* provides a disturbing profile of those who choose exile because they defy by their sheer numbers all attempts at classification: they are rich and poor, young and old, single, separated and married, professionals, white collars, blue collars and so on. Some emigrate through official channels, others illicitly, some are healthy, others are sick, some are virtuous others are nymphomaniacs . . . However, one trait unites them all and that is the distance they create between themselves and their homeland. Little by little they neglect their loved ones, forget their friends and their foes. For those left behind, depression, poverty, and frustration define their daily lives and limit their social mobility, given the enormous drain of human resources. Undoubtedly for many Haitians, entry into the United States or France represents a safe refuge but the discourse of the author insists on the misleading or false images that they project.

In all the short stories of *Le Chant des sirènes*, the author encourages her readers to identify the motives of her characters, the myriad of reasons that force so many Haitians to leave the country. In each of her short stories, Colimon-Hall provides an intimate portrait of her characters, their joys, their pains, their hopes, and their despair. The theme of each short story remains unresolved: the revenge never takes place, the trip to New York is constantly postponed, the parents' solutions to their children's problems destroy rather than unite the family, and the daughter's best wishes to her mother never reach the latter. The void is never filled and this impacts on the individual and collective identity of her characters. Consequently, the nation is further impoverished, for the price of exile is costly to those who leave as well as to those who are left behind.

From the outset, *Le Chant des sirènes* warns readers against the snares and dangers of the siren's song. If the Duvalier regime is at the root of Haitian emigration, she also shows that American ideology is a strong magnet for many Haitians. In particular, she represents characters whose beliefs in the American Dream ruin their lives while impoverishing both morally and materially their loved ones. The first short story, entitled "La Revanche," describes Adrienne Sarty's hope for a better future in America. The reader is given an internal glimpse into the psychology of this character through her correspondence with her best friend Silotte. As depicted in her letters, before she has even been granted a visa, we find Adrienne glowing with happiness at the prospect of being able to find work that would secure her a better living for herself and her daughter. Unfortunately, once in America, she finds an altogether different El Dorado than the one of her dreams. In order to survive in the urban jungle, she must exercise ingenuity and endure many hardships. Once in New York, her reality changes and so does her expression, which becomes more and more hybrid. In her letter to Silotte, her French expression is replete with English words "Lever 5h du matin; bain, déjeuner rapide, snack bar, le bureau jusqu'à 1h; lunch rapid au subway, passage au market une ou deux fois par semaine ou au drugstore du coin."[25] Her expression translates the weight of her economic and linguistic realities in America. In her letters to Silotte, she describes the fragmentary moments of her life in New York which consists of a series of menial jobs. One hears the implicit voice of the author in Silotte's reply to Adrienne in which she questions her voluntary separation from her child, her friends, and her homeland in order to be a housekeeper and a blue-collar worker.[26]

In Colimon-Hall's text, the repertoires of classical Greek and French literatures are the basis for innovation.[27] Each short story starts with a brief recognizable excerpt that serves as a starting point for literary interaction. Using the seductive song of the sirens that Ulysses and his companions heard as the basis of her text, she expounds the lures which entice many Haitians to leave or simply disappear. The parallel between the Mediterranean and the Caribbean, between Ancient Greece and Haiti reactivates and subverts the authority of classical myths which continue to define "empires." Just as Ulysses benefited from Circé's counsel to protect his crew from the seductive song of the sirens, Colimon-Hall seeks through her narrative voice to warn her readers by providing them with varied testimonies on those who were seduced by the American Dream. Each short story attests to the exorbitant cost of each human life and through repetition, the evocation of the American dream is always associated with some tragic story. References to beasts and monsters take on mythological proportions and perpetuate allusions to the myth of Ulysses, with the exception that there is no return for those who fall prey to their seductive songs. At each loss, the narrator lends her voice to rekindle hope. The recurring metaphorical allusions to the siren's song in all her short stories are aimed at showing the recurring myths and illusions that trap Haitians abroad and leave their families in Haiti scrambling for subsistence, protection and affection.

It is interesting to note that Colimon-Hall's characters in *Chant des sirènes* appear transparent but through the course of the narrative one discovers their zones of opacity. Each short story presents characters who think they know their husband, their wife, their lover, their child . . . but they are dismayed to discover their "illusion." In "La Revanche," Silotte could not have imagined the form of Adrienne's revenge. In "Le Plat de lentilles," Simon will probably never discover that he married Aglaé instead of Euphrosine. In "Actuellement à New York," Arnold's wife cannot accept her husband's betrayal and abandonment. In "Le Rendez-vous," the dying mother will never know why her children were not at her deathbed just as they will not know what she wanted to tell them before dying. In "La Solution" the parents' decision in regard to their children ends in the fragmentation of the family; all their children are based elsewhere and the parents are left to fend for themselves. Finally in "Bonjour, Maman! Bonne Fête, Maman!, Dulcina will never understand why her parents, especially her mother, have not taken steps to bring her to the United States. The one underlying sentiment which unites all the stories is uncertainty.

Le Chant des sirènes invites readers to reject simplistic assertions on the Haitian situation. Although one can clearly see the idealization of "l'autt bô," the dichotomies between here and there, them and us, present themselves at several levels. An American or European reader would see a critique of emigration but a Haitian reader would simply view emigration as a fact of life, his/her reality. In order to live, one has to work and more often than not the work is based "l'autt bô" (the other side of the ocean), in other words, elsewhere. Her characters are victims and executioners, subjects and objects of internal and external political discourses. Her emphasis on the conflicts and at times severance of relationships between two or three generations of women, where there was once a continuity of values and solidarity among them, underscore, the detrimental effects of emigration on kinship. "Le Rendez-vous" describes the last moments of a mother on her deathbed who cries out to her children, who are nowhere to be found. Another example is Dulcina's profound dismay that she will never leave her perceived infernal existence in Haiti for the United States, her paradise. This last short story sounds the death knell for Haiti's future, for even the new generation of young women desires to live elsewhere.

The last short story, "Bonjour Maman, Bonne Fête Maman!" goes full circle with the first short story. The author once again broaches the mother-daughter relationship but this time from the daughter's perspective. The short story focuses on the reality for those who remain in Haiti while their family members leave to create new lives for themselves in America. Dolcina Désilus was left in the care of her grandmother when she was just a child and has been waiting to rejoin her family in the United States for almost fourteen years. Dolcina does not remember her parents, nor does she really know them, since her parents left Haiti for economic reasons when she was just a baby. Dolcina is so anxious to rejoin her mother that she leaves the one person who truly loves her, her grandmother, in order to live in the city. But Dolcina's dream never materializes and her despair is so great that not even her grandmother can ease her pain. Deprived of a maternal figure, Dolcina is an exile in her homeland, and like all exiles, she is always searching for her roots. Her name, closely related to Dulcinea del Toboso in *The Man from La Mancha*, subverts the pragmatic nature of her predecessor by underlining the quixotic folly of Dolcina's vision and projection of America as paradise. Dolcina ignores all moral lessons from those around her, fearing that they will counter her longing desire to join her mother. At the end of the short story, the reader feels the character's frustration with her mother's indifference. She doesn't understand that her parents are working in America without visas and that to bring their daughter to the United States would jeopardize their present situation. The two short stories come full circle and the reader is left wondering how this maternal absence will affect Adrienne's daughter Suzy and now Dolcina. How will the daughters of tomorrow embrace their motherhood and will they too abandon their homeland? Dolcina's dreams show that when one cannot escape the physical constraints of the island, then one tries to compensate for the loss at a psychic level. Given that in Dolcina's view America and not Haiti is the generator of satisfiers, it is most unlikely that she will choose to stay in Haiti. This begs the question of how to counter the drain of Haiti's human resources. Although the author doesn't answer the question, she invites her readers to reflect on the form of development that may nurture Suzy's and Dolcina's present so that their human needs are deemed a priority. In Colimon-Hall's view, turning a blind eye or neglecting the problem would endanger the very future of the nation. In order to destroy the monsters within and outside Haiti, Marie-Thérèse Colimon-Hall prescribes like Dalembert a form of individual humanism. Her writings point to the need to explore new ideas and invent new weapons which will allow Haitians to deafen the song of the sirens and rail against the economic and moral decay of the country. Although implicit, it becomes apparent that Colimon-Hall criticizes the political upheaval that forced many Haitians to leave but there is also the gnawing absence of international organizations and policies to aid those in dire need of basic subsistence.

Breath, Eyes, Memory: Call-Response to *Le Chant des sirènes*

Whereas in Colimon's text the disintegration of the family is imminent, Edwidge Danticat's *Breath, Eyes, Memory* proposes an alternative view, one of hope for family connections and solidarity. Like Colimon's *Le Chant des sirènes*, the novel examines the personal lives of ordinary people. Sophie's quest for personal fulfillment is twofold: she struggles for liberation from social constraints whilst seeking in the same breath reconciliation with her mother. Undoubtedly these challenges entail critical reflection, challenges and transformation on a personal scale. Danticat's novel revisits socially constructed myths that are degrading to women and places Sophie's burden of having been emotionally scarred by the invasive *test* designed to make her an acceptable bride in a patriarchal society. In breaking this familial tradition whereby mothers verify their daughter's virginity, Sophie liberates herself and her daughter from its harmful effects.

In *Breath, Eyes, Memory*, motherhood is important to Sophie but her role is not bound to it as she tries to heal herself of the legacy of the *test* while reaffirming her female sexuality. No longer is she able to accept the objectification of women as recipients of male sexual desire. It is noteworthy that Sophie's relationship with her mother is tense; having grown up physically and emotionally distanced from her, she has little recollection of her mother Martine who left Haiti for the United States shortly after her birth. Raised by her Aunt Atie, Sophie tries to come to terms with the separation. Even after being reunited with her mother, Sophie identifies herself as "my mother's daughter and my Tante Atie's child."[28] Her feeling of estrangement grows as she matures and discovers that she was the child of her mother's rape. In this novel, storytelling unites women but also has the capacity to instill anxiety and fears. Aunt Atie tries to prepare Sophie by recounting her own experience of the tests but this sharing of experience does little to alleviate Sophie's inner turmoil.[29] The test left very painful emotional scars on Sophie as well as on other women in her close and extended family. On a personal level, the humiliation lingers on, and it affects negatively her relationship with her own body. The test also has impacts on her sexual relationship with her husband Joseph. In an act of defiance and liberation, Sophie breaks her own hymen which she describes in terms of political oppression. For her, . . . it was like breaking manacles, an act of freedom."[30] It is relevant that Sophie doesn't blame her mother for her complicity in the test but lays blame on socially constructed myths that both men and women play a role in perpetuating. "Women tell stories to their children both to frighten and delight them. These women, they are fluttering lanterns on the hills, the fireflies in the night, the faces that loom over you and recreate the same unspeakable acts that they themselves lived through. There is always a place where nightmares are passed on through generations like heirlooms. Where women like cardinal birds return to look at their own faces in stagnant bodies of water."[31]

Mothers who have internalized the dominant society's idea of purity uncritically pass the suffering of the test on to their daughters. Men benefit from the social mythology surrounding the test because it gives them greater control of women's reproductive potential, ensuring the continuation of paternal lineage, as is evident in Sophie's recollection of Tante Atie's life lessons:

> *Haitian men, they insist that their women are virgins and have their ten fingers.*
> According to Tante Atie, each finger had a purpose. It was the way she had been taught to prepare her to become a woman. Mothering. Boiling. Loving. Baking. Nursing. Frying. Healing. Washing. Ironing. Scrubbing. It wasn't her fault, she said. Her ten fingers had been named for her even before she was born. Sometimes, she even wished she had six fingers on each hand so she could have two left for herself.[32]

Tante Atie limits herself to taking care of others (Sophie and her grandmother) but this altruism doesn't fulfill the void she feels. Resigned to her station in life, she confesses to Sophie that "We must graze where we are tied."[33] In her view, she relegates women's role as equivalent to an animal whose freedom has been lost. Sophie realizes the difficulties her mother endured and offers forgiveness and reconciliation.

In *Breath, Eyes, Memory*, Danticat is concerned with the inner gaze of her characters as it collides with the external gaze. Sophie's poor self-esteem is the result of externally constructed myths imposed upon her. She reads a letter written by another woman at her sexual phobia therapy group which echoes her own feelings toward her mother and her family. "It would be easy to hate you, but I can't because you are part of me. You are me . . . I knew my hurt and hers were links in a long chain and if she hurt me, it was because she was hurt, too."[34] In order to break these negative images reflected as in a house of mirrors, Sophie takes stock of her life and assumes the responsibility of breaking the pattern of degradation that has been passed down in her family along with the test. "It was up to me to make sure that my daughter never slept with ghosts, never lived with nightmares, and never had *her* name burnt in the flames."[35] In engaging in critical reflection, she saves her daughter from its trauma and heals the whole family in the process. She reinforces this in building bridges between the generations of women in her family through private conversations, storytelling and photography.[36] These three methods of documenting family history are complementary as they provide the youngest generation, symbolized by Brigitte, with a genealogical history from which she can draw wisdom and strength. Through photography, she can inscribe in her living memory a physical portrait of her great-grandmother. Brigitte is herself described as a living document of the family history. When Sophie's grandmother looks at Brigitte, she thoughtfully notes: "The tree has not split one mite. Isn't it a miracle that we can visit with all our kin, simply by looking into this face?"[37] Ultimately it is the diversity of approaches to preserving memories that allow for the successful preservation of family history. Danticat emphasizes the interdependent nature of family life, the solidarity and the strength that can be drawn from knowing and being involved with one's collective history.

In *Breath, Eyes, Memory*, Danticat portrays Guinea and by extension Africa, as an idealized land of creation myths, ancestors and happiness. It is, like heaven, the place where one goes to die. It is the place where one rejoins other family members and rests in peace. When Sophie is young, Tante Atie tells her wondrous stories about a group of people in Guinea: "They are the people of Creation. Strong, tall, and mighty people who can bear anything. Their Maker, she said, gives them the sky to carry because they are strong. These people do not know who they are, but if you see a lot of trouble in your life, it is because you were chosen to carry part of the sky on your head."[38] This passage is meant to signify that strength and resilience come with adversity. The image of Guinea that one derives from this story is one of strength, beauty and wisdom. Danticat draws on this reference to Africa to give added weight to Atie's perspective of the world where Haiti's rich cultural legacy can be a weapon of empowerment in times of need.

In Danticat's novel, memory is also a tool of survival in the harsh social and political realities of Haiti, as this passage clearly reveals: "In our family, we had come to expect that people can disappear into thin air. All traces lost except in the vivid eyes of one's memory."[39] History is an inescapable element of individual and collective identity. Haiti is a place where "you carry your past like the hair on your head."[40] One's history is as much a part of an individual as his or her physical features. However the burden of history remains daunting. History is not sought and told simply for the sake of history: it is a way of cultivating understanding for one's identity, one's distinctiveness in midst of social unrest and transformations; it is also a way of restoring one's dignity through awareness of unequal power relations across race and gender lines.

Sophie, Brigitte, Martine, Atie, and Sophie's grandmother represent four generation of women whose life experiences enrich and bind them together. Sophie's individual strength and identity are drawn from the collective history of her entire family. Danticat symbolizes family solidarity among the Caco women when they all divide ownership of the family's land equally between them. Tante Atie feels the need to make a link with future generations by including her name in the town archives. Here, Danticat depicts the tension between written records and memory as depository for the family's history. Sophie's grandmother prefers to preserve people in memories rather than written words.

On a final note, Danticat does not confine her characters to Haiti. The novel divides its time between Haiti and New York, and this bridging of communities is aimed at collapsing spatial divides between the island and the continent. Danticat underlines the importance of New York as a place in the Haitian diaspora.[41] Martine left Haiti because she was trying to escape the emotional trauma of being raped as a young woman in Haiti. The norm of social respectability prevented her from seeking justice and reparation. Her flight and exile in the United States do not help her heal as she still experiences horrible nightmares many years later. Martine goes back to Haiti to reconcile with Sophie and the rest of her family. But ultimately the psychological burden of the rape is too much for her to bear. Unable to resolve her inner turmoil, she commits suicide. Sophie is left to confront and overcome the ghosts that haunted her mother and in doing so she heals herself and allows Martine to rest in peace. At the end of *Breath, Eyes, Memory*, Sophie prepares to leave Haiti, but in leaving, she has integrated her family into herself. This is a departure from other Haitian women writers such as Marie-Thérèse Colimon-Hall whose writings depict most often family members' sentiments of abandonment and solitude. In Danticat's novel, Sophie officially owns a share of her family's land. She goes away from Haiti not as an exile but as an empowered woman, capable of expanding the geography of Haitian experience beyond the narrow confines of the island itself.

In conclusion, Haitian literature is seeking to cross borders, to extend its parameters to include the voices of compatriots near and far, in the fold or in the *kadans*. Haiti's national past is both complex and violent and its varied responses have contributed to the wealth of its aesthetic expressions. Haiti's present is unfolding in a world where frontiers are rapidly changing and disappearing. Marie-Thérèse Colimon-Hall and Edwidge Danticat draw attention to these issues at thematic and symbolic levels. Louis-Philippe Dalembert and Émile Ollivier have inveighed against political repression and zombification, highlighted how in a regime where all forms of expression are closely monitored, oral forms of communication can be both a weapon of oppression or inversely of liberation, depending on how the dynamics of unequal power relationships affect meaning. Alongside images of resistance and of social transformation capable of counteracting political repression and zombification, are portraits of human beings: their beauty, their spirit, their weaknesses, their strengths, their truths and their illusions. Colimon-Hall, Dalembert, Danticat and Ollivier all focus on those moments when the scales of human suffering and tragedy are unevenly weighted by patterns and discourses of domination. As this study has emphasized, these writers do not limit themselves to conventional forms of literary and social discourse but use them as starting points for literary interaction and innovation. In crossing boundaries across the disciplines, in attuning their reader's ears to the oral/aural quality of their texts, Haitian writers hope to create a space where freedom, diversity, creativity and dialogue can restore some balance, some measure of mutual appreciation for the interdependence of peoples and interconnectedness of life in our global communities.

Notes

1. On fugitive slave resistance and maroon communities in the Caribbean, see Joan Dayan, *Haiti, History and the Gods* (Berkeley: California University Press, 1995); Jean Fouchard, *Les Marrons de la liberté* (Paris: Éditions de l'école, 1972); C.L.R. James, *The Black Jacobins* (London: Allison & Busby, 1980); and Richard Price, *Maroon Societies* (New York: Anchor/Doubleday, 1973).

2. This is a version of my article, "History, Literature and Cultural Indentity," published in *International Journal of Francophone Studies* 5, no. 1.

3. This study does not claim to exhaustivity or to representative selection but attempts to offer an overview of Haiti's rich literary legacy.

4. Namely, *Le Chant des sirènes* by Marie-Thérèse Colimon-Hall, *Le Songe d'une photo d'enfance* by Louis-Philippe Dalembert, *Breath, Eyes, and Memory* by Edwidge Danticat, and *La Discorde aux cent voix* by Émile Ollivier.

5. The corpus of these writings includes perhaps the oldest texts in Haitian literature since it can be traced back as early as 1749. The first work, *Lizet kité laplenn*, is attributed to a French settler, Duvivier de la Mahautière. Oswald Durand's *Choukoun* and George Sylvain's *Cric Crac* are among the most cited examples of Haitian Creole writings before 1944. After 1944, linguists sought to standardize the Haitian language, implement it in its school curriculum and encourage its literary expressions.

6. According to Max Dominique, "La génération de *La Ronde* appartient à la période de notre histoire qui va de 1888 à 1915 et qui voit le déclin (1888–1908) et la crise généralisée (1908–1915) de l'ancienne Haïti." *L'Arme de la critique littéraire* (Montreal: CIDHICA, 1988), 65. For an in-depth analysis on the question of ideology and subversion in the works of these poets, see chapters 4 and 5.

7. Christophe Charles, "Le Paysage politique et poétique sous la dictature des Duvalier," *Prestige* 3, no. 2 (1996), 25–26.

8. On the literary history of Haiti, see Raphaël Berrou and Pradel Pompilus, Max Dominique, Léon-François Hoffmann and Maximilien Laroche among others.

9. Jacques Roumain (Washington: Howard University Press, 1980) as well as Roger Dorsinville's *Jacques Roumain* (Paris: Présence africaine, 1981). Jean-Baptiste Cinéas' *Le Drame de la terre* (Cap-Haïtien: Impr. du Séminaire Adventiste, 1933) and *L'Héritage sacré* (Port-au-Prince: Henri Deschamps, 1945), as well as Marie Chauvet's *Fonds-des-nègres* (Port-au-Prince: Henri Deschamps, 1960) are also representative of the genre which attracted many writers.

10. See his article "Le Réalisme merveilleux des Haïtiens" *Présence africaine* 8, no.10 (1956), 245–71.

11. For literary representations of the Duvaliers, see René Depestre's *Le Mât de Cocagne* (Paris: Gallimard, 1979), Roger Dorsinville's *Mourir pour Haïti, ou Les Croisés d'Esther* (Paris: L'Harmattan, 1980), Gérard Étienne's, *Le Nègre crucifié* (Montreal: Éds. francophone & Nouvelle Optique, 1974), Franck Fouchés *Général Baron-la-Croix* (Montreal: Leméac, 1974), Jean Métellus's *L'Année Dessalines* (Paris: Gallimard, 1986), Félix Morisseau-Leroy's *Roua Kréon* (Dakar: Jardin Kreyol, 1978), Émile Ollivier's *Paysages de l'aveugle* (Montreal: P. Tisseyre, 1977), Anthony Phelps's *Mémoire en colin maillard* (Montreal: Nouvelle Optique, 1976).

12. Louis-Philippe Dalembert, *Songe d'une photo d'enfance* (Paris: Serpent à Plumes, 1993), 18.

13. For in-depth analyses on Duvalier's assault on Haitian culture, see Laënnec Hurbon's *Culture et Dictature en Haïti* (Paris: L'Harmattan, 1979) and Maximilien Laroche's *L'Avènement de la littérature haïtienne* (Quebec: GRELCA, Université Laval, 1987).

14. Louis-Philippe Dalembert, *Songe d'une photo d'enfance*, 110.

15. Dalembert, *Songe*, 116.

16. Dalembert, *Songe*, 116–17.

17. Dalembert, *Songe*, 126.

18. The short story "L'Authentique histoire de Tikita-Fou-Doux" is an exemplary case of identity reconstruction through polyphonic interactions. There are so many stories about Tikita-Fou-Doux that the word "authentic" can only be explained through a deliberately ironic stance. The same is true of Macaron in "Macaronade" in which numerous versions defy any attempt at reconstructing a "true" portrait of the man. Like Tikita-Fou-Doux, his identity remains elusive and mysterious.

19. Émile Ollivier, *La Discorde aux cent voix* (Paris: A. Michel, 1986), 80.

20. Ollivier, *La Discorde*, 82.

21. Ollivier, *La Discorde*, 232.

22. Laënnec Hurbon, *Culture et dictature en Haïti* (Paris: L'Harmattan, 1979), 190.

23. Ollivier, *La Discorde*, 163.

24. Ollivier, *La Discorde*, 168.

25. Marie-Thérèse Colimon-Hall, *Le Chant des sirènes* (Port-au-Prince: Éditions du Soleil, 1979), 19.

26. Colimon-Hall, *Le Chant des sirènes*, 18.

27. In "Le Rendez-Vous," the author combines the conventions of writing with a manipulation of the oral tradition. Colimon-Hall presents the story of Maman Ya through the voice of her friend Madame Victorin while Mme Dubourg and the readers listen to her attentively. However, the structure of the narrative implies a desire to retain possession of her history.

28. Edwidge Danticat, *Breath, Eyes, Memory* (New York: Soho Press, 1994), 49.

29. Danticat, *Breath*, 60.

30. Danticat, *Breath*, 130.

31. Danticat, *Breath*, 233–34.

32. Danticat, *Breath*, 150.

33. Danticat, *Breath*, 136.

34. Danticat, *Breath*, 203.

35. Danticat, *Breath*, 203.

36. On the question of censorship and social taboos affecting Haitian women's writings see Paulette Poujol Oriol, "La femme haïtienne dans la littérature: problèmes de l'écrivain," *Journal of Haitian Studies* 3, no. 4 (1997–98): 80–86 and Miriam Chancy's full-length study *Framing Silence: Revolutionary Novels by Haitian Women* (New Brunswick, N.J.: Rutgers University Press, 1996).

37. Danticat, *Breath*, 105.

38. Danticat, *Breath*, 25.

39. Danticat, *Breath*, 170.

40. Danticat, *Breath*, 234.

41. New York has a strong Haitian community and has attracted well-known writers such as Frantz Bataille, Georges Castera, Pierre Carrié and Marie Vieux Chauvet, among others. It is also the base of *Haiti Observateur*, founded in 1971. In a conversation with Dany Lafferrière in February 2001, the prolific writer commented on the marketing strategies and financial rewards of inserting New York or Manhattan in the title of one's books. Nevertheless Frantz Bataille's essay *La Vie haïtienne à New York* (Port-au-Prince: Fardin 1977), Pierre Carrié's novel *Bonjour New York* (Ville Saint-Laurent: Journal Offset, 1970) and Jean-Claude Charles' novels *Manhattan Blues* (Paris: Barrault, 1985) and *Sainte Dérive des cochons* (Montréal: Nouvelle Optique, 1977) underline the harsh realities (racism, poverty, unemployment) and the experiences of insularity (isolation, marginalization, silence) felt by Haitians based in New York.

IV
NORTH AMERICA

17

The Quebec Novel

Jacques Allard

THE PERSONIFICATION OF THE QUEBEC NOVEL as a rather melancholy yet humorous French-speaking North American provides an illuminating insight into Quebec literature. This chapter is a rapid sketch of "the Quebec novel," which it seeks to describe in technical, precise terms.[1] Describing the Quebec novel as North American implies that it is "of mixed race." part of the ever-changing hybrid that the title "Canadian" suggests: a patchwork of the "savage" and the "civilized," of Native American, French and British traditions (that is, English, Scots and Irish), enriched since 1960 by significant waves of immigrants at a time of demographic decline in Quebec. To expand the image, north of the forty-fifth parallel there is a multicolored fabric fluttering in a wind that blows from the United States. So it is that the Quebecois is born of the Northern American, knotting together a whole host of cultures from the New World. This geographic term has lost its rather Utopian overtones along with its European origins, but Quebec and its literature, which, like America itself, were once children of the Renaissance, still preserve their European traits even more than other continentals.

Although the history of the Quebec novel begins in 1534 with the arrival of Cartier and the writing of *Relations*, it is still a young literature: it would take a further three hundred years before creative writing appeared—the first collection of poetry in 1830 and the first novel in 1837. More than four centuries of episodic fresh starts, or rather 160 years of slow productivity, do not make this a venerable literature by European standards. Not only is there still a limited corpus, but even experimentation in form and language is recent. In Quebec the period of apprenticeship (that is, of imitation) lasted until about 1965, during which time a population that was 6,000 in 1660 and 60,000 in 1760 has now become approximately 6 million. Sustained creative innovation arrived only as a result of the efforts of twelve generations.

Commentators and essayists of the nineteenth and twentieth centuries noted melancholy as a central characteristic. The predominant tendencies in the Quebec novel of the 1990s could be qualified as meditative rather than active. The Romantic, Nordic and intuitive character of Abbé Henri-Raymond Casgrain still holds true, as does that of the internal exile in the country of clerics, Arthur Buies. This melancholy could be described as Nordic and Celtic, like that of a native people who were constantly migrating: nomadic communities with their sense of nationhood are historically and culturally mutant.

The characteristic of humor emerges less from a hypothesis than from the sustained reading of the works of the last forty years. But since the beginning of written expression (1764), as in the oral tradition before it, traces abound of the self-deprecating humor that is typical, it seems, of groups that experience tribulation or domination. The considerable number of stand-up comedians in Quebec today (that is, monologists who have taken the place of popular singers and their songs), demonstrates the rise of comic tone and expression in Quebec society since 1960.

Since the beginning of colonization (which includes the colonization of literary output) Canadian speech[2] has always involved speaking French. After the conformist pressure of Canadian clerical doctrine (in the nineteenth century), echoed by the associations for the advancement of "proper French" during this period,[3] there remains today only the feeling that in Quebec standard French is a language people love to hate (a feeling aptly expressed by the Neo-Quebecois novelist, Sergio Kokis). More precisely, it is a language that people love to *put in its place* with all the violence that such an expression supposes, that is to say to place it at a distance, which is the function of all regional idioms in relation to the language that has been consecrated as the norm in the mother country. One may thus see the whole linguistic history of Quebec as one of progressive creolization, leading to a composite language, a kind of pidgin, with French grammatical structures and a mixed English-French vocabulary. But this has not yet come to pass, and the reference or norm for writers (if not for other speakers) remains French and Parisian.

The Primitive Novel (1534–1904)

This historical overview is both thematic and aesthetic, focusing on three stages: the primitive novel (1534–1904), the modern novel (1904–1965) and the new or postmodern novel (1965–2000). Examples will be taken from landmark texts like *Les Anciens Canadiens*, *Trente arpents* and *Prochain épisode*. These three novels each give narrative form to their own relation to history, thereby showing a continuity in the quest for meaning through aesthetic liberation.

The whole group of works discussed here will be presented as a history of narrative freedom. This endeavor to sketch a history of narrative forms moves from primitive (colonial and Canadian) expression, which was generally more utilitarian than artistic, to formal hedonism, characteristic of the new novel of the second half of the twentieth century. It departs from the traditional critical perspective, which was primarily clerical and generally downplayed any innovations that emerged on the grounds that such works were lacking in literary merit.

Colonial Narrative

Two groups of texts provide the themes and forms of the primitive novel: the grand colonial narrative (1534–1837) and the Canadian novel (*le roman canadien*, 1837–1904). The first, a considerable fore-text of official prose, narratives and correspondences, unfolds in two well-defined stages: the first marked by Jacques Cartier's *Relations* (1534), the second by the introduction of the printing press to Quebec in 1764, which also marks the beginning of the English colony. In the sixteenth, seventeenth and eighteenth centuries, i.e., from Cartier onwards, reports of explorers, religious men and colonizers of all kinds transposed their own time and space into discourse and narrative. These practical and descriptive works are not fiction as such, but they play an important role by constructing the first characters in Quebec literature: Nature and its natives, the Amerindians.

As regards narrative form, Cartier's *Relations* mark the arrival of a genre—the founding narrative. Following his work, and that of Champlain, many more such founding narratives appeared, among them the valuable writings of the Jesuits.[4] There followed the amateur historians, such as Pierre Boucher de Boucherville, and authors of correspondences—some mystical, like Marie de l'Incarnation, and others worldly, like Élisabeth Bégon. Whether official or intimate, these direct accounts vividly conjure up both correspondent and reader: both of them self-effacing in their relation to the King, but alive and visible when addressing God or their loved one.

Canadian-born authors, such as Élisabeth Bégon, soon began writing in this all-encompassing narrative form. Born of the *Voyageurs* of the Renaissance and the seventeenth and eighteenth centuries, its function was to report and its voice was French-Canadian. Such writing contained the promise of a true American-French literature. Instead, the British conquest (Treaty of 1763) brought about a folklorization of Canada: most of the educated French returned to France, leaving behind a majority of peasants, their priests, a few *seigneurs* and a very rich oral tradition. Hence the importance of legends. The legend of Cadieux, the *coureur de bois*, is typical. Mortally wounded by Amerindian enemies, he is said to have written the account of his last moments on some birch bark before lying down forever in the hollow he had dug for himself. Certain songs also played a major role, such as "À la claire fontaine," which the *Voyageurs* sang wherever they went. These popular narratives in the oral tradition, whether brought from France or invented in Canada, left many traces in the newspapers printed from 1764 onwards. The newspapers became all the more important to readers during the winter, when the ships no longer brought news from Europe. All these texts deserve to be studied in their own right. The colonial text is of great interest and significance, as much for its genre as for its subjective or imaginative perceptions. The myths it recounted were to sow the seeds of the future Canadian novel, while the charm of archaic French lent a literary charm to even the prosaic documentary writings.

The Canadian Novel (1837–1904)

This second type of novel, originally labeled Canadian but soon to be called French-Canadian, bears the marks of the colonial narrative: the elements of adventure and discovery, the familiar voice, and the constant references to Europe. *L'Influence d'un livre*,[5] although based on a local news item, moves into a world of folktales and legend, while the narrative voice—very close to the author's—refers at every turn to the great works of European literature. The title, in fact, purports to mock the famous book of alchemy attributed to Albert le Grand and to make fun of the havoc it wreaks on a self-taught peasant. However, the novel finally shows that higher spheres of knowledge can be attained by seeking out the wisdom of simple folk. In addition, it demonstrates that the so-called realist novel can be reached via the fantastic (in this case, the Gothic).

L'Influence d'un livre followed in the footsteps of *Le Canadien*, the newspaper established in 1803 through which a handful of people educated after 1763 aired their views. Already Canadian in spirit and content, it was to be complemented in its ideological aims by agriculturist novels such as *La Terre paternelle* and *Charles Guérin* (1846), which established what was to be the largest-lived sub-genre of the Quebec literature. After these came historical and adventure novels that sang the glories of the past and of New France.

The Canadian novel, which began in the fanciful spirit of a genre much scorned by the establishment of the time, acquired an increasingly ideological slant, spelled out from the 1840s in numerous author prefaces and later in the 1860s by Abbé Henri-Raymond Casgrain and his circle. The Catholic clergy formulated a literary doctrine that prescribed the defense of language and faith, and favored local subjects, rural life and the heroic past before the English regime. All this was done in the manner of French religious Romanticism, which eschewed modern realism and its naturalist successors.

The best synthesis of this other facet of the primitive novel in Quebec history is to be found in *Les Anciens Canadiens*. This does not mean that the historical novel is also a novel of homesteading or rural life, or a sustained defense and illustration of the French language and the Catholic faith. Nor is it the pure novel that certain readers longed for, referring back to the nineteenth-century canon, whether their interest was in Balzac or the Victorians. This desire for the "pure novel" expressed their displeasure with the mixing of memories and hard facts and a style in which everything is commented on in the text itself, in footnotes and even in a final section of "Notes and Explanations."

Les Anciens Canadiens is "impure," as the author himself takes care to point out in the first chapter, which also serves as a preface. In the manner of Cervantès or Diderot, the author speaks to his readers without explicitly referring to them, exhorting them to "promptly throw away this unfortunate book," as they will find "a thousand defects" in it. Avid readers will have understood that *Les Anciens Canadiens* was, after all, a true, pure novel. It conforms perfectly to the great tradition of primitive European narrative, playing on reality and its representation through the important roles assigned to the author and his own historical period, and pretending all the while to be describing another epoch.

Like all learned or cultivated writers, Philippe Aubert de Gaspé in effect goes against the grain of the doctrine that was well on its way to becoming established, pursuing his own pleasure above all. He tells of the good old days, songs and dances, peasant and religious rituals, and of great battles, but does not forget his own misfortunes or those of his noble family, which was ruined by the English conquest. To this end, as narrator, he strongly emphasizes his humiliated nobility, all the while also taking care to portray himself in the guise of the transparent character of a deposed *seigneur*, whose story he purports to tell only in passing. At the beginning of the second part, he places himself right in the center of the novel with Sieur Egmont, as if the better to show that history begins at home. History begins with ourselves, with familiar things, petty stories, regional myths and beliefs, before leading to grand destinies and culminating in great exploits, here represented by those of Archibald Cameron of Locheill and Jules d'Haberville. This is the story of two childhood friends who, by a cruel twist of fate, are forced to fight against each other during the Seven Years' War at the Battle of Quebec in 1759 and the Battle of Levis in 1760.

This then is a tale of the Canadian hybrid that, in its rich ambiguity, founds the fictional character of Quebec. The fact that it was written by a seventy-six-year-old man, the friend of the best writers of his time, says much about the late maturity of literary expression in Quebec. The fact that this book has been translated into English and Spanish and reprinted constantly in Quebec since its publication in 1863 also says a great deal about the reception given to the only novel by Aubert de Gaspé.

After *Les Anciens Canadiens* many historical novels were to appear in which the personal voice and the freedom inherent in the primitive genre were to fade away, as is evident in the works of the other important writer of the Canadian novel, Laure Conan. Of all her historico-religious works, only *Angéline de Montbrun* falls outside the prescriptions of the clergy. This novel is largely autobiographical, giving it a vibrancy that was to make it the most moving novel of the Canadian series. The story is that of an eighteen-year-old girl who wishes to devote herself to good works after her father's death and her beau's change of heart. It breaks with the formal expectations of its time, with the intervention of the subject in the clericalized object. The author turns the *angelism* required by her pre-programmed mandate into a disturbing mirror of female desire, women being almost entirely absent from nineteenth-century writing. This is the culmination of the long apprenticeship in narrative form undertaken since the time of New France and still so often apparent in Laure Conan's own text. It is a far cry from the clerical novel that predominated in the writing of her contemporaries and the rest of her own work. The constraints of the Canadianist doctrine were felt most keenly in the last quarter of the century, by which time the ultramontanist ideology had almost eliminated the liberalism of the beginning of the century. This can be seen in the journalistic narrative that the militant Christian novel ultimately became.[6]

The Modern Novel (1904–1965)

The historical-rural-Catholic model was to hold sway for a long time to come and did not truly disappear until the 1930s, with works such as *Trente arpents*. However, before discussing the novels of the 1930s it is necessary to focus briefly on a novel that appeared in 1904 and upset the established model. Like *L'influence d'un livre*, it proved despite its imperfection to be a landmark text,[7] foreshadowing the new developments that were to follow: in this instance, modernity. *Marie Calumet* is a typically French-Canadian novel, popular in origin, inspired as it was by a folksong, and using familiar language. The action takes place in the middle of the nineteenth century in the house of a rural curé.

The reversal of tradition is brought about by the radically new, irreverent treatment of the subject, and by the confusion between high and low, which accords with Auerbach's proposition in *Mimesis* that realism invaded classicism with the arrival of Molière, and his new use of language, irony and mockery. In this primitive tale, which at first seems merely to be a humorous piece in the style of Jean Richepin, the journalist Rodolphe Girard tells a story about the curé's housekeeper taking charge—in 1904, the simple fact of telling the story at all is extraordinary.

The outrageous treatment of a religious subject includes mention of the visiting bishop's urine and of the clumsy Marie's bottom when she exposes herself on her wedding day. It also describes the whole wedding party running bare-tailed into the fields, struck by diarrhea after the wedding breakfast. This famous final scene is preceded by a long quotation from the Song of Songs, which was particularly sacrilegious as Catholics of the period were not permitted to read the Old Testament except under the supervision of a priest.

Such an entrance into the new century broke completely with the venerable literary contract of the past. This was perhaps "the return of the repressed," a reaction against the refusal to acknowledge realism and a leap into the naturalist garden and into carnival. Three other novels follow in the same anticlerical and modernist vein. *Le Débutant* relates the behind-the-scenes realities of newspaper and city life in 1914, the very year of *Maria Chapdelaine*. *La Scouine* followed in 1918 with its cruel scenes of rural Catholic life. In 1922 came an industrial, secular viewpoint in *Marcel Faure*, the first novel of Jean-Charles Harvey, followed in 1934 by *Les Demi-civilisés*, in which the Establishment as a whole (religious, political, academic, etc.) is accused of ignorance, stupidity or dishonesty.

Banished to the Index, *Le Débutant* and *La Scouine* had only a few hundred readers. In Canada the regionalist fashion in Europe legitimized the artificial survival of nineteenth-century doctrine, and the general hostility toward all forms of outward-looking "exoticism" and modernism.

However, in the 1930s the bishop's proscription of *Les Demi-civilisés* almost made it a best-seller in Montreal. Clerical doctrine was giving way more and more under the onslaught of modernity.

In 1938 Dr. Philippe Panneton (who wrote under the name of Ringuet) struck the final blow by setting out the boundaries of rural Canadian territory in the very title *Trente arpents* and demonstrating at last the inevitability of the modernist aesthetic that had so long been held at bay by Church doctrine. He did this thanks to his mastery of classical realism. Suddenly, the language of the novel was precise, and the narrative logical and richly informed on every level—social, linguistic, historical and even mythological. This had been partly true of some traditional, regionalist works, but Ringuet's first novel brought together all the qualities of a good novel of the period (according to the European canon), and also benefited from the critical dimension characteristic of modernity. This was a rather conventional modernity, obviously closer to Zola than to Sartre, but, for the French-Canadian ideology of the period, the leap was considerable.

His novel spans the four seasons of the life of farmer, Eucahriste Moisan. During Spring and Summer he is successful, a faithful servant of his religiously venerated land. But his submissiveness ultimately takes on such preposterous proportions that he experiences a rapid decline in the Autumn of his life, and real destitution in the Winter of old age. At the end of the novel, he who had spent his quiet life in the great outdoors on good Catholic soil has become a night watchman in a foreign country, the United States of America. He even owes his job to the favors bestowed by his Anglo-American daughter-in-law or the employer of his son Ephrem, who has lost the land he inherited. Most probably Eucahriste does not even understand his grandchildren, who speak to him in English. In his total stupidity, he is betrayed by nature and the cult he has made of it, and is inevitably cheated by his notary and his own son, finally becoming an American migrant.

The skilfulness of the novel is manifold. The action takes place between 1887 and 1932, with appropriate references to world events. The Catholic faith has become pagan—echoing Greek mythology—which indicates that the clerical city is dying. It has closed in upon itself and is unaware of the values of the modern world, particularly the values of the city and of the other, as is the simplistic *Terre paternelle*, which opened the cycle of rural novels in 1846. The great dream of a French nation on American soil presented by *Jean Rivard* (1862–64) fails here, even in a part of the United States to which Quebec had lost a million citizens since 1850.

Written during the Great Depression, the last of the rural novels also speaks of the internal, cultural crisis of the era. It is understandable that Ringuet was the first Quebec writer to attract so much attention from the French press, since he was portraying the total contradiction of the myth, already obvious in 1914–16, of Maria Chapdelaine choosing the land rather than the city and the States. Ringuet's narrative pokes holes in the Utopian discourse that had been built up over a hundred years and combines in one great panorama of the seasons all the moralizing, stereotypical petty scenes of the past that were still to be found in recent works, such as those by Claude-Henri Grignon (*Le Déserteur et autres récits de la terre*, 1934). The grand narrative metaphor of the seasons would appear to be classical, but its primitive character betrays the reductionist version of history that had been accepted by an entire agricultural society.

At last urban realism was free to express itself, as in *Au pied de la pente douce* (Roger Lemelin, 1942) and *Bonheur d'occasion* (Gabrielle Roy, 1945). In the next decade there was a blossoming of psychological (or spiritual) realism, in which fictional events were colored to a very large extent by a meditative dimension (for example: *Mon fils pourtant heureux*, *Le Temps des hommes*, *La Bagarre*).

The French-Canadian novel had suddenly caught up with its time, becoming urban, involving itself in ideas and the realities of modern life. No longer colonial or rural, it had become analytic and critical. Formal innovation followed on psychological realism. *Le Libraire*, first published in Paris because of fears as to way this story of a dissident world would be received in Quebec, perfectly illustrates this phase. It follows the musings of casual diarist, the alter ego of the writer, who ponders existential matters and in so doing changes the traditional form of Quebec fiction. The tone is Sartrian, although there are some traces of Camus and the absurd.

The central character, Hervé Jodoin, a former teacher, cannot get on quietly with his journal of provincial exile and immobility. As he describes his release into the community of forbidden literary work,[8] he is carried away by his own narrative. The vocabulary and rules of composition are always respected, yet constantly criticized, and the emotional tirades he unleashes get the better of reason. However, they do not get the better of the dictionary—there are no neologisms—or of narrative grammar—there is no formal break with standard sentence or paragraph structure and no stream of consciousness. There are no traces of the new modernity, yet to come, of the postmodern novel, merely a highlighting of the cracks in the last remaining laws of fictional illusion, still so recently in evidence in Quebec's fictional space but which Bessette had already begun to question in his first novel, *La Bagarre* (1958).

The Postmodern Novel (1965–2000)

It was not until 1965 that the new modernity burst onto the scene, and that the new term "Quebec Novel" was adopted following its use in the review *Parti Pris*, for works such as Bessette's *l'Incubation*; Marie-Claire Blais's *Une saison dans la vie d'Emmanuel*; Jacques Ferron's *La Nuit*, and Hubert Aquin' *Prochain épisode*. At this stage the Francophone novel in Quebec was representative of a North-American synthesis of forms, integrating particularly the experimental forms that had been developed since Proust and Joyce, including the French *nouveau roman*. This undertaking was original in that the new Quebec novel maintained its readability and referentiality. None of these writers[9] completely adopted either Joyce's stream of consciousness, Simon's labyrinthine style, still less the minimalism of Robbe-Grillet or the theoretical exercises of Ricardou—except for Aquin in *Trou de mémoire*.

Prochain épisode is an excellent example of the new novel and its aims: to invent itself, to be independent and no longer to be content with mere reproduction. The emphasis is on improvisation, stylistically rather like a jam session. Events unfold in an associative, cinematic manner. Hence the fragmentation of content, the multiplication of points of view, the low angle shots and the indirect approach. But, beyond these breaks in the narrative structure and narrative voice, the quest for meaning and the social dimension are almost never absent.

Hubert Aquin relates the story of an anonymous Montreal revolutionary who, finding himself in a psychiatric clinic after an aborted coup, discovers his vocation as a writer. Like Jodoin in *Le Libraire*, he endeavors to overcome his boredom by projecting himself into the novel, on this occasion a spy novel set in Switzerland and ending in Montreal. Typically postmodern in its use of narrative and montage and also its self-referential account of its own genesis, *Prochain épisode* is the textual representation of a whole literary and political theory of a philosophy of the novel where Aquin's literary and political beliefs are narratively expanded to the dimensions of Quebec itself.

The playfulness and inventiveness of the new novel continue in the 1970s. Important works include: *Kamouraska* (1970), a historico-fantastical novel by Anne Hébert; *D'Amour P.Q.*

(1972), a good-humored novel typical of the flower-power generation by Jacques Godbout; *L'Euguélionne* (1976), a feminist manifesto by Louky Bersianik; and *Les Anthropoïdes* (1976), a great epic work by G. Bessette that relates the birth of humanity and narrative in North America. The formal element is very strong in this novel, as in the rest of Bessette's work. Along with Aquin, he is the most important Québécois narrative theoretician.

The influence of these new directions taken during this period can be seen in popular novels such as *La Grosse femme d'à côté est enceinte* (Michel Tremblay, 1978), and later publications in the 1980s: *Le Matou* (Yves Beauchemin, 1981) and *L'Ombre de l'épervier* (Noël Audet, 1988). Writers turn with increasing frequency to magic realism (Tremblay's three fairies), the play on the signifier (see the quotation mark that kills in the work of Beauchemin), or the representation of the author in his fiction (in N. Audet). A return to linearity and history (encouraged by the referendum of 1980) is noticeable in Louis Caron, who launched his series *Les Fils de la liberté* in 1981. Henceforth there was nothing left to prove except that one can benefit from accumulated fictional capital. The output of the 1990s continued this trend (perhaps to an even greater degree), as accessibility became essential and experimentation took a back seat. A preference for neo-realism spread, becoming ever more visible, but taking advantage of the fact that readers were by now more competent and knowledgable about contemporary literature, of which the Quebec writer is now a part. He is no longer a theoretician comparable with the one in *Prochain épisode*, but remains the seeker of form and meaning subsequently found in *Le Semestre* (Bessette, 1979), *Volkswagen Blues* (1984), or later, in *Frontières ou Tableaux d'Amérique* (N. Audet, 1995), *Choses crues* (L. Bissonnette, 1995) and *Le Milieu du jour* (Y. Rivard, 1996).

The extraordinary development in the short story since 1980 also needs to be acknowledged, and the importance of various popular narrative forms and children's literature. The multifaceted nature of writing in Quebec today proves that a certain maturity has been attained, not only by the novel, but also by the publishing industry and the Quebec literary establishment as a whole.

Notes

1. For most of the texts please refer to *Dictionnaire des auteurs de langue française en Amérique du Nord* (Montreal: Fides, 1989), 1364. For more recent texts, see *Panorama de la littérature québécoise contemporaine* (Montreal: Guérin, 1997), 822.

2. Defined from 1965 on as Québécois.

3. After the scandal of "joual," promoted by the contributors to the review *Parti Pris* and then in *Les Belles-Soeurs* by Michel Tremblay.

4. Forty volumes over several decades.

5. Philippe Aubert de Gaspé, Jr.

6. Jules-Paul Tardivel, *Pour la patrie, roman du XXe siècle*, 1895.

7. Despite its imperfections.

8. Voltaire's *Essai sur les moeurs*.

9. This is also true of writers like Anne Hébert and Noël Audet.

18

Québécois Drama: Bordering on Intimacy

Marie-Christine Lesage

WITH THE ARRIVAL OF THE 1980S, the dominant social and political tone of the theater of the 1960s and 1970s (that of Jean-Claude Germain, Robert Gurik and Francoise Loranger, for example) gave way to a drama that veered away from questions of ideology in order to explore, most notably, territories more intimate in nature. It would be an obvious oversimplification to include all Québécois plays in such a homogeneous trend, as there actually are several young authors, like Yvan Bienvenue and Jean-Francois Caron, who reaffirm the need for a politically committed theater. Nonetheless, the works that left their mark on the 1980s and 1990s exhibit certain structural characteristics in common, such as a propensity for the soliloquy and a contamination by recent forms of narrative. This aesthetic is not unique to Québécois theater, as the French, with authors like Eugene Durif, Philippe Minyana, Nathalie Sarraute and Valere Novarina, exhibit a decided taste for the monologue in their plays.[1] Certain critics classify this dramatic writing as non-representational theater or theater of the word, theater to be spoken or listened to. These texts revive the act of listening, as the spectator becomes the silent interlocutor for characters who tell their story by bringing snatches of their past to the surface. Memory and the past are at the heart of this drama, in which characters fall prey to a *mal de vivre* that is singularly unromantic, witness rather to the progressive dissolution of the self undergoing an exhaustive examination. As Michel Corvin has described it, "au théâtre traditionnel on vit, au théâtre contemporain on a vécu."[2]

The failure of the 1980 Quebec referendum on sovereignty became, in the recent history of Québécois theater, a symbolic border dividing two imaginary territories, the one characterized by the affirmation of a collective identity,[3] the other intimate and creative and bearing the imprint of the subject. With the advent of the 1980s, Québécois drama began an aesthetic and thematic shift by resorting, initially, to various modalities of metatheater. *Mise en abyme*, reflexivity and self-referentiality are signs of a theater that, throughout these years, sought new forms freed from the constraints of plot, psychological realism and the search for a collective identity that so marked the sixties and the seventies.

The question of identity shifted from the outside (the social space) to the inside, and a more intimate and introspective drama came into existence. New authors have been responsible for this renewal, led by René-Daniel Dubois and Normand Chaurette, particularly with *Province-town Playhouse, juillet 1919, j'avais 19 ans*[4] and *26 bis, impasse du Colonel Foisy*,[5] plays that have become emblematic of a change in paradigm readily apparent from today's vantage point. These intricately structured texts revive an emphasis on the imaginary, without reference to Québécois reality. The question of collective identity has shifted toward that of a sexual,[6] artistic and, in a larger sense, intimate identity. By employing various techniques of fragmented dramatic narrative, notably making the voice of the artist (writer or director) audible during the creative process, these plays in fact lead us to the source of all performance, which is located in the subjective consciousness of the characters. Several authors later adopted this approach, including Michel Tremblay, the most famous Québécois playwright, who was able to renew his writing and follow the change of direction that took place in the 1980s. His plays *Albertine en cinq temps*[7] and *Le Vrai Monde?*[8] employ *mise en abyme* and mirror-like structures that address the characters' inner space as well as the role of the artist. The first play features a woman, appearing at five different ages in her life, who interacts with these inner figures from her past in order to take stock of her existence. The second deals with the responsibility of a creator toward those who have inspired him, the relationship between the autobiographical and the imaginary. Immersed in self-referential examination, these plays signal the turning inwards of the author as subject. The redeeming aspect of this inward tendency was, however, that it gave birth to drama that was no longer exclusively devoted to the transposition of Québécois references and subjects. From a "théâtre-miroir fondé sur la reproduction minutieusement caricaturale de stéréotypes sociaux,"[9] Québécois theater shifted to writing more refined in nature as far as its formal and literary structures are concerned: speech lent itself more to the artificial and lyrical than the vernacular (it has become a theatricalized speech), and the contents of the plays touched upon a poeticized reality.

A new generation of texts extended this exploration of the inner world, but without recourse to metatheatrality. One of the principal characteristics of a number of texts written during the nineties is their intermingling with modern narrative structures, as exemplified by the short forms favored in contemporary fiction. Andrée Mercier has defined this form in the following terms: "Le récit partage, en effet, bien des traits de la production narrative des vingt dernières années dont, au premier chef, la fascination du je et de ses doubles et les jeux entre autobiographie et fiction. Mise en scène de soi, recours aux diverses formes de l'autobiographie (journal intime, lettre, mémoire, etc.), discours introspectif, le récit n'échappe pas à l'émergence très significative de l'écrit intime et de ses avatars fictionnels."[10]

This has had several consequences, one of which is the heightened importance of the single speaker, to the detriment of the dialogue, even to the point of a quasi-absence of plot and action. This crossing of dramatic and narrative forms, however, is only an external manifestation of a more profound change indicative of the spirit of the time. This will be illuminated by looking at the formal characteristics of the plays of two playwrights, Daniel Danis and Normand Chaurette, as they reveal, every bit as much as the actual content of the plays, the sense of change observed in the writing itself. The importance of the soliloquy, for instance, attests to a shifting of the search for identity toward the subject's inner self. Yet it is with the subject in crisis and in search of new values that this drama concerns itself.

The Subject in Crisis

Authors like Normand Chaurette, Daniel Danis and others, such as Michel Tremblay, Carole Fréchette and Larry Tremblay, to name but a few, have written dramatic texts constructed in mosaic form that emphasize an "I," exploring, by way of soliloquy, the inner recesses of the memory and the self. If, since the end of the nineteenth century, the novel has often resorted to the use of the interior monologue or stream of consciousness, when it comes to theater it is mostly contemporary writers who have used this narrative form. Their contribution has been such that it has led to the development of a distinct form of dramatic monologue now recognized as a genre in itself. The monologue usually offers up an individual, reflexive, organized discourse; it is the voice of logos, the process of rational thought that organizes, explains and ensures coherence of the self. The monologue usually parallels an affirmation of the personality of the character. However, the long narrative monologues that are found in the work of Danis, Chaurette and Tremblay do not exhibit this type of discursive logic; on the contrary, they tend to express inner feelings and oppressions that interfere with any structured discourse. Moreover, these monologues, delivered in unorganized fragments, do not constitute a homogeneous narrative. In fact, they tend to represent an individual's weaknesses, those that cause the self to disintegrate and crumble under the weight of memories and inner searching.

This is why it appears essential to distinguish between the different natures of the two types of discourse. In an excellent article Jean-Jacques Delfour explains the main difference between monologue and soliloquy in theater: "Si le monologue est l'effort d'un individu qui restaure son unité en se faisant savoir à lui-même le contenu de ses pensées, le soliloque, à rebours, signifie la faiblesse de l'individu coupée d'une indispensable main manquante relation à un autre qui, comme destinataire biffé, rend fragile, voire dérisoire, la parole proférée."[11] The monologue is the guarantor of the self and the voice of logos, whereas the soliloquy expresses the rupture of the self and an immersion into what Sarrazac calls an "intrasubjectivité," meaning the "relation du personnage avec la part inconnue de lui-même."[12] This unknown part of the self, drawing upon buried memories and the unconscious, gushes forth in explosive speech, dense, sinuous and often strongly metaphorical. In consequence, the soliloquy offers a discourse less organized and more erratic than the monologue. It also testifies to the solitude of the character, who is not speaking to anyone onstage. The spectator therefore becomes the privileged interlocutor of an inner space that is being unveiled, shamelessly bared. Here the soliloquy appears to constitute the dramatic form of the inner self, that is "ce qui est le plus au-dedans et le plus essentiel d'un être ou d'une chose, en quelque sorte l'intérieur de l'intérieur,"[13] to return to the words of Sarrazac. A particular feature of the intimate narrative is its ability to deliver subjective feelings at the same time as facts, offering a view from the inner self.

Fragments of Soliloquies

The importance of the soliloquy indicates that "l'introspection a remplacé la critique des valeurs collectives"[14] in contemporary Québécois drama. This introspection leads, however, to a split in identity, as if a unity of consciousness was being re-evaluated. Thus, the plays of Danis—like those of Chaurette and Tremblay's latest work—echo this split in the very structure of texts that combine long narrative passages and fragmentation. On one hand, the characters' narratives are presented in a freer, more lyrical form. The soliloquies do not always follow the usual syntagmatic axis of a story, but mix narratives from the past and digressive thoughts, performing analogical jumps, as one image calls up another. On the other hand, each subjective narrative is interspersed with that of another character, creating a highly discontinuous dramatic structure. This juxtaposition of soliloquies is not always chronological, as the narratives frequently jump in time. Finally, in the plays of Daniel Danis, characters are sometimes heard to speak after their physical or psychological death. This is the case with Coco and Clermont in

Cendres de cailloux,[15] and the mother in *Celle-là,*[16] in which narratives suddenly appear from an abstract, unspecified space. Rather than speaking to each other, the characters meet in a time-less, perhaps metaphorical, place.

Dramatic tension is be felt by the audience on another level when intimate recollections from different times and places are superimposed. The past does not appear as a continuous whole, but emerges instead in bits and pieces that follow the disorderly changes in direction of every-one's thoughts. The theatrical dynamic then arises from the arrangement of segments of mem-ories that, by way of a kind of metadialogue, allows the spectator to reconstruct a vision of the characters' common past, all the while aware of the gaps between subjective perceptions. This metadialogue is, in fact, an artificial montage of soliloquies composed of remnants of past events, images revisited that return to life with all the weight of the physical sensations that originally structured the memory. The stage is no longer "le lieu qui déclenche une action, elle est plutôt le lieu privilégié de l'introspection d'un sujet qui ressasse les événements d'un passé demandant à se réincarner."[17] If the plot seems to suffer, it is in the interests of a tension con-tained in the writing itself that restores depth to the memories. As opposed to a scene contain-ing dialogue in which conflict explodes, a scene constructed around a soliloquy offers up an inner density, the dramatic effect of which is more a matter of implosion. Soliloquies implicitly call upon the complicity and attentiveness of an audience, who are no longer anxiously await-ing the resolution of a plot. Reemphasizing the importance of listening, this drama creates enig-matic situations, fragmented stories that the spectator is invited to complete.

Cultural Recycling

The plays of Daniel Danis, *Celle-là* and *Cendres de cailloux,* in particular, are emblematic of this dramatic form. They are structured in a similar manner: instantaneous moments of thought are juxtaposed in the form of soliloquies. In *Celle-là* the three characters pass through a series of photographic clichés that click on and off in their memories, allowing them to "revoir leur vie ensemble." In *Cendres de cailloux* each scene reveals the voice of a character recounting a seg-ment of his or her past. Each of the plays is put together in reverse, which is to say that each protagonist concentrates on rebuilding a past that has been marked by a tragic event. This work on memory, rebuilding the past by recalling painful images and feelings, is also a response to the need to take the present into account. These are universes that examine human and social values, and behaviors that have led to failure and suffering, both mental and physical. *Celle-là* summons up and recycles some of the familiar mythology about Quebec, particularly that con-cerned with the oppression of religion and the taboo imposed on sexuality, but in a way that provides a perspective on how these moral constraints might have nourished and accentuated the darker side of the urges in an individual's imagination. In other words, this play *à rebours* is concerned with the retroactive effects of the past on the present. The soliloquy of the mother's character, which unfolds during her death throes, recounts the extent of the ravages inflicted on this woman, the victim of ostracism in a closed society, by a body too long sup-pressed. Her past life has oscillated between the desire and joy related to childbirth, and an urge for destruction: during a fit of rage she stabbed her son with her scissors. In her memories, the blood of childbirth mixes with the blood of this violent act, uniting pain and joy into insepa-rable realities in her mind: "Le sang rouge partout salissait la chambre du logis. / Autour de l'en-fant de moi, le silence était arrivé. / Quand l'enfant Pierre / c'était sorti de moi tout rouge / la joie de partout / quand l'hôpital l'ont couché entre mes seins."[18] It is not a drama that heaps shame upon a collective past, but rather attempts to uncover the marks left by this past on the subjective consciousness, all the while stressing individual responsibility amidst devastating chaos. In this way, the soliloquy imposes a time to pause and reflect that allows the consciousness to search through images of the past sealed up in the memory and free itself from them, just as the mother says: "Les choses, faut que ça finisse par sortir / sinon on meurt avec. / On s'étouffe."[19] But is it not society as a whole that runs the risk of suffocating if it seeks to bury and forget a past of which it is ashamed?

This is the conclusion to which this author's plays seem to lead, anchored as they are in the bedrock of the individual memory, which reveals a great deal about the collective memory. The agony and death of the mother, for instance, might very well represent the death of a certain state of society, insofar as this character is at once a victim and carrier of the values of "l'ancien monde." This scenario reconnects with an age-old function of theatre that consists in destroying whatever society has outgrown onstage, in order to create space for the values of the future. It is just as revealing that it is young people who have broken into the mother's apartment to kill her, without any apparent motive: is it not this arbitrary violence that threatens a society from within when it has yet to assimilate its past? Without memory, existence falls prey to chaos, and what is under threat, basically, is the individual and collective soul. "Sans mémoire, le sujet se dérobe, vit uniquement dans l'instant, perd ses capacités conceptuelles et cognitives. Son monde vole en éclats et son identité s'évanouit. Il ne produit qu'un ersatz de pensée, une pensée sans durée, sans le *souvenir* de sa genèse qui est la condition nécessaire à la conscience et à la connaissance."[20] An impressive number of contemporary Québécois plays portray memory by the use of the soliloquy.[21]

In the other play, *Cendres de cailloux*, Daniel Danis brings to the stage tormented souls symptomatic of a society caught between two worlds, one in the process of dying, the other as yet unformed. Four characters, Shirley, Coco, Clermont and his daughter Pascale, mentally pace the territory of their common past. If their words invoke the closed horizons of a rural Quebec, the author manages to transcend this reality by raising it to the level of myth. Ordinary human beings become goddesses, monstrous creatures, mythical animals inhabiting a space larger than life. In a scene entitled "L'Amazone sur un quatre-roues," Shirley, the girl with the word "macchabée" (corpse) tattooed on her breast, appears as a wood goddess possessing destructive powers. She and her friends invent rituals, dig up the dead, enter into trances and perform sacrifices on nights when the moon is full. One of them, Coco, who has a savage beast named Gulka gnawing at him from inside, performs a rite of self-destruction by gulping down all the waste in the world in a rebellious gesture toward a sterile society: "Après, j'vas aller avec Dédé pis Flagos / dans le dépotoir municipal. . . . J'vas me mettre les deux pieds / dans les puanteurs de la ville morte. . . . J'vas crier: / 'Gulka! / Attaque!' / La gueule encore en sang / j'vas ramasser à pleines mains / des déchets en décomposition. / La gueule grande ouverte / Gulka va manger."[22]

In effect, the play as a whole presents a generation in their thirties, saddled with dark energies, whose activities consist of destruction and self-destruction, engendered by despair: "Un rêve pour de l'espoir / C'est là pour que les gens / s'inventent un paradis. / Nous autres de ma génération, / on essaie de vivre de nous autres. / Sans dieu nulle part. / Sans job nulle part. / On regarde la vie comme a l'est. / Sans l'enjoliver. / On est pas nés dans la bonne période."[23] The play presents the desolate landscape of a lost generation, sacrificed and stuck between two worlds, one in which dying gods are no longer able to reassure the soul left alone with its fate, the other in which heaven needs to be repopulated with new dreams.

The structure of the play, with the first scene featuring a gruesome dance and the last presenting Pascale, the youngest member of the group, dancing in celebration of life, reveals the meaning of an exploration of the memory that enables new values to rise from the ashes of the past. What is interesting to note in this mythical transposition of Québécois reality is a process of valorization and poeticization that applies as much to territory as to the imaginary. The description of bodies, for instance, outlines the contours of an inner identity forged from the very landscape of Quebec's wilderness: Shirley has had her hair dyed green in order to have a "tête d'épinett," and insolence runs through her veins like "une rivière sur une terre de colon." Once again, by recycling figures from the past and worn-out images, the author brings about a transmutation at once lyrical and detached: indeed, this past is recounted to the audience, a move that prevents any process of psychological identification.

Soliloquies provide a lyrical articulation of each character's inner drama, one that mirrors forces at work in society. This lyrical articulation rests upon the very color of the Québécois language, which is used as the poetic material from which the author invents a language of his own, at once raw and innocent, that echoes the chaotic flux of the discourse found within the consciousness. For instance, the son, in *Celle-là*, recalls a moment from his past in the language of the five-year-old child he once was: "Le noir du soir me faisait avancer. Je courais dans l'hiver qui était en neige tout autour. Mon corps est entré dans l'Hopital. . . . J'arrête devant une porte. Une madame me regarde son manteau sur le dos avec un enfant malade dans ses bras pour l'urgence et un bébé plus loin qui pleure avec l'écho des corridors."[24] In a way that accounts for the characters' inner perceptions, this writing is informed with intense bodily feelings, thus endowing the orality of the language, which distinguishes Québécois theater, with a new poetic sonority.

The Dissolute Identity

The drama of Normand Chaurette features no cultural recycling, reflecting neither the reality of Québécois life nor the particular sonorities of its language. His texts are arranged like musical scores that demand close attention from an audience. *Le Passage de l'Indiana*[25] is structured like a quartet: four voices respond to each other, as a duo from one scene to the next, then as a quartet in others. The quartet scenes involve two duos performing simultaneously, the meaning of the words being overshadowed by the rhythm and interplay of the sonorities. One of Michel Tremblay's latest plays, *Messe solennelle pour une pleine lune d'été*,[26] also conforms to a musical structure: it is composed like a mass, its various sections entitled *De Profondis, Libera Me, Sanctus, Agnus Dei*, etc. These plays for several voices employ a repetitive interplay of motifs, phrases and themes that creates a modulated, cyclical form. They are written as musical scores, and an important aspect of their performance lies in the rhythm and its poetic effects.[27] In *Le Passage de l'Indiana* Chaurette depicts the ambivalence of consciences seeking to unravel a story of literary plagiarism: a young writer named Éric Mahoney may have copied eighty-three lines from the novel of a famous writer, Martina North. In fact, this situation is only a pretext that allows the author to tie together a complex group of connections that cloud the meaning of a plot resembling that of a psychological thriller: what at first seems central to the puzzle, the plagiarism, remains an enigma. The spectator is jolted from one set of leads to another, each of them finishing in a dead end: Was the plagiarism intentional? Or was it rather an improbable accident that caused a page from North's novel to slide into Mahoney's while the two writers' manuscripts were on the desk of Dawn Grisanti, his publisher? Or yet, could it be that, in the full swing of writing, Mahoney's prodigious memory unconsciously regurgitated this passage previously encountered in North's book? After all, he swears he knows all of her novels by heart. Another hypothesis, more mystical in nature, would have it that the two writers had simply written the same passage:

> Il y a parfois dans la tête des gens, souvent dans mon cas, une musique qui revient sans cesse. On ne sait pas d'où elle vient, à quand remonte la dernière fois qu'on l'a entendue, qui l'a composée. . . . Or cette musique est en nous. D'où vient-elle? Si moi je l'entends, pourquoi d'autres ne pourraient-ils pas aussi l'avoir entendue? Et pourquoi n'en serait-il pas de même avec les mots, avec le passage entier d'un roman?[28]

The interplay of hypotheses strewn throughout the text makes the play a kind of puzzle with which the spectator tinkers about in search of a meaning. Immersed in the odds and ends of interwoven thought that flow from one scene to the next, one's intuition alone allows for a reconstruction of a coherent vision of the drama. Nonetheless, the meaning of this work lies more in the interplay of questions than in the resolution of the plot.

Even if the play brings together a series of scenes containing dialogue, assembled around the motif of plagiarism, their content serves mainly to reveal the characters' inner nature. This is more implied than explained, but it gradually emerges as the heart and soul of the play: personalities seem to dissolve as disputes are resolved, as if a truth based on external factors were less valuable than one veiled in a subjective consciousness confronting the porousness of the borders defining an intimate self. "Qu'importent nos pauvres personnalités?" repeat Martina and Éric, each having been stripped of what appeared to hold their identity intact. The passage lifted from North's novel conceals within it the autobiographical core running throughout both her work and her life, the death of her parents during the wreck of *l'Indiana*: "On m'a volé mes parents, on m'a volé *l'Indiana*, on m'a volé ma tasse, on m'a tout volé,"[29] she cries. As for Mahoney, his creative identity has crumbled under the influence of Caroubier, her publisher, who might have written everything himself: "Un pharaon vous mène droit aux enfers. . . . Vous ne pouvez plus vous en délivrer car il vous séquestre, vous suffoquez, il vous tient. Il devient si puissant que tout se passe comme au temps de la sorcellerie. C'est lui qui écrit à votre place."[30] If, in the plays of Danis recycling the memory acts as a guarantor of the identity, in *Le Passage de l'Indiana* the search for identity loses its meaning and individual creation discovers its raison d'être in the fact that it connects with universal tendencies. Throughout the play, the question of literary plagiarism gives rise to reflections on the notion of individual artistic property. Éric Mahoney and Dawn Grisanti counter the hypothesis of plagiarism with that of the anonymous circulation and constant reinterpretation of works of art. Thus, Grisanti answers Caroubier, who has accused her of copying a text that he himself has written: "Que faites-vous de l'école flamande? Tous ces élèves qui ont copié les maîtres? . . . Et les cantates de Zobrovika, copies conformes de Zimoviez?"[31] Zimoviez, it soon becomes apparent, is a performer of Bach. Moreover, faced with the accusation of plagiarism, Éric Mahoney states that he feels a certain pride in being compared to an author of such renown. Defending this position, he quotes a sentence then asks his interlocutor if she is aware of who wrote it:

> En fait, explique-t-il, cette phrase existe dans un roman publié récemment chez Elmers, mais je me suis souvenu que ce passage existait aussi dans un long poème de Harrison Lester, qui se trouvait mot à mot chez Andrew Edmitt, lequel l'avait lu chez Augustin Moser, qui le tenait de Byron, et l'on sait que Byron l'avait empurunté à Southampton qui l'avait volé à Shakespeare qui le tenait d'Aristote, qui avait copié Hénoch, qui lui-même l'avait lu dans l'Ancien Testament. Or aucun de ces auteurs n'a été cité en justice pour avoir repris les mêmes mots d'un siècle à l'autre.[32]

In other words, art is a constant reinterpretation of art, and before universal genius the claim of individual genius is but vanity.

The question of identity is explored through the discussion of plagiarism:[33] Martina North feels literally robbed of her identity when a passage is taken from her book and printed without quotation marks. Her character goes from the "réaction panique devant le v(i)ol de son texte à un détachement qui la conduit au-delà du texte: à l'indicible qui ne peut être ravi."[34] This passage is one that moves from the individual to the universal, as the writer, in accepting her detachment from the object of her creation, puts it back into free circulation and admits that the work does not determine identity. This question seems extremely pertinent at a time when recycling, pirating, wholesale borrowing and collage are more than ever characteristic of contemporary art; these second-hand processes of creation call into question the notion of artistic property: elements of various works may circulate freely in a contemporary creation. But has not artistic creation always been founded upon the reinterpretation of existing works? As Mahoney exclaims, "Qu'importent nos pauvres personnalités? Qu'importe la susceptibilité de Martina North? Il lui arrivera de publier des choses qui avaient été dites avant elle, à défaut de quoi on lui érigera un temple. Les écrivains n'ont-ils pas droit par moments à un répit? Pourquoi faudrait-il que chaque page qu'ils noircissent soit une innovation ou une prophétie?"[35]

Chaurette's play addresses the question of personal identity from an unusual angle, dismantling its most intimate borders in order to put the accent less on the individual than its connections to the universal. It has been said of the play that it is not rooted in the soil of Quebec: "L'histoire est intemporelle et les personnages, dans leur grandeur toute triviale, ont quelque chose d'universel. Cette pièce n'est pas sans couleur, mais elle est sans couleur locale, elle fait voyager d'un bout à l'autre du globe dans des contrées dont il n'est pas important de savoir qu'elles existent."[36] One could extend this comment to include Chaurette's entire repertoire, which is not directly anchored to a specific cultural space.

The strength of this writing lies in its capacity to explore the crisis of the subject, a postmodern question if ever there was one, in a literary language tinged with poetry. In the work of this author, as with that of Danis, Québécois drama perhaps rediscovers a certain sense of the transcendent and the sublime, which is to say that it tends to go beyond an immediate social reality in portraying a vision that champions a single territory, that of mankind's spiritual condition in the world of today. This is certainly one of the reasons why Daniel Danis and Normand Chaurette are among the contemporary playwrights most widely produced abroad (after Michel Tremblay, obviously). Their approach to identity touches upon essential human values and, within the context of the history of Québécois drama, highlights just how much of the authentic search for identity is directed inwards. From a drama both demonstrative and discursive based on orality, there has been a shift to allusive writing, at once musical and poetic. This trend in contemporary Québécois drama is also related to studies of language that reclaim a space for listening and restore poetic value to an intimate territory informed by the sensitive and the sublime.

Notes

Translations by Richard Lebeau.

1. See Georges Schlocker, "La parole affolée. La propension au monologue du théâtre francais comtemporain," *Jeu* 72, (1994): 104–8.

2. Michel Corvin, "Otez toute chose que j'y voie. Vue cavalière sur l'écriture théâtrale contemporaine," in *Théâtre contemporain en Allemagne et en France*, ed. Wilfried Floeck (Tübingen: Francke, 1989), 13.

3. Again, it would be an oversimplification to include all Québécois plays in such a homogeneous trend, as the theater of Michel Tremblay, for instance, can be read from different points of view. Also, women's theater is, in a way, participating in the same collective affirmation of identity as well as inaugurating a movement toward the subjective quest for feminine identity. The theater of Pol Pelletier, Jovette Marchessault and Lise Vaillancourt, for example, is completely new, and is breaking ground that will be explored by other playwrights, some in affirming a homosexual identity on stage.

4. *Provincetown Playhouse, juillet 1919, j'avais 19 ans* (Montreal: Leméac, 1981).

5. *26 bis, impasse du Colonel Foisy* (Montreal: Leméac, 1983).

6. Many playwrights have explored the question of homosexuality. The plays of Michel Marc Bouchard, *La Contre-nature de Chrysippe Tanguay, écologiste* (Montreal: Leméac, 1984) and *Les Feluettes ou la répétition d'un drame romantique* (Montreal: Leméac, 1987), deal with the question of sexual identity by the intervention of theater within theater, cross-dressing, and gender and role exchanges by the characters.

7. *Albertine en cinq temps* (Montreal: Leméac, 1984).

8. *Le vrai monde?* (Montreal: Leméac, 1987).

9. Paul Lefebvre, "La dramaturgie québécoise depuis 1980," *Théâtre/Public* 117, (1994): 46.

10. Andrée Mercier, "Poétique du récit contemporain: négation d'un genre ou émergence d'un sous-genre?" *Voix et Images* 69 (1998): 466. See also Guy Poirier and Louis Vaillancourt, eds., *Le bref et l'instantané. À la rencontre de la littérature Québécoise du XXIè siècle* (Orléans: Les Éditions David, 2000).

11. Jean-Jacques Delfour, "Du fondement de la distinction entre monologue et soliloque," *L'Annuaire théâtral* 28, (2000): 124–25.

12. Jean-Pierre Sarrazac, *Théâtres intimes* (Arles: Actes Sud, 1989), 19.

13. Sarrazac, *Théâtres intimes*, 20.

14. Mercier, "Poétique du récit contemporain," 471.

15. Daniel Danis, *Cendres de cailloux* (Montreal and Arles: Leméac and Actes Sud, 1992).

16. Daniel Danis, *Celle-là* (Montreal: Leméac, 1993).

17. Schlocker, "La parole affolée," 104.

18. Danis, *Celle-là*, 63.

19. Danis, *Celle-là*, 23.

20. Joël Candau, *Anthropologie de la mémoire* (Paris: Presses Universitaires de France, 1996), 3.

21. For instance, all the plays of René-Daniel Dubois portray memory in different ways (see M.C. Lesage, "La dynamique de la mémoire: fragmentation et pensée analogique," in *Le bref et l'instantané*, 173–203). We also find this association between memory and soliloquy in some of Larry Tremblay's plays: *Le Déclic du destin* (1989), *Leçon d'anatomie* (1992), *The dragonfly of Chicoutimi* (1995), *Le Génie de la rue Drolet* (1994); in some plays by Carole Fréchette: *Baby Blues* (1990), *Les Quatre Morts de Marie* (1995), *La Peau d'Élisa* (1998); some works by Michel Tremblay: *Albertine en cinq temps* (1984) and *Messe solennelle pour une pleine lune d'été* (1996); one play by Abla Farhoud, *Jeux de patience* (1997) and one work by Hélène Pedneault, *La Déposition* (1988).

22. Danis, *Cendres de cailloux*, 47.

23. Danis, *Cendres de cailloux*, 90.

24. Danis, *Celle-là*, 34.

25. Normand Chaurette, *Le Passage de l'Indiana* (Montreal and Arles: Leméac and Actes Sud, 1996).

26. *Messe solennelle pour une pleine lune d'été* (Montreal: Leméac, 1996).

27. Another article would be needed to explore this formal characteristic properly. With reference to Normand Chaurette, see the study by Denyse Noreau, "*Le stabat Mater II*, un oratorio de la douleur," *Voix et Images* 75 (2000): 471–85.

28. Chaurette, *Le Passage de* l'Indiana, 77.

29. Chaurette, *Le Passage de* l'Indiana, 85.

30. Chaurette, *Le Passage de* l'Indiana, 24.

31. Chaurette, *Le Passage de* l'Indiana, 14.

32. Chaurette, *Le Passage de* l'Indiana, 26–27.

33. On the question of plagiarism, see Jean-Luc Hennig, *Apologie du plagiat* (Paris: Gallimard, 1997); Christian Vanderdorpe, ed., *Le Plagiat* (Ottawa: Presses de l'Université d'Ottawa, 1992); Annick Bouil-laguet, "Une typologie de l'emprunt," *Poétique* 80 (1989): 48–497.

34. Pierre L'Hérault, "Passages," *Spirale* 153, 23.

35. Chaurette, *Le Passage de l'Indiana*, 52.

36. Sylvie Bérard, "Hiatus," *Lettres Québécoises* 87 (1997): 37.

19

Reflections on the Figures of a Nation in *Les Anciens Canadiens* by Philippe Aubert de Gaspé Père

Micheline Cambron

O NE OF THE TRAITS CHARACTERIZING THE genesis of the idea of nation as it appears in Québécois literature throughout the nineteenth century was that it brought to the fore several representative national figures. Beginning with the establishment of the newspaper *Le Canadien* in 1806, the definition of the Canadian "race" (the word 'race' had yet to acquire the connotations it carries today and the term "Canadian" then referred exclusively to the "Français nés au Canada") took shape against a background of what one might describe as ethnic multiplicity. A large part of the newspaper's arguments was aimed at unraveling the erroneous homogeneity of the "we" proposed by the Anglophone newspapers, which were prompt to affirm "We Englishmen,"[1] regardless of the actual diversity of British immigration, something that was underlined by *Le Canadien* in its insistence on the sometimes divergent interests of the Scottish and Irish immigrants. This use of the other for argumentative purposes was not unique to *Le Canadien*, as Anglophone newspapers also exhibited a tendency to compose an image of the Canadians that served as a foil in the demands they directed toward London and justified the implantation of a truncated parliamentary regime in the Province of Quebec. Very early on, these various images of the nation, the Canadian, the English, the Scottish and the Irish, would be constructed one against the other in a comparative relationship that Weber would not have disavowed, but that, as the era would have it, owed a great deal to the "theorie des climats"[2] and to the classificatory paradigms that would serve as the foundations of ethnography.

It is considered good form to omit from scrutiny all these "excesses" of discourse, under the pretext that racial prejudices are an individual matter. This is no doubt true. Nevertheless, with the nation first constructing itself within discourse, it is important to understand how these portrayals of nationality, as prejudiced as they might be, contribute to the slow sedimentation of an imaginary of the nation itself, nourishing what Paul Ricoeur calls the narrative identity of a collectivity.[3] This chapter will obviously not propose an interpretation of national stereotypes encountered in passing, nor otherwise elaborate upon the reflections pursued by Alan Dundes on the strange stability of these stereotypes in time and in space.[4] Instead, the analysis will focus on a text that presents four national figures, the English, the Scottish, the Canadian, and the *Sauvage* (native—to use the modern term), in a story structured around paradigms of memory and of truth.

The novel *Les Anciens Canadiens* by Philippe Aubert de Gaspé père,[5] in which this story is found, constitutes one of the richest nineteenth-century Québécois texts in that it contains

several narratives of seminal significance in the literary or political realm: one describing Corriveau's trial,[6] another the shipwreck of the Auguste,[7] yet another Blanche d'Haberville's refusal
to marry one of the conquerors, a Scot named Archibald Cameron of Locheill,[8] and still others,
largely utopian, with the customs of a seigneurial system presented as the veritable golden age
of Canadian society.[9] These stories are combined with various others that are either historical
("La Bataille des Plaines d'Abraham" for instance) or anecdotal ("La Sortie du collège," "La
Débâcle," etc.) and loosely joined together by a plot device based on the passage from the
French Regime to the English Regime, a changeover that was almost immediately followed by
another rupture, one that plunged the empire of the *Ancien Régime* into the modern era. The
whole comprises a work that is difficult to classify according to genre,[10] which, when you think
of it, is certainly the best definition of the mid-nineteenth-century novel. The flimsiness of their
linkage gives each of these stories an autotelic dimension while, simultaneously, their con-
comitance creates cross-references that extend their ramifications. One of the most revealing of
these stories, "Une Nuit avec les sauvages," is situated at the heart of the narrative sequence of
the novel: it reveals that the fate of certain characters is intertwined. The plot is simple. After
having been compelled, by virtue of his status as a British officer, to burn down the house and
the mill of the d'Habervilles (the Canadians who at one time had welcomed him as a son),
Archibald Cameron of Locheill is taken prisoner by "Sauvages" allied to the French and awaits
certain death. Believing that one of the three *Sauvages* presently in camp could be a Frenchman,
the prisoner calls out to him for something to drink. This *Sauvage* turns out to be Dumais,
whom Locheill once heroically rescued from drowning. Dumais manages to save the prisoner's
life by means of lengthy palaver in which the drunkenness of one of the *Sauvages*, the history
of the English-Scottish wars, the generosity of the other *Sauvage*, the heroism of the Scot and
Dumais's sense of honor are all discussed in succession. The apparent fragmentation of the narrative (the sequence of stories in the night, near the fire that gives to the scene the air of a storytelling session) is redeemed by the cohesive, pragmatic intent of these brief narratives,
strongly illustrating the power entailed in storytelling.

A Ritual of Storytelling

Let us then examine these negotiations, introduced as they are by Dumais, who, after a brief
verbal exchange with Locheill, pretends to relate the words of the prisoner in translation: "Le
prisonnier remercie les peaux-rouges de lui faire souffrir la mort d'un homme; il dit que la
chanson du visage-pâle sera celle d'un guerrier."[11] Here Dumais acts as a veritable medium,
translating the culture every bit as much as the language. Talamousse and Grand-Loutre, the
two Abenaquis who have captured the prisoner, however, immediately challenge his utterance.
Without trying to take advantage of them, Dumais eats, and then offers Talamousse some
brandy,[12] adding that he knows Grand-Loutre doesn't drink. Grand-Loutre then recounts how
long ago the Great Spirit loved him enough to inspire in him disgust for it. Dumais adds a short
anecdote to that of Grand-Loutre: he recounts how the Great Spirit loves him as well and has
spoken to him, enjoining him to buy back the prisoner. Grande-Loutre accuses him of lying
"comme tous les visages-pâles."[13] As for Talamousse, he quickly feels the effects of the alcohol,
and Dumais easily manages to purchase his share of the prisoner in exchange for what is left in
the bottle. It remains to convince Grand-Loutre. Dumais explains to him that he wishes to buy
the prisoner in order to resell him to Captain d'Haberville, "qui le fera pendre pour avoir brûlé
sa maison et son moulin."[14] Grand-Loutre answers that the captain would be better avenged if

the prisoner was burned at the stake, as that was much more painful. Dumais, however, replies that the prisoner would endure the torment by fire like a warrior and that the noose alone "le fera pleurer comme une femme."[15] Grand-Loutre once again accuses Dumais of lying and pre-emptively states: "Il n'y a que le guerrier sauvage qui préfère le bûcher à la honte d'être pendu comme un chien."[16] The terms of the argument are established. From this point on, Dumais will try to show, by various rhetorical means, that the Scot truly is a savage warrior, and that it is therefore suitable, in seeking revenge, to deprive him of his "chant de mort," which is to say the opportunity to die with dignity.

In order to accurately measure the complexity of the cultural transcoding at work (in a trans-lation of a European tale into terms appropriate for the "savage," a translation destined for Canadian readers),[17] it is important to recall some of the circumstances of the story. The whole discussion is conducted in the Abenaquis language, which Dumais speaks "avec facilité."[18] Locheill, therefore, understands nothing that is said on his behalf, and it is all reported to us by an omniscient narrator, who, as convention dictates, would be Philippe Aubert de Gaspé.[19] Du-mais is a good Canadian, a farmer and a trapper who is very respectful of the social hierarchy, but who, without his foxskin hat, could be mistaken for an Indian. As for Grand-Loutre, he is an ally of the French, who give him a bonus for each enemy scalp. The dialogue between the two interlocutors is presented as rigorously homogeneous in terms of form, as if the two par-ticipants shared the same cultural universe, that of the Indian: an abundance of comparisons on each side, a recourse to anecdotes to establish the veracity of facts, the use of conventional phatic and conative formulas that testify to the existence of an imaginary within the Indian id-ioms, and repetitive references to the conflict between the paleface and the redskin. One also notes the systematic use of the third person in addressing the interlocutor (for instance, "Que mon frère écoute"), which creates an apparent distance, though this is contradicted by the des-ignation "mon frère," which introduces most of the responses. The dispute between the two in-terlocutors is certainly carried out indirectly by means of the reactivation of clichés opposing the paleface and the redskin, but it is particularly apparent in the series of comments on truth and falsehood that punctuate the dialogue. Even if de Gaspé includes a note referring to the idiom "menteur comme un sauvage,"[20] the reader does not really know how to decide between the voices on this matter: whereas the discourse delivered by Dumais seems a ruse aimed at sav-ing the prisoner, the *Sauvage* appears right away to have a greater affinity with the truth.

In this way they argue about the identity of the prisoner, who would behave like a savage war-rior, states Dumais, because the captured Englishman is really not an Englishman at all, but a Scot; and it so happens that "les Écossais sont les sauvages des Anglais."[21] In fact, he continues, the Scots are in every way just like the Indians. To begin with, Dumais compares the clothes (likening the kilt to the "brayet"), then their beliefs (he bestows upon the Scots the native belief that if a hanged man "visitait le pays des âmes la corde au cou, les guerriers sauvages ne voudraient pas chasser avec lui").[22] These arguments fail to convince Grand-Loutre: "Mon frère ment encore."[23] For him, even if the Scots are "savages," they are still palefaces. Dumais then throws himself into an account of the story of the English-Scottish wars, transforming the clans into tribes, the battles into guerrilla warfare and the ensuing negotiations into meetings around the peace pipe. Some of the "translations" are certainly amusing, such as the description of the English parliament as a "grand wigwam,"[24] or the passage where the clans' chieftains, who are seeking to free Wallace,[25] say to the "Grand Ononthio des Anglais,"[26] i.e., the king: "Nous désirons enterrer la hache de guerre."[27] Yet, essentially, despite a proliferation of allegories, the elements of a heroic Caledonian history are present, with the hanging of Wallace as the high-light of the narrative. Grand-Loutre is almost convinced, but it still remains to be explained why the Scots became allies of the English. Once again Dumais goes back to his story, insisting on the courage of the Scots, whom it was only possible to conquer by an act of treason: "La guerre durerait encore sans un traître qui avertit les soldats anglais que neuf grands chefs écossais, réunis dans une caverne pour y boire de l'eau-de-feu, s'y étaient endormis, comme notre frère Talamousse."[28] Commenting on this betrayal, which seems to him to establish an immeasurable distance between the Scots and the "savages," Grand-Loutre states: "Les peaux-rouges ne sont jamais traîtres à leur nation: ils trompent seulement leurs ennemis, jamais leurs amis."[29] Taken, nevertheless, by this latest episode of the story ("on fit un festin [lors de la signature du pacte entre les Anglais et les Écossais] qui dura trois jours et trois nuits, et où l'on but tant d'eau-de-feu que les femmes serrèrent les casse-têtes, car, sans cela, la guerre aurait recommencé de nouveau") and by a conclusion containing a dose of irony that escapes him ("Les Anglais furent si joyeux qu'ils promirent d'envoyer en Écosse, par dessus le marché, toutes les têtes, pattes et queues des moutons qu'ils tueraient à l'avenir"), Grand-Loutre enthusiastically exclaims, "C'est bon ça, les Anglais sont généreux!"[30] However, he does not wish to sell his share of the prisoner, but would rather plead his own case, which means telling the story to the tribe, who will then decide upon Archibald's fate. Faced with this rebuff, Dumais is briefly tempted to attack Grand-Loutre, but changes tactics: he reminds Grand-Loutre that long ago he had taken care of him and those close to him when they were stricken with smallpox. Grand-Loutre replies that he would have done as much for Dumais and his family but that he would not have reminded him of his debt. The Abenaquis concludes, "Que mon frère emmène le prisonnier: le peau-rouge ne doit plus rien aux visages-pâles."[31]

Technically, the story could have ended here: the ransom negotiations apparently concluded. Yet Dumais cannot bear to see their friendship destroyed. He would prefer a gift to an economic exchange, however symbolic in nature. He thus reveals the truth to Grand-Loutre, who gives a great cry and springs to his feet before drawing his knife and rushing at the alarmed prisoner, cutting his bonds, grasping his hands in delight, and pushing him toward Dumais. The episode ends with Dumais recounting an anecdote intended to demonstrate that political morality supersedes that of the individual during a time of war, which in some fashion excuses the fact that Locheill has burned down the house and the mill of the d'Haberville family.

Let us look at the story from a slightly different angle. A fake Indian helps a fake Englishman to escape from real Indians thanks to negotiations that are initially undertaken in a strictly economic sense (half of a prisoner for half a bottle of brandy, which are the terms of the exchange with Talamousse) but will later be seen as a dialogue extending forwards and backwards to include a series of gifts. Four national figures are heavily thematized throughout the dialogue: the "Savage," the Scot and the Englishman, while that of the Canadian is discernible interspatially. This dialogue is punctuated with questions about the truth of the constituent elements of the arguments delivered by the fake Indian, questions rendered more troubling by the recurrent presence of the motif of betrayal in the narratives. The story is certainly about saving the life of Archibald Cameron of Locheill, but no one will deny that the discourse also examines the question of identity and the distance between appearance and reality, truth and falsehood. The various voices in the text find themselves inextricably mingled in this search for identity: those of the storytellers heard in the night, the voice of the narrator unable to decide between two contradictory proverbs ("Menteur comme un Sauvage,"[32] "Mon frère ment comme un Français"[33]), the voice of the one who remains silent whose story told by others (Locheill), and, finally, that of the Canadian reader, also silent, called upon to decide between what is true and what is false.

National Figures: The Noble Savage, the Proud Scot and the Indolent Englishman

De Gaspé's novel is dense with commentary on characteristics of "race," as it was referred to at the time. The first chapters provide, moreover, the opportunity to contrast Canadian customs with those of the Scots, customs that the young d'Haberville never tires of mocking. *Les Anciens Canadiens* appeared on the heels of the *Soirées canadiennes*, in which the idea was to "raconter les délicieuses histoires du peuple avant qu'il ne les ait oubliés,"[34] and Philippe Aubert de Gaspé associated with Canadian "antiquaires" interested in popular practices in the process of disappearing. The evident influence of Walter Scott on his work no doubt partly explains this fascination with folklore: nostalgia for the *Ancien Régime* mingles with the desire to describe the "races" through ethnographic traits, tales and legends, religious practices and rituals, and customs of eating and dressing. This gives rise, in this story, to the explicit thematization of three of the representative national figures. In examining them, it is necessary to be aware that, from de Gaspé's perspective, the individual can only embody the traits of his "race."

In the story "Une Nuit avec les sauvages" this thematization is rendered particularly visible by the effect of comparisons. The Scot and the Indian are represented as being free, the form of their clothing seeming to refer to the quality of the being; by contrast, the Englishman is constrained at once by his clothing ("[il] étouffe . . . dans ses habits")[35] and his way of conducting battle (he does not have the agility needed to pursue the Scots when they flee into the mountains).[36] Furthermore, the English are mercenary, their decisive victories made possible by the use of traitors who sell information, while the Scots win thanks to their courage and physical prowess (they have "la jambe forte comme l'orignal et sont agiles comme le chevreuil").[37] Though they lack these physical qualities, the English are certainly "grands et robustes,"[38] but they have "la jambe molle et le ventre gros."[39] Evidently this contrast, *jambe forte/jambe molle*, must refer to another paradigm of comparison, which states without hesitation that "les Anglais sont riches et les Écossais sont pauvres,"[40] inasmuch as everyone knows that ease engenders indolence, which paves the way to degeneration. This idea serves an enthymematic function in the text, and de Gaspé does not shy away from describing the Spartan life of the young Locheill or the frugality of the seigneurial lifestyle as the sources of his courage. But it is also placed in juxtaposition with the contrast, free body/constrained body, directly referring to the image of the "Noble Savage" established during the Enlightenment: that of a free individual who is as he appears to be, without adornment or artifice,[41] and who situates himself beyond any mercenary consideration.[42] The national representation of the Scot and of the Englishman thus appear as syncretic and opposed: the English are rich, venal and degenerate; the Scots are poor, incapable of calculation (if you exclude the traitors) and natural. Moreover, these two syncretic representations are defined dialectically by recourse to the third figure of a nation, that of the Indian who is portrayed as the ideal. Certainly, this is partly due to the pragmatic intent of the stories Dumais chooses to tell: he wants to convince Grand-Loutre that the prisoner is his counterpart and for this reason must be punished in the most fitting, i.e., the cruellest possible, manner: hanging. From an illocutionary point of view, it then appears normal that Dumais presents a positive image of the Indian, an image upon which doubt is cast by the words of Grand-Loutre: "Mon frère ment comme un Français . . . il ment comme tous les visages-pâles."[43] However, this reduction of Dumais's discourse to its apparent illocutionary functions (and in this way to a type of white lie) is not sustainable under analysis, as other elements of the discourse elude this interpretation and provide an equally favorable image of the Indian. For instance, as the plot unfolds it becomes clear that the *Sauvage* is the truthful man, as he is the only one whose appearance matches his being and who reveals his true motives in his argumentation. Talamousse makes no attempt to hide the fact that he prefers the immediacy of the brandy to the subsequent reward promised by the French; Grand-Loutre maintains that he wants to keep his word toward his tribe and so initially refuses to sell the prisoner, even when Dumais offers to pay six times the amount of the expected reward. Furthermore, at the end of the story, Grand-Loutre provides Dumais with a lesson in friendship, reminding him that it is based on a gift given without expectation of return rather than the calculations of a symbolic exchange.[44] This portrait of the Indian closely matches the image of the "Noble Savage" (lack of dissimulation and calculation, courage, the beauty of a body freed from the constraints of occidental clothing, and a natural goodness of the soul).

In the verbal exchange, the Canadian is represented negatively: to begin with, Dumais seems to be a man given to dissimulation. Not only does he appear to be an Indian on account of his clothing and his language, but, what is more, he attempts to convince Grand-Loutre with specious logic: he translates the story of Scottish history, but in doing so he betrays it as well (the irony contained in his conclusion about the sheep's tails is evidence enough of that). Nevertheless, despite their illocutionary dimension, these narratives are not as fanciful as they might seem, as the description of the conflict between the English and the Scots is evidently based on supposedly true prejudices nourished by the topoi of Scott's novels.[45] If the story of the battles between England and Scotland seems strongly influenced by its pragmatic intent (Dumais wants to convince Grand-Loutre that Locheill is a true *Sauvage*), it can be read, nonetheless, as the Indian translation of the popular version of the history of the Scottish nation, whose antagonistic sentiments toward England were running high in the middle of the nineteenth century. This popular history adapts well to the symbols proposed in the dialectical construction around the figure of the Noble Savage: the kilt, which is the emblem of the cohesion of the clan, becomes at once an image of freedom and a testimony to authenticity; the barbarity apparent in certain traditions becomes stylized or dramatized, as the "chants de morts" and the libations from the skulls of victims become strong images, testifying to authenticity. Besides, the very definition of barbarity, which essentially constitutes the dark side of the image of the Noble Savage, is adapted in the novel in relation to Archibald's critical error when, following his irreparable action, he exclaims:

> Voilà donc les fruits de ce que nous appelons code d'honneur chez les nations civilisées! Sont-ce là aussi les fruits des préceptes qu'enseigne l'Évangile à tous ceux qui professent la religion chrétienne, cette religion toute d'amour et de pitié, même pour des ennemis. Si j'eusse fait partie d'une expédition commandée par un des chefs de ces aborigènes que nous traitons de barbares sur cet hémisphère, et que je lui eusse dit: "Épargne cette maison, car elle appartient à mes amis, j'étais errant et fugitif et ils m'ont accueilli dans leur famille, où j'ai trouvé un père et des frères," le chef indien m'aurait répondu: "C'est bien, épargne tes amis; il n'y a que le serpent qui mord ceux qui l'ont réchauffé près de leur feu."[46]

Here the usual symbols have been reversed, making the English rather than the Indians the incarnation of barbarity.

This complete valorization of the image of the Indian (because here Talamousse serves only as a foil), modifies and renders more complex the fourth figure, that of the Canadian. The Canadians, who dress like the "savages," speak their language, and ultimately conform to the same code of honor, are, in this way, like the Scots, in contrast to the English, who thus find themselves isolated in a "non-savagery" that, as the text would have it, is perhaps the real barbarity. This exercise in applied ethnology seems to fall back on a political analysis and propose a natural alliance between the Canadian and the Scot against the Englishman.

It must not be forgotten that the assimilation of the Canadians with the "savages" is a permanent feature in the English-language texts that followed the Conquest. This assimilation was based on well-established images: the Canadians of New France preferred the Indian style of doing battle, they fought side by side with their indigenous allies and even adopted their more convenient style of dress. One need only think of the young aristocratic emissary, Jumonville, referred to in the novel's notes, who was killed by George Washington when he arrived at Fort Nécessité under the pretext that he was dressed as a *Sauvage*, an excuse "qui n'a rien de vraisemblable . . . parce que Washington ne pouvait ignorer que non seulement les soldats mais les officiers même de l'armée française portaient le costume des aborigènes: capot court, mitasse, brayets et souliers de chevreuil. Cet accoutrement souple et léger leur donnait un grand avantage sur des ennemis toujours vêtus à l'européenne."[47]

Whatever the case might be as regards these images, the English-language newspapers also sought to present the Canadians as savages in order that they be denied their status as fully fledged British subjects, and, like the members of the Indian tribes, considered as aboriginals without political status and thus incapable of exercising their civic rights.[48] The presentation of the figure of the Canadian as homologous to that of the Indian is therefore an endorsement of an old topos[49] and an inversion of the symbol, since the positive image is not that of the Indian, but that of the Englishman. Nevertheless, in the story, far from being shameful, this assimilation appears glorious. Even the narrator, as dignified as he is, finds his discourse influenced by Indian turns of phrase, appropriating, in moments of intense emotion, expressions such as "ces chiens de français" or "se lamenter comme des femmes."[50] Thus, the figure of the *Sauvage* is utilized in a sense close to that established during the Enlightenment, blurring the lines between the Self and the other and giving to the word *avec* in the title "Une Nuit avec les sauvages" an unforeseen sense of community.

To move from the text to its reception, it is important to recall that its readers were Canadian. Each intertwined representation they were offered was a story that contributed to the construction of their narrative identity. In that sense, if the Canadians resemble the Scots and the Indians, each in opposition to the English, is it not because, in the dialogue, their narrative identity is expressed through the same paradigms?

Truth and Falsehood

However, this is not a political treatise, and the various traits that permit de Gaspé to sketch these national figures can only be understood in the sequence of narratives that make up the dialogue. This dialogue, however, is distinguished by being stretched between four terms that comprise two oppositions: one between what is remembered and what is forgotten, and the other between what is true and what is false. The movement between these four terms is at once what motivates the discursive action and what enables the construction of an ethical model that transcends the categories embodied by the representative national figures.

From the beginning, recollection is the motor of the action, both discursive and "real." Dumais, remembering the voice of Cameron of Locheill, responds to his call. Talamousse remembers that "l'eau-de-feu délasse les jambes,"[51] and therefore decides to forget his original agreement and sell his share of the prisoner. Grand-Loutre remembers that the paleface does not know how to confront the tortures of the stake and will therefore accuse Dumais of lying. Dumais remembers the stories told to him by Locheill during his recovery after having nearly drowned, a fate he avoided due to the efforts of the young Scot; he draws from these stories the versions of Scottish history discussed above. Finally, the memory of the tangible signs of their mutual friendship allows Grand-Loutre and Dumais to escape from the sordidness of the ransom negotiations. Recollection is the source of discourse and, in "Une Nuit avec les sauvages," it is discourse that carries the action along. Recollection and its recitation have, in this case, a performative value. This aspect of the text gains significance if it is realized that the principal point from which the action of the novel springs, the order given to Archibald to burn down the property of his friends, also stems from a recollection (that of Montgomery, the Englishman who remembers the hereditary hatred that his family bears against the Camerons of Locheill) resulting in an act of vengeance, and that its denouement, which finds Blanche d'Haberville acquitting herself of a debt toward her country by refusing to marry Archibald, is also based on memories, of battles lost and sacrifices owed to her race.

However, it is not only the narrative sequences that owe much to recollection. One could make a long list of "sections" in the novel derived from the memory of one or another of the protagonists recalling either a song or a forgotten event. Within the very conception of the work Philippe Aubert de Gaspé gives a performative dimension to the act of recollection. Even if this novel appears to be pure fabrication, it is expressly presented as a chronicle containing "quelques épisodes du bon vieux temps, quelques souvenirs d'une jeunesse hélas! bien éloignée."[52] It is from this perspective that the abundant notes containing supplementary information or archival documents must be viewed. The dialectic created between what is remembered and what is forgotten here takes on the appearance of a structural opposition: Though there will be general agreement that in this case recollection is performative, questions have to be asked about the author's illocutionary intentions. Why remember?

"Une Nuit avec les sauvages," which explicitly adds the tension between the remembered and the forgotten to that existing between truth and falsehood, enables us to glimpse an answer that, without refuting the usual motives attributed to de Gaspé (the glorification of the virtues of the Canadian aristocrat in order to defend the seigneurial system), suggests a pragmatic intent wider in scope. In the "storytelling ritual" that "Une Nuit avec les sauvages" resembles, the successive narratives are presented as evidence awaiting judgment. "Cela est vrai" and "mon frère ment" are utterances that punctuate various sections of the dialogue, which from then on serves as the site for the laborious unveiling of the truth that, in being recounted, defines the image of the Scot and, by virtue of the dynamics of the system, defines the other national figures involved. This truth ultimately gains Locheill his freedom. The eloquence is thus not only performative, it is axiological in that it reveals the dividing line between the truth and the lie, illustrating the distinction between giving and selling one's word (the most striking example of venal exchange being the betrayal of Wallace, the chieftain of the Scottish clans, for money), which at the same time distinguishes, brings together and contrasts the Self and the other.

In this axiology the Scot and the Canadian are ambiguous figures. When Dumais chooses to reveal the identity of Archibald Cameron of Locheill by insisting on his kinship with the image of the Indian, his rhetorical guile does not completely misrepresent the truth. He does not betray the essence of Archibald's life, which has been devoted to scorn, if not hatred, for the English since the battle of Culloden. Even before the occurrence of the event necessitating the negotiations, Archibald himself had proposed a comparison between the Indian and the Scot,[53] had complacently accepted being treated indirectly as a *Sauvage* (Jules d'Haberville states that Scottish cooking is "primitive"),[54] and had been described by the narrator as seeming to delight in a "vie sauvage et vagabonde."[55] The discourse delivered by Dumais is deceitful only in appearance; his narrative reveals the very essence of the portrait of the Scot in the order of the novel; it is a matter of "lying truly," synthesising the real by way of a fiction.

Moreover, Grand-Loutre is not fooled by the rhetorical component of what Dumais has to say. After Dumais has spoken of Scottish mountains so high that halfway to the summit one already has a white beard,[56] Grand-Loutre mockingly says: "Les Français sont toujours fous, dit l'Indien, ils ne cherchent qu'à faire rire: ils mettront bien vite des matchicotis (jupons) et iront s'assoir avec nos Squaws (femmes) pour les amuser de leurs contes."[57] Dumais concedes: "Mon frère doit voir que c'est pour lui faire comprendre combien sont hautes les montagnes."[58] Dumais is a liar who holds his mask in his hands. Even his way of dressing is not, properly speaking, a disguise: he is not trying to pass for an other and it could only fool those who are complete strangers to the Canadian/Savage alliance. Instead, his way of dressing exposes him by revealing the complexity of his identity. He most certainly lies by omission and initially hides the motives of his discourse from Grand-Loutre, but the acknowledgment of his friendship with the *Sauvage* leads him to reveal everything: he too is incapable of betraying his friends. His feelings of solidarity are triple: with the Canadians, the Scots and the "savages."

As for the figure of the Scot, despite Archibald's uprightness, it remains explicitly sullied by the shadow of betrayal: the one that delivered up Wallace and the one that led to the forced alliance with England. But it would be wrong to see here a strong difference between the representation of the Scot and that of the Canadian. A good many nineteenth-century texts bear witness to the loyalty of the Canadians, a loyalty called into question by the English: the shadow of the traitor also hovers over the figure of the Canadian.[59] This shadow profoundly transforms the representation of the nation, as the traitor is the one who casts doubt upon identity, the one who, disjunctively, is the Self and the other at the same time, and who, because of this, turns the narrative upside down. From this point of view, only the figure of the *Sauvage* appears totally coherent: When it comes to Grand-Loutre, appearance and reality are one and the same thing, and, despite the circumstances, his discourse is presented as being transparent; the Indian is therefore the true ethical model proposed by the story.

What about the Englishman? He cuts a sorry figure. He is the one who buys the word of another, so, to a certain extent, is the real liar, the one who corrupts the rules of verbal exchange. Moreover, what he has to say does not follow the discursive modalities proposed in the story: He has no story to tell, he refuses to be involved in the dialogue (for example, in the story that Dumais recounts, during the negotiations with the Scots, the English refuse to discuss, they "execute"). The Englishman is thus also, in his own way, in the performative register. Yet his identity remains elusive, for it can only be read in the oppositions upon which the other figures are based: The Englishman is the only one who is denied an active participation in the diegesis. In order to discover the complexity of this image of a nation, it is necessary to return to Locheill's critical error. For despite the absolution granted by Dumais, the Scot's act of obedience proves debilitating: Blanche d'Haberville will not marry him.[60] Yet Archibald himself has a good idea of the nature of his error. He should have refused to obey the orders without fearing dishonor, since English law would have allowed him to appear before a military tribunal: "J'aurais été éloquent en défendant mon honneur,"[61] he says. Archibald Cameron of Locheill is punished for having underestimated the power of speech. This power is not represented in de Gaspé's text as belonging only to the Indian, the Canadian and the Scot; with his courts and his parliamentary system, the Englishman possesses it as well. This representation is certainly peripheral and is based on an abstract approach to the theme, a kind of *a posteriori* rationalization: numerous passages exhibit de Gaspé's desire to glorify the benefits of the British system of government. They are, however, outside the diegetic order and even outside the scheme of the novel, since they are not founded on an act of recollection. In this circuitous manner, the four national figures come together in a common representation of ritualized speech, but remain pulled between two poles:

that of fiction or auto-fiction, which are drawn together by memory, and that of commentary, which is subject to reality and therefore evades axiological complexity. On one hand, there are the figures of the Scot, the *Sauvage*, and the Canadian; on the other, that of the Englishman. Through the frictions between these figures, the diegetic pathways reveal something repudiated by the explicit discourse of the novelist: that speech and its powers will not be limited to the rules of parliamentary debate as established by the English Government in Canada.

Nevertheless, it is important to remember that these four national figures were conceived for the Canadian reader, who would then ensure their integration. Ultimately, the paradigms that served to distinguish each of these figures: clothes, beliefs, history, movement between the remembered and the forgotten, and between what is true and what is false, are the very ones the reader is offered to use in defining himself. The almost transcendental integration achieved by the discourse is therefore particularly significant. The narratives strung together like pearls in "Une Nuit avec les sauvages" warn us: The word may conquer, but it is also deceitful; it can be just, but its magic circle did not prevent the erosion and ultimately the disappearance of the Indian nations, a point echoed discreetly in the novel by the reference to the end of the lineage of the Camerons of Locheill (Archibald remains a bachelor and is the "dernier de sa race").[62] Despite an ostensibly happy denouement (Jules d'Haberville marries an Englishwoman and has a son named Arché d'Haberville), the spectre of the dissolution of the representative national figures is present throughout the novel. The way in which these various figures are intertwined by the act of remembering and forgetting bears witness to this presence. The narrative identities of collectivities, like those of individuals, must always come to terms with that most radical and absolute other: death.

Notes

Translated by Richard Lebeau.

1. As late as 1849, this was still the discourse upheld by Ferres, editor-in-chief of the newspaper *The Montreal Gazette*. See Marie-Paule Remillard's (unfortunately) unpublished master's thesis, "La construction d'une polémique: l'annexionnisme dans deux journaux montréalais, *L'Avenir et The Montreal Gazette*," (M.A., Études françaises, Université de Montréal, 1998). The first half of the nineteenth century had nevertheless been marked by massive Scottish and Irish immigration.

2. This theory originated with Montesquieu (*De l'esprit des lois*, ed. P. Brèthe de la Gressaye, 4 vols., 1950–61) and was to profoundly influence Madame de Staël.

3. Paul Ricoeur, *Temps et récit. Le temps raconté* (Paris: Seuil, 1985), 352–59; "Le Soi et l'identité narrative," in *Soi-même comme un autre* (Paris: Seuil, 1990), 167–98.

4. Allan Dundes, "Slurs International: Folk Comparisons of Ethnicity and National Character," *Southern Folklore Quarterly* 39, (1975): 15–38.

5. Philippe Aubert de Gaspé père, *Les Anciens Canadiens*; the unabridged text conforms with the 1864 edition (Montreal: Bibliothèque Québécoise, 1994). The page numbers of the references throughout the text are taken from this edition.

6. Marie-Josephte Corriveau was sentenced to death by the English justice system for the murder of her husband. Her corpse was placed in a metal cage and hung at the crossroads of Pointe-Lévis. This episode gave rise to a great many scholarly works on the justice system, several legends and modern versions, including Victor Levy-Beaulieu's *Ma Corriveau* (followed by *La Sorcellerie en finale sexuée, théâtre*) (Montreal: V.L.B., 1976), and *La Cage*, a play by Anne Hébert (followed by *L'Île de la Demoiselle*) (Paris/Montreal: Seuil/Boréal, 1990). Philippe Aubert de Gaspé presents it as an amusing story within the body of the text (Corriveau is a witch who wishes to attend a witches' sabbath) and recounts the original event in the notes with the support of legal documents.

7. This story is taken from an older work that was subsequently recopied and republished, *Journal du voyage de M. Saint-Luc de la Corne, écuyer, dans le navire* l'Auguste, *en l'an 1761*, written by a witness to the drama, Saint-Luc de la Corne. This event has given rise to an abundance of commentary by historians. See Pierre Lespérance, "La Fortune littéraire du *Journal de voyage de Saint-Luc de la Corne*," *Voix et Images* 50 (1995): 329–46; Bernard Andrès, "La Génération de la conquête: un questionnement de l'archive," *Voix et Images* 50 (1995): 270–93.

8. This refusal of a Canadian woman to marry one of the British conquerors soon became a topos of Québécois novelistic tradition.

9. It has been correctly suggested that, in his work, Philippe Aubert de Gaspé sought to glorify the Canadian nobility of the *Ancien Régime* in order to defend the recently abolished (1854) seigneurial system. He implicitly opposed the historian François-Xavier Garneau, who saw the structure of the French Regime in Canada only as a source of difficulty and a brake on the development of the colony. A biased rereading of Garneau's *Histoire du Canada* would tend to present the period of New France as the golden age of the colony. By expanding the explanatory notes and archival documents, Philippe Aubert de Gaspé, who prided himself on his knowledge of the historian's craft, effectively nourished this utopian rereading of the past.

10. Moreover, de Gaspé states that we can classify it as we wish: "Que les puristes, les littérateurs émérites, choqués de ces défauts, l'appellent roman, mémoire, chronique, salmigondis, pot-pourri: peu importe," 27.

11. *Les Anciens Canadiens*, 236.

12. In the original text this alcohol is referred to as "eau-de-vie."

13. *Les Anciens Canadiens*, 238.

14. *Les Anciens Canadiens*, 239.

15. *Les Anciens Canadiens*, 239.

16. *Les Anciens Canadiens*, 239.

17. In fact, there were two groups of readers, as the English translation, *The Canadians of Old*, appeared the following year. Rainier Grutman accurately notes that the pragmatic dimension found itself radically changed: "On s'imagine par ailleurs comment a été lu . . . tel . . . rappel des bienfaits de la cession: nous vivons plus tranquilles sous le gouvernement britannique que sous la domination française," 346. Here the British reader finds a confirmation of his prejudice, and the Canadian, a contentious statement open to discussion, *Des Langues qui résonnent* (Montreal: Fides, 1996), 111–12. The present chapter concentrates on the likely responses of the Canadian reader, that is, Canadians of French ancestry, following a well-established semantic usage (at this time in the process of being transformed) that de Gaspé endorses without question.

18. *Les Anciens Canadiens*, 234.

19. According to his own account, de Gaspé knew many of the characters in the stories that he tells but, in all likelihood, they did not speak Abenaquis. That his translations are presented as being self-evident reveals the existence of a particularly active heteroglossia in this work. See the illuminating analysis by Grutman, *Des Langues qui résonnent*, 108–25.

20. *Les Anciens Canadiens*, 238.

21. *Les Anciens Canadiens*, 239.

22. *Les Anciens Canadiens*, 239.

23. *Les Anciens Canadiens*, 240.

24. *Les Anciens Canadiens*, 242.

25. William Wallace was the Scottish hero who defeated the English at the Battle of Stirling Bridge in 1297 during the "War of Independence." He was one of the first symbols of Scottish resistance. Captured as a result of betrayal, he was convicted of betraying England: "décapité, coupé en quartiers qui furent envoyés dans les villes d'Écosse pour l'exemple" (*Petit Robert des noms propres* [Paris, 1989], 566); he became a martyr for the Scottish cause. See Janet R. Glover, *The Story of Scotland* (London: Faber and Faber, 1960), 67–68. During the 1860s, Wallace made the headlines when a monument was erected in his honor at Stirling amid much controversy.

26. *Les Anciens Canadiens*, 242.

27. *Les Anciens Canadiens*, 242.

28. *Les Anciens Canadiens*, 243.

29. *Les Anciens Canadiens*, 243.

30. *Les Anciens Canadiens*, 244. The quotations in this sentence are all found on the same page. In the footnotes De Gaspé adds that the Indians were particularly fond of the heads and feet of dead animals, and perhaps enemies. In the preceding chapters, the young d'Haberville mocks Caledonian eating habits: "on ajoute alors au premier plat ['un ragoût d'avoine'] une tête, des pattes et une succulente queue de mouton à la croque au sel: le reste de la bête manque en Écosse," 51.

31. *Les Anciens Canadiens*, 248.

32. *Les Anciens Canadiens*, 238.

33. *Les Anciens Canadiens*, 238.

34. In this case, Nodier's words have been substantially modified, as what he said was: "Hâtons-nous d'écouter les délicieuses histoires du peuple avant qu'il ne les ait oubliées." See Jeanne Demers and Lise Gauvin, "Le Conte écrit, une forme savante," *Études françaises* 12, nos. 1–2 (1976): 4, and Luc Lacoursière, *Cahier des dix* 32, 224–25.

35. *Les Anciens Canadiens*, 239.

36. *Les Anciens Canadiens*, 241.

37. *Les Anciens Canadiens*, 241.

38. *Les Anciens Canadiens*, 241.

39. *Les Anciens Canadiens*, 241.

40. *Les Anciens Canadiens*, 241.

41. It must be noted that in this case indolence and fatness refer to an operation of addition, with respect to a naked, healthy, and therefore svelte body, which finds itself masked by the fat. Moreover, the image of reprehensible fat is found elsewhere in the novelistic discourse of the nineteenth century.

42. The most conventional representation is that of Adario, in the *Dialogues* of Lahontan, stating his refusal to distinguish between yours and mine. See Lahontan, *Oeuvres complètes*, ed. Réal Ouellet and Alain Beaulieu, "Bibliothèque du Nouveau Monde" (Presses de l'Université de Montréal, 1990), 801–5.

43. *Les Anciens Canadiens*, 237–38.

44. In this action, Grand-Loutre breaks with the logic of the mercenary exchange, embracing instead the logic of the gift, as described by Marcel Mauss, in which the giver, as well as the recipient, is in a position of obligation. See "Essai sur le don," *Sociologie et société* (Paris: Quadrige/Presses universitaires de France, 1950), 1923–24.

45. Numerous elements in the novel, including some epigraphs, indicate a knowledge of Scott's work. See the commentary by Rainier Grutman, *Des Langues qui résonnent*, 108–25.

46. *Les Anciens Canadiens*, 227–28.

47. *Les Anciens Canadiens*, 418–19. This episode, which actually occurred, has provided much material for Canadian and American historians. Note the reversal of the symbols. According to Rousseau, clothing hides the individual, while in the case of the Canadian/Savage assimilation, clothing (Indian) reveals the individual.

48. Beginning in 1806, the newspaper *Le Canadien* reprinted texts from English-language newspapers tending toward this view of the matter. This idea endured and was still current at the end of the nineteenth century.

49. Let us recall the heroic figures proposed by Voltaire (*L'Ingenu*) or Lesage (*Les Aventures du commandant de Beauchesnes*), which make the 'primitivized' Canadian a symbol of the free man.

50. Both quotations in this sentence come from the notes on chapter 14, 418.

51. *Les Anciens Canadiens*, 236.

52. *Les Anciens Canadiens*, 27.

53. Referring to Scottish mothers who followed the Indian custom of throwing "leurs enfants nouveaux-nés dans un lac, ou dans une rivière, leur laissant ensuite le soin de gagner le rivage. C'est une première leçon de natation," 111. It is after having saved Dumais that he offers this comparison in the hope

of providing a modest explanation *for* his actions. According to this logic, Dumais owes his life to an Indian tradition followed by Scottish mothers!

54. *Les Anciens Canadiens,* 50–51.

55. *Les Anciens Canadiens,* 35.

56. *Les Anciens Canadiens,* 240.

57. *Les Anciens Canadiens,* 241.

58. *Les Anciens Canadiens,* 241.

59. One has only to think of the mythification of the Battle of Chateauguay (1812), presented as proof of the loyalty of the Canadians to their new motherland. Beginning in 1806, in *Le Canadien,* one finds recurrent protests against what was said by certain "anti-Canadians" who denied the loyalty of the Canadians: "Le Canadien en sera le nom [du journal]. C'est celui dont l'honneur est à venger" (*Prospectus,* 13 November 1806).

60. Rainier Grutman sees this as an indication that, despite their similarities, the Scot would never be considered as a Canadian. *Des Langues qui résonnent,* 122.

61. *Les Anciens Canadiens,* 229.

62. *Les Anciens Canadiens,* 246.

20

Antonine Maillet's Rewriting of Acadian History

Jean-Luc Desalvo

W̶HILE LITERARY CRITICS HAVE DEVOTED A great deal of attention to the notion of the carnival in Maillet's works and have focused either on the historical or non-fictional aspects of her writing, or, conversely, on their fictional counterpart, the Acadian "Conte," this chapter examines the interplay between history and storytelling, and explains how and why she intentionally blurs the distinction between fictional and non-fiction texts, and, likewise, the roles she assigns to her various narrators and characters, as well as to herself as author as her works rewrite Acadian history. This chapter also specifically examines the underlying tension this creates in her works between history and storytelling, which has been ignored or underestimated for the most part till now as it relates to the (his)story timeline and the world-upside-down *topos*.

Given that storytelling is at the heart of Antonine Maillet's project to safeguard in writing Acadia's oral patrimony, while at the same time remaining faithful to this form of communication and its particular lexical, syntactic and morphological characteristics, one of the most obvious ways to explain the manifest conflict or tension in her works between history and storytelling and, similarly, between writing and orality, relates to the detrimental role that history has played in the view of the Acadian people. There also exists a conflict between history and storytelling in her works because she succeeds precisely in creating a confusion between history and storytelling, blurring the normally well defined boundary between the two. Maillet refers to this as the "réel imaginaire."[1] Moreover, Maillet exploits the inherent ambiguity of the French word "histoire" which means both "history" and "story."

Pitfalls of History

Although one of Maillet's most important aims as a writer is to introduce Acadia's name into the pages of history, she also critiques writing and history in her books because she is conscious that, even in the most favorable circumstances, they paint at best an incomplete or partial portrait of Acadian existence. Furthermore, by elevating storytelling to a status equal to that of history, Maillet's narrators are free to interpret and vary historical outcomes. Correspondingly, there are several excellent examples in her works of attempts to reverse the course of history and fantasies about such an act. This is what the narrator in *Par derrière chez mon père* refers to as "virer les vents de l'histoire" so that these "vents" or events are more heroic or less tragic, a project that entails the rewriting of Acadian history. It is at this point that one begins to gradually realize the correlation between storytelling's great worth, as opposed to that of history, and the presence of the world-upside-down *topos* in Maillet's works. Storytelling, in fact, makes it possible to turn reality or history upside down in several ways so as to turn the world right side up. The refusal on the part of many of Maillet's narrators to follow chronological or historical time in their attempts to go back historically in time or "remonter l'histoire à rebours" as they relive certain glorious periods in Acadian history, their chronological jumps and their stopping of time are evidence of their adherence to a carnivalesque notion of time that, as in the storyteller's tale, does not conform to conventional conceptions of space and time.

One of the best examples of a reality being turned upside down or a historical outcome being reversed is found in *Pélagie-la-Charrette*. In her article on *Pélagie-la-Charrette*, Karolyn Waterson also takes account of Maillet's desire to reverse history through the use of the tale and storytelling. She describes the episode in which Pierre à Pitre and the giant P'tite goule are imprisoned on a British ship up until the time they decide to flee on a whale's back. In contrast with the biblical story of Jonah, who is swallowed up by a great fish, Maillet's characters are swallowed up by Beausoleil's schooner. Waterson rightly points out that the recreation of a myth, the elements of which are transposed, is symptomatic of Maillet's desire to reverse the course of history.[2] Furthermore, it is possible to consider Pélagie's and her people's dramatic return to Acadia as portrayed in *Pélagie-la-Charrette*, which represents an epic "à l'envers," as a reversal of history. This struggle to reverse history's course is expressed perfectly, in fact, in *Pélagie-la-Charrette*: "Mais en attendant le pays, son pauvre peuple payait très cher sa résistance aux George d'Angleterre et au revirement de l'Histoire."[3] In addition, with regard to the opposition between life and death and the great confusion existing between history and storytelling in Maillet's works, Kathryn Crecelius correctly notes that when "la Charrette de la Vie" beats her counterpart, "la Charrette de la Mort," this division or mirror effect is reversed.[4] The invincible "charrette" is beaten, signifying a victory by the weak over the strong. Crecelius also sees this same phenomenon taking place throughout the rest of Maillet's novel thanks to the use of storytelling, hearsay and legends: "Des contes, des ouï-dire, des légendes, racontés une fois au cours du récit reparaissent plus tard comme des événements attestés de l'histoire: la reprise du conte comporte toujours un renversement qui lui permet d'avoir un effet concret sur l'histoire."[5] As a result, Acadians find consolation in this story or version of history, as Maillet has pointed out in an interview.[6]

It is also evident in *Les Confessions de Jeanne de Valois* that the narrator/character hopes genuinely to reverse or, at least, correct the damage, "les maux (mots)," of history: "Puis je me suis frotté les mains, comme si je venais de reconquérir les Plaines d'Abraham."[7] Marc Czarnecki is correct to point out that the deportation of the Acadians, the "Grand Dérangement," is historically and symbolically equivalent to the Québécois experience at the Plains of Abraham.[8] Furthermore, these two tragic events in the history of Francophone Canada occurred at nearly the same time. Whereas the deportation of the Acadians took place in 1755, the Québécois's defeat at the Plains of Abraham, which marked the end of the French military presence in Canada, occurred four years later in 1759. In other words, the Acadians and Québécois both suffered a great, historical defeat that changed forever their political and cultural status in Canada.

In addition to having a concrete effect on history, Maillet's narrators and characters often rely on storytelling, because it is better suited to turning reality or history topsy-turvy in space and time. It therefore offers more flexibility to rewrite history and, ultimately, to turn the world back right side up. In fact, everything connected to storytelling and fantasy, such as giants and monsters, is pertinent to the discussion of the presence and role of the world-upside-down *topos* in Maillet's works in that, as Maillet explains herself in *Rabelais et les traditions populaires en Acadie*: "La seule introduction d'un géant dans un univers donné, renverse toutes les lois de cet univers et fait éclater sa réalité."[9] Likewise, there is no shortage of giants or colossal figures, especially female ones, in Maillet's works. The overturning of laws and shattering of reality are most obvious spatially and temporally in her works to the extent that storytelling brings about a subversion of the laws of space and time that creates, rather like the carnival, what Anne Élaine Cliche refers to as a breaking up of spatial-temporal categories.[10]

Overthrowing the Laws of Space and Time

In order to better understand how storytelling succeeds in overthrowing the laws of space and time, it is, first of all, helpful to examine the space-time continuum in Maillet's carnivalesque texts. In her article "Le temps sacré et le temps profane chez Antonine Maillet," Mathé Allain makes an important distinction between two different conceptions of time, reiterating the historical notion of time as opposed to that of the carnival and of storytelling:

> Le temps profane est celui de la vie quotidienne et individuelle. C'est un temps historique, par là-même dépourvu de signification, un temps-flèche, héraclitien, où on ne se baigne jamais deux fois dans la même rivière. . . . Le temps-flèche, irréversible, se déroule inexorablement vers la mort et la dégradation, emporté par l'entropie vers une dégradation croissante. Le temps sacré, par contre, est celui des mythes, des rites, de la vie collective. C'est un temps-roue, rythmé par les fêtes et les saisons qui se répètent inlassablement, un temps parmidien, immuable et cyclique, formé par une succession d'instants éternels.[11]

Furthermore, many critics have spoken about the cyclical nature of Maillet's works,[12] which is due in large part to her use of tales that run from one work to the next and sometimes are even repeated within the same text. For example, Jonah's tale in the whale's stomach and variants of this tale represent prime examples of this phenomenon in her works.

Emmanuel Le Roy Ladurie's research on the carnivalesque notion of time is also very helpful in understanding Maillet's attitude to time in her tales because it demonstrates that, contrary to linear or historical time, the carnivalesque notion of time is cyclical and represents a timewheel in opposition to linear time or the Heraclitean notion of time.[13] Furthermore, LeRoy Ladurie's research shows that carnivalesque time sometimes even runs backwards.[14]

Many of Maillet's narrators subscribe to this carnivalesque notion of time, which, like the storyteller's tale, eludes the space-time continuum, as Maillet herself explains in *Rabelais et les traditions populaires en Acadie*: "Le conte qui s'efforce d'expliquer le mystère, de la création du monde à la destinée et au comportement des hommes, appartient à l'*in illo tempore* et échappe à notre spatio-temporel. . . . Il n'en va pas tout à fait ainsi de la légende. Celle-ci naît dans un temps et un lieu déterminés, et sort d'un fait historique."[15] In other words, one of the tale's most important and appealing characteristics, according to Maillet, is its ability to diverge from historical time or, at any rate, to resist the effects of time because, as Maillet again points out, "le conte, se situant dans un *in illo tempore*, les gestes du héros n'ont pas à se glisser dans le temps."[16] There is an excellent illustration of this phenomenon in *Le Huitième Jour* when one of the characters notes that "Ils sont rentrés chez eux, mon frère, dans le conte et la légende, dans les plis de l'histoire et du temps d'où on les a sortis."[17] In addition to their conformity with the notion of time found in the tale, Eva-Marie Kröller offers a very perceptive explanation to account for the rupture of spatial-temporal categories so frequent in Maillet's works or, at least, for her narrators' and characters' manipulation of the space-time continuum. If her stories seem to advance and, likewise, move backwards in time by leaps and bounds instead of following linear time, this reflects the specific characteristics of Acadian history, which proceeds laterally rather than directly as a result of the "Grand Dérangement":"Separation of close family members during the Grand Dérangement, dispersion over vast territories, isolation in the woods, no official recognition of their separate identity forced Acadians to modify their sense of time and place; like other peoples in diaspora—Jews, Mennonites, the French-Canadians."[18]

Given the disastrous role that history has played from the Acadian perspective, it is easy to imagine why Maillet calls upon the tale to escape linear time, which, as Maillet has so often repeated through her narrators and characters, serves as an obstacle[19] and, moreover, is destructive and fatal to Acadia.[20] In this respect, Mircea Eliade's research on the importance and value of myths in the modern world in *Mythes, rêves et mystères* explains perfectly the tale's function in Maillet's works. Eliade points out that, especially during a period of anxiety with regard to historical time, it is humanity's desire to destroy time's homogeneity and return to a period when time was "glorious, primordial and total" that best accounts for the popularity and appeal of myths in modern times.[21] More importantly, Eliade also notes that this wish to release oneself from time often goes hand in hand with the desire to rewrite history.[22] In his commentary on Maillet's second version of *Les Crasseux*, Pierre L'Hérault recognizes the importance and function of resorting to the "Il illo tempore" of the tale in this play: "*Il illo tempore*, voilà le temps privilégié d'Antonine Maillet, celui du conte, celui où se situe l'action des *Crasseux*. C'est un drame intemporel (aucune notation de temps, sinon celle de la date de composition). . . . L'espace est de même irréel et impossible: non pas 'L'action se passe *quelque part* en Acadie,' mais *L'action se passe en Acadie*."[23]

The character "Jour en Trop" in *Le Huitième Jour*, who also goes by the name of "Hors du Temps," is probably the best personification of the notion of "in illo tempore" in Maillet's works.[24] In fact, it is noteworthy that this highly symbolic character, who was born outside time, attacks the embodiment of Time and Death, "la Faucheuse," who represents, in Allain's very own words: "Le temps-flèche, irréversible, [qui] se déroule inexorablement vers la mort et la dégradation": "Quand Jean de l'Ours l'apercevra le cul en l'air, il lui attrapera les chevilles et la tiendra ferme dans cette position jusqu'à ce que le petit Hors du Temps achève l'œuvre de leur vie."[25] There is also a similar, epic battle in *Pélagie-la-Charrette* between the forces of Pélagie's "la Charrette de la vie" and Bélonie's "la Charrette de la Mort." Furthermore, it is worth noting again that the carnivalesque notion of time associated with the world-upside-down *topos* is one outside time.[26]

Of course, Maillet's narrators and characters also refer to the timelessness associated with the tale in order to destroy time's homogeneity. They seek to release themselves from time by attempting to "fix" history's glorious and heroic periods and, conversely, avoiding its tragic moments. As it happens, in an interview Maillet clearly expressed her desire to "fix" time, as well as her characters, in her works:

Je suis toujours très préoccupée par la notion du temps; ce qu'est le temps, comment nous pouvons presque le prendre dans nos mains, comment nous luttons contre le temps, comment le temps devient un anti-destin. Même le seul fait d'écrire, c'est un anti-destin. C'est essayer, comme disait Proust lui-même, de figer, de fixer l'instant présent. J'ai toujours ce besoin d'empêcher le temps de me voler mes idées, de me voler mes personnages. Alors je les fixe.[27]

More recently, in another interview, she has reiterated this wish with regard to two of her later novels:

> Toute ma vie j'ai été hantée par la recherche du temps perdu. Cela a été un de mes leitmotifs et c'est sous-jacent à tout ce que je fais. C'est sûr que l'écrit pour moi est un anti-destin qui lutte contre le temps, contre la mort. Le temps signifie la mort finalement et l'écriture est un anti-destin. Alors, dans ce sens-là, il y a toujours eu ça et ça s'est plus révélé dans *Les Confessions*, mais c'est toujours ça. Ça l'est aussi dans *Le Chemin Saint-Jacques*.[28]

The title of Maillet's novel *Le Chemin Saint-Jacques* clearly represents her own particular vision of the universe. At the same time, this universal vision projects toward the past, by returning to her ancestors and the events surrounding her own birth, or what she even refers to in certain books as her "pré-naissance,"[29] as well as toward the future. In addition, this title illustrates the tale's considerable power and influence over Radi, Maillet's alter ego. It is the tale's ability to immortalize and transcend the present that is, above all, glorified by the epigraphs at the beginning of each part of the novel: Jules Renard's declaration that "Le bonheur serait de se souvenir du présent" and Marcel Proust's phrase, "Éterniser l'instant présent."[30] Like poets, Radi is able to immortalize time by transgressing the laws of space and time: "Elle a tenté un instant de relier l'Arcadie grecque à l'Acadie du Nouveau Monde, transgresser la loi du temps et de l'espace."[31] In other words, *Le Chemin Saint-Jacques* ultimately represents a voyage in space and time that links together mankind's entire history.[32]

Furthermore, given the fact that Acadia is not a "fixed" country, Maillet's narrators and characters naturally long for a normalization and stabilization of their status, even though they are aware that this is nearly impossible. For example, one of the characters in *Cent ans dans les bois* emphasizes the idea that Acadia's status is uncertain or indefinite by making the following point: "Comment voulez-vous vous agripper à une idée fixe dans un pays comme celui-là!"[33] For better or worse, writing is one of the best means of "fixing" space and time. The only drawback to writing, as opposed to the oral tradition associated with the tale, is that once it is written it is extremely difficult to rewrite or vary historical outcomes.

These attempts on the part of Maillet's narrators and characters to "fix" or stop time reflect Maillet's obsessive fear of Time and Death. One way of stopping time in order to conserve Acadia's good old traditions, values and beautiful language is to freeze the characters and their speech in time. The following example taken from *Pélagie-la-Charrette* points not only to Maillet's obsessive fear of Time and Death, but also to the effectiveness of this means of preservation: "Comment durant un quart de siècle ils [Beausoleil et les autres matelots] avaient été les témoins immobiles mais conscients de la vie qui fige et du temps qui s'arrête; comment des vents les ayant poussés dans des courants chauds, le dégel les avait rendus au temps et à la vie, les livrant comme tous les mortels à l'usure et au pourrissement."[34]

Although Maillet's play, *Les Drôlatiques, Horrifiques et Épouvantables Aventures de Panurge, ami de Pantagruel*, supposedly takes place during one of her favorite historical periods at a time when Acadia was still intact, in this work Maillet is, nevertheless, still curiously preoccupied with the notion of "Paroles gelées" or speech that has been frozen in time. The presence in this play of certain "Paroles gelées" is that much more paradoxical if one fails to take into account the tale's timelessness, because these words are anachronistic, some of them belonging to the twentieth century.[35] Nevertheless, these words frozen in and from time seem designed, as in *Pélagie-la-Charrette*, to preserve Acadia's good old traditions, values and beautiful language, recalling its glorious past to withstand the natural wear and tear brought about by the passing of time: "Nous approchons d'endroit où furent conservés en froidure et salure nos plus vieux mots et antique parlure de pays."[36] In consequence, it is not surprising to encounter once again a character "congelé dégel," frozen and thawed, in *Le Huitième Jour*, Messire René, who regains his original speech and accent, which date back to the distant past and are coveted by Maillet herself, as well as her narrators and characters. Likewise, Maillet possibly gives the name "Gélas" to several of her characters, notably her heroine Mariaagélas, because this name symbolizes the preservation of traditional Acadian traditions and values. This hypothesis appears to be even more plausible given that, unlike the Cormiers, Leblancs and others who are often present in Maillet's texts, this family name is conspicuously absent from the detailed list of Acadian names that Maillet gives in *L'Acadie pour quasiment rien*.[37] In any case, the information provided by Maillet in *Rabelais et les traditions populaires en Acadie* supports the hypothesis as to the positive role of the cold. As she herself says, the role of "la froidure," the cold, is similar to that of the oral transmission of tales: "Dans un conte du type 1920, on a tenté ainsi d'expliquer la transmission des mots.—Chez nous, dit l'un, il a fait tellement froid que le thermomètre s'est cassé et le zéro se promenait dans le chemin.—Chez nous, répond l'autre, il a fait tellement froid que les paroles nous gelaient dans la gueule. Qu'ils nous soient parvenus par la réfrigération ou par la transmission orale, les 'mots de gueule' de Rabelais nous restent."[38]

However, there is a counterexample in Maillet's works to show that speech frozen in time is not always necessarily good. This example seems to lessen somewhat the great worth that her narrators and characters place on tradition as a whole. Just like the oral tale, which needs to continually evolve so that its lessons remain valuable and topical, it is natural, without diminishing the importance of tradition, that words also evolve and are not forever static. However, references in Maillet's works pointing to the harmful role played by Malherbe and the French Academy are excellent examples of speech frozen or "fixed" in time that do not serve a positive function.[39] In other words, being highly conscious of the existence, on the one hand, of a highbrow, and on the other, of a low-brow Acadian language, Malherbe is to a certain extent responsible, according to Maillet, for imposing an official, high-brow language purged of all its dynamic features. This particular accusation appears in several of Maillet's texts. For example, in "la lettre d'Antonine Maillet," which serves as an epilogue or afterthought intended to frame and guide the reader's understanding of *Christophe Cartier de la Noisette dit Nounours*, rather like the prologue and epilogue to *Huitième Jour*, the narrator addresses the following reproach directed at Malherbe: "Si la France l'a perdu [le mot 'prime'], c'est la faute à Malherbe qui l'a déclaré trop vieux et désuet. Il ferait mieux, le grammairien, de ne pas approcher son nez des dents primes de Nounours."[40]

As well as the cold, another means of stopping time or protecting against the natural deterioration brought about by its passage involves "la salure," the preservation of the memory of Acadia's glorious past in salt. Maillet's characters are undoubtedly conscious of salt's great powers as a conserving agent and symbol of incorruptibility. For instance, the heroine in *Évangéline Deusse* points out: "C'est le sel qui empêche le sang de se gâter."[41] A similar observation is made in *Cent ans dans les bois*: "Vous trouvez peut-être que les genses de l'Île savont point trop ben parler. C'est par rapport aux bouffées de sel qu'ils avalont chaque jour et qui leur pavouèsont le gorgoton. Mais comme contont les vieux, le sel ça empêche un houme de se gâter et ça le garde frais longtemps."[42] In most likelihood, this explains why there are repeated references in several of Maillet's books to the biblical account of Edith's metamorphosis into a pillar of salt.[43] It is, however, probable that this reference is also directly related to Maillet's denunciation of patriarchal discourse that portrays women in rigid or fixed positions.[44] Furthermore, although salt appears to play a positive role in Maillet's works, one should not forget that salt is by nature corrosive.

In addition to fixing or stopping time to conserve Acadia's traditions, values and beautiful language, Maillet finds the notion of time associated with the tale appealing and useful because, by contrast with history's linear approach to time, it allows her to jump chronologically. Furthermore, as discussed above, the tale is not subject to history's spatial constraints insofar as it need not be situated in a well-defined or absolute place. For example, even though the title *Par derrière chez mon père* appears only to refer to a place, it is, in fact, at the same time both a spatial and temporal reference: "Le monde est grand par derrière chez mon père. Le monde, c'est tout l'espace et tous les temps. On peut rentrer chez soi par le jardin[45] ou par la rue; mais on peut aussi venir de l'été ou des autres saisons. Parcourir le monde, c'est remonter l'histoire. Et dans l'histoire se jouait la vie de nos pères."[46]

The notion that one can come from time as well as travel in time, which the narrator in *Le Chemin Saint-Jacques* calls her "longue expédition dans le temps et l'espace," probably explains the presence of numerous references in Maillet's works to the yearly round of events, such as the seasons and the holidays. Moreover, Maillet points out that "Le rythme des saisons et les temps forts du calendrier sont la respiration des petites gens."[47] It also becomes evident at this point that the first two paragraphs in *Par derrière chez mon père* refer not only to a place ("Par derrière chez mon père, il y a un pommier doux"),[48] but, more importantly, refer back to the time of Adam and Eve. In other words, the narrator attempts, with the aid of her memory, to go back as far as possible in time, "plus loin que derrière chez mon père, mais chez le grand-père du grand-père du grand-père."[49] It becomes evident at this point that she is no longer relying solely upon her own memory and therefore needs to call upon the talents of an extremely important individual in her works, the storyteller, who is responsible for passing on to her these events or stories. It is also obvious that the title of this book represents disorderly flights backward in time that do not conform to history's linear notion of chronology, but rather to the tale's non-linear understanding of time. These flights in time allow the narrator to go back to Acadia's glorious, collective past, beginning with the era of Adam and Eve before the Fall;[50] then the magical time of the narrator's childhood, which offers, from this point on, greater flexibility to visit various places and times, "l'enfance éternelle, lourde de souvenirs et grosse de tous les rêves des hommes";[51] and finally Acadia's glorious past when it was still a [French] colony, up until the time she evokes as Paradise Lost and the ensuing tragic events that lead up to the "Grand Dérangement" and the difficult one-hundred-year period which follows, "les cent ans dans les bois." It is worth noting that it is precisely at this moment that, in order to bear the weight of these tragedies, the narrator in *Par derrière chez mon père* experiences the need to resort to the use of fantastic tales and legends "pleines . . . de comédies, de romans picaresques et de contes fantastiques, que l'histoire ne suffisait plus à la raconter et devait faire appel à la légende."[52] Obviously failing to recognize the great value of myths, tales, legends and all imaginary or fantastic discourse, a critic of Maillet's works has gone so far as to say, for example, that her novel, *Pélagie-la-Charrette*, is as historically relevant to Acadia as Disneyland is to the real world.[53] It is equally evident that this same critic neglects to take into account the cathartic role that Disneyland plays and the beneficial effects it has on its visitors.[54] Moreover, Maillet's narrator at the end of this section seems no longer to want, or be able, to distinguish again between the boundaries associated with the tale or legend and those of the real world: "La petite cousine dormait. Toute la maisonnée était figée comme dans le sommeil de la Belle au Bois Dormant. Et je sortis de la maison de terre brune au toit d'ardoise qui abritait mes aïeux, sans fermer la porte et sur le bout de mes pieds, en me demandant si vraiment j'y étais entrée."[55]

Likewise, the same notion or perception of time is present in *L'Acadie pour quasiment rien*, the title of which emphasizes, probably ironically, the fact that even though Acadia was had for cheap[56] and that it no longer officially exists today, the narrator is being generous by offering what is left. The narrator invites the reader to travel back in time in order to visit Acadia rather than visit it spatially: "Je vous conseille de ne pas calculer, de ne pas prendre de rendez-vous au retour, mais de partir dans le temps et non vers un lieu.[57] Parce que l'histoire ['folklorique, ethnique, culturelle . . .' de l'*Acadie*] n'est pas spatiale, elle est temporelle. Et l'*Acadie*, c'est une histoire."[58]

In other words, the narrator wants the reader to travel in time because she knows beforehand that, upon return, Acadia will no longer exist spatially as a defined and recognized territory. In fact, the narrator points out that Acadians can be chased away from a place, but not from time: "L'Acadie, c'est là où il y a des Acadiens. Or partout où ils passaient, on les chassait. . . . On les a chassés de Grand-Pré, chassés de Virginie, chassés à leur retour d'exil, chassés de partout. Mais . . . et là ils vous ont eus! on n'est pas parvenu à les chasser hors du temps. Ils n'étaient plus nulle part, mais ils étaient."[59] Thus, with the aid of the "conteurs" and "conteuses," the male and female storytellers, and, likewise, the "défricheteurs ou défricheteuses de parenté," the unofficial, Acadian genealogists, the Acadians are able to take their revenge on what Maillet's narrator calls "l'histoire juridique" in the only way they know. The tale becomes, in effect, a weapon used against historical or official time: "Vous verrez l'Acadie des contes et de la chronique se dessiner sur la toile de fond de l'Acadie historique. Ainsi armé, vous pourrez poursuivre le voyage dans le temps: jusqu'à Beauséjour où l'Acadie achèvera de tomber aux mains des Anglais; jusqu'à Memramcook, berceau de la nouvelle Acadie sortie du bois."[60] Furthermore, the numerous references in her works to explorers of the New World, such as Christopher Columbus, Marco Polo, Sebastian Cabot and Jacques Cartier,[61] among others,[62] should not be ignored, given the fact that Maillet's ancestors were themselves explorers, and that she encourages her readers to "explore" Acadia in time. It is possible that Maillet refers particularly often to explorers of Acadia because she wishes ardently to return to this magical or paradisiacal time and place when Acadia was discovered and Acadians had not yet been driven out of the "Garden." Certainly, the need to rediscover the moment when Acadia was discovered or born is present throughout her works.[63]

There are also excellent examples of the chronological leaps associated with the tale in *Le Huitième Jour*. For example, Messire René is capable of jumping four centuries of history: "Il vient lui-même de sauter quatre siècles d'histoire, [et] hoche la tête dans la direction des rescapés d'une plus antique antiquité."[64] As discussed above, the narrator/character in *Les Confessions de Jeanne de Valois* does not abide by the rules of linear time when she recounts anecdotes or fragments of Acadian history as seen from her point of view. In fact, Maillet has admitted in an interview that she starts off with a single character in a particular context, or rather with a character who has practically been carved out of space and time.[65] In any case, the narrator/character in *Les Confessions de Jeanne de Valois* obviously rules out the need to follow chronological time: "Mais je m'égare, car je ne suis pas rendue là dans mon récit chronologique. Chronologie? mais qui m'impose de suivre la chronologie?"[66] In other words, Maillet's narrators and characters love to defy time's logical progression, or what is referred to as chronology.[67]

Conclusion

Maillet is attracted to storytelling and the tale in particular because they offer the opportunity and the means to master time by jumping chronologically or stopping time in order to rewrite Acadian history, making the necessary corrections and additions, and righting the wrongs of history. She succeeds in rewriting Acadian history primarily by adhering to a carnivalesque notion of time that, like the storyteller's tale, does not conform to conventional ideas of space and time and makes it possible to turn reality or history upside down so as to turn the world right side up again.[68] In the end, Maillet's project of rewriting Acadian history clearly serves a cathartic function for her and for those readers longing for a glorious vision of the Acadian past in which nearly all the social and political injustices suffered by the Acadians have been avenged or reversed.

Notes

1. Simone LeBlanc-Rainville, "Entretien avec Antonine Maillet," *Revue de l'Université de Moncton* 7 (1974): 14. In a more recent interview, Maillet reiterates this notion when she says: "L'histoire raconte tout ce que l'on sait ou croit savoir. Le conte raconte tout ce que l'on voudrait qu'il soit vrai. Alors, moi, je suis beaucoup plus proche du conte que de l'histoire en ce sens que je raconte le monde comme je le voudrais. Or, je me rends compte à un moment donné que le monde se met à ressembler à mes livres. À force de dire à l'Acadie ce que je crois qu'elle est, elle finit par l'être. . . . Alors, oui, j'ai dans mes histoires du conte et dans les contes il y a l'histoire bien sûr." Jean-Luc Desalvo, "La vision globaliste d'Antonine Maillet: Entretien avec Jean-Luc Desalvo," *Women in French Studies* 6 (1998): 102.

2. Karolyn Waterson, "The Mythical Dimension of *Pélagie-la-Charrette*," *Francophone Literatures of the New World* 2, (1982): 48.

3. Antonine Maillet, *Pélagie-la-Charrette* (Montreal: Leméac, 1979), 193.

4. Kathryn Crecelius, "L'histoire et son double dans *Pélagie-la-Charrette*," *Studies in Canadian Literature* 6, (1981): 214.

5. Crecelius, "L'histoire et son double."

6. Antonine Maillet, and Liano Petroni, "Histoire, fiction et vie; langue, forme, mémoire: un entretien sur *Pélagie-la-Charrette*," *Francofonia* 2 (1982): 16.

7. Antonine Maillet, *Les Confessions de Jeanne de Valois* (Montreal: Leméac, 1992), 323.

8. Marguerite Maillet and Judith Hamel, *Réception des œuvres d'Antonine Maillet* (Moncton, N. B.: Chaire d'études Acadiennes, 1989), 276.

9. Antonine Maillet, *Rabelais et les traditions populaires en Acadie* (Québec: Presse de l'Université Laval, 1971), 183.

10. Anne Élaine Cliche, "Un romancier de carnaval?," *Études françaises* 23 (1988): 45.

11. Mathé Allain, "Le temps sacré et le temps profane chez Antonine Maillet," *Québec Studies* 4 (1986): 320.

12. See, for example, James de Finney, "*Maariaagélas* [*sic*], ou l'épopée impossible," *Revue de l'Université de Moncton* 8 (1975): 45; Barbara Thompson Godard, "Maillet's *Don l'Orignal*," *Atlantis* 5 (1979): 55; Micheline Herz, "A Québécois and an Acadian Novel Compared: The Use of Myth in Jovette Marchessault's *Comme une enfant de la terre* and Antonine Maillet's *Pélagie-la-Charrette*," in *Traditionalism, Nationalism, and Feminism: Women Writers of Quebec*, ed. Paula Gilbert Lewis (Westport, Conn.: Greenwood, 1985), 173.

13. For an excellent example of the opposition between linear time and Maillet's cyclical notion of time, see *Le Chemin Saint-Jacques* (Montreal: Leméac, 1997), 366.

14. Emmanuel LeRoy Ladurie, *Le Carnaval de Romans* (Paris: Gallimard, 1979), 338.

15. Maillet, *Rabelais*, 57.

16. Maillet, *Rabelais*, 35.

17. Antonine Maillet, *Le Huitième Jour* (Montreal: Leméac, 1986), 281.

18. Eva-Marie Kröller, "Landscape, History and the Child: *On a mangé la dune*," *Québec Studies* 4 (1986): 258.

19. For example, time is represented as a wall that one must jump over in *Le Chemin Saint-Jacques*, 284.

20. See, for example, *Christophe Cartier de la Noisette dit Nounours* (Montreal: Hachette/Leméac, 1981), 86–88; *Le Chemin Saint-Jacques*, 71, 318.

21. Mircea Eliade, *Mythes, rêves et mystères* (Paris: Gallimard, 1957), 34.

22. Eliade, *Mythes, rêves et mystères*.

23. Pierre L'Hérault, "*Les Crasseux* ou le Mythe du retour aux origines," *Revue de l'Université de Moncton* 7 (1974): 52. There is also a note at the bottom of this page in which L'Hérault is correct in pointing out that, "Fait significatif et qui pourrait appuyer ce que j'avance: la première version de la pièce portait la mention: Ici maintenant, n'importe où, n'importe quand."

24. Maillet's heroine in *Crache à Pic* also probably personifies the notion of "in illo tempore." The narrator in this novel remarks, for example: "En deçà de deux ans, Crache à Pic, fille de rien, sortie de nulle part, s'était payé cinq fois la tête du maître du golfe," 205–6.

25. Maillet, *Huitième*, 249.

26. Jean Lafond, and Augustin Redondo, *L'Image du monde renversé et ses représentations littéraires et para-littéraires de la fin du XVIe siècle au milieu du XVIIe* (Paris: Vrin, 1979), 183.

27. Maillet and Petroni, "Histoire, fiction et vie," 16.

28. Jean-Luc Desalvo, "La vision globaliste d'Antonine Maillet: Entretien avec Jean-Luc Desalvo," *Women in French Studies* 6 (1998): 109.

29. See, for example, *Le Chemin Saint-Jacques*, 221.

30. A comparative study of Maillet's and Proust's works would prove fascinating, especially with regard to the ways these two authors recall the(ir) past. For obvious personal reasons, Maillet undeniably has a greater need to undertake this voyage "à la recherche du temps perdu" in the name of the Acadian people. Moreover, the Proustian notion of involuntary memory is present in *Les Confessions de Jeanne de Valois* 25 and *Christophe Cartier de la Noisette dit Nounours*, 96. See also Melvin Gallant, "Épopée, fantaisie et symbole dans *Don l'Orignal*," *Québec Studies* 4 (1986): 291; Martine L. Jacquot, "Je suis la charnière: Entretien avec Antonine Maillet," *Studies in Canadian Literature* 13 (1988): 259; Desalvo, "Vision," 109.

31. Maillet, *Chemin*, 345.

32. Maillet, *Chemin*, 346–47.

33. Maillet, *Cent*, 18.

34. Maillet, *Pélagie*, 184–85.

35. Antonine Maillet, *Les Drôlatiques, Horrifiques et Épouvantables Aventures de Panurge, ami de Pantagruel*, (Montreal: Leméac, 1983), 130.

36. Maillet, *Les Drôlatiques*, 132.

37. Antonine Maillet, *L'Acadie pour quasiment rien* (Montreal: Leméac, 1973), 64–66.

38. Maillet, *Rabelais*, 132.

39. Maillet has expressed her opinion on this point succinctly in an interview. See Françoise Collin, "Antonine Maillet: Interview," *Cahiers du GRIF*, nos. 12–13 (1976): 41.

40. Maillet, *Christophe*, 107; see also 109; *Acadie*, 48; *Confessions*, 70, 181, 213.

41. Antonine Maillet, *Évangéline Deusse* (Montreal: Leméac, 1975), 24.

42. Maillet, *Cent*, 348; see also 126.

43. See, for example, *Don l'Orignal* (Montreal: Leméac, 1977), 136; *La Veuve enragée* (Montreal: Leméac, 1977), 80; *Le Bourgeois gentleman* (Montreal: Leméac, 1978), 105; *Cent*, 199; *Oursiade*, 203; *Confessions*, 114.

44. For a further discussion of this topic, see Jean-Luc Desalvo, *Le Topos du mundus inversus dans l'œuvre d'Antonine Maillet* (Bethesda: International Scholars Press, 1999), 525.

45. There is also an obvious reference to the Garden of Eden.

46. Antonine Maillet, *Par derrière chez mon père* (Montreal: Leméac, 1972), 8.

47. Maillet, *Rabelais*, 71.

48. Maillet, *Derrière*, 7.

49. Maillet, *Derrière*, 9.

50. There is also a reference to going back to Adam and Eve before the Fall in *Le Chemin Saint-Jacques*, 35.

51. *Le Chemin Saint-Jacques*, 8–9.

52. *Le Chemin Saint-Jacques*, 11.

53. Maillet and Hamel, *Réception des œuvres*, 142.

54. See Desalvo, "Vision," 102.

55. Maillet, *Derrière*, 11.

56. The same idea is presented in *On a mangé la dune* when Radi realizes that Acadia is "À vendre!" 99.

57. Likewise, when Maillet dedicates *Emmanuel à Joseph à Dâvit* to her sister Claudette, "À Claudette qui s'est trouvée, elle aussi, au rendez-vous," it is, in most likelihood, a "rendez-vous" in time rather than in space.

58. Maillet, *Acadie*, 15.

59. Maillet, *Acadie*, 19.

60. Maillet, *Acadie*, 32.

61. This explorer is presumably either Christophe Cartier's long-lost relative or a mixture of "Christophe Colomb" and "Jacques Cartier" in *Christophe Cartier de la Noisette dit Nounours*. In fact, Maillet's narrator asks herself in this work whether Nounours is named after either or both Christopher Columbus and Jacques Cartier. However, she rightly points out that these two explorers were not contemporaries of one another: "Cartier et Colomb étaient séparés par au moins quarante ans et ne pouvaient, par conséquent, être confondus en un seul," 12. In other words, Maillet's main character represents yet another example of her deliberate attempt to create an anachronistic confusion that turns linear or historical time topsy-turvy.

62. Likewise, in *Les Confessions de Jeanne de Valois*, is it mere coincidence that one of Maillet's characters is named "sœur Magellan"? See 43.

63. It is also interesting to compare the circumstances in which Acadia and Maillet were born. For example, if one accepts the notion that it is the peculiar birth of the female narrator that is being presented, it is possible to associate the narrator's birth, as well as the sudden appearance of "l'Île-aux-Puces" in *Don l'Orignal*, with the hope for the creation of a better world. Is it mere coincidence that the island's birth occurs, like Maillet's, at noon with the female mayor's declaration? "Puis, à midi, la mairesse frissonna, agita son chignon emplumé, et déclara le fond de sa pensée en face du bourg rassemblé.—C'est une île de foin, dit-elle," 21.

64. Maillet, *Huitième*, 187.

65. André Major, "Entretien avec Antonine Maillet," *Écrits du Canada Français* 36 (1973): 24.

66. Maillet, *Confessions*, 279.

67. See, for example, *Le Chemin Saint-Jacques*, 250, 311.

68. For a general discussion of the importance of the world-upside-down *topos* in Maillet's works and a complete bibliography of her works, see Jean-Luc Desalvo, *Le Topos du mundus inversus dans l'œuvre d'Antonine Maillet* (Bethesda: International Scholars Press, 1999).

21

"Raconte-moi Acadie": The Competing Voices of Acadia in Jacques Savoie's Novel *Raconte-Moi Massabielle* and His Film *Massabielle*

Tony Simons

The Theoretical Background

JOSEPH YVON THÉRIAULT INDICATES the difference between the Acadian potential for national identity and that of Quebec:

> Au Québec, la politisation de la vieille nation-culture a pu se greffer à un nouveau projet national qui vise autour du Québec français à créer un État moderne. . . . Une telle modification permet d'espérer maintenir, sinon accroître, le niveau d'historicité de la nation. Hors Québec un tel projet 'national' s'avère une impossibilité pratique. La politicisation a eu comme effet de propulser les communautés minoritaires dans le champ provincial, accentuant par ce fait le caractère minoritaire de leur réalité.[1]

Thériault distinguishes between the Acadians of New Brunswick, with their demographic strength, and Acadians in other parts of Canada whose sense of being a minority is overwhelming. There is therefore not one contemporary Acadian experience, but many, based nevertheless on a shared knowledge of a historical and a mythical past.

There are two theoretical positions offering an underpinning to a study of the novel and the film, and giving a framework for the different discourses. They are both explored by Thériault and concern the problem of how to retain a separate identity within the dominant discourses at play in political participation.[2]

The first framework introduced by Thériault outlines concepts explored by Jürgen Habermas. These concepts are based on the notion that there are two types of social activity. First, there is rational, purpose-oriented activity, for example, the sphere of work, and, secondly, there is communication-oriented activity based on the sharing of values and norms. The first relates to modern, capitalist nation-states; the second relates to traditional societies, to ethnic groupings rather than nation states.[3] These two concepts are at the heart of the works studied, and they are at the heart of the debates about the nature of the Acadian identity.

A further issue explored by Habermas is that of the public sphere, a place beyond or outside the realm of the two activities discussed above. Rick Roderick summarizes the issue thus: "Citizens meet as part of a public sphere when they come not as subjects of the state or as private economic actors concerned with matters of individual interest, but rather as a free and open public body to discuss matters of general interest."[4] Such a discussion, based on Habermas's principle of "discursive will-formation," would lead to "consensus on political questions under conditions of open and free discussion without dogmatic appeal to authority or tradition."[5] As Roderick indicates, the public sphere gradually becomes depoliticized, being increasingly influenced and manipulated by external forces: "The commercialization of the public media, the increase in state intervention in the economy, the increase in large economic enterprises and the expanding influence of science and technology all furthered the process of the depoliticization of the public sphere."[6]

The second framework is taken by Thériault from Michel Wieviorka,[7] who represents the issue in the form of a triangle of ethnicity.[8] At the apex are individualism and universal values. At the bottom left is subjectivity and at the bottom right the sense of community. The individual remains within the triangle, subject to the tensions between the three poles. The apex implies total integration into the dominant culture and socioeconomic situation. The individual aligns himself with universal values rather than specific ones and loses his identity, retreating into anomie. The community pole is that of a closed set of relationships to the cultural and historical past. The issue here is the nature of the ethnic characteristics, how far the individual restricts himself to a narrow set of qualities and rejects those he perceives as not belonging to them. The third pole is that of subjectivity, the way in which a community or an individual responds actively and responsibly to economic, social and political demands, creating rather than responding negatively. These three poles and the interplay of discourses between them, given expression by the voices of the three main characters, represent the range of different attitudes toward the nature of Acadia, from political and socioeconomic integration to political and socioeconomic independence.

The Basic Plot of the Novel and the Film

The plots of the novel and the film are broadly similar. The principal character is Pacifique Haché, the last remaining inhabitant of Massabielle. He is the self-styled king of the village, having set up home in the church. The remaining inhabitants have all been moved to Bathurst by a mining company. The company sends a lawyer to try either to encourage Pacifique to leave Massabielle or to prove that he is mad and therefore legally be able to remove him. Pacifique resists all the temptations of the lawyer and the threats made by him. A woman, Stella, arrives from a nearby village and forms a relationship with him. The lawyer brings him a television set as a present. He is initially very interested in it but eventually destroys it.

In its bare outlines such a plot could be relevant to any context relating to alienation and anomie in the twentieth century, or even further back. Reginald Martel writes of the novel that it evokes Saint Anthony in his desert retreat.[9] However, it is made specific to the Acadian experience by its direct geographical and socioeconomic allusions. As such, it is distinct from the Quebec experience, while having similarities. Ginette Michaud argues that, though the issues of the historical drama are the same as those of a Francophone in Quebec in relation to Canada, the reading experience for someone living in Quebec is that of an outsider. It presents an "alliance de deux tendances de la littérature acadienne actuelle: d'une part, être à l'écoute de la voix des ancêtres—à ce titre, le récit de Savoie n'est pas sans rappeler au lecteur québécois la leçon nationaliste d'un certain Menaud—afin de rassembler, de rapailler les traditions du patrimoine culturel ; d'autre part, rendre compte d'un quotidien aliéné avec la lucidité, et parfois l'amertume, qui s'imposent, et ce, malgré tout projet politique."[10]

The triangle of opposing discourses presented by Wieviorka is therefore set firmly within the Acadian experience. The lawyer may be seen as representing the dominant socioeconomic universal forces. He is noticeably not given a name, emphasizing the global nature of his position. Stella, the woman, represents the community pole. Her name and its associated sets of connotations will be examined later. Finally, there is Pacifique Haché, the subjective pole, whose name in French represents not only a conflict of characteristics—peaceful versus a symbol of violence—but also refers back to one of the founders of Acadia, Michel Hache dit Gallant. The church that is the setting for most of the dialogue and action begins as a conflictual environment in which the external economic, social and political forces are dominant, but shifts into becoming Habermas's public sphere of open dialogue by the end of the works. The discourses set up in the dialogues and actions will be examined and the differences between the novel and the film explored.

The plots of the novel and the film, while being broadly similar, do, however, have significant differences. The novel encompasses a wider range of events. There are more characters and consequently more voices articulating a wider range of discourses. The novel is more exploratory. It starts negatively and ends with a message that is less positive than that of the film.

The Novel

The novel opens with a description of loss, separation and solitude evoking the image of widowhood representing the disrupted family, and the single child representing the incomplete family. Even the old family homes are nothing more than the foundations marked by cellars. They are empty and, rather than offering an image of potential development, the impression is one of abandonment evoking "Le Grand Dérangement."

The first dialogue takes place in the church between the lawyer and Pacifique Haché. It centers on Pacifique's argument for the necessity of "Le travail, la famille et l'ordre!"[11] in order to give the inhabitants their dignity and self-respect. Recalling the Vichy motto, the replacement by "ordre" of the word "patrie" is significant. Pacifique may be the self-styled king of Massabielle, and act out being its priest in its church, but he does not perceive himself as being the leader of a nation-state. Rather, he sees his domain as a collection of individuals, each with their own identity, dignity and self-respect bestowed by the defining characteristics of work. Indeed, actual ownership of the land is unimportant. In the ensuing dialogue, he says he sees no need to provide the deeds of his land to the lawyer in order to prove that he belongs there.

Pacifique's attitude is problematic. On the one side, he supports work—the purpose-oriented activity of Habermas signifying the modern capitalist nation-state—and would appear therefore to be aligning himself with the dominant discourse represented by the lawyer. But he resists the lawyer. Pacifique is in an ambiguous, midway situation, having no new discourse of his own with which to counter the argument of the lawyer. This new discourse only emerges when he meets Stella. For the present, the two can only engage in a provisional set of actions.

The lawyer tempts Pacifique with presents and the offer of a new house built by the mining company. This could be in Massabielle, as long as Pacifique leaves his current home, the church. He is being tempted by a solution that would give him material well-being, but would deny him his present identity. Pacifique turns the tables on the lawyer by ironically tying him up in pink toilet paper, one of the presents brought by the lawyer. He then, on a different occasion, pretends to have hanged himself, and sees the lawyer searching for the deeds. The representative of the law has become a potential thief. The lawyer becomes more threatening and states that the company will bring in bulldozers to demolish the church.

It is clear that the universal, external values represented by the lawyer can destroy the subjective, creative values represented by Pacifique. References are made to the fate of the original inhabitants of Massabielle and the Indians. In effect they have all been put into protected reserves, in which their identities are stripped away as they sink into idleness and drunkenness. Indeed, the fate of the ex-inhabitants of Massabielle is a potential copy not only of the fate of the Indians, but also that of the Acadians in 1755, excluded from an environment that they had created as their own: "C'était là qu'ils avaient atterri, les gens de Massabielle. Dans de belles maisons qu'on leur avait faites, juste pour eux. Semblables, pareilles et ressemblantes. On avait mis les Indiens en réserve, cent ans plus tôt, presqu'au même endroit, et ils s'étaient dilués. Dissouts. On refaisait la même chose aux gens de Massabielle. L'histoire se recopiait."[12] This comment leads into a section of dialogue between the ex-inhabitants of Massabielle in their "tribunal de la taverne" and their lawyer. This is a different form of Habermas's public sphere. In the public sphere of the church the discourses are actively at play. There is still a future since resolutions to the competing voices have not yet been found. The lawyer has not yet succeeded in dispossessing Pacifique. All that is shown in the tavern, however, is the result of such an outcome, that of integration into the dominant discourse. The inhabitants are only too aware of their fate, and refer to themselves as "les 'bourbons,' les traîtres de Massabielle,"[13] who accepted the offers made to them, but resent living in an English environment on "Welfare Street," rather than in a French-speaking town. This episode focusing on defeat is followed by one focusing on resistance. One of the ex-inhabitants, Dieudonné, talks to Pacifique about his resistance and the relationship between resistance, cunning and madness. Subsequently, the lawyer arrives in a lorry with three surveyors. Pacifique has created a number of scarecrows representing a religious procession. He forces the lawyer and the surveyors to kneel before the scarecrow priest. The lawyer notices that, as decoration, Pacifique has used the deeds to his land. They blow meaninglessly in the wind.

The following episode introduces Stella. She arrives in a Cortina. Pacifique is intrigued when she takes the battery out of her car in order to keep it in full working order for her departure. He is not, however, welcoming, suspecting that she is the lawyer's wife come to tempt him. She denies this, saying that the mines have raped her: "Sais-tu comment s'est fait les mines? C'est une grande cheminée, Pacifique! Avec un diable noir derrière. Si tu veux voir, j'va te montrer la marque qu'a m'a fait, la mine, quand a m'a violée. Une grande cicatrice de la longueur de la cheminée."[14] Pacifique is now, however, no longer alone and the emphasis shifts to communication based on the sharing of values and norms. He and Stella discuss their situation, referring in particular to the "Festin des fous," an ancient tradition in which the king and his jester (also "madman" in French) exchange roles for a day. She also takes his photo with a Kodak camera, "capturing" and fixing his image. This concerns him, since it turns him from being a changeable, open person able to shift roles, into a single person. The force of external, universal values is still there, but it has become one part of the discourse—that of communication, rather than being the whole of the discourse seen in the episode with the lawyer.

His relationship with Stella develops. They fall in love, but they are also divided by mistrust. Stella explains this as the lack of agreement that is fundamental to membership of the same race, one that finds it difficult to come to a common, agreed position: "Des fois, j'l sens, tu m'haïs comme du monde d'la même race s'haïssent sûrement ... on est d'une race qui s'accorde pas encore."[15] Progressively, Pacifique's world becomes more full, evoking the rebuilding of Acadia after "Le Grand Dérangement." Other characters are introduced from La Dauversière, the same village that Stella comes from, and their family histories are given. Massabielle is filled with children and Pacifique introduces the notion of marrying Stella. The voices no longer represent separate discourses, but have become multiple.

Then the television set arrives. It is linked to the idea of giving birth, a symbol of a new be-ginning, since, when it appears on the steps of the church in a box making the sounds of a baby crying, Pacifique thinks that it is an abandoned newborn baby. Stella shows him how to use the television set, in particular how, by pressing the appropriate button, he can change not only from one image to another, but from French to English and vice versa. Pacifique assumes that the television set is a present from the lawyer, whom he has not seen for a long time. This causes mental confusion. He finds it increasingly difficult to differentiate between reality and imagi-nation, seeing Stella and the lawyer on the television. His favorite program is a quiz show, *The Price is Right*. Initially he feels sympathy with the losers, but gradually begins to react in a more materialistic way, siding with the winners. The dominant pole of universal values appears to be winning. As Stella says: "Je sais maintenant qu'on lui a bien aligné le cerveau sur ce qu'est le bonheur de gagner, et il ne reste plus qu'à organiser la scène finale."[16] Pacifique finds it increas-ingly difficult to separate life on the television from real life. The films he watches seem more interesting than his own dreams. Gradually, the television set takes over his life, not only his mental condition, but also his physical environment. It appears to grow larger and larger as Pacifique seems to grow increasingly insane. Stella is still in love with him, but she realizes that the television set now means more to Pacifique than she does. She now feels alone. Pacifique neither loves her nor hates her. He is indifferent to her, and she decides to leave.

Once she has left, Pacifique realizes how much he has lost. It is not only her, but his author-ity and his link to a community. He begins violently to break up the statues in the church with an axe, a wordplay on his surname Haché, and a double wordplay on his first name Pacifique. Stella returns, however, her car having broken down. She sees that he has destroyed the televi-sion set, leaving only its frame, which he has attached to the door of the confessional. It is now the fifty-first day of September. They have decided that it will remain September until spring comes. They will place themselves, as it were, out of real time, able temporarily to be themselves with their own identities, awaiting the return of conflict with the dominant discourse of uni-versal values. This is not an optimistic solution, but rather a form of escape or self-imposed exile. Though similar to the end of the film, it is very different in its message.

The Film

The film version, at twenty-five minutes long, naturally contains less material than the 153 pages of the novel. It is also more tightly structured and more focused. By limiting the sets of discourses, the message is clearer. The film explores the issues, but it also offers a form of reso-lution. It opens with a pan across a deserted shoreline. The camera focuses in on a scarecrow. This is greeted by Pacifique as he passes, playing his harmonica, carrying a fishing line and the fish he has caught, and accompanied by a dog. The camera tracks him back through the same empty landscape seen previously, as he makes his way to a distant village in which a church can be made out. There is no need for the long description given in the novel of the solitude of Massabielle. It is evoked on the screen, but here it is linked to positive images of contentment resulting from the sense of Pacifique being in control of his everyday life. There is none of the sense of loss and abandonment described in the novel.

The next scene is that of the lawyer arriving in an estate car. The estate car is initially seen as a blurred image behind a translucent screen, and then is seen clearly, the camera focusing on the words "Panda Mining Inc." displayed on the side of the door. Pacifique ignores him. He greets more scarecrows before entering the church, which is decorated with car hubcaps around the door. These may represent an ironic expropriation by Pacifique of one part of a significant icon of the power of Western economies—the car—turning it to aesthetic use. He has divided the icon, creating himself a form of dispersal—an inversion of "Le Grand Dérangement"—and has collected the dispersed elements for his own use.

The dialogue covers broadly the same material as that given in the novel, but it focuses almost totally on Pacifique's expressed desire not to be thrown out of Massabielle and the church in which he has made his home, and the arguments of the lawyer representing the mining company. Replacing material in the novel concerning the ex-inhabitants of the village is a visual stress on violence on both sides. On the one side are the threats of the lawyer. On the other side, Pacifique wields a potentially lethal knife as he cuts up his fish. He also appears to be about to smash the windshield of the estate car. However, the visual signifiers of Pacifique's violence do not link to signifieds of violence. His violence only *appears* to be so. He is wielding the knife as an everyday object, used for cooking and other activities: it appears threatening, but actually is merely functional. Similarly, the scene in which he appears to be about to smash the windshield turns out to be the sprinkling of "holy" water on the screen. Material is also included in the dialogue concerning family values. The lawyer is married, but has no children. Pacifique offers him the eyes of the fish as an aid to helping his wife to become pregnant. Fish are a powerful symbol as an aid to childbearing among Jewish peoples, in particular, but also for others, such as Nordic, Icelandic and Breton populations. Pacifique is looking to the myths of the past, but his attitude is ambiguous, since he chops off the head of this phallic symbol, ironically offering a worthless part of the myth to the lawyer.

After the lawyer has driven off angrily, another truck is seen arriving, playing loud music and flashing the lights on its roof. It is Stella. As in the novel, Pacifique thinks she is connected to the lawyer, but she says she is not. She also stresses the fact that Stella is the only name she has. Their relationship develops very quickly, from hostility and indifference to a solid relationship, especially when she tells him she comes from La Dauversière. As in the novel, she takes his photo, this time with a Polaroid camera, creating an image that appears before his eyes. He has the same reaction as in the novel, amazement turning to anger at having been fixed. As in the novel, she tells him they are both of the same race.

The final stage of the film is the arrival of the television set. This time it is brought openly by the lawyer, rather than being mistaken for a crying abandoned baby. This leads quickly to the end of the film, where the credits are shown over a series of still photographs of Stella and Pacifique's life together, Pacifique watching the television, and Stella looking increasingly sad. The credits stop as we see film of Pacifique throwing the television into the sea. Then the credits resume over stills of Stella becoming pregnant, and the two of them surrounded by an increasing number of children. This is interrupted with a short clip of the lawyer expressing his astonishment at their growing number. The film ends with a triumphant sound-track of choral music, film of Stella and Pacifique's children playing, and an archetypal sunset over the hills beyond the water.

It is clear that the film, by cutting much of the material of the novel, and by focusing on the triangle of discourses (the lawyer and television set representing universal values, Stella community values and Pacifique the subjective), gives a much more focused and optimistic picture of the potential future of Acadian life. It does not, however, close off the discourses. It sets them out and demonstrates one set of conclusions, but, by hiding them beneath the credits at the end, it hints at a situation that will continue beneath the apparent sets of discourses. It hints also at subversion, the life of the growing family happening underneath the fixed convention of film credits, a form of universal values within the genre of cinema.

There are other indications not only of subversion, but also forms of resistance in the novel and film concerning each of the three poles. Each of the poles has, associated with it, sets of signifiers that complete the picture of the discourses.

Taking first the pole of universal values, leading to the integration of the individual into the dominant discourse, it is interesting to note that the lawyer works on behalf of a mining company. In the novel this is Noranda Mining Ltd. Klein and Pena, in their study of Canadian multinational companies, indicate the monopolistic and colonialistic aims of Noranda, from its beginnings in 1922 with the financial backing of U.S. companies such as Dupont, U.S. Steel and Rockefeller, and it subsequent backing by Canadian financial companies based in Ontario.[17] Its mining activities have had a considerable influence on the economy and society of New Brunswick, not only under its own name, but in the form of other companies with different names, such as the Bathurst Mining and Smelting Co., that it partially or wholly controls. As such, while it created secondary-sector industry-based employment in some of the urban areas, its activities have been seen as a threat to rural primary-sector activities, such as agriculture and fishing. Encouragement by the government to move to towns has not always been a success: "Cette attitude de la population du Nord-Est d'éviter les centres urbains et de s'attacher à son milieu rural est vite perçue comme un obstacle de taille par les planificateurs de la région qui avaient grandement misé sur la mobilité des ruraux pour réduire la pauvreté dans les campagnes et fournir une main d'œuvre abondante aux quelques centres désignés pour le développement industriel."[18] It is interesting that the company lawyer invokes the government, making the expropriation official:

> —Logiquement si tout le monde à Massabielle a déménagé à Bathurst, y a cinq ans, y a pas de raison que leurs terres leur appartiennent encore. Pas plus qu'y ne t'appartiennent à toi!
> C'est écrit sur tous les papiers officiels du gouvernement!
> Pacifique replies:
> —Le gouvernement? J'le connais pas, lui? Y a jamais cultivé de terre à Massabielle, le gouvernement! Je l'ai jamais vu se pencher pour ramasser des roches dans les champs icitte. J'vois pas ce qu'y aurait à dire là-dedans, lui?[19]

This dialogue from the novel, with its differences in accent and syntax, demonstrates the lack of mutual understanding between the two sides. On one side are the lawyer, the government and their economic and legal reasoning expressing in a rather more standard French the world of universal values, and on the other side is Pacifique, the individual with his experience of working on the land at Massabielle, representing with his own natural, local use of language the creative, personal set of values. Ironically, Pacifique is able, when he so decides, to switch to a more universal language than that used by the lawyer, Latin. At the end of this section he speaks as the priest of his local church, saying: "Omnipotens Deus et Pater noster Massabielle et Confiteor Deo Amen!"[20] The lawyer has, however, gone to sleep, but repeats the "Amen" on being woken up. He has not even listened to Pacifique. He is only interested in his own voice.

It is interesting to note that, while in the novel the lawyer works for Noranda, this is changed in the film to the almost homophonous Panda Mining Inc. and a panda logo is displayed. Such a name is doubly ironic. Elsewhere in the world, the panda represents ecological balance and the protection of endangered species. Here the company is the threat, endangering the Acadian rural way of life. It does so, however, in a reassuring manner, like a panda, at least on the surface. In fact it displays the iconic virtues on the surface while having the aggression of the real animal underneath. The lawyer brings presents, but his real aim is to dispossess Pacifique.

The second aspect of the pole of universal values represented by the lawyer is the television set that is given to Pacifique by the lawyer. The television is a voice from afar, but also one that appears to be present. It appears to be talking personally to Pacifique, but, in practice, is speaking to a vast audience composed of anyone who happens to be listening. In the novel, the first time Pacifique switches it on, he thinks it is the lawyer he can see talking. He is unaccustomed to seeing television and is confused. The television is clearly a gift relating to the set of universal values. While the information it gives is in French, the information itself is not specific to Acadia, at least on the surface. He watches a news broadcast that begins with Vietnamese refugees, continues with the death of children in Managua as a result of the Sandinista uprising, then the death of thousands in Pakistan as a result of the drought. It finishes, almost as an afterthought, with the profits of Noranda: "Au pays, enfin, la compagnie minière Noranda a fait des profits de l'ordre de un point deux milliards de dollars cette année."[21]

The parallels are clear. The Acadian experience of dispossession is not unique when considered on a global scale. The Vietnam War created a dispossessed people—the refugees. In Nicaragua, the Somoza regime saw increasing movements of people from the countryside to towns, either voluntarily or under duress, leaving many with no job, no means of supporting themselves and without their original identity. Equally, Pakistan is an example of a country split historically and geographically. These all allude to aspects of the Acadian situation, but, of course, they are not the Acadian situation. The parallels only reinforce the global picture and offer nothing but a pessimistic future. The irony is that the only allusion that might refer to Acadia is to Noranda, and this is prefaced by the neutral "Au pays."

Pacifique does not appear to be interested in any of this, but nevertheless is taken over by the television. Its power as a set of universal values is hegemonic. He watches it and becomes, in the novel at least, totally involved in "The Price is Right." This echoes the role of money alluded to earlier in the novel. The former inhabitants of Massabielle had been offered a good price for their land and had sold out to Noranda. Their price had been right. Now, as Pacifique watches the game show, he starts by feeling empathy with those who lose, but eventually cheers the winners. He is seen to have sold out to the lure of money, albeit vicariously. At the end of the novel Pacifique does destroy the television, but the final episode describes him dressed up like a grotesque priest with his head in the only remaining part of the set, the frame in the door of the confessional. He has been "captured" by it, and, although he has destroyed the television, it has destroyed him. The final image from the novel is therefore significantly more negative than the one at the end of the film, in which the television plays a smaller part. Pacifique ends the film in control of it, destroying it totally rather than submitting to it.

The second pole of the triangle, that of the community, is represented by Stella and its discourse is exemplified in her relationship with Pacifique and the mutual understanding of their heritage. Stella comes from a small village nearby called La Dauversière. These are two important sets of information for the building up of interpretation. Stella is the only name given to the woman and is thus accorded especial significance in an area where the genealogy of family names is so important in tracing a person's Acadian roots. Her name refers clearly to the Acadian flag, the design of which was adopted by the second national Acadian Convention held at Miscouche in 1884. The Acadian anthem "Ave Maris Stella" was adopted at the same time: "Comme marque distinctive de la nationalité acadienne on placera une étoile, figure de Marie, dans la partie bleue, qui est la couleur symbolique des personnes consacrées à la Sainte Vierge. Cette étoile, Stella Maris, qui doit guider la petite colonie acadienne à travers les orages et les écueils, sera aux couleurs papales pour montrer notre inviolable attachement à la Sainte église, notre mère."[22]

The star, in papal yellow and representing the star that guides the sailor safely home, set within the French tricolore has become a powerful symbol of Acadian identity, even though there were those at the time and later who would have preferred a "fleur-de-lys" included, symbolizing the ties with pre-Revolutionary France. The anthem chosen at the time, with its reference to the Virgin Mary, may have enjoyed less support, especially from the 1960s onwards. For example, at the New Brunswick Francophone convention held at Fredericton in 1972, 58.7 percent of the members attending wanted it to be replaced. Thus, at the time of these two works, while the name Stella had very strong associations with Acadia, its function as a symbol was not undisputed.

In addition to this link with the Acadian community, Stella comes from the deserted village of La Dauversière, introducing another set of connotations which, on examination, have a strong connection with Quebec, but also extend to Acadia. Jérôme Le Royer de la Dauversière was an important figure in the history of Quebec. Early in the seventeenth century he believed himself called by God to undertake the evangelization of the island of Montréal and found a hospital there. This he did, forming a company to help establish the settlement at Ville Marie. Place de la Dauversière is a recognized landmark in Montréal. He also founded the Religious Hospitallers of Saint-Joseph. The Religious Hospitallers remained in Montreal for two hundred years, but then moved outwards. Acadia was one of the early sites they chose for their work. Significantly, in the second half of the twentieth century, when these two works were created, the Religious Hospitallers were more involved in social problems such as homelessness, injustice and violence, central themes of these works about Acadia. Stella's village is now, however, deserted, implying an ending to the link with the Quebec past implied by its name.

Stella also introduces another set of discourses by referring to the "Festin des Fous." This is the tradition whereby the king takes the place of the jester and viceversa, the most dominant person exchanging with the one who has no power. The discourse of domination is clear in both novel and film. However, if the word *fou* is translated as "mad" and then put into the context of the novel and film, a different picture emerges. In his *Madness and Civilization: A History of Insanity in the Age of Reason*, [23] Foucault explores questions relating to the treatment of the mad. Before the seventeenth century, madness and reason were both forms of experience of knowledge, madness being almost privileged as a form of sacred experience offering insights into life. The eighteenth century, however, saw the rise of institutions containing not only the insane—those who acted differently from the rest of society and who could not be understood by it—but also the unemployed and the poor, those who were seen as a threat to the economic growth of the country and its general well-being. They were divided off from the rest of society, excluded from it in institutions. [24]

The allusions to Acadian life are clear. Indeed, the text goes back to the fate of the Indians who lived on the same territory. They spoke a different language. Their voice could not be understood and they were excluded: "Les Indiens qui ont habité là avant, nommaient les choses avec d'autres mots que les nôtres. Ils n'y sont plus d'ailleurs, parce qu'on ne les comprenait pas." [25] Their fate, to be excluded from society in reservations, is the same as the ex-inhabitants of Massabielle, excluded from their village and put into new houses in Bathurst. Just as the mad were dominated and excluded in the discourse of reason versus insanity, so the Acadians were excluded in a political discourse of French versus English, or an economic one based on capitalist values.

Yet Pacifique finally transcends this discourse by subverting it. Firstly, he can compete against the expropriation of his land by claiming madness. Anything put to him by the lawyer is based on argument or reason. Proclaiming insanity means that he can circumvent the argument since he does not offer an opposing discourse. What he does is play at opposition or resistance. He ties up the lawyer in pink toilet paper, and he gives the appearance of aggression. It is not resistance, but an alternative way of proceeding, and as such can never be countered by dominating forces.

Second, he can play at being the king of his territory, a dominating force, but he is king of nothing, only his own destiny and identity. As such, this form of domination is meaningless. He is therefore free to explore his relationship with the community values represented by Stella as they create a life together in the knowledge of their common heritage.

The film denotes this more clearly than does the novel. The short clip of the lawyer at the end of the film between the credits shows his astonishment. His rational arguments and universal voice have failed. Pacifique is able to produce a family, but in a more subversive manner, underneath the credits, where he is free. This may be seen as a positive message. It puts to one side the fixed nature of the discourses about Acadian identity, Acadia as a nation and Acadia as an ethnic grouping, and opens up the debate on a different level, that of an openness, the freedom to choose and to create one's own sets of discourse in response to external factors.

The film therefore has a rather different message from that of the novel. The novel explores the issues and offers negative conclusions, highlighting the characters' inability to ensure the permanent continuation of Acadian identity. The only means of survival is escape into a world out of time, a self-imposed exile that is little different from the exile of "Le Grand Dérangement." The film, however, explores the issues and offers a solution, that of enabling Massabielle and its Acadian identity to grow alongside the dominant discourses, creating a new public sphere. The opposing voices will still be there, but, as a couple and then as a family, Pacifique and Stella will be able to grow and strengthen their identity beyond the dominating discourses. This is not escapism, since the space they inhabit can only exist alongside the dominant discourses. Their awareness of the power of external voices will ensure that their space retains its authenticity. They will not give in to them, but will remain open to engagement with them at any time.

This reflects the political climate of the early 1980s. The film made in 1983 has moved on from the dead end of escape suggested by the 1979 novel version, with its connotations of "Le Grand Dérangement." Both works explore the issues surrounding the place of the individual and the community in relation to integration or independence within the triangle of competing discourses, but the film offers a real solution for Acadia. It can be seen as a fictional representation of the notion of community dualism of the kind introduced by the New Brunswick government of Richard Hatfield in Bill 88 of 1981, in which there would be separate linguistic (and ethnic) communities living side by side, each having access to their own autonomous institutions. However, such a solution is still not a complete one. As a form of ethnic community with access only to its past rather than active engagement with the present, the public sphere created by Pacifique and Stella is outside the sphere of political identity and political responsibility. The weakness is that, while such a public sphere could theoretically open up to engagement with the national, the federal or some other community at any time, it might not do this because it is essentially outside the discourse of politics. Its position in the film, beneath the final credits, underpins such a view. It is not formally part of cinematic discourse, just as the public sphere that is depicted is not part of political discourse.

The film, while appearing to offer a solution to the issue of Acadian identity, offers it rather as a subject for debate about discourse, as one solution among many. It is not the dead end of the novel, but an invitation to discuss further, to find a future that faces up to the reality of political choices for Acadia in present-day Canada within the discursive framework of the possible solutions that have been proposed and explored. As Thériault states, and as the film demonstrates, the parameters of the debate are now perfectly clear. There is a choice of routes for the future of Acadia, and Thériault concludes that its future lies not in one of the old solutions, but in a synthesis of them: "Ni l'autonomisme politique des années 1970, ni le dualisme communautaire (ethnique), ni l'intégration institutionnelle nous sont apparus des voies qui portent à elles seules une réponse à la question du politique en Acadie (la mise ne forme d'une société) et son rapport à la politique (la vie politicienne). N'en concluons pas pour autant une impasse, car ces réponses partielles sont des indicateurs nous permettant de comprendre autour de quels axes gravite la question acadienne. . . . C'est dans leur synthèse que semblent résider les possibilities les plus riches de la reunification du politique et de la politique en Acadie."[26]

Notes

1. Joseph Yvon Thériault, *L'Identité à l'épreuve de la modernité*, (Moncton: Éditions d'Acadie, 1995), 266.

2. Thériault, *L'Identité à l'épreuve*, 25.

3. Thériault, *L'Identité à l'épreuve*, 57–58.

4. Rick Roderick, *Habermas and the Foundations of Critical Theory* (London: Macmillan, 1986), 42.

5. Roderick, *Habermas*, 42.

6. Roderick, *Habermas*, 42–43.

7. Michel Wieviorka, *La Démocratie à l'épreuve: Nationalisme, populisme, ethnicité* (Paris: La Découverte, 1993), 125.

8. Thériault, *L'Identité à l'épreuve*, 114–16.

9. Reginald Martel, "Livres d'artistes ou non," *La Presse*, Montreal, 3 May 1980, D3.

10. Ginette Michaud, "La Version acadienne d'une double expropriation," *Le Devoir*, Montreal, 22 November 1980, 26.

11. Jacques Savoie, *Raconte-moi Massabielle* (Moncton: N.B., Les Éditions d'Acadie, 1979), 13.

12. Savoie, *Raconte-moi*, 35.

13. Savoie, *Raconte-moi*, 40.

14. Savoie, *Raconte-moi*, 68.

15. Savoie, *Raconte-moi*, 81.

16. Savoie, *Raconte-moi*, 129.

17. Juan-Luis Klein and Orlando Pena, *Compagnies multinationales et espaces géographiques. Noranda Mines, une étude de cas* (Rouyn: Collège d'Abitibi-Témiscamingue, January 1984), 3.

18. Donald J. Savoie, and Maurice Beaudin, *La Lutte pour le développement* (Sillery, Québec: Presses de l'Université de Québec, 1988), 120.

19. Savoie, *Raconte-moi*, 11.

20. Savoie, *Raconte-moi*, 13.

21. Savoie, *Raconte-moi*, 115.

22. Marcel-François Richard, reported in *Le Moniteur Acadien*, Shediac, 28 August 1884.

23. Michel Foucault, *Madness and Civilization: A History of Insanity in the Age of Reason* (London: Tavistock Publications, 1977).

24. Barry Smart, *Michel Foucault* (London and New York: Tavistock Publications, 1985).

25. Savoie, *Raconte-moi*, 34.

26. Thériault, *L'Identité à l'épreuve*, 49.

V
EUROPE

22

Communication, Language and Silence in *Suisse Romande*

Joy Charnley

Un Bon Étranger Est un Étranger Invisible[1]

CRITICS AND EVEN WRITERS THEMSELVES have made much of their tendency toward introspection and retreat from the affairs of the world, in contrast to their counterparts in *Suisse alémanique*. Thus Francillon declares that "l'écrivain de Suisse française . . . ne s'engage guère,"[2] Fornerod speaks of "le caractère très peu engagé de notre littérature contemporaine,"[3] while the writer Jean-Pierre Monnier (1921–98) felt that "il s'agit . . . non pas d'une superbe nonchalance à l'égard de tout ce qui constitue le pouvoir civil, mais d'une réelle difficulté à lui accorder la moindre importance."[4] More recently, however, Daniel de Roulet (1944) has criticized previous generations of writers for not being sufficiently "engagées"[5] and he has contributed his own criticism of the Swiss state in books such as *Double*, which deals with the early-1990s scandal dubbed the "Affaire des Fiches."[6]

While it is true that writers in *Suisse romande* have on the whole not displayed the militancy or "engagement" of a Frisch or a Dürrenmatt,[7] communication and the difficulty of achieving real understanding between human beings are important themes for many of them[8] and ones that are now being explored in relation to foreigners in Switzerland. That this change is relatively recent is made manifest by the fact that even comments made only fifteen years ago are no longer entirely valid: ". . . nos lettres semblent se référer de moins en moins à la réalité romande et on s'étonne, par exemple, de constater que des sujets aussi importants et aussi brûlants que les travailleurs étrangers, les immigrés, . . . n'ont pratiquement jamais été traités par des romanciers de chez nous."[9] This is certainly no longer the case; from being silent and invisible, foreigners have in fact moved toward center stage in the literature of the six cantons of *Suisse romande*, either writing about their experiences or being written about by others. This gradual "prise de parole" is important and has been foregrounded by writers in different ways. Gabrielle Chambordon (1944), of Spanish and Swiss parentage,[10] has attempted to write through a child's eyes about the experience of not having access to the language needed to defend oneself adequately. In *La Suisse des autres*, for example, she says: ". . . sans le vocabulaire c'est toujours les riches qui ont pu acheter les livres pour savoir tous les mots qui auront raison pour embêter ceux qui ne savent pas. . . . Je voulais apprendre des mots, ça c'était sûr, parce que les pauvres comme nous, on en avait besoin pour sortir de là."[11] Significantly, however, it is the child's fascination for words and the frank, unguarded comments she makes to a teacher about her unorthodox home life that start off the cycle of domestic problems, state intervention and separation. The child learns that language can mean power but it can also spell danger if used unwisely.

The denial of access to language and the power it bestows, the desire to take control of one's life through words and awareness of the need to use words carefully are once again illustrated by Adrien Pasquali's *Le pain de silence*.[12] Published literally days before his suicide in March 1999, Pasquali's work, posthumously described as "sa dernière tentative pour sortir de son exil intérieur,"[13] illustrates the weight of silence that had to be overcome by this writer, critic and translator who worked so closely with *words*. Perhaps Pasquali's entire life can now be seen as in some sense a battle against that terrible silence. For indeed he emphasizes the pressure placed on immigrants such as his parents *not* to use language, not to play too prominent a role, not to be too visible, not to annoy the neighbors. *Le pain de silence*, in which silence becomes a real and menacing presence, leaves one with an overwhelming sense of the exclusion felt by these "spaghettis, maguts, maccaronis, capians"[14] who were not important or integrated enough in the 1960s to be allowed to be heard.[15] Silence and retreat from the world become the best defences: ". . . il résulta sans doute ce 'parlez plus doucement,' pas entendu, pas vu, pas pris, pas de commisariat, même si nul besoin d'être entendu, d'être vu pour être dénoncé."[16] Denied the possibility of public expression, a sense of acceptance and a real role in society, Pasquali thus concludes that his parents' attitude, passed on to him, was "tant qu'à faire autant rentrer chez soi, pilules et cigarettes, et si ça explose autour de la table de la cuisine plutôt que sur le palier, la place publique, n'en pas parler."[17]

The following analysis will look at various manifestations of migrants and exiles in *Suisse romande* literature, concentrating, in particular, on the issues of language, silence and communication in three types of writing: fiction in which Swiss writers portray foreigners, autobiography and biography recounting the lives of immigrants and *récits de vie* involving either collaboration between a Swiss writer and an immigrant or writing in which a foreigner "speaks for herself." Questions to be asked include: who is writing and who is at the center of the narrative? What role do the non-Swiss play and how are they portrayed? How are the themes of language, communication and silence explored in each work?

Fiction

Three recent texts by Swiss writers have attempted to portray the lives of foreigners living in Switzerland: In the short story "Les frontières de ton corps"[18] Janine Massard (1939) brings together a Kurd established in Switzerland and a Swiss woman; in *Le Miroir aux alouettes*[19] Benoîte Crevoisier (1938) imagines an encounter between a young Turkish man and an older Swiss woman, while Anne-Lise Thurler (1960) turns to "requérants d'asile" from Zaire for her representation of the mental stress and fragility which can be caused by the experience of exile.[20]

In "Les frontières de ton corps" both central characters are looking for something—intimacy, acceptance—which for a while they find in their ultimately doomed relationship. "Aziz" craves some kind of refuge in this foreign land, telling Olga "qu'elle était son pays retrouvé"[21] and in turn he makes her feel loved and desired. They manage for a time to love and understand one another, but, as in so many other accounts of exile in *Suisse romande*, communication, comprehension and trust eventually become impossible, and they are driven apart. Massard, who has often written about poverty in Switzerland, here once again grounds her story in an element drawn from reality—this time the presence of many Turks and Kurds on Swiss soil—but her story is told resolutely through the eyes of Olga. While indicating, with the story of the wife and children that Aziz has in fact left behind, that she is only too aware of what it means to be a Kurd in Turkey, Massard does not attempt to delve too deeply into Aziz's life and motivation. She is, it would seem, much more interested in her central female character, her perception of the relationship and her disappointment once she discovers that "elle lui avait servi d'abri et de nid contre une réalité qu'il niait."[22]

The difficulty of facing reality, the problem of communication and the impossibility of a "happy ending" are also hinted at right from the start in *Le Miroir aux alouettes*, the title of which bears a triple significance: "la Suisse qui attire fallacieusement les réfugiés, la jeunesse de l'homme qui éblouit la femme mûre, l'illusion d'un bonheur encore possible."[23] Here again Crevoisier imagines the friendship that grows up between two people of very different backgrounds who attempt to cross the barriers and understand one another better. Like Massard, Crevoisier has grounded her novel in a reality of modern Switzerland, the presence in many towns and villages (here in the Jura) of "requérants d'asile" who live alongside communities rather than being part of them. As her central female character Marie recognizes, few of these refugees will ever be allowed to remain permanently,[24] and her efforts to help them assimilate by teaching them French are thus unlikely to be of any real use. Just as in Massard's work there was a suggestion of an "exchange" between the two main protagonists, something for each of them in the relationship that develops, the idea of "give and take" between the Swiss hosts and their foreign guests, so it is here. Marie offers friendship, a home and in return is flattered by the attentions of Dogan and the important role she plays in his life.

At the outset Marie feels just as lost as the refugees since she is in the process of divorcing and her life has been turned completely upside down; it would seem that she is thus capable of feeling greater sympathy for the refugees than those whose comfortable lives have never been threatened. In addition, while recognizing her own cultural prejudices, which can be hard to combat, Marie mentally multiplies the points of connection between herself and Dogan, from wondering how it would feel to be a refugee in Turkey—"on s'imagine exilé dans leur pays à eux et ce qu'on ferait à la nuit tombée"[25]—to drawing parallels between the wars elsewhere that bring refugees to Switzerland and "le gentil combat de libération du Jura,"[26] which suddenly seems quite tame in comparison.[27]

Significantly, in both of these works it is women who already feel like outsiders who make contact with those who are even more different, even more excluded; being already on the fringes of society, they are drawn to those who are completely outside it. The same can be said for Anne-Lise Thurler's *Le crocodile ne dévore pas le pangolin*, which once again draws elements from reality, being dedicated "aux 1907 requérants d'asile zaïrois refoulés par la Suisse en 1992 et aux 12 dont la demande a été acceptée." The focus is different since the central character is this time a young man from Zaire and, as the title and the glossary of French words used in Zaire indicate, there is a clear desire here to describe and understand the African context. Unlike Massard and Crevoisier, Thurler describes in some detail the situation from which the central character Lumina is attempting to escape, and thus makes his presence in Switzerland seem entirely logical. To this end, Thurler alternates chapters set in Switzerland, describing Lumina's encounters with officials and his steady decline and breakdown, with chapters that take us through his life in Zaire from 1974 onwards. In this and in the use made of references to Swiss realities—the fact that only about 1 percent of refugees from Zaire were given leave to remain in 1992, the 71 attacks on asylum centers in 1991, the survey that revealed that 60 percent of Swiss openly expressed a dislike of foreigners[28]—*Le crocodile* is perhaps rather more clearly "engagé" than either Massard or Crevoisier's work. In centering her writing on Lumina rather than on a Swiss character, adopting a *va-et-vient* between Switzerland and Zaire, and charting so graphically the stress and psychological breakdown that can accompany invisibility and rejection, Thurler gets closer to enabling Swiss readers to understand the experience of the refugee. She is not so interested in describing the reaction of the Swiss toward these wanted or unwanted guests and has shifted the focus from the "insiders" to the "outsiders."

Those who are on the outside and generally have few opportunities to express themselves have also figured in recent biographical and autobiographical writing in which the themes of the difficulty of communicating and the need to break the all-pervading silence are again evident.

Autobiography/Biography

The focus is on Kosovo and Kurdistan with Liliane Perrin's *Un Marié sans importance* and Serge Bimpage's *La seconde mort d'Ahmed Alesh Karagün.*[29] Perrin (1940–95), a novelist[30] and journalist at *Radio Suisse romande*, emphasizes the change that has taken place regarding immigrants in Switzerland when she comments that "les Italiens ne sont plus les petits, comme dans son enfance . . . mais les patrons qui 'micmaquent' avec ceux qui viennent ensuite, par ordre d'entrée dans l'univers suisse."[31] Through her characters "Doris L." and "Slam" she depicts elements of her own marriage to a young Albanian Kosovar, but this is not a purely autobiographical account, for Perrin transforms some of the details of her own life to fit the story she wishes to tell. Thus the young Kosovar, in reality a writer of poetry, becomes here the more stereotypical immigrant struggling to communicate accurately, and Doris L., rather than facilitating her husband's integration, secretly sabotages his attempts to find work.

The action, centered in Switzerland and recounted through the eyes of the Swiss journalist, leaves little room for the voice of the young Kosovar; he evokes Kosovo and his childhood memories, but this is essentially Doris's account of her encounter with "l'étranger." She is terribly ambivalent about her feelings and motivation: while she of course wants to help Slam stay in Switzerland by marrying him, she also wants to remain in control of the situation and seems fearful that he may become too independent and "escape" her. While he is unemployed and to some extent dependent upon her for help, she dominates him; she has her job, financial security and the safety of a Swiss passport, he has nothing but his youth. Thus once again an exchange of sorts is effected: marriage and potential security in return for the company of an attractive young man who will, however, remain subordinate and not become too demanding.

For all her supposed desire to help Slam, Doris's motivation remains obscure. Unlike Perrin herself, who translated and edited her husband's poetry,[32] she does not evince much interest in his background and culture, and is unable either to communicate to him her ambivalence or explain her strange desire to sabotage all moves toward independence. Ultimately though, she has to accept that marriage without any greater commitment is not enough, and that she bears some responsibility for the misunderstandings between them. Her selfish actions have serious consequences, and she eventually recognizes her failure to do more to help Slam integrate into Swiss society successfully. Her sad conclusion that "la Suisse n'avait rien à offrir à Lam Ajeti,"[33] confirming his status as "un marié sans importance," unimportant to Switzerland, for whom he is just one more refugee, and perhaps even for her too, could doubtless apply to many more like him.

Death is the outcome in Perrin's (semi-auto) biographical work (although not in real life), as it very nearly is in Bimpage's reconstruction of the life of a Kurd who, in desperation at the refusal of his request for asylum, set fire to himself in Geneva in 1982 but survived with 60 percent burns. With the main actor of this drama unable or unwilling to cooperate actively with the project, it is left to Bimpage (1951), like Perrin a journalist, to attempt to piece together what happened and why. If Perrin has deliberately chosen to alter certain details, Bimpage is highly aware of his need for hard facts, since he never really knew the man he is writing about, having only met him twice and having only discovered his fate through a "fait divers" in the newspaper. However, his account is very "engagé"; he comes down clearly on the side of the Kurdish refugees and against both the Swiss authorities, who seem unwilling to take their claims seriously, and the Turkish regime responsible for their persecution. Like Thurler, Bimpage incorporates facts and statistics into his reconstruction, and attempts to bring together two different kinds of writing: on the one hand, journalistic information about the political situation in Turkey and, on the other, the literary presentation of what may have been Ahmed Atesh Karagün's feelings and experiences.

La seconde mort could be described as a "biographie romancée," since Bimpage has to rely so heavily on his own imagination and any information he may have managed to extract from reticent Kurdish refugees. He recognizes the limitations of his approach and the problems posed by attempting to speak for someone else and relate an individual's story without his active participation, telling us straightaway that "ce récit sera celui du silence. Car nous avons parlé à la place de Karagün,"[34] and admitting that "jamais nous ne saurons ce qu'a pensé ou ressenti Ahmed Atesh Karagün."[35] However, when Bimpage talks of silence he does not just mean the silence of the taciturn Kurd Karagün and his wary fellow countrymen, which makes it more difficult than he had hoped to reconstitute the man's story,[36] for the Swiss too, as Pasquali remarked, think very highly of silence. Indeed, Bimpage declares that "de façon générale, dans cette affaire comme dans toute autre, nous autres Suisses nous distinguons par notre silence."[37] He remarks on the failure of many Swiss to discuss and be aware of why these refugees are arriving, and is critical of the duty of discretion and silence that the Swiss impose not only on foreigners (as indicated by Pasquali) but also on themselves, the obligation to "ne pas trop dire, ne pas trop voir, ne pas trop entendre."[38] Like the other books discussed here, Bimpage's account is thus a clear attempt to break that silence and get at the truth, ploughing through the tons of officialese to express the so far unheard and bring the invisible out into the light.[39]

This need to express certain truths has been an important part of the writing of immigrants who have themselves become writers; some have made their experiences central to their writing and return to them constantly, whereas others have moved on to deal with other issues and produce other kinds of writing. Thus Mireille Kuttel (1928), descendant of Italian immigrants, has written novels such as *La Malvivante*,[40] *La Pérégrine*[41] and *La Maraude*,[42] which all concentrate on the problems encountered in Switzerland by Italians, women in particular. Similarly, Anne Cuneo (1936), also of Italian origin, explored this subject in her earlier autobiographical works,[43] but has since preferred different modes of writing—for example the historical novel, with *Objets de splendeur: Mr Shakespeare amoureux*,[44] and the detective novel, with *Âme de Bronze* and *D'Or et d'Oublis*.[45] Both Kuttel and Cuneo have written about the postwar years when Italians, far from being the "patrons" described by Perrin, were arriving in Switzerland in large numbers to take up jobs, but had not yet been well accepted by the population, and both describe the alienating effects of living with rejection in a foreign country. These feelings are similar to those found in some *récits de vie*, which are valuable precisely because they recount the lives of what might be called "ordinary people," that is, women who are *not* writers and whose simple stories of hard work and sacrifice are a useful response to those who deny or ignore the positive contribution made to Switzerland by immigrants.

Récits de vie

Thus in two recent works Italian immigrants were helped to tell their stories: in *L'Emigrée*[46] Carla Belotti (1924) thanks "Claire Masnata-Rubattel, qui m'a écoutée, qui a mis en forme ce texte et sans laquelle il n'aurait peut-être jamais vu le jour," while on the flyleaf to *L'Italienne*[47] Sylviane Roche tells us that "j'ai écrit cette histoire d'après le récit que mon amie Marie-Rose De Donno m'a fait de sa vie. C'est ce qu'elle m'a dit, et c'est aussi ce que j'ai entendu. Nos mots se mêlent. C'est une oeuvre commune." She remarks in her introduction that "les gens ont tendance à penser, assez généralement, que leur vie est un roman" and admits that "d'habitude, je m'enfuis aussi poliment que possible," but here the close collaboration between the two women has led to a finely observed account from one of Switzerland's "outsiders." These accounts by Belotti and De Donno (1950) are clearly different from the writing of women such as Cuneo and Kuttel, who have reworked their and their families' experiences, made them part of a literary project and moved on to other stories. Belotti and De Donno, like Bimpage's Karagün not lucky enough to get much schooling, only have one story to tell, "l'histoire d'une vie," and by bringing it into the public domain they provide real insight into the lives of a category of worker who has not often been heard in Swiss writing, and whose role has not always been recognized.[48]

These *récits de vie* bring us back once again to the issue of language and the power that it either bestows or denies, for both Belotti and De Donno come originally from very poor Italian families and, never having studied, they lacked the confidence (and perhaps the contacts) to tell their story without help from a "professional."[49] Their texts, which naturally have a strong "oral" feel about them, remain closely focused on their own experiences and neither attempts any real analysis or generalization of the situation. However, Belotti does hint that, perhaps thanks to her experiences, perhaps in part due to her "nouvelle passion, la lecture,"[50] she now realizes that "notre révolte personnelle avait des causes sociales."[51] Although she may not previously have either understood it nor had the words to express her feelings, she now knows that she was exploited simply "parce qu'ils savaient très bien qu'ils pouvaient le faire,"[52] and she is finally able to verbalize her realization that "il ne faut pas dire que l'argent que la Suisse a donné aux étrangers, elle l'a donné sans les faire suer."[53]

A further step toward finding one's voice and speaking one's own story is taken by Leyla Chammas (1964), who, unlike Belotti and De Donno, had the advantage of education and origins in a Francophone country, Lebanon. She takes full responsibility for her text, as they were not able to do, and gives it a more personal identity with the title *Leyla*.[54] This account follows a familiar pattern: she tells of her childhood and adolescence in Lebanon, the outbreak of war, the decision to leave for Europe, clandestine entry into Switzerland and problems faced there, the sense of being "un simple dossier parmi d'autres . . . de l'encre noire sur du papier blanc."[55]

The leitmotiv encountered elsewhere of a contact and exchange, however tenuous, with someone in the Swiss population is also present here, since Leyla is supposedly writing her account for a friend she calls Simone, but just as in most of the other works studied, she experiences Switzerland as a country that, despite being prosperous and efficient, is unwelcoming to foreigners. She recalls her naïve belief that "nous gagnerons la Suisse, le pays de l'humanitaire, le pays du coeur. Là-bas ils essuieront nos larmes et soulageront nos souffrances"[56] and declares bitterly that in fact "la Suisse est devenue un autre enfer, plus civilisé, un enfer qui fait souffrir mais en silence."[57]

Conclusion

Just as for so many others, both real and imagined, the result of Leyla's journey to Switzerland is negative: despite their best efforts, she and her family are not allowed to stay and are grateful to be offered asylum in France. For others too the outcome is at best disappointing, at worst traumatic, even fatal: Perrin and Bimpage tell the stories of men for whom the journey to Switzerland ended in death or serious injury; Massard and Crevoisier bring together a man and a woman from each "camp" between whom communication becomes impossible and whose relationships founder; Thurler recounts an exile's experience of depression and mental breakdown; Belotti and De Donno have had to endure lives of hard work, deprivation and loss before arriving at some hard-won sense of belonging.

These different types of writing illustrate the various ways in which the immigrant experience has been explored in *Suisse romande* literature, portraying both the attempts to build bridges and the inevitable divisions, and all in their own way bring us back to the central issue of language: its possibilities and limitations, the ways in which it brings people together or drives them apart, the different ways in which language can be used to express a reality or occupy space. Aziz and Olga are brought together by a newspaper advertisement and divided by the incontrovertible evidence of dishonesty contained in a letter from Turkey; Marie the schoolteacher recognizes the importance of helping Dogan with his French and unselfishly helps him, only to lose him; Doris the journalist, a manipulator of words, realizes that Slam is handicapped by his limited French, but does nothing about it, and in a perverse way his dependance seems to suit her; Thurler reminds the reader that although Lumina (or "Etienne" as he subsequently dubs himself in his confusion and desperate desire to fit in)[58] comes from Francophone Africa, his world is very different from Switzerland, where he is not always "understood." The Swiss in control of the writing here are journalists (Perrin, Bimpage) and teachers (Roche, Crevoisier), their subjects more often than not are people with little formal schooling who have picked up French as well as they can (Belotti, De Donno, Karagün), but all the works—novels, short story, *récits de vie*—contribute in different ways to breaking the silence, the "sacro-sainte modération" as Bimpage calls it,[59] imposed on Swiss and non-Swiss alike. They tell of the work immigrants do, their attempts to fit in and make contact or form relationships with the Swiss, their despair when things do not work out, just as they also tell of the Swiss who show an interest in these immigrants, but do not always fully understand them, and whose attempts to help are often inadequate or ineffectual.

Pessimistic judgements on the experience of migration and exile abound, and the generally negative tone of much of the writing studied here would seem to fit into this vein. Many of these writers would doubtless agree that "pour beaucoup l'émigration devient une maladie chronique et plus d'un y succombe,"[60] or that "la migration isole les personnes où qu'elles atterrissent, dévore leurs ressources psychologiques."[61] However, given that the theme is still a relatively recent one in *Suisse romande* literature, one that it would seem is being increasingly discussed and exploited, and that is not about to disappear from Swiss society—after all, a fifth of the population is not Swiss—it seems likely that new points of view and new ways of looking at the issue will emerge in time. The vision of Switzerland with which these texts leaves one is unfortunately overwhelmingly negative, but it is very much to be hoped that in future more voices will be heard, and more writers, both Swiss and non-Swiss, will add their contributions to the ongoing debate on living in, belonging to, feeling accepted by and making a positive contribution to this particular multicultural society.

Notes

1. Uli Windisch, *Xénophobie? Logique de la pensée populaire. Analyse sociologique du discours des partisans et des adversaires des mouvements xénophobe* (Lausanne: l'Âge d'Homme, 1978), 104.

2. Roger Francillon, "Dans le sérail helvétique. Le guerrier, l'ivrogne, le berger et l'eunuque," in Roger Francillon, Claire Jacquier and Adrien Pasquali, *Filiations et filatures. Littérature et critique en Suisse romande* (Geneva: Zoé, 1991), 11–88.

3. Françoise Fornerod, "Enseigner la littérature romande?" *Études de Lettres* 1 (1988), 35–40.

4. Jean-Pierre Monnier, *Écrire en Suisse romande entre le ciel et la nuit* (Vevey: Galland, 1979), 136–7.

5. In "Eloge de mes grands-parents," *Écriture* 51 (printemps 1998), 211–16.

6. Saint-Imier/Frasne: Canevas, 1998.

7. Gérard Froidevaux, *Ecrivains de Suisse romande* (Zug: Klett und Balmer, 1990), 10–55. Writers such as Gaston Cherpillod (1925) and Janine Massard (1939) have, however, written more "militant" texts about the working class in Switzerland.

8. Yvette Z'Graggen (1920) is a good example of a *romande* writer whose writing turns a great deal around the question of communication. In a Postface to a recent re-edition of *La Preuve* and *Un long voyage* (Geneva: Zoé, 1995), Sylviane Roche remarks that very often Z'Graggen's characters "sont murés dans une solitude intérieure terrifiante, due à la totale impossibilité à se faire entendre d'autrui. Même si l'espoir de briser ce mur de silence et de solitude surgit parfois, il est de courte durée," 44.

9. Yves Bridel, "Y a-t-il une littérature romande aujourd'hui?" in *Vous avez dit "Suisse romande?"* ed. René Knusel and Daniel Seiler (Lausanne, Institut de Science politique, 1984), 125–37 . For an example of a writer who did notice and refer to these "travailleurs étrangers," see Alice Rivaz's *Traces de vie*, first published by Galland in 1983 and re-edited by Aire in 1998, 207, 220–21.

10. Until the introduction into the Constitution of the concept of equality of the sexes in 1981 and the subsequent reform of marriage laws in 1988, a foreign woman could become Swiss by marriage whereas a foreign man could not. A Swiss woman who married a foreigner lost her nationality and acquired that of her husband, which, of course, meant that only Swiss men married to a foreigner could transmit their nationality to their children. The situation has now been equalized and the acquisition of Swiss nationality has become harder for both sexes. See Philippe Bois, "Nationalité et naturalisation," and Micheline Centlivres-Demont/Laurence Ossipow, "La naturalisation comme rite de passage," both in *Devenir Suisse*, ed. Pierre Centlivres (Geneva: Georg, 1990), 13–46 and 187–209. The advantage of being Swiss thanks to her father fails, however, to impress Chambordon's child character in *La Suisse des autres* (Geneva: Zoé, 1981; references from the 1988 edition) since her nationality does not enable her to avoid problems and she is led to remark that "si Miguel avait des ennuis comme étranger moi j'en avais comme Suisse et ça suffit bien," 128.

11. *La Suisse des autres*, 56–61. She continues the theme in *Les enfants c'est comme les éléphants* (Geneva: Zoé, 1982) and *Les mots disent plus rien* (Geneva: Zoé, 1985). All three texts were re-edited together by Zoé in 1988. The theme of working-class children achieving social success through study is also dealt with by Janine Massard, for example in *Christine au dévaloir* (Geneva: Éditions Éliane Vernay, 1981).

12. Geneva: Zoé, 1999.

13. Isabelle Falconnier, *L'Hebdo*, 1 avril 1999.

14. *Le pain de silence*, 93.

15. Pasquali was born in the Valais in 1958.

16. *Le pain de silence*, 93.

17. *Le pain de silence*, 120.

18. In *Trois mariages* (Vevey: Aire, 1992), 119–84. Massard returns to the theme of displacement in *Ce qui reste de Katharina* (Vevey: Aire, 1997), the story of a German woman living in Switzerland.

19. Vevey: Aire, 1994.

20. In *Le crocodile ne dévore pas le pangolin* (Geneva: Zoé, 1996).

21. "Les frontières de ton corps," 145.

22. "Les frontières de ton corps," 177.

23. Catherine Dubuis, "Chronique des livres," *Écriture* 46 (automne 1995), 261–71.

24. *Le Miroir aux alouettes*, 22.

25. *Le Miroir aux alouettes*, 22.

26. *Le Miroir aux alouettes*, 69.

27. It was only in 1979 that the Canton of Jura came into existence, after many decades of fighting for independence from the mainly germanophone canton of Bern. See Steinberg, 89–98.

28. *Le crocodile ne dévore pas le pangolin*, 119. In 1998 9.5 percent of all requests for asylum were accepted (figure from the *Office des réfugiés* quoted in *La Tribune de Genève*, 28 May 1999, 3).

29. Genève: Metropolis, 1994; Genève: Zoé, 1986.

30. Under the name Hélène Perrin she published *La Fille du pasteur* (Paris: Gallimard, 1965) and *La Route étroite* (Paris: Gallimard, 1967).

31. *Un Marié sans importance*, 36. Just as the Swiss themselves had previously gained "social promotion" by the arrival of the Italians; in the words of Alice Rivaz (1901–1998) "nous voici passés dans la race des patrons, des seigneurs." *Traces de vie*, 207.

32. Shemsi Makolli, *Ne pleure pas* (Lausanne: Perrin, 1995).

33. Makolli, *Ne pleure pas*, 129.

34. *La seconde mort d'Ahmed Atesh Karagün*, 21.

35. *La seconde mort d'Ahmed Atesh Karagün*, 73–4.

36. *La seconde mort d'Ahmed Atesh Karagün*, 124.

37. *La seconde mort d'Ahmed Atesh Karagün*, 102.

38. *La seconde mort d'Ahmed Atesh Karagün*, 84.

39. Indeed, Bimpage's account appears in Zoé's "Collection Cactus," which precisely aims to publish polemical texts for "le voyageur perdu dans le grand désert du mutisme helvétique" (backcover).

40. Lausanne: l'Âge d'Homme, 1978.

41. Lausanne: l'Âge d'Homme, 1983.

42. Lausanne: l'Âge d'Homme, 1986.

43. For example *Les portes du jour* (Vevey: Galland, 1980) and *Le temps des loups blancs* (Vevey: Galland, 1982). On Cuneo and Kuttel see Joy Charnley, "Four Literary Depictions of Foreigners and Outsiders in French-speaking Switzerland," *Occasional Papers in Swiss Studies* 1 (Bern: Lang, 1998), 9–28.

44. Yvonand: Campiche, 1996.

45. Yvonand: Campiche, 1998; Orbe: Campiche, 1999.

46. Genève: Éditions Grounauer, 1981.

47. Orbe: Campiche, 1998.

48. For a discussion of these two texts as reflections of the vision of Switzerland as a utopia, see Joy Charnley, "J'aime bien ma Suisse: some Italian reactions to the Schwarzenbach Initiative (1970)," *Occasional Papers in Swiss Studies*, 3 (Bern: Lang, forthcoming).

49. On the question of language, it is interesting to note that just as Thurler includes a glossary of Zairean French words, Roche provides a glossary of "suisse romandismes" to help readers unfamiliar with this particular version of non-standard French.

50. *L'Émigrée*, 142.

51. *L'Émigrée*, 64.

52. *L'Émigrée*, 149.

53. *L'Émigrée*, 148.

54. Genève: Zoé, 1997.

55. *Leyla*, 131.

56. *Leyla*, 103.

57. *Leyla*, 125.

58. Some cantons still require candidates for Swiss nationality to display their degree of assimilation by changing their names, if their original names are considered difficult to pronounce or spell. See Centlivres-Demont/Ossipow, *Devenir Suisse*, 194.

59. *La seconde mort d'Ahmed Atesh Karagün*, 84.

60. André Siniavski quoted in "La littérature et l'exil," *Magazine littéraire* 221 (juillet/août 1985), 14–65.

61. Bolzmann and Musillo, 82.

23

The Paradox of Linguistic Specificity and Dependence on Central Norms in the Belgian Regionalist Novels of Arthur Masson

Emmanuelle Labeau

ARTHUR MASSON MAY BE SAID TO BE A MAN who only had one book in him, as there is a great deal of unity in both his themes and his characters. Some examples of recurrent characters are: the fat good-tempered man who appears in the *Toinade* and *Le cantonnier opulent*; the unruly boys, such as Hilaire in *Le grand Gusse* or Hector in *Ulysse au volant*; the pacifist in *Un homme pacifique, Un joyeux garçon* and the short story "Le soleil et la neige" in *Prosper en paradis*. For the sake of simplicity, this study will focus on a series of six books, of which Toine Culot, a humble gardener from Trignolles,[1] is the hero. These books—*Vie du Bienheureux Toine Culot, obèse ardennais; Toine, maïeur de Trignolles; Toine dans la Tourmente* (2 volumes); *Toine, chef de tribu* and *Toine Retraité*—start with Toine's birth in 1888 and finish in the 1960s. They tell of the main adventures of Toine's simple life: his childhood and youth, his marriage and mayoral responsibilities, and finally his involvement in the Second World War.

The novels' main interest is their polyphony. The narration is written in a polished French in which lexicon and syntax often verge on affectation, while most of the village characters—at least in the first few volumes, and only the old people in the later ones—use a Walloon dialect, their mother tongue, in daily conversation. In exceptional circumstances the characters have recourse to a hybrid language or "dialectal French." The characteristics of this literary language reflect a sociolinguistic conception of society in which peripheral varieties of French are depreciated. The concept of dependence on a central norm in French is central to the work of Arthur Masson.

This dependence on central linguistic norms has existed since the very first texts in French. As early as the twelfth century, Guernes de Pont-Saint-Maxence claims legitimacy for his language by saying: "Mis langages est buens, car en France sui nez;"[2] while in 1180 Conon de Bethune complains about being ridiculed at Alix de Champagne's court for using words from his native Artois. In the *Ballade des dames de Paris*, François Villon summarized the peripheral linguistic inferiority complex in a well-known sentence: "Il n'est de bon bec que de Paris." If regional words and phrases were encouraged by the Pléiade[3] in the sixteenth century, the later doctrine of the "Honnête homme"[4] and the refined language of the classical period discriminated against peripheral linguistic practices. At the end of the eighteenth century the homogenization of the French language became a political program for the Revolutionaries, who thought, as stated in the famous Grégoire report, that words are the links of society—that a shared language would create political unity. From that time onwards there was a systematic depreciation of non-central usage, and it was not until the second half of the twentieth century that an interest in regional languages resurfaced as a result of the Deixonne Law of 11 January 1951. This law made possible the teaching of regional languages and heritage at every level of education in France.

While this peripheral linguistic inferiority complex was prevalent in France, it seemed even stronger in Belgium, the "terre de grammairiens," where much attention has been devoted to linguistic accuracy by Grevisse, Hanse and the like. The embarrassed Belgians apparently wished to cure their so-called linguistic pathologies by turning to reference works with revealing titles that illustrate the linguistic inquisition to which the Belgians subjected their own language. The most famous are the *Chasses aux Belgicismes* by Hanse, Doppagne and Bourgeois-Gielen, but there were many other *Corrigeons-nous, Consultations grammaticales* and countless columns on good usage.

This repressive, institutionalized attitude seemed to fade away after the 1980s and signs of this new, freer approach have appeared in the ways that the French language is perceived. For example, the "Quinzaine du bon langage,"[5] a title evocative of the prescriptive approach, was changed into the "Quinzaine de la langue française," while since 1995 the "Conseil de la langue française" has been organizing "La langue française en fête," a title that implies a freer celebration of the language.

However, though the official position seems to have changed, the attitudes of ordinary Belgian Francophones have not always evolved accordingly. In 1991 Lafontaine conducted a survey entitled *Les mots et les Belges*, which examined the ways that speakers in the three biggest Belgian Francophone cities, Brussels, Liège and Charleroi, perceived their own linguistic behavior. The results showed that, despite some manifestations of a rejection of standard French, it still remained the model that was followed: "La conclusion principale qui se dégage, ce mélange d'admiration et de rejet, cet attachement à distance pour le 'modèle' français paraît suffisamment solide, et conforme à ce que l'on connaît par ailleurs de situations analogues, pour qu'on la retienne—provisoirement—comme caractéristique en attendant que d'autres enquêtes viennent la confirmer."[6] She concludes that "L'heure du 'Belgian is beautiful' n'est pas près de sonner,"[7] and although Belgians associate some positive connotations of friendliness or musicality with their own language, there is an overwhelming feeling that the French speak "quand même mieux." The existence of a dominant central linguistic variety implies dominated varieties and creates a linguistic insecurity among those who speak them, as defined by Swiggers: "L'insécurité linguistique peut être définie comme un sentiment socialisé d'aliénation: d'une part, par rapport à un modèle qu'on ne maîtrise pas/plus, et d'autre part, par rapport à sa propre production qu'on veut refouler ou forclore."[8] This situation therefore involves a double alienation from, on the one hand, a model that is not mastered (any more) and, on the other, one's own undervalued production. The speaker stands in between and cannot identify with any of the varieties.

Linguistic Insecurity and Literature

The concept of linguistic insecurity goes back to the work of Labov,[9] who studied the social stratification of the phoneme /r/ in New York. He noticed a gap between the auto-evaluation of pronunciation and speakers' actual performance, a difference that he called linguistic insecurity. It is indicated firstly by hypersensitivity to stigmatized features of the language used by the speaker himself or herself; then by an inaccurate perception of one's own discourse; and finally by a stylistic variation that implies repeated corrections of the speaker's production and hypercorrection (in other words, the erroneous overgeneralization of features that characterize the standard variety). While Labov worked in a monolingual context, Gueunier, Genouvrier and Khomsi[10] extended the concept to diglossal situations when they studied attitudes toward the use of speakers' mother tongues and a linguistic norm. The survey they conducted in four French cities—Tours, Lille, Limoges and St Denis de la Réunion—showed that the use of a linguistic variety different from the politically legitimized form could lead to linguistic insecurity.

In the studies discussed above linguistic insecurity appears at a phonological level. Bourdieu notes that it can also show on the lexical and syntactic levels:

> Mais [la reconnaissance du pouvoir symbolique d'une variété linguistique] n'est jamais aussi manifeste que dans toutes les corrections, ponctuelles ou durables, auxquelles les dominés par un effort désespéré de correction, soumettent, consciemment ou inconsciemment, les aspects stigmatisés de leur prononciation, de *leur lexique* (avec toutes les formes d'euphémisme) et de *leur syntaxe*; ou dans le désarroi qui leur "fait perdre tous les moyens," les rendant incapables de trouver leurs mots, comme s'ils étaient soudain dépossédés de leur propre langue.[11]

This broader conception focuses not only on pronunciation, as in Labov, but also on particularities of vocabulary or even sentence structure. Another contribution is Francard's survey in the rural region of Lutremont in Belgium. It shows that linguistic insecurity depends more on an awareness of the norm, which is linked with schooling, than on the use of a less valued variety of the language. Francard quotes four aspects of the concept in Francophone Belgium: the unquestioned supremacy of the French variety of the language, a low opinion of one's own linguistic production, especially in speech, and the recourse to compensatory strategies.[12] These are attitudes that have been translated into literature.

There is a general depreciation of autochthonous literature in Belgium. Klinkenberg mentions "l'auto-dépréciation littéraire globale"[13] in Belgium, where French literature constitutes the bulk, if not the entirety, of literature taught in the education system and the national literature is optional in the training of future French teachers. Publishing is also highly dependent on Parisian circles. Only 1.7 percent of the books published in Belgium are classified as general literature and just 15 percent of Belgian publications are exported to France.[14] The reaction to this situation may be either a scrupulous respect for the central norm, what Klinkenberg calls "purism,"[15] or, conversely, what he calls "surécriture," the overemphasis of specific regional features: "Nombre d'auteurs ont pu ainsi convoquer dans leur oeuvre l'archaïsme et le flandricisme, comme chez Charles de Coster, le néologisme, chez des auteurs aussi différents que Verhaeren, Lemonnier ou Michaux, la création imitant le langage enfantin ou l'argot, comme chez Norge, le mot savant et le wallonisme force, comme chez Jean-Pierre Otte; en un mot le style carnavalesque-au sens bakhtinien du terme-, qu'illustre bien Jean-Pierre Verheggen."

Belgian literature is characterized by unusual linguistic practices. It uses various forms of expression, such as the recourse to aspects of its historical heritage, archaisms or words borrowed from the country's dialects. It also explores the boundaries of the language by using childlike expressions, slang and erudite words. However, allegiance to the central norm is evident in a number of Belgian works, such as *St Germain ou la négociation* by Francis Walder:

> En 1958, le Prix Goncourt couronne, en la personne de Francis Walder, un récit *St Germain ou la négociation* qui dégage une admirable musique de la langue et qui révèle une limpidité plus grande que celle de Mme de la Fayette; son classicisme est plus épuré que celui de Marguerite Yourcenar. L'auteur provient du milieu des armes. Ses pairs, ce sont les grands grammairiens normatifs de la langue, les Hanse et les Grévisse [sic]. Ils ont aimé cette étrange mère, toujours proche et toujours lointaine, au point d'en vouloir dire, à l'intention d'autrui, tous les secrets et les détours.[16]

This category of book shares the implicit desire of grammatical works to expurgate from the language anything that would mar its classical purity. In the other category of "surécriture" there are works that draw the reader's attention to regional features. The language of Brussels in *Le mariage de Mlle Beulemans* and *Bossemans et Coppenolle,* and of Wallonia in the novels by Masson are good examples. However, the Parisian influence is problematic. Arthur Masson's *Toinade*—a series of six novels revolving around the character of Toine Culot—offers an opportunity for the study of the relationships to the French norm expressed by the attitudes of the characters and the author's own narrative style. Although the narrative and dialogues are representative of Walloon culture, there are obvious and implicit signs of dependence on the Parisian French norm in the language of both the author and his characters.

Attitudes Toward Central French in Masson's Works

Masson's characters are mostly uneducated, rural people living during a period[17] in which dialects were still very much alive. Walloon is therefore the principle means of communication between them; French is valued as a sign of refinement and social achievement, but it is hardly ever mastered by Masson's characters. French, or a tentative version of French, is used by Masson's characters to address people higher in the social hierarchy or in particular circumstances that will be detailed below. However, French does occur in daily intercourse.

Firstly, French is used in familial or familiar relationships to express higher feelings, as during the episode in which Toine, who is about to celebrate his fiftieth wedding anniversary, reiterates his commitment to his wife: "C'est drôle, Hilda. V'là que nous sommes vieux tous les deux et c'est comme si on retrouverait nos vingt ans. Je vous vois encore arriver au château de Monsieur à la saison des confitures. Vous m'avez 'plaît' au premier coup d'oeil et. . . ."[18] Solemn circumstances require a nobler means of expression than the simple vernacular, and French is the medium of such communication. It also appears in serious conversations, for example, when Phanie, one of Toine's daughters, becomes alarmed by her husband's frequent absences and fears that he is unfaithful. Toine knows, in fact, his son-in-law is working for the Résistance and wishes to reassure her daughter: "Ma fille, trancha le gros Toine, *en attrapant aussi son français,* je suis t'au courant et je n'ai qu'une chose à vous dire. . . . M'fiye, dit gravement le père Toine, dont *le discours français avait épuisé toutes les réserves stylistiques.*"[19] This shows that, for Masson's characters, French expresses a greater degree of solemnity; but this passage also indicates that the use of French is a difficult and unnatural exercise: it stretches the characters' linguistic abilities. This reminds us of Bourdieu's ideas about the feeling of loss that users of peripheral varieties have in relation to language.

French also represents a pedagogical enterprise, because it is seen as a passport to education and social achievement. Toine tries to teach his grandchildren to use French: "Et les trois enfants d'Antoinette, épouse Evenepoel, ne connaissent vraiment bien que le wallon du cru, *malgré les efforts de Toine pour leur inculquer la langue de Voltaire.*"[20] The phrase "la langue de Voltaire" is further evidence of the alienation of French-speaking Belgians from their own language.

In addition to these uses in the context of the family or a rural community, French is also used with people of a higher social rank or the better educated. In the *Toinade* several groups of people are deemed worthy of the linguistic tribute of French. Firstly, there are those who work in education (local primary school teachers or school inspectors), then members of the clergy or leading citizens like doctors and politicians. Toine's son-in-law is a doctor and Toine always addresses him in his French: "Disez un peu, Ugène, est-ce que vous n'aureriez pas, dedans toutes vos droques que vous recevez comme échantillons des choses des machins enfin qui pourraient me soutenir le coeur si quéqufois y venait à me manquer. C'est que je connais mon émotionabilité, moi, et ma suspectibilité."[21] This use of euphemisms by speakers of non-standard French is indicative of a keen desire to use correct terms, a desire that in fact leads to the coinage of new words.

French is also the medium of communication with strangers. It is used with people outside the local circle, whatever their social rank. For instance, Toine's first conversations with his future wife, a Fleming, are in dialectal French: "Faut m'excuser, Mam'zelle Hilda. Quand j'ai-t-été vous rattende, je n'avais pas eu le temps de m'approprier. Et d'ailleurs, je croyais que ça serait core Raphaïlte qui aurait venu."[22] The ageing Toine fails to recognize King Baudouin when the monarch asks him for directions. As a stranger, the king is addressed in Toine's best French, and Toine confides in him how much he misses his late cousin.[23] This use of French with strangers is particularly noticeable when Masson's characters have contact with French people, whose language is seen as superior. In the following passage Toine takes pride in having French grandchildren whose language is seen as exemplary:

> Il se rengorge le gros Toine, lorsqu'il entend ses petits-enfants de France parler *avec un accent qu'il estime être celui de la bonne société* et même avec une virtuosité qui ne recule pas devant l'argot ni l'irrévérence. "L'pépé Toine, l'est marrant" qu'ils disent à chaque visite. "L'est même tellement qu'y a des fois qu'on se demande si y a pas un papillon sous la toiture. Et quand il a ses paturons dans ses sabots, tu parles d'une paire de péniches! L'a toujours l'air d'attendre le remorqueur." Toine, qui *admire sans bien comprendre*, profite de ces occasions pour recommander à ces autres descendants: *Écoutez vos petits cousins de France comme y causent bien le français. Vous deveriez tâcher de les imiter.*[24]

Here the French of France is clearly presented as a higher variety to be admired and imitated. However, it is clear from the quotations inserted that this variety of French is not closer to the standard; rather the excerpts above suggest slang French. The preference for the French varieties of speech shown by Masson's character reveals an irrational self-deprecation common among users of less legitimate varieties of French.

However, despite this respect for French as a sign of social distinction, it is not always invested with a positive human image. The use of French in familiar and familial communication is seen as a sign of pride and an unwelcome desire to show superiority. In the following example a cattle dealer compares the good administration of Trignolles, Toine's village, with the incompetence in his own village, where the mayor is better educated and fluent in French but unable to deal with practical business:

> Le maquignon, qui, décidément, détestait son beau-frère, recommença ses critiques, très acerbes.
> —[...] Ici, au moins, le Toine, avec ses airs bonasses, y pense à ses administrés, n'a p'tête pas beaucoup d'instruction, mais à quoi ça sert l'instruction, quand on n'a pas d'avisance? Mon beau-frère, tiens, il a fait son école moyenne *et y vous fignole des fois le français qu'on le prendrait pour quéqu'un de bien.* La même été sous-officier. Faut l'entendre, aux distributions de prix! L'instruction, qu'y dit ç't'imbécile, c'est la plus belle des richesses.[25]

In contrast, an ability to use the patois is highly valued in informal circumstances, as in the case of "Cousine Sylvie," an old maid whose inheritance could have brought Baby Toine lifelong prosperity had she not married against all the odds. She deserves to be addressed in French as a primary school teacher whose disdain for incorrect language is much dreaded by her less educated family and as a wealthy relative. So her willingness to use patois is received as an exceptional token of kindness: "Tandis que le Choumaque et sa Phanie [Toine's parents] s'acharnaient à estropier le français, elle, la cousine Sylvie, *elle s'était mise à parler en wallon*, 'à cause l'plat patwès, comme ti et mi', mais oui, comme tout le monde. 'C'es-t-in bia p'tit valet' qu'elle disait en parlant de Toine. *Pourtant, elle 'en' avait.*"[26] It is also obvious from this passage that a mastery of French is directly associated with social achievement in the minds of French dialect speakers. There is an ambivalent attitude toward French. On the one hand, it is highly valued as a sign of distinction and social achievement; yet, on the other hand, specific regional language varieties are preferred for sentimental reasons.

Having studied the attitudes of Masson's characters toward French, it is necessary to move on to the author's attitude toward this language. Unlike most of his characters, Masson was highly educated and had studied French and French literature at a high level. Nevertheless, he seems to express a deep inferiority complex toward France and its language, which would corroborate Francard's conclusions about linguistic insecurity and its links with schooling. He is pernickety about syntax, even though specific Belgian features appear in the course of his writing, as in the following example, where the position of the adjective before the noun seems to echo either a Dutch or Walloon structure:[27] "C'était un *grand laid* bougre, d'une maigreur que le jeune Flamand jugea musculeuse."[28]

Masson uses features of official Belgian French, what Pohl has called "statalismes or words linked with state structures, such as "septante," "nonante" and "bourgmestre." He deploys dialectal words like "maïeur," "fournias," "fôfe," but, at the same time, his French vocabulary is highly sophisticated and bears witness to his constant search for accuracy. The introduction to one chapter in *Toine, maïeur de Trignolles*, "Solitude,"[29] includes the following words: "fredons," "poissarde," "perchis," "falourde," "hart," "fascine" and "affouage." The words of a former pupil suggest that this was a feature of Masson as a man and teacher:

> Quand j'évoque l'artisan, c'est aux leçons de vocabulaire que je songe. Inlassablement, il nous a initiés à polir et à repolir nos phrases, rejetant tour à tour le style plat et le style pédant, veillant à ce que nous utilisions le terme propre, bannissant ce qu'il appelait des mots "passe-partout."[30]

In 1949 Masson published the manual *Pour enrichir son vocabulaire*, which shows his concern for lexical accuracy.

Masson's work combines two apparently antagonistic concepts of literature that have been alluded to above. His writing usually exemplifies the tendency toward purism, while showing some features of overwriting when regional words are used, but above all when illustrating his characters' language.

While Masson's writing implicitly pays tribute to standard French, there are also explicit acknowledgments of an allegiance to France. The speech of the French characters is shown to be superior, as in this description of the influence of French children in the school on the border:

> Mais depuis quelques années, trois ou quatre ménages franco-belges, . . . étaient venus planter leurs pénates à Trignolles. Affaire de commodités et de petits avantages personnels. Si bien que les rejetons de ces ménages-là, nés en Belgique, conféraient à la classe du papa Dardenne un coloris dont il ne songeait pas du tout à se plaindre, parce qu'il n'aimait pas la monotonie et qu'au surplus, *il arrivait à ces petits gaillards de donner à leurs condisciples, sans qu'ils le soupçonnassent, l'exemple du terme propre agrémenté d'un accent qui avait son charme.* Le malheur, c'est qu'à la longue, *ce bel accent de France s'aliénait de tout ce que le dialecte indigène contenait de pittoresque, bien sûr, mais aussi de désolante cacophonie.*[31]

This highlights the ambiguity expressed by users of peripheral French varieties toward a production that is invested with amusing qualities, as opposed to a lack of linguistic distinction. Here, the French children are shown to be superior in their phonological production as well as in their mastery of the language's resources. The irony of this is of course the high quality French used by the Belgian author (imperfect subjunctive for example) to express a deprecatory judgment on his own countrymen!

This unconditional admiration for the French use of the language is coupled with a dubious generalization of the superiority of the French spirit, which is summed up by their cheek:

> Par sa mère, Zidore était quelque chose comme *un demi-Français et cela se sentait autant à son caractère qu'à son langage.*
>
> —Allez, monter, maïeur, fit-il avec une joviale impertinence. Ça ne m'en fera toujours qu'un de plus [de porcs], un peu gros, mais le moteur est solide.[32]
>
> Pensif, le Choumaque contempla le tableau un long moment, et ce qu'il vit, figures, gestes, façons de rire et de fumer,bref, *ce qui fait la touche gauloise*, eut pour effet, probablement, de ranimer au fond de sa vieille cervelle des souvenirs curieusement conservés dans leur longue léthargie.[33]

'Frenchness' is also associated with distinction, as in the first description given of one of Toine's future son-in-law: "Son pas surtout, révélait d'emblée *le Français, et de bonne souche.* C'était un pas rapide, régulier, correct, un pas de défilé."[34] This positive judgment includes indulgence toward French chauvinism, which is quite justified in Masson's eyes. There is an interesting example of this in the radio report on Aloys Verluysen (another of Toine's sons-in-law to be) when he wins one of the legs of the Tour de France:

> Le second, c'était le Français Pascaillou. C'est d'ailleurs lui que la foule acclamait le plus. Et le speaker expliqua devant le micro que c'est lui qui devait vaincre, si l'autre ne l'avait pas empêché.[35]
>
> Mais trêve de commentaires sentimentaux, chers auditeurs, et fermons cette parenthèse gentiment idyllique en concluant que, somme toute, l'exploit de Verluisant[36] s'il est une victoire belge, c'est encore et surtout la victoire de la rose, de la rose cueillie dans un jardin de chez nous, de la rose, fleur de France.[37]

This shows nothing of the harsh criticism of other nationalities and ethnic groups, such as Germans or Gypsies, found in some of Masson's other novels. His attitude is one of unconditional admiration for standard French, and this leads him to indirectly depreciate the social value of regional varieties of French spoken by his characters, while simultaneously pursuing an ideal classical variety of the language in his writing.

Conclusion

Masson's novels present a fundamental linguistic ambiguity. On the one hand, they are explicitly located in an area where a non-legitimized variety of French is spoken. It is not only a provincial region, it is also a different country from the one that possesses linguistic legitimacy: France. It is worth noting that a positive image—relying on affective and non-linguistic qualities—is given of this peripheral region. On the other hand, the novels are intended to obtain literary recognition by exploiting the exoticism of this milieu.

While the regional variety of French is associated with the positive characteristics of simplicity, good humor and expressiveness, it is also looked down on in comparison to standard

French as it lacks sophistication and seriousness. This devaluation openly shows in the characters' attitudes: they are clearly conscious of their linguistic imperfections. Devaluation is also a feature of the narrative, which includes explicit negative comments about regional linguistic markers, while central French is valorized.

Masson's work is thus a good illustration of the feelings of insecurity and alienation felt by educated Belgians toward central French. In his writing, Masson manages to convey the ambivalent attitude of educated Francophone Belgians: regional varieties of French are felt to have positive affective features but lack sophistication. By dividing his writing between two areas—his characters' language, which unashamedly uses regional features, and his own language, which aims at neutrality—Masson tried to resolve the tensions of a national linguistic inferiority complex.

Notes

1. Trignolles is a fictitious village on the French border inspired by the real village of Treignes.

2. In this context "France" means the Île-de-France.

3. A group of seven authors (Pierre de Ronsard, Joachim du Bellay, Jean-Antoine de Baïf, Pontus de Tyard, Étienne Jodelle, Rémi Belleau and Jacques Peletier du Mans) who rejected the rigid poetical forms of the Middle Ages.

4. For an "honnête homme" the most important consideration was the desire to be understood by all. His language therefore had to avoid any type of language that would not be generally understood, either because it was too specialized or purely regional.

5. The "Office du bon langage," a private body, was founded in 1962 and has organized fortnights of events based around the French language ever since. The change of name, which indicates a less prescriptive attitude, occurred in 1992.

6. Dominique Lafontaine, "Les mots et les Belges," *Français et Société* 2, Communauté française de Belgique (March 1991): 8–9.

7. Lafontaine, "Les mots et les Belges," 33.

8. Pierre Swiggers, "L'insécurité linguistique: du complexe (problématique) à la complexité du problème," *L'insécurité linguistique dans les communautés francophones périphériques*, ed. Michel Francard (Louvain-la-Neuve: Cahiers de L'Institut de Linguistique de Louvain, 1993), 23.

9. William Labov, *The Social Stratification of English in New York* (Washington, D.C.: Center for Applied Linguistics, 1966).

10. Nicole Gueunier, Émile Genouvrier and Abdelhamid Khomi, *Les Français devant la norme* (Paris: Champion, 1978).

11. Pierre Bourdieu, *Ce que parler veut dire: L'économie des échanges linguistiques* (Paris: Fayard, 1982), 38 (emphasis added).

12. Something that has been discussed by Lafontaine when she refers to the positive connotations attached to regional varieties of French and the lack of regard for developments in the language.

13. Jean-Marie Klinkenberg, "Insécurité linguistique et production littéraire: le problème de la langue d'écriture dans les lettres francophones," *L'insécurité linguistique dans les communautés francophones périphériques*, ed. Michel Francard (Louvain-la-Neuve: Cahiers de L'Institut de Linguistique de Louvain, 1993), 73.

14. M. Van Renterghem, *Belgique, côté francophone*, *Le Monde* supplement, 15 September 1998.

15. Klinkenberg, "L'insécurité linguistique," 75.

16. Quaghebeur, Marc, "Belgique: la première des littératures francophones non françaises," *La Belgique francophone: lettres et arts*, ed. R. Pop (Cluj-Napoca [Romania]: Studia Universitatis Babes-Bolyai [philologie 1–2], 1991), 10.

17. Mainly during the first half of the twentieth century.

18. Arthur Masson, *Toine retraité* (Brussels: Racine, 1995), 44.

19. Arthur Masson, *Toine dans la tourmente* (Brussels: Racine, 1995), 296 (emphasis added).

20. Arthur Masson, *Toine chef de tribu* (Brussels: Racine, 1995), 13 (emphasis added).

21. Masson, *Toine chef*, 185.

22. Arthur Masson, *Toine Culot obèse ardennais*, (Brussels: Racine, 1996), 151.

23. Arthur Masson, *Toine chef de tribu* (Brussels: Racine, 1995), 198.

24. Masson, *Toine chef*, 13 (emphasis added).

25. Masson, *Toine chef*, 35 (emphasis added).

26. Arthur Masson, *Toine Culot obèse ardennais* (Brussels: Racine, 1996), 35 (emphasis added).

27. See Louis Chalon's comment in his analysis of Remy's language: "Conformes à l'usage du français parlé dans la région—calqué sur celui du dialecte—sont les relatives en cascade et la redondance des relatifs (où que), de même que l'antéposition des épithètes distinctives: un grand long bennai, un petit comique tablier." Marcel Remy, *Les ceux de chez nous* (Brussels: Labor, 1997), 307.

28. Arthur Masson, *Toine maïeur de Trignolles* (Brussels: Racine, 1995), 127.

29. Masson, *Toine maïeur*, 74–83.

30. Marcel Lobet, *Arthur Masson ou la richesse du coeur* (Brussels: Vanderlinden, 1971), 26.

31. Arthur Masson, *Toine chef*, 15 (emphasis added).

32. Arthur Masson, *Toine retraité*, 41.

33. Arthur Masson, *Toine dans la tourmente*, 30 (emphasis added).

34. Masson, *Toine chef*, 169 (emphasis added).

35. Arthur Masson, *Toine maïeur*, 146.

36. Amusing French pronunciation of a Flemish name, Verluyzen, as /vœrlœjzœn/.

37. Arthur Masson, *Toine maïeur*, 154.

24

Linguistic Profit, Loss
and Betrayal in *Paris-Athènes*

Susan Stuart

FRENCH LITERATURE HAS WELCOMED, and honored, many writers not born in the Hexagon who have chosen to write in French: the Irishman Samuel Beckett, the Romanian-born Ionesco, and a great number of writers in the current generation of North African and Caribbean origin. The phenomenon of the errant or emigrant Greek reaches back to Odysseus. The Greek diaspora has included many writers: Constantine Cavafy (1863–1933), the great Greek poet, spent much of his childhood in England and his adult life in Alexandria; the Greek-born Jean Moréas (1856–1910), who wrote the manifesto for the symbolist movement published in *Le Figaro* of 18 September 1886, was a friend of yet another Greek poet who lived in France, Yannis Psycharis (1854–1929). The writer Nikos Kazantzakis (1883–1957) studied in France and spent much of his life away from Greece. The more recent poets George Seferis (1900–1971) and Dimitris Saloumas have captured in their writings the experience of diaspora that is, according to James Pettifer, "central to Greek experience."[1]

Vassilis Alexakis is one of these intellectual migrants. He is a Greek who grew up and went to school in Greece. However, his higher education and subsequent professional career as a writer have largely taken place in France. Although in his own writing he expresses doubts about the acceptability of his activities as a writer in French, there is ample evidence that he has had considerable success. When the first edition of his autobiographical work *Paris-Athènes* appeared in 1989, the Moroccan writer Tahar Ben Jelloun ended his review thus: "Ce Grec qui doute et écrit en français est en effet un grand écrivain."[2] His novel *La langue maternelle* won the Prix Médicis in 1995 (sharing it with Andreï Makïne, a Russian-born writer). In a review of his collection of short stories, *Papa*, he is referred to as "ce délicieux rêveur grec";[3] and he was awarded the Prix de la Nouvelle de l'Académie Française for this collection. He appears frequently on cultural programs broadcast by French radio and is regularly invited to speak at literary events.

Vassilis Alexakis[4] is a Greek who has written mainly in French. He left Greece in 1961 at the age of seventeen to take a course at the school of journalism in Lille. At that time there was no such course in Greece, and it was fully his intention to return on completion of his studies. He remained in France and has made a career in journalism, both print and television. He has also published several novels in French, besides *La langue maternelle*.

Paris-Athènes is far from being an attempt at a full autobiography. It may be described more accurately as an autobiographical essay in which Alexakis gives an account of some aspects of his life, in particular the experiences of changing countries and acquiring a new language, and the issues of identity they raise. This chapter will focus on these themes. The titles of two of his novels point to two of his principal preoccupations: *Contrôle d'identité* (1985) and *La langue maternelle* (1995). Chronology is subsidiary to theme. It is the work of a man who, having reached his middle years, has become seriously preoccupied with the questions: "Who am I?" and "Where do I fit in?" Although such questions generally first arise in adolescence, "people are working on their life stories, consciously and unconsciously, throughout their adult years" and in the middle years they "recast and revise their own life stories so that the past is seen as giving birth to the present and the future, so that beginning middle and ending make sense in terms of each other."[5] The writing of an autobiographical work in the middle years is clearly an example of this process being conducted in a public arena.

Language

Before embarking on the writing of this memoir, Alexakis has to decide in which language to write, and throughout the book he chronicles his relationship with the French language: how he learns, the gaps that remain, the attitudes of native French speakers to his work, his altering aspirations and evolving attitude to his second language. He presents his relationship with the French language in terms of a love affair, employing the rhetoric of love, obligation, doubt, betrayal and separation.

Having to make a decision about which language to use means that he has to spend some frustrating time in front of a "page blanche," because he must, in order to write about the difficulty of choosing which language to write in, make the choice. The idea of writing about his Greek mother in French is uncomfortable; the difficulty is compounded because his children are French: "Comment peut-on choisir entre la langue de sa mère et celle de ses enfants?"[6] In fact, he resists the possibility of writing about Greeks in French, believing that they would seem like caricatures of European Community officials, and similarly hesitates to describe his French life in Greek. In his French-language novels he writes about French people who communicate in French. While at a conference in Quebec he takes notes in French because he is in a French-speaking environment. A few days later he converses with Greeks in New York; his notes are in Greek. More than half of his life has been lived bilingually. Perhaps he might have preferred the solution of the folksong "All aboard des Etats,"[7] which passes freely between French and English. He does in fact include a few phrases in Greek in the text. The most cursory reader will know the meaning of *dèn xero* by the end. It is evident that a bilingual text is no solution for a writer who wants to be published. A device that may be considered an interesting curiosity—or simply one that works, and is natural in a bilingual context—in a song, is simply not possible in a commercially published book. Alexakis may not necessarily aim for the widest possible readership—he does eventually write a novel in Greek—but his work must be accessible to a sizeable community of readers.

Alexakis consciously associates language with the affective. He recalls sitting in the grass with his mother as she taught him the Greek alphabet and remembers her exasperation with his difficulties: "la langue maternelle n'est après tout que la première des langues étrangères qu'on apprend."[8] He feels a personal relationship to the French language and repeatedly personifies the language as a woman: "L'idée que je pourrais être amené un jour ou l'autre à *rompre* avec le français m'a bouleversé";[9] ". . . j'avais besoin d'une explication avec la langue française, . . . j'avais besoin de converser sereinement avec elle";[10] "je me sentais en froid avec le français . . . j'avais besoin du français."[11] The French language is a living entity that he needs, that he wants to talk to, to argue with, that he can feel cool toward and with which (or whom) he may break off relations; it is a mistress. It is somehow a force with a direction of its own: "j'ai parfois l'impression pendant que j'écris, que le français songe déjà à la suite du texte, qu'il va me faire des suggestions. . . ."[12]

This personification extends also to Greek: he writes of the changes that have occurred in Greek "depuis que je l'avais quittée."[13] On writing in both French and Greek he reflects: "Je n'avais le sentiment ni de me trahir, en utilisant deux langues, ni de les trahir." He says of another foreign writer who lives in Paris, that he is "fidèle à sa langue maternelle."[14] The comparison is made explicit when he writes about the difficulty of sustaining a relationship at a distance: "On ne peut pas aimer une langue, pas plus qu'une femme d'ailleurs, longtemps à distance."[15] In a note at the beginning of a 1997 collection of short stories Alexakis characterizes languages thus: "Les langues sont des maîtresses très exigeantes et très jalouses, même du passé."[16] In brief, his two languages are in competition with each other for his affections.

He is aware of the complementary gaps in his French and his Greek. When his children go to nursery school, he learns for the first time many words designating trees, flowers and birds.[17] He becomes familiar with the register used by adolescents in French but realizes that he has little idea of the equivalent language in Greek. He learns many technical terms in French, for which he knows no equivalent in his native tongue.

There is an evolution in Alexakis's relationship with French, and the motivation that drives his progress. At first it is simply a language that he learns at school. When he goes to live in France he finds his schoolboy French inadequate and he works tremendously hard to improve it. At first he wants to learn as fast as possible in order to complete his studies and return to Greece; at this stage his motivation is certainly instrumental. As his proficiency increases he wants to deploy his new skill—a clear case of resultative motivation. When he is looking for work in Paris it becomes very important to sound like a native speaker of French, but this "mimétisme" is a temporary phase.

> Au temps où je cherchais du travail à Paris, j'imitais assez bien l'accent français, de sorte qu'on ne devinait pas toujours que j'étais étranger. Plus tard j'ai désapprouvé mon mimétisme et je n'ai plus tenté de dissimuler mes difficultés de prononciation. Je parle avec de plus en plus d'accent: les animateurs de l'émission de France-Culture à laquelle je participe se posent même des questions sur mon compte, ils se demandent si je n'en rajoute pas.[18]

There is a moment (he is unable to identify precisely when) when Alexakis begins to answer the telephone in Greek rather than in French. On examining his notebook, he finds he uses both languages, slightly more Greek than English;[19] when he calculates he does so in Greek; when he speaks in his sleep, his wife tells him, he speaks in Greek. Although it would be exaggerated to suggest that he suffered from a fear of assimilation, there was a recognition of serious loss, a loss that took him a number of years to make good. As early as his first years in France he felt a sense of isolation that was the result of living in a country where his language was not spoken: "La France fut une sorte d'orphelinat, où l'on ne parlait même pas ma langue."[20]

The return to Greek is partly motivated by an awareness of a partial loss of his mother tongue: he has to search for the right word, he has difficulty in finding the correct form, and there are gaps in his knowledge created by language change over his years of residence in France: "il a donc fallu que je réapprenne en quelque sorte ma langue maternelle: ça n'a pas été facile, ça m'a pris des années, mais enfin j'y suis arrivé";[21] "j'avais failli oublier le grec."[22] In the course of working as a freelance journalist in Paris, where long hours were required to make a living, he considers that French "s'est substitué à ma langue maternelle."[23] Writing in French has become a natural act: "Je n'ai nullement eu le sentiment . . . d'accomplir une performance en écrivant ce roman directement en français."[24] The fact that he does not experience this act as a performance suggests that he has naturalized the act, that this feat has simply become a competence among others. At a certain point in his life writing in French has become more natural than writing in Greek. The reception of this writing, however, raises issues that will be discussed below.

Identity

This awareness of the possibility of performance raises the doubt in Alexakis about the integrity of his identity, another major theme of the book. The most obvious index of identity is a person's name, and, reflecting his concern, Alexakis relates a number of anecdotes concerning names. At a *colonie de vacances* he tries to refuse to give his first name to the leader, as an expression of his displeasure at being there. He mentions that the father of one of his friends is known as Georges, rather than by his Greek name Yorgos, because his French wife has a dressmaking business patronized by the Athenian bourgeoisie.[25] Alexakis himself chooses a pseudonym, Cyrano, with which to sign his articles on the wall newspaper at primary school. When he goes to live in Lille he is known as Basile: at that time Greek first names were not transliterated into the Roman alphabet on passports, but translated into the French equivalent. As a result, he is initially known in France as Basile, a name he abandons when he leaves that city. If names can be so easily altered and disposed of, this suggests that the identity of those they identify may be endangered.

Alexakis is an acute observer of the linguistic practices and shifting identities of others. With his awareness of the potential fragility of identity, he recounts meetings with those who have experienced such difficulties. He encounters some Greek immigrants in Montreal who speak "en quelque sorte, deux demi-langues," semi-linguals,[26] one might say; on the same trip he hears of Cretans dressed as Indians selling moccasins in Canada. He writes of Vietnamese neighbors who speak Vietnamese to each other, but French to the stray cat they have adopted.[27] His interest is also in the immigrant experience, and that of the next generation of these families. He has great sympathy for his friend Yamina, the child of Algerian parents, who feels bound to France by her childhood experiences, yet who is embarrassed by her acquired French nationality;[28] he sees the children of Greek immigrants to Germany as people who no longer have a home country to dream of.[29] The parents can yearn for their homeland, and dream of a return that is not likely to take place. The children, however, have been culturally displaced. Alexakis writes at some length about these children, whom he sees as "tiraillés entre deux cultures qu'ils ne possèdent le plus souvent que partiellement." He is always alert to the predicament of those whose identity seems to be endangered. On a boat trip to Tinos he hears a woman of about sixty telling of her discovery that her parents were not her real parents, that her name, her birthday and her age are not what she believed them to be.[30]

In each of these cases there is a partial mirroring of his own experience or fears of the worst: changing his name, not being fully competent in his first or second language, feeling ties to the place where he grew up, being pulled between two cultures. Yet, although he experiences these anxieties both directly and through his empathy with the experiences of others, there is in his case no real problem. The partially imposed use of a French version of his own name is abandoned when he goes to Paris; he is professionally successful in a milieu in which his competence in French is essential; he takes positive steps to recover his Greek; his visits to Greece become more frequent; and he does in the end reach a satisfactory equilibrium.

He is, no doubt, drawn to these life stories because, as an immigrant, he feels that there is a possibility of shared experience. However, he has not been part of a group or chain migration: he is an individualistic migrant. Cornwell and Hartmann characterize the individualistic migrant thus: "Individualistic migrants in general tend to be opportunistic, responding to the *pull* of economic or social opportunity rather than the *push* of economic disaster or political persecution."[31] Some of Alexakis's anxiety may be attributable to an over-identification with others who seem to be in a similar situation—they are all immigrants—but the real comparability is limited since his exile is entirely voluntary. He has responded to a "pull" rather than a "push." His initial arrival in France was motivated by an educational opportunity; his second, after the rise of the colonels in Greece, was the exercise of a preference in response to that situation.

Alexakis does, however, recognize the possibility of integrity of identity in those who migrate: he refers to the Greek poet Cavafy, a man who also spent his life in different countries. "Cavafy parle d'un homme qui se sent bien malheureux dans sa ville et cherche à s'en aller vivre ailleurs. Il n'y a pas d'ailleurs, lui dit le poète. Ta vie, telle que tu l'as faite te suivra partout. Où que tu ailles, la ville te suivra."[32] No doubt Alexakis recounts this anecdote for its potentially therapeutic value. It suggests that migration may not necessarily be damaging, that, although things may change outwardly, geography does not affect the inner core of self. Elsewhere he refers to another Greek writer, Kazantzakis,[33] who also lived in France and wrote in French— yet certainly continued to be considered a Greek writer. Alexakis's identity as a Greek may be safe after all.

The Right to Speak

Another part of his identity is as a writer in French, and it is here that there is a real external challenge to his sense of self. His need to become fluent in French quickly is externally determined: only in Lille is the kind of course he wants to do available. When he moves to Paris he quite soon marries a French woman, partly, he believes, as a result of his sense of isolation in Lille. She suspects him of marrying her for her value as an editor: "Ma femme, qui est professeur de français, m'a toujours soupçonné de l'avoir épousée parce que j'avais besoin de quelqu'un pour corriger mes fautes d'orthographe et de français."[34] In order to get work he must operate as a French person, linguistically at least. His children are French. These factors combine to make his daily environment French. Yet there is a tension between what he is able to do (make his living as a writer of French) and the responses of others: French people are often incredulous at his undertaking: "Ah bon? Vous écrivez en français? . . . Ça doit être difficile. Il y a tellement de nuances!"[35] "On se réjouit que le français conquière des étrangers mais on n'est nullement convaincu que ceux-ci puissent à leur tour conquérir la langue."[36] Essentially, he is perceived by some as engaging in an illegitimate activity, as an impostor. Despite his fluency in the language, this critical reception means that he has not gained full acceptance. Bourdieu considers the "right to speech" as an essential component of linguistic competence that is demonstrated when "those who speak regard those who listen as worthy to listen and those who listen regard those who speak as worthy to speak."[37] The right to speak implies the right to be heard. By writing in French, Alexakis asserts and acts out his right to do so; but, by criticizing this activity, others challenge the legitimacy of his action. It may even be appropriate to see him as functioning from a "negative position in the culture" as do women, black minorities and poor people.[38] As Nancy Huston, a Canadian novelist who writes in French, put it, speaking of the reaction to the performance of non-native French speakers, "Les Français guettent."[39]

Alexakis's publisher doesn't quite know how to categorize his novels: are they foreign or French literature? He does not conform to the popular expectation of the foreign writer: "on leur demande surtout des nouvelles de leurs pays."[40] It is considered surprising that he writes in French "et que je ne parle pas nécessairement de la Grèce."[41] There is a great tension here: Alexakis operates successfully in French, successfully enough to earn a living through his writing and to win one of the major French literary prizes. His publisher recognizes, as he does, that his bilingualism is problematic. He does not note the objections stated specifically, though it is reasonable to suppose the tenor of the remarks enumerated above is representative, and he claims not to be particularly troubled by them, considering them to derive principally from the French lack of interest in foreign languages. Nevertheless, these opinions are so painful to Alexakis that he thinks of leaving France, even wondering whether he should forget French.

Two encounters, one at the beginning of his career in Paris and one at the literary conference in Quebec once he has become a successful writer, rankle particularly. He tells of a telephone conversation with the secretary of a magazine editor. He used the expression *à tout hasard* with a liaison. This was the response: "Elle s'était tue. Puis, telle une institutrice, s'adressant aux plus arriéré de ses élèves, elle avait répété 'à tout' et avait observé un long silence avant d'ajouter hasard."[42] At the conference in Quebec he is angered by a famous linguist who maintains that an original work can only be written in the mother tongue of the writer.[43] Alexakis is caught in a cultural difference here: he maintains that in Greece a knowledge of foreign languages is considered to represent openness and progress,[44] but in France "les étrangers d'expression française" are regarded with suspicion.[45] He feels marginalized by the critical establishment, and this reaction is significant in his commitment to renewing his involvement in things Greek.

Two Selves?

From his earliest memories Alexakis recalls having had to act a part that was not truly his own. At school he had the sense of having created a new identity in his efforts to gain good marks: "Je m'étais forgé une nouvelle identité, à l'opposé de celle qui était réellement la mienne. Je me reconnaissais dans tous les personnages de roman qui ont deux visages. Je fus le docteur Jekyll."[46]

He frequently presents himself (or others) as a double or image. On the day of his departure from Greece he seems to remember his shadow on the quay. He lives "à cheval sur deux pays";[47] he travels "d'un pays à l'autre, d'un moi à l'autre";[48] he refers to "les deux moitiés de ma vie."[49] The French view him as a Greek author, and it is as such that he is invited to attend the conference in Quebec. Greeks see him as a French author. He has written novels in the first person, one autobiographical in which "il m'est arrivé de me déguiser en femme."[50] He considers that he has examined himself, but only through a mask . . . on this occasion the mask is off, and he is not sure he likes what he sees.[51] He recounts being dressed up as a parrot as a boy, reciting a poem at the French Institute in Athens; sensing that he plays a part when he goes to a business meeting; feeling obliged to pretend to be a French person in Greece; being mistaken for Cavafy himself at the Frankfurt book fair.

Alexakis is a man in perpetual dialogue with himself. He refers to "grandes conversations muettes avec moi-même"[52] on the subject of his return to France when the colonels took power in Greece. From the beginning of the memoir he is aware not only of writing for himself, but in some sense writing to himself: "J'écris pour avoir de mes nouvelles";[53] "Je crois que c'est à moi-même que je m'adresse d'abord."[54] He cuts out and keeps all the reviews of his work, "comme si je cherchais encore à travers les comptes rendus favorables, à me reconcilier avec moi-même."[55] It is not only in the process of writing that he identifies two selves. When on a trip to a conference in Quebec he is irritated by his own company: "la présence des autres ne m'ennuyait pas. C'est plutôt la mienne qui me gênait."[56] In writing a memoir, Alexakis accepts the possibility of two selves. As Hayes suggests, "if autobiography is also a fiction, the author of that fiction must be another subject, a self split from the subject whose life is being told." [57] While not accepting the word fiction for Alexakis's work with the degree of invention that this implies, he is certainly the teller, and therefore the shaper, of a tale in which he is the central character. He is conscious of his life as a narrative, and senses that the book he is writing began perhaps twenty-five years previously when he left Greece.[58]

Although he does not experience writing in French as a performance, he is sometimes aware of playing a role in France: "A Paris je m'étais si bien installé dans la peau de mon personnage que la plupart du temps je n'avais pas l'impression de jouer la comédie."[59] Nevertheless, the presence of his parents in Paris makes him feel uncomfortable, because he then has to play two roles, and this is difficult.[60] On hearing a recording of a broadcast he had made, his mother exclaims, "Mais tu es français!" When he makes his first phone call in French on return from a trip to Greece he says, "j'ai . . . l'impression d'entendre quelqu'un d'autre parler à travers moi, utiliser ma voix: je me fais l'effet d'un acteur qui se voit à l'écran en version doublée."[61] While at the conference in Quebec he is aware that the writers play the part of writers in the course of the conference: "la nuit mettait un terme à nos comédies d'auteurs."[62]

Bridging the Gap

Alexakis is always alert to his "identité d'immigré."[63] At one point he almost goes through the process of becoming a French citizen.[64] He senses that the attitude toward immigrants will harden after the first petrol crisis—but he cannot bring himself to do it. He walks round the préfecture where he has gone to start the administrative procedures; the sky is grey, the blackish wall of the building reminds him of unhappy days in Lille. He returns home without entering the building. His loyalty to the ethnos, the imagined cultural community of Greece, is too great to allow him to join the demos, the political state of another ethnos.[65] The advantage of administrative convenience is not enough to overcome loyalties to the place of his childhood: "On appartient fatalement au lieu de son enfance."[66] Becoming a French citizen would add a formal aspect to the dual or double identity he already fears insofar as it may imply no identity, a state of anomie. The blank page he faces at the beginning of this project expresses his situation exactly.[67] His French identity is incomplete, for no one in France remembers him as a child.[68] This refusal to become a French citizen clarifies the site of his ultimate loyalty: he is too Greek to become French.

Despite his belief that he has arrived at a tolerable perspective on his situation, there are still anxieties: "Alors que j'avais cru trouver un équilibre entre deux pays et deux langues, j'ai eu la sensation que je marchais dans le vide. Comme dans un cauchemar, je me suis vu en train de traverser un gouffre sur un pont qui, en réalité n'existait pas."[69] This image is particularly telling for a man who suffers from vertigo. He describes the sites of a number of vertiginous episodes, describing his feelings thus: "J'ai le sentiment que le vide me guette, qu'il m'attend, qu'il m'appelle: il doit avoir sûrement des choses à me dire."[70]

He has observed this in the case of poor Greeks he met in Canada: "Ils avaient quitté les rives d'une culture sans jamais atteindre celles d'une autre. Ils naviguaient vaillemment sur un radeau."[71] On a raft one is exposed and vulnerable, and the mere effort of keeping afloat absorbs a great deal of energy. A similar image is used to describe his feelings of directionlessness as he embarks on the writing of this text: "J'ai l'impression d'être sur un bateau sans moteur, qui se déplace au gré des courants, au gré du vent."[72] As Coulson observes, "There are figures, who, by choice or necessity, distance themselves from one culture as they approach another, and are, or become, strangers to both."[73] This is plainly Alexakis's fear, but his awareness of the danger protects him from it. He finally casts anchor on the Greek side.

As a writer who has been translated in both directions between Greek and French, he wonders whether the intermediary between his translators might not just disappear and the translators would somehow be able to make do without him. This surrealistic fantasy shows his fears, but again his alertness to the possibility of a problem acts as a shield against any phenomenon that might erode his sense of self. Yet he has also translated himself, and found it less problematic than he expected: "Il m'a semblé néanmoins que j'avais trouvé dans l'une comme dans l'autre [langue] les mots qui me convenaient."[74] Writing in a second language is less of a drama for Alexakis than it is for his critics. Indeed, he takes this activity for granted in a way that has not been possible for some other writers. When Julien Green, for example, had begun to write his autobiography *Quand nous habitions ensemble*, he translated the early passages into English with the intention of continuing in that language, but realized that he was writing a different book, sensing that his perspective on life changed according to the language he used.[75] Of Assia Djebar, the Algerian novelist whose French-language book *L'amour, la fantasia* is built on a combination of her life story and Algerian history, Hayes writes: "The language of the life story being different from that of the life, the story alienates its storyteller who can no longer identify with herself as the story's referent and must then read her own autobiography as outsider."[76] Djebar herself says: "L'autobiographie pratiquée dans la langue adverse se tisse comme fiction."[77] It seems worthwhile to linger on the experience of these other translingual writers, because their differences show clearly the diversity of ways in which it is possible to respond to, and experience, an act—writing autobiographically in a language other than one's first language—that can be described in identical terms. The experiences of the various writers are all quite different. In the case of Green, there is the sense of different (but equal) selves for different identities; in the case of Djebar, there is a separate persona in the French text, obviously created by, but not identical with the writing self; in Alexakis, there is a cooler more nonchalant approach in spite of his anxieties: writing in a second language does not cause fracture.

The question of identity becomes a problem for Alexakis, particularly at the time when he realizes that he has lost full command of his first language and therefore feels he can no longer claim Greek identity: part of being Greek is speaking Greek. Yet he is not French. So what is he? The inability to fit neatly into categories leads to negative responses in a social context;[78] and this helps to account for both the negative response of critics and Alexakis's own anxiety. The creation of identity is largely a process of defining boundaries that mark difference. Part of the meaning of being Greek is simply not being of other nationalities, not being Italian, not being Turkish, not being French. Alexakis had to come to terms with making the boundary fuzzy or elastic, or eliminating it altogether.

Alexakis resists being member of a group. As a child he resists the group experience of the *colonie de vacances* by becoming ill; when he goes to Canada he arranges not to travel too closely with the group.[79] When he goes on holiday with friends he needs to keep a private space. This is more evidence of his desire to be individual, not to be subsumed under a group heading. The price of this individualism is that he no longer fits into an obvious single group.

He is troubled by some aspects of French life: the writers with whom he lunches over decades, for instance, who impart no personal information; reticence because "je viens d'un pays où l'on expose volontiers ses états d'âme, ses doutes et ses blessures."[80] He has not become like them, he has not gone native.

Continuities and Return

His residence in France has had a positive effect on his attitude to Greece: "Je n'ai jamais autant aimé la Grèce qu'après l'avoir quittée."[81] It is in France that he begins to read the Greek classics, in French of course, because at the time his main aim is to learn French as quickly as possible.

Finally, he writes a novel in Greek, which seems to resolve a number of difficulties: "Il [the novel] m'a réconcilié avec la Grèce et avec moi-même. Il m'a rendu mon identité grecque. Je pouvais désormais me regarder sereinement dans la glace."[82] The past has weighed heavily on Alexakis because he has not known how to integrate, or recognize the actual integration of, what seem to be two parts of his identity. His mother returns to him two large bags full of the letters he wrote to her when he was in Lille. This is how he describes carrying them away from his parents' house: "En traversant le terrain vague qui sépare la maison de mes parents de la route, j'ai ressenti une grande fatigue."[83] This weight is also the burden of the past, which he manages to lighten through the process that is the writing of this memoir. "Je cherche une sorte d'apaisement. Chaque paragraphe achevé me procure une certaine paix."[84] Writing is a means of ridding himself of excess mental baggage. He says of his studio in Paris: Je ne dispose pas d'assez de place, dans mon studio parisien, pour laisser les choses s'accumuler à l'infini."[85] The impulse to write this memoir seems to have been motivated by a similar desire for a clear-out.

In a number of respects, Alexakis clearly resembles his own parents. Emigration has not cut the continuity of inherited identity. He is impatient when attempting to teach some Greek to one of his sons, just as his mother had been impatient when teaching him the Greek alphabet. Like his own father, he is largely absent from his own children, although they occupy the same living space, describing himself as a "faux bon père"; like his father the actor he moves between worlds, and is acutely aware of elements of performance in his own life.

In the years that Alexakis has lived in France, the distance between Athens and Paris has diminished. At first it was a three-day journey by boat; taking the airplane was inaccessibly expensive. Now the gap has closed: the journey is only a matter of a few hours. At the same time "la distance entre les deux villes . . . paraît énorme";[86] the telephone rings differently, and the washing takes longer to dry. But the journey is easier, and he makes it more often. The "distance" now is psychological. Paris is merely his place of work, "un immense bureau traversé par un fleuve."[87] Greece is his psychological home. Coulson suggests that "the exile and the migrant must live between identities, negotiating with a strangeness that is both within and around them."[88] This may be the migrant experience in some cases, but it depends on a view of identity as a discrete bounded area. Alexakis succeeds in integrating the diverse elements of his experience and achieving a sense of himself as an integrated whole.

In an interview recorded in *Sites*, Serge Doubrovsky identifies an "entrecroisement de l'écriture et de la vie" in the writing of Chateaubriand.[89] Writing is a developmental experience; the activity of thinking about aspects of his life and the mental processes he goes through as he gives an account of, and accounts for, his experiences brings Alexakis to a particular view of his life. Of itself, this view colors the nature of these experiences.

The writing of the book was a learning and healing experience. Its genesis may have been the "turn" that Sturrock identifies in much autobiographical writing.[90] The "turn" in *Paris-Athènes* is surely the point at which Alexakis begins seriously to question the effect on his identity of his engagement with the French language. Alexakis is returning home after a long journey, and some elements of the outward journey are echoed in the return. As he reacquaints himself with the Greek language he uses the same device as he had used when learning French: he records conversations for later study, becoming an ethnographer in his own country. This journey could be conceived in traditional, folk terms. A young man sets out on a journey in search of something. He has a number of adventures, and returns having gained maturity and identity. It is true, in a sense, that the self that sets out is not the self that returns, because every individual human evolves over time. The final geographical destination is not clear: Alexakis expects that he will die in Paris or Athens, but does no know which. Despite this, in the end Alexakis knows who he is.

Notes

1. James Pettifer, *The Greeks* (Penguin, 1984), 228
2. Tahar Ben Jelloun, *Le Monde*, 8 September 1989, 19
3. Josyane Savigneau, *Le Monde*, 27 June 1997, 4
4. Vassilis Alexakis, *Paris-Athènes* (Paris : Fayard, 1997). All references in this chapter not given in notes refer to this edition. An earlier edition published by the Editions du Seuil appeared in 1989.
5. Dan R. McAdams, *The Person*, 2nd ed. (Harcourt Brace, 1994), 764.
6. Alexakis, *Paris-Athènes*, 45.
7. Alexakis, *Paris-Athènes*, 47.
8. Alexakis, *Paris-Athènes*, 66.
9. Alexakis, *Paris-Athènes*, 20.
10. Alexakis, *Paris-Athènes*, 45.
11. Alexakis, *Paris-Athènes*, 21.
12. This and some other aspects of Alexakis's linguistic experiences are shared by Alice Kaplan and recorded in her memoir *French Lessons* (Chicago: University of Chicago Press, 1993).
13. Alexakis, *Paris-Athènes*, 14.
14. Alexakis, *Paris-Athènes*, 218.
15. Alexakis, *Paris-Athènes*, 19.
16. Vassilis Alexakis, *Papa* (Paris: Fayard, 1997), 9.
17. Alexakis, *Paris-Athènes*, 98.
18. Alexakis, *Paris-Athènes*, 97.
19. Alexakis, *Paris-Athènes*, 21.
20. Alexakis, *Paris-Athènes*, 109.
21. Alexakis, *Paris-Athènes*, 14.
22. Alexakis, *Paris-Athènes*, 19.
23. Alexakis, *Paris-Athènes*, 218.
24. Alexakis, *Paris-Athènes*, 218.
25. Alexakis, *Paris-Athènes*, 67.
26. Semi-lingualism is "a lack of complete fluency in either language," see John Edwards, *Multilingualism* (London: Penguin, 1995), 58.
27. Alexakis, *Paris-Athènes*, 23.

28. Alexakis, *Paris-Athènes*, 59.

29. Alexakis, *Paris-Athènes*, 95.

30. Alexakis, *Paris-Athènes*, 117.

31. Stephen Cornwell and Douglas Hartmann, *Ethnicity and Race* (Thousand Oaks, Calif. and London: Pine Forge Press, 1998).

32. Alexakis, *Paris-Athènes*, 126.

33. Alexakis, *Paris-Athènes*, 20.

34. Alexakis, *Paris-Athènes*, 96.

35. Alexakis, *Paris-Athènes*, 15.

36. Alexakis, *Paris-Athènes*, 16.

37. Pierre Bourdieu, "The economics of linguistic exchanges," *Social Science Information* 16, no. 6 (1977): 648.

38. Julia Swindells, ed., Introduction to *The Uses of Autobiography* (London: Taylor and Francis, 1995), 4–5. She draws here on the work of Sidonie Smith.

39. Personal communication at the conference La Langue Maternelle, University of Paris 7, 19 March 1999.

40. Alexakis, *Paris-Athènes*, 16.

41. Alexakis, *Paris-Athènes*, 17.

42. Alexakis, *Paris-Athènes*, 96.

43. Alexakis, *Paris-Athènes*, 15.

44. Alexakis, *Paris-Athènes*, 20.

45. Alexakis, *Paris-Athènes*, 17.

46. Alexakis, *Paris-Athènes*, 84.

47. Alexakis, *Paris-Athènes*, 13.

48. Alexakis, *Paris-Athènes*, 14.

49. Alexakis, *Paris-Athènes*, 18.

50. Alexakis, *Paris-Athènes*, 27.

51. Alexakis, *Paris-Athènes*, 26.

52. Alexakis, *Paris-Athènes*, 12.

53. Alexakis, *Paris-Athènes*, 26.

54. Alexakis, *Paris-Athènes*, 27.

55. Alexakis, *Paris-Athènes*, 85.

56. Alexakis, *Paris-Athènes*, 39.

57. Jarrod Hayes, "Rachid O. and the Return of the Homopast," in *Sites* 1, no. 2 (1997): 502.

58. Alexakis, *Paris-Athènes*, 9.

59. Alexakis, *Paris-Athènes*, 225.

60. Alexakis, *Paris-Athènes*, 226.

61. Alexakis, *Paris-Athènes*, 11.

62. Alexakis, *Paris-Athènes*, 39.

63. Alexakis, *Paris-Athènes*, 28.

64. Alexakis, *Paris-Athènes*, 158.

65. James Donald refers to Habermas's distinction in "The Citizen and the Man about Town," in Stuart Hall and Paul du Gay, *Questions of Cultural Identity* (London: Sage, 1996), 173.

66. Alexakis, *Paris-Athènes*, 58.

67. Alexakis, *Paris-Athènes*, 11.

68. Alexakis, *Paris-Athènes*, 13.

69. Alexakis, *Paris-Athènes*, 21.

70. Alexakis, *Paris-Athènes*, 104.

71. Alexakis, *Paris-Athènes*, 50.

72. Alexakis, *Paris-Athènes*, 26.

73. Anthony Coulson, Introduction to *Exiles and Migrants: Crossing Thresholds in European Culture and Society* (Brighton: Sussex Academic Press, 1997), 3.

74. Alexakis, *Paris-Athènes*, 15.

75. Michael O'Dwyer, "Julien Green—Expatrié et Sudiste" in *Exiles and Migrants*, ed. Anthony Coulson (Sussex Academic Press, 1997), 185–92.

76. Jarrod Hayes, "Rachid O. and the Return of the Homopast," in *Sites* 1, no. 2 (1997): 502.

77. Hayes, "Rachid O."

78. The work of Mary Douglas among others is referred to by Stuart Hall in *Representation: Cultural Representations and Signifying Practices* (London: Sage, 1997), 236.

79. Alexakis, *Paris-Athènes*, 38.

80. Alexakis, *Paris-Athènes*, 30.

81. Alexakis, *Paris-Athènes*, 39.

82. Alexakis, *Paris-Athènes*, 246.

83. Alexakis, *Paris-Athènes*, 26.

84. Alexakis, *Paris-Athènes*, 27.

85. Alexakis, *Paris-Athènes*, 52.

86. Alexakis, *Paris-Athènes*, 271.

87. Alexakis, *Paris-Athènes*, 187.

88. Coulson, "Introduction," 4.

89. Roger Célestin, "Interview with Serge Doubrovsky," in *Sites* 1, no. 2 (1997), 399.

90. John Sturrock, *The Language of Autobiography* (Cambridge: Cambridge University Press, 1993), 289.

25

Of Earthquakes and Cultural Sedimentation: The Origins of Post-Colonial Shock Waves in Azouz Begag's *Zenzela*

Michael O'Riley

WITH THE RECENT FILM ADAPTATION OF HIS successful novel *Le Gone du Chaâba*,[1] Azouz Begag joins other popular "Beur"[2] novelists, such as Mehdi Charef and Farida Belghoul,[3] whose artistic interventions query the definitions of French and Maghrebian cultural identity alike. Readers familiar with these authors' works are attuned to the identity quests performed on both the narrative and diegetic levels by children of Maghrebian immigrants, whose comic and at times strident voices contemplate, ironize and dislocate essential notions of Maghrebian and French national identities.[4] For his part, Begag has sought an aesthetics that would "porte l'accent sur les turbulences de ces deux éléments," and scrutinize "la topologie, les distances qui séparent et unissent les deux mondes."[5] Searching out a tertiary space of identity, independent of the notion of a fixed cultural homeland, Begag's writings have almost exclusively focused on the relations (or absence thereof) between the Algerian and French spheres within France. Converging on the darkly humorous childhood worlds of Azouz "le gone" or of Ben Abdallah in *Béni ou le paradis privé*,[6] Begag's sensibilities attain a universal quality in their tracking of the role of ethnic minorities in the France of the post-colonial era.

Much of Begag's appeal might be attributed to his tendency toward a phantasmal exploration of identity construction that visits the subterraneous and portentous borderline of reality, the threshold of "magical realism." The final scene of *Béni ou le paradis privé*, for instance, concludes with a *deus ex machina*: A strange shadow beckons Béni to fly away from his unattainable yet beloved France, into the netherland, an alternative space that delivers the subject from the cultural dilemma of choosing between a French or Algerian heritage. Yet, just as textual "otherworlds" of this kind seem designed to curtail critically the idea of a singular or dominant cultural identity, of a cloying assimilation, they are also predicated on the evasion of the specific cultural spaces they interrogate.

While Begag's recent work, *Zenzela*,[7] continues to explore the realm of intercultural identity through the topos of covert, supernatural forces, it departs from previous works in its use of these forces to advance the vision of a postnational reality in both France and Algeria. By tapping the geological sources of an earthquake, Zenzela, "une ogresse seismique," Begag's narrative seeks to displace the densely constructed ideological foundations that divide (within) Algeria and France as it unites the material and organic impulses of multiple cultural territories in the instance of writing. As an author with a Franco-Algerian background living in France,

Begag's cultural location between the cultural territories and histories of the former colony and metropolis strategically positions him to both critique and unite the two countries. The discursive or interventionist endeavor that finds the author interpreting the mutually determined histories of nationalism within the two territories as a rejection of the other, the outsider, constitutes a performance of sorts through which the imaginative and artistic enterprise prescribes a change in the actual material or lived structure of cultural relations. Performance, in this sense, signifies an attempt to enact this change through the imaginative and discursive processes that derive from a hybrid, multicultural vision of cultural relations between and within France and Algeria. Julia Kristeva's formulation of multicultural discursivity as an acute awareness of the interconnection of the symbolic and organic domains expresses the anchoring of Begag's writing in cultural territory. As Kristeva suggests in the context of the multicultural psyche, the alignment of "telles forces maléfiques seraient un tressage du symbolique et de l'organique: peut-être la pulsion elle-même."[8] Begag's text resonates with Kristeva's weaving of the symbolic and organic realms in that, derived from the organic source of seismic activity, the symbolic drive of *Zenzela* seeks to dissolve the edified underpinnings of Maghrebian and French cultures. Begag's text uses the figure of the monster to underscore the shifting dynamics of cultural relations. As Mladen Dolar argues, the monster is always at stake in ideology. "The point where the monster emerges," says Dolar, "is always immediately seized by an overwhelming amount of meaning. . . . It has immediate social and ideological connotations. The monster can stand for everything that our culture has to repress."[9] Zenzela's force points to the performative emergence of a subaltern[10] multicultural reality in both France and the Maghreb, and suggests a dismantling of cultural claims to hierarchy and supremacy. As a monster, Zenzela's emergence from underground constitutes a literal performance by a subaltern or subterranean force that emerges to disrupt the natural order of territory and cultural relations in the text by creating a disaster that forces a radical rethinking of the established order. The parallels, then, to the emergence of the text as a post-colonial narrative—written by a child of formerly colonized Algerian immigrants—that forces the rethinking of established cultural (b)orders are quite striking. Metaphorically, the appearance of Zenzela can be understood as an emergence of the colonial era—the colonial unconscious—within the post-colonial period, demanding a reconsideration of the conventional divisions that order colonial and post-colonial temporality, as well as cultural relations, in the usual understanding of nationalism in the post-colonial period. This performative shifting of relational dynamics across cultural borders finds resonance in Edouard Glissant's "poétique de la relation," which is characterized by the tumultuous aesthetics "de la rupture et de la suture . . . du variable et du continu, de l'invariable et du discontinu."[11] The resultant aftershock of Zenzela accounts for the mutually determined histories of Algeria and France, and provides a vision of cultural territory that points beyond the orientalist and nationalist paradigms characteristic of Franco–North African history.

As a metaphor for a cultural revolution in relations between and in Algeria and France, Zenzela's trembling inscribes itself in a rich series of what one might term a literature of post-colonial shock waves. For Frantz Fanon, the enslaved consciousness of the colonized is figured by a static, immobile state, signature of the hegemonic nature and physical as well as psychological control of colonial power. Writing of the colonized's discovery of selfdom in this colonial relationship, Fanon notes the deeply disruptive shock of the assertion of a post-colonial identity: ". . . cette découverte introduit une secousse essentielle dans le monde. Toute l'assurance nouvelle et révolutionnaire du colonisé en découle."[12] For Fanon, this disruptive shock signals the assertion of the colonized's formerly dormant identity. Fanon uses the seismic figure to represent the act of physical revolt required of the colonized in order to seek liberty and reconnect with the

organic nature of physical territory. The fixity of the colonial world, the intransigence of the hierarchical structure in this "monde de statues" is shaken in Fanon's *Les Damnés de la terre* by the
moment of insurrection.[13] "[L]a solidité du système colonial," and "[la] pseudo-pétrification"
of the colonized tremble under "la rencontre de deux forces congénitalement antagonistes."[14]
The performative culturequake that follows this inevitable encounter, argues Fanon, levels the
material and ideological infrastructure of the colonial world: "Comme on le voit, c'est tout un
univers matériel et moral qui s'écroule."[15] The dismantling of the Manichean divisions of the
colonial world introduces an enunciatory shock of liberation into a world once dominated by
static patterns of domination. Yet, writing on the eve of Algerian Independence, Fanon recognizes that, having "suivi le craquement de plus en plus essentiel des vieilles sédimentations culturelles," his work must first take account of the paradoxical need for an emergent and potentially dangerous nationalism, the "expression d'une nation."[16] The active liberation required to
break the hold of colonial control is necessarily accompanied by the formation of a nationalism predicated on an exclusionary ideology, and rooted in the binary principles of enmity and
control as means of revolt. While Fanon's work attempts to temper this phase, it notes that the
performance of newfound nationhood threatens with its mimicry of the abusive and internally
inconsistent structure of the old colonial model. As national consciousness reclaims territory, a
burgeoning fundamentalism permeates the newly liberated psyche, anchoring the nation to
singular claims. Such territorialist impulses, which ultimately replicate the territorialism of
colonial culture, emerge as reactionary and protectionist defenses against the image of an imperialist other. To achieve a degree of autonomy, these forces attempt to control and homoge-
nize culture from within. The aftershocks of Fanon's shifting cultural forces, then, can only extend so far, ultimately reinstating "ce mouvement immobile,"[17] the static cultural sign of an
internally corrupt state.

Much like Fanon, Roland Barthes identifies a seismic moment in the cultural structure of his
L'Empire des signes: "'réveil devant le fait,' saisie de la chose comme événement et non comme
substance."[18] Writing, argues Barthes, is concurrent with the Zen phenomenon of a *satori*: "le
satori (l'événement Zen) est un séisme plus ou moins fort (nullement solennel) qui fait vaciller
la connaissance, le sujet."[19] The symbolism of cultural tradition and its potential to transmit a
monolithic value system of "superimposed layers of meaning" is shattered as the *satori* "efface
en nous le règne des Codes."[20] As a performative event, the *satori* permits us to "éprouver la secousse sans jamais l'amortir, jusqu'à ce qu'en nous tout l'Occident s'ébranle et que vacillent les
droits de la langue paternelle, celle qui nous vient de nos pères et qui nous fait à notre tour,
pères et propriétaires d'une culture que précisément l'histoire transforme en 'nature'."[21]

Barthes's literary moves suspend the transmission of patriarchal values upon which, as Edward Said has argued, national traditions of colonialism were established.[22] Through an invo-
cation of the Orient—as critique of the Occident—Barthes imagines a toppling of the West.
The Orient becomes the seismic generator located outside institutionalized orders of social
symbols and practices in the West. This Barthesian mid-career valorization of Oriental culture
is an attempt to dismantle the logic of the symbolic semiological system. By situating the Zen
occurrence within Western culture, Barthes seeks to shake 'the very root of meaning,'[23] the territorial foundations built by "natural" versions of ethnicity and cultural identity, so presciently
underscored by Fanon's work, which quickly become exclusionary. However, in creating binary
divisions between Occident and Orient, Barthes's identification of the performative seismic
moment fails to unite the cultural territories of East and West and, much like Fanon's culturequake, envisions cultural space as something circumscribed by intransigent borders that ultimately reinstate cultural divisions.

Zenzela's Emergence and the Challenge to Cultural Fixity

Begag, too, places the Zen occurrence at the root of his text, but its shock waves ripple through the cultural symbols of Barthes's West as well as Fanon's East. *Zenzela* is constructed on a narrative fault line that breaks the text into alternating fragments narrated by the novel's protagonist, Farid, and events in Sétif and El Asnam in Algeria, and in Lyon. The novel sets up a series of oppositional forces from its outset, deriving its force from their deliberate collision: Farid's parents' dream home is located in Sétif, and although they live in Lyon, they hope to return there one day. Despite his mother's intention to wed him to an Algerian woman and his own visit to an Algerian prostitute during a stay in Sétif, Farid is in love with a French girl named Anna. Farid also imagines that a member of the OAS (*Organisation armée secrète*), a terrorist group of right-wing vigilantes opposed to Algerian independence, is secretly following him, a supporter of the FLN, the Algerian independence movement, even though more than twenty years have passed since Algerian independence. This fact alone signals the lingering cultural tensions both between the French and Algerian cultural spheres, and within the politically factious Algeria of the post-independence period, suggesting that the legacy of the Algerian War remains an important repository of cultural memory both within and outside Algeria and France. Moreover, the first signs of Zenzela appear to Farid in Lyon while he is "sur l'un des deux bords, entre cauchemar et réalité, avec ma voix au milieu qui faisait le messager entre le temps d'hier et le temps de demain, essayant de coller les deux bouts."[24] He dreams of belonging to the soccer team whose members and coach Gaston ask, "De quel bord es-tu?"[25]—implicitly linking ethnicity and territorial loyalties; yet the dream also emerges from the tension between opposing cultural heritages. Here, just as in the previous series of oppositions, Farid's struggle is cut through by a temporal and spatial gap that divides Algeria and France, the depths of Farid's own cultural subconscious. The novel's juxtapositions, all characterized by a deep-seated territorial impulse, are punctuated by the monstrous emergence of Zenzela from the depths of darkness: "Un tremblement de terre sur mon matelas . . . il s'agissait d'un séisme . . . je voyais seulement la terre s'ouvrir et aspirer dans une énorme crevasse tout ce qui se trouvait à sa surface. . . ."[26] The dream turns out to be a premonition of an earthquake at El Asnam in Algeria, the force of which dislocates the connection between territory and identity, and levels asymmetrical power relations between and within cultural territories as "des fondations s'enfoncent dans le néant."[27]

The quake itself is ambiguously located in time and space, having simultaneously shaken, it seems, the cultural foundations of Lyon, El Asnam, and Sétif. Farid says: "mes sensations étaient confuses, mais elles me renvoyaient à une dizaine d'années auparavant, lorsque j'avais vécu un séisme dès le premier jour de mon arrivée dans la maison à Sétif. Mon corps avait enregistré ces ondes sur son sismographe."[28] *Zenzela*'s negative force levels the hierarchical distinctions between past and present, Algeria and France, signaling the acute performative enactment of the minority status of all cultural territories as the established order disintegrates in the apocalyptic moment: "J'avais le vertige et la chair de poule. Je ne sentais plus l'ordre des choses . . ."[29] As Homi Bhabha notes, "negating activity is . . . a bridge where presencing begins because it captures something of the estranging sense of the relocation of the home and the world—the unhomeliness—that is the condition of extraterritorial and cross-cultural initiations."[30] Bhabha celebrates negative attempts to capture the nomadic condition of post-colonialism as a means of critiquing the essentialist and territorialist conceptions of culture and space that are the signature of imperialist tendencies. In espousing the destruction of fixed conceptions of cultural territory by negative force, Bhabha seeks to hollow out a hybrid, cross-cultural space, in which post-colonial cultures might convene.

Congruent with Bhabha's dismantling of fixed correspondences between culture and space, territorial oppositions and hierarchies fold under the emergent force of Zenzela's performative enactment as an initial step toward a hybridized reality.

The novel's principal voice, Farid, registers these shifting cultural dynamics on his body. Of the earthquake at Sétif he remarks, "Oui, mon corps avait enregistré ces ondes pour toute la vie. Ce sont elles, exactement, qui dix ans plus tard revenaient à la surface de mon cauchemar."[31] The subaltern emergence of leveling forces is imputed to him in signs: "Je recevais des décharges électriques. Mes ampoules allaient toutes griller. . . . J'avais vu l'accident géologique en direct et mon corps était transi à cause du choc."[32] The body becomes the epicenter, and by extension, the translator of change: "J'étais devenu marabout, voyant, troisième œil."[33] Farid's mother is convinced that he has been sent "un message à déchiffrer."[34] The waves of information radiating from the oppositional shocks and subterranean variances are inscribed on Farid's body as he becomes their interpreter. Much like the author himself, conscious of ethnic minorities "qui ouvrent des horizons nouveaux et créent des valeurs nouvelles," Farid deciphers the material signs of transformation emitted by Zenzela's shifting of cultural territory.[35] He proclaims, "Zenzela! Zenzela! Elle est venue."[36] As an enunciative agent, an announcer of the transcultural event, Farid mirrors the performative engagement of the text as a sign of the emerging power of a multicultural literature. Farid's engagement with Zenzela thus reproduces the author's own artistic movements, his participation in the emergence of an "underground" literature, published, coincidentally in this case, by *Editions du Seuil*. While Begag's text certainly does not constitute an "underground" text in the conventional sense of a censored tract, it nonetheless represents an intervention in the widely discussed cultural questions of multiculturalism and post-colonial identity. As a post-colonial subject in France, one generation removed from colonialism and immigration, Begag represents one voice of the colonial unconscious that speaks or performs through post-colonial narrative, which is still just beginning to emerge in full force in France and elsewhere and is therefore poised on the threshold of these cultures. The appearance of post-colonial voices in this way figures the emergence of a repressed colonial unconscious in France and Algeria—a past that remains lodged within post-colonial territory and history—and that emerges from a sort of subterranean space through the performance offered by authorship and readership.

No cultural territory escapes Zenzela's power. Her fault line reveals all the deeply rooted structural weaknesses of French and Algerian society, sending citizens "hors de portée des failles seismiques."[37] Zenzela issues from deep within the roots of civilization where the organic nature of social relations has been disturbed by an internal malady: "des confins du monde, la terre s'est mise à bourdonner, elle était en colère."[38] The totalitarian fundamentalism that has divided contemporary Algeria is the first movement to be crossed by Zenzela's leveling trajectory. All the signs point to embedded corruption and a bloodstained core within the recesses of Algerian society: "L'Algérie est en deuil," a man confesses to Farid, and "les fondations sont pourries."[39] Begag's transcription of Algeria thus participates in what Assia Djebar has called "une Algérie sang-écriture," which writes "Pour l'instant, l'Algérie de la douleur."[40] Deciphering the shocks of Zenzela in Sétif, Farid remarks, "je voyais bien qu'il y avait un truc qui ne tournait pas rond dans cette démocratie forcée. Des odeurs de soufre jaillissaient des canalisations défoncées."[41] The social turmoil and intestinal disharmony that have plagued the core of Algerian society and engender Zenzela must be examined for posterity's sake: "Il faut analyser les causes scientifiques des tremblements de terre pour éliminer définitivement de la surface de la société ces risques d'explosion sociale majeurs."[42] The fundamentalism and political factionalism that have seen the deaths of thousands of Algerians at the hands of fellow citizens in the wake of Algerian independence and during the search for Algerian identity, political as well as cultural, are viewed as subterranean forces capable of bringing about disaster. The covert, subterranean formulation of such civil disorder points to the repressed, reactionary nature of the contemporary violence in relation to unresolved anti-colonial sentiment of the past. The fundamentalist violence and political factionalism to which the text makes reference have their roots in the struggle to assert a pure, essentialist identity against the looming image of a colonial other. Moreover, the internal and civil nature of this condition suggests the lingering desire of a certain section of the formerly colonized psyche to inflict punishment upon itself for its past condition of colonial imprisonment. The seismic waves of Zenzela are thus seen as a postcolonial agent capable of locating such repression and transforming its energies. Zenzela's explosive force is viewed as a means of restructuring the petrified, corrupt administrative and social structures of Algeria: "Finalement, à regarder de plus près, une bonne Zenzela 'numéro 9 de Richter' ne détruisait-elle pas les fondations de la société et n'offrait-elle pas une excellente occasion de repenser l'organisation d'une véritable démocratie populaire et socialiste?"[43]

The cataclysmic power of Zenzela resides in her ability to unite society in the stark face of the unadulterated disaster. Her apocalyptic tone[44] reveals an underlying element of truth. Following Farid's interpretation of the power of the earthquake, Zenzela displaces sedimented divisions between different groups within Algerian society: "Il n'y avait plus de règles strictes, plus de barrières, les gens réalisaient qu'ils vivaient hors jeu, hors du temps—la Zenzela n'annonçait-elle pas, après tout, l'occurrence d'une mort imminente à quelques degrés de Richter près?"[45]

The "fissure noire"[46] to which the quake transports the community challenges monolithic forms of identity; it creates what Bhabha calls a "cleavage in the language of culture" that displaces fixed sociological structures, impenetrable sites of intolerance leading to exclusionary distinctions between groups.[47] Bhabha conceives of this symbolic splitting in narrative in terms of the tension between the opposing cultural forces of a nation's iconic image of totalitarian authority, "an a priori historical presence" or "pedagogical address," and a performative, "enunciatory present."[48] In a disruptive movement, the "intervention of the performative" breaks down the sedimented image of internal national boundaries, and "ensure[s] that no political ideologies . . . claim transcendent or metaphysical authority for themselves."[49] Bhabha's narrative dynamics engage the sources of dissenting cultural voices, pitting them against the images and codes of authoritarian, nationalist voices. As an enunciative practice that emerges within the context of conflictual differences in narrative itself, the performative is conceived as a challenge to homogenizing or organic notions of culture. It emerges within the context of the linguistic instability of enunciation and therefore functions as a performance of sorts, replete with uncertainty and spectacle, destabilizing the authority of culture as intransigent knowledge or history. Performance, for Bhabha, is profoundly linked to the ambivalence of cultural authority that derives from the instabilities of the enunciative moment and therefore provides an interesting theoretical parallel to the performative emergence of Zenzela, which destabilizes the very foundations of the cultural territories from which it emerges. Conceived in narrative terms, however, Bhabha's conception of a hybrid, performative intervention cannot account for slow processes of cultural sedimentation since it continually confronts and undermines them in a synchronic movement. Nor can it account for the limitations of narrative as a performative and disruptive agent in processes of historical secretion outside discursive forms. Zenzela, however, reveals these petrified sites and explores both the force and limits of performative intervention. The space of cultural signification hollowed out by Zenzela's collision with the institutionalized image of Algeria favors the dissolution of internal factions and the relational nature of the event as a potential unifying experience. Zenzela privileges the reception of the cultural shock waves produced by its performance and so points a way out of the static world of social relations in contemporary Algeria through the communicative act, while suggesting that such communication is only a potential social narrative that will have to confront deep-rooted sites of historical tension. Furthermore, the text's emphasis on the emission and reception of shock waves between the Algerian and French spheres suggests a dissolution of cultural barriers and the existence of a potential communicative link rooted in the mutually determined movements of Algerian and French cultural territories.

In France, Zenzela's shock waves penetrate the division between private and public space, and reconfigure the conceptual construction of peripheral territory within the urban frontier. Waves of information announcing Zenzela's arrival penetrate private residences across France.[50] In Lyon the towering social housing projects, *les HLM*, where Farid's family and many other families of Maghrebian origin reside on the borders—or *banlieu*—of the city,[51] are hit by the tremors. The conceptual reconfiguration of social space in this way is intended to transform the social and material mobility of many Maghrebian immigrants and their children, who, even after numerous years of residence in France, continue to reside on the peripheries of urban territory, apparently distanced from access to central metropolitan structures and the opportunities they promise. Farid remarks: "Une sacrée Zenzela qui mettrait à genoux cette dizaine d'immeubles hauts de quinze et dix-sept étages, y compris la tour panoramique hexagonale. Une belle Zenzela qui ensevelirait dans un remblais de béton armé près de vingt mille habitants."[52] The hierarchical division of social space that places many ethnic minorities on the margins of France's urban social structure is shaken, bringing down the symbolic surveillance tower from which ethnic minorities can be observed and kept to the edges of society. The monumental quality of the hexagon, which has long been a symbol of France, is threatened at its foundations by the imagined enactment of Zenzela's performance. Transformative shock waves lurk beneath the surface of all sedimented forms of cultural territory within France, as they do in Algeria, pointing to imaginative subjunctive worlds, alternative futures, which shake the hills of Lyon so that "on avait presque envie de tendre la main pour suivre leur oscillation."[53]

If the strict correspondence between national soil and ethnic identity is threatened in France, it falls apart in Algeria. As a result of a series of aftershocks Farid's family home in Sétif slowly crumbles to the ground, and with it his parents' mythic dream of an originary homeland, so common a feature of the literature of and by children of Maghrebian immigrants, is quickly if painfully displaced.[54] While the dislocation of the mythic return displaces the divisions between French and Algeria by delegitimizing the symbolic figure of fixed cultural territory, the borderline of cultural identity to which Farid's family and others of Maghrebian origin are relegated is critically examined: "cette faille . . . c'était ça, une ligne blanche qu'on n'osait pas franchir . . . une maison qu'on bâtit et qui s'écroule, un temps passé qui se noie, un autre à venir qui ne vient pas, avec nous, présents, au milieu du gué."[55] Suspended between two impossible homelands, minorities of Maghrebian descent in France live their cultural nomadism, the text signals, as a function of a very real, densely configured border zone that the symbolic force of Zenzela may be able to cross but cannot possibly erase.

Though Zenzela is not able to penetrate the material foundations of contemporary antagonisms, her trembling does cut through the residual colonial divisions between Algeria and France lodged in the depths of historical consciousness. In Algeria, Akila, a "rescapée du temps de la colonie française" accords Zenzela a French provenance, naming Farid a carrier of the disaster: "Tu as vu? Elle est venue, hein? C'est toi qui l'as amenée de France."[56] France, and its citizens of Algerian descent, such as Farid, stand accused of exporting hostile forces to Algerian territory. As Farid remarks, "Elle aussi faisait de la Zenzela une ogresse qu'elle connaissait bien."[57] Old antagonisms of the colonial era thus surface in new forms. In France, these forces are portrayed in a simulated war between Farid and M. Oas, the representative of the *Organisation armée secrète*, as the two talk on a bus. Summing up their encounter, Farid remarks, "*j'avais lu* dans son esprit ce qu'il s'apprêtait à invoquer: que si les Français étaient restés en Algérie, il n'y aurait pas eu de tremblement de terre."[58] Zenzela's origin is once again situated in the colonial encounter, though localized this time in Algeria and blamed on Algerian independence. As a cultural phenomenon that shakes the Manichean divisions of the colonial world and blurs the boundaries between the former metropolis and its satellite, Zenzela is seen as a threat to the compartmentalized distinctions between Algerian and French culture. Although both French and Algerian factions attempt to bend her force to their respective agendas, Zenzela's energy defies appropriation by any single constituency. Fanon's colonial "monde compartimenté" is suddenly menaced by Zenzela's international movement, as both France and Algeria are hit by successive waves of shocks.[59] As Farid mentions when talking about the earthquake's scope and magnitude, "il faut s'attendre à une autre secousse . . . l'une ne vient jamais sans l'autre."[60] Zenzela's emergence penetrates the lingering colonial distinctions that eclipse the mutually determined histories of Algeria and France. Moreover, defying appropriation by any single cultural constituency, Zenzela points to the synchronized movements of a cross-cultural post-colonial world divested of territorialist impulses emanating from imperialist interests. Cutting across boundaries, Zenzela demonstrates the emergence of a post-colonial historical moment that accounts for the colonial past while reshaping the form of its lingering quarrel in the present.

Beyond Orientalist History in France and Algeria

The imagined divisions between Orient and Occident that subtend the history of French and Algerian relations also tremble with Zenzela. As a feminized space, "penetrated, worked over, taken hold of," in Said's words,[61] Algeria has figured as an orientalized location in the history of Western thought; exotic and sensuous, it is penetrated by the masculine psyche. Playing a central role in an orientalist imaginary in France, Said argues, Algeria came to be physically and materially possessed as a colony.[62] In *Zenzela*, too, an orientalist tradition is identified, but only as a means of dislocating its axiomatic underpinnings. The text reveals orientalist impulses in a series of movements: first, Algeria is constructed as a feminized space to be exploited; second, the sensuous Algerian space is associated with the exotic and placed in an imaginary tradition of orientalism; third, the images of a feminized Algeria and France are superimposed and become intertwined, essentially reproducing the phallic structure of orientalism and projecting it onto French territory; lastly, the entire project deconstructs to reveal its essential impotence and structural flaws.

In Sétif, Farid decides to visit a bordello in order to learn how best to please his true love, Anna, in France. The Algerian space is, at first, viewed only as a rich resource of sensual energy from which to profit: "apprendre à faire l'amour doucement, respirer profondément, retenir l'énergie, l'expulser au moment propice, penser d'abord à Anna. Tout ce que j'allais apprendre ici allait un jour lui servir là-bas."[63] Algeria is constructed as a reserve from which to extract the energy required to thrive in France. Casting his glance as he wanders past the brothels, Farid evokes the exoticism that circulates in the orientalist imagination, inscribing the bordello within the literary tradition of orientalism: "Elles avaient le même caractère que les harems que j'avais imaginés dans Les Mille et Une Nuits."[64] After choosing a prostitute, Farid superimposes the feminized image of Algeria upon that of France: "J'ai transporté son image dans une chambre du troisième étage d'un immeuble en face du mien, sur une femme blonde, belle, droite et fine."[65] Essentially transferring the phallic structure of orientalism to the imagined space of France, Farid reproduces the orientalist dynamic. In a reverse movement, Farid then transports the center to the feminized space of the harem: "Mes yeux étaient plantés entre ses cuisses. C'était la capitale où il fallait que j'aille, mon Arc de Triomphe."[66] In an ironic twist, the French edifice is remembered at the height of passion; dislocated, it becomes a sexualized place of entry through which the institutionalized tradition of orientalist practice is reversed and reapplied. Yet, the reversal and perpetuation of the discriminatory practice come crashing down in the scene's telling finale. Unable to perform, Farid measures his own seismic movements in "le temps d'une ou deux Zenzelas, pas plus,"[67] recording Zenzela's deconstruction of the scene of desire. As if touched by Zenzela, Farid remarks, "Pour qui allait-elle me prendre, la dame si j'avais fini avant d'avoir commencé, si je m'écroulais comme un château de paille."[68] The edifice of desire that sustains and perpetuates the discriminatory underpinnings of orientalist tradition is erected, only to be revealed as an impotent weapon. The scene mimics the phallic structure of orientalism, turning it against France, only to reveal finally its internal weaknesses and delegitimize its authority and tradition. As Bhabha argues, "Under cover of camouflage, mimicry . . . is a part-object that radically revalues the normative knowledges of the priority of race, writing, history. . . . [It] mimes the forms of authority at the point at which it deauthorizes them."[69] *Zenzela* revisits the sedimented sites of the French and Algerian historical imaginations to break their grasp and point to the prospects opened up by postorientalism.

It is with the instance of writing that such restrictions are ultimately overcome in *Zenzela*. Back in France, Farid realizes that his pursuit of Anna, the subtextual territorial drive of which, in many ways, structures the novel, is fundamentally flawed. With the sensations of Zenzela reverberating within his core, he renounces his quest, closing the narrative with a rhetorical, "A quoi ça servait, tout ça?"[70] Farid's remarks illustrate the fatuous nature of the masculine quest in writing; equally, they point to the essential flaw in attempts to reverse the underlying orientalist principles that have victimized Algeria by turning them back on the French cultural sphere. Just as putatively visceral divisions between and within Algeria and France are shaken by Zenzela, so too do discursive oppositions between an essential feminine or masculine essence ultimately tremble. The text seems to suggest that territory, be it material, physical, or an idyllic human image, cannot be possessed exclusively without engendering a culture of divisive practices.

As its force derives from the trembling of cultural models, from the grating that occurs between overlapping areas and the vestigial spaces between and within them, Begag's text mobilizes the frequently inchoate and dangerous energies released by shifting configurations of identity and place in the post-colonial world. Undoubtedly inspired by earthquakes in El Asnam and in Agadir in the 1960s, the natural disaster becomes Zenzela's subtextual shadow, eerily reminiscent of the catastrophe that looms when friction between territorial borders increases: "Trente mille morts à Agadir en 1960 . . . Et après?"[71] *Zenzela* draws on the natural disaster in Algeria in order to preclude social disasters in Algeria and France resulting from past and present territorial intersections. It is no coincidence that one of the novel's closing vignettes takes us from the disaster zone to the *Zone diplomatique*, an area where outer and inner borders are shaken, a space of which Farid, perhaps speaking directly for Begag, remarks, "j'aimais cet endroit, c'était chez moi."[72] The text's geological underpinnings help to shape this space, borrowing from the material and organic impulses of the natural world to form a new reality in cultural relations between groups. The privilege *Zenzela* accords to territory and its disconnection of the relationship between cultural identity and natural space place the narrative within the nascent field of ecocriticism, a mode of consciousness that couples ecological sensitivity with cultural critique. In Begag's *Zenzela* the performative dismantling of sedimented nationalist and international barriers and the relational quality of the event create the power of this continuously evolving literature, shaping new conceptions of French, Algerian, and world culture that reflect the changing landscape of the era of de-colonization.

Notes

1. Azouz Begag, *Le Gone du Chaâba* (Paris: Seuil, 1986).
2. While many young people of Maghrebian descent have embraced the term, others dislike it.
3. Both Mehdi Charef and Farida Belghoul have seen two of their works through to the screen. They are, respectively, *Le Thé au harem d'Archimède* (1985) and *Miss Mona* (1987), and *C'est Madame la France que tu préfères?* (1981) and *Le Départ du père* (1983).
4. Christiane Achour, "Ancrage, identité et dérision: L'humour dans le récit beur," in *Humour d'expression française* (Nice: Z'Editions, 1990), 202–8; Martine Delvaux, "L'ironie du sort: Le tiers espace dans la littérature beure," *French Review* 68, no. 4 (1995) : 681–93; Alec Hargreaves, "Resistance at the Margins: Writers of Maghrebi Immigrant Origin in France," in *Post-Colonial Cultures in France*, ed. Alec Hargreaves and Mark McKinney (London, Routledge, 1997), 226–29.
5. Azouz Begag, *Ecarts d'identité* (Paris: Seuil, 1986), 19–20.
6. Azouz Begag, *Béni ou le paradis privé* (Paris: Seuil, 1989).
7. Azouz Begag, *Zenzela* (Paris: Seuil, 1997).
8. Julia Kristeva, *Étrangers à nous-mêmes* (Paris: Fayard, 1988), 274.
9. Mladen Dolar, "I Shall be with You on Your Wedding Night: Lacan and the Uncanny," *October* 58, (1991): 75.
10. On subalternity, see Gyatri Spivak, "Can the Subaltern Speak?" in *Colonial Discourse and Post-colonial Theory: A Reader*, ed. Patrick Williams and Laura Chrisman (Hemel Hempstead: Harvester Wheatsheaf, 1993), 66–111. The subaltern is a figure for the post-colonial subject that has been subjected to the forces of imperialism and subsequently placed outside the realms of power. He or she is consequently subaltern by virtue of his/her placement below and outside the realm of Western power. Within the text, Zenzela emerges as a subaltern figure—formed and lodged within the recesses of colonial dynamics—thereby conveying a certain colonial consciousness that informs contemporary post-colonial relations both in France and Algeria.
11. Edouard Glissant, *Poétique de la relation* (Paris: Gallimard, 1990), 165–66.
12. Frantz Fanon, *Les damnés de la terre* (Paris: Gallimard, 1991), 76.
13. Fanon, *Les Damnés*, 82.
14. Fanon, *Les Damnés*, 84–66.
15. Fanon, *Les Damnés*, 74.
16. Fanon, *Les Damnés*, 293.
17. Fanon, *Les Damnés*.
18. Roland Barthes, *L'empire des signes*, ed. Albert Skira (Geneva: Editions d'Art, 1970), 103.
19. Barthes, *L'Empire*, 11.
20. Barthes, *L'Empire*, 99.
21. Barthes, *L'Empire*, 13.
22. Edward Said, *Orientalism* (New York: Vintage Books, 1979), 204.
23. Barthes, *L'Empire*, 75.
24. Begag, *Zenzela*, 25.
25. Begag, *Zenzela*, 17.
26. Begag, *Zenzela*, 25.

27. Begag, *Zenzela*, 23.

28. Begag, *Zenzela*, 26.

29. Begag, *Zenzela*, 29.

30. Homi Bhabha, *The Location of Culture* (London: Routledge, 1994), 9.

31. Begag, *Zenzela*, l.

32. Begag, *Zenzela*, 24–29.

33. Begag, *Zenzela*, 30.

34. Begag, *Zenzela*, 31.

35. *Ecarts*, 106.

36. Begag, *Zenzela*, 20.

37. Begag, *Zenzela*, 68.

38. Begag, *Zenzela*, 28.

39. Begag, *Zenzela*, 70–66. Begag's vision of the earthquake as a cure for the social ills of Algeria has echoes in two other works that speak directly to the Algerian cultural order. Rachid Boudjedra's novel, *Le Démantèlement* (Paris: Denoèl, 1982), draws on the 1954 earthquake of Orléansville to create a more colonial, Fanonesque, variant of the earthquake as a metaphor for cultural revolution, identifying the geophysical trembling of late 1954 as a precursor of the Algerian uprisings in 1955: "Le tremblement de terre du 9 septembre 1954 portait dans sa généalogie et dans sa géologie les signes de la guerre qui allait se déclencher deux mois plus tard," 266–67. In the contemporary context of Algeria, Maïssa Bey's recent *Nouvelles d'Algérie* (Paris: Grasset, 1998), also draws parallels between death and mourning, and the earthquake at El-Asnam.

40. Assia Djebar, *Le Blanc de l'Algérie* (Paris: Editions Albin, 1995), 275.

41. Begag, *Zenzela*, 37.

42. Begag, *Zenzela*, 36–37.

43. Begag, *Zenzela*, 36.

44. The expression "an apocalyptic tone" is taken from Jacques Derrida's *D'un ton apocalyptique adopté naguère en philosophie* (Paris: Galilée, 1983), in which Derrida argues that the apocalyptic tone reveals a moment of emergent truth, 77.

45. Begag, *Zenzela*, 35–36.

46. Begag, *Zenzela*, 33.

47. Bhabha, *The Location of Culture*, 163.

48. Bhabha, *The Location of Culture*, 147.

49. Bhabha, *The Location of Culture*, 148.

50. Begag, *Zenzela*, 43.

51. For a study of housing and the North African community in France as reflected in literary works, see Mireille Rosello, "North African Women and the Ideology of Modernization: From Bidonvilles to Cités de Transit and HLM," in *Post-Colonial Cultures in France*, ed. Alec Hargreaves and Mark Mckinney (London, Routledge, 1997), 240–54.

52. Begag, *Zenzela*, 37.

53. Begag, *Zenzela*, 50–51.

54. Alec Hargreaves, *Voices from the North African Community in France: Immigration and Identity in Beur Fiction* (New York: Berg, 1991), 148–52.

55. Begag, *Zenzela*, 139.

56. Begag, *Zenzela*, 34.

57. Begag, *Zenzela*.

58. Begag, *Zenzela*, 43.

59. Fanon, *Les Damnés*, 82.

60. Begag, *Zenzela*, 43.

61. Said, *Orientalism*, 211.

62. Said, *Orientalism*.

63. Begag, *Zenzela*, 78.

64. Begag, *Zenzela*, 80.
65. Begag, *Zenzela*, 90.
66. Begag, *Zenzela*, 89.
67. Begag, *Zenzela*, 91.
68. Begag, *Zenzela*, 90.
69. Bhabha, *The Location of Culture*, 91.
70. Begag, *Zenzela*, 140.
71. Begag, *Zenzela*, 71.
72. Begag, *Zenzela*, 113–14.

VI

THE INDIAN OCEAN AND
SOUTHEAST ASIA

26

How Appropriate Is the Term "Post-Colonial" to the Cultural Production of Réunion?

Peter Hawkins

IN ORDER TO UNDERSTAND THE PIQUANCY OF THE QUESTION, it will be necessary to elucidate some points about the particular status of the island of Réunion. Originally uninhabited, this mountainous island in the southwest Indian Ocean was first populated in 1649 by mutineers sent there as a punishment from the French trading post of Fort Dauphin in Madagascar. They prospered, and this led to the establishment of French colony on the island in the 1660s, then named Bourbon in honor of King Louis XIV. The colony soon developed into a slave-owning plantation economy devoted in the first instance to the cultivation of coffee, and subsequently sugar cane. The revolutionary government changed the island's name to Réunion in 1792, but was unable to impose the eradication of slavery, which persisted until 1848. Then, as in other neighboring islands such as Mauritius, the slaves, mostly of African or Malagasy origin, were replaced on the plantations by indentured laborers brought in principally from southern India. In the late nineteenth century further waves of immigration from China and what is now Pakistan diversified the population of the island still further.

This history has left the island with a complex, mixed-race population of about 700,000 inhabitants, in which the boundaries between the various communities are often blurred. The original French settlers brought with them Malagasy partners, which made the island's initial land-owning class often of mixed-race origin. As in other plantation economies, the lack of a common language among the slave population led to the growth of a local Creole language, based on French—often the provincial dialect of the slave-masters—and a variety of African and Malagasy languages. Creole has survived as the mother tongue of most native Réunionese, and since the 1970s has been the object of a cultural revival, with the earliest attempts to use it as a vehicle for literary expression.

Thus far, nothing suggests that the island has been anything other than a colony of France, but the change of status in 1946 to that of an overseas department of the French Republic, along with Guadeloupe, Martinique and Guyane, complicates the issue. This has been described as a "de-colonization by assimilation" since the population of the island are now full French citizens, and the island is politically governed and represented just like the departments of mainland France. It is hard to deny, even so, the vestiges of the island's former colonial status, if only in its extremely mixed-race population and its continued economic dependency on mainland France.

This complicates somewhat the use of the term "post-colonial" with reference to the island. It certainly has a colonial history, but after 1946, is it still a colony? Or does it have the status of a former colony, thus authorizing the prefix "post." It is difficult to determine, and this very ambivalence is what makes the use of the term "post-colonial," with its baggage of theorizing, particularly interesting and revealing.

Theoretical Perspectives

For the sake of argument, we shall assume that the label is indeed appropriate. After all, according to the definition given by Ashcroft, Griffiths and Tiffin in the introduction to *The Postcolonial studies reader*, any cultural product marked by the influence of colonialism can be identified as "post-colonial" regardless of the particular social or political context in which it was formulated.[1] In the light of this, one of the founding fathers of Réunionese literature, the eighteenth century poet Evariste de Parny, can be considered a post-colonial writer, inasmuch as some of his writings are clearly inspired by the mixed-race society of his native island,[2] and many of his declarations are intended as a denunciation of the slave-owning character of its plantation economy. This does not, however, foreclose the discussion, as the question of the positioning of the literary text within a post-colonial discourse is of primary importance. The situation of the early twentieth-century colonialist ideologues and novelists Marius and Ary Leblond, for instance, would not necessarily be the same as that of Parny. The same would be true of the critical discourse that takes such authors as its subject matter: to what extent does it deal with the issue of colonialism and how does it resolve the thorny question of its relation to political or aesthetic judgments of the works in question?

This kind of questioning is a feature of many of the discussions incorporated into *The Postcolonial Studies Reader*. To what extent is it possible to develop a critical discourse, which is not based on eurocentric or Western preconceptions? In the creation of a body of post-colonial criticism it is extremely difficult to escape from the closed circuit of a university discourse inseparable from some form of colonial project, whether it be French, British or even American, that is to say in some way neo-colonial. The exploration of these questions takes place to a very large extent in that context, and it often appeals to philosophical traditions which have for the most part remained aloof from questions about the nature of colonialism. All this constitutes an almost insurmountable obstacle to the creation of a post-colonial discourse outside the major intellectual centers of Western culture, a situation which perpetuates the same inequality, the same relations of dominance and submission, that this discourse is supposed to be questioning. Among the most influential positions, that of Edward Said is probably the most pessimistic on this issue, since he goes so far as to doubt whether such a discourse is possible outside the humanist norms of the Western university system, and concludes that it is indispensable to relativize and adapt this discourse in the direction of a recognition of its silences, of its political and cultural pre-suppositions.[3] After his work in *Orientalism* [4]on the constitution of the Orient as an object of Western discourse, as an "other" weighed down with the orientalist discourse of Western university centers, Said has more recently turned his attention to the arrogance of Western literary canons in *Culture and Imperialism*, revealing the hidden colonialist aspects of classic works such as Jane Austen's *Mansfield Park* or Gide's *L'Immoraliste*, not to mention the more obvious examples of Camus' *L'Étranger* and *La Peste*. His standpoint is explicitly that of a Palestinian exile who nevertheless benefits from the privileged environment of a liberal North American university.

More directly relevant to this discussion and to the situation of Réunion is the strategy of Homi K.Bhabha in his 1994 collection of essays, *The Location of Culture*. Through an astute application of the concepts of French post-structuralist theorists such as Barthes, Foucault or Derrida, Homi Bhabha has developed a sophisticated rhetorical analysis which seeks to adapt their identification of gaps and fissures in the texture of Western discourse to the recognition of a hybrid discourse which is elaborated in the interstices, as it were, of Western philosophical positions. Among the more striking moments of this analysis, one might mention the distinction he establishes between the banal notion of "cultural diversity"—which obscures the relations of power and dominance between cultures—and the recognition of "différance," spelled with an a, in the manner of Derrida, which designates the domination of Western logocentrism and the necessary supplementarity of the discourse of the "other." In this way Bhabha establishes a theory of the hybrid text, which roots itself in the fissures of the Western text, undermining it from within, as it were. In the light of these notions, he undertakes a brilliant analysis of the work of Salman Rushdie,[5] among others, as well as that of Frantz Fanon, which he regards as indispensable.[6]

Another debate that is prominent in the pages of Homi Bhabha's essays as well as those of the *Post-colonial Studies Reader* is one which seeks to determine the links between post-colonialism and post-modernism. There are various points of view on the question, but it is clear from what we have already seen that post-colonial theory is at the very least one aspect of post-modernism.[7] This can be recognized in the emphasis placed on the fragmentation of discourse, on the questioning of the "grand narratives" that underpin national cultures, in the rejection of the universalist pretentions that have often served to mask the colonial or neo-colonial projects of economic domination and cultural hegemony. Both movements reject all-embracing discourses, and the arguments they deploy are often similar. The attention paid to marginality, to subaltern status within the hegemonic Western discourse takes its impetus from the recognition of the relativity and partiality of this discourse, which is a characteristic of postmodern sensibility.

Even more than Said, then, Homi Bhabha can be seen as the theoretician of a hybrid discourse that seems to correspond to the situation of Réunionese literary and cultural production. This participates on the one hand in the literary and cultural life of metropolitan France, while at the same time displaying a subversive "différance" in relation to the norms it imposes. Even more than in the latent nationalistic revolt that it all too often betrays, it is perhaps in this notion of hybrid cultural production that the Réunionese work shows its wider relevance and its true identity.

One may wonder what distinction might be drawn between this hybridity and the all too familiar notion in French culture of literary and cultural "métissage."[8] This idea, in spite of its prestigious literary associations (in the writings of Léopold Sedar Senghor, for instance), is nonetheless defined in racial terms, implying the involuntary mixing of genetic identities which are perhaps appropriate to human types, but less so to literary and cultural products. The notion of hybridity, on the other hand, implies a deliberate choice, and as in the domain of horticulture, a chosen combination of characteristics with a view to certain desired results, certain new characteristics. The features of a hybrid cultural activity would thus be those of several recognizable categories, without being clearly identified with any one of them.

Hybridity in Réunionese Cultural Production

This does seem to correspond to the particular interest of Réunionese literature as well as other forms of cultural production. Thus it is that a Réunionese writer such as Axel Gauvin writes novels in a French colored by the regional idioms of Réunion, while enjoying the prestige of being published by a Parisian institution such as Le Seuil and at the same time publishing with a local Réunionese publisher versions in Creole of the same novels.[9] In this way Gauvin is able to participate in the literary life of mainland France, securing a place in the Parisian literary scene, while maintaining his identification with the Creole language. He operates in a hybrid way, taking advantage of the most beneficial features of both situations.

Other examples of hybrid productions are provided by the best-known theater groups of the island, the Théâtre Vollard and the Théâtre Talipot. The writers, who are also the directors of these two companies, Emmanuel Genvrin and Philippe Pelen, are both originally from metropolitan France. They have both chosen to situate their works in the context of Réunion, while maintaining an openness to external influences. In the case of Vollard, their most successful recent productions in metropolitan France have been plays with a strongly Réunionese content: *Lepervenche*, which for all its reference to the origins of trade-unionism on the island, nonetheless appealed to metropolitan audiences;[10] and *Sega Tremblad*, which centered on the Réunionese diaspora in the Paris region while celebrating the typically Réunionese musical style of the Sega.[11] One of their most popular local productions in recent years has been *Votez Ubu Colonial*, an adaptation into Creole of a play by a Réunionese exile, Ambroise Vollard, which itself was a development of the farce by his metropolitan French friend Alfred Jarry, *Ubu Roi*, one of the classics of French theater.[12] In all these cases we are dealing with productions that are situated in both metropolitan French and Réunionese traditions, using the Creole language but also recognizably part of a popular burlesque theater in France.

In the case of Philippe Pelen, author/director of the Théâtre Talipot, he has theorized his approach to the company's multicultural productions under the label of "métissage,"[13] but in practice these are the result of a similar strategy of cross-fertilization, refusing to limit themselves to a single theatrical convention. In *Ma*, a multicultural and multimedia production, Pelen has attempted to create a synthesis of the characteristics of several traditions present in the Indian Ocean area: the island culture, the African and Malagasy animist heritage, Hindu beliefs and traditions, and a certain Western conception of experimental theater, involving music, mime and dance The whole production was placed under the auspices not of any national cultural body, but a supra-national one, UNESCO. The use of a kaleidoscope of languages in the play, including Réunionese Creole, Hindi and Malagasy, as well as French, symbolizes the intention to go beyond any one national or linguistic tradition, while remaining accessible to several. Pelen has thus sought to go beyond the frame of reference of any one local or national culture, by drawing inspiration from a range of traditions present in the island's culture. Thus both of the two most representative theater groups from the island illustrate very well in their different ways the creation of a hybrid cultural production.

The same can be said of the lively and diverse musical production of the island, which often presents a multicultural aspect. The indigenous music and dance form of the Maloya was often presented when it was rediscovered some thirty years ago as a style of purely African origin, linked to the cult of ancestor worship, transmitted through the propagation of the animist rituals of Madagasacar, the "servis kabaré," and as such a musical inheritance of the early slave population of the island. More recently, however, the possible influence of the "sacred drumming" of the Tamil religious rituals has been identified, which would make Maloya not a purely African form, but a hybrid incorporating Malagasy and Indian influences. It is clear that some of the best known and most successful exponents of the style, such as the groups Ziskakan[14] and Baster,[15] practice a poetic and lyrical form of Maloya, which incorporates the international influences of world music into the rhythmic patterns and percussion effects characteristic of the style. Most often it is a musical style which is not confined to one particular tradition, however authentically Réunionese it may be, but incorporates the resources of a deliberate musical hybridity. In this way one can hear in the background of some recordings of Ziskakan the sounds of Breton pipes, Corsican polyphonic choral singing, or the throaty Islamic voice of a Senegalese griot, not to mention an electric guitar solo in the style of progressive rock.[16] This practice can be interpreted as the desire not to be restricted to one cultural tradition but to assimilate and adapt the resources of the dominant musical culture, that of Anglo-American pop music, so as better to subvert it by putting it to use in the defense of a marginalized Creole culture.

Post-colonial theory allows us to situate in an international aesthetic and philosophical context this diversified kind of cultural production that refuses to be contained within a national style or genre. Thus far, however, the post-colonial critics involved in the extensive theoretical debates that run throughout the pages of the *Post-Colonial Studies Reader* have not as yet elaborated a critical method which might be deployed in the analysis of the kind of hybrid works we are considering here. In order to fill this gap, one might consider borrowing in a tentative and experimental way an adapted version of the approach of Pierre Bourdieu, outlined in his 1992 volume *Les Règles de l'art*.[17] Bourdieu's socio-literary approach is influential in the Anglo-American schools of Cultural Studies and not very far removed from the post-colonial movement, inasmuch as they are both concerned to analyze national cultures marked by a colonial heritage. Thus far the Bourdieusian approach has been restricted to a "field" such as a national literature so as better to identify the investment of "cultural capital" likely to bring the best returns in "symbolic value" in a competitive situation marked by "symbolic violence" and the effects of the "habitus," the conservative values of a certain cultural establishment.[18] This sociological kind of approach will, if applied to a hybrid cultural production, require the identification of not one but several "fields" which will then need to be differentiated and hierarchized. To illustrate the operation of the approach I shall apply it to a typically Réunionese work which shows the characteristics of cultural hybridity. This is the novel *Bleu nuit*,[19] the last in a series of historical novels by Daniel Vaxelaire, all situated in the islands of the southwest Indian Ocean.

An Example of Post-Colonial Analysis: A Novel by Daniel Vaxelaire

The choice of this text may seem surprising. Vaxelaire is a writer not widely known in mainland France but is a familiar figure in Réunion. He is not Réunionese by birth, but originates from mainland France: he has lived on the island for the last twenty years, however, and made it his home. He has published seven historical novels, usually fairly traditional in construction, which dramatize certain crucial moments in the colonial history of the region. In this way his works develop into a panoramic deployment of the myths which might serve to underpin a sense of identity in the Francophone Indian Ocean, by means of "grand narratives" that would appear to reflect a kind of epic ambition on the part of their author. The list includes *Chasseur de noirs*,[20] the story of an eighteenth-century hunter of runaway slaves; *L'Affranchi*,[21] about the social and economic ascension of a freed slave in nineteenth-century Réunion; *Chasseurs d'Epices*,[22] the story of the eighteenth-century botanist and spice trader, Pierre Poivre, a colonial administrator of the Ile de France, now Mauritius; *Grand Port*[23] and *Cap Malheureux*,[24] the saga of the British conquest of Mauritius during the Napoleonic wars; and finally *Les Mutins de la* Liberté,[25] a work that will be referred to subsequently, which recounts the adventures of the French pirate Olivier Misson and his companion, the former monk Angelo Carraccioli, in the Comoros Islands and in northern Madagascar, where they founded the utopian community of Libertalia.

The seventh and last novel in the series, *Bleu nuit ou les sept vies du moine*, is constructed very differently from the previous six. It is no longer a romanced historical drama, but a work both more serious and more playful, with a less traditional and more ironic structure. The principal narrative thread concerns a contemporary figure, Florence, a primary school teacher and occasional journalist who, on the evening of the millennium, summons the spirits by means of a ouija board borrowed from her fortune teller, and lands on the ghost of an unfrocked eighteenth-century monk turned pirate. This turns out to be Angelo Carracioli, the hero of the preceding novel *Les Mutins de la* Liberté, and the founder of the ephemeral and utopian republic of Libertalia, on the site of the present-day city of Diego Suarez or Antsiranana, on the northern tip of Madagascar. This soul awaiting reincarnation has a privileged access to the spirit world and a gift for storytelling: Could he be the *alter ego* of the author? While communicating with the heroine Florence on a sort of cosmic wave radio, he seems to be in touch with several lives as well as hers.

This improbable and jokey invention is the structure that allows Vaxelaire to weave together several narrative threads that link together, juxtaposing different periods in the colonization of the island of Réunion, including the present day, represented by the love affairs of Florence and the contacts of an unhappy wife and neighbor of Florence with a scheming witch doctor who promises help in reviving her relationship with her estranged husband. The characters in which the monk is reincarnated in his "seven lives" include a young stowaway on a sixteenth-century ship en route for India; a Malagasy woman, companion of one of the first French settlers on the island; an eighteenth-century runaway slave; a Creole "slave hunter" from the same period; a Creole woman who becomes the wife of a rich Indian merchant at the end of the nineteenth century; and a young Réunionese conscript soldier on his way to fight in the First World War. Everything appears to be orchestrated so that the author can illustrate the mixture of diverse populations brought together on the island, and also the different religious beliefs that are practiced there.

In what "field" or "fields" might one situate this multifarious work, clearly hybrid and postmodern in both its form and its content? It is aimed first of all at an audience, at a particular clientele, at a Réunionese literary field. Secondly it alludes constantly, through nods and winks to the well-informed reader, to the field of the social and political situation of contemporary Réunion, and the heavy influence of its past. Finally it attempts to impose itself in the literary field of mainland France, through a major French publishing house, in this instance Flammarion. Already in the operation of these three fields we can distinguish the workings of a hierarchical prioritization: the literary milieu is merely one aspect of the social and political field of Réunion; and both represent a marginal, exotic domain for the metropolitan French reader. At the same time this marginality, this otherness questions and undermines the parameters of the French literary milieu, and the sociopolitical assumptions of metropolitan France. One can already see the way in which a hybrid work such as this is constituted as a supplement, as a subversive and marginal appendage to a certain mainstream of historical or exotic literature, in the way that Homi Bhabha has theorized it.

Having identified three main elements in the hybrid situation of the work, it remains to establish the relation of the work to these three points of reference. The first task is to situate the novel in its Réunionese literary context. An initial observation about the linguistic characteristics of the work confirms the almost exclusive use of standard French, but which is not averse to the use of a familiar or slangy register, no doubt for the sake of realism, and occasionally resorts to phrases in regional French and Creole. So the witch doctor speaks to his client half in French, half in Creole: "N'aie crainte. Tu n'oses pas parler? . . . Le z'homme, c'est barre d'fer, femme c'est do feu la forge."[26] This is far removed from the authentically creolized dialogue in Axel Gauvin's almost exactly contemporary novel *Cravate et fils*,[27] quite apart from a hypothetical future version entirely in Creole. It is clear that Vaxelaire is not aiming at that particular audience, but rather at a metropolitan French audience not necessarily familiar with Creole.

The work does position itself even so in a Réunionese context by its broad vision of the historical development of Réunionese society from its origins to the present day, and situated in relation to the dynamics of the region: the Malagasy influence, the presence of a Hindu community, the colonial influence, both powerful and distant, etc. etc. With its almost epic range of reference, and yet never taking itself too seriously, the novel seems to want to encompass all the multifarious historical influences that make up the particular identity of Réunion. In this respect it seems to reveal a greater literary ambition than most of its contemporaries, a broader vision than is usual in Réunionese novelists: In this respect the contrast with the small-scale social dramas recounted by Axel Gauvin could not be more striking.

The third characteristic that situates the novel in a Réunionese literary context is its sense of humor, its irony, very close to the "moucatage" or banter typical of the Creole community, but without employing the local language. Vaxelaire practices the nod and wink to the reader in a very assured manner, worthy of a former journalist, not only in the fanciful inventions of his unlikely central premise, but also in the allusions to familiar events in the history of the island: the arrival on the island of the first French settlers[28] or the declaration of the abolition of slavery by Sarda Garriga in 1848;[29] the allusions to the defects of Réunionese society, such as political violence;[30] or the evocation of everyday life in Réunion, such as the particular atmosphere associated with the imminent arrival of a tropical storm. It is a discreet and quite subtle humor, but comparable even so to the coarser humor of Emmanuel Genvrin in his *Votez Ubu Colonial*, which exploits a similar sense of complicity.

It is no great step to move on to a consideration of the position of the novel in relation to the sociopolitical context of Réunion. In the first instance it describes the world of local journalism, through the part-time work of the heroine Florence. The business community is also sketched in, through the relationship between Florence and the son of the rich proprietor of a local newspaper. Her work as a primary school teacher is also brought in through the personal encouragement and private lessons she gives to one of her young pupils from an underprivileged background. All this gives a varied picture of contemporary middle-class life in the island's capital, Saint-Denis. In parallel, the story of the "woman from across the canal," unknown to her neighbor Florence, but recounted, presumably, thanks to the all-seeing monk, is a little less than convincing. The misfortunes of the woman with her unfaithful and violent husband, who becomes the driver and minder for a local politician, are reasonably convincing, but her attempts to rekindle her married relationship with the help of an unscrupulous witch doctor seem rather grotesque and sensationalized. Similar things could be said of the rather melodramatic ending, in which a child is to be sacrificed, and turns out to be the private pupil of the heroine. One wonders if this aspect of the work does not pander to the worst nightmares of the expatriate middle classes of Saint Denis, in making a villain of the witch doctor, who represents a marginalized non-Christian culture, and in reviving the myth of child sacrifice.

On the other hand the sketches of the past life of Réunion, through the stories of characters representing a range of different elements of a very mixed-race society, show a narrative and imaginative inventiveness that give a fuller historical perspective to the novel. In these "reincarnations" of the ghost of Angelo the monk at different periods in the populating of the island, the author gives free rein to his storytelling gifts, and endows his novel with a poetic and epic quality, a kind of "history of the origins" of Réunionese society. In this way he provides a kind of "founding narrative," admittedly fragmented, but broadly convincing, of the social history of the island; and in doing so, he is responding in his own fashion to the constant questioning of the islanders about their identity. Similarly, the higher sphere inhabited by the monk seems to be a deliberate mixture of the different transcendent visions associated with several of the island's religious beliefs—Christian, animist, Buddhist, Hindu—with as an extra ingredient a kind of science-fiction fantasy that allows the heroine Florence, not without some irony, to communicate with this higher plane. But as we have seen, the caricature of animist beliefs in the figure of the witch doctor suggests the limits of this religious syncretism, which in any case is not treated very seriously.

The final aspect of the situation of the novel in relation to the island's sociopolitical field is that of a certain republican utopianism, which is shown by the further evocation of the myth of an egalitarian and mixed-race society, already described in *Les Mutins de la* Liberté, and which symbolizes the hope of creating in Réunion a more durable example of the same kind of ideal community. This utopian dream is confirmed by the proposition on the very last page that the next incarnation of the monk Angelo, the philosopher and founder of Libertalia, would be the child Florence is carrying, the fruit of a casual sexual relationship with her colleague, a wayward journalist, which rounds off the central love story of the heroine. Here too the author's irony comes into play, and we are not expected to believe too strongly in this idealized perspective.

Drawing as it does on the imaginative sensibility of the island and on its historical background, on its beliefs and superstitions, how does this novel fit into the highly competitive literary field of metropolitan France? Rather than attempt an analysis of the way the novel was received, it would seem more appropriate to make some general comments. *Bleu nuit*, coming as it does after the six other historical novels of Daniel Vaxelaire, is clearly situated in the first instance in that particular genre, which is probably regarded as a minor one amongst literary critics, and one which appeals to a broad, middle-of-the-road audience. While it illustrates some of the typical features of the genre—a well-crafted plot, larger-than-life characters, etc., the novel blows apart the conventional norms of the previous works. No linear narrative, a proliferation of subplots, a ghostly narrator figure, an ironic relationship with the reader, all these features make the work a kind of postmodern version of the genre. The same is true of the other minor genres where one might consider placing it: the regional novel, travel writing, fantastic literature, the last two being clearly signaled by the "Gulliver" series in which the publisher Flammarion has decided to place it. *Bleu nuit* represents an attempt to go beyond these categories, by exposing through a process of proliferation and juxtaposition some of the tricks of this kind of fiction, while maintaining a relationship of ironic complicity with the reader.

At the same time the novel does appeal to a certain exoticism, evoking as it does places, situations, behavior somewhat different from those familiar to a well-informed metropolitan French reader. It is set in a milieu that is rather different from mainland France, even if it has almost always been under French jurisdiction. The play of "différance," in the Derridean sense, is evident in the disparate and disjointed subject matter, which allows us to situate it in the context of the hybrid, post-colonial works we are concerned with. The different historical narratives juxtaposed in the novel all take place outside the mainstream of French history as it is usually taught, which is evident if only in the obvious example of the narrator, an eighteenth-century Neapolitan monk who becomes a utopian pirate. It is indeed an attempt to go beyond these conventionally minor genres, so as to situate the novel and its author in a new perspective, that of a hybrid, postmodern literature, with cross-cultural resonances.

Conclusion

The purpose of this analysis was to show the usefulness of the new theories and approaches labelled "post-colonial" in relation to the cultural production of Réunion Island. It is clear that they allow us to situate this production in relation to a broader phenomenon of hybridity, which encompasses such well-known figures as Salman Rushdie, Edward Said or Frantz Fanon. This tendency, which one can also link with that of postmodernism, with its questioning of the "grand narratives" that constitute national cultures, is also one that is typical of the "globalization" of cultural exchanges at the level of the whole planet. It presents a considerable methodological challenge, however, to the literary and cultural critic: how does one deal with the multiplicity of cultural references which are brought into play? Some kind of response is offered by an adaptation of the cultural analysis of Pierre Bourdieu to deal with a situation that is more complex than that of a single national culture. The example of Vaxelaire's novel *Bleu nuit* provides a convenient way of testing this approach by applying it to a typical example of Francophone cultural production from the island of Réunion, usually itself regarded as a marginal and peripheral zone in relation to mainstream Francophone culture. A lot remains to be done, however, in further refining and developing this approach—itself a hybrid one—in relation to other areas of cultural production.

Notes

1. Bill Ashcroft, Gareth Griffiths and Helen Tiffin, eds., *The Post-colonial Studies Reader* (London: Routledge, 1994) "General Introduction," 2.

2. Such as the *Chansons madécasses*, for instance.

3. Cf. Edward W. Said, *Culture and Imperialism* (London: Chatto and Windus, 1993) "Challenging Orthodoxy and Authority," 367–408, in particular 386–90.

4. Edward W. Said, *Orientalism* (London: Routledge, 1978).

5. See Homi K. Bhabha, *The Location of Culture* (London: Routledge, 1995) 166–9, 223–9.

6. See Homi K. Bhabha (1995), "The Other Question," 75–84.

7. See Homi K. Bhabha (1995), "The Post-Colonial and the Post-Modern," 171–97; and Ashcroft, Griffiths and Tiffin (1994), "Postmodernism and post-colonialism," 117–47.

8. The notion of "métissage" is difficult to translate into English: it literally means "racial mixture" but is often used in a figurative sense, unlike its English equivalent.

9. See, for instance, Axel Gauvin, *Faims d'enfance* (Paris: Seuil, 1987), and Axel Gauvin, *Bayalina* (Saint-Denis: Grand Océan, 1995).

10. Emmanuel Genvrin, *Lepervenche* (Saint-Denis: Théâtre Vollard/Grand Océan, 1996), performed by the Théâtre Vollard in Vitry-sur-Seine as part of the festival *Paris Quartier d'été* in 1997.

11. Emmanuel Genvrin, *Sega Tremblad*, performed by the Théâtre Vollard at the Divan du Monde, Paris, September 2000.

12. Emmanuel Genvrin, *Votez Ubu Colonial* (Saint-Denis: Théâtre Vollard/Grand Océan, 1994).

13. In an essay "Théâtre et métissage" included as a post-face in Philippe Pelen, *Ma* (Saint-Denis: Grand Océan, 1996).

14. See CD: Ziskakan, *Ziskakan* (Paris: Island/Mango, CD 514 974–2, 1993).

15. See CD: Baster, *Mon Royom* (Réunion: Oasis/ Sonodisc, CD 33473, 1995).

16. As in Ziskakan, *Soley* glasé (Paris: Sankara/Mercury, CD 532 410–2,1996).

17. Pierre Bourdieu, *Les Règles de l'Art* (Paris: Seuil. 1992); English translation available: *The Rules of Art*, trans. Susan Emanuel (Cambridge: Polity Press, 1999).

18. This provides a brief summary of the main terms of Bourdieu's analysis, which he applies to French literature and culture of the late nineteenth century. For further discussion of their implications, see Bourdieu (1992), "Questions de Méthode," 249–53, and "Le point de vue de l'auteur," 321–26.

19. Daniel Vaxelaire, *Bleu nuit ou Les sept vies du moine* (Paris: Flammarion, 1996).

20. Daniel Vaxelaire, *Chasseur de noirs* (Paris: Lieu Commun, 1982). Republished (Paris: Gallimard, Folio, 1991).

21. Daniel Vaxelaire, *L'Affranchi* (Paris: Lieu Commun, 1984); republished (Paris: Phébus, 1996).

22. Daniel Vaxelaire, *Les Chasseurs d'épices* (Paris: J-C Lattès, 1990).

23. Daniel Vaxelaire, *Grand Port* (Paris: Phébus, 1992).

24. Daniel Vaxelaire, *Cap Malheureux* (Paris: Phébus, 1993).

25. Daniel Vaxelaire, *Les Mutins de la* Liberté (Paris: Phébus, 1995).

26. Vaxelaire, *L'Affranchi*, 48.

27. Axel Gauvin, *Cravate et fils* (Paris: Seuil, 1996).

28. Vaxelaire, *L'Affranchi*, 122.

29. Vaxelaire, *L'Affranchi*, 363

30. Vaxelaire, *L'Affranchi*, 466–67.

27

The Poetics of Mixed
Marriage in Le Clézio's *La Quarantaine*

Robert Alvin Miller

JEAN-MARIE GUSTAVE LE CLÉZIO PUBLISHED his first novel in 1963 and is today, after publishing more than thirty books, enigmatic and difficult to place in any one geographic framework. Although some may view his fiction, set in as widely varied places as the Indian Ocean, Africa, Switzerland, Palestine and North America, either as a new exoticism or a late-twentieth-century version of travel literature, the dominant narrative voice of Le Clézio's fiction seems to imply a viewpoint that interiorizes the perspective of a cosmopolitan or global other. This may occur through varying narrative processes having as a common goal the construction of this "altered" point of view, which makes it difficult to determine whether Le Clézio should be seen as a French, French Francophone or Francophone French author, or whether these labels are themselves inadequate to the new worlds that arise out of Le Clézio's fiction. One such narrative process is narration attributed to the other: Laïla telling her own story as an errant African woman in *Poisson d'or*. Another is the juxtaposition of two narrative voices that implicitly question and rephrase each other's rhetoric in relation to the oppression and destruction of the other they both claim to love: this is true of John of Nantucket and Captain Scammon in the novella *Pawana*.

La Quarantaine is one of the most difficult and fascinating cases of this cosmopolitan enigma. A small group of Europeans and a larger group of people of East Indian origin were quarantined together in 1891 by the British-Mauritian authorities on a small island near Mauritius.[1] One of the Europeans (all passengers of the *Ava*, a ship on which one passenger and a crew member had contracted smallpox), named Léon Archambau, falls in love with an Indian woman he calls Suryavati. His brother Jacques still hopes to be accepted by the Mauritian elite from whom the Archambaus are descended and so warns his brother the marriage will not be accepted. When the quarantine is lifted, Léon and Suryavati disappear together, never to be heard from again. The story is told by Jacques's grandson Léon Archambau, who recognizes the incompleteness of his own consciousness on account of the family's fateful separation in 1891. The result is a complex series of imbricated invented narratives: an imagined Léon of the 1980s imagining a Léon of the 1890s and then inventing (or allowing the earlier Léon to invent) a saga of Suryavati's mother traveling as a little girl with an adopted Indian mother from India to Flat Island decades before.

The alterity of the *La Quarantaine* is thus not dependent on any one narrative process. The earlier Léon's youthful subjectivity and innocence, the expanding role of Suryavati and her mother as focalizers of their own story, the constant play of the enigma prompted by the later Léon's inability to understand his truncated self as a product of a racially broken past, all contribute to the construction of a "mixed" world view. These multiple processes may be brought together by a complementary structural and interpretive approach that considers both problems of narration and spatial poetics. The narration is located in a geographically and historically specific space while the reader's perception of that space is founded on the problematic of representing a decentered cosmopolitan world-view. As an interpretative, and structural, approach, this study will consider the implications of such a poetics in relation to *métissage*, whether as an expression of a changing global consciousness or as an ideological construct.

Mixed Marriage as a Narrative of *Métissage*

Le Clézio uses the representation of interracial and inter-ethnic sexual relationships, in *La Quarantaine* and to a lesser extent other works,[2] not only to evoke the breaking down of barriers in an imaginary "post-colonial" world, but also to generate a spatiotemporal narrative form in which barriers, frontiers and boundaries *stand for* constraining and often contradictory structures governing relationships within and between societies. Characters meet, separate, reunite and dream of reuniting in a way that is not only determined by these signifying space-time structures, but that also comments on, reflects on and even in its imagination transforms these structures, without ever ultimately being able to confirm the finality or success of such a struggle against the boundaries that it so passionately desires to subvert. It is because of this ambiguity at the subjective level of the poetic thrust of *La Quarantaine* that it is necessary to look more closely at the process of narration at work in the text: what or who is this narrative voice that leads into the labyrinth of separation inspired by the practice of the quarantine and, at the same time, withdraws from that world by suggesting it to be a purely imaginary, if not chimeric, reconstruction of a past and almost unknowable chapter of history?

However, before returning to the problem of narration, it may also be apposite to look at the far horizon and reflect on what the "mixed marriage" might lead to in terms of a referential, interpretative understanding of interracial marriage in Le Clezio's work. Beyond some kind of vague moral endorsement of mixed marriage, does Le Clézio's vision of this "practice" reflect a specific commitment of a politics of *métissage*?[3]

Taking an essentially Barthian approach, Roger Toumson offers an incisive critique of the notion of *métissage*, more as an ideology than as a concrete political agenda: "Laboratoire humain, l'Amérique a incarné depuis 1492 l'avenir d'une illusion lyrique. Les races et les peuples s'y sont métissés mais sans se mélanger: hybrides mais séparés. Les interdits s'y sont accrus, multipliés, aggravés. C'est donc bien par ce que l'utopie du mélange des sangs et de la réunion des âmes ne s'est pas réalisée que le métissage demeure une 'valeur-refuge' d'avenir, un mythe d'actualité."[4]

Le Clézio's *La Quarantaine* does, in fact, seem to contribute to the construction of the *métissage* myth as a "valeur-refuge" of a world that mixed without mixing up. However, by taking what Paul Ricoeur has seen as the long route through the semantics of language,[5] in this case, through the narrative and semiotic structure of the text, it may be shown that Le Clézio's vision of mixed marriage is both the lyrical construction of a utopian rhetoric and the expression of a haunting, ambiguous doubt, according to which the mixed marriage, formed as a union of marginalized individuals, leads strangely back to a new, lost generation still dreaming more of past unity than anything clearly pointing toward the future.

To speak of narration in *La Quarantaine*, one has to think about who the narrator is and where he comes from. Léon Archambau makes only a few passing references to his own marriage and to the medical profession in which he works at the time he tells the story (present of narration). The reason for this is that the narrative is largely based on the story of his ancestors, and especially ancestors about whom he has very little information: Their ethnic identity, language and race are among the few bits of knowledge on which Léon will base his narrative.

The first of Léon Archambau's paternal line was the Patriarch, Alexandre Archambau, who got rich in the sugar industry and was a member of the Mauritian elite. He is the uncle of Léon's grandfather Jacques. The Patriarch's half-brother, Antoine, marries Amalia, the "Eurasian," "as she was called in our family," says Léon.[6] Of the two sons of the marriage, which was already a source of conflict with the Patriarch, the older Jacques moves in the direction of fanonian *lactification* by marrying a white Réunionaise, Suzanne. Jacques and Suzanne are the grandparents of Léon. But Jacques's younger brother was also named Léon Archambau, and apparently this Léon (referred to below as Léon I) married an Indian woman during a period of quarantine on Flat Island in 1891. After Jacques's warning that such a "misguided alliance" would be rejected on their return to Mauritius, Léon I and his spouse disappear forever at the end of the quarantine period.[7] Léon II's narrative is a largely imaginative reconstruction of this period of quarantine, during which the narrative voice passes from Léon II to Léon I. It thus appears to be Léon I who invents the name Suryavati (the Indian spouse): "En revenant vers le Diamant, à la fin de l'après-midi, j'ai vu pour la première fois celle que j'ai appelée ensuite Suryavati, force du soleil. Est-ce vraiment son nom? Ou est-ce le nom que je lui ai trouvé, à cause de la reine du Cachemire, à qui fut racontée l'histoire de Urvashi et Pururavas, dans le livre de Somadeva, traduit par Trelawney, que je lisais à Londres, l'été qui a précédé notre départ?"[8] On the other hand, it is difficult to imagine that Jacques and Suzanne could have transmitted to their grandson Léon II so much detail about the quarantine, and especially Leon I's doubts, which make even the origin of the name Suryavati uncertain. If Léon I is the true narrator (and not more of a focalizer promoted to the status of narrator by Léon II, who could then be seen as the fictional and fiction-building source of the narrative voice) he seems to tell his story in a strangely distanced manner, as if he himself is remembering an encounter from the distant past, and yet the book ultimately gives no clear picture of what Léon's fate was after the 1891 quarantine.

The narrative work of the two Léons thus seems to be mixed up in one story-telling act: Léon I and Léon II become, in a sense, one complex voice, even though they represent two different moments of historical existence. In his prologue-like first part of the narrative, Léon II says: "Parfois il me semble que c'est moi qui ai vécu cela. Ou bien que je suis l'*autre* Léon, celui qui a disparu pour toujours, et que Jacques m'a tout raconté quand j'étais enfant."[9]

The relationship between Léon I and Léon II puts in place an initial problem of *métissage* that could be formulated as follows: since Léon II is a descendant of the "white" branch of the Archambaus, of Jacques and Suzanne, he will attempt, by assuming the voice of his great-uncle and namesake, to reconstitute the mixed marriage that divided the family at the moment of its departure from Flat Island. But he also recognizes that a mixed marriage had already determined the mythic bifurcation of the fraternal couple Jacques/Léon I, as if Léon I had chosen to complete the *métissage* that his brother seemed to want to sweep under the carpet. Through this bifurcation Léon II manages to conceive of an imaginary narrative reunification between himself and his great-uncle at the very moment of the separation, during the 1891 quarantine. He believes he can relive that critical moment while he dreams of re-establishing the Archambau family on new foundations: "Je reviendrai, et ce ne sera pas pour posséder la fortune des sucriers, ni la terre. Ce sera pour réunir ce qui a été séparé, les deux frères, Jacques et Léon, et à nouveau en moi, les deux ancêtres indissociables, l'Indien et le Breton, le terrien et le nomade, mes alliés vivant dans mon sang, toute la force et tout l'amour dont ils étaient capables."[10] Léon dreams of restoring an already mixed unity that has been lost. One possible answer to this dream may be found in the character of Anna, a direct descendant of the Patriarch and the last of the Archambaus living on Mauritius, whom Léon goes to see before leaving Mauritius.

To the extent that Anna is named after the former property of the Archambaus and that her father had been forced off that property by the manipulations of the Patriarch, one could interpret the character Anna as the end-product of a process of *métissage*, as the sign of the persistence, and yet at the same time the loss, of this dream of unity evoked by Léon II and just as forcefully present in the narrative work of Léon I as he describes the time of quarantine. Léon II persistently refers to Anna's "Indian face" and ends his narrative with a discussion of a manuscript left by Anna in which she speaks of a childhood friend named Sita, whose friendship with Anna had been forbidden by Anna's furious father—apparently another "true" Archambau like his father Jacques, although the text reveals very little about him. For a very brief time, Léon II conceives of the notion that Sita might be the daughter of Léon I and Suryavati. Such an unlikely and speculative connection calls for further interpretative work:

> Tout à coup, tandis que je regarde le cahier jauni que m'a donné Anna, dans l'avion qui vole au-dessus de l'ocean, je découvre cette certitude: Sita, la jeune fille indienne dont Anna était amoureuse, et qui est sortie un jour de sa vie sans retour, c'est elle, l'enfant de Surya et de Léon, conçue dans le désert de l'îlot Gabriel. La rencontre de Sita et d'Anna n'était pas le résultat du hasard. Elle était préméditée depuis leur naissance. Il est probable qu'elle ne l'ont jamais dit. Mais Sita le savait, et c'est pourquoi après s'être mariée elle ne devait plus la revoir. Anna l'a-t-elle su, l'a-t-elle deviné? Sinon pourquoi aurait-elle gardé ce cahier tout au long de sa vie, comme son souvenir le plus précieux? Pourquoi me l'aurait-elle donné? En me donnant ce cahier, elle m'apportait, à sa manière ironique et profonde, la réponse à tout ce que je suis venu demander à Maurice.[11]

Anna has been set adrift. She is comparable to the Rimbaud whom Jacques and Léon I had seen briefly, hospitalized in Aden. This parallel is emphasized by the detail that both Rimbaud and Anna are associated with the practice of poisoning dogs. For the Patriarch, Anna's race and culture constituted an impossible contradiction. Anna was perhaps not the only one to be left in this state, but the others had managed to leave Mauritius and live out their contradictions in a more vague and dispersed world, a world characterized by the fin-de-siècle consciousness of Léon II. Anna is, as her name suggests, attached not only to the insular space of her "fatherland," but also to the memory of her race-without-race, that is, the last of the Archambaus of Mauritius, without being exactly a pure Archambau. She needed Sita in order to know the other of *métissage* who exists only in unity. Here the two Léons' dreams of unity correspond precisely (though this is not necessarily the implied author's last word on the subject) with Toumson's analysis of the ideology of *métissage*: "La base d'appui de l'idéologie du *métissage* demeure un concept du sujet par opposition du *Même* et de l'*Autre*. *Se dire Métis*, c'est se vouloir être un *Autre* du *Même* sans cesser d'être un *Même* de l'*Autre*, c'est vouloir fondre l'*Autre* en soi sans cesser d'être soi. *L'idéologie du métissage* implique une négation de l'altérité."[12]

In *La Quarantaine*, the issue of alterity continues stubbornly to reassert itself. From the point of view of what is left of the Archambaus long after the disappearance of Léon I and Suryavati, the other has to be disposed of immediately it is perceived or even conceived: For the Archambaus the mixed is always the beginning of a process of exclusion, contradiction and disintegration. Thus, the gaze of the Archambaus is always an ironic response: the lightning-quick recognition of a contradiction about to disappear. Léon I is himself a dream of *métissage* in the mind of the one who prolongs in the present this gaze of the "pure race" (something that proves in the end to be more illusory than the dream of *métissage* itself), which momentarily finds in the other its own non-sense. For example, Suryavati had come to Gabriel Island to treat Suzanne, who was suffering from smallpox, but shortly before the passengers of the *Ava* are rescued from the quarantine, Jacques reminds his brother that the family on Mauritius will not be able accept Suryavati. At that moment, Léon I reflects: "Jacques se méprend sur mon silence. Il m'entoure de son bras, dans un geste faussement protecteur. Est-ce qu'il a oublié que Surya a sauvé sa femme?"[13] On the one hand, this question reflects the critical point of view of someone who, having conceived of his existence as being elsewhere, comes to realize his irrevocable separation not only from his brother Jacques, but also from his whole lineage. On the other hand, the question also reflects the gaze of Jacques's legitimate descendant (Léon II, Jacques's grandson, who "reproduces" him symbolically by becoming a doctor) trying to understand, from within the irony of this question, the existential and moral absence that has determined his own existence.

It might be admitted that the mixed marriage of Léon I and Suryavati is at the center of the process of questioning and self-questioning undertaken by Léon II. But the dream of Flat Island could also be read as a critique of the notion that an alliance pure and simple between two "peoples" can happen in a world of collisions and ruptures that have being going on for a long time. Surya's father, about whom little is said—only that he worked in the sugar fields on Mauritius,[14] and that he "was a Christian from Ville-Noire"[15]—was probably of Indian origin, while his mother Ananta had been the daughter of English parents killed at Campore in the 1857 Sepoy Revolt. Surya's "grandmother" had pulled the five-year-old Ananta from the arms of her dead nurse and brought her up as her daughter, bringing her to Mauritius in search of a new existence. Ananta constantly dreams of a mythical England she has never seen, and is at the same time the mysterious, silent leader of the doubly if not triply isolated pariahs of the Indian community of Flat Island. This blond woman "does not want to meet any white people," her daughter says. The *métissage* of Léon I and Surya becomes ultimately elusive in the sense that the cultural identities to be brought together either do not really exist or at best disintegrate as quickly as Léon II tries to sew them together.

The Spatial Poetics of *Métissage*

Therefore, the unity of association that happened on Flat Island in 1891 and that divided once and for all both the lineage and the consciousness of the Archambaus was not simply a racial and cultural alliance motivated by love, although that love may well have been as Léon II seems to sincerely believe. What took place was rather an imaginary, poetic, inter- and intra-textual reconstruction, on the basis of the stories and recited poetry of the white grandmother Suzanne, of a space rendered problematic by the question of *métissage*. This space thus has a number of specific poetic characteristics.

The first of these characteristics is that the notion of the quarantine generates an unusual variant of the Manichaean division of mother-country and colony.[16] As colonized space, Flat Island reproduces the divisions of class and race that reign on Mauritius, while adding new elements. The "Whites," the "grands mounes," are temporarily exposed to the same threat of contagion as the Indians on the other side of the island. Thus they too are excluded from the center: this is an obsessive interdiction for all the passengers of the *Ava*, and especially for Jacques who, while claiming to have rejected the Patriarch who ruined his parents, desperately desires to take back his place in the hierarchy of his homeland.

The fear of contagion becomes a macro-structural metaphor for the fear felt by the White Man of losing his place in his homeland because of relations with, or even proximity to, the other. Following Toumson's remarks discussed above, it could be suggested that contagious sickness and *métissage* have this underlying question in common. On the one hand, the fear of "contamination" puts the transgressor on the other side of the social fence in relation to those around him or her. On the other hand, illness/mixing up forces individuals to question their own identity as a part of something inherently complete and self-contained. To succumb to illness, for someone like Suzanne, implies a disloyal and suspicious surrender not so much to the other's culture—none of the Europeans other than Léon I makes any real effort to have connections with the Indians—but rather to the state of otherness and exclusion that the quarantine poses as a possibility and an existential question: Could it be that you yourself are an other? The strange lucidity that Léon I notices in the eyes of the smallpox victims and Sarah Metcalfe's antisocial insanity after John's death add to the urgency of this question by separating out selected individuals from the racial group to be alone and beyond the understanding and communication of their compatriots.

The second element of the novel's spatial poetics is the symbolic boundary put in place to separate the part of the island occupied by the immigrants from the part where the Europeans are quartered. Already intuitively sensed by the passengers of the *Ava* ("Les bâtisses de La Quarantaine paraissaient des forts, construits pour résister aux attaques des Indiens"[17]), this boundary is formally instituted as a sanitary measure in a document signed by Sirdar Shaik Hussein and his lieutenant, on the one hand, and by Véran, Bartoli and Jacques, on the other hand: "une frontière est instituée dans l'île entre la partie est et la partie ouest, afin de limiter le mouvement de ses habitants et le risque de diffusion des épidémies."[18] Léon concludes: "Ainsi, l'île est coupée en deux par une ligne imaginaire."[19] But this severing is interpreted in several different ways by different characters. The botanist John Metcalfe, for example, had nothing to do with the declaration and ignores the boundary in his search for the wild indigo-plant: "le spécimen qui manque à la chaîne, et qui unira Plate à Maurice et à Madagascar et au-delà, au continent austral."[20] Metcalfe's delirious quest, foreshadowing his premature death from smallpox, is emphasized in the text by interspersed passages taken from his journal, where vegetal cosmic space fills the world at the expense of all the racial and social divisions that otherwise determine the disposition of the island's occupants.

For Jacques, the fact of having signed the declaration, on the surface a simple act of prudence on the part of a conscientious physician, becomes in his brother's eyes the beginning of a long desired return to the Archambau fold as he gives in to Véran's interpretation of the world: "Julius Véran a tout perverti. Il s'est installé au milieu de nous, lui qui n'est rien, il a réussi à nous rendre semblables à lui-même."[21] Since this judgment hardly applies to the Metcalfes, nor to Suzanne, who continues to dream of a heroic role resembling the life of Florence Nightingale, nor to Léon I himself, who was never a party to the edict, this judgment can only really apply to Jacques—the only one who dreams of finding again his hereditary place in a society of racial purity.

It is through the absurdity of a quarantine separating two peoples suffering from the same epidemic that Léon presents the situational irony of his brother's dreams of purity: "En voulant se préserver du contact avec les Indiens pour quitter plus vite La Quarantaine, les passagers de l'*Ava* se sont enfermés dans leur propre prison."[22] It is here that Léon II's voice begins to be heard in the background, because the Quarantine as an illusory defense against illness (the cold goddess, the foreign woman) serves as an analogy for the preservation of a race. That is to say that Léon II is the ultimate captive of a prison built by his ancestors, a prison never "sheltered" from a process of *métissage* that is always already too deeply rooted to be torn out without self-destruction.

But for Sirdar Hussein, the edict is a game, perhaps a subversive one in relation to whites like Véran and Jacques. In his dealings with them he seems passive, yet presents them without their knowledge to the Indians as the true source of contagion. When Léon I asks Surya if Shaik Hussein has forbidden the immigrants contact with the others, she answers: "Non, il n'a rien interdit. Il dit seulement que nous ne devons pas approcher des grands mounes, parce que chez vous il y a des hommes qui sont morts de la maladie."[23] This answer suggests for Léon I a troubling reflection: "La frontière instituée par Véran et par Bartoli n'existe pas? N'est-ce pas Shaik Hussein qui l'a voulu?"[24] The poetic function of the interracial relationship of Léon I and Suryavati is thus also revealed to be more subversive than reconciliatory, a way of reminding the reader of the cold gaze of the racial other constructed in the very process of establishing cultural communities.

Thus the problem of the imaginary boundary becomes for both Léon I and Léon II, and finally for the novel's readers, a barrier and a limit, the legitimacy, reality and truth of which depend on the abstract authority of someone's signature. Who is it in fact who seeks to isolate us from each other? Do our isolation and captivity come from others or from ourselves, from their distrust or from our own imagined fears? Véran must have conceived of the boundary in order to prevent Suryavati from coming to the beach, Léon I believes.[25] The latter's decision to transgress the limits of the quarantine constitutes both a refusal of the authority of the edict as an act and a passionate personal interpretation of its meaning. The same imaginary line that claims to imprison him is also the opening of his desire, a fact which is marked in the narrative by the reorganization of the characters' movements. If Surya can no longer come to fish near the beach during the day, Léon will have to go during the night to discover in secret that from which the others are hiding. He discovers not only the hidden life of Suryavati herself, but also a set of cultural practices connected with her. These discoveries open the imagining narrative work to movements in space and time that will be completed in his own creative understanding— an understanding that has to be negotiated between Surya, her mother Ananta and himself.[26] These spatial poetics may be further interpreted in reference to the small, rocky Gabriel Island, separated from Flat Island by a narrow channel. Gabriel is the quarantine of the quarantine in that it accommodates the contagious and the dying from both sides of Flat Island and unites them in a sort of improvised community on the margins of a larger but severed "society" incapable by itself of forming any kind of community.

It is in fact Gabriel, in the narrative's symbolic language, that brings about the union of Léon I and Suryavati. The first time Léon sees Surya, she is walking upright in the sea between Flat and Gabriel: "Elle avançait le long du rivage, un peu penchée en avant, comme si elle cherchait quelque chose, et de là où j'étais, sur l'embarcadère, en face de l'île Gabriel, j'avais l'impression qu'elle marchait sur l'eau. . . . J'ai compris qu'elle marchait sur l'arc des récifs qui unit Plate à Gabriel à marée basse."[27]

Léon and Surya's relationship functions in reference to the elements brought together on Gabriel—sun, water, stone and fire (the fire of the burnt bodies and the circulation of the image of fire in the plumage of the pailles-en-queue birds) in order to present itself, in the mind of the two Léons, as a mythic act of re-creation, the beginning-again of the world, in a center where the forbidden, artificially drawn, but no less real racial boundary of Flat Island (by extension Mauritius and the modern world) is short-circuited by its own implied end: death, madness and the possibility of a return to life. These elements are reproduced elsewhere in the quarantined space, for example in the funeral pyres on the beach at the Palissades, in the volcano, in the basalt that is both a refuge for the couple and an old cemetery, and in the final scene on Flat Island, after the departure of the Europeans. Even in the description of this moment, Léon continues to take Gabriel as a point of reference: "Quand je me couche l'oreille contre le sol, j'entends toujours la vibration. Je la connais bien, c'est celle que j'ai perçue chaque nuit, sur Gabriel. Quelque chose de vivant, d'éternel, tout près de la surface du monde, juste au bord de la lèvre du volcan, sur la frange de la mer."[28] This symbolic value of Gabriel (biblically the angel bearing good news) suggests two other observations. Firstly, since Suryvati never approaches the buildings of the Quarantine that house the Europeans, but comes freely to Gabriel, risking her own life, not only to join her husband, but also to come to the aid of Suzanne, the mixed marriage is no longer, in the context of Gabriel, a transgression of the patriarchal law that had pretended, or desired, to govern the destiny of the Archambau family, but rather the beginning of a separate existence at the expense of any sense of completeness or even identity the descendants of the Archambaus, like Anna and Léon II, might imagine. Secondly, this context suggests a double meaning in a troubling statement of Léon I: "[Véran] soupçonne Jacques de vouloir cacher quelque chose de plus sérieux, pour épargner à sa femme le voyage à l'îlot Gabriel."[29] Given the significance of Gabriel, Jacques's concern was not only to spare his wife the more than probable death implied by such a journey, but also to "spare" her (in a sense perhaps less edifying for him) the experience of this space of new creation where racial purity loses its meaning. Suzanne, who pictured herself as a new Florence Nightingale to the Indians, will survive with the help of an Indian nurse (Surya) whose mother was culturally Indian, a pariah, and racially an Englishwoman dreaming of an impossible return to an England no less mythical (for her and her daughter) than the Gabriel fixed in the mind of both Léon I and Léon II.

The quarantine can, in fact, be interpreted as a temporal as well as spatial boundary. In this sense, Léon II's desire to know the "passé métissé" of his great-uncle parallels the further imaginary journey in India of Giribala, Ananta's adoptive mother, down the river to the sea and on to the Flat Island of a previous quarantine. The same is suggestively present in the imagined/imagining characters' dream-quests, but never available to them beyond the boundaries of those dreams. The passages imagining Giribala's journey, because of the indentation that distinguishes them from the Flat Island narrative of Léon I, cannot in fact be definitively attributed to either of the two Léons: the narrator who says "C'est comme si j'avais vécu cela, comme si je l'avais rêvé hier,"[30] could be one or the other (or even both). This symbolic organization and the general rhetoric of the text, mediated by a narration that in turn depends on the unifications and ruptures associated with mixed marriages, also represents a set of referential geopolitical problems: transmigration, the violence of the colonialist world, the suffering and exploitation of the sugar plantations. *La Quarantine* is a love story, but also a dream of world culture and *métissage*. Why does Léon I say, when the other passengers of the *Ava* are impatiently waiting for their liberation from the quarantine: "Et moi, je suis comme l'homme d'Aden, que j'ai vu couché dans son lit, le regard durci par la souffrance. Je n'ai rien que les souvenirs et les rêves. Je sais que je ne peux rien attendre en dehors de cette île."[31] The mention of Rimbaud again suggests (even if the term "homme d'Aden" implies the consciousness of Léon I, who apparently did not know the identity of the patient he and Jacques visited in Aden) a joining of the two narrative voices. It is Léon II who reports the bar scene at the beginning of the novel, who retraces the last days of Rimbaud in Paris and who sees a reflection of the poet in Anna, who poisons stray dogs in the market of Mahébourg. Thus the statement "I have nothing but memories and dreams" describes a transhistoric state characterized by a sense of dispossession that can be compensated only by an imaginary or poetic process of reconstruction. It is between these two poetic forms (that of the colonialist wanderer Rimbaud and that of Léon I defying his racial quarantine) that the ambiguous value, in Le Clézio's poetic universe, of both mixed marriage and *métissage* would have to be situated: on the one hand, the man of Aden and Anna poisoning dogs; on the other hand, Léon and Suryavati coupled on a bed of basalt.

Conclusions

An exploration of this value will have consequences for any understanding of Le Clézio's work in general. Is Le Clezio a French author continuing, as Bruno Thibault has suggested, a parodic deconstruction of the exoticist novel of the colonial period, with perhaps a discrete attempt to preserve something of the pleasure that genre sought to procure? Thibault connects Le Clézio with authors like the Alain Robbe-Grillet of the "African novel" in *La Jalousie* and Michel Tournier's rereading of the Robinson Crusoe story in *Vendredi ou les limbes du Pacifique*.[32] Yet the reader intuitively senses something other than parody (though some kind of parody there must be) in Le Clézio's vision of *métissage*. Bénédicte Mauguière, in a recent comparison of Tournier's *Vendredi* and Le Clézio's *Le Chercheur d'or*,[33] sees a more feminist, even feminine openness to the other in Le Clézio's image of the union-communion of Alexis and Ouma. Could it be that Le Clézio marks the beginning, because of his own cosmopolitan experience, of a transition from the new novel to a more open Francophone novel that shows a community of consciousness more directly connected with recent African, Caribbean or Pacific novelists, for example? Should French novelists be called Francophone simply because they write in French, or should the term Francophone draw together voices of a heightened awareness of both the significance and the deceptiveness of a "post-colonial" world view? The ideology of *métissage* is always present and the dream of the post-colonial can be self-deceiving for descendants of colonized and colonizer alike. It is necessary for the reader to be at least as guarded as Le Clézio's characters, who leave "for the other end of the world" still carrying their doubts with them.

Notes

1. Mauritius was occupied by the British in 1810 and was officially under British administration from 1814 to 1968.

2. There are other examples of interracial relationships in Le Clezio's novels, such as those of Alexis and Ouma in *Le Chercheur d'or* and Laïla's many involvements in *Poisson d'or*.

3. Chris Bongie makes the point that Édouard Glissant gradually substituted the term *créolisation* for *métissage* in his theoretical work because of criticism of the latter term for its presupposition of originally separate racial identities. However, Bongie also points out that the notion of *métissage* is still present in the definition of *créolisation* as "*métissage* without limits." *Islands and Exiles: The Creole Identities of Post/colonial Literature* (Stanford, Calif.: Stanford University Press, 1998), 67.

4. Roger Toumson, *Mythologie du métissage* (Paris: Presses Universitaires de France, 1998), 24–25.

5. See Paul Ricoeur, *The Conflict of Interpretations: Essays in Hermeneutics*, ed. Don Ihde (Evanston: Northwestern University Press, 1974), 11.

6. J. M. G. Le Clézio, *La Quarantaine* (Paris: Gallimard, 1995), 17.

7. Thompson stresses the importance of this disappearance as a determining absence within the succeeding generations of the Archambau family: "He will disappear forever from their lives, immobilized as a composent of their past." William Thompson, "Voyage and Immobility in J. M. G. Le Clézio's *Désert* and *La Quarantaine*," *World Literature Today* 71, no. 4 (1997): 715.

8. Le Clézio, *La Quarantaine*, 75.

9. Le Clézio, *La Quarantaine*, 20.

10. Le Clézio, *La Quarantaine*, 457.

11. Le Clézio, *La Quarantaine*, 459–60.

12. Toumson, *Mythologie*, 260.

13. Le Clézio, *La Quarantaine*, 354.

14. Le Clézio, *La Quarantaine*, 115.

15. Le Clézio, *La Quarantaine*, 155.

16. "[T]he colonial project and its anticolonial double were founded upon certain legitimizing narratives—most notably, perhaps, authoritative narratives about progress that were indissociable from categorical and categorizing assertions of (racial, ethnic, national) identity; but these narratives were themselves subject to a rewriting made possible by the specifically hybrid conditions that the colonial enterprise inevitably promoted and that were always-already in the process of eroding its Manichean world view." Bongie, *Islands and Exiles*, 13–14.

17. Le Clézio, *La Quarantaine*, 67. (Thompson, "Voyage and Immobility," 715) also emphasizes this cultural siege mentality in the Europeans undergoing quarantine: "The primitive barracks in which the travelers spend their quarantine is not only a source of revulsion but, ironically, of comfort, . . . for it is the only location remotely resembling the Western society with which they are familiar, and the only place where survival seems possible."

18. Le Clézio, *La Quarantaine*, 120–21.

19. Le Clézio, *La Quarantaine*, 122.

20. Le Clézio, *La Quarantaine*, 133.

21. Le Clézio, *La Quarantaine*, 121.

22. Le Clézio, *La Quarantaine*, 123

23. Le Clézio, *La Quarantaine*, 128.

24. Le Clézio, *La Quarantaine*, 128.

25. Le Clézio, *La Quarantaine*, 121.

26. After the couple's first meeting, Suryavati says: "Maman m'a donné sa bénédiction. Elle m'a dit que je pouvais être ta femme. Elle va aller à Vindavan maintenant" (Le Clézio, *La Quarantaine*, 278). The mixed marriage is thus presented as a pact and as the integration of Léon into Ananta's movement from Campore through Mauritius and into death.

27. Le Clézio, *La Quarantaine*, 75.

28. Le Clézio, *La Quarantaine*, 401.

29. Le Clézio, *La Quarantaine*, 147.

30. Le Clézio, *La Quarantaine*, 157.

31. Le Clézio, *La Quarantaine*, 123.

32. Bruno Thibault, "Le *Livre des fuites* de J. M. G. Le Clézio et le problème du roman exotique moderne," *The French Review* 65, no. 3 (1992): 425–26.

33. Bénédicte Maugière, "Figure du double dans *Le Chercheur d'or* de J. M. G. Le Clézio et *Vendredi* de Michel Tournier," paper given at the World Congress of the Conseil International d'Études Francophones (Lafayette: Louisiana, 28 May 1999).

28

A Vietnamese Voice in the Dark:
Three Stages in the Corpus of Linda Lê

Emily Vaughan Roberts

L INDA LÊ, ONE OF THE FEW CURRENT WRITERS to be accepted in France as both a French and a Francophone writer, fled Vietnam when she was fourteen years old, during the great exodus of 1975.[1] In a short parable published in 1995, Lê addressed the condition of the exile, using one powerful image to express the impossibility of achieving union with the homeland following departure: "Nelly Sachs disait, Un étranger porte sa patrie dans les bras comme une orpheline pour laquelle il ne cherche rien d'autre qu'un tombeau. La réconciliation est impossible, impossible le retour."[2]

In a recent work, Lê reinterprets this same image. This time the orphan represents the semi-autobiographical narrator's own suffering: "Je portais ma souffrance comme une femme porte une orpheline pour laquelle elle ne cherche rien d'autre qu'un tombeau."[3] The evolution of Lê's use of this image expresses the centrality of the symbolic or literal figure of the exile to her corpus and its connection to human suffering. The figure of the exile, and the space that the exile both creates and comes to occupy, will operate as a metaphor for Lê's bleak vision of the human condition.

The term "exile" denotes a person who is in a "state of being expelled" from his or her native land.[4] This state of banishment (*exilium*) can result in a sense of confusion concerning the location of the place of "home."[5] In terms of the diasporic peoples of the world, who are often forced to exile themselves not only from their homeland but from their culture, this can produce an "in-between class."[6] For the purposes of this chapter, the exile will be understood as a displaced person, bereft of a clear sense of belonging, possessed by a profound sense of confusion and duality, in an "in-between" position socially and culturally. In Lê's corpus, this condition is mirrored in the creation of a narrative space that the exile occupies. Both this space and the condition of the exile, encompassed in this chapter by the term "the state of the exile," are extended in significance beyond the compass of a literal consideration of the situation of the exile to act as a metaphor for the human condition.

This chapter will contend that Lê's novels largely operate in a hybrid in-between space that exists between the speaker and the interlocutor, the writer and the muse, the diegetic world and the world outside the text, and the homeland and the sanctuary. This is reminiscent of Bhabha's "third space," in which cultural difference is negotiated through the meeting and mixing of cultures during the colonial encounter.[7] It will also be related to Bakhtin's definition of the characteristics of the "dialogic" or "polyphonic" novel: "There is nothing merely thing-like, no mere matter, no object—there are only subjects. Therefore there is no word-judgment, no *word* about an object, no secondhand referential word—there is only the word as address, the word dialogically contacting another word, a word about a word addressed to a word."[8] The narrative exists somehow between the signifier and signified, but not in a way that represents fusion or the resolution of the semantic bind. This in-between space will be examined as "the state of the exile" in terms of the space that the exile occupies and the condition of the exile. The two are inextricably linked, as the exile figure ironically seeks to resolve an overwhelming sense of duality and isolation through entry into this amoral, ambivalent space.

This chapter will examine seven of her works in terms of their portrayal and expression of the position and condition of the exile. Two pivotal points in the development of her novels to date will be pinpointed. This first stage in Lê's corpus witnesses her initial foray into the "state of the exile," the signifier for the human condition. The second stage of Lê's corpus marks an increasingly confident use of an original narrative form and style. *Les Trois parques* (1997) marks the most recent turning point in Lê's corpus. The novel directly addresses the state of the French Vietnamese. It constitutes the swan song of the second stage, and the inspiration behind her two further works, which indicate an increasingly overt use of autobiographical detail. Linda Lê's last two novels mark a move toward a peaceful, hopeful future that simply was not possible in the constant purgatorial present of her previous works. In his assessment of Lê's corpus, Yeager claimed that Lê "creates her place within the French language as a means of bypassing conceptions of Frenchness 'based on linguistic and cultural purity.'"[9] Whereas Yeager identifies the establishment of Lê's narrative "homeland" relatively early on in her corpus, this chapter will argue that the "state of the exile" only truly becomes a home, in the sense of the site of the familiar and a sense of belonging, in her most recent works, with the 1999 text suggesting a possible resolution of the fraught dialogic state of the exile.

Stage One: Entering the "State of the Exile"

Linda Lê's first novel, *Un si tendre vampire*,[10] contains no reference to Vietnam, or to any Vietnamese characters, a fact that Yeager deems to signal Lê's reluctance to be associated solely with a Francophone literary tradition.[11] The novel is told in part by an omniscient third person narrator, privileging the dialogue and interior monologues of Philippe and Xavière. It begins at the moment of re-encounter between the author Philippe and the man who took the credit for his first novel, the cruel and manipulative Louis. Louis provided the lived matter that formed the substance and inspiration for Philippe's first novel; Philippe provided the craft and skill of creative composition. This past relationship of muse and writer is brought into the present. As a result of Louis's reappearance, Philippe meets Xavière, Louis's former lover, and the two engage in a dialogue of memories interspersed with flashbacks. Xavière discusses her sexual obsession with the man who left her for her abusive mother, who was stricken with nervous exhaustion and took to her bed when she was in her turn abandoned by Louis. As both Philippe and Xavière recognize, Louis brought about the circumstances of their dialogue, as well as its content.

The circularity of the text, ending as it begins, gives the impression that the narrative is constructing itself. *Un si tendre vampire* therefore acts as a sequel to Philippe's fictional first novel, providing a fictional account of its own genesis. The open-ended narrative is self-replicating and self-perpetuating, never moving closer to resolution through union with the desired object. The two protagonists are drawn into the obsessive dialogic narrative space that they have created between them, but remain isolated and alone. Their narrativized, mythologized experiences appear to have more substance than their lives as they are lived. Their relationship embodies the ambivalence of the yearning for fusion, always combined with a conflictual, competitive edge, that is the nature of human relations.

The link between dialogic relationships and the "state of the exile" is clarified further in Lê's 1988 novel, *Fuir*.[12] The Vietnamese content of the novel bears witness to Lê's familiarity with Vietnamese culture. The Vietnamese narrator flees from the North of Vietnam, as the victim of superstition and familial rejection. This stems from the failure of a tree symbolically planted at his birth to thrive. The stunted tree comes to represent the narrator's rejection and isolation, the fatuity and power of superstition, and the rigidity of Northern Vietnamese society. The narrator feels himself to be in exile before his physical departure from Vietnam: "Exilé, je l'étais déjà dans mon pays."[13] The narrator's continuing rootlessness is embodied in the image of his movement across a barren land:

> J'avais beau gratter la terre sous mes pieds, je ne trouvais pas un os à ronger. Rien à moi: ni patrie ni famille. Orphelin par un caprice du sort, exilé par lâcheté, marié par hasard, cocu comme tout le monde. J'étais un bohème qui ne comprenait rien à la poésie de l'errance. J'avais le don d'attirer des parasites, des importuns qui se collaient à moi et ne me lâchaient plus. Naguère ma tante avec son humilité de veille maîtresse. Aujourd'hui Vinh avec ses minauderies de coquette.[14]

The narrator perceives himself as an orphan, bereft of familial, social or national ties. As an exile, his roots have been severed, preventing him from establishing territorial allegiances elsewhere. Despite his continual state of isolation, however, the narrator nonetheless attracts fellow exiles from humanity throughout his life, a process that culminates in his simultaneously collaborative and conflictual dialogue with the Japanese beggar. The beggar and the narrator both vie for each other's attention, seeking the symbolism and importance of their lives and identities in the eyes of their interlocutor. Yet, as one speaks, the other is preoccupied with his full bladder; when the other begins, his listener is paying more attention to his own digestion.[15] The dialogue as duel is one indication of the universal human desire to seek self-definition in the eyes of others. Dialogue, however, does not result in true connection; their narrative is both a means of communication, and, paradoxically, an obstacle to its full achievement. Yet the potential for dialogic fusion is tantalizing and compelling. The narrator functions both as a "spectateur" and an "adversaire," an indication of the ambivalent relationship that he enjoys with the beggar.[16] Having found his double and engaged him in a dialogue, the beggar commits suicide. Through the act of killing himself, he has both ensured the attention of his dialogic other half, and freed himself from the yoke of judgment.

Lê's incorporation of the act of telling into the fabric of the narrative itself thematizes the sting of the human condition: namely, the unattainable grail of perfect union and harmony, and the brute reality of conflictual relationships that form the basis of human interaction. The dialogic protagonists attempt to resolve their duality through some sort of fusion. Ironically, in their attempt to resolve their sense of isolation through dialogue, they are seduced into an intermediary dialogic space fraught with confusion, ambivalence and ambiguity. They open up a negatively "hybrid" space that is neither one nor the other, but do not manage to make themselves "hybrid" in the positive sense of being a fusion of both one and the other. Both the characters' solitary condition and this shifting, codeless space that they occupy are embodied in the term "state of the exile." The expression of this state is developed in the next stage of Lê's corpus through a clear "move away from an emulative aesthetics of composition and style."[17]

Stage Two: Expressing the "State of the Exile"

Lê's collection of short stories, *Les Evangiles du crime*, explores a number of narrative positions and frameworks.[18] According to Jack Yeager, Linda Lê first claimed to have "raised" her "authentic voice" in this text.[19] Despite the presence of first-person narrators who lend narrative coherence and structure to each story, the narratorial position is complicated by the inclusion of a number of "faceless" voices in the shape of telephone conversations, letters and diaries that are read or interpreted by a first-person narrator. There is a sense of circularity inherent in these polyphonic stories, as the first person narrator is often drawn into acting upon or replicating what has happened to others. The stories "can be understood more as a process that never achieves a resolution."[20]

Although this work is primarily remarkable for its deft handling of complex narrative positions and forms, the use of the symbolic nickname is also significant. This device can be related to the innate symbolism of Vietnamese names. In this way, Lê weaves her Vietnamese cultural knowledge into her French narrative. These names are rooted in the present, linked to the defining characteristics of the protagonists; they are not based on the character's national or familial heritage. Firm social and territorial affiliations are replaced with descriptions, as befits a "dialogic" or "polyphonic" space. This device places the narrative within the "state of the exile," which does not encourage the growth of roots in the shape of clearly defined allegiances and loyalties.

The first dialogue recounts an obsessive romantic relationship ending in suicide during the 1950s. It is retold in a series of telephone calls between an unknown man and the first person narrator, a woman nicknamed "Douleur Muette," following a chance encounter in the street. Her calm is disrupted by the addictive flow of his words on the telephone as he offers her "une belle douleur."[21] "Douleur Muette" and her interlocutor are united by a sado-masochistic relationship. They recognize each other as complementary/conflictive halves united through the story of Reeves C. and his wife Carson: "Sur le moment, je ne savais pas encore que j'éprouverais une telle volupté à prononcer le nom de Reeves C., et qu'à travers lui, j'avais retrouvé mon jumeau, mon saboteur, ma face mutilée, mon moi déglingué, mon frère belliqueux, mon ennemi trop aimant."[22] The relationship between husband and wife in the 1950s sees the wife, Carson, absorb all her husband's forces. Reeves lives intensely, whereas Carson observes and writes, thereby assuring her reputation and posterity. The relationship between the narrator and the stranger mimics this destructive collaboration of muse and writer, the stranger acting as the "Reeves" to the narrator's "Carson." She scribbles down his words as he speaks on the phone, absorbing and reconstituting both his narrative and the lives of others. She thus becomes drawn into the narrative, integrated into it as she reconstructs it, away from her steady, uneventful life.

The second short story, entitled "Prof T.," is told through a series of interviews with acquaintances of the professor's family, the "enquêteur's" own perspective, and excerpts from the diaries of the professor and his alter ego, "Plus-dure-sera-la-chute." It forms an investigation into the Professor's death following his son's suicide and his wife's institutionalization. It transpires that the professor had two separate personalities; the sanctimonious, vindictive, bullying professor, dominating his wife and son, and "Plus-dure-sera-la-chute," who countered the professor's moral sermons with an unflinching obsession with the corporeal and the carnal. Sex, masturbation, suicide and madness figure strongly in this narrative. This is characteristic of the extremity of Lê's "state of the exile." This space is productive through its encouragement of chaos and anarchy, challenging the boundaries of acceptability, but it is also destructive for the same reason.

The dialogue between the professor and "Plus-dure-sera-la-chute" does not result in a negotiated resolution, but in mutual destruction. As a result of his investigation, the "enquêteur" comes to repeat the Professor's actions and assume his madness. Once again, a reconstructed dialogue from the past results in destructive emulation in the present, an indication of the cyclical nature of the human condition.

The primary dialogic relationship in the third short story is between mother and daughter. The manipulative mother, nicknamed "Mad Eyes" by the first person narrator, mentally abused her daughter as a child and destroys her daughter's relationships as an adult through a series of slanderous anonymous letters, denouncing Klara to her lovers. The mother's dialogic relationship with the daughter precludes satisfactory union with another person. When her mother dies, Klara assumes the role of sending the letters. Letters, which figure prominently in *Les Trois parques*, *Voix*, and *Lettre morte*, act as another form of dialogue: "The letter, like a rejoinder in a dialogue, is addressed to a specific person, and it takes into account the other's possible reactions, the other's possible reply."[23] Although the letters are addressed to Klara's lovers, they are actually between Klara and her mother. The protagonist subjugates herself and her own happiness to these letters, which assume a life of their own. This provides yet another example of the danger and power of creating a narrative. Klara denies herself a sense of belonging or stability through her continuing compulsive dialogue with the past—a predicament that often affects an exile.

The final story of the collection, "Vinh L.," bridges the distance between France and Vietnam, focusing on a literal exile. The center of this narrative is the self-recrimination of Vinh L., one of the many Vietnamese boat people who fled the Communist regime. During this voyage he killed and ate a fellow traveler in order to survive, thereby violating one of the ultimate human taboos. As a result, he finds himself isolated from the rest of humanity as if he has "dévoré le cordon ombilical qui me relie à l'humanité."[24] He is the foetus responsible for his own destruction and alienation.

Vinh identifies with first person narrator, a plagiarizing author, as he is committing a more socially acceptable form of "anthrophagie."[25] The comparison of plagiarism with cannibalism portrays the written word as a living entity. This parallel is supported by the author's acknowledgment of the inadequacy of his revised version of Vinh's original letters, which he has since destroyed: "En réécrivant la première fois, les lettres de Vinh L., j'avais voulu le manger. Je dus me résoudre à me laisser manger par lui."[26] This integration of one human body into another challenges "the confines of the body and the outer world,"[27] in keeping with the challenge mounted to corporeal boundaries by the grotesque: "The events of the grotesque sphere are always developed on the boundary dividing one body from the other, and, as it were, at their points of intersection. One body offers its death, the other its birth, but they are merged in a two-bodied image."[28] The incorporation of one body into another, the inversion of the ideal of fusion, destroys the possibility of true union with another, the unattainable ideal of the dialogic relationship. Lê's use of excess and the grotesque focuses on the intimate interface of two bodies, two voices, two protagonists. The duality of her texts mirrors the duality that is both the cross borne by the exile, and the origins of the state of the exile.

The story concludes with Vinh L. deciding to seek redemption in his homeland with his fatalistic and stoic mother: "J'ai vécu désincarné, je me réincarne."[29] Having destroyed his link with humanity, he decides to return to his origins in order to recreate his identity. Vinh abandons his fate to his forebears, who can teach him to accept his destiny without struggle,[30] silencing the multiple voices of his conscience. An existentialist acceptance of the contingencies of fate and responsibility for one's own acts, and a corresponding abandonment of the practice of endlessly negotiating the meaning of the act, leads to the resolution of his predicament and position. In this respect, the short story acts as a precursor of Lê's most recent novels.

Whereas *Les Evangiles du crime* explored the possibilities and symbolism of a largely dialogic narrative form, *Les Dits d'un idiot* pushes the boundaries of narrative style.[31] The novel's use of ellipsis, notably at the beginning and the end, suggests the continuation of the events described within the narrative beyond the confines of the book itself. This has the effect of disrupting the illusion of narrative linear progression toward an inevitable end, which could indicate a degree of narratorial control over the events described. This is mirrored in Lê's sparse use of syntax within the novel. It is stripped of the punctuation that normally divides texts into logical and manageable parts, compartmentalizing and controlling the release of information. Lê plays with language in a way that shows she does not accept its meanings or patterns as fixed and un-alterable. This fits with Yeager's interpretation of Lê's corpus as constituting a challenge to any homogeneous conception of Frenchness. The "stream of consciousness" effect that this engenders is mirrored in the narratorial voice of the text. The narrator, the disabled philosopher son of a domineering mother nicknamed "Mandragore," lacks the authority of an omniscient third person narrator, as he assumes the voices of others into his own. His mother's voice is incorporated into the flow of words, thoughts and associations. As a result of the narrator's intrinsic polyphony, the text becomes a hybrid construction, in Bhabha's sense of the term: "What we are calling a hybrid construction is an utterance that belongs . . . to a single speaker, but that actually contains mixed within it two utterances, two speech manners, two styles, two languages, two semantic and axio-logical belief systems."[32] The narrator internalizes his mother's perception of himself, readily assuming the voice of his mother: "J'ai beau jeu de la regarder de haut je ne suis que le fruit monstrueux de sa serre chaude un croisement de ratage et de l'indifférence."[33] If he is the monstrous hybrid product of her failure and indifference, she is the product of the union between life and death. The circumstances of the mother's conception and the destructiveness of her interaction with others explain the narrator's choice of nickname. Mandragore's father committed suicide; her husband died in a car crash. The mandrake, a plant with legendary medicinal qualities, can cause death if ingested in large quantities. It is associated with the hanged, supposedly growing near the site of the hanging, and, according to legend, emits a deadly scream when uprooted. It is therefore rooted in death and transgression, existing on the boundary between life and death.

When Linda Lê read an excerpt from this work at an American conference, she was questioned about the "inaccessibility of her literary world" and its excesses. "For the listeners, her voice seemed to represent the legendary scream of the mandrake pulled from the ground."[34] The barely concealed cynicism and hate of the narrator, expressed in language stripped of the controlling mechanisms of syntax, expresses the anguish of the displaced, the unbelonging. This squares with the conception of Lê's diegetic world as being that of the uprooted exile. The characters are exiled into this space of grotesque excess, flux, and endless possibilities. This is the space of the "unheimlich," of "everything that ought to have remained secret and hidden, (that) has come to light."[35]

Once again, *Les Dits d'un idiot* contains one character who is literally exiled, a woman of Vietnamese nationality. Morte-saison is locked in a dialogic relationship with a man from her homeland, referred to only as "le jumeau," but is denied the possibility of union with him. This embodies the exile's relationship with the homeland. She is also a solitary figure in the host country. She is a transgressive figure, related to the supernatural through her description as a "petit lutin saboteur," and a secret murderer of the elderly and vulnerable. Her individual transgression is in keeping with the general tenor of the book, which flouts stylistic, structural and syntactical norms. It is appropriate that Morte-saison also acts as a prototype for La Manchote, the exiled narrator of Lê's debatably most powerful novel, *Les Trois parques*. In the in-between, hybridized space of Lê's corpus, characters transcend the division between novels.

The seeds of *Les Trois parque's* genesis have been sown throughout Lê's corpus.[36] It is the first direct treatment of the position of the exiled French Vietnamese in terms of their relationship with the homeland in the texts discussed here. The three women at the center of the *Les Trois parques* are never given first names, but are given nicknames according to their characteristics. The elder daughter, L'Aînée, is also referred to as "Le Ventre," as she is heavily pregnant. The youngest daughter is referred to as Belles Gambettes, as she is physically attractive and has good legs. Their female cousin is denoted as La Manchote, as she is missing a hand. She is a grotesque figure, always dressed in ill-fitting black clothes, scratching her stump and predicting all manner of misfortunes. She has a tic of muttering "ilnestpasfou" under her breath, and repulses the two sisters.[37] All three are in the elder daughter's house near Paris, awaiting the visit of the two sisters' father from Vietnam. The father is referred to as Le Roi Lear throughout the narrative.

The author combines the first person narration of La Manchote with omniscient third-person narration using the *style indirect libre*, which allows for a privileged access to the innermost thoughts, feelings and memories of the protagonists. The tone of ironic, humorous detachment that pervades the novel undercuts the use of the first person by the narrator, effectively splitting the voice. The narrative is interspersed with parodies of the telephone questionnaires that Belles Gambettes conducts for a living. In this way, voice is layered upon voice to create a confused cacophony. The past, present and future are similarly jumbled together, one leading seamlessly to the consideration of the next. The narrative transcends the geographical distance between Vietnam and France. This chaotic yet omniscient narrative style is reflected in the use of the Vietnamese ghosts and witches, who bring the past into the present and whisper predictions of approaching disaster. This chorus, which appears to pass judgement on the exiled sisters, is foreshadowed in a reference to a Vietnamese legend in *Fuir*:

> Comme les montreurs de foire qui ne sortent jamais sans leur perroquet juché sur leur épaule, l'homme qui quitte sa patrie est condamné à porter sur son dos un lutin chargé de lui rappeler sa trahison. Vient le jour où le mauvais esprit saute à terre pour désigner du doigt le rénégat avant de disparaître en fumée. Privé du seul bien qui le rattachait à ses origines, l'exilé se laissera dépérir de remords.[38]

The polyphonic narratorial voice, which demonstrates the confused boundaries of the "state of the exile" both as a narrative space and as a way of being, is cleverly explained and linked to the supernatural as the novel reaches its climax. It transpires that La Manchote is a witch. According to the legends told by the Vietnamese grandmother, a witch's hand falls free from her body and wanders the night, looking for a soul to capture. Witches who fall in love with their human double lose their hands and their powers, and their human double loses his mind. This sheds light upon the previous revelation that La Manchote, at a very young age, made love with her twin brother, who was sent to a mental asylum soon afterwards. This explains her verbal tic of "ilnestpasfou." Other aspects of La Manchote's behavior—her refusal to eat at her cousin's wedding, her habits of scratching her stump—begin to fall into place:

> Les sorcières amoureuses étaient bannies de leurs tribus, condamnées à se mêler aux mortels, où elles vivaient en parias, se nourrissant du souvenir de leur main morte sur le coeur de leur moitié humaine. Elles comprenaient la langue des fantômes et les fourmillements de leur moignon les avertissaient des catastrophes, mais il n'était plus en leur pouvoir d'en accélérer le mouvement ni d'en détourner le cours.[39]

La Manchote has insight into people's innermost thoughts because of her supernatural powers. The significance of her control of the narrative is widened when the female characters move from constituting stereotypes of womanhood—the earth mother, the bimbo and the mad, bitter spinster—to becoming figures of tragedy and allegorical representations of the three regions of Vietnam: Tonkin, Annam and Cochinchina. This association becomes clear at the end of the novel, as the various strands of the complicated narrative come together. The following description of post-independence Vietnam elucidates the implied link between the three female characters and the geopolitical landscape of Vietnam: "Le sommeil l'avait quittée à petits pas l'année où la terre en S avait été sectionnée juste sous la veine jugulaire S, un collier de barbelés séparant la tête, rouge de fièvre communiste, du tronc gringalet, arc-bouté sur sa nostalgie des courbettes devant le dernier empereur et dédaigneux de ses jambes qui couraient au-devant de la soldatesque étrangère en bons valets de l'impérialisme."[40] Once again, Lê's trademark density of metaphors and idiosyncratic use of syntax assert their presence. The "body" of Vietnam is distorted and grotesque, the feverish head separated from the torso, with its back braced against tradition and the legs furiously pumping away. The exiles act as representatives of the homeland and as a grotesque distortion of it. L'Aînée, with her adherence to her heritage, represents Annam, the old imperial center of Vietnam. Her pregnant belly fits her for the role of "torso" to the former French colony. Belles Gambettes represents the loud, blousy South of Saigon and its sex shops, the "*modern girl*" who is pragmatic in her response to dominant systems of power. La Manchote represents the Communist "head," assuming control. Her polyphonic narratorial voice reflects Communist infiltration of the individual's private space. Le Roi Lear, in contrast, is a simple, modest figure. He is denied union with this hybrid figure, a parodical vision of the homeland pulled out of shape by exile.

The two sisters and their cousin do not enjoy a harmonious or happy relationship, and are never reunited with the representative of the homeland, Le Roi Lear. When the novel is placed within the context of Lê's other works of prose fiction, it can be seen to function both as a description of the state of the French Vietnamese exile and as an allegory of human condition. There is no possible shelter from this basic truth; there is no safe "home" for the individual. Everyone is isolated and ostracized, in the past, present and future.

At the end of the novel, in a post-scriptum, Linda Lê contextualizes the novel in terms of her own life. It was written in isolation. She originally intended to publish it under a pseudonym, which suggests the personal import of the text. Its completion was followed by "trois mois de stupeur et de confusion." A contemporary review of the novel draws parallels between the content of the novel and Lê's own life. "Le Roi Lear" never arrived in France:

> Comme n'est jamais venu le père de Linda Lê, émigrée vietnamienne à l'âge de quatorze ans et qui, juste avant de commencer Les Trois parques, avait reçu du Vietnam un télégramme. Le roi Lear, le vrai, venait d'y mourir, sans avoir pris le temps de les rejoindre un jour en France, elle, sa mère et ses trois soeurs, envoyant des centaines ou des milliers de lettres à travers l'océan, devenant la muse pudiquement remerciée dans la postface: "L'absent, dont le murmure sut dominer cette 'voix épouvantable' qu'on appelle ordinairement le silence."[41]

The incorporation of figures and experiences from Lê's own life into the narrative is further evidence of the slippage of the text into an "in-between" space, in between fixed identities, in between fact and fiction, in between cultures. The third and most recent stage of Lê's corpus has seen an increasingly overt use of autobiographical material, as a sense of the familiar and "heimlich" is incorporated more and more into "the state of the exile."

Stage Three: Accepting "The State of the Exile" as Home

Voix, written in 1998, focuses on the narrator's descent into hallucination following the death of her father.[42] A contemporary review highlights the factual basis of the account: "La folie, ici, n'est plus seulement mimée, mise en forme: elle est d'abord vécue, puis portée sur la scène de l'écriture."[43] The work begins with treatment in a mental asylum, and ends at the climactic point of Lê's illness, prior to treatment. The first person narrator has been committed because of what appears to be an acute persecution complex accompanied by delusions. The text then moves back in time to the initial stages of her illness. The narrator's illness is implicitly brought about by her remorse concerning her deceased father, and this is compounded by the fact that she burns his letters in accordance with the directions of the "Organization," her imaginary persecutors. The Organization manifests itself in a chorus of disembodied heads and voices that judge the narrator.

As the grip of mental illness tightens, the novel gradually expands into the outside world and culminates in a vast expanse of snow in the French countryside. After immersing herself in the confused turmoil of her inner world, the narrator seeks peace in complete isolation, as the final words of the novel indicate: "Je cherche en vain dans la neige la trace qu'auraient laissée les têtes coupées. Je suis seule. Je ramène les pas de mon manteau. Je m'allonge dans la neige. J'écoute siffler le vent. Je regarde le ciel bas. Une profonde paix descend en moi."[44]

The voices are silenced and syntactical order is restored in this landscape of grief, white being the color of mourning in Vietnam. As the novel effectively begins at the end, however, it is clear that this is a momentary respite for the narrator. From her tumultuous inner world, the narrator emerges into the cacophony of the asylum, finding herself to be equally isolated. The passivity and silence of the narrator is juxtaposed with the constant stream of noise and action provided by her fellow inmates. The only escape from the polyphonic world she occupies is death, which provides the possibility of full union with her father (and by extension the homeland) and atonement for her neglect.

Whereas *Voix* details the author's experience of mental illness, Lê's 1999 novel, *Lettre morte*, focuses more on the roots of this illness. The novel is a response to her father's dying letter to her, never received: "Cette lettre que je n'ai pas reçue, j'y réponds maintenant en te parlant."[45] The narrator contemplates the immediate circumstances that brought about the onset of her illness, namely, her father's death and her doomed affair with a selfish married man. She also revisits the memories of her Vietnamese childhood, always addressing herself to a silent yet sympathetic listener, Sirius.

It is made clear that guilt concerning the circumstances of her father's death—he died alone, in Vietnam, waiting for her long-promised visit—is responsible for her descent into mental illness. When the narrator attends her father's funeral in Vietnam, she feels as if she is silently accused of neglect by other mourners. Yet the funeral signals her rebirth: "Les mots de ses lettres sont comme des notes célestes qui jouent une douce mélodie. J'entends venir la vie."[46] The narrator's resolution of her relationship with the past and her father is signaled by his funeral, and her release from an unsatisfactory, guilt-ridden dialogic relationship with him conducted through letters. The ghost of the guilt of the exile is laid to rest, and the vision of the world generated by trauma fades. The exile's return to her roots heralds a new era of optimism. This renaissance of hope is reminiscent of the decision to return to the homeland undertaken by Vinh in *Les Evangiles du crime*. It appears as if the decision to accept the guilt that accompanies exile and to embrace and incorporate one's past into the present may help Lê's protagonists to reconcile themselves to "the state of the exile." In the instance of *Lettre morte*, this ability to envisage a brighter future is also attributable to the demise of the destructive dialogic relationship with "Morgue," her married lover.

Lettre morte employs an overt and acknowledged use of autobiographical material, revealing the autobiographical basis of many of Lê's stock characters in previous novels. The claustrophobic atmosphere of Lê's earlier works and the motif of madness can in large part be explained by the autobiographical narrator's childhood experiences:

> Il me semble parfois, Sirius, que, toute mon enfance, j'ai vécu enfermée dans la chambre d'un asile, avec ma mère qui me sortait de ses langeurs que pour se lamenter, assise sur le lit, les cheveux et les vêtements en désordre, l'oncle qui se terrait dans un coin, de peur que les bêtes velues échappées de l'enfer ne le dévorassent, et mon père, placide, tel un infirmier qui gardait la tête froide entre une neurasthénique et un fou furieux.[47]

The narrator's uncle is clearly delusional and is pelted by children when he leaves the house, as was the Japanese beggar in *Fuir*. He is her mother's brother, yet has a much closer relationship with her father; this was also the case of the relationship between the narrator and his brother-in-law in *Fuir*. The mother spends entire days in bed, as did Klara's mother in the third story of *Les Evangiles du Crime* and Xavière's mother in *Un si tendre vampire*. The father paints the uncle in a multi-colored coat, surrounded by flames, after the uncle has set fire to the house. This is very close to the image of the father clothed in a coat of flames in *Voix*. The effect of the reoccurrence of these characters across the corpus is to lend the characters a symbolic value and a significance that transcends the confines of the individual text. One of the effects of the overt use of autobiographical material in the novel is the establishment of a "heimlich," or familiar, space within the state of the exile. This integration of the scarcely fictionalized into the narrative space allows the author/narrator to establish a foundation for a stable position within the "state of the exile."

The novel ends on a positive note, as the narrator appears to embrace the outside world beyond the confines of her mental illness and pain: "Adieu, Morgue, gué de la mort, amer amour, amour tu, amertume, tumeur de l'amour. . . . Le jour se lève, Sirius. Ouvre donc cette fenêtre. Laisse pénétrer la fraîcheur de l'aube."[48] The pre-elliptical words witness Lê's ludic, irreverential approach to the French language. They are associated with her mental breakdown and disastrous love affair. After the ellipsis, however, the style becomes more syntactically conformant. It is stripped of linguistic flourishes and brought back down to basics. The simplicity of the style is combined with a direct address of Sirius, who represents hope for the future. But this is a dialogue emptied of guilt and confusion, conducted between a defined "I" and "you." The flux, ambiguity and confusion that once characterized the dialogic relationship reached its climax in the accounts of the autobiographical narrator's mental illness, and has been replaced with a sense of certainty, rootedness and purpose that accompanies the establishment of a "heimlich" space within the state of the exile.

Conclusion

Lê's quest for an authentic literary voice has led to an experimentation with form and style, and a recent movement toward a more overtly autobiographical content, blurring the boundaries between fact and fiction, memory and imagination. Her unique style probes the possibilities of the French language. Her interest in the possibilities of the paradigm of dialogue permeates her narrative at every level. Until her most recent works, she expressed the impossible desire for union and the essential isolation of the individual in a multitude of ways. Her "state of exile" has been one of shifting, barren ground and uncertain meanings, a world trapped in a continuing present that can never achieve resolution. This is a space where taboos are meaningless and meanings are negotiated. Lê's recent novels have hinted at a resolution of the problematic dialogic "state of the exile." Almost against expectations, the evolution of the corpus leads to the state of the exile becoming a homeland in its own right, through her acceptance of her Vietnamese past, which, through a painful and dramatic process, comes to be integrated into her present rather than juxtaposed against it. Linda Lê's texts ultimately express the harmonious resolution of the duality and uncertainty of the "state of the exile."

Notes

1. Marion Van Renterghem, "Le sabbat de Lady Lê," *Le Monde des livres*, 31 October 1997, 1. Marion Van Renterghem's article establishes that Linda Lê, who was thirty-six when she wrote *Les Trois parques* in 1997, emigrated when she was fourteen.

2. Linda Lê, "Les pieds nus," in *Littérature vietnamienne: La Part d'Exil*, ed. Le Huu Khoa (Aix-en-Provence: Université de Provence, 1995), 58.

3. Linda Lê, *Lettre morte* (Paris: 1999), 77–78.

4. Definition taken from *The Concise Oxford Dictionary* (Oxford: Clarendon Press, 1995).

5. Bill Ashcroft et al., eds., *Key Concepts in Post-Colonial Studies* (London: Routledge, 1998), 93.

6. Ashcroft et al., eds., *Key Concepts*, 93.

7. Homi K. Bhabha, *The Location of Culture* (London and New York: Routledge, 1994).

8. M. M. Bakhtin, "The hero's monologic discourse and narrational discourse in Dostoevsky's short novels," in *Bakhtinian Thought: An Introductory Reader*, ed. Simon Dentith (London: Routledge, 1995), 194.

9. Jack A. Yeager, "Culture, Citizenship, Nation: The Narrative Texts of Linda Lê," in *Post-Colonial Cultures in France*, ed. Alec Hargreaves and Mark McKinney (London: Routledge, 1997), 265.

10. Linda Lê, *Un si tendre vampire* (Paris: Editions de la Table Ronde, 1987).

11. Yeager, "Culture, Citizenship, Nation, 257.

12. Linda Lê, *Fuir: roman* (Paris: Editions de la Table Ronde, 1988).

13. Lê, *Fuir*, 15.

14. Lê, *Fuir*, 148–49.

15. Lê, *Fuir*, 144.

16. Lê, *Fuir*, 179.

17. Yeager, "Culture, Citizenship, Nation, 264.

18. Linda Lê, *Les Evangiles du crime* (Paris: Julliard, 1992).

19. Yeager, "Culture, Citizenship, Nation, 264.

20. Simon Dentith, *Bakhtinian Thought: An Introductory Reader*, 44.

21. Lê, *Les Evangiles du crime*, 51.

22. Lê, *Les Evangiles du crime*, 17.

23. M. M. Bakhtin, "The Hero's Monologic Discourse and Narrational Discourses in Dostoevsky's Short Novels," in *Bakhtinian Thought: An Introductory Reader*, 159.

24. Lê, *Les Evangiles du crime*, 199.

25. Lê, *Les Evangiles du crime*, 176.

26. Lê, *Les Evangiles du crime*, 178.

27. M. M. Bakhtin, "The Grotesque Image of the Body," in *Bakhtinian Thought: An Introductory Reader*, 227.

28. Bakhtin, "The Grotesque," 230.

29. Lê, *Les Évangiles du crime,* 227.

30. See Neil Jamieson, *Understanding Vietnam* (Berkeley: University of California Press, 1993), for a discussion of the importance of Confucianism to traditional Vietnamese society.

31. Linda Lê, *Les Dits d'un idiot* (Paris: Christian Bourjois, 1995).

32. M. M. Bakhtin, "Heteroglossia in the Novel" in *Bakhtinian Thought: An Introductory Reader,* 200.

33. Linda Lê, *Les Dits d'un idiot,* 161.

34. Yeager, "Culture, Citizenship, Nation, 264.

35. Bhabha, *The Location of Culture,* 10.

36. Linda Lê, *Les Trois parques,* (Paris: Christian Bourjois, 1997).

37. Lê, *Les Trois parques,* 15.

38. Linda Lê, *Fuir,* 53.

39. Lê, *Les Trois parques,* 238.

40. Lê, *Les Trois parques,* 219.

41. Marion Van Renterghem, "Le sabbat de Lady Lê," *Le Monde des livres,* 31 October 1997, 1.

42. Linda Lê, *Voix: une crise* (Paris: Christian Bourjois, 1998).

43. Patrick Kechichian, "La voix des démons," *Le Monde des livres,* 18 September 1998, 3.

44. Lê, *Voix,* 68.

45. Lê, *Lettre morte,* 47.

46. Lê, *Lettre morte,* 104.

47. Lê, *Lettre morte,* 73.

48. Lê, *Lettre morte,* 105.

VII

THE PACIFIC OCEAN

29

New Caledonia:
An Emerging Literature as Social Project

Peter Brown

NEW CALEDONIA IS A FRENCH TERRITORY[1] in the southwest Pacific, a thousand miles east of Australia and twelve thousand miles from Europe. It is today characterized by great ethnic, cultural and linguistic diversity (28 Melanesian languages are spoken there), and has a finely balanced demography (Melanesians, 44 percent; European settlers, often known as "Caldoche," 33 percent; Polynesians, 15 percent).

Austronesian migrations from Southeast Asia first populated the island some three thousand years before it became known to Europeans when Captain James Cook sailed there in 1774.[2] Annexed by France in 1853, New Caledonia became a penal colony in the second half of the nineteenth century. Under colonial rule, the indigenous Melanesians (also known as Kanaks), whose culture is based on their relationship to the land, were often removed from their customary lands and resettled on reservations.

The Fourth Republic repealed the "régime de l'Indigénat" in 1946, making Kanaks full French citizens and New Caledonia itself a Territoire d'Outre-Mer. By about 1960, however, demographic change had resulted in a redistribution of the relative size of the various ethnic communities, such that the indigenous Melanesians became, for the first timer, a minority in their homeland. The 1970s saw the beginnings of the independence movement, and the following decade witnessed sharpening divisions between the communities, producing the strife-ridden years known euphemistically as *les événements* (1984–88).

A political compromise was achieved with the signing of the Matignon Accords in 1988. This restored peace and made some attempts at social and political "rééquilibrage." Despite the tragic assassination of the independence leader Jean-Marie Tjibaou in 1989, the Matignon Accords held good and, in 1998, a further agreement, the Nouméa Accord, was signed. This provided for a devolution of certain state powers over the next fifteen years, increased recognition of indigenous culture and greater integration of the Territory into its regional context.

Jean Mariotti: New Caledonia as Paradox

New Caledonia started to appear in *récits de voyage* from the end of the eighteenth century, such as the account by La Billardière of d'Entrecasteaux's expedition. There was, however, little "literary" work about the island until the late nineteenth century, when adventurers such as the engineer Jules Garnier (*La Nouvelle-Calédonie, côte orientale*, 1871) and others recorded their impressions. The Communard Louise Michel was the first and most notable among the convict population to write about the island that was her imposed "home" for eight years after 1873.

The first "local" voice of note was Georges Baudoux (1870–1949), who combined tales of colonial life, stockmen, and *la brousse* with attention to Melanesian stories in such works as *Légendes canaques*. A generation later Alin Laubreaux (1899–1968) wrote novels dealing in a polished and critical way with the colonial society of the island (e.g., *Le Rocher à la Voile*); as did Jean Mariotti (1901–75),[3] who remains the most significant writer to have been produced by New Caledonia. His expatriate vision of life in the Territory is often fearful, even apocalyptic, as well as nostalgic, even if in some of his works Melanesians become characters in their own right for the first time after so many years as human décor or sources for transcribed folk tales.

Mariotti's novel *A bord de* l'Incertaine (1942) could be seen as emblematic of troubled Caledonian identity of the day. Set around 1900, it shows a world out of joint in which people are not at ease with either their time or place. Melanesian culture is in decline, and the chief's son Téhin, deprived of power and replaced by "pantins,"[4] realizes that the days of glory are gone and that his kinsmen have become "des êtres incomplets."[5] Even their gallicized names are a mockery of their heritage: "Api, Yuya et Mamembroc avaient troqué leurs noms canaques contre ceux de Bouton, République et Guerré."[6] Nor is there hope in revolt. Biha, the *sorcier*, may foment trouble, but it is clear that this will inevitably lead to defeat and that the imminent uprising of 1917 will suffer the same fate as the suppressed insurrection of 1878. On the European side, Marcellin, the ex-*bagnard*, can never be truly worthy of New Caledonia, yet he has nowhere else to go. The *petits blancs*, represented by M. Savinien, struggling to survive between the dual threats of the *Canaques* and their bankers, seem destined to yield to uncompromising, exploitative colonial interests. Their demise will be the end of the special relationship that they have been developing with the Canaques. Yet the example of Bertrand *père*, who had his head cracked open, shows the danger of an over-indulgent attitude. Even the seemingly invincible stockman Darne, "le Blanc,"[7] tireless in his efforts to tame nature, is forever chasing his (self-created) demon in the form of the "Taureau bleu," a rampaging figure from the bush that will surely turn against the hunter and bring him down.

The very title of the work indicates the degree of ambiguity and irony that characterize it. *L'Incertaine*, the shipwrecked boat lying off the coast of New Caledonia, appears as a martyred, Christ-like figure. It is an image of the island itself—close and seemingly available, but also mysterious and finally inaccessible, an enticing symbol of death: "L'île s'allongeait démesurément, en avant et en arrière, comme un navire immense dont on ne pourrait apercevoir ni l'étrave ni l'étambot, tranchés par l'horizon lointain et bleu. Une *Incertaine* géante que l'on pouvait chevaucher dans l'infini."[8] The emptiness, uncertainty and anguish of this world are all portrayed as being in proportion to its immense attractiveness and potential. Set half-way between the Canaque revolts of 1878 and 1917, at a time when the memory of the first uprising was still alive enough to make people aware of the possibility of another one, it is myth more than history that determines the tone and underlying phenomenology of the story, which is full of Romantic foreboding.

Nowhere is this tension felt more acutely than in the Third Republic schoolroom. The teacher, Madame Bourbignan, is a caricature of the misplaced colonial project, trying to force the young locals not to believe their most real and immediate experience (e.g., for her, winter is in December, whatever the Antipodean temperature outside). But, however comically out of touch with this wild colonial environment, the schoolroom is always there to recall the children back to the world enclosed by its walls. The novel may well offer a critique of European rationality, at least as universal, but such rationality does end up representing the values of adulthood and inevitably relegates the child's experience of New Caledonia—primeval, all-powerful and mysterious—to the domain of recollection and nostalgia.

The experience of Bertrand *fils* brings all this to a head: having spent his formative years on the island, he returns to it after a long absence in Europe with the intention of making it his home. At first, he appears to be successful in beating back and taming nature, restoring order, constructing a dwelling, apparently giving life back to the land. But he finally discovers that he is out of place here, a "colon maladroit." In this respect, it is, ironically, the ludicrous colonials, Madame Bourbignan and her administrator husband, who are perhaps the only souls who are not ultimately lost in this world, as they are sure of their values, which are not located in New Caledonia. They are merely *de passage*, with no desire to assimilate or settle. They do not attempt the impossible synthesis. There is no need to understand the other. They have right on their side.

Jacqueline Sénès: New Caledonia and the Dream of "Deux Couleurs, Un Peuple"

Another "historical" novel dealing more with myth than history is *Terre violente* by Jacqueline Sénès, one of the writers who have contributed to the renewal of Caledonian literature over the past two decades. A career journalist, she spent thirty years in the Territory from the early 1950s through to the mid-1980s, before returning to metropolitan France. In New Caledonia she presented a weekly radio program reporting on events from all walks of life for many years and published books relating day-to-day traditions of Territorial life that were in the process of disappearing.

Terre violente, written in the midst of *les événements* of the 1980s, nostalgically evokes the 1950s' ideology of the Union Calédonienne—a political movement calling for greater local autonomy and interracial harmony—and its motto "deux couleurs, un peuple." The story follows the adventures of the Sutton family on its *station* (farm) south of Nouméa through virtually the whole period since colonization, depicting the vicissitudes of their lives as small farmers eking out an existence in a land more hostile than welcoming. But the *station* also represents the adventure of the whole island—its economic, political and human possibilities. It is both a line of demarcation separating races and creating antagonisms, and a place of meeting, indeed of the possible unification of opposites. It is therefore a suitable place in which to play out the drama of Caledonian history and identity.

The vicissitudes of life on the farm may be many, but they are governed by an implacable binary logic in which hope alternates with disaster: crops fail, nature is uncertain and harsh, and John Sutton is killed by a plague. His wife Helena valiantly carries on the work of the farm and, despite much adversity, manages to raise her two children, one of whom later adopts a Melanesian orphan, Kahahéné. A symbolic representation of the pro-independence leader, Jean-Marie Tjibaou, Kahahéné—now Moses, now Christ—goes from being Jean-Chrétien, the model student of the Catechism, to discovering his genealogy, his origins, his body and flesh. He finally takes the inevitable decision to renounce his vocation as a priest and work in the secular sphere for the betterment of his fellow Melanesians, who live in a general state of decline, ignorance and neglect: "entre jeunes et vieux, on ne s'écoute plus."[9] while "la coutume, à présent, c'est l'argent et le whisky."[10] When he finally returns to the family property to reclaim his land—in the name of his people, more than for himself—he finds himself wanted for subversion when the *station* goes up in flames, probably due to the anger and frustration of Wanatcha, the *métis* caretaker of the property who had also grown up on it and loved it as his own, without ever being able to own it, and who felt excluded from both white and black society in New Caledonia.

Beyond its historical reconstruction, the work also has a metaphysical dimension, in which the era of colonialism merges with that of myth, both Western and indigenous. The station may well have been defined in the epigraph as the "première concession coloniale ouverte à l'aventure de l'Occident sur la terre mélanésienne,"[11] but the novel constantly strives to attenuate its historical and political significance by positing settlement on the land, both Kanak and colonial, as an atemporal constant, something outside history. Sénès uses the Suttons' farm to give a mythical, if not mystical status to the European settler population: "chevaliers d'un domaine . . . ils se savaient maintenant cimentés par un même code, par une même sagesse, par une même quête . . . la station, lieu de paix, royaume secret de la permanence."[12]

This land offers cosmic potential (the term "sacré" recurs as a leitmotif): good settlers and indigenous Melanesians will work together to build a New Babylon founded on an assumed original "pacte," the betrayal of which—the separation of *colon* and *coutume*, Western and indigenous culture—is presented as having betrayed the island itself: "Ce caillou est maudit. . . . à partir du jour où . . . on n'a plus respecté le pacte."[13] Héléna, the settler heroine of the text, is in particular able to achieve such reconciliation of opposites since "dans une rétrospective ardente, elle allait au nœud de l'énigme"[14] to the point where she ends up becoming N'Dorong, the magical tortoise of Melanesian myth, "demeure d'un totem toujours présent."[15] Furthermore, myths and history are only reflections of each other, since, at its best, the island integrates universal symbols, religion, song, sex and nature into a coherent whole: "Au fond des âges, cette terre à sortilèges, fragment d'un continent perdu, que représentait-elle? . . . Légendes et Histoire s'enlaçaient en un long chant de plaisir."[16]

Ideologically, therefore, Sénès shifts the historical disputes of the island away from the settler/Kanak axis—showing that the two can get on very well together—to the situation of *métis* "ballottés dans le vide."[17] Despite her ambivalence, Sénès seems to be trying to show that it is only by recognizing *métissage* as a doubly inclusive rather than exclusive category, seeing it as a chance for enrichment, as energy and will to live rather than as a handicap, that New Caledonia will be able to find its way forward into the future.

If Sénès's novel is a landmark in the literary production of New Caledonia, the troubled years of the 1980s saw a burst of literary activity by other writers, some expatriate "metropolitans," some native authors. The expatriates were particularly active in the production of thrillers with political overtones (e.g., Baudouin Chailley's *Nouméa, ville ouverte*; A.D.G.'s *Joujoux sur le cailloux*) in which the island served as the backdrop for catastrophe, even universal apocalypse. This vogue could not expect to outlive its heavily charged ideological moment. On the other hand, however, the acute social unrest and repositioning of this period also gave rise to a new generation of local writers, notably the Kanak Déwé Gorodé, Wanir Wélépane and Pierre Gope; the settler descendants Nicolas Kurtovitch, Frédéric Ohlen and Catherine Régent; and French writers attempting to assume a local perspective, such as Claudine Jacques and Laurence Leroux. In their different ways, these writers from various communities are thus striving to assess the implications of political conflict and social polarization, and their place in the new dispensation following first the Matignon Accord (1988) and now the Nouméa Accord (1998).

Déwé Gorodé and the Resurgence of Kanak Cultural Consciousness

In the context of Melanesian tradition, in which orality has had a rich and vital role to play over the course of the past three thousand years, the production of written literary texts is a relatively recent, and still largely exceptional, phenomenon. Hence the great interest presented by the publication of works by the Kanak author Déwé Gorodé (1949–), who is currently also vice-president and minister of culture in the new territorial government. The foremost if not "the first Kanak writer," Madame Gorodé published a book of poetry, *Sous les cendres des conques* (1985), in the midst of the troubled years of the *événements* of the 1980s and, more recently, two collections of short stories, *Utê Mûrûnû, petite fleur de cocotier* (1994) and *L'Agenda* (1996), as well as a small collection of poems with Nicolas Kurtovitch, *Dire le vrai* (1998).

If *Sous les cendres des conques* reveals both the lyricism of nature and a strong political commitment—the latter having resulted in Gorodé's internment for several months in the Camp Est prison of Nouméa when she took her views onto the streets during the first wave of demonstrations by the Kanak independence movement in the early 1970s—*Utê Mûrûnû*, which appeared roughly midway between the Accords de Matignon (1988) and the Nouméa Accord (1998), is a more sustained piece of writing, a deepened reflection on the past and future alike, and a much more elaborate textual construction.

The collection contains five stories, four of which deal with daily life in a Melanesian setting, while the fifth concerns a meeting of women from the developing world in Sydney, Australia. From the outset the work deals with major themes—memory, tradition, the land, kinship relations and the role of women. The first story, after which the collection is named, encompasses, as it were, the entire history of New Caledonia from the beginning of colonialism in the mid-nineteenth century until the dawn of the twenty-first century through a series of relationships between grandmothers and granddaughters, all called Utê Mûrûnû. These are the bearers of Melanesian culture, which is intimately bound up with the earth. It is quite literally a matter of life and death: "Seule la terre demeure. . . . Nous ne pouvons pas vivre sans elle et nous la saignons un peu plus chaque jour."[18] The text is made the more complex by the fact that Kanak pro-independence discourse is projected onto the situation of women through the metaphor of the land, thereby transforming, by analogy, Kanak men into the colonizers of women. The story creates new traditions and a new or renewed sense of history, both through the interplay of female genealogies and through the use of the rhetorical device of the *mise en abyme*.

Written by a university-educated Melanesian from an oral cultural tradition, these stories are innovative precisely because, through their interplay with tradition, they try to reconcile custom and modernity by reinstating suppressed practices and creating other traditions that hold promise for the future. And while this discursive (at least) reappropriation of history by its dispossessed and those who are doubly dispossessed on account of being both female and Kanak, certainly takes place in French, it is a French in which the reader is obliged to adopt Kanak images and perspectives, and even to some extent vocabulary and verb tense in order to gain proper understanding.

Modernity and tradition, women's liberation and custom, political action and explorations of being, these are all at stake for Déwé Gorodé in this text. Through its *mises en abyme*, its anticipations and flashbacks, its transformed repetitions and returns of various kinds, the text is constantly echoing itself, forever weaving past and future into each other, into a patchwork or composition of cultural *métissage*, establishing its own traditions in the workings of a very (post)modern form of writing that features a plurality of voices. In this text, which ultimately rewrites the future more than the past, Gorodé exploits myth and traditional cultural settings, but her figures are literary tropes devoid of traditionalist essentialism.

However, if history is anti-essentialist, unequal to itself, what is culture other than a constant process of *métissage*—a phenomenon given greater, albeit distorted, focus under the influence of colonialism? *Métissage* has long been one of the taboo subjects in New Caledonia, but it would seem that in this story, through the interweaving of tradition and modernity, myth and literature, oral and written practices, Kanak culture and colonial history, Kanak perspectives and—indeed expressed in—the French language, Déwé Gorodé has created a prime example of a cultural artifact of *métissage* that may well be a precursor of a more general cultural awareness in New Caledonia, as the island continues on its path of self-reassessment.

Gorodé's next work, *L'Agenda*, concentrates more on the encounter with the other. It presents moments of Kanak life *en tribu*, yet these moments of memory, of the past captured as tradition in an extended present, are themselves inserted into the flow of history. Thus both "La Case" and "Une dame dans la nuit" deal with attachment to the traditional hut, "case," but also with the encounter between Kanaks and Europeans and the generational shifts in attitudes that have taken place over the past quarter of a century. In addition, they portray a mythic reversal of fortune in which revenge is wreaked on history, as women take back their bodies, their lives and their land (e.g., in the story "Où vas-tu Mûû?").

Yet this very reversal of history raises the question of identity in a place where boundaries can seem blurred, and the difference between dream images and reality unclear. The familiar is also the uncanny ("Le Passeur"): "un visage familier que j'ai peut-être moi-même imprégné de mystère vu mon état, vu la nuit, vu l'ambiance alentour."[19] An aura of unreality, or what might be described in another context as "magic realism," pervades the text. Artificial or altered states seem to intersect with real ones in this world, but at the same time there is a political overlay to this atmosphere of the "étrangement familier,"[20] in which one colonization (of Indochina) is identified with another (New Caledonia). The "passeur" is both associated with death as a figure of the Styx, but is also seen as someone overcoming death, turning defeat into victory. In fact, he is the memory of place and person, the rhythm of tides and seasons, and extends beyond a Melanesian context to the vitality of other cultures, here Vietnamese.

The most complex story in the collection is "Affaire classée," which metaphorically recounts New Caledonian colonial history through three different eras, all times of conflict, each featuring a central male protagonist from a different background: a young settler about to go off and be killed in the Great War; an American soldier stationed in New Caledonia during World War II who will lose his life at Guadalcanal; and a Kanak NCO parachutist with the French army stationed back in the Territory during *les événements* of the 1980s. Each of these soldiers on foreign soil, including the Kanak in his "peau de traître . . . cet uniforme de renégat"[21] (a throwback to the betrayal committed by some Kanaks in the 1878 insurrection), is entranced, "médusé,"[22] by a beautiful young woman under a Banyan tree dressed in flowing white gown, each time different and yet always the same as Marguérite, Margaret and Maguy. Accompanied by her grandfather, a fisherman, she wears long white gloves covering her burnt fingers—hence her name, Doigts-Calcinés—and bears each time an uncanny resemblance to the soldiers' own beloved. This resemblance is so great that each one bequeaths his fortune to her before going off to his death. It turns out that the identity of this young woman, who subsequently appears dressed in black, is the same as that of "une jeune Mélanésienne d'autrefois"[23] burned alive when her parents' house was set alight during the Kanak uprising of 1878. She is therefore a haunting symbol of Kanak resistance, of innocence persecuted, of retribution—"un sourire triomphant sur les lèvres"[24]—and of the land, given that she seems to be part of the vegetation, even merging with the Banyan tree. Kanak memory, inscribed in text, is here more than cultural artifact or nostalgia. It is put in the active service of a contemporary political project.

Nicolas Kurtovitch: European Settler in Accord with "Matignon" and "Nouméa"

Nicolas Kurtovitch (1955–), whose maternal family has been in New Caledonia from the beginning of European settlement a century and a half ago, is another of the Territory's leading contemporary writers, and in 1997 became the first president of the newly founded Association des Ecrivains de Nouvelle-Calédonie. His 1998 play *Le Sentier* opened the Tjibaou Kanak Cultural Center, demonstrating the Center's forward-looking approach, given that all the actors but one—a European woman—are Kanak, a situation that would have been barely imaginable just a few years before.

Enacted in a Melanesian tribal setting, with echoes of Greek tragedy, and respecting French classical conventions regarding the unity of time, place and manner, it concerns the discussions that take place over the fate of a young European woman, taken prisoner by some of the tribe's impetuous youths at a time of heightened antagonism between Kanak and whites reminiscent of the *événements* of the 1980s. The chief must decide if the woman is to be freed or to die—not for any misdemeanor on her part, but for the sins of her forefathers, who took the land and destroyed Kanak culture. Into the equation comes the fact that the woman is the lover of the chief's son, himself trapped in the struggle against oppression by the woman's clan, i.e., "les Blancs." The son momentarily denies and denounces her, before surreptitiously freeing her one night and guiding her to safety. Love therefore triumphs over misguided and abstract hate presented as "duty" in the form of political struggle, and averts an otherwise tragic outcome. It can hardly be coincidental that this play, produced to general acclaim the month following the official signing of the Nouméa Accord, highlights the theme of reconciliation as it legitimizes the European presence and phantasmatically projects love across the racial divide as its central relationship.

This reaching out to the other, here consonant with the spirit of the Nouméa Accord, has long been a concern of Kurtovitch, as witnessed, for instance, in his post–Matignon Accords collection of short stories, *Forêt, terre et tabac* (1993), in which some of the characters are, or could be, Melanesian, mostly on journeys of self-discovery via encounters with the other. This 'identification' with Kanak 'experience' reaches an idealized plane in "Femmes au marché," in which two generations of fishermen and their wives realize their lives of fidelity, happiness, indeed completeness.

The most interesting story in the collection is "A bord de l'eau," in which a young white man on the very European Promenade Pierre Vernier in Nouméa—an image perhaps of European settlement in New Caledonia on a thin strip of land between the mountains and the sea—asks a Melanesian woman, the "propriétaire" of the field opposite, to excuse him for having trespassed on her land. In doing so, the narrator is sensitive to the irony of the Kanakization of urban life: "Ainsi, les familles kanakes colonisent-elles les moindres espaces verts de la ville comme une sorte de revers à l'histoire récente de ce pays."[25] Yet, the woman's field is invisible from the road behind the bushes, and the young man had believed that he could penetrate onto it unseen and without disturbing anything. Although mistaken in this, he shows himself prepared to learn as an "étranger."[26]

In this tale, the two cultures are presented as living in close proximity to each other, but hidden from each other as if they were not destined to meet. The curious narrator, "excentrique,"[27] driven each night to delve further, defers his desire for encounter to the following day. But a need to feel at peace with himself more even than curiosity finally draws this young European man to meet his counterpart, his other (older, Melanesian, woman) in a kind of secret harmony, intimacy, entente.

The projected and yet deferred meeting of "neighbors" is again the problematic of "Au bord de l'eau II," "même si nous ne nous connaissons pas, nous sommes tout de même là, ensemble,

presque chaque jour!"[28] Indeed, there is a sense that both share the same goal and expectation—including the fact that each is waiting for the other to make a gesture, the first move. Yet
it is this very expectation that prevents contact, the meeting so desired and seemingly so natural, given the convergence of interests in the same physical space and the same attitude to life,
"la même allure, la même absence."[29] The realization, the resolution that "c'est à moi de l'abor-
der le premier"[30] suffices to bring about in return—but also in anticipation—the sought-after
contact with the neighbor, as they both sense that they long for the same boat, "cette barque au
loin,"[31] (on) this strip of land, this Pacific island, this New Caledonia.

The imagined dialogue with the other—one's neighbor, one's brother, oneself—is pursued
and inflected in "Intérieur" on several metaphorical levels at once, as the narrator overhears a
conversation in a bus: "Je me sentais de plus en plus concerné par ce que j'entendais[32] . . . sa
voix. Elle était comme un rythme cardiaque, le battement des joies et des souffrances d'un
cœur . . . il me semblait que nous nous rencontrions en un endroit précis de l'espace qui nous
séparait. Nous allions à la rencontre l'un de l'autre et nous nous trouvions."[33] In a series of *dé-
doublements*, past and present, dream and reality converge in a phantasmic expiation of guilt at
betrayal, including the unwitting betrayal of a brother "coupable de son emprisonnement,
coupable de sa solitude."[34] However, it is this recognition of betrayal and fraternity that is also
the means of redemption.

Claudine Jacques: New Caledonia as a New Society Beyond the Nouméa Accord?

Multiracial projection into the future is the theme of the novel by Claudine Jacques (1951–), *Les
Cœurs barbelés*. Published in the year of the Nouméa Accord (1998), it tells the story of a failed
love affair between a *Caldoche* (European settler) woman and a pro-independence Kanak man.
In doing so, it recounts the personal impact of *les événements* of the 1980s, the rise of Kanak political consciousness and the ensuing polarization between the communities. Nevertheless, important as such a period was, the author is skeptical of politics, which can be obsessive and serve
as an excuse for the promotion of personal interests and investments in power relations. In the
process, the work deals with issues such as the convict heritage, mixed racial descent and inter-
marriage—taboo subjects in a closed society: "derrière les apparences tranquilles, il y a l'univers
clos . . . la pensée secrète, oublieuse des mots, bloqués dans le non-dit, sans possibilité d'éva-
sion."[35] *En passant*, the novel draws in other voices from the past as well as the present: that of
the *bagnard* crying out his sense of humiliation and neglect; that of the *Caldoche* West Coast
stockman, fiercely attached to his land—"Ils n'auront jamais mes terres. Ça jamais."[36] The
work's purpose is to explore the tragedy of two cultures sharing the same space without ever really coming to terms with each other, without being able to overcome mutual mistrust, and this
despite often enjoying the same contact with nature: "Enfants, ils cueillaient les crevettes au bord
des creeks, couraient les bambounières . . . inséparables, puis ils ont grandi."[37]

The separation of communities is a widespread and endemic social phenomenon in this universe. Parallelism involves exclusion: "il fallait se rendre à l'évidence, dans l'île la plus proche du
paradis l'intimité raciale était jalousement gardée de part et d'autre. Ni Kanak, ni Calédoniens,
ni Zoreilles, ni Javanais, ni Wallisiens, ni Tahitiens ni ni ni n'en partageaient une once. La jolie
mosaïque ethnique décrite dans les dépliants touristiques cachaient des mondes fermés, qui se
côtoyaient en lisière sans se comprendre."[38] The irony is that neither side can see the similarity
of their situation. Thus the main protagonist Malou may well ask "quelle est la couleur du
cœur?"[39] But in this world everyone, or nearly everyone, tries to deny their own concrete his-

tory of interaction in the name of, or in search of an essentialist identity, leading to intransigent or self-indulgent behavior and disregard of others based on preconceptions, albeit politically understandable ones. Thus Malou's lover Séry "l'avait emprisonnée dans son avenir."[40] And yet this partitioning flies in the face of biological reality and individual aspiration beyond the narrow definition of history: "J'aime Rimbaud et Picasso, murmurait Séry. Leur œuvre m'appartient aussi."[41] Breaking out of the straitjacket is no easy task, however, even when the other appears ready to offer, and lovingly, the opportunity to do so. Ingrained social experience and historical memory, petrified into psychological reflexes, are hard to overcome, given the internalization of the way others view oneself, the "fameux complexe colonial."[42]

The novel shows that, despite a certain social evolution, the hour has not yet come for New Caledonia to put into practice, at least not at the interpersonal level, the "destin commun" promoted by the new political framework. The island is here presented as having engaged for too long in self-inflicted suffering—a biblical self-sacrifice in a colonial bubble economy—"Christ au regard fixe sur chromo de mauvais goût."[43] The text itself is presented in binary form, divided as it is into parts, "Destins croisés" and "Un si grand amour." The ambiguity expressed by "Destins croisés" would appear to have achieved a happy resolution in "Un si grand amour." However, this proves not to be the case, the hearts of Territorians still being too "barbelés" for inter-ethnic love to prevail. Even so, in the end some hope does emerge for the future through a *métissage* in which body will take the place of mind. This will, however, have to wait until the next generation, as it is recognized that "il faut du temps pour se libérer de ses chaînes."[44]

Claudine Jacques is concerned to promote the spirit of the Nouméa Accord, and her text is ultimately a call for openness, a call to the other, a recognition that *métissage*, both biological and cultural, is the way of the future, even if that future will not come about tomorrow. She makes Séry's Melanesian mother recognize this, contradicting her son's feelings: "Tu t'es métissé mon fils, avec cette femme d'ailleurs. T'es l'image de l'homme de demain, celle de ton propre fils."[45] His *métis* offspring is literally the key to the future, a sign of reconciliation and forgiveness. But this moment of forgiveness has not yet come, even if there is an apparent realization that love can overcome the differences separating people: "leurs différences n'étaient rien dans l'élan qui les avait poussées l'un vers l'autre."[46] Indeed, reconciliation may seem all the more difficult in this land because it is so passionate. Although the condition for forgiveness set by Malou is indeed the end of passion, Séry rejects such indifference, seeing reconciliation as restitution of love. It is this realization, announced with a sense of urgency, this desire to be with the other—the other—that has freed him, or so he believes, of the troubled past, and provided an open future full of promise: "sans le savoir tu as fait de moi un homme libre, je te rendrai l'espoir."[47]

Conclusion

This hope may or may not be fulfilled. Presented as "l'île la plus proche du paradis" in the tourist brochures, New Caledonia has clearly not always been so for its diverse populations. Colonization, the penal settlement and racial divisions have all produced dislocations and left a heavy legacy of which the island is by no means yet free, even if recent political arrangements have eased social tension and pointed the way forward. In any event, New Caledonian literature, which for a long time was a dormant manifestation of the difficulty of (self-) expression and affirmation, or remained in the extended colonial shadow of the motherland, has, in recent times, been accompanying, indeed often anticipating, the course of social and cultural change in the Territory—in Jacqueline Sénès's novel, for example, the figure of Kahahéné is a tragic premonition of the fate that was to befall Jean-Marie Tjibaou, his model, within two years of its publication. Nevertheless, if history, even in its painful forms, is revisited and taboos lifted or mythologized, whether they be *Caldoche* (the racial separation of "neighbors" in Kurtovitch's texts); Kanak (the place of women in Gorodé); or metropolitan (*les événements* for Sénès and Jacques, who, despite their differences, both situate this conflict as internal to the Territory, the role of France being muted), there is in each case an attempt at, or glimpse of, the transcendence of the limitations of history—toward a dialectic of tradition and modernity (Gorodé), self and other (Kurtovitch), black and white (Jacques), Kanak and Western myth (Sénès).

A quarter century after his death, the quality of Jean Mariotti's prose may still see him laying claim to the mantle of foremost New Caledonian writer. But the expatriate problematic that defined his life is no longer dominant among contemporary authors who, whether pro- or anti-independence, see this South Pacific island as their home rather than as a place of exile. In particular, over the past twenty years, despite or because of the tragedy of *les événements*, they have increasingly given themselves a shot at the future as much as being concerned to restore the often buried past. In so doing, they are playing an active role in the self-redefinitions that the Territory is presently undergoing. Their contribution is likely to become more important in the years ahead, as this island society grapples with the implications of its political settlement. And the future, in New Caledonia more than in most places, remains an open book. Writer and reader alike can look forward to considerably more on the subject.

Notes

1. With the constitutional changes brought about by the *Accord de Nouméa* (1998), New Caledonia is no longer, technically, a French Overseas Territory (TOM). It has become, "simply," *la Nouvelle-Calédonie*, and its constitutional status has shifted from that of a *Territoire d'outre-mer* to that, uniquely, of a *Pays d'outre-mer* (POM). For convenience, and given the unresolved nature of the latter term in many respects, the term "Territory" is still used in this chapter to designate New Caledonia.

2. The received view is that Cook, finding that the inhabitants had given no general name to the island, called it New Caledonia, as the impressive hills he saw on the east coast supposedly reminded him of parts of Scotland. In a similar vein, on the same voyage he named the neighboring islands, now known as Vanuatu, the New Hebrides. The first known French navigator to visit New Caledonia was d'Entrecasteaux in 1792, although it is also possible that La Pérouse did so in 1788, before embarking on his final, fatal voyage.

3. The publishing house, Grain de Sable, has recently produced a critical edition of Mariotti's collected works in thirteen volumes (1996–2001).

4. Jean Mariotti, *A bord de* l'Incertaine (1942) (Nouméa: Editions Grain de Sable, 1996), 41.

5. Mariotti, *À bord de*, 42.

6. Mariotti, *À bord de*, 34.

7. Mariotti, *À bord de*.

8. Mariotti, *À bord de*, 57.

9. Jacqueline Sénès, *Terre violente* (Paris: Hachette, 1987), 305.

10. Sénès, *Terre violente*, 310.

11. Sénès, *Terre violente*, 10.

12. Sénès, *Terre violente*, 168.

13. Sénès, *Terre violente*, 307.

14. Sénès, *Terre violente*, 213.

15. Sénès, *Terre violente*, 314.

16. Sénès, *Terre violente*, 319–20.

17. Sénès, *Terre violente*, 138.
18. Déwé Gorodé, *Utê Mûrûnû* (Nouméa: Éditions Grain de Sable, 1994), 34–35.
19. Déwé Gorodé, *L'Agenda* (Nouméa: Éditions Grain de Sable, 1996), 48.
20. Gorodé, *L'Agenda*, 49.
21. Gorodé, *L'Agenda*, 38.
22. Gorodé, *L'Agenda*, 32.
23. Gorodé, *L'Agenda*, 27.
24. Gorodé, *L'Agenda*, 34.
25. Kurtovitch, *Forêt, terre*, 47.
26. Kurtovitch, *Forêt, terre*, 41.
27. Kurtovitch, *Forêt, terre*, 41
28. Kurtovitch, *Forêt, terre*, 56.
29. Kurtovitch, *Forêt, terre*, 57.
30. Kurtovitch, *Forêt, terre*, 58.
31. Kurtovitch, *Forêt, terre*, 59.
32. Kurtovitch, *Forêt, terre*, 76.
33. Kurtovitch, *Forêt, terre*, 77.
34. Kurtovitch, *Forêt, terre*, 79.
35. Claudine Jacques, *Les Cœurs barbelés* (Nouméa: Éditions du Niouli, 1998), 69. (Subsequently published: Paris: La Table Ronde, 1999.) All quotations are from the first, Nouméa, edition.
36. Jacques, *Les Cœurs*, 56.
37. Jacques, *Les Cœurs*, 66.
38. Jacques, *Les Cœurs*, 118.
39. Jacques, *Les Cœurs*, 84.
40. Jacques, *Les Cœurs*, 82.
41. Jacques, *Les Cœurs*, 118.
42. Jacques, *Les Cœurs*, 126.
43. Jacques, *Les Cœurs*, 6.
44. Jacques, *Les Cœurs*, 6.
45. Jacques, *Les Cœurs*, 194.
46. Jacques, *Les Cœurs*, 232.
47. Jacques, *Les Cœurs*, 233.

Appendix: Summaries
of Selected Creative and Critical Works

À Bord de *l'Incertaine by Jean Mariotti*

Set at the turn of the twentieth century, this is a novel of settler representations of New Caledonian identity, showing a world where people are not coherent with either their time or place. Melanesian culture is in decline, puppets replace the old chiefs, and there is no hope in revolt. Biha, the sorcerer, may foment trouble, but this will inevitably lead to defeat. On the European side, the ex-convict Marcellin is not worthy of New Caledonia, and yet he has nowhere else to go. The misplaced colonial project is caricatured through the Third Republican schoolteacher, Madame Bourbignan, trying to convince the young locals that December is winter whatever the antipodean temperature. The *petits blancs*, represented by M. Savinien, struggle to survive between the dual threats of Canaques and bankers, and even the seemingly invincible stockman Darne is forever chasing his own demon in the form of a rampaging "bull." The "Incertaine" of the title is a shipwrecked boat lying off the coast of New Caledonia that appears as a Christ-like figure, an image of the island itself, in this work of foreboding without promise of redemption.

Atipa *by Alfred Parépou*

Although *Atipa* is subtitled "roman guyanais," it is hard to endorse the identity of the book as a novel per se, but rather, as a satirical chronicle of a slice of a Guianese man's life in Cayenne. Atipa walks around the city, goes to the market, and during his peregrinations, encounters twelve of his friends with whom he stops to chat or share a meal. Most of the book reports these conversations, during which Atipa shows his humor, his philosophy, and his at times bitter criticism of the people in power, and of society in general. Written in Creole, the book provokes all sorts of questions not simply about its own genre, but about its intended audience at the time, for instance.

Baara *by Souleymane Cissé*

Baara (Mali, 1978. Color, 90 mins., Bambara) is written and directed by Souleymane Cissé, with original music by Lamine Konté. Cinematography by Etienne Carton de Grammont and

Abdoulaye Sidibé. Editing by Andrée Davanture. Cast members Balla Moussa Keita (the Factory Owner), Baba Niare (the Porter), Boubacar Keita (the Engineer), Oumou Diarra (the Engineer's Wife), Ismaïla Sarr (the Senior Worker). Filmed on location in Bamako and produced by Cissé films. Winner of three awards: Ernest Artaria Award for cinematography, and Prize of the Ecumenical Jury, at the 1978 Locarno International Film Festival; Grand Prize Etalon de Yennega at the 1979 Ouagadougou Panafrican Film and Televsion Festival (FESPACO). *Baara*, made with non-professional actors, explores class interactions in modern, industrialized Africa. It stresses the role of the individual in the collective, and its powerful cinematography presents in heroic terms the struggle of African workers for basic rights. Balla Diarra, a "baara" (a porter with his own handcart) who works the streets of Bamako, meets the young progressive Balla Traoré, who befriends him, and helps him find better employment in the textile factory where he works as an engineer. Traoré is involved in the workers' struggle with their oppressive factory owner for better conditions. The factory boss, a monstrous representative of the rich African elite, has murdered his wife on suspicion of adultery and has Traoré killed for his encouragement of the workers' attempts to unionize. Traoré's death provokes a general revolt by the workers, but justice may be going to be done: the police arrive and the factory boss is arrested and driven away.

Batouala: véritable roman nègre *by René Maran*

The author was employed by the *Ministère des Colonies* and worked in West Africa. In the preface to the novel, he denounces the evils of imperialism, the violence done to the people of West Africa, and the atrocities and various forms of abuse in which the French colonial authorities indulged in that region of the world. The novel itself is the complaint of Batouala, hunter, warrior and chief, and what happens to him and his clan. Written in lyrical, often poetical style, it is also an extremely violent text, showing both the existence and force of a pre-colonial civilization and culture, and its clash with the colonial invader. This first "véritable roman nègre" is considered a major work foreshadowing the *négritude* movement.

Borom Sarret *by Ousmane Sembène*

Borom Sarret (Senegal, 1963. Black and white, 18 mins., French) is written and directed by Ousmane Sembène. Assistant director: Ibrahima Barro. Cinematography by Christian Lacoste. Editing by André Gandier. Cast members: Ly Abdoulaye (Borom Sarret the carter), Albarah (the horse). Filmed on location in Dakar and produced with aid from the *Ministère de la coopération*. The first professional film to be made in African and directed by an African, the short *Borom Sarret* recounts a day in the life of a poverty-stricken carter in post-independence Dakar. Made with non-professional actors and with Sembène's own voice-over commentary in French giving the interior monologue of the carter, the film's simple structure belies the complexity of its analysis. Borom Sarret's profession is a peripatetic one, which allows Sembène to give a panorama of contemporary Dakar and its population. Thus in the course of the film Borom Sarret traverses rich and poor districts, picks up rich and poor people, and is solicited by a crippled beggar and an itinerant griot (professional story-teller). The climax of the film comes when Borom Sarret's livelihood—his cart—is impounded because of his unauthorized excursion into the smart bourgeois districts of Dakar to drop off a rich passenger. Borom Sarret has no choice but to return home empty-handed to his wife and children. Sembène uses the voice-over to allow the carter—and the audience—to extrapolate from his encounters the fundamental causes of the poverty in which he and others are trapped, and the film draws a clear line of continuity be-tween divisions in urban Senegal pre- and post-independence.

Calomnies *by Linda Lê*

In this novel, the inmate of an asylum receives a letter from his niece, who acts as the sec-ondary narrator. The niece, a Parisian-based writer, implicitly of Vietnamese origin, has been told by her mother that the man she believed to be her father may not be a blood relation. Her blood father was apparently her mother's lover, a foreign soldier. The novel weaves together an account of the niece's past and present, and the uncle's memories of his dysfunctional and ma-terialistic family. The novel ends in tragedy, as the uncle kills himself, surrounding by the trap-pings of knowledge, in the form of books.

Caméra Afrique *by Férid Boughedir*

Caméra Afrique (Tunisia/France, 1983. Color and b/w, 95 mins., French and English) was produced, written and directed by Férid Boughedir. Cinematography by Sekou Ouédraogo and Charly Meunier. Editing by Andrée Davanture. English narration by D. Bouchoucha, R. M'Ra-bet and M. Harrison. This first major documentary by the Tunisian filmmaker and academic Férid Boughedir covers twenty years of film production by Africans in Africa, commencing with Sembène's Borom Sarret and ending with the second generation of filmmakers from the 1980s such as Gaston Kaboré. The film focuses primarily on filmmaking in Francophone Africa, and stresses the importance of the festivals *Les Journées cinématographiques de Carthage* and FESPACO in encouraging exchange and creativity in the cinema industry across the conti-nent. The film addresses issues such as the practical difficulties of independent film distribu-tion in Africa, the ambiguities of state aid schemes, and the role of the filmmaker in contem-porary African society. Substantial clips from eighteen films are given, as well as extracts of interviews with eight African filmmakers, including Sembène and Cissé.

Camp de Thiaroye *by Ousmane Sembène*

Camp de Thiaroye (Algeria/Senegal/Tunisia, 1987. Color, 150 mins., Wolof and French) is written and directed by Ousmane Sembène and Thierno Faty Sow with original music by Is-maël Lo. Assistant directors Ouzid Dahmane, Clarence Thomas Delgado and Amadou Thior. Produced by Mustafa Ben Jemja, Ouzid Dahmane and Mamadou Mbengue. Cinematography by Ismail Lakhdar Hamina. Editing by Kahena Attia. Cast in alphabetical order: Sigiri Bakaba, Hamed Camara, Philippe Chamelat, Moussa Cissoko, Ismaila Cissé, Eloi Coly, Innocence Coly, Camara Med Dansogho, Eric Dudoit, Marcel Duplouy, Marie-Ève Duplouy, Charles Estifian, Laurent Kuntz, Pierre Londiche, Ismaël Lô, Lamine Mane, André Massoni, Gerard Maxent, El Hadj Ndiaye, Thierno Ndiaye, Oumarou Neino, Daniel Odimbossoukou, Pierre Orma, John Peterson, Leopoldine Robert, Adama Samboa, Ibrahim Sane, Jean-Daniel Simon, Gustave Sorgho, Ababacar Sy Cissé, Gabriel Zahon, Koffi Saturnin Zinga, Casimir Zoba. Filmed on lo-cation in Senegal and produced by the *Société nouvelle de production cinématographique*. Win-ner of Grand Special Jury Prize at the 1988 Venice Film Festival. Based on an actual but sup-pressed event from the colonial past, the French massacre in 1944 of *tirailleurs sénégalais* awaiting repatriation in a transit camp at Thiaroye, just outside Dakar. When the French au-thorities go back on their promise of back pay, civilian clothes and a demob allowance for each soldier, mutiny breaks out. The camp commander is taken hostage but released when he promises to negotiate compensation for the soldiers. His release allows the French authorities to send tanks and artillery in the dead of night to quash rebellion in the camp. The camp is razed to the ground and many of the *tirailleurs* lose their lives. The film highlights the hypocrisy of France's colonial project through a nuanced but damning exposé of relations between colonizer and colonized in the later stages of colonialism, mediated in particular through the carefully drawn characters of the highly educated, classical-music-loving Sergeant Diarra and the traumatized private "Pays."

Catacombes de soleil *by Elie Stephenson*

This book opens with a preface by Bertène Juminer and a poem by Stephenson dedicated to Léon Gontran Damas. It contains three groupings of poems qualified by Juminer in the following manner: "'Feux sur la savane' traces the agony of an entire people undermined by humiliation and despair; 'Catacombes de soleil' awakens people to the light even when they are underground; finally, 'Textes sauvages' exhorts people to take up the fight while not forgetting to glorify the Mother, source of tenderness, courage, and dignity" (p. 6). Although written in French, the poems include features of oral literature, such as the repetition of the "Massak/ Kam" ritual formula to start an evening of "dolos" (or guessing games) in "Le poème des enfants suppliciés."

Ceddo *by Ousmane Sembène*

Ceddo (Senegal, 1977. Color, 120 mins., Wolof and French) is written and directed by Ousmane Sembène with original music by Manu Dibangu. Cinematography by Georges Caristan. Editing by Florence Eymon. Cast members: Tabata Ndiaye (Princess Dior), Moustapha Yade (Madir Fatim Fall), Ismaila Diagne (the Kidnappper), Matoura Dia (the King), Omar Gueye (Jaraaf), Mamadou Dioumé (Prince Biram), Nar Modou (Saxewar), Ousmane Camara (Diogomay), Ousmane Sembène (a *Ceddo* renamed Ibrahima). Filmed on location in Senegal and produced by Sembène films. Winner of the Interfilm Award in the Forum of New Cinema at the 1977 Berlin International Film Festival. A critique of cultural colonialism, *Ceddo* is set during the scramble for conquest of sub-Saharan Africa by Islamic North Africans, around the late eighteenth and early nineteenth century. The local king and some subjects have converted to Islam, but the Imam insists that everyone convert, and the king complies by punishing those who resist. The resisting *ceddo* (non-Muslims) kidnap the king's daughter in protest, but the king dies and the Imam installs himself as head of the village. European traders look on, engaging unchallenged in slaving activities. Conversion to Islam is enforced, and Princess Dior is recovered by the Imam who will marry her to ensure his position of power. Amidst mass conversions, Princess Dior shoots the Imam. The princess's pivotal role radically challenges Islamic doctrines about the position of women in society, and the film as a whole is openly critical of religious ideologies that mask the naked pursuit of power. *Ceddo*'s contentiousness is clear from the fact that under the Christian president (L.S. Senghor) of Muslim-dominated Senegal, it was banned for eight years.

Cent ans dans les bois *by Antonine Maillet*

Referring to the difficult hundred-year period of silence and isolation Acadians spent "in the woods" between 1780 and 1880, this novel serves as a logical and historical sequel to *Pélagie-*

la-Charrette beginning where *Pélagie-la-Charrette* left off. Whereas this earlier novel recounts the triumphant return of the Acadian people to their homeland, *Cent ans dans les bois* chronicles how through their determination and bravery these people survive, settle down and are scattered all over what used to be Acadia. Much like *Pélagie-la-Charrette, Cent ans dans les bois* makes great use of anecdotal accounts drawn directly from the tale and from the best Acadian oral literature has to offer. It is more specifically the story of Pélagie-la-Gribouille, Pélagie-la-Charrette's great granddaughter. The novel ends with the Acadians "coming out of the woods" in 1880, which also marks the advent of the Acadian National Conferences and a growing political consciousness on the part of Acadians.

Chemin d'école *by Patrick Chamoiseau*

Chemin d'école tells the story of its young hero's passage through the first years of school in such a way as to provide a precise allegorical double of Martinique's struggle to establish its cultural identity. From the unstudied, insular embrace of Mam Ninotte, to the first, somewhat bewildering exposure to European culture provided at Mam Salinière's preschool, to the harshly Eurocentric values of the boy's assimilated grade school teacher, to the militantly Afrocentric values of a Césairian revolutionary who serves for a while as a substitute teacher, each of the young boy's teachers symbolizes a phase in the island's cultural development. Chamoiseau's *négrillon* is able to derive some benefit from all of these pedagogical experiences, but when, the novel seems to ask, will the Martinican school system learn to accept the Creole culture that predominates in the day-to-day experience of the young boy and the majority of the island's populace? The answer to this question is left unanswered.

Christophe Cartier de la Noisette dit Nounours *by Antonine Maillet*

As a seemingly harmless children's book whose main character is a stuffed teddy bear whose name, despite the historical time discrepancy, is derived most likely from combining the names of Christopher Columbus and Jacques Cartier, it is a highly allegorical tale reminiscent of Swift's *Gulliver's Travels*. Like so many of Maillet's other fantastic characters, who are clearly identified with Acadia or the Acadian context, Nounours denounces and fights injustice and defends the rights of the downtrodden under the revolutionary banner of "liberty, equality and fraternity." Not surprisingly, there are numerous social-historical and political references to Acadia, the ill-treatment of Acadians and their eventual coming out of hiding.

Cinquante ans de journalisme *by Ernest Mallebay*

A major figure in turn-of-the-century colonial culture in Algeria, Ernest Mallebay recounts in this autobiographical works the historical and anecdotal details of the development and diversification of the colonial press in the second half of the nineteenth century. By virtue of his role in the creation of a number of late-nineteenth-century reviews and journals like *La Revue algérienne illustrée* and *Le Turco*, Mallebay was in a position to discover local writers and provide for them a major forum of expression without having to test their talent in the literary circles of the Metropole. Also included in this work are important accounts on the works and careers of, for example, the writer Stephen Chaseray and the illustrator and caricaturist Assus.

Comme des gouttes de sang *by Elie Stephenson*

Like his other poetic works, *Comme des gouttes de sang* incites to wake up, and go from oppression to freedom, from the old to the new, from sleep to clear consciousness. In order to do this, the people need a man, perhaps a prophet-poet (much like Victor Hugo) whose poetic voice will arouse consciousness: "Viendra-t-il enfin un Homme / viendra-t-il un Homme / un seul! / pour avoir—ô mon peuple / de l'histoire une virgule" (p. 15). Stephenson, maybe in the footsteps of Baudelaire and Hugo, sees the role of poet as savior of his people and perhaps even of mankind.

Contrôle d'identité *by Vassilis Alexakis*

A man in the Troyes-Paris train has forgotten the purpose of his journey; moments later he realizes he does not know his own name and cannot recognize himself in a café mirror. His identity card supplies essential information. Has he lost his memory, has he gone mad? His girlfriend confirms that he is from Yugoslavia. He tries to reconstruct his personal history from the documents in his flat. That night at a dinner party at the flat of his boss an apparently diverse company (including a homeless gate-crasher) assembles. The preoccupations and problems of the guests are rehearsed; questions of memory and identity are shown to be significant not just for the man who has lost his memory. Finally it is revealed that the narrative is a draft for a novel by a writer, many of whose experiences are those of the characters in the novel.

Coquelicot du Massacre *by Evelyne Accad*

Evelyne Accad traces the journey of several main characters, each with his or her own story to tell. Nour wanders through the surreal city of Beirut in a desperate attempt to cross the line of demarcation to the peaceful side, where she and her child, Raja, will be sheltered from the violence. She encounters various inhabitants of the city along the way who offer her courage, advice, food and shelter. The journey is fraught with danger. However, by attempting to cross the city she is defying the violence of the war. She is also defying the restrictions placed upon her by rejecting and breaking the walls of tradition and silence. Najmé is a young university student who must face a bleak future as the war destroys her country and its youth. In order to deal with the chaos, she expresses herself and traces her story by keeping a journal. Through her writings, she questions the social, political and religious powers that are destroying her future. Hayat, a university professor, returns to her home country Lebanon where she battles the absurdity of the war in her writings and her discussions with her lover Adnan, a philosopher. Her words trace the social, political and religious problems that are at the basis of Lebanon's vulnerability and its eventual destruction.

Crache à Pic *by Antonine Maillet*

Even though this epic novel recounts similar events of everyday village life as in *Cent ans dans les bois*, serving to a certain extent as a sequel to this earlier novel, the narrative techniques of using several layers of narration and an informant resemble more those found in *Pélagie-la-Charrette*. Set against the backdrop of the 1930s and Prohibition, the story revolves primarily around the great rivalry which pits the iconoclastic and less privileged heroine Crache à Pic, who comes from a long line of giants, sorcerers and sailors, against her less able and ingenuous male counterpart Dieudonné, the great capitalist smuggler. True to her outlaw status, she goes about turning the world upside down by serving as captain and commanding men. As one of Maillet's notable heroines, Crache à Pic represents the classic example of the "woman on top" who questions male superiority based solely on patriarchal tradition.

D'Chimbo du criminel au héros. Une incursion dans l'imaginaire guyanais
by Serge Mam Lam Fouck

The character of D'Chimbo is well known in Guiana, explains the historian, but not his factual history. Hence Mam Lam Fouck draws a useful and clear picture of Guiana at the time of D'Chimbo's life (its economics, its social strata, its representations of the Negro in post-slavery times, its colonial status, its geography), and, gathering archival work from the press at the time of the D'Chimbo affair and from the trial proceedings, retells the story of the criminal in an attempt to clearly separate fact from fiction. The second part of the book traces the representation of the character in the D'Chimbo narratives (analyzed above) and in the tales of the Guianese oral tradition, and concludes that D'Chimbo has become a hero. Illustrated, this book also provides the reader with useful annexes such as the prosecutor's report, the text of the court's condemnation and the report of the execution. Although a little succinct, it provides insight into the folktales woven around D'Chimbo which endow him with magic powers.

Den Muso *by Souleymane Cissé*

Den Muso (Mali, 1974. Color and B/W, 95 mins., Bambara) is written and directed by Souleymane Cissé, with original music by Wandé Kuyaté. Assistant directors Abdoulaye Séki, Karimu Daramé. Cinematography by Abdoulaye Sidibe. Editing by Andrée Davanture. Cast members Dounamba Dany Couibaly, Fanta Diabate, Omou Diarra, Ball Moussa Ketia, Ismaïla Sarr. Filmed on location in Bamako and produced by Cissé films. *Den Muso* deals with the difficulties faced by the young generations of modern, urban Malians, and with the injustices that women suffer as second-class citizens in African society. Sékou is a worker in a factory owned by the father of Ténin. Sékou and other prospectless youths form a group who attract girls from good homes (amongst them Ténin, who is mute) to ride with them on their mopeds, go dancing, and swim in the Niger. On one trip to the river, Sékou takes advantage of Ténin's muteness to rape her. Ténin's pregnancy is discovered, and despite her mother's pleas her father throws her out for dishonoring the family, warning other family members not to take her in. Sékou refuses to acknowledge that he is the father of Ténin's child. Ténin's father discovers that his own parents have taken her in. He chases after Ténin in fury but collapses suddenly and dies. Ténin's distraught mother blames her for the family's misfortunes and throws her out herself. Ténin goes to confront Sékou and finds him sleeping with another girl. She secures the door of his house and sets fire to it, then returns home and ends her own life with an overdose.

Don l'Orignal *by Antonine Maillet*

Very similar in content to Maillet's dialectal drama *Les Crasseux*, in this highly allegorical fantasy tale having profound social implications by mirroring closely Acadian historical events, including the social strife or conflicts between various clans and the Deportation, a reversal of fortunes takes place after much heated debate and conflict between the two opposing groups. On the one hand, there are the Continentals who implicitly are identified with their bourgeois professions and who are led by the village maîtresse who is intent on annihilating or, at the very least, chasing the other group away. On the other hand, there are the "filthy," lower class characters, the Puçois, who occupy an island, which has recently and miraculously sprung up, and who keep to themselves and mean harm to no one. The conflict is resolved at the end of the novel through the creation of a paradisiacal island where the "Shakespeareanesque" Romeo and Juliet couple, Adéline and Citrouille, each from opposing camps, settle down.

Douceurs du bercail *by Aminata Sow Fall*

Douceurs du bercail is the story of Asta Diop, a forty-five-year-old divorcee, educated in France, sent to Paris as a Senegalese representative to the Conference of Economic World Order. Found suspicious for all the hand luggage she's carrying (gifts for her daughters who live in Paris, and fresh fish for her friend Anne), she is searched by a customs officer and reacts violently when this search turns into an improper bodily probe. She is arrested and taken to a depot, awaiting deportation. Over half of the novel takes place in this depot where Asta spends eight long days in abject conditions, along with two hundred other "illegal aliens," four of whom become her friends. Eventually, Asta's anger turns into introspection and a resolution to change her life. Upon her return to Senegal, she buys a plot of land, and with the help of her new friends, against all odds, develops it into a successful agricultural operation, called "Douceurs du bercail."

Elissa, la reine vagabonde *by Fawzi Mellah*

The book tells the story of Elissa, the founder of Carthage, as inscribed in a letter allegedly found on Punic stelae discovered among the ruins of the old city and translated into French by the narrator. The Phoenician queen recounts her journey from Tyre, her stops in Cyprus, Libya, and Hadrumet and the circumstances surrounding the establishment of her kingdom in Carthage or Quart Hadasht. She dwells on her dreams, motivations and politics. There is a hint that she was not motivated by politics alone and that she may have fled the temptation of a forbidden relationship with her brother Pygmalion. A good deal of the book is devoted to discussion of the problem of language and representation, and self-representation. The book responds to Virgil's version of Dido's story in the *Aeneid* from a non-Western perspective by portraying Elissa completely outside the frame of reference of the Roman Empire.

Éloge de la créolité *by Jean Bernabé, Patrick Chamoiseau, Confiant Raphaël*

In this lyrical and theoretical essay, the authors define "créolité" (not to be confused with the Creole language) as a Caribbean essential quality, in an attempt to express what constitutes the distinctness of Antillean literature and culture. They claim that "créolité" is at the basis of each Antillean self and urge authors and other creators to explore the self and use its resources for inspiration first, before revisiting the past and rewriting its history. A postmodern notion, the term both combines and transcends Aimé Césaire's approach, which privileged introspective moments of self-revelation and Édouard Glissant's celebration of multiple origins. "Créolité" becomes a rallying Caribbean cry meant to influence its artistic production, a quest for "a more fertile way of thinking, for a more accurate means of expression, and for a more genuine aesthetics" which would be neither European nor African, nor Asian, but Creole.

Emmanuel à Joseph à Dâvit *by Antonine Maillet*

A novel whose full title refers to a "nativity in Acadia" and which celebrates the biblical and genealogical link between the past and the present by recounting the early beginnings of a poor but proud coastal Acadian fishing village community, inspired by accounts and scenes reminiscent of Jesus' own nativity. The novel also links the Acadian Deportation to the annual Christmas time celebration by evoking the notion that Acadians are being forced to leave the intimacy of their villages to relocate to the cold and impersonal city. However, at a time when all seems hopeless, several miracles take place, which represent hope for the creation of a brighter future. The older couple, Élisabeth and Zacharie, will finally have a son. Likewise, Mârie and Joseph have a son by the name of Emmanuel who is visited by three wise men and who symbolizes a second chance, the promise of a new beginning for the Acadian people.

Évangéline Deusse *by Antonine Maillet*

A play set in a public park in Montreal where four uprooted characters or exiles converge: Évangéline Deusse or the Second, whose name serves as an historical parody of Longfellow's poem about Evangeline the First; a nostalgic eighty-year-old Breton who still fondly remembers his Brittany; a wandering Jewish Rabbi who longs to die in Israel; and a character by the name of Stop who recently has moved to Montreal to look for work and just happens to be at that intersection. The pretext for their meeting is a little fir tree from Acadia which Évangéline Deusse has decided to plant in the park. It should be noted that, unlike the rest of Maillet's Acadian heroines, Évangéline Deusse is the only character who remains uprooted. As the Rabbi correctly points out, however, this highly symbolical fir tree represents Évangéline's Deusse very own Acadian soul which she is transplanting and which will take root in the Montreal soil.

Femmes d'Alger dans leur appartement *by Assia Djebar*

This is a series of short novels in which Djebar combines historical narratives of colonization, orientalist tableaux and fictions of female everyday life experiences. This apparently fragmented text is in fact clearly organized into three different chapters: "Aujourd'hui" (Today), "Hier" (Yesterday) and finally a postscript which, more than just a conclusion, is the core of Djebar's text. In this final chapter, Djebar discusses in length the famous painting by Delacroix after which her book is entitled: *Femmes d'Alger dans leur Appartement*. First, Djebar acknowledges that Delacroix, probably unknowingly, was the first artist to offer a feminine representation of the Orient. Partially influenced by Picasso's own rendition of Delacroix's masterpiece, Djebar offers to develop this feminine gaze on the Orient by substituting her writer's point of view. In her various stories covering many centuries of female alienation and seclusion in the harem, Djebar delivers a series of portraits which depict emancipated women. All the women imagined by Djebar share the same ambition: to be recognized as liberated women, in others words as "femme-voix," femme-mouvement and ultimately "femme-regard." Despite its brevity, this work reflects the major struggles experienced by these Algerian women in search of their freedom of speech, movement and sight ("droit de regard").

Finye *by Souleymane Cissé*

Finye (Mali, 1982. Color, 100 mins., Bambara) is written and directed by Souleymane Cissé. Cinematography by Étienne Carton de Grammont. Editing by Andrée Davanture. Cast members: Omou Diarra, Goundo Guissé, Balla Moussa Ketia, Fousseyni Sissoko. Filmed on location in Mali and produced by Cissé films. Awarded the Grand Prize Etalon de Yennega at the 1983 Ougadougou Panafrican Flm and Television Festival (FESPACO). *Finye* deals in both realist and mythical modes with the situation of young people in modern Mali, critiquing the morally bankrupt military regimes of contemporary Africa and meditating on the role of traditional beliefs in moving Africa forward. Batrou, daughter of the local military governor, and Bâ, grandson of Kansaye who is versed in traditional lore, become involved with each other and with a group of politically active students who distribute tracts against the military regime. Batrou and Bâ are arrested in a police raid on the student headquarters, and refuse to renounce their fight for justice. The young people are sent to a harsh correctional camp. Kansaye consults the ancestral spirits for guidance, and, told to rely only his own initiative, he confronts the military governor with apparent impunity. In retribution his home is ransacked, and he passes the baton of resistance on to the politically committed students. The national government is unhappy with the local levels of unrest, and the military governor is pressured into resigning his post. The young people who were arrested are released.

Forêt, Terre et Tabac *by Nicolas Kurtovitch*

This post-Matignon Accords collection of short stories all show encounter with the other, or at least a longing for such, even to the point of idealization, and can be seen as a fictionalized instantiation of those Accords (1988) on the way to becoming the *Accord de Nouméa* (1998): in "A bord de l'eau," for example, a young white man in a very European part of Nouméa asks pardon, as an *étranger*, of a Melanesian woman for intruding onto her nearby field. In this collection, some of the characters are, or could be, Melanesian, mostly on journeys of self-discovery, leading to transformed vision. In "Veillée," the hero discovers that a physical journey home to one's place of origin is less important than a spiritual one. Kurtovitch reminds Kanaks of the importance of the old ways, to the point of idealization ("Femmes," in which two generations of fishermen and their wives realize their lives of fidelity and simple happiness.) Even though there may be destruction of the natural habitat through urbanization ("Au bord de l'eau III"), as "Un arbre" shows, there is always the chance for resurgent life bearing hope after cataclysm.

Fuir: roman *by Linda Lê*

An unnamed French Vietnamese narrator recounts his miserable life in Vietnam to an unknown Japanese beggar on the streets of Paris. He was abandoned by his parents, forced to live with his socially ostracized aunt, corrupted by a profligate tutor, and eventually compelled to leave North Vietnam in haste, after attempting to strangle a promiscuous village girl who rejected his advances. When in South Vietnam, the narrator reveled in his own degradation. He was eventually noticed by a wealthy doctor, who married him to his pregnant daughter. He subsequently found himself the object of his wife's and father-in-law's scorn, and his brother-in-law's affections. The beggar and the narrator recognize each other as kindred spirits, fellow exiles from humanity. At the end of their dialogue, the Japanese beggar commits suicide.

Guelwaar *by Ousmane Sembène*

Guelwaar (France/Germany/Senegal, 1992. Color, 125 mins., Wolof and French) is written, directed and produced by Ousmane Sembène with original music by Baaba Mall. Cinematography by Dominique Gentil. Editing by Marie-Aimée Debril. Cast members: Abou Camara, Marie Augustine Diatta, Mame Ndoumbé Diop, Moustapha Diop, Lamine Mane, Babcar Mbaye, Belle Mbaye, Coly Mbaye, Papa Momar Mbaye, Thierno Ndiaye, Myriam Niang, Joseph Baloma Sane, Omar Seck, Samba Wane. Filmed on location in Senegal and produced by Channel 4, Films Domirev, FR3, Galatée Films, New Yorker Films, WDR. Awarded the President of the Italian Senate's Gold Medal at the 1992 Venice Film Festival. Deemed politically inflammatory, *Guelwaar* has not yet been screened or released in Senegal. Pierre Henri Thioune, a Christian political activist known as "Guelwwar," is buried by mistake as a Muslim in a Muslim cemetery. The attempt to negotiate the return and reburial of Guelwaar's body is marred by the religious fanaticism of both the Muslims and the Christians involved. The film cuts to include flashbacks of Guelwaar's political speeches, which decry the weakening of Africa through international food aid. It is suggested that Guelwaar has been done away with because of his political agitation. Guelwaar's three children in the film represent potential responses to the contemporary economic impasse of Africa. One son, an image of shattered post-independence hopes, has an accident that cripples him so that he depends on others to survive. The older son has nothing by contempt for Africa, having left for a better life in France. Guelwaar's daughter works as a prostitute in Dakar supporting the family, as her father's political activities have never provided as steady income. The fracturing of contemporary African society is thus depicted, but the film posits a valid response to this as the two opposed communities finally work together, and a group of young people overturns a lorry of food-aid.

Guyane pour tout dire, *suivi de* Le mal du pays *by Serge Patient*

These two collections of poems published in the same book seem to focus around the theme of acculturation and its dangers, and attempts to exorcise it. The poet sings of a country that has been robbed of its history and memory, torn between anxiety over the past and the present and hope for the future, being and non-being. The poet writes about Cayenne as an ambiguous town, "bâtarde," and schizophrenic like the people who inhabit it. The poet resorts to antonyms to describe the multiple personality of the place and the people, caught between "la réalité Créole" and "l'occidentale fiction," "l'alpha de la négritude" and "l'oméga de la schizophrénie." In *Le mal du pays*, his poems are love declarations to a Guiana that no longer is, and a virulent attack on colonialism.

Guyane. Traces-mémoires du bagne *by Patrick Chamoiseau and Rodolphe Hammadi*

This photographic and literary essay brings to the forefront the issue of monument, commemoration, memory and traces of the past. Both the visual medium and the text complement each other in showing what the "bagne" de Cayenne—i.e., various islands where prisoners were incarcerated—has left behind and how to read its traces. Hammadi's photography reveals the graffiti of a prisoner; a church entirely decorated by another; vegetation having taken over the door to an old cell; the odd perspective drawn between the place of death (where the guillotine used to stand) and the place of nourishment (the kitchens behind). Meanwhile, Chamoiseau's text circles around and defines the notion of "trace-mémoires" as the space left out by official histories, official memories, and belonging to an oppressed memory and/or history, and which, somehow, preserves it. And yet, the same "trace" can also contain the superimposition of various memories and histories in time, becoming ever fainter and difficult to read as time and memories pile up on it. The Guianese "bagne" is an exemplar of such traces that needs to be preserved (not renovated) so that it can keep evoking / retelling the past.

Histoire Générale des Antilles et des Guyanes *by Jacques Adelaide-Merlande*

This bird's-eye view of history of the Caribbean isles and Guyanas introduces the novice reader to this region of the globe from pre-Colombian times to the Cuban revolution. This historical panorama of the whole region clearly reveals how the Arawaks disappeared from the larger islands under the shock of the Spanish colonization; how various European nations started to settle in the smaller islands from the Seventeenth century onwards, discusses the economy of the region, slavery, the slave revolts, the various abolitions of slavery (depending on the colonizing nation), and the more recent influence of the United States on that region. Because of the daunting scope and complexity of the task, every effort was made to make the reading clear: the work is clearly divided in chronological chapters, themselves divided into sub-sections along the geopolitical lines of colonization. This format allows for several possible selective readings in which one can follow the fate of Guiana, Haiti, etc. Each chapter closes with a document section, which contains either texts from the time evoked, or large excerpts of books treating of specific subjects (e.g., acts on the better treatment of slaves in the Anglophone Caribbean, articles on natural catastrophes in the region, religion, languages, hiring procedures in Guiana).

Introduction à la Littérature Guyanaise *by Biringanine Ndagano and Monique Blérard-Ndagano*

Probably the most useful to a new reader in French Guianese literature, this didactic anthology presents Guianese literature from its beginnings to the early 1990s. Its introduction indicates the problem of defining Guianese literature (Who writes it? In what language? etc.). A first part is dedicated to oral literature: tales, legends, fables that form the various traditions of Guiana (Amerindian, Creole, Bushinenge et al.), and how they have been either transcribed or rewritten in French. The second part explores narratives and features the travelers' tales (and includes an excerpt of Frédéric Bouyer's narrative) as well as the first Guianese novel by Parépou, *Atipa*, in Creole, and Patient's rewriting of D'Chimbo alongside René Maran and Bertène Juminer's texts around questions of identity. Novels, plays and poetry are also amply discussed and illustrated with numerous excerpts. It is an anthology—not an essay—and, as such, has the weaknesses of its strengths: it cannot be exhaustive, and the choice of canonical texts is perhaps debatable, as is the case with many anthologies. But it is the only anthology of Guianese literature known to this author at the time of writing, and as such, is immensely precious.

Justine *by Catherine Régent*

The "hero" of the novel *Justine* (1995) is a sympathetically portrayed reformed convict, François, who has a love affair with Justine, the daughter of a well-to-do bourgeois in Third Republican New Caledonia. While the affair is doomed, in secret they pledge their sacrificial love to eternal friendship. The past is redeemed from shame by assimilation into free settler society, the latter having ideally abandoned the capital, Nouméa, for the bush, thereby lyrically marrying the land. In this environment, and after the death of her father, Justine finally takes as her own the child of the ex-convict, ex-orphan François by another ex-convict, an ex-prostitute who died in childbirth. In the process, Justine elevates her own soul as she liberates the future for the convict descendants. Written between the Matignon and Nouméa Accords by the descendant of a free settler, *Justine* mythically projects a "common destiny" for New Caledonia's diverse (European) inhabitants whose fate, chosen or imposed, is wedded to the island. Set at the beginning of the twentieth century, it thus anticipates the future in the past, a future parallel to the one that New Caledonia is projecting for itself a century later with respect to all its racial communities.

L'Acadie pour quasiment rien *by Antonine Maillet*

As a personal travel guide or tour, comical for the most part, of Acadia, the title is a tongue-in-cheek reference to the fact that Acadia was had for cheap. There are other caustic remarks throughout the work when the narrator refers, for instance, to Acadia no longer existing as such. The title also refers to the narrator's willingness as a guide to generously present all she knows about Acadia and the Acadian people so that the reader/traveler can have a better grasp and appreciation of Acadia's glorious past and oral literature. Similarly as in *On a mangé la dune* and *Par derrière chez mon père*, there are themes and archetypes in this work that reappear in Maillet's future works.

L'Agenda *by Déwé Gorodé*

L'Agenda (1996) is concerned with encounter with the other. It presents moments of Kanak life *en tribu*, yet these moments of memory, of the past captured as tradition in an extended present, are themselves inserted into the flow of history. Thus, there are stories that deal with attachment to the traditional hut ("La Case," "Un dame dans la nuit") or idealized natural environment of the ancestral village ("Rencontres"). Others present the encounter between Kanaks and Europeans in the city and the generalized shifts in attitudes that have taken place over the past quarter-century in New Caledonia and their attendant social problems ("Benjie, mon frère"). There is also a portrayal of a mythic reversal of fortune, where revenge is wreaked on history, as women take back their bodies, their lives and their land ("Où vas-tu Mûû?"), or where Kanaks achieve allegorical retribution in a story recounting New Calaedonian colonial history over three generations ("Affaire Classée"). Yet, identities can also be blurred and the familiar uncanny ("Le Passeur"), with an aura of unreality, or "magic realism" pervading the text about an old river-barge man.

L'Amour d'un monstre: Scènes de la vie créole *by Frédéric Bouyer*

This serial novel published in the Parisian newspaper *L'Événement* is actually the very first text of fiction elaborated around the figure of D'Chimbo. However, the narrative focuses not on him, but on the trials and tribulations of Maurice, a young French white naval officer fresh from a French boat in Guiana, and Julienne, a very pale and exceptionally beautiful mulatta. As they reveal their chaste amorous feelings to each other, D'Chimbo spots Julienne and falls in lust with her. The lovers are separated: Maurice's seafaring keeps him away from Julienne's bucolic house in the middle of the woods. Their relationship becomes epistolary for a while. Meanwhile, D'Chimbo has been going on a criminal rampage and is feared by every damsel and lady. Maurice's friend, Lionel, has taken on the role of Julienne's protector. Finally, Maurice's ship is back in Cayenne. But between the time he lands and the time he gets to his sweet Julienne, the latter is attacked and raped by D'Chimbo in the woods. She loses her mind. D'Chimbo is arrested and she recovers her spirits when she recognizes him in court, enough at least to be a prime witness: he is condemned and executed shortly thereafter. However, very soon after these terrible events, Julienne dies, in great piety, to the sadness and strange relief of Maurice whose love for her had been greatly hampered by the unfortunate loss of her virtue to a "savage."

L'Amour, la fantasia *by Assia Djebar*

The first of a quartet that explores the relationship of the narrator to her various and conflicting Arab, French and Berber ancestries. Her two films, "La Nouba des femmes du Mont-Chenoua" (1978) and "La Zerda et les chants de l'oubli" (1982), were crucial to this autobiographical novel. They provided her with a way back to writing after a ten-year silence. The intertwinement of her voice with those of the women she had interviewed for her films allowed her to write more intimately about herself. *L'Amour* is set in three parts: the first two are a mix of personal episodes and a rereading of French colonial documents. The third part engages in dialogues between herself and the women-fighters of the Algerian war. *L'Amour, la fantasia* is a very complex narrative that once again blends autobiographical fictions with historical accounts of the French colonial conquest of Algeria which started in 1830. While chronology seems to irremediably separate these two dimensions of the text, Djebar unveils a series of scenes connecting the historical drama of colonization and de-colonization to the more subjective struggles that Algerian women face in their everyday life. This historical and autobiographical intertextuality enables Djebar to ultimately envision a troubled, fragmented but real Algerian identity that would nonetheless allow silenced female memories and identities to resurface. In order to gain access to this identity, the women described by Djebar have to map out their own body and their own language. In this attempt to reconcile the individual and the collective, the feminine and the historical, Djebar imagines a new cultural space where Algerian women would break away from their silence and their isolation in the secluded space of the harem.

L'Appel des arènes *by Aminata Sow Fall*

L'Appel des arènes is the call of the wrestling arena that twelve-year-old Nalla listens to instead of doing his homework. At home, he hears the call of Western ideas from his Europeanized parents, Diattou and Ndiogou. From his friends André and Malaw, both wrestlers, he hears the call of tradition, magical and compelling. In the struggle between the two worlds, Diattou champions the cause of blind modernity and severs all ties with her African heritage; in the process, she loses her family, her job, and her sanity. The wrestlers champion the cause of a simple life rooted in ancestral values. Mr. Niang, Nalla's tutor, champions the cause of wisdom as he tries to mix tradition (the wrestling chants) and modernity (French grammar!). The winner is Nalla, who is able to draw his father to the wrestling match and makes a pact with him at the end of the book: they will go to the arena of tradition together, but they will also do the homework of modernity together.

L'Aventure ambiguë *by Cheik Hamidou Kane*

Cheikh Hamidou Kane's novel tells the story of Samba, a young member of the Diallobé people of Senegal. Samba begins the novel as a devout pupil at an Islamic school. As the most talented member of his generation he soon becomes a pawn in a political debate as to whether the Diallobé should send their children to the colonial schools. This debate explicitly contrasts the pragmatic but secular knowledge of the West with the Islamic spirituality of the Diallobé. It is feared that in acquiring the former they must inevitably lose the latter. It is decided that this risk must be taken and Samba is sent first to the French colonial schools and then to be educated in Paris. While in France Samba becomes politicized and feels increasingly deracinated; this throws his faith into doubt. When he is summoned back to the Diallobé Samba finds himself the object of great attention, particularly from "le fou." an old soldier who has gone mad during a trip to Europe. "Le fou" believes Samba to be a reincarnation of the Islamic master, but when he finds out that Samba has lost his faith, he murders him. The novel ends with Samba's death.

L'Enfant noir *by Camara Laye*

L'enfant noir is an autobiographical story of a childhood spent among the Mande of Haute-Guinée. It paints a vivid picture both of the general beliefs and practices of the Mande and of Laye's own domestic life. As the novel progresses two strands become apparent in Laye's life. The first of these is his immersion in traditional society, a bond cemented by his close relations with his family and by his initiation into the rituals pertaining to adulthood. The second is his education in the colonial schools, an education in which he is very successful and which creates a relation to European knowledge and practices. Eventually Laye goes to Conkary to complete his studies. There he is offered a scholarship to study in France. This brings the two sides of Laye's life into open conflict, as he is forced to choose between life in the village and education abroad. Despite his mother's opposition Laye chooses, with the blessing of his father, to go to France and the novel closes with him leaving to start his new life.

L'Esclavage en Guyane. Entre l'occultation et la revendication *by Serge Mam Lam Fouck*

This essay by a historian traces the representation of slavery in French Guianese society in post-slavery times, between 1848 (the abolition of slavery) and 1977. Mam Lam Fouck distinguishes two main moments: a) from 1848 to the mid-1950s, Guiana was trying to erase traces of slavery in several ways and for different purposes. First the ruling ideology was that of "réparation," which insists that the Republic no longer exclude part of its population from the sacrosanct republican belief in "liberté, égalité, fraternité"; then the mulatto class, eager to take power, resurrects the fear of slavery in order to win over white political opponents; finally, from 1875 to the mid-1950s, the politics of assimilation are triumphant and slavery is represented only as the subtext of emancipation. b) Since the 1950s (a few years after Guiana becomes a "département français"), slavery has been interpreted as a significant site for the construction of the Creole identity, although its representation is far from monolithic.

L'Oursiade *by Antonine Maillet*

As a fable of "Acadian" bears that take on human traits, this novel recounts the trials and tribulations of a bearish clan. Revenant-Noir serves as clan leader and is paired with Simon le Métis, an orphan raised by bears. Nounours, Revenant-Noir's cub, is paired with Tit-Jean. Oursagénaire is paired with Ozite, Simon's neighbor and a hundred-year-old, life long neighbor of bears. A forest fire, a famine, being hunted and harassed by authorities over the village dump, reminiscent of the events portrayed in Maillet's pivotal play *Les Crasseux* are among the challenges which the Acadian-like "bears" are forced to deal with. The underlying ecological message or moral of this work underscores the need for humans and animals to all get along through peaceful and harmonious coexistence.

Le Commencement des douleurs *by Sony Labou Tansi*

In *La commencement des douleurs*, Labou Tansi intensifies the fantastic atmosphere of his previous novels. Like *Les sept solitudes de Lorsa Lopez*, this novel is set in a coastal town in a fictional or unidentified post-colonial African nation. Hondo-Noote is a small quiet town where nothing much ever happens, until one day Hoscar Hana, an elderly bachelor, kisses Banos Maya, a young girl. The kiss is intended as part of a ritual, but it goes too far and Banos Maya falls passionately in love with Hoscar Hana. It is decided that he must marry her, but he refuses to do so and the issue divides the community for many years. After several false starts Hoscar Hana and Banos Maya eventually marry. He falls in love with her but dies shortly afterwards. Their son goes on to become a world-famous doctor, and Banos Maya eventually remarries a millionaire. As in *Les sept solitudes de Lorsa Lopez*, Labou Tansi uses a single event to act as the catalyst that forces the members of a small community to consider their relationships with each other and the outside world.

La Contrebandière *by Antonine Maillet*

In this theatrical version of Maillet's novel, *Mariaagélas*, similar also in content to her novel *Crache à Pic*, the feminine outlaw figure once again takes center stage and turns everything topsy-turvy by assuming the role and authority reserved or assigned traditionally only to men. As do many of Maillet's heroines, Mariaagélas effectively challenges and transgresses in this play the laws of the Father. This play also pits the prudish, holier-than-thou-character, La Veuve à Calixte, against the impious Mariaagélas, who is clearly identified with the carnival and the "gens d'En-bas." In fact, as in nearly all of Maillet's works, an irreverent, carnivalesque atmosphere, where role reversals are not uncommon between men and women, the rich, the "gens d'En-haut," and the poor, the "gens d'En-bas," also prevails throughout the play.

La Guyane entre maux et mots. Une lecture de l'oeuvre d'Elie Stephenson *by Biringanine Ndagano*

This critical essay on Elie Stephenson presents the latter as a poet, a playwright and a politically engaged author. The book starts with a discussion of *guyanité* as it applies to the thinking of Elie Stephenson and raises such issues as: in which language to write? for whom? The political engagement of Stephenson being indistinguishable from his work, Ndagano presents his plays and poetry alongside his reflections on the Guianese history from colonization to French department. The poetry is often perceived here as a cri de guerre trying to rally the troops, who appear singularly passive. The theatre is described as historical rewritings (of the D'Chimbo legend, for instance) or as the dramatization of the seduction France exerts, like a siren, on the Guianese only to assign them to a bitter form of exile. Beyond and through the study of Elie Stephenson's work, the essay poses questions about the identity of Guiana, its possible future, the myth or realistic possibility of Guiana's independence.

La Langue maternelle *by Vassilis Alexakis*

After spending twenty-four years in Paris, Pavlos returns to his native Greece. He reflects on his personal history, both Greek and French: he writes of his childhood, his family, the death of his mother, his relationships with women, and draws attention to the cultural differences between

Athens and Paris. He observes the changes that have taken place in Greece since his departure, and the old ways he had forgotten. Throughout, he is searching for the significance of epsilon, the Greek E: he notes words, muses on their meanings, and takes pleasure in the process of reacquaintance with his mother tongue. Much of the novel seems to be autobiographical and many themes and preoccupations of *Paris-Athènes* are echoed here.

La Littérature des Antilles-Guyane françaises *by Jack Corzani*

This six-volume presentation of the literature of the Francophone Caribbean (and Guiana) is written like an old-fashioned French academic essay, which delineates periods from the birth of a world and literature (with historical references to the discovery and peopling of that region of the globe) to what he calls "le désarroi contemporain." Out of the six volumes, the first one covers the period from the landing of Christopher Columbus to 1900 and never mentions the first Guianese novel (Parépou's *Atipa*, 1885); the five others are devoted to the twentieth century. Unfortunately, one can find only very few pages on Guianese literature. The work remains a likely solid reference for readers who need to have a well-documented view of the Francophone literature of the Caribbean and understand how it differs from Guiana's. A few solid chapters on the Harlem Renaissance and negritude give a welcome image of both the connections between the literatures of the New World and the global dimensions of the négritude movement.

La Littérature nord-africaine *by Arthur Pellegrin*

A long-standing resident of the French protectorate of Tunisia and the creator of the Cagayous-like Ragabouche in the late 1890s, Arthur Pellegrin was one of the major theorists and commentators on what some critics had begun to call the North African school of writers. In this work, he outlines the favorable cultural context of North African societies, extols the virtues of French culture as a civilizing force, and traces the roots of the North African school to writers like Musette, Stephen Chaseray, and Louis Bertrand whose work began to emerge in the late nineteenth century. The final section of the book includes the printed responses to an inquiry soliciting from fifty leading North African writers and critics their opinions on the present and future of a North African school of literature in French.

La Noire de . . . *by Ousmane Sembène*

La Noire de . . . Senegal/France, 1966. B/W, 65 mins., French. Written and directed by Ousmane Sembène. Produced by André Zwoboda. Cinematography by Christain Lacoste. Editing by André Gaudier. Cast members: Mbissine Thérèse Diop (Diouana), Anne-Marie Jelinek (Madame), Robert Fontaine Jr. (Monsieur), Momar Nar Sene (Diouana's fiancé), Ibrahima Boy (Boy with mask), Toto Bissainthe (Voice of Diouana), Robert Marcy (Voice of Monsieur), Sophie Leclerc (Voice of Madame). Filmed on location in Dakar and Antibes and produced by Films Domirev and *Les Actualités françaises*. Winner in the 1966 Cannes Film Festival Semaine de la Critique. Based on a real event from 1958, the first feature-length film to be made in Africa by an African, *La Noire de . . .* is a stinging indictment of colonial mentalities. Diouana has been nursery maid for a family of French *co-opérants* in Dakar, and leaps at the chance to continue working for them in Antibes when they return home to France. Dreaming of the fine sights and experiences she will have in France, Diouana parts lightly from her fiancé and family. Once in service in Antibes, however, she is exploited as an unpaid skivvy by Monsieur and Madame and virtually imprisoned in the small apartment. Friendless, she spends her time cooking, cleaning and clearing up after Monsieur and Madame, who are uncomprehending of her increasing distress. Diouana increasingly refuses to carry out her duties as she is expected to, incensing the petulant Madame. Unable to see a way out of her situation, and cut off from her family in Dakar, Diouana commits suicide.

La Nouvelle légende de D'Chimbo *suivi de* Massak *by Elie Stephenson*

La nouvelle légende de D'Chimbo, written in Creole (with its French translation in the same volume) situates the action in 1804. D'Chimbo has a two-year-long criminal record and he is seen talking with Elena (a woman he has kidnapped) in his carbet. Both protagonists give different versions of D'Chimbo's life. Elena is the vox populi accusing him of all sorts of crimes. D'Chimbo responds that he has committed some of them but not all, that he has been a scapegoat for all the evil doings of the Guianese, and blames his criminal record on the racism to which he fell victim after his arrival in Cayenne. He is presenting himself as having been framed by the white boss of the gold exploitation company as well as—and even more so—by the people of color in Guiana, who see in him the blackness they are struggling to escape. Taking advantage of his inebriation, Elena has him reveal to her the secret of his invincibility, and, when he awakes from his slumber, he is arrested and taken to Cayenne. The last scene shows him haranguing the crowd gathered to witness his execution. D'Chimbo throws back accusations to all present.

La Parole des femmes *by Maryse Condé*

La Parole des femmes examines womens' voices—and their lack thereof—in the Antilles Islands. Condé argues that women in the Antilles are bound to cultural mores in which the man plays the dominant role—as a result, wives tend to make excuses for their husbands, mothers for their boys. These women are hesitant to challenge the men who mistreat them—to the point of not even acknowledging the men's faults. Frustrated, Condé concludes that the women often perpetuate their own condition of subordination and voicelessness in the Antilles.

La Quarantaine *by J. M. G. Le Clézio*

La Quarantaine is about a small group of Europeans and a larger group of people of East Indian origin who were quarantined together in 1891 by the British-Mauritian authorities on a small island near Mauritius. One of the Europeans (all passengers of the *Ava*, a ship one passenger and a crew member of which had contracted smallpox), named Léon Archambaud, falls in love with an Indian woman he calls Suryavati. His brother Jacques still hopes to be accepted by the Mauritian elite the Archambaud's are descended from and so warns his brother the marriage will not be accepted. Thus, when the quarantine is lifted Léon and Suryavati disappear together never to be heard from again. The story is told by Jacques' grandson Léon Archambaud who recognizes the incompleteness of his own consciousness because of the family's fateful separation in 1891. The result is a complex series of imbricated invented narratives: an imagined Léon of the 1980s imagining a Léon of the 1890s, and then inventing (or allowing the earlier Léon to invent) a saga of Suryavati's mother traveling as a little girl with an adopted Indian mother from India to Flat Island decades before.

La Revue africaine

Subtitled the *Journal des travaux de la société historique algérienne* and initially edited by Louis-Adrien Berbrugger, *La Revue africaine* began to appear on a monthly basis in September 1856. *La Revue africaine* sought to write the recent history of the colony with articles on noteworthy events that had taken place since the arrival of the French in 1830 as well as provide information on indigenous folklore, history, and culture. While the first issues are a mix of historical articles, poetry, and editorials, the orientation of the journal increasingly became dominated by pre-colonial indigenous subjects, particularly in relation to pre-Islamic archaeology in North Africa.

La Revue algérienne illustrée

Inaugurated with the April 15, 1888, issue, *La Revue algérienne et tunisienne*, renamed *La Revue algérienne illustrée* in 1893, was a major journal appearing on a weekly basis that sought to represent the cultural landscape of the colony by publishing the fiction of local writers, short pieces on indigenous culture and folklore, literary and social columns, and political cartoons. *La Revue algérienne illustrée* also provided substantial editorial commentary in the weekly "Chronique algérienne," which discussed topical cultural and political issues of interest to a colonial reading public. Ernest Mallebay served as the editor of *La Revue algérienne illustrée* and one of its major contributors until 1898, after which Joseph Angelini took over the responsibilities of its direction.

La Revue algérienne

Published by the *Société des Beaux-Arts, des Sciences et des Lettres d'Alger* in monthly issues from November 1877 through March 1878, the short-lived *La Revue algérienne* was intended as an instrument for the enrichment the cultural life of the colony of Algeria. While the journal reported on lectures and cultural events that the *Société* had sponsored in Algiers, it also included literary efforts that were primarily extensions of metropolitan themes and styles rather than examples of an emergent culture specific to the colonial Algerian idiom or experience.

La Veuve enragée *by Antonine Maillet*

As a theatrical version of Maillet's novel, *Les Cordes-de-Bois*, the main character after whom the play is entitled represents one of Maillet's most constant and high-profile characters. The widow is one of Maillet's most visible representatives of the prudish well-to-do (also seen in *Mariaagélas, La Contrebandière* and *Garrochés en paradis*) who look down on the not-so-fortunate—*les gens d'en-bas*—and are, in this play, collectively called "the Mercenaire." Putting *les gens d'en-bas* against *les gens d'En-hant* once more, this play centers more precisely, however, on exposing the Veuve's religiously hypocritical behavior with regard to her dealings with the Mercenaire who threaten and disturb her haughty religious principles. In the end, it is ironically the Mercenaire who are shown to be more generous or charitable than the Veuve herself.

La Vie et demie *by Sony Labou Tansi*

Sony Labou Tansi's first novel tells the story of the fictional African state of Katamalanasie, which is ruled by a despotic line of dictators, the Guides Providentiels. The rebel leader Martial, who is brutally murdered at the beginning of the novel, opposes them. After his death his cause is pursued by his daughter Chaïdana and granddaughter, also called Chaïdana. The sons of the second Chaïdana and one of the Guides found the secessionist state of Darmellia. The conflict between the two countries eventually embroils the Western superpowers and leads to an apocalyptic war. By framing his story in hyperbolic and grotesque terms Labou Tansi is able to combine elements of comic satire with a shocking evocation of the horrors of despotism, which is shown to be as absurd as it is brutal. This sense of the absurdity of violence allows the novel to affirm and celebrate humanity despite its dystopian ending.

Le Bal du Gouverneur *by Marie-France Pisier*

Le Bal du Gouverneur is a novel published on the eve of the crisis years of the *événements* (1984–88) and in the midst of calls for independence. It is a nostalgic look at the past, via the story of the rites of passage of Théa, a high-school girl growing up in Nouméa in the 1950s, as the author herself did, the daughter of a high-ranking metropolitan *fonctionnaire*. The novel portrays her difficult relationship with her mother, who is a worldly but frustrated and decadent woman, unable to realize love and finally humiliated by her imperious husband. Théa's parents thus represent the values of colonial France, whereas Théa herself is a symbol of New Caledonia on the verge of "maturity," identified with the island's passage from its status as "colony" to that of *Territoire d'outre-mer*. While she is sad to see her best friend, Isabelle, return "home" to France, her family being expelled on charges of corruption within the Governor's bureaucracy, Théa stays on in New Caledonia, which seems to be her home at novel's end. Despite the twin insecurities represented by the convict heritage and the disquieting presence of Melanesians, the novel expresses implicit faith in France's ability to ensure a successful de-colonization.

Le Baobab fou *by Ken Bugul*

Le Baobab fou is the autobiography of Mariétou M'Baye, forced by Les Nouvelles Editions Africaines to use a pseudonym, for fear that some African readers might be scandalized by the life she depicted in this novel. The name she chose, Ken Bugul, is the name given by mothers to a child born after a number of stillbirths. It means, "nobody wants it" and is supposed to protect the child from death (Bernard Magnier, 1985). This turns out to be very symbolic in the book. Abandoned for a while by her mother, Ken leads a solitary childhood. She finds refuge in the French schools where she excels, receives a scholarship to pursue her studies in Belgium, but while trying to find her identity in the midst of two contradictory cultural realities, she slowly loses her soul to drugs and prostitution. She finds herself the victim of racial prejudice and discrimination. She is drawn into an increasingly bohemian milieu, but finds that she is regarded only as an exotic sexual object. All of which are presented as an attempt to obliterate awareness of herself and her non-belonging. She gets to the point where "nobody wants her." But she is somehow protected from death and returns in time to her village in Africa, where the old baobab tree awaits. Her level of satisfaction as the novel closes is, to say the least, ambiguous.

Le Bourgeois gentleman *by Antonine Maillet*

Although inspired by Molière's play, *Le Bourgeois gentilhomme*, Maillet has reworked considerably this comedy into a parody of his play in order to better reflect her aesthetic and literary affinities. As the bilingual title suggests, it is the dramatic dilemma of every French speaker,

Québécois and Acadian alike, who for economic and social reasons is confronted with the choice of employing French or adopting the colonizer's language in order to feel superior and succeed in life. The comedic aspect of the play stems from the juxtaposition of the culturally assimilated bourgeois figure, Monsieur Bourgeois, who suffers from an inferiority complex and whose sole ambition, as a result, is to belong to the English-speaking class "d'En-haut," and his lowly, proud French-speaking (Acadian) servant, Joséphine, who is shown to be morally and in every other respect superior to him. At the end of the play, Monsieur Bourgeois comes to accept through a cathartic, comedic process who he really is.

Le Brigand D'Chimbo, dit le Rongou. Ses crimes, son arrestation, sa mort *by Frédéric Bouyer*

This first D'Chimbo narrative recounts the crimes of D'Chimbo from a French traveler's perspective. D'Chimbo has escaped from the company that had hired him and taken refuge in the forest, where he has built his "carbet." He steals food from the baskets of women who go and visit their friends on Sundays, and attacks them if they put up any resistance. He escapes the police all the time, which leads to various beliefs in his supernatural powers. The search for him lasts for two years during which he commits more and more crimes, rapes and murders, including an infanticide. Finally a fellow Rongou (i.e., a man from the river Gabon's banks) manages to capture him. He is then brought to justice in Cayenne, where he undergoes a trial according to the French justice system and is executed shortly thereafter.

Le Chemin Saint-Jacques *by Antonine Maillet*

Divided in two parts, the first part of the novel is highly autobiographical recounting the main character's childhood adventures. Going by the name of Radi, Maillet's childhood alter ego and the same character as in Maillet's earlier novel *On a mangé la dune*, she reaches the age of fourteen as the first part ends. The second part of the novel deals with the same character who is now an adult who goes by the name of Radegonde. This part is much less autobiographical and can be described merely as the "autobiography of Maillet's soul." The novel's title refers to Maillet's cosmic view of the universe where differences between past, present and future seem to disappear and, correspondingly, where the laws of space and time can be transgressed. The juxtaposition of Radi's and Radegonde's vision of the universe and the differences in their perspectives, account for the originality and interest of this novel.

Le Code Noir ou le calvaire de Canaan *by Louis Sala-Molins*

This essay is actually an annotated edition of the Black Code written by Colbert and Louis XIV in 1685. In the introduction, the author depicts its history, argues about its essential paradoxical—absurd—nature, and his own relationship with this text. In the first part, he deconstructs the Code and gives his interpretation of it as closely linked to the theological debate of the Catholic colonizing powers (whether Africans have souls or not), and ardently justifies his re-edition of the Code as a document never to forget (keeping the memory of it alive might prevent present and future generations from feeling a "scandalous nostalgia" for eras gone by). The second part is the re-edition of the Code itself, each of the sixty articles presented with an accompanying gloss by the editor. The third part presents other texts on slavery: writings by slaves themselves (More Lack, Cugoano), by thinkers and philosophers such as Montesquieu or

Rousseau, and, finally, an essay on the "Société des Amis des Noirs" exposing all its complexities and paradoxes. Clearly and passionately written, this book is essential to understand the official French discourse on slavery.

Le Conclave des pleureuses *by Fawzi Mellah*

A journalist is assigned to investigate alleged rapes in an unnamed town. The city, however, is a thinly disguised Tunis, Tunisia, where the Red Mountain neighborhood is located and where the statues of President Bourguiba and the historian Ibn Khaldun are erected. The family accused of perpetrating the rapes is run by a matriarch (Aïcha-dinar) and comprises six brothers, one of whom is a saint (le saint de la parole), and one sister. The sister makes the journalist draw the New Quarter into the investigation. When a civil servant residing in the New Quarter dies, a conclave of professional mourners is held and conflict within the community is uncovered. The journalist uses the investigation to settle his personal history with the matriarch who is responsible for his expulsion from the company of women at a young age. The narrative gives a number of versions of events mixed with autobiographical detail and thoughts on history, myth and writing.

Le Huitième jour *by Antonine Maillet*

Referring to a time and place outside of history, where the impossible is possible, limited only by the writer's imagination, the eighth day represents the opportunity for mankind to complete God's incomplete Creation. This autobiographical novel by Maillet's own admission recounts the tales or exploits of four heroes whose names are taken directly out of the storyteller's book but who are modeled after Maillet's own great grand-parents—"Jean de l'Ours," "Gros comme le Poing," "Messire René" and "Jour en Trop." They set about exploring the world in the hope of finding "Paradise Lost" and combat injustice along the way in a "Cervantesque" manner reminiscent of the adventures and follies of Don Quixote.

"Le mouvement littéraire en Afrique du Nord" *by Robert Randau*

The leader and primary theorist of the *Algerianiste* movement in the 1910s, Robert Randau had been an active participant in emerging colonialist culture since the 1890s. In this article, Randau surveys the achievements of colonial Algerian literature in French at the turn of the century by discussing, among others, Musette, Stephen Chaseray, Louis Lecoq, Louis Bertrand, Pierre Mille, among many others. The stated goal of his discussion is to convey the originality, variety, and high quality of colonial literary production in Algeria and to demonstrate its divergence from metropolitan culture.

Le Nègre du gouverneur *by Serge Patient*

Subtitled "Chronique coloniale," this novel locates the story around 1802, when slavery is reinstated in Guiana, and Victor Hughes is governor. Slave-traders raided D'Chimbo's native village in Africa; Natéké, his wife was raped under his very eyes, and he has been forcibly taken to Guiana. Once there he wants to know the secret of the white people's power and does everything he can to master every possible white code (be they verbal or amorous). His social ascension is irresistible: he uses his sexual appeal to advance his cause with women, while his strength, intelligence and hard-working habit do not go unnoticed by the governor. The latter hires him to infiltrate maroon groups, command a group of soldiers and kill rebellious slaves. D'Chimbo ends up thinking he has mastered the white power and has, in effect, liberated himself from the shackles of slavery—he can even envisage a marriage with beautiful, innocent, white Virginie. He has done what the master has always prohibited: to know a white woman and to recover his human dignity.

Le Petit prince de Belleville *and* Maman a un amant *by Calixthe Beyala*

These two novels are told from the point of view of Loukoum, the young son of an immigrant family in the Belleville quartier of Paris. They portray the situation of the African community as a whole—subjected to menial employment, racial prejudice and police harassment—and the domestic drama of Loukoum's own family. The main focus of the two novels is the relationship between Loukoum's mother M'am and his father. At the beginning of the sequence the father is portrayed as a despotic patriarch, keeping his two wives in a state of domestic servitude while he works intermittently to support his philandering and gambling. At the same time, however, we see how difficult he finds it to relate to European life and how emasculating he finds his failure to be successful in French society. At the same time M'am becomes increasingly independent, she learns to read and eventually starts up her own business, which is very successful. A brief affair with a French man builds up her self-esteem and when she returns to the family a new consensual balance of domestic power is attained.

Le Sentier *by Nicolas Kurtovitch*

In this play which premiered during the inaugural season at the Tjibaou Kanak Cultural Centre in 1998, all actors but one—a European woman—are Kanak, a situation that would have been barely imaginable just a few years before. Set in a Melanesian village, it concerns the discussions that take place over the fate of a young European woman, taken prisoner by some of the tribe's impetuous youths at a time of heightened antagonism between Kanaks and whites, reminiscent of the *événements* of the 1980s. The chief must decide if the woman is to be freed or to die—not for any misdemeanor of hers, but for the sins of her forefathers, who had taken the land and destroyed Kanak culture. Into the equation comes the fact that the woman is the lover of the chief's son, himself trapped in the struggle against oppression by the woman's clan, i.e., *les Blancs*. The son momentarily denies and denounces her, before surreptitiously freeing her one night and guiding her to safety. Love therefore triumphs over misguided and abstract hate presented as "duty" in the form of political struggle, and averts an otherwise tragic outcome.

Les Anciens Canadiens *by Philippe Aubert de Gaspé père*

A young Scot, Archibald Cameron of Locheill, becomes an intimate friend of Jules d'Haberville, a young Canadian, the son of a *Seigneur*. As the war of conquest continues, the friends find themselves in opposing camps: the foundation of their friendship is severely shaken. Although reconciled following the cessation of hostilities, the two friends experience a different fate. Jules marries an Englishwoman, while Archibald is rejected by Jules's sister, who is unwilling to accept one of the conquerors as her spouse. Interspersed with this loosely woven historical plot is a lively and empathic portrait of the seigneurial regime and its customs.

Les Coeurs barbelés *by Jacques Caludine*

This novel published in the year of the *Accord de Nouméa* (1998) treats the "impossible" relationship between a young Caldoche woman, Malou, from a very conservative rural background, and her pro-independence Kanak lover, Séry, the father of her child. In doing so, it recounts the personal impact of *les événements* of the 1980s, the rise of Kanak political consciousness, the recognition of the importance of Kanak culture after 1974 and the ensuing polarization between communities. The irony is that neither side can see the similarity of their situation. In this world, nearly everyone tries to deny their own concrete history of interaction in the name of an essentialist identity, leading to intransigent or self-indulgent behaviour toward others. The novel shows that, despite a certain social evolution, the hour has not yet come for New Caledonia to put into practice, at least not at the interpersonal level, the *destin commun* promoted by the new political framework. However, beyond the present separation of communities, the novel posits, in the spirit of the Nouméa Accord, a multiracial future for New Caledonia, through the *métis* offspring of the doomed lovers.

Les Confessions de Jeanne de Valois *by Antonine Maillet*

In this (auto)biographical novel based on the religious experiences of a Catholic sister, Maillet's literary alter ego, whom she once knew and who was influential in her life, religious confessions serve as a pretext to recount official and non-official historical events as seen through the eyes of a ninety-year-old Acadian sister. These recollections chronicle to a large extent events in Acadian history long forgotten or ignored by historians. Serving as a direct witness and bridge to Acadia's glorious past as well as a collector of Acadian stories and legends, Sister Jeanne sees herself in the privileged position and obligation to pass along this knowledge and heritage to future Acadian generations. Literate, well-educated and outspoken, she turns her attention, however, not only toward the past but also toward the present and the future when discussing a wide range of topics, such as religious, feminist and minority issues, race relations, pedagogy and ecology.

Les Crasseux *by Antonine Maillet*

A pivotal play dating back to 1968 which Maillet has revised twice and which probably best characterizes and sums up her aesthetic affinities and entire literary creation. In fact, the vast majority of the themes and archetypes dear to her heart can be found in this dialectical, Manichean dramatic comedy, which pits the well-to-do, the "gens d'En-haut," against the less fortunate "Crasseux," the "gens d'En-bas." The playwright's sympathies are clearly on the side of the "Crasseux" whose social, political and minority status resembles closely that of a certain segment of the Acadian population, exploited and oppressed by those who are socially or economically above them. Notable characters in this play, such as Don l'Orignal, la Sagouine, la Sainte and la Cruche, reappear in future works of hers. The play ends on a positive or hopeful note, as do most of Maillet's works, with the resolution of the symbolic opposition between the two groups. Whereas the "gens d'En-haut" invade and occupy the Crasseux's world, the Crasseux settle down in their new home vacated by the "gens d'En-haut."

Les Dits d'un idiot *by Linda Lê*

This novel is remarkable for its innovative style. It rejects the illusion of linear narrative progression, and dispenses with rules of syntax and punctuation. The narrator is a wheelchair-bound philosopher, locked in an unhealthy relationship with his manipulative mother. The mother figure, nicknamed "Mandragore," requires constant proof of his affection for her, yet is never satisfied with the results. The narrator intersperses the narrative of their relationship with an account of the life of one of his friends, "Morte-saison," who appears to be of Vietnamese descent. A shadowy, introverted character, Morte-saison awaits the arrival of a man from her home country, who never comes. She initially works for a misanthropic, possessive employer, before moving to a company that allows former stars to recapture their glory days.

Les Drôlatiques, horrifiques et épouvantables aventures de Panurge, ami de Pantagruel *by Antonine Maillet*

Based on several of Rabelais's works, such as *Gargantua, Pantagruel* and, especially, the *Tiers Livre* with regard to its particular story line, this play includes notable Rabelaisian characters, such as Panurge, Pantagruel, Frère Jean and Gargamelle. Although inspired greatly by Rabelais's carnivalesque view of the world to which Maillet subscribes entirely, Maillet has succeeded in several ways to give an Acadian flavor to her play as well as her characters. Set in the New World during the sixteenth century, one of Maillet's favorite time periods, there are numerous anachronistic references to Acadia when, for instance, the character Frère Jean declares allegorically that they are not yet "out of the woods," Furthermore, when recounting the somewhat misogynistic episode taken from the *Tiers Livre* where Panurge is searching for a faithful woman to marry, Maillet rewrites this episode to place women in a more favorable light.

Les Évangiles du crime *by Linda Lê*

The four short stories of *Les Évangiles du crime* dwell upon the darker side of human nature. The first story depicts a man and a woman drawn together through the narration of a tragic 1950s love affair. The second pieces together the circumstances leading to Professor T.'s apparent suicide through his diary and the journal entries of his alter ego, "Plus-dure-sera-la-chute." The third story begins with a random encounter between the male narrator and the mysterious Klara V., who subsequently commits suicide. An examination of the contents of her handbag yields evidence of her promiscuous lifestyle and her destructive relationship with her mother. The final story sees Vinh L., a former Vietnamese boat person, unburden himself to a plagiarizing author, as he struggles to come to terms with the fact that he once killed and ate a fellow boat person in extreme circumstances.

Les Pieds nus *by Linda Lê*

This short parable tells of a six-year-old girl forced to flee her home in great haste. She forgets her shoes, and when her father returns with them, she finds that he has given her one of her own shoes, and a shoe belonging to her sister. She learns to walk in odd shoes. Lê applies this image to herself; as an exile incapable of speaking her mother tongue, she has learned to walk in odd shoes, but can never return home as a result.

Les Sept solitudes de Lorsa Lopez *by Sony Labou Tansi*

Labou Tansi's magical, burlesque novel tells the story of the people of Valancia, the coastal province of a fictional African state. At the beginning of the novel Lorsa Lopez, a prominent figure in the community, murders his wife. In protest, the formidable matriarch Estina Bronzario leads the women of the city in a sex strike. This unleashes a series of increasingly bizarre, occasionally supernatural events, as the inhabitants of Valancia attempt to work through the consequences of this crime and to come to terms with their history and identity. This process brings then into conflict with the authorities of Nsanga Norda, the capital. Eventually these authorities have Estina Bronzario assassinated, but on the very day on which that murder is committed a flood engulfs Nsanga Norda. Valencia is left with the autonomy and status it has desired. Lorsa Lopez returns from his self-imposed exile and the novel closes in a mood of redemption.

Les Trois parques *by Linda Lê*

This novel, once more notable for its experimentation with narrative form and style, is largely set in the "cuisine rutilante" of a heavily pregnant French woman of Vietnamese origin, married to a German Buddhist. She has summoned her sister and one-armed female cousin to discuss the impending visit of her father from the homeland. The theme of filial betrayal is introduced by the sustained reference to the father as "Le Roi Lear." The novel becomes increasingly surreal as the wheels of tragedy, set in motion by the invitation to the father, moves the narrative toward the father's death in Vietnam.

Lettre morte *by Linda Lê*

In this autobiographical novel, Linda Lê reminisces about her Vietnamese childhood with her beloved alcoholic father, neurasthenic mother and mentally ill uncle. Her memories are prompted by the death of her father, the novel acting as a response to the unsent letter that he wrote to her on his deathbed. She also dissects her miserable affair with a selfish married man and the mental illness that she has endured. The words of the narrator are addressed to a silent listener, Sirius, who guides her toward a more positive vision of the future.

Lettres créoles. Tracées antillaises et continentales de la littérature 1635–1975 *by Patrick Chamoiseau and Raphaël Confiant*

This essay on Antillean and Guianese literature reclaims the territory of the study of "belles lettres" and clearly defines its own approach to this corpus as a "marronnage" of all previous academic discourse on the topic. The authors want to free it from the strictures of such academic terminology and attempts at classification that have tried to box this literature in coarse conceptual categories such as "littérature négro-africaine," "littérature noire d'expression française," or "littérature afro-antillaise." They give it a new name, "littérature créole," and ask that both literature written in French and literature written in Creole be considered part of it. The book is illustrated, written in a narrative fashion rather than a dry essay or an anthology. Yet it efficiently introduces the literature of the region set against a presentation of history, geography, arts, and beliefs. It is in itself a Creole book in its structure and way of addressing the reader in a call-and-response fashion (using the "tu" form). The Creole texts are quoted and translated into French.

Massabielle *by Jacques Savoie*

This film (ONF/NFB, 1983) by Jacques Savoie is based on *Raconte-moi Massabielle*, the novel by Jacques Savoie. Pacifique Haché lives alone in an abandoned church in the deserted village of Massabielle in Acadia. A mining company has moved the previous inhabitants to Bathurst. A company lawyer tries to entice him into leaving Massabielle, but Pacifique resists. A local woman Stella joins him and they form a relationship. At the end of the film, Pacifique receives a television set as a present and becomes wholly absorbed by it. He eventually destroys the set when he realizes that it is making him mad. The film ends with rapid images of the growing family produced by Pacifique and Stella.

Massak *by Elie Stephenson*

Massak is a rewriting of Serge Patient's novel, *La nouvelle légende de D'Chimbo* in which D'Chimbo has become Kalimbo. Victor Hughes, who trusts him, has sent him to meet Pompée, the leader of the maroons, to offer him and his group a deal: if the fugitive slaves surrender their weapons and go back to the Isle of Cayenne, they will not be prosecuted. Pompée refuses. The dialogue between both men shows two opposing figures: Pompée is a mulatto who claims his African roots and is ready to die, fighting for his freedom, whereas D'Chimbo is what Pompée calls a "Nègre-Blanc," a man and who has adopted the white man's values and is eager to compromise. D'Chimbo sees himself as a survivor and a trickster who wants assimilation. In the end, however, Hughes betrays D'Chimbo and throws him in jail for treason. While he waits the morning of his execution, D'Chimbo realizes Pompée's way to freedom is the only possible one.

Métisse blanche *by Kim Lefevre*

In this poignant story of her childhood and adolescence Kim remembers the pain of being rejected by the country and culture she loves. Born of a Vietnamese mother and a French father, Kim narrates the first twenty years of her life in Vietnam and her threefold displacement in Vietnamese society—as girl, "métisse" and illegitimate offspring. She relates how she was shunted between places and families from Hanoi to Saigon to Tuyen Quang back again to Hanoi. From there she went to Sam Sôn, Nam Dinh, Van Xa, Tuy Hoa, Quan Can, Nha Trang, Dalat and finally to Saigon. Placed for a while in an orphanage, ignored by her stepfather, rejected by her legitimate siblings, her nationalist uncle and her more sophisticated cousins, the narrator survives, proves her self-worth by succeeding at school and eventually leaves for France in 1960 to pursue further studies. In a narrative that locates her métissage in "white space," Lefevre challenges colonizer-colonized binaries, blurs boundaries of race and constructs a creative world in the margins.

Moi, Tituba *by Maryse Condé*

Ghost-mothers accompany Condé's character Tituba, as oppressors successively wrench her from her native island and the people she loves. These figures foreshadow Tituba's own life-after-death and her continuing humane presence among the tortured victims of puritanical righteousness and slavery. Although throughout her tumultuous life, Tituba struggles to maintain long-term personal relationships, her selfless attitude and humble self-disclosure serve to create friendships that are not bounded by the normal constraints of time and space. When she is held in prison as a witch, for example, she joins her sorrows with those of a fellow inmate, Hester Prynn, thereby linking her fate with a young white woman and her story to Nathaniel Hawthorne's *The Scarlet Letter*. Against a backdrop of more militant voices, Condé emphasizes Tituba's unique indiscriminate empathy for fellow sufferers, regardless of their race, sex, or religion, modeling a multicultural community.

Mythologie du métissage *by Roger Toumson*

This essay examines the roots of our postmodern ideology of "métissage" and traces them back to the various historical stages of the discourse on identity. The author first describes the most significant changes in sociological, ideological and symbolic frames of reference and representation through his reading of texts such as the Bible, the Black Code, and the French philosophers from the Enlightenment, to name but a few. He also looks at archetypes of the mixed race myths (Odysseus, Oedipus, Caïn) and ends up describing the historical sites of "métissage" as mythical. Finally, he proposes an analysis of neighbouring yet very distinct concepts such as *antillanité, guyanité, créolité*, the discursive strategies through which the "métis" is no longer an erring signifier in quest of identity, but embodies the critique of the very notion—and signifier—of identity.

O Mayouri *by Elie Stephenson*

This play was written in Creole (published alongside its French translation) and inspired by Haitian author Jacques Roumain's novel *Gouverneurs de la Rosée* (1944). The Haitian protagonist, Manuel from Roumain's novel, finds a soul mate in Guianese protagonist Frédéric from Stephenson's play, as they are both humanist militants and consciousness raisers. The play opens with Frédéric coming home after ten years abroad, most of them in France, and a brief passage in Algeria, fighting for the French. His time away has taught him to love his country and he now wants to serve it (rather than France). Upon his return, he finds his country untilled, the rural areas deserted, and a general feeling of abandonment. He decides to create a type of traditional "mayouri" (a cooperative aiming toward self-sufficiency), which would be efficient and economically viable, and fit in the modern development projects. He envisages it as part of modern development projects, and designed by united people, away from any political party. In the village, his opponents are the mayor and other mediocre people who feel threatened by Frédéric whom they see as a rival. Frédéric will end up killed over amorous and political rivalry. At his wake, the villagers understand their collective responsibility in his murder. Frédéric's message was one of love and hope for a future built communally. His death heralds the end of idealism.

"Of Mimicry and Man" *by Homi Bhabha*

In this article, Homi Bhabha elaborates his theory of mimicry which attempts to account for psychological phenomena in colonial subjects in situations where they are forced to, or strategically choose to, imitate colonials. Mimicry describes the process by which colonial subjects may challenge colonial authority through dissimulation: behind the mask of repetition, an independent psyche may safely evaluate and subordinate colonial sources of power. This is described as "partial representation" and describes dynamics in which colonial subjects independently assimilate, subvert colonial intention, and mock colonial authority without any visible manifestation perceptible to the colonial observer.

Ombre sultane *by Assia Djebar*

In *Ombre sultane* Assia Djebar parallels the lives of two women married to the same man. Despite their shared husband, these two female characters lead radically different and even antagonistic existences. While Isma, the main narrator of *Ombre sultane*, is an emancipated woman who is in control of her destiny, Hajila is isolated in her silence and her submission to her abusive husband. Throughout her narration, Isma accompanies Hajila in her quest for emancipation. After several secret outings in the Forbidden City, Hajila slowly discovers her new identity as a free woman, in other words, a woman who has the power to go out. This liberation remains nonetheless dramatic. Her husband cannot tolerate that she has the audacity to leave the house, take off her veil and allow men on the streets to witness her newly gained nudity. Violently confronted by her husband who attempts to punish her sin by blinding her, Hajila is going to take control of her destiny for the first time. Instead of returning home to her life of submission and abuse, Hajila has the courage to leave everything behind her. After sharing one husband, Hajila and Isma meet in the outside space of the city where they can, at last, freely drift.

On a mangé la dune *by Antonine Maillet*

As tales about children, namely, her seven older brothers and sisters and her childhood friends, Maillet's second novel, written much like her first novel, *Pointe-aux-Coques*, in a French academic style (unlike her later works, which take full advantage of the particularities and originality found in the popular Acadian vernacular), is an autobiographical and often idyllic portrait of her childhood. The novel takes place in a small Acadian village reminiscent of Bouctouche, New Brunswick, where Maillet grew up at the beginning of the Second World War, and as seen for the most part through the eyes of the eight-year-old narrator, Radi. An adult voice or narrator closely tied to that of Maillet's occasionally steps in to offer her views. As is evident in Maillet's future works, the children's power of imagination to transform reality by breaking the laws of space and time takes center stage.

Orphée Dafric *by Werewere Liking*

Orphée Dafric is a complex combination of verse and prose that relocates the Orpheus myth to an African setting and tells it through a series of tableaux inspired by the initiation rituals of the Bassa people. Their families oppose the marriage of Orphée and Nyango. In order to prove their love and obtain permission to marry, they undertake the challenge of crossing a torrential river in a flimsy canoe. They successfully complete this task and are married. The story is immediately retold, however, and this time Nyango is drowned. Orphée descends to the underworld to look for her. He undergoes six tests, based on Bassa initiation rituals. At the end of his ordeals, which last for nine months, he realizes that there is more to his journey than a search for Nyango and he receives an ecstatic vision of the potential future of his country. He is then reunited with Nyango and returns to the surface. Orphée then awakes and realizes that the whole experience has been a dream on his wedding night. Liking leaves us in no doubt, however, that the "dream" experience is every bit as real as the waking one.

Où est le droit? *by Pierre Gope*

This is a play that confronts the subject of sexual abuse and cover-up in contemporary Kanak society. Corilen, the virgin daughter of Chief Cango, is bashed and raped by her drunken kinsman Sérétac one night on the outskirts of the village. The latter acknowledges his action and receives forgiveness from the assembled customary elders conservatively upholding "tradition." Cango himself subsequently admits that his daughter had to be sacrificed for the common good, although he is torn by contradictory feelings. Corilen remains dissatisfied, however, with "customary justice" and decides to take legal proceedings in the court of the "whites." There, Sérétac pleads irresponsibility for his actions due to being drunk at the time, but the white man's court does not accept this as a mitigating circumstance and he is sentenced to eight years' imprisonment. Years pass, and Sérétac serves out his prison sentence. Upon release, he comes back to the village to look for Corilen and again ask her forgiveness. But she has gone to the cemetery where her mother is buried. Overwhelmed by her own suffering and the indifference of the clan, she stabs herself as Samy arrives. He and Sérétac are unable to prevent Corilen's killing herself, but in a final gesture of reconciliation, Samy accepts Sérétac's forgiveness and asks him to do likewise.

Où est le droit? *and* Cendres de sang *by Pierre Gope*

In his plays, Pierre Gope explores sensitive, taboo issues in Melanesian society, such as rape, incest, corruption and the silence that conspires to cover them up. The plays confront the authority, if not the wisdom, of the "elders" with the voice of the innocent victim (principally in the form of a girl), and reveal a society undergoing profound change.

Papa et autres nouvelles *by Vassilis Alexakis*

This is the first collection of short stories by Alexakis to be published in France. The themes of identity and memory and occasional excursions into the fantastic that are characteristic of his novels reappear in these shorter works: a man is approached by a child in a park who believes him to be his father; another waits to meet the daughter he did not know he had; a writer creates a fiction inspired by a household mail order catalogue; a film director launches a film, wonders whether he is in love, visits his mother in hospital and renovates an old rocking horse; a husband recounts the manifestations of his obsessive jealousy; other obsessives are the man whose whole life is watching a faded video of a Platini goal, the elderly academic who observes a young girl, the man with a pair of tweezers who removes all manner of objects from every orifice of his body. All but one of these narratives is told in the first person.

Par derrière chez mon père *by Antonine Maillet*

As a collection of picturesque, folkloric and often humorous portraits and sketches frequently (auto)biographical in nature, this work is a spatial and temporal reference to the glorious Acadian past going as far back as to the biblical account of Adam and Eve. This seminal work which celebrates, similarly as in *On a mangé la dune*, the children's power of imagination to create fantastic worlds that do not conform to the laws of space and time lays the groundwork for recurring themes and archetypes found in many of Maillet's future works. Allusions to notable characters, such as Évangéline, la Sagouine, Don l'Orignal and even Pélagie, abound. The binary opposition between "the haves," the "gens d'En-haut," and "the have-nots," the "gens d'En-bas," the great importance and worth of the storyteller and his or her tales, and Acadia's long period of silence and isolation are among the historical and social themes discussed in this work.

Pélagie-la-Charrette *by Antonine Maillet*

Published in 1979 on Acadia's 375th anniversary, this Goncourt Prize–winning epic novel, which draws heavily upon the oral tradition, recounts the tragic but heroic events following the deportation by the English in 1755 of thousands of French-speaking Acadians from their homeland. After spending fifteen years as exiles in Georgia, Pélagie Leblanc and her compatriots decide to return to their homeland, the "Promised Land." Pélagie's "charrette" soon comes to symbolize and serve as a metaphor for Pélagie's and her people's determination and courage to return to their rightful home. Their ten-year "odyssey" from 1770 to 1780 through Virginia, Maryland, Pennsylvania and the New England states comes to an end when the "Mother Courage" figure or heroine and her followers return to the birthplace of (New) Acadia.

Rabelais et les traditions populaires en Acadie *by Antonine Maillet*

Published in 1971 and based on her doctoral thesis presented at the Université Laval the previous year, Maillet seeks to demonstrate and highlight this detailed study, as the title suggests, the link or relation between Acadia's rich linguistic heritage and traditions and those of sixteenth-century France as presented by Rabelais. She lists, for instance, over five hundred archaisms from the Touraine and Berry regions of France still in use in what are today the Maritime Provinces of Canada. The work also covers a wide range of other subject matters, such as tales, folklore, legends, customs, beliefs, superstitions, pastimes, proverbs and sayings, which Rabelais's sixteenth-century France and modern-day Acadia still both have in common.

Raconte-moi Massabielle *by Jacques Savoie*

This novel received the Prix de l'Association Francophone Internationale. The central character is Pacifique Haché, who lives alone in an abandoned church in the deserted village of Massabielle in Acadia. The Noranda Mining Company has moved the previous inhabitants to Bathurst. A company lawyer tries to entice him into leaving Massabielle, but Pacifique resists. A local woman Stella joins him and they form a relationship. Pacifique receives a television set as a present and becomes wholly absorbed by American game shows. He eventually destroys the set when he realizes that it is making him mad, but its frame remains, fixed by Pacifique to the door of the confessional. He and Stella decide to remain in Massabielle.

Retour à la saison des pluies *by Kim Lefevre*

In Lefevre's second book the narrator takes up the story of her life thirty years after her departure from Vietnam. During these years Kim has lived in Paris, avoided fellow Vietnamese and never intended to return to Vietnam. The success of *Métisse Blanche* brings her into contact with old friends and acquaintances. She gets in touch once again with her family in Vietnam and she picks up enough courage to return to meet them. The narrative is divided into two sections, the fantasized return and the actual voyage to Vietnam. As she listens to her mother, who speaks candidly to herself about her daughter's childhood, Kim gradually gets over the hurt and pain of rejection. During her trip she is able to retrieve only some very rare images of her past. The contact with her country of origin and her family makes her realize the importance of living in the present. The book provides the reader with a new dimension to the rhetoric of displacement.

Sitt Marie Rose *by Etel Adnan*

Etel Adnan bases her novel on an actual event in order to portray the horror of the war. Marie Rose is a mother and teacher who braves the line of demarcation in order to cross the city to go to work. Her refusal to adhere to political or geographic restrictions is an act of defiance against such divisions erected by a country taken over by various political and military factions. She is kidnapped and taken prisoner in her school, where representatives of society interrogate her: three militiamen and a clergyman. She is accused of betraying her country, her religion and her people for pursuing the cause of the Palestinians in Lebanon and for defying the traditional role of a woman. As a result, she is tortured and executed. Adnan portrays a society that leaves no room for defiance and whose rules are enforced through violence and horror. Any resistance is met with severe punishment. It is a society that is collapsing and its authority disintegrating as a new resistance gains strength, as is represented by Marie Rose, whose words prove to be more powerful than her executioners' weapons of destruction.

Surveiller et punir: naissance de la prison *by Michel Foucault*

This essay on the history of incarceration, and the practice of watching, punishing, and disciplining criminals (and children, colonized people, outcasts of all sorts) does not only take a good look at what made French society a disciplinary one. It also analyzes the body as the object of incarceration and punishment, and as a body which needs to be corrected (from bent to straight, from unfit to fit): hence the French "maisons de redressement." The body is then posited as a political entity. This essay, although it is not at all its goal, is useful to further understand the perception of the slave as body.

Terre violente *by Jacqueline Sénès*

This is a novel that follows the adventures of the Sutton family on its *station* south of Nouméa through virtually the whole period since colonization. Despite establishing a foundational "pact" with Melanesians, the family's life on the land is governed by an implacable binary logic in which hope alternates with disaster. Following John Sutton's death by plague, his wife Helena valiantly carries on the work of the farm, and despite adversity manages to raise her two children, one of whom later adopts a Melanesian orphan, Kahahéné. A symbolic representation of the pro-independence leader, Jean-Marie Tjibaou, he goes from being Jean-Chrétien, the model pupil of catechism, to renouncing his vocation as a priest and working for the secular betterment of his people, whose life is everywhere in a state of decline. When he finally returns to the family farm to reclaim his land, he is wanted for subversion as the station goes up in flames, probably due to the anger and frustration of Wanatcha, the *métis* caretaker of the property who had also grown up on it. He had loved this land as his own, yet without ever being able to own it, thereby feeling excluded from both white and black society in New Caledonia.

Terres mêlées *by Elie Stephenson*

The same militant revolutionary themes haunt this collection of poems. The poet wants to wake up an indolent people, who have fallen prey to inaction, which is imaged as sleep, death, inebriation, or fear: "le peuple joue à l'insomnie dans les carrefours / d'alcool" (p. 10); "le peuple est fort mais il a peur" (p. 71). The poet also writes in a condensed lyrical style odes to a woman, in "Autour de Yolande": "L'amour aussi a l'habitude d'aller toute nue / sur les presqu'îles / verticales et chantent nos pas / sur les tapis de coquillages miroitant / sous les flambeaux / de la mer / jetée telle une cape sur tes épaules / de fraîcheur." (p. 64) His colorful images are of striking originality : "Les flamboyants égrennent / des notes de sang / dans l'air vert et pastel." (p. 13)

Texaco *by Patrick Chamoiseau*

Chamoiseau's novel *Texaco* offers what is no doubt the most complete novelistic realization of the theory of Creolity, as presented in such texts as the *Éloge de la Créolité* (written with Raphaël Confiant and Jean Bernabé), and *Lettres Créoles* (written with Confiant). In *Texaco*, the shantytown that lends its name to the novel serves as an emblem of Creole culture as a whole. The novel revolves around the stories of Marie-Sophie Laborieux, who recounts the histories of the Creole *quartiers* that she has known personally or through the stories passed on to her by friends and relatives. These stories focus on the contentious relations between the Creole *quartiers* and the cities (or "*en-villes*") around which they have formed and upon which they depend for their economic survival. In her telling of these stories, Marie-Sophie manages to relate the whole history of Martinique, from the slave days through to the present moment. The history of the *quartiers* is inseparable from the history of Creole culture, and understanding the history of Creole culture, according to Chamoiseau, is the only legitimate way to understand the history of Martinique as a whole.

Toine chef de tribu *by Arthur Masson*

This novel shows a mature Toine at the head of a numerous family that includes Flemings, French people and Trignollais. The duet with T. Déome now reaching one hundred is a motor of the story. In this volume as in the following, we are presented with a modern world where the village life starts losing its former importance.

Toine Culot obèse ardennais *by Arthur Masson*

Arthur Masson initiates a series of six books of which Toine Culot is the hero. This first volume recounts the early years of Toine. It starts with his birth in Trignolles, a fictive Walloon village that has been identified as Treignes, a village at the French border; Toine was born in the home of Le Choumaque, an ageing shoemaker, and his wife Phanie. Late fruit of the marriage, Toine will have an overprotected childhood, punctuated by minor accidents and many happy times. This does not prevent his parents from thinking that Toine is not lucky. The late marriage of a well-off cousin that deprived Toine of her inheritance or a fall in the dough persuades the couple that Toine "n'est pas bâti pour la chance." Fortunately, the good humour and the mischievous temper of Le Choumaque's cousin, T. Déome, a seeds dealer and a cantor, keep everybody with their feet on the ground. After a schooling where much more application than talent is shown, Toine tries out several trades. He finally chooses gardening, an activity that suits his pacific temper and precocious stoutness. While working for the village mayor, Mr Du Verger des Sprives, Toine meets his wife-to-be, Hilda, a Fleming who will give him five children.

Toine dans la tourmente *by Arthur Masson*

This is a much more serious part of the series. The story is set during the Second World War and Toine becomes an unwilling hero by being made prisoner by the Germans for his "political activities." The general tone of the two books is graver than the rest; they obviously contain a fair bit of the author's autobiography (he also was incarcerated during the war) and show a fiercely anti-German attitude.

Toine maïeur de Trignolles *by Arthur Masson*

Toine maïeur de Trignolles recounts Toine's accession to the post of village mayor. His limited abilities are luckily compensated by the shrewdness of his communal secretary, T. Déome. Among other things, the volume describes the conflicts with his political enemy, Pestiaux, a pseudo-scientist, who happens to be the owner of the hardware shop. In this volume also appears Joseph, Toine's only son, who came long after his four sisters and just after his first nephew.

Toine retraité *by Arthur Masson*

Shows the old days of Toine who has transmitted his mayoral functions to his son-in-law. Although T. Déome is dead, he still appears in the story as a voice that Toine can hear from heaven. Masson's set of books, sometimes called the "Toinade," witnesses the changes of society throughout the first half of the twentieth century: wars, technical progress and life. While offering a pleasant and somewhat nostalgic image of village life in bygone times, the novels present a strong linguistic interest. The novels are indeed polyphonic as three levels of language can be found: standard French in the author's writing, Walloon in the characters' informal relationships and a mixed literary language, that we have called "dialectal French" when the same characters address certain categories of people and when they find themselves in solemn circumstances. The use of these different linguistic levels are sociolinguistically significant as they betray a hierarchy of languages in both the characters' and the author's attitudes. This is reinforced by an inferiority complex toward the central French norm, typified by the variety of French used in France.

Tu écriras sur le bonheur *by Linda Lê*

In this work, Linda Lê celebrates her love of the written word, particularly of prose fiction, through a collection of articles and prefaces covering authors as diverse as Kôbô Abê, Franz Werfel, Henry James and Marina Tsvétaéva.

Tu t'appelleras Tanga *by Calixthe Beyala*

Calixthe Beyala's second novel tells the story of an encounter in an African prison cell between Anna-Claude, a middle-aged French woman, and Tanga, a seventeen-year-old African girl. Tanga has been tortured by the police and is dying. As she dies she tells Anna-Claude the story of her life. Abused by her father and prostituted by her mother, Tanga has become her family's main breadwinner at an early age. Eventually she rebels against her exploitation and gives up prostitution. This rebellion brings her into conflict both with her family and with society at large. After a series of misadventures, Tanga falls in with a gang of counterfeiters and it is this involvement that has led to her imprisonment. As she tells Anna-Claude her story, Tanga passes on her identity, so that she might continue to live. As the novel ends, Anna-Claude is in some sense transformed into Tanga. Through this device Beyala is thus able to explore the exploitation of women and children in Africa, while suggesting that this oppression also carries a global dimension and that it is possible to think in terms of a non-localized feminism.

Un si tendre vampire *by Linda Lê*

The first of Linda Lê's novel, *Un si tendre vampire*, contains no Vietnamese characters and is set mainly in Paris. It recounts the relationship between the cruel and manipulative Louis, and two of his victims, Philippe and Xavière. At university, Louis encouraged Philippe in his literary ambitions, and then persuaded Philippe allow him to take credit for the authorship of the novel. At around the same period, he slept with first Xavière and then her mother, before returning to Xavière. Despite the waning of his affections, Xavière finds herself incapable of leaving his side. Philippe and Xavière, who meet as a result of Louis's re-eruption into Philippe's life, are locked into a dialogue centering on their memories of Louis, proof that they remain in his thrall.

Une flèche pour le pays à l'encan *by Elie Stephenson*

This collection of poems is prefaced by Serge Patient, who sums up Stephenson's vision of the Guianese people when he describes his fellow countrymen as "un peuple étrangement placide, résigné peut-être, qui ne braille ni ne gesticule." The poetry has similar militant themes and political engagement as Stephenson's theatre: he accuses the Guianese of having settled for compromise and sleep, and he lashes out against the Creole bourgeoisie. He concludes his poem "Le peuple des races bout à bout" with the following lines which epitomize the whole collection: "Nous avançons en regardant derrière / pour voir en quel point le néant prend sa source / mais le vide c'est nous / statues de vase brûlée / que les corbeaux dédaigneront."

Une Vie de boy *by Oyono, Ferdinand*

This novel, written in the form of a journal, portrays the plight of a young boy named Toundi in colonial Cameroon who becomes a "boy" or domestic servant for both a white missionary and an officer in the French colonial administration. Toundi's coming of age coincides with a reflective deconstruction of the racial, social and political myths that surround him. His inability to identify with one of two diametrically opposed cultural communities eventually leads to his death at the hands of the colonials. This novel is emblematic of racial tension and collapsing power struggles at the end of the colonial period in Cameroon.

Utê Mûrûnû *by Déwé Gorodé*

Utê Mûrûnû appeared at roughly midway between the Matignon Accords (1988) and the Nouméa Accord (1998). Set mostly in a Melanesian context, the collection, containing five stories, deals from the outset with major themes: memory, tradition, the land, kinship relations and the role of women. The first eponymous story, nearly half the length of the book, encompasses, as it were, the entire history of New Caledonia from the beginning of colonization in the mid-nineteenth century until the dawn of the twenty-first century, through a series of relations between grandmothers and granddaughters. Subsequent stories deal with the possible reconciliation of indigenous and Western traditions, via the tale of a grandfather that is presented from multiple narrative perspectives ("La Cordyline"); a woman's life in a tribal village in which we see the difficulties of her lot, as well as those of her people stemming from growing Kanak consumerism and the imbalance between traditional life and the demands of modern living ("On est déjà demain"); an allegory of power relations exploiting superstition to the exclusion of a woman ("La Saison des pommes kanak") and finally, set in Sydney, Australia, women in the

Third World revolutionary scene, where they are independent actors, albeit at the price of exile and possible death ("Dos montes . . .").

Voix: une crise *by Linda Lê*

This short autobiographical novel begins with a description of the characters that the narrator encounters in a mental asylum. It then traces her own descent into mental illness, which manifests itself in the eponymous voices of the "Organization," her imaginary persecutors. The voices, often accompanied by bloody and grotesque hallucinations, ridicule her literary endeavours, urge her to injure herself and force her to burn the letters sent by her beloved and deceased father.

Waati *by Souleymane Cissé*

Waati (Mali/France, 1995. Color, 143 mins., English, French, Bambara) is written and directed by Souleymane Cissé with original music by Bernard Coulais. Cinematography by Jean-Jacques Bouhon, Vincenzo Marano, and Georgi Rerberg. Cast members: Sidi Yaya Cissé (Solofa), Mariame Amerou Mohamed Dicko (Nandi at six years), Balla Moussa Keita (the Teacher), Martin Le Maître (the Farmer), Eric Miyeni (Father), Nakedi Ribane (Mother), Niamanto Sanogo (the Rastafarian prophet), Linéo Tsolo (Nandi), Mary Twala (Grandmother). Filmed on location in South Africa, Namibia, Côte d'Ivoire and Mali, and produced by Carthago Films, Cissé Films, Erato Films, La Sept, Renn Productions. Nominated for a *Palme d'or* at the 1995 Cannes Film Festival. *Waati* ranges widely in time and space, and concerns itself with investigating African solutions to Africa's problems. The film follows the fortunes of Nandi, a young black South African who, growing up under apartheid, kills her father's oppressors and flees the country. Nandi finds refuge in Francophone Africa, learns new languages, and enrolls at the University of Abidjan, where she eventually receives her doctorate in African Civilization. Subsequently, Nandi goes to live and work with the poverty-stricken Touareg of northern Mali. She takes under her wing an orphaned boy, and when she leaves to return to post-apartheid South Africa, she takes him with her. Nandi finds that post-apartheid South Africa differs only little in mentality from the South African she left behind as an adolescent.

Xala *by Oumane Sembène*

Xala (Senegal, 1975. Color, 119 mins., Wolof and French) is written and directed by Ousmane Sembène with original music by Samba Diabara Samb. Cinematography by Georges Caristan, Orlando L. López, Seydina D. Saye and Farba Seck. Editing by Florence Eymon. Cast members: Thierno Laye (El Hadj Abdou Kader Beye), Miriam Niang (Rama), Seune Samb (Adja Awa Astou), Younouss Seye (Oumi N'Doye), Dieynaba Niang (N'gone), Fatim Diagne (the Secretary), Iliamane Sagna (Modu, the chauffeur), Makhouredia Gueye (President of the Chamber of Commerce). Filmed on location in Dakar and produced by Films Domirev and Ste. Me. Productions de Sénégal. *Xala* is a biting satire of the *mores* of the African elites in the immediate post-independence period, which casts a critical eye also on neo-colonialism, polygamy and the role of women in African society, and class conflict. El Hadji Abdou Kader Beye is a member of the post-independence Chamber of Commerce, the first of which Africans are in charge. To the chagrin of his two other wives and children, he takes a young third wife, N'gone, but finds himself impotent and cannot consummate the marriage. His compromised virility compromises him in the eyes of his new wife's family and his business partners, and he goes to comic lengths to get to the bottom of the *xala* (curse of impotence) and reverse it, ruining himself financially in the process. El Hadji is forced to face up to his corruption and hypocrisy in an excruciatingly humiliating scene at the end of the film, when it is revealed that the cause of the xala is a beggar whose ancestral lands had been stolen by El Hadji.

Xala *by Ousmane Sembène*

Xala, published in 1973, after the early optimism of the independence era had given way to the disillusionment and disappointment of the 1970s, reflects the general impression characteristic of this period that the newly empowered Dakar (and implicitly African) bourgeoisie was essentially a self-serving, unfruitful and unprogressive minority. The novel's hero, who represents this group, El Hadji Abdou Kader Beye, is prevented from consummating his third, extravagant, marriage with a nineteen-year-old because he is suddenly and mysteriously struck with a curse of sexual impotency. While desperately searching, both from European-trained doctors and African traditional healers and seers, for a cure for this *xala*, El Hadji neglects his commercial empire and quickly falls into bankruptcy, again suggesting the bankruptcy of the new bourgeoisie and the neo-colonial society in which it attempts to function. He finally discovers that the sender of the *xala* is a beggar he was determined to ignore and even reduce to silence. The beggar reveals at the end of the novel not only his act of imposing the curse, but also his identity as a victim of the expropriation of a communal land on which El Hadji's wealth had been founded. The beggar had in fact been one of the few victims to publicly denounce El Hadji, an act that had led to the beggar's imprisonment through El Hadji's political influence. The story ends with the ceremonial humiliation of El Hadji by the beggar and his fellow underclass individuals, all under the ominous threat of imminent police action against them. This ending implicitly and symbolically announces the advent of one-party and military tyranny that would soon come to dominate many African states through the 1980's and 1990's.

Yeelen by Souleymane Cissé

Yeelen (Mali, 1987. Color, 105 mins., Bambara and French) is written and directed by Souleymane Cissé. Cinematography by Jean-Noël Ferragut and Jean-Michel Humeau. Editing by Andrée Davanture. Cast members: Issiaka Kane (Nianankoro), Aoua Sangare (Attou, the Peuhl woman), Niamanto Sanogo (Soma, the father/Djigui, the twin), Ball Moussa Keita (the Peuhl king), Soumba Traore (Mah, the mother), Ismaila Sarr (Bofing, the uncle), Youssouf Tenin Cissé (Attou's young son), Koke Sangare (the head of the Komo cult). Filmed on location in Mali and produced by Cissé films. Awards: Golden Rosa Camuna, 1987 Bergamo Film Meeting; nominated for a *Palme d'or*, and winner of Jury Prize and Prize of the Ecumenical Jury, special mention, at the 1987 Cannes Film Festival; nominated as best foreign film at the 1989 Independent Spirit Awards. *Yeelen* has been much misunderstood in the West as a poetic, apolitical fable with quasi-anthropological value; but Cissé maintains the film's contemporary relevance. Set in the powerful Mandé empire of thirteenth-century Mali, *Yeelen*'s action centers on the conflict between generations, the dissemination of knowledge and power, and the ethical responsibilities of those with power. Soma, a powerful and competitive sorcerer of the Kore initiation society, is in pursuit of his son Nianankoro, whom he intends to kill for stealing the secrets of the Komo, or divine knowledge. On his mother's advice, Nianankoro journeys in search of his uncle, his father's twin brother, who was himself blinded and banished because he asked his own father to reveal the Komo secrets so that all could benefit from the knowledge. Nianankoro undertakes this journey, traversing Peuhl territories and finding a wife, and finally reunites the eye of Kore (a gemstone) with the wing of Kore (the sceptre of the Komo). This restores the wing's power and enables Nianankoro to face his father in an encounter in which both are destroyed by the power of the Komo symbols.

Zenzela *by Azouz Begag*

Zenzela, the Arabic term for a seismic ogress, wreaks havoc on both Algeria and France. Farid Belgacem, the son of immigrant Algerians in France, a "Beur," explores the cataclysmic movements engendered by the earthquake, taking readers on a humorous and enlightening journey into the subterranean cultural depths of French and Algerian societies. The sixth novel of author Azouz Begag, himself a child of Algerian immigrants, *Zenzela* tarries with the regimented obstacles of both France and Algeria, which preclude a multicultural dialogue within and between both countries. The novel examines the weight of troubling movements lodged within the cultural subconscious as a means of enjoining a post-colonial sensibility that values the vitality of a cross-cultural reality.

Glossary

Acadia. Referring to the seventeenth-century name for the French Atlantic seaboard in the New World, corresponding today to the Maritime Provinces (q.v.) of Canada, Acadia was the first permanent French settlement in North America. Acadia was relinquished to the British in 1713, fifty years before Quebec (q.v.) was; it had been in existence since 1604. Acadia has a cultural and linguistic character distinct from that of its neighbor Quebec. In addition to having their own flag and national holiday, Acadians identify themselves more readily with the sea.

Acadian National Conferences. Series of nationalist conventions begun in 1881 in Memramcook (q.v.) bringing together all the major Acadian leaders to voice their pride and solidarity as a people, culminating in the social and political demands and unrest of the late 1960s and early 1970s at the University of Moncton (q.v.).

Acadie /Acadia /Acadians. Acadia, initially inhabited by Amerindian tribes, was France's first colony in North America, being set up in 1604 in what is now Nova Scotia. Gradually, however, France began to concentrate its efforts on Quebec to the northwest and surrendered Acadia to the British in 1713 under the Treaty of Utrecht. Acadie/Acadia was the source of many Franco-British conflicts in the eighteenth century, the main one of which was the enforced deportation of the French in *Le Grand Dérangement* of 1755.

Accad, Evelyne, b. Lebanon 1943. A professor at the University of Illinois, Champaign-Urbana since 1974 in French, comparative literature, African studies, women's studies, Middle East studies. Other activities include writing the music and lyrics to songs and performing at various concerts in the United States and abroad. Her body of work includes over eight books, thirteen chapters in books and fifty-seven articles. Through her writing, Accad exposes the destructiveness of exclusionary nationalism and oppression and celebrates difference and diversity. She is an advocate of peace and actively pursues resistance to hate, injustice and oppression.

Accord de Nouméa. Agreement signed in Nouméa in May 1998 between FLNKS, RPCR and the French State on New Caledonia's future constitution. This averted the need for a referendum, foreshadowed by the *Accords de Matignon*, on independence, the latter being deferred until at least 2013. The accord provides for gradual devolution of certain state powers (e.g., in education, employment) from France to the Territorial Congress in New Caledonia.

Accords de Matignon. Agreement signed in June 1988 by Jean-Marie Tjibaou (FLNKS), Jacques Lafleur (RPCR) and Michel Rocard (French Prime Minister) aimed at restoring social peace in New Caledonia after years of unrest known as *les événements* (1984–88). These accords divided New Caledonia into three provinces (North, South and Loyalty Islands) and also provided for a referendum on independence to be held in 1998.

actant. In Paris School semiotics, the actant represents a position or role in the abstract underlying structure of a narrative text. This role may be filled by a person or group of persons, an animal, an inanimate object or an idea. The six *actants* of Greimas' "actantial model" are subject, object, sender, receiver, helper and opponent.

ADCK, *Agence de Développement de la Culture Kanak*. Agency set up in the wake of the Accords de Matignon (q.v.) to promote Kanak cultural heritage and contemporary expression. Since 1998 it is housed in the Centre Culturel Kanak Jean-Marie Tjibaou, designed by Renzo Piano. In October 2000, the Centre was one of the main venues for the 8th Pacific Arts Festival.

Adnan, Etel, b. Lebanon 1925. A poet, novelist and artist, she has also worked as a teacher, a journalist and an art editor. She was first published in 1966 with *Moonshots* and continues to write both in French and in English. Her work also includes texts of two documentaries about the civil war in Lebanon. She left Lebanon after receiving death threats for writing *Sitt Marie Rose* (1978). She is an advocate for peace and justice for all and has given a voice to those oppressed into silence, particularly women, in the Arab political context.

Affaire des fiches. Name given to the scandal caused in 1990 when it emerged that for many years the Swiss state had been spying on some of its citizens, having suspects (often left-wing activists or anti-nuclear protesters) followed and their phones tapped. These revelations led to outrage in the country and writers' boycott of the 1991 commemoration of Switzerland's seven hundred-year existence. Modified versions of files held by the authorities were subsequently made available to the individuals involved.

Albert 1er, b. Belgium 1875, d. 1934. Third king of Belgium, nicknamed *le roi chevalier* (the knight king) for his heroic behavior during the First World War. He granted universal suffrage to all male citizens in 1918, increasing the weight of the more numerous Flemish population in the nation's political life.

Alexis, Jacques Stephen, b. Haiti 1922, d. 1961. Militant Haitian writer who joined the communist party founded by Jacques Roumain at the tender age of sixteen. He was an active participant in politics and traveled extensively around the world. Impressed with the Negritude movement, he sought to define his voice within the Caribbean context. His manifesto on "marvellous realism" delivered during the First Congress of Black Writers and Artists in Paris (1956) is a case in point. With hopes of quashing François Duvalier's regime, he founded and led a new party, but he disappeared after his arrival in Haiti. The mysterious circumstances around his death are still abuzz today. His literary works, from *Les Arbres musiciens* (1957) to *Romancero aux étoiles* (1960), all have a militant but human tone to them. He is most concerned with a new national consciousness that will empower the Haitian peasantry.

Algeria. North African state bordered by Morocco, Mauritania, Mali, Niger, Libya, Tunisia and the Mediterranean sea. The three main invasions of Algeria are: the Arab conquest in the eighth century, the Ottoman control in the seventeenth century and finally French colonization starting in 1830 with the conquest of Algiers. After eight years of war against the French, Algeria finally gained its independence on March 18, 1962 with the signature of the Evian Treaty.

Algerian heritage. This term refers to the traditions and culture that are exported to France and transmitted to children of Algerian immigrants referred to as "Beurs." While this heritage is complex and diverse, it nonetheless remains a point of tension between Algerian immigrant culture in France and Beur culture.

Algerian independence. Official in 1962 after the cease-fire of the Evian accords in March, Algerian independence can be traced back to the 1930s with Islamic reform and nationalist sentiment. In 1954 official rebellion was witnessed in Grande Kabylie and in the Aures, leading to de Gaulle's eventual proclamation of the Algerian right to autodetermination in 1959.

alienation. State of separation from social reality experienced by an individual. Marxists focus on the way in which workers in capitalist society are unable to relate to their work, and, by extension, to those around them.

analepsis. The telling, in the linear progression of a narrative text, of events that the reader understands to have occurred at an earlier time than the events of the present moment in the story as it unfolds.

anomie. A social condition, first introduced by Emile Durkheim in his book "The Division of Labor in Society" (1893) describing the individual's sense of inability to attain a meaningful existence within a society perceived as unstable and disorganized.

Arab-Israeli War of 1967. In 1967, due to increasing tensions between Israel and Arab states, Egypt closed the straits of 'Aqaba to Israeli shipping. On June 5, 1967, and for the next six days, hence the name the Six Day War, Israeli warplanes bombed airfields in Egypt, Syria and Jordan, destroying the Arab air forces. On June 10, the Egyptian, Syrian and Jordanian troops were defeated and Israel held the Sinai Peninsula, the west bank of the Jordan River, the Golan Heights and Jerusalem.

Aron, Raymond, b. 1905, d. 1983. Central figure in journalism, philosophy and sociology. Strongly influenced by Weber, Tönnies, Benjamin and Pareto, Raymond Aron wrote a series of influential books that mostly opposed the then dominant use of Marxism in social sciences. Professor of sociology at both the Sorbonne and later the Collège de France, Raymond Aron questioned in his numerous books the nature of industrial society, the problem of totalitarianism as well as issues of international relations.

assimilation. In the French colonial system, Africans were ostensibly "in training" to become French citizens. Through intense acculturation and an oppressive educational and administrative system, African traditions, languages, and cultures were belied in order to favor and promote French and European models of behavior, systems of value and meaning, and cultural practices.

autobiographical novel. A fusion of fact and fiction; a fictionalized account of true events. Philippe Lejeune applies this term to all works of fiction "dans lesquels le lecteur peut avoir des raisons de soupçonner, à partir des ressemblances qu'il croit deviner, qu'il y a identité de l'auteur et du *personnage*, alors que l'auteur, lui, a choisi de nier cette identité, ou du moins de ne pas l'affirmer." See Philippe Lejeune, *Le Pacte autobiographique* (Paris: Editions du Seuil, 1975).

Bachelard, Gaston, b. 1894, d. 1962. Influential philosopher of science, Bachelard revolutionized his discipline by demonstrating that scientific progress is more the result of radical breaks and ruptures than a linear accumulation of scientific knowledge. In addition to his epistemological research, Bachelard played a very important role in literary criticism. Throughout various close-readings of poetical texts, Bachelard established the idea that poetry is mostly rooted in the four fundamental elements of nature: air, earth, fire and water.

bagnards. Convicts sent to New Caledonia between 1864 and 1897, numbering close to thirty thousand. This included an important contingent of several thousand Communards, deported following the popular uprising in 1871, the vast majority of whom left New Caledonia after an amnesty was granted in 1880.

bagne. Penitentiary. The term comes from the Italian *bagno* (bath), after the nickname given to the first institution in Livorno, located in ancient baths. The *bagne* in French Guiana made it a penal colony from 1854 to 1945.

Bakhtin, Mikhail, b. 1895, d. 1975. Russian critic best known for his *Problems of Dostoyevksy's Poetics* (1929) and *Rabelais and His World* (eventually published in 1965). Bakhtin identified the subversive powers of the carnivalesque and the transgressive qualities of the grotesque and explored the concept of the heteroglossia and the dialogic novel, a text that engaged in a dialogue with the reader.

banlieu. The French term for suburb or urban periphery, *banlieu* carries a special weight in French and Francophone cultures because it signifies the residential area where many post-colonial immigrants and their children reside. A place of great ethnic tension, the banlieu also is attached to numerous stereotypes of immigrant life in the metropolitan centers of France such as Paris, Lyon, and Marseille.

baobab tree. A large sprawling tree that grows in the African plains. It rarely grows over sixty feet tall, but its trunk can be thirty to fifty feet in diameter. The fruit of the baobab, called monkey bread, and its leaves are used for culinary and medicinal purposes, while the bark is used to make hammocks. Along with Aimé Césaire's "Kaïlcédrat," the baobab tree is often used in African literature as a symbol of Africa.

Barbançon, Louis-José, b. New Caledonia 1950. New Caledonian historian and teacher, descendant of "bagnards." His writings on "taboo" subjects such as the penal settlement (on which he wrote a monumental *thèse* for the University of Paris in 2000) and race relations have been the subject of much controversy in New Caledonia. The title of his first book, *Le Pays du Non-Dit* (1993), has passed into the local language, as social tensions eased during the 1990s.

Barthes, Roland, b. France 1915, d. 1980. One of the most influential cultural critics of the post-war period in France. A generator of new theoretical approaches to the study of culture and society, Barthes engaged with Marxism and existentialism in the 1940s, with structuralism in the 1950s, semiology in the 1960s and post-structuralism in the 1970s. Never a politically committed intellectual in the mould of Sartre or Foucault, Barthes assaulted most intellectual discourses to demystify them when they became entrenched in academia.

Baudouin 1er, b. Belgium 1930, d. 1993. The fifth king of Belgium, crowned in 1951, following his father Leopold III's abdication, provoked by the latter's controversial involvement with the Germans during the war.

Baudoux, Georges, b. France 1870, d. 1949. The first "local" voice in New Caledonian literature, who combined tales of colonial life, stockmen, and "la brousse" with attention to Melanesian stories in such works as *Légendes canaques* (1928).

Beauséjour. Acadian village associated with Acadia's greatest tragedy, the "Grand Dérangement" (q.v.), and the year 1755 when began the deportation of thousands of French-speaking Acadians from their homeland.

Bernabé, Jean, a linguist who, along with the novelists Raphaël Confiant and Patrick Chamoiseau, published *Éloge de la Créolité* where they present a (French) Creole-centered perspective on Caribbean identity and literature, advocating the representation of the poorer population of the French Caribbean and defending the use of Creole.

Béti, Mongo, b. Cameroon 1932. Noted writer whose first novel, *Ville Cruelle*, was published under the name Eza Boto in 1954, launching a new era of possibility for Cameroonian writers.

Beur literature. Literature of and by the generation of children of North African immigrants. Beur literature is profoundly influenced by the questions of identity related to being of Maghrebian heritage and of French nationality since most "Beurs" are French citizens with ties to Maghreb through their parents. Azouz Begag, Farida Belghoul, and Mehdi Charef are perhaps the three most popular contemporary Beur authors.

Bhabha, Homi K., b. India 1949. Influential theorist of cultural transformation and colonial/post-colonial social systems and their consequences, notably in the area of identity formation. Bhabha's important collection of theoretical essays, *The Location of Culture*, is concerned with the notion of hybridity and the "third-space" of cultural identity, in which binary notions dissolve, creating a conceptual space for post-colonial identity.

Boukman, Daniel, b. Jamaica. A legendary opponent to slavery who waged a campaign of terror against the French colonists of Saint-Domingue in the late eighteenth century. Well versed in Vodou, he used it to inspire and mobilize slaves to revolt against French plantation owners. There are many historical and literary accounts surrounding the *Cérémonie du Bois Caïman*, the rallying site of the first concerted slave rebellion, at which he officiated on August 14, 1791. In this context, *cérémonie* refers to a complex of rituals of the voodoo cult.

Bourdieu, Pierre, b. France 1930, d. 2002. Director of Studies at the *École des Hautes Études* and director of the *Centre de Sociologie Européenne*. A major theorist in the field of sociology (particularly the sociology of education) and literary and cultural theory. Bourdieu's work argues that cultural practices are an integral part of the struggle between dominated and dominant sectors of society, using the terms "cultural capital" and "symbolic capital" to help explain the logics of cultural and social practice.

Bourguiba, Habib, b. Tunisia 1903, d. 2000. Politician and leading figure in the nationalist movement in Tunisia. He was the first president of the Republic of Tunisia from 1957 until 1988. Bourguiba maintained close ties with Europe and defended the nation-state model rather than pan-Arab nationalism, at least in practice. Bourguiba created a climate in which "liberal" ideas were able to take hold, especially with regard to women and the cultural outlook of the country, and laid the foundation of bilingualism.

boy ("Boy"). In French colonial households, this term was used to designate a servant regardless of his (or her) age.

Bugul, Ken, b. Senegal 1948. Novelist whose real name is Mariétou M'Baye and whose first novel, *Le Baobab fou* (1982), created quite a stir in Senegalese society, where women are supposed to be known for their "jom," i.e., dignity and social reserve, rather than their outspokenness. In *Le Baobab fou*, Ken Bugul reveals all, the good and the bad, the acceptable and the shocking in the life of a black woman, herself, seeking her identity in all the wrong places. She continues to tell all in *Cendres et braises* (1994) and especially in *Riiwan ou Le chemin de sable* (1999), where she recounts her experiences as the twenty-eighth wife of a Muslim religious leader, a marabou. Ken Bugul now lives in Benin, where she directs the Centre de Promotion et de Vente d'Oeuvres Culturelles, d'Objets d'Art et d'Artisannat.

Cabot, Sebastian, b. Venice 1482, d. 1557. Italian navigator, explorer and cartographer credited with exploring the southern Labrador coast of Newfoundland or Cape Breton Island (q.v.).

Cacos. Peasant guerrilla forces which militated against the American Occupation.

Caldoche. Name commonly given since 1970s to European settler population of New Caledonia, particularly of convict origin. Previously pejorative, the term is now often adopted by members of the younger generation in search of their identity.

Cameroon. West African state bordered by Equatorial Guinea, Gabon, Congo, the Central African Republic, Chad, and Nigeria, and the Atlantic Ocean. A German protectorate from 1884, Cameroon was divided between France and Britain following World War I, in 1922. British Cameroon made up one-fifth of the territory, and the rest was French Cameroon. Gained independence in 1960, and East and West Cameroon operated as a federation until 1972, at which time a single state was created.

Cap-Breton / Cape Breton Island. Originally named Île Royale by the French, it corresponds to the northeastern region of Nova Scotia and is surrounded by the Gulf of St. Lawrence and Cabot Strait. It is believed to be the first land visited by Italian navigator and explorer John Cabot and his son Sebastian Cabot (q.v.). Maillet (q.v.) reminds her readers in *L'Acadie pour quasiment rien* that "Cap-Breton is Acadia."

Carnival. Festive event and concept referring to the period of feasting and merrymaking immediately preceding Lent during which masks, role reversals and, more generally, world-upside-down imagery are commonplace and are thought to play a cathartic (q.v.) function.

Carthage. Founded in 814 B.C. by the Phoenicians, Carthage became the leading city in the region. It conquered Spain and sent expeditions as far as Britain and Senegal. It threatened the Roman Empire so seriously that the Romans invaded and destroyed it more than once. It was then rebuilt by the Romans themselves and used as their capital during their prolonged rule of North Africa. The Christian leading figure St. Augustine and the writer Apolius both studied in Carthage.

Cartier, Jacques, b. France 1491, d. 1557. French navigator and explorer credited with exploring the North American coast and the St. Lawrence River as early as 1534, laying the groundwork for later French claims to Canada.

Cathartic. Adjective derived from the Greek word *katharsis*, meaning literally "purgation" or "purification." It was a metaphor used originally by Aristotle in *Poetics* to describe the effects of true tragedy on the spectator. More generally, the term describes the healthful and humanizing effects of literature, art and film on the spectator or reader.

Cent ans dans les bois. Title of Maillet's (q.v.) 1981 novel, which serves as a sequel to her 1979 Goncourt Prize–winning (q.v.) novel *Pélagie-la-Charrette*. The expression refers to the difficult and highly symbolic one hundred-year period of "hibernation," which followed the "Grand Dérangement" (q.v.), during which Acadians hid out in the woods away from the English for fear of their life.

Césaire, Aimé, b. Martinique 1913. Poet and playwright, he also coined the word "négritude" in the 1930's and was one of the main proponents of this literary movement with Léopold Sédar Senghor (Sénégal) and Léon Gontran Damas (French Guyana). His *Notebook of a Return to the Native Land* (1939) is a founding text of Caribbean and Francophone literature. He has since published a number of collections, including *Les Armes Miraculeuses* (1946), *Soleil cou coupé* (1948), *Ferrements* (1960) and *Moi, Laminaire . . .* (1982), as well as plays, including *Et Les Chiens se taisaient* (1955), *La Tragédie du Roi Christophe* (1963), and *Une Tempête* (1969). Césaire also played a major political role in Martinique as mayor of Fort-de-France and deputy to the French Parliament.

Christophe, Henri, b. Haiti 1767, d. 1820. Renowned Haitian leader who fought against the French expeditionary forces and with Pétion's help defeated Dessalines in 1806. Whereas Pétion became president of the southern part of the island, Christophe became king of the northern part. As a symbol of Haiti's powerful presence in the Caribbean and as a warning to the French, he constructed under dire conditions the Laferrière Citadel, which still stands today. This historical figure inspired many writers, most notably, playwrights Aimé Césaire (Martinique) and Bernard Dadié (Ivory Coast).

Cissé, Souleymane, b. Mali 1940. A politically committed filmmaker who trained in Moscow and has been imprisoned for his work, Cissé's films analyze the society and politics of modern urban Mali, and critique the corrupt, post-colonial ruling elites of contemporary Africa. The strong influence of Bambara oral traditions in his films suggest Cissé's response to present impasses in African society through an imaginative reconnection with the roots of African culture and myths.

Citizenship. The administrative and bureaucratic mode of belonging to a particular nation. Citizenship, versus cultural identity, is defined by juridical means and enforced by the construction of borders and other State governing institutions.

Code Noir. Series of sixty articles written in 1685 by Colbert and Louis XIV, officially designed to legislate the behavior of masters toward slaves and ensure the exclusive presence of the

Catholic religion in the colonies. The Code briefly disappeared in 1794, was reinstated in 1803, and finally abolished in 1848 (at the French abolition of slavery).

colonial mandate. The desires and policies of a colonial administration or ideology.

colonial subject. A person subjected to a colonial power or ideology.

Columbus, Christopher, b. Genoa 1451, d. 1506. Italian navigator and explorer most closely identified and credited with discovering "America."

commercial cinema. Cinema made for profit above all else. Seeking primarily to entertain audiences rather than challenge them, commercial cinema tends to rely on conventional, tried-and-tested formulae for its plots, characters and film style.

Communauté française de Belgique. The organization responsible for cultural affairs since the first reform of the state in 1970, where three communities (French, Flemish and German) were established. The second reform in 1980 extended its competence to what is known as *matières individualisables.*

community. A grouping of people who share common political, religious or other allegiances or beliefs.

Condé, Maryse, b. Guadeloupe 1937. Left Guadeloupe at sixteen to study in Paris. Lived in Guinea from 1961 to 1966 with her Guinean husband. She worked in London and Dakar before completing her Ph.D. at the Sorbonne in Paris. She has contributed to several journals and magazines, published numerous anthologies, studies, short stories, and novels and three plays. She has written several essays challenging the focus on the island-home and its poorer inhabitants in French Caribbean literature, proning instead a more open and inclusive definition which encompasses all social classes and diasporic trends.

Conteur / conteuse. Male / female storyteller. In Maillet's (q.v.) works, s/he is a cross between a historiographer and a storyteller whose tales are associated with the "réel imaginaire" (q.v.).

cultural identity. Different from national identity, cultural identity signifies one's relationship to culture or cultures rather than to a particular national entity. Cultural identity thus becomes a rootless affiliation related to diverse modes of group belonging.

cultural space. A term frequently employed in post-colonial and cultural studies theory, cultural space signifies the conceptual or material space that subjects occupy or address as a means of positionality. With vast colonial and post-colonial migrations, cultural space is itself reconfigured by the gatherings of cultures and diverse cultural subjects.

de Certeau, Michel, b. 1925, d. 1986. De Certeau was a historian with a solid background in philosophy, classics and theology, who also drew from anthropology, linguistics and psychoanalysis. Among his diverse contributions, his work on contemporary cultural practices and especially his insight into the productive activities of consumers has been very influential. In particular, his distinction between opposition and resistance and tactic and strategy, has been adopted in recent criticism. See for instance, Mireille Rosello's *Littérature et identité créole aux Antilles* (1992), and *Infiltrating culture* (1996), as well as Richard D.E. Burton's *Afro-Creole* (1997).

de Coster, Charles, b. Belgium 1827, d. 1879. Belgian writer, author of *Légendes flamandes* (1857) and *La légende d'Ulenspiegel* (1867), sometimes seen as the founding book of Belgian literature.

défricheteur/défricheteuse de parenté. From Old French meaning literally "land clearer," it is Maillet's (q.v.) term for her male or female, unofficial Acadian genealogists in her works.

demystification. The dismantling of superstitious or inflated appreciation of someone or something.

départementalisation. Term used to refer to the granting of the status of Département to Martinique, Guadeloupe, Guyane and Réunion in 1946. The status enabled their inhabitants to enjoy most of the same social rights and privileges as metropolitan French people. Césaire's role in encouraging *départementalization* in order to secure a better living standard for overseas residents has been criticized as having opened the doors to greater assimilation.

Depestre, René, b. Haiti 1926. One of the most militant poets of his generation. Influenced by Jacques Roumain and Aimé Césaire, Depestre embraced communism and sought to promote his political vision and humanism in his poetry. Forced into exile, he sought refuge in Cuba (1959–78) where he taught at the University of Havana, and then settled in Paris where he worked for UNESCO. He has written a number of essays where he states his position on negritude and the role of art in transforming social conditions and empowering individuals and peoples. Highly polemical, his collections of short stories, *Alléluia pour une femme-jardin* (1980), *Eros dans un train chinois* (1990) and his novel *Hadriana dans tous mes rêves* (1988), explore the complex relationship between politics, voodoo and eroticism.

Dessalines, Jean-Jacques, b. Haiti 1748, d. 1806. The first head of the Republic of Haiti on January 1, 1804. Also a legendary Haitian leader who served as Toussaint L'Ouverture's lieutenant. He successfully expelled the French from the island in 1803. He declared himself emperor Jacques 1st (1804), ruled with an iron fist but died in 1806 in the insurrection led by Pétion and Christophe.

devoir-faire (Eng. having to do). Also referred to as *deontic modality*, a modality of obligation involving practical necessity, legal coercion, moral duty, or a combination of these different forms of obligation.

dialogic novel. A Bakhtinian concept, hinging on the idea that the text always assumes an addressee, and anticipates a response. The text is the site of an interaction between different points of view or languages, with words existing in a relativistic sense. This makes the novel open-ended, dependent upon interpretation for its existence and function.

diaspora. Term referring originally to Jewish settlements dispersed throughout the world as a result of the Jewish people's exile from their homeland of Israel. The term connotes, more generally, the notion of exile and dispersion of all peoples, as in the context of the *Grand Dérangement* (q.v.) or the Acadians' deportation from Acadia.

discourse. Language that has an object and that is directed at an object, utterance as a social practice having intentions. Thus not all language is discourse. *Ideological* discourse may be understood as sets of utterances occurring across society (in law courts, school rooms, newspapers, advertising hoardings) that enact particular understandings of the world in order to legitimate particular forms of social organization. "The concentration on *discourse* in Francophone studies derives from insights gained from twentieth century French studies that have led to the development of critical tools that enable the student to analyse the way phenomena are categorized in colonial and post-colonial politics and subsequent aesthetic and linguistic conceptions and formulations that these categorizations give rise to. The Francophone discourse also shows an interest in the strategies that have become the new canon and include modernism, deconstructionism and absurdist approaches to narrative. The informing principle in Francophone studies, therefore, is the idea that French colonial/post-colonial history, politics, literatures and cultural production are interpretative discourses that reshape the languages from where they arise, revealing much about the culture of the former colonial powers and challenging post-colonial cultural and political histories. Francophone studies in the Anglo-Saxon world, are ways of introducing the outsider to a Francophone discourse and helping those who study canonical French Studies to see that the dispossessed do, in fact, possess a language (French), the alienated can be decentred from discourses of power (colonial / post-colonial), especially by the possession of another language/culture, and the disempowered have recentred themselves in their empowering Francophone intellectual literature. Those unacquainted with these literary and linguistic strategies tend to skirt the closed interpretative frames of French histories of the 'other' in and outside France, while

Francophone writers, who have their own discursive centers, have created visions of new, pluralist forms of politics and art." (cf. Kamal Salhi, *Francophone Studies: Discourse and Identity*, Elm Bank, 2000).

Djebar, Assia, b. 1936 in Cherchell (Algeria). Central figure of contemporary Algerian and Francophone literature. Assia Djebar, a historian by training, started writing novels in 1957, with La Soif. Her two following novels, *Les enfants du nouveau monde* (1962) and *Les Alouettes Naïves* (1967), focus on the problems of Algerian women and the Algerian war. In 1980, she published a collection of short stories, *Femmes d'Alger dans leur appartement* (1980), the title of which alludes to a painting by Delacroix. With her quartet that includes *L'amour, la fantasia* (1985), *Ombres Sultanes* (1987) and *Vaste est la prison* (1995), her writing becomes a textual interrogation of the multiple layers of personal and collective memory, and instantiates a dialogue between the narrator and her conflicting ancestors (the Arab, the French and the Berber). The tragic events taking place in Algeria pushed her to interrupt her quartet at various moments and also publish circumstantial works, *Le Blanc de l'Algérie* (1996) and *Loin de Médine: filles d'Ismaël* (1991). She has also published *Chronique d'un été algérien: ici et là-bas* (1993), *Nuits de Strasbourg* (1997) and *Ces voix qui m'assiègent: en marge de ma francophonie* (1999) as well as co-written a play with Walid Carn, *Rouge l'aube; pièce en 4 actes et 10 tableaux* (1969) and a collection of poetry, *Poèmes pour l'Algérie heureuse* (1969?). She has also written and produced two films, *La Nouba des Femmes du Mont Chenoua* (1979) and *La Zerda et les chants de l'oubli* (1982).

é-cri-tu-re. The word écriture, spelled in such a way, conveys two fundamental dimensions of Assia Djebar's writing, but could also be used to describe other texts. É-cri-ture emphasizes texts that are able to register, even if unconsciously or unwillingly, the voices of those whom they are misrepresenting and whose humanity they are undermining. It refers both to the colonizer's texts that Djebar "listens to" in order to recover the cries of her murdered ancestors, as well as to her own writing practice of such recovery. Écri-tu-re on the other hand, by highlighting the second person pronoun, conveys a writing practice that evolves from an intimate dialogue with other people, for instance, the women that Djebar interviews, but it also refers to a writing that is dialogical in other ways, for instance, the alternance of the narrative voice in *Ombres Sultanes*.

Eliade, Mircea, b. Romania 1907, d. 1986. Romanian-born novelist and religious historian who conducted extensive research on the notion of sacred time and space and the role of myths. He argues most notably in *The Myth of the Eternal Return* that whereas some cultures view time as history or as a one-way progression, others highlight the cyclical or repeatable nature of time which is reactivated by ceremonies preserved in myths, thereby periodically abolishing history.

Elissa. Known in Roman sources as Queen Dido or Sidonian Dido, she is the sister of Pygmalion, the king of Tyre, located in modern-day Lebanon. Elissa is said to have devised a cunning plan to build Carthage, the most important power in the Western Mediterranean for centuries. Legend has it that Elissa chose to throw herself in a pyre rather than marry a local king.

enfumades. Practice of the French military used during the colonial conquest of Algeria. They asphyxiated whole groups that had taken refuge in caves by blocking the entrances and exits in order to fill them up with smoke.

énoncé (Eng. utterance). The utterance itself (the language sequence actually produced) as opposed to the act or process of producing that sequence (see énonciation).

énonciation (Eng. uttering). A semantic term referring to the act of producing an utterance in a natural language (as opposed to the utterance itself as a product of that act). This distinction was elaborated by the French linguist Émile Benveniste, and focuses attention on the processes involved in using language in a situation of communication. Elements of this situation include: the relationship between speaker and audience, meanings implied by the context, and pragmatic intentions on the speaker's part.

ethnicity. The quality of belonging to a group who share common racial, religious, cultural or other characteristics.

ethnocentric. A worldview in which the particulars of one's own ethnicity are seen to be at the center of meaning, truth, and possibility.

ethnographic film. Ethnography, born in the nineteenth century and devoted to the "scientific" study of human "races," has always been closely involved with photography. Still photography allowed the physical attributes and cultural practices of humans to be recorded and measured, its aura of truth providing both evidence and proof for ethnography's claims. Moving film enabled ethnographers to record cultural practices more "truthfully" as sequences in time. Portions of ethnographic film and/or its stylistic conventions are often used in Western *commercial cinema* (q.v.) to authenticate the representation of other cultures.

eurocentrism. Beliefs and practices predicated on the view that Europe is at the center of worthwhile knowledge and civilization.

exile. From the Latin *exilium*. Denotes a state of banishment, from a place formerly known to the exiled individual as home. According to some exponents of post-colonial theory, "exile" can displace the exiled to the point where they cannot achieve a sense of belonging in their adoptive country.

Fall (the). Christian doctrine referring to the Original Sin or the eating of the forbidden fruit in the Garden of Eden by Adam and Eve in defiance of God, leading to mankind's alienation from God and Paradise.

Fanon, Frantz, b. Martinique 1925, d. 1961. Psychiatrist and theorist of anti-colonial struggles. Fanon's writings from the 1950s and 60s analyze the practical and psychological effects of colonialism on colonizer and colonized. Informed by the methodologies of Marx, Hegel and Sartre, Fanon's approach is a dialectical one. It fundamentally rejects the essentialist categories justifying colonialism, which also featured prominently in contemporary anti-colonial philosophies such as that of *Négritude*. Fanon's insights have strongly influenced later theorizations of colonialism and "post-colonialism," in work by Edward Said and Homi Bhabha, for example.

fantasia. The fantasia is both a musical form and a war tactic, and is used by Assia Djebar in her novel *L'amour, la fantasia* as a metaphor for her writing. As she herself explains: "Qu'est-ce que c'est que la fantasia? Ce sont des cavaliers qui s'initient à la guerre par le jeu de la guerre. . . . Dans la fantasia, vous avez un premier galop de cavaliers qui courent, courent, courent; à un certain moment ils tirent en même temps. Une fois qu'ils sont partis, le deuxième galop va se faire plus rapide, et ainsi de suite."

Faucheuse. Meaning literally the "Grim Reaper" and as the embodiment of Time and Death, the term refers to the inexorable march in time toward death.

FCCI, *Fédération des Comités de Coordination des Indépendantistes*. Political grouping formed in 1998 by certain dissident members of the FLNKS (including the then président of the Province Nord, Léopold Jorédié), in opposition to the FLNKS's call for independence, judging such a step "premature" for New Caledonia. As a consequence, the FCCI became to some extent aligned with the RPCR.

Feraoun, Mouloud, b. 1913, d. 1962. Trained as a high school teacher, Mouloud Feraoun started a literary career in the early 1950s with the encouragement of fellow writers like Emmanuel Roblès and Albert Camus. Feraoun's "ethnographic" writings, often influenced by his childhood memories, mostly question the rural and Kabylian identity. Killed by the OAS in March 1962, Feraoun both symbolizes the desire for the Algerian people to reconnect with their roots and the fraternal dream of dialogue and reconciliation between the French community and the Algerian people.

field. As used by Pierre Bourdieu, an area of cultural production characterized by strategic positions of influence defined in competitive relation with each other.

Flemish movement. After the unity shown by the Flemish and French linguistic groups in 1830 to gain independence from Holland, some voices started to rise in the 1830s, initially among Flemish intellectuals claiming cultural recognition for Flemish. The claims evolved throughout the nineteenth century to include equivalence of both languages in all aspects of public life.

FLNKS, *Front de Libération National Kanak et Socialiste.* Pro-independence coalition formed in 1984, whose first leader was Jean-Marie Tjibaou. It became a major political force during the period known as *les événements* beginning in 1984, when it proclaimed itself the provisional government of an "independent" *Kanaky.* It still represents the majority of Kanaks politically, and was one of the three institutional signatories (along with the French State and the RPCR) to the *Accords de Matignon* (1988) and the *Accord de Nouméa* (1998). Of late, however, particularly since 1998, it has been subject to internal tensions, which have given rise to the rival Kanak political grouping, the FCCI (*Fédération des Comités de Coordination des Indépendantistes*).

focalizer. The character in a narrative text through whose eyes or from whose perspective the narrative voice describes the events and situations of the fictional world being represented.

Foucault, Michel Paul, b. France 1926, d. 1984. Leading French post-structuralist philosopher strongly influenced by the philosophy of Friedrich Nietzsche and professor of the history of systems of thought. His works include *Madness and Civilization: A History of Insanity in the Age of Reason* (1961), in which he explores questions relating to the treatment of the insane. Before the seventeenth century, madness and reason were both forms of experience of knowledge, madness being almost privileged as a form of sacred experience offering insights into life. The eighteenth century, however, saw the rise of institutions containing not only the insane—those who acted differently from the rest of society and who could not be understood by them—but also the unemployed and the poor, those who were seen as a threat to the economic growth of the country and its general well-being. They are divided off from the rest of society and excluded from it in institutions. Based on a series of isolated case studies of madness, medicine, prisons and sexuality, Foucault linked throughout his career the questions of power and knowledge by analyzing the importance of discursive formations in the construction of social control. His "micro-physics of power" still influences a growing number of academic fields, including history, art, sociology and literary criticism.

Fouchard, Jean, b. Haiti, 1912, d. 1990. Historian, politician, ambassador, Jean Fouchard occupied each of these roles fully committed to promote Haiti's legacy to world history. Editor-in-chief of many scholarly journals, he traveled extensively to Europe, Africa, United States, and Latin America. His writings center on Haitian history and culture and he worked tirelessly to show Haiti's remarkable artistic activity in the fields of theatre, dance, painting and literature. His voluminous works have been reedited by Henri Deschamps.

Francophone Lebanon. In 1880 Onésime Reclus first coined the expression *francophonie* to refer to French-speaking populations. In Lebanon, the use of French was first introduced in the nineteenth century and became widespread in the twentieth century, particularly as a direct influence of the French Mandate (1920–47). To this day, Lebanon remains a bilingual country. The Lebanese system of education is still based on the French system and the use of the French language is widespread in the media and among the people. Lebanese literature in French is also thriving.

French Academy. Institute founded in 1635 by Cardinal de Richelieu, minister to Louis XIII, and whose original purpose was the "development, unification and purification" of the French language.

French Indochina. Established in stages in the late nineteenth century. During the period of French Indochina, Vietnam comprised Tonkin in the north, Annam—the Vietnamese imperial center—in the center, and Cochinchina in the south. The south, popularly known as "the rice bowl," contained Saigon, the commercial center. France bowed out of the Vietnamese arena in 1954, following a humiliating defeat at the hands of the northern Communist forces. The United States stepped in on the side of the capitalist south. The Communists gained control of Vietnam in its entirety in 1975, promoting an exodus of southerners, intellectuals and capitalists.

French mandate (1920–1946). France created Greater Lebanon in 1920, a move which allowed them to establish a strong presence in the Middle East thanks to their allies, the Christian Lebanese, more specifically the Maronites. The Maronites, on the other hand, benefited from France's protection in the face of rising Arab nationalism in the Middle East and an ever-increasing Muslim minority in Lebanon. In 1943 the Free French government granted Lebanon its independence but tried to recapture Lebanon in 1945 by sending in French troops. In the face of Lebanese nationalism which united Christians and Muslims, the last French soldiers left in 1946.

French Vietnamese. First or subsequent generation French citizens of Vietnamese origin.

Golden Spurs battle. Battle fought between the King of France and the Count of Flanders, Guy de Dampierre and his communal militia on the July 11, 1302. The count of Flanders was victorious and that date has been set as the anniversary for the Flemish Community.

Gope, Pierre, b. New Caledonia 1957. Kanak poet and playwright from the Loyalty island of Maré, whose plays *Où est le droit?* (1996) and *Cendres de sang* (1998) explore sensitive, taboo issues in Melanesian society, such as corruption, rape and incest.

Gorodé, Déwé, b. New Caledonia 1949. Kanak writer and politician. Jailed for her pro-independence militancy in the 1970s, she is currently "minister" of Culture and Youth Affairs in the New Caledonian "government." Her work ranges from politically engaged and lyrical poetry, for example, *Sous les cendres des conques* (1985), to short stories such as *Utê Mûrûnû* (1994) and *L'Agenda* (1996) of realism and "magic realism" dealing with Kanak life in New Caledonia. Her first play, *Kanaké 2000*, on the life of Jean-Marie Tjibaou, was premiered at the 8th Pacific Arts Festival in Nouméa in October 2000.

Grand Dérangement, Le. Meaning literally but euphemistically "Great Disturbance," the term describes the deportation by the British of the majority of the French-speaking inhabitants of Acadie in 1755. The expatriation from their homeland of thousands of French Acadians unwilling to swear allegiance to the king of England, in order to make room for their English-speaking neighbors, was Acadia's greatest tragedy. The French population at the time was approximately 15,000. Of these, between ten and twelve thousand were forced to leave. The Treaty of Paris of 1763 enabled a slow return, and there are nowadays about 300,000 francophone Canadians living in the maritime provinces of Canada, the majority—about 200,000—in New Brunswick and the east coast. There are about one million people of Acadian descent across the world, of which a substantial proportion, the Cajuns, live in Louisiana. There are many other groups elsewhere. The enforced exile, causing the splitting-up of families and significant loss of life, has been seen as a form of ethnic cleansing, and is still remembered with bitterness and anger.

Grande Terre. Name given to the New Caledonian Mainland, to distinguish it from the Loyalty Islands and other islands that form part of the territory of New Caledonia.

Grand-Pré. Acadian village, along with Beauséjour (q.v.), closely identified with the "Grand Dérangement" (q.v.). Scene of the tragic romance of Gabriel Lajeunesse and Evangeline Bellefontaine who were engaged to be married but were accidentally separated, recounted in Henry Wadsworth Longfellow's narrative poem "Evangeline."

Grégoire, Henri, b. France 1750, d. 1831. Revolutionary priest, who carried out an investigation into the knowledge of French in France. He presented his results in a report to the national convention in 1794. He came to the conclusion that at the time only 3 out of 25 million of French citizens could speak "pure" French, 6 million did not know it at all and another 6 million had too limited a knowledge to have a sustained conversation in French.

Grevisse, Maurice, b. Belgium 1895, d. 1980. Grammarian who in 1936 published "Bon usage," a reference French grammar. His work was taken over by his son-in-law, André Goosse, the secretary of the Académie de langue et littérature belges.

grotesque. Mikhail Bakhtin explored the transgressive productivity of the grotesque, which challenges bodily taboos and blurs the inside/outside, acceptable/unacceptable bodily boundaries.

Guadeloupe. Formerly named Karukera, area 1,779 sq. km, population about 400,000 inhabitants. Discovered by Columbus in 1493, it was occupied by France in 1635. The last Carib Indians left the island in 1658. The island was occupied by the British from 1759 to 1763. Thanks to the support of the black population, Victor Hughes was able to oust the British in 1794 but the island fell under British domination again in 1810, 1814, 1815 and 1816. Slavery was abolished in 1848, and Guadeloupe became a Département d'Outre-Mer in 1946 and a Région in 1974.

Guyane. This South American territory borders Brazil and Suriname. Its official language is French, its capital Cayenne. A French province since 1676, it became a penal colony with the construction of its famous *bagne* (1854–1945). In 1945, it became a French D.O.M (Département d'Outre Mer), and Kourou became a space-shuttle launching base for France and Europe. The Guianese population of 150,000 includes Creole, Amerindian, Bushinenge, Arabic, Asian, South American (particularly Brazilian), Haitian, and French communities.

guyanité. Shorthand term to express the idiosyncratic features of French Guianese identity, as distinct from "créolité" or "antillanité."

Habermas, Jürgen, b. Germany 1929. Habermas was a student of Theodor Adorno and a member of the Frankfurt School of critical theory. In one of his first works, *Strukturwadel der Öffentlichkeit* [The Structural Transformation of the Public Sphere] (1962), he explores the interrelationship between types of social activity and communication, how rational discourse may legitimize political authority, and whether there can exist other forms of discourse that are free of political authority, or which can survive for long without being influenced by external forces of authority.

habitus. The accepted norms habitually operating within a given field.

harem. Term defining a house, or an isolated part of a house, where women are secluded and where access to outsiders is strictly controlled and often forbidden. Even if the harem is not a pure product of Islam, the Koran played a very important role in the development of this habitat. Nowadays, especially in Western countries, the word *harem* is not limited to the definition of a closed space: it also symbolizes the group of women who live with one man.

hegemonic. The systemic and pervasive nature of power and its operative forms within cultural spheres. Hegemonic refers to the unseen and totalizing nature of dominant forms of culture, race, ethnicity, and political power and is first analyzed by the Italian Marxist critic Antonio Gramsci.

Heraclitean time. Linear notion of time associated with historical time.

heteroglossia. Umbrella term for Bakhtin's theory of the dialogic novel, containing words with negotiable meaning.

hijab. Arabic term coming from the verb *hajaba* which means "to hide from view," "to conceal," "to seclude," "to mask," Hijab can be both translated as "veil" (as a piece of clothing) or "curtain." The original seven Koranic references to the Hijab as a curtain separating unbelievers from believers and wrongdoers from the righteous have been slowly replaced by a more gendered and conflictual definition emphasizing the (necessary) separation between men and women.

homologation. A semiotic application of Lucien Goldmann's socio-critical premise that a correspondence or homology exists between the narrative structure of a novel and the structure of exchange in a capitalist economy. In the case of homologation, a one-to-one correspondence is established between the movements of fictional characters in space and the evolution of their relationships with social and economic power structures.

hors du temps. Meaning literally "outside of time," that which does not abide by the laws of space and time.

hudud. Central and polysemic term in Muslim theology originally expressing an idea of "frontier," "limit" and "geographic delimitation." In addition to this topological meaning, the notion of hudud is associated in the Koran to the ideas of prohibitions and punishments. Thus, the hudud refers to the mandatory punishments against specific crimes listed in the Koran as crimes against religion. These fundamental crimes are adultery, false allegations of adultery, fornication, theft and highway robbery.

hybrid (-ity). Literally, the offspring of two plants or animals of different species or varieties. Used widely within colonial discourse to denote a person of mixed racial or cultural origin. This concept is now largely associated with the critic Homi K. Bhabha. According to his definition, hybridity is the process through which "new transcultural forms," emerging from the complex interplay between concepts of sameness and difference, recognition and disavowal during the colonial encounter, negotiate, translate or reinterpret the foundation blocks of colonial discourse.

Ibn Khaldun, Abd al-Rahman, b. Tunisia 1332, d. 1406. The most prominent Arab historian, he studied in Tunisia but traveled and worked in Spain, Algeria and Egypt. He is most famous for devising a theory of history based on the idea of solidarity and a cyclical view of the rise and fall of nations. His sociological and historical theories are included in his prolegomena (*al-Muqaddima*), which introduces his comprehensive history of North Africa up to his time.

in illo tempore. Latin expression referring to a place or action situated outside of time.

infiltration. Mireille Rosello develops this concept in her *Infiltrating culture* (1996) in order to suggest how people without a territory of their own (women, minorities, immigrants, children) momentarily play with and escape the laws of oppressive orders.

intervention/interruption. Notion developed by Gayatri Spivak to describe cultural practices that are inscribed within a dominant system such as capitalism, but can nevertheless produce moments that "interrupt" or momentarily break this dominant logic.

Islam. The term *Islam* comes from the Arabic root s-l-m which means "submission" or "peace." Second largest religion in the world, Islam was founded in Arabia in the seventh century by the prophet Muhammad before spreading to the rest of the Arab world and ultimately to the rest of the world. Even if Islam is still associated with the Middle East, the largest Muslims communities are found in Asia (India, Pakistan, Bangladesh and especially Indonesia) as well as in Africa (Morocco, Algeria, Tunisia, Somalia, Mauritania, Niger and Mali).

Jacques, Claudine, b. France 1951. Writer and publisher born in metropolitan France who has lived in New Caledonia since her adolescence. After writing collections of short stories dealing primarily with Caldoche life on the west coast of New Caledonia, she published in 1998, the year of the *Accord de Nouméa*, a novel, *Les Cœurs barbelés*, concerned with race relations.

jour en trop. Meaning literally "surplus day" as in the "Eighth Day" of God's creation, the term also designates that which is outside of time.

kadans translates literally as beat or dance. This term often refers to music and dance with African rhythms (most often calypso, mazouk and biguine). There are also different types of kadans (dous, pampa, rampa). Radio Kadans and the musical group Kadans also contribute to the popularity of this music form.

Kanak (see Melanesian). Originally a Polynesian term, "Kanaka," meaning "man," was adopted by missionaries and others in the nineteenth century. Gallicized as *Canaques*, it became a pejorative designation used by European settlers. The term was readopted in the 1970s as *Kanak* (invariable form) by Melanesians as a gesture of cultural reappropriation and political affirmation linked to the independence movement.

Kanaky. Name given by FLNKS to New Caledonia as a self-proclaimed "independent" state in 1980s. The term can still be found as a reference point of the independence movement, but it no longer has the same currency.

Kurtovitch, Nicolas, b. New Caledonia 1955. Writer and teacher, and founding president (1997) of the New Caledonian Writers' Association. A descendant of European settlers, whose maternal family has been in New Caledonia since before French occupation in the nineteenth century, he attempts in his works to bridge the racial divide that has for so long characterized New Caledonian society.

L'Ouverture, Toussaint, b. Haiti 1743, d. 1803. Perhaps the most legendary leader of the Haitian Revolution (1791–1800). After he vanquished Napoleon's troops, he declared the independence of the island and became president of the Republic in 1800. However Napoleon sent troops under General Leclerc and L'Ouverture was defeated in 1802. Imprisoned in France, he died in exile in 1803. His name "L'Ouverture" alludes to his talents at breaking the ranks of enemy troops, thereby creating an opening for his men. Among many other African and Caribbean writers, Aimé Césaire, Bernard Dadié and Édouard Glissant have written on the legacy of this legendary figure.

La Revue phénicienne. A literary magazine founded by Charles Corm in 1920. It provided a forum for writers, the majority of whom were French-educated Maronites, who heralded Lebanon's Phoenician heritage as opposed to their Arab heritage.

lactification. Term coined by Fanon to designate the choice of a lighter-skinned person as a partner to ensure that children born will inherit a light skin, thereby having "la peau sauvée."

Lafleur, Jacques, b. New Caledonia 1935. Wealthy New Caledonian businessman and politician. Like his father, the *Sénateur* Henri, before him, he represents New Caledonia, as a *député*, in the French Parliament. In 1978, he founded the anti-independence political party, the RPCR (*Rassemblement pour la Calédonie dans la République*) of which he is still the leader. He was one of the signatories of the *Accords de Matignon* and the *Accord de Nouméa*.

Laubreaux, Alin, b. New Caledonia 1899, d. Spain 1968. Journalist and writer who spent his pre-war adult life in France working for the far-right press (e.g., *Je suis partout*) in the 1930s. Condemned to death *in absentia* in 1945, he sought refuge in Spain, where he remained in exile until his death. His novels dealing with New Caledonia, written from abroad (e.g., *Le Rocher à la voile*, 1930), can be seen, despite their multiple contradictions, as a settler's critique of colonialism.

le boom. The years of dramatic economic expansion (1969–72) in New Caledonia, largely due to exploitation of mineral resources, particularly nickel. New Caledonia is one of the world's leading producers of nickel, which accounts for about 90 percent of its export revenue.

Le Clézio, J.-M. G., b. Nice, France 1940. French novelist whose cosmopolitan background, interest in travel narratives and acute consciousness of the "elsewhere" have led him to create a vast fictional universe of cross-cultural exploration, wandering (French: *errance*), and uprooted individuals with an ambiguous longing for collective memory and identity combined with an impassioned revolt against conventional identity, racial purity and the complacency of "rootedness."

Le Roy Ladurie, Emmanuel, b. France 1929. French historian whose research on the carniva-lesque notion of time in *Le Carnaval de Romans* highlights its cyclical nature which represents a time wheel in opposition to linear or the Heraclitean notion of time (q.v.).

Lê, Linda, b. 1961. French Vietnamese writer who fled Vietnam when the Communists took control of the whole country in 1975 and settled in Paris. Wrote her first novel, *Un si tendre vampire* (1987) and later *Les Trois parques* (1997), after which she had a much-publicized mental breakdown.

Lebanese Civil War. Civil war erupted in Lebanon in 1975 between numerous factions including Muslim fundamentalist and secular movements; various Christian militia, including the Lebanese Forces and the South Lebanon Army; and militant organizations representing Palestinian refugees in Lebanon. The complexity of the war was intensified when it assumed international proportions with the direct participation of Israel and Syria, and the indirect involvement of the major powers. The signing of the Taif Accords officially brought an end to the war in 1989 but fighting continued well into 1992.

Lefebvre, Henri, b. France 1901, d. 1991. French Marxist intellectual whose writings from a lengthy career have influenced philosophy, geography, cultural studies, political science, and literary criticism. Lefebvre's readings of Marx delve deeply into Marxism's Hegelian ancestry. In particular, Lefebvre views dialectical materialism as transcending both materialism and idealism, and orienting the dialectic toward a resolution in practical activity or "praxis." Lefebvre's Marxist humanism opposes him to theorists such as Althusser and is apparent in his extensive work on the sociology of everyday life.

les événements. Period (1984–88) of heightened social tension and violence in New Caledonia as pro- and anti-independence factions became increasingly radicalized. Social peace was restored with the signing of the *Accords de Matignon* in June 1988.

Line of Demarcation / Green Line. The dividing line between Muslim West Beirut and Christian East Beirut which claimed the lives of those who attempted to cross this no-man's-land.

Loi-cadre. Also known as *Loi-Defferre*, after the then French Overseas Territories Minister, Gaston Defferre. It refers to the French administrative law which granted a certain internal autonomy to New Caledonia in 1956, creating a local parliament (*Assemblée Territoriale*) and integrating Melanesians into political life for the first time. It was abrogated in 1963.

Longfellow, Henry Wadsworth, b. USA 1807, d. 1882. American whose epic poem "Evangeline" recounts the tragedy of *Le Grand Dérangement*. It tells of the two lovers Gabriel and Evangeline, who were separated when ten to twelve thousand Acadians were forced into exile by the British in 1755.

Louis Delgrès, Mulatto, he led a revolt in 1802 against the reinstitution of slavery and committed suicide along with three hundred of his men at the Matouba stronghold by detonating some dynamite.

Low Countries. The Low Countries were set up by the Madrid Treaty. The present Belgian provinces (except for the independent principality of Liège) were part of a group of seventeen provinces, including Holland, under Spanish rule. In 1581, the union was split into two groups that correspond largely to modern-day Belgium and Holland.

Loyalty Islands. Group of New Caledonian islands to the east of the *Grande Terre* (Mainland). Comprised of Lifou, Maré, Ouvéa and the barely populated Tiga, the Loyalties represent ten percent of New Caledonia's population. They are mostly Protestant (due to the influence of the London Missionary Society in the nineteenth century), unlike the predominantly Catholic *Grande Terre* (due to the influence of the French Marist missionaries).

Maghreb. The ensemble of the three countries of Northwest Africa, Marocco, Algeria, and Tunisia. The Grand Maghreb covers, in addition, Libya and Mauritania. In 1989, these countries formed the economic union called the Union of the Arabic Maghreb. The term itself remains contested, accepted by some and rejected by many people of North Africa due to the Arabic connotation of the West and the stigmata of colonization that it continues to convey.

Maghrebian immigrant. A person, formerly from the Maghreb, who has immigrated. In France, most Maghrebian immigrants arrive from Algeria, given the complex colonial history the two countries share. These immigrants take up full residence in France, eventually becoming French national citizens.

Maghrebian. The adjective attached to the noun Maghreb. Maghrebian is frequently used to identify Algerians or people of Algerian heritage in France. The terms collapses the specific cultural and national distinctions of peoples of North Africa and thus becomes a marker of the region itself.

magical realism. A form of narrative which borders between the real and the unfathomable. A genre best known in Latin America and associated with the works of Garcia-Marquez, magical realism contains a mystical quality related to a beyond and thus tarries with the spiritual and natural domains of the imaginary.

Maillet, Antonine, b. Canada (Acadia) 1929. Acadia's most well-known and celebrated author or "ambassador." No single author's works better epitomize the struggles that Acadia and the Acadian people have endured and overcome than hers. Recipient in 1979 of the prestigious Prix Goncourt (q.v.) for her novel *Pélagie-la-Charrette*, which recounts the return from the United States of exiled Acadians to their homeland.

Makandal, François, b. Haiti. Haitian resister against slavery who waged a campaign of terror against the French planters of the colony of Saint-Domingue in the eighteenth century. The endless stories of how Makandal would miraculously escape from his enemies by transforming himself into a bird, a fly, or a wolf are legendary in Caribbean historiography and oral traditions.

Malherbe, François de, b. France 1555, d. 1628. French poet considered to be the first major theoretician of French classical poetics, best known for his role in reforming the French language.

Manichean division. In the context of post-colonial theory, the absolute division between the world of the colonized and the world of the colonizer created by the violent oppression and repression of the former by the latter. This division was effectively described by Frantz Fanon in *The Wretched of the Earth*.

Manichean view of history and identity. Going back to the Greek philosophy that believed in the objective and separate existence of good and evil, this view of history and identity has been harnessed by colonial and anti-colonial ideologies to justify their own power structures. For instance, the colonial self-definition can be said to be Manichean, in that it defined itself against an other that it constructed as the negative image of itself (i.e., as inhuman, inferior, immoral). Abdul Jan Mohammed has used this term to describe the aesthetics of colonialist literature in his essay, "The Economy of Manichean Allegory: The Function of Racial Difference in Colonialist Literature."

Manichean. A concept which divides everything into dualisms by which one half is considered superior and the other half a complete negative. The terms stems from the religion of Mani founded on a strict system of dualisms opposing good and evil. The religion itself was a missionary rival to Christianity until the Middle Ages.

marabout. In African Muslim cultures, a man respected for his Koranic as well as traditional knowledge, often consulted for what are considered to be his powers of divination.

Mariotti, Jean, b. New Caledonia 1901, d. France 1973. Foremost New Caledonian writer who produced over a dozen novels. Although raised in the New Caledonian "bush," he spent most of his adult life in metropolitan France, where, in 1962, he became vice-president of the Société des Gens de Lettres. His works express both a longing for an idealized New Caledonia and a rejection of its reality.

Maritime Provinces. Canada's three adjacent Atlantic-seaboard provinces of New Brunswick, Nova Scotia and Prince Edward Island.

maroons. Slaves who escaped plantations to live in the hills. They either lived on their own or formed communities in the Caribbean islands and in Guiana. Marooning was more important in hilly islands than in territories such as Barbados where forests were soon cleared to make way for plantations.

Mauritius (Fr. Île Maurice). A state consisting primarily of the Indian Ocean island Mauritius which forms part of the Mascarene archipelago. Visited by the Portuguese in 1505, occupied by the Dutch until 1710, the island was a French possession (known as Île de France) from 1715 till 1810 and was under British rule until its independence in 1968. A multicultural, multi-ethnic society with an economy based largely on sugar cane production.

Maximin, Daniel, b. 1947 Guadeloupe, is a professor of literature. Collaborates regularly to various reviews and has held various political positions in Guadeloupe with regard to defending Guadeloupean culture and literature.

Meddeb, Abdelwahab, b. Tunisia 1946. Novelist, poet, translator and editor. He studied literature and history of art and archaeology in Tunis and in France and lives in France. His work is an example of self-reflexive narrative where thoughts on the writing process are part of the narrative. He tends to use complex references to various languages and cultures, in particular, Islamic Sufism.

Melanesian (see Kanak). Term coined by French navigator Dumont d'Urville in the 1830s to designate the indigenous population of New Caledonia and other islands of Melanesia (Papua New Guinea, Fiji, Vanuatu, the Solomons). Austronesian migrations from Southeast Asia first settled in New Caledonia nearly 3,000 years B.C. Important traces of their early culture, known as Lapita, are scattered throughout the island.

Mellah, Fawzi, b. Syria 1946. Studied literature and philosophy in Tunis and law in Switzerland and now lives between Switzerland and Tunisia. Mellah writes novels, plays, essays and journalistic reports. Mellah's engagement with Western as well as local representations of history marks most of his work. His essays explore both personal and national identities and his narratives often mix philosophical ideas with ethnographic observations.

Memmi, Albert, b. Tunisia 1920. Albert Memmi is a novelist, essayist and researcher of Jewish origin. He studied philosophy in Algeria and in France and has held many academic positions. His analysis of the situation of the colonized and the colonizer, *Le Portrait du colonisé* (1957), has been very influential in addressing the role of culture in the colonial situation. In his other works, he has studied various forms of domination, including the "condition juive" in *Portrait d'un Juif* (1957) and *La libération du Juif* (1962), the problems of dominance and dependence in *L'homme dominé* (1968) and *La Dépendance* (1979), and racism in *Le racisme* (1982). He developed the notions of *heterophobia* (fear of the other which causes aggressivity) and *judéité*. Some of his novels are: *La Statue de sel* (1953), *Agar* (1955), *Le Scorpion* (1969) and *Le Nomade immobile* (2000). Memmi's influence is largely linked to his essay on the psychological effects of identity formation under colonialism. His early novels portray inter-community relation in his native Tunisia while stressing personal issues. His work is widely available in English.

Memramcook. City located in New Brunswick not far from Bouctouche where Maillet (q.v.) was born, and considered the birthplace and cradle of New Acadia after the difficult 100-year period of "hibernation" following the *Grand Dérangement* (q.v.). It was the scene in 1881 of the Acadian nationalist revival movement and where the Acadian National Conferences (q.v.) first took place.

métissage. Originally, biological term designating the offspring of the union of different ethnic or racial elements. Long denied as a biological reality in New Caledonia, it has recently become fashionable to use the term figuratively, in defining examples of *métissage culturel*, the artistic productions of a society striving to redefine itself in the wake of the Accord de Nouméa (q.v.) (1998). A danger and source of degeneration for racial purists, an illusion of universal culture for some post-colonial critics such as Roger Toumson (see *Mythologie du métissage*), and an inadequate term for Édouard Glissant, who prefers *créolisation* to describe cultural relationships in the West Indies (and in modern to post-modern times in general). Françoise Lionnet has developed this term in her *Autobiographical Voices: Race, Gender and Self-Portraiture*, to convey the concept and practice of "solidarity which demystifies all essentialist glorifications of unitary origins, be they racial, sexual, geographic, or cultural." Lionnet draws on the connotations (braiding, *mètis*) of this term in order to analyze how texts from different geographical and cultural locations all offer new, non-essentialist ways of conceiving identity, that have in common a "dynamic model of relationality." She also uses it to indicate a reading practice that brings together "biology and history, anthropology and philosophy, linguistics and literature."

metonymy of presence. A concept linked to mimicry, in Homi Bhabha's (q.v.) terms, which has the consequence of requiring the subject to become or to imitate in a way that substitutes a part for the whole (assimilation).

metropolitan citizenship. A particular type of citizenship which permits, in particular, formerly colonized Francophone subjects to reside within metropolitan France, frequently known as the Hexagon because of its geometric form.

metropolitan identity. This form of identity refers in particular to the identity of metropolitan France and its administrative and bureaucratic centers. Opposed to the identity of France's overseas departments and former colonies, the term marks a specific delineation of French identity within the metropolis and is frequently used to refer to post-colonial immigrants' adoption of a "French" form of identity within France, the country of residence.

Michel, Louise, b. France 1830, d. 1905. Revolutionary, writer and teacher who, as a *Communarde*, was exiled to New Caledonia (1873–80). The first notable European to take an interest in the Melanesian world, whose tales and legends she transcribed and embellished in several works, such as *Légendes et chansons de geste canaques* (1875/1885).

mimicry. Involving that part of the colonial project which encourages or requires partial, but not complete, imitation of the imperial by the subjected. Homi Bhabha has written about this process and its consequences in *The Location of Culture* (1994).

mission civilisatrice. Based on the idea that non-Europeans were at a lowly stage of development and could be morally and physically improved through contact with European values. The concept of the European's "Civilizing Mission" abroad was used to justify Europeans' presence in the colonies and the reorganization of societies and lands for European profit. Secular and religious forms of the "civilizing mission" co-existed.

Montréal / Montreal. The largest city in Québec/Quebec, Canada. The majority of the inhabitants are French-speaking.

Mujahida, Pl. Mujahidat. The women who fought in the Algerian war of independence.

narrative dynamics. The means by which a narrative functions, including the movement of the plot as well as the relationship between reader and writer, character and imagination. Narrative dynamics also refers to the actual structure of narrative, the energy by which the narrative acquires its ability to create a cohesive or unitary (albeit frequently fragmented) vision for the reader.

narrative space. Narrative is an oral or written discourse telling of an event or series of events, real or fictitious, that are the subjects of this discourse. Narrative discourse is produced by the action of telling an addressee. The works of Linda Lê occupy an in-between narrative space, between the text and the reader, and within the novel, between the diegetic narrator or speaker and the interlocutor, or the writer and the muse.

Natif natal. Term used by Césaire in *Le Cahier* to evoke his island-home.

neo-colonialism. Meaning literally "new colonialism," the term neo-colonialism is used to highlight the continuation of colonial domination by Europe and the West, particularly in the areas of trade and economics, in former colonies even after the formal end of colonial administrations. "Neo-colonial," which stresses the continued domination in the new world order of former colonies by the former colonial powers, is sometimes used in opposition to the term "post-colonial," which tends to suggest that there is a perceptible end to colonial domination.

New Caledonia. French Overseas Territory, which became a *pays d'outre-mer* (q.v.) in 2000. It is situated in the southwest Pacific, a thousand miles east of Australia and over ten thousand miles from Europe. Capital Nouméa. Population 200,000 (44 percent Melanesian; 34 percent European; 12 percent Polynesian; also Indonesian, Vietnamese and others). Melanesians occupied the land for three thousand years before James Cook "discovered" it in 1774. Annexed by France in 1853, the island served as a penal colony 1864–97 and an important American military base in the Second World War.

nomadism. A form of wandering, be it physical or metaphorical, in which the nomadic subject encounters a variety of conceptual or geographical spaces. Nomadism, while sterotypically related to desert nomads and early migrations, is also related to a post-colonial theoretical concept of deterritorialization or the fact of being displaced or diasporic, roaming either physically or psychologically. Nomadism is frequently adopted in post-colonial theory as a positive mode of uprooting the fixed nature of identity and culture.

non-lieu. Meaning literally "non-existence," in addition to referring to a geographical vacuum or "no man's landm" the term connotes that which has no legal status.

Nouméa. Capital of New Caledonia, in the largely European and wealthy Southern Province. The phenomenon of urbanization, particularly over the past decade, has seen the population of greater Nouméa grow to become nearly two-thirds of that of the entire country.

Nouveau Roman. Alain Robbe-Grillet, Nathalie Sarraute, Michel Butor, Claude Simon, Jean Ricardou et al. argued for a new aesthetics of the novel based on the systematic deconstruction of the classical model. In the Nouveau Roman, plot is often a series of repetitions and variations while characters are loci of signs and clues to be organized and interpreted by the reader. Realistic description is replaced by minute observations reflecting either the narrator's subjectivity or maniacal objectivity. In the process, chronology is dissolved. Nouveau Roman has had considerable influence on Francophone North African literature.

OAS (Organisation Armée Secrète). A clandestine movement that attempted to oppose itself to Algerian Independence through violence and terrorism after the failure of the military putsch of Algers between 1961 and 1963. The organization was directed by the generals Salan and Jouhaud until their arrests.

opposition. See strategy and De Certeau.

othering. A term coined by post-colonial scholar Gayatri Spivak, meaning the process by which power dynamics, or a colonial system of subordination, creates an other of the colonial subject and a Self defined against that other.

Oyono, Ferdinand, b. Cameroon, 1929. Known as a literary artist for his biting irony and caricatural techniques in three anticolonial novels *Le Vieux nègre et la médaille* (1956), *Une vie de boy* (1956), and *Chemin d'Europe* (1960). When he was young, he worked as a "boy" for European missionaries. He later earned a doctorate in law in Paris, and he has since been active as a diplomat for Cameroon in several capacities, including as delegate to the United Nations and as ambassador in various countries around the world.

Pays d'Outre-Mer. The administrative status of New Caledonia within the French Republic since January 1, 2000, following the *Accord de Nouméa* (1998), a status deemed to reflect the increasing autonomy, *émancipation* in the New Caledonian vocabulary, proposed by this accord.

performative. A theoretical term best associated with the gender theorist Judith Butler, the performative is seen as a subversive means of performing within a dominant order. The term was first launched in the 1950s by the philospher and linguist J. L. Austin and later a target of Derridean deconstruction. Frequently the performative is understood as an ambivalence which destabilizes the fixed terms of hegemonic or dominant forms of identity and authority and thus serves a subversive purpose.

Perle des Antilles françaises translates literally Pearl of the French Antilles (West Indies) and refers historically to the colony of Saint-Domingue, France's most important and wealthiest overseas territory, on account of its rich plantations of sugar cane, coffee and cotton. The term is now appropriated by Haitian artists and intellectuals to counteract the negative images of Haiti.

Phoenicians. Settlers along the Lebanese coast in 2800 B.C. whose origin is yet to be determined. They referred to themselves as Canaanites but were given the name Phoenicians by the Greeks after the purple dye they were known to have discovered and sold. They were also known for their sailing expertise and by 1100 B.C. dominated the trading routes across the Mediterranean and along the Nile. In 335 B.C. they were massacred and sold into slavery by Alexander the Great and his army. Today, the Phoenician legacy is still evident in Lebanon among the ruins found in the cities of Tyre, Sidon and Byblos.

Pisier, Marie-France, b. France 1946. Actress, writer and filmmaker. The daughter of a highranking French civil servant posted to New Caledonia, she grew up in Nouméa in the 1950s and wrote a fictionalized account of this experience in her novel *Le Bal du gouverneur* (1984), which she subsequently adapted to the screen (1990).

Plains of Abraham. Situated just outside the fortified walls of old Quebec, it was the scene of the decisive battle and defeat in 1759 of French forces under the command of Montcalm by British forces under the command of Wolfe. The battle served as a prelude for complete French military withdrawal from Canada under the terms of the Treaty of Paris (q.v.) in 1763.

Plisnier, Charles, b. 1896, d. 1952. Belgian writer, author of *Mariages* (1936), *Faux-passeports* (1937) and *Meurtres* (1939–41). He went to live in France and hoped that Belgian French speakers would eventually be incorporated into France.

Polo, Marco, b. 1254, d. 1324. Medieval Italian traveler credited with being the first European to cross the entire continent of Asia and to recount in *The Travels of Marco Polo* what he observed. He was particularly impressed with China's civilization, which he considered more culturally and technologically advanced than Europe.

polyphony. From the Greek "poly," "many," and "phone," "voice, sound." Literally "many voices."

post-colonial agent. A post-colonial subject who intervenes in the dominant discourses to challenge the formerly colonial worldview of a dominant colonial culture and dominated colonized culture. A post-colonial agent emerges wielding power in a belated gesture which siezes the terms of power and brings the notion of a dominant or dominated group or identity into question. Frequently such post-colonial agency emerges using the very terms of the former master.

post-colonial literature. Literature from the period following the independence of formerly colonized countries, written by authors from post-colonial states or engaging with post-colonial discourse or problematics.

power relations / *rapports de force*. Relationships between individuals, societies, states and nations which are based on unequal distributions of power. This power may be economic, social, cultural and political, or any combination of these. Pierre Bourdieu (q.v.) analyses the operation and reproduction of power relations in society in much of his work.

Price-Mars, *Jean,* b. Haiti, 1879, d. 1969. One of the most influential thinkers of his generation. Anthropologist, historian, diplomat, politician, Dr. Price-Mars encouraged Haitian intellectuals to turn their gaze inwards and celebrate their multiple heritage and the wealth of their culture. Haitian voodoo, Creole, everyday practices were given special treatment as they provided insight into the collective un/consciousness. His impact has also been felt in literature and many intellectuals and literary critics today consider him a precursor of the Negritude movement. Price-Mars received a Doctor Honoris Causa by the University of Dakar (Cheikh Anta Diop) and has been given many more prestigious tributes not only from Haiti but also from Latin American and African countries.

prolepsis. The telling, in the linear progression of a narrative text, of events that will occur later than the present moment in the story as it is unfolding.

proust, Marcel, b. France 1871, d. 1922. Renowned twentieth-century French novelist and critic. Author of *À la recherche du temps perdu,* also known by the English title *Remembrance of Things Past.* Both Proust and Maillet (q.v.) place great importance on recalling the(ir) past and the notion of involuntary memory.

purism. The attitude that rejects any linguistic form that is not attested in the variety of the language recognized as the norm.

Québec / Quebec. The largest province of Canada. The majority of the inhabitants are French-speaking. Founded in 1608, four years after Acadia (q.v.) was established, by Samuel de Champlain, Quebec remained a French colony as part of New France up until the Treaty of Paris (q.v.) in 1763, at which time it became a British colony, thereby ending completely France's military presence in Canada.

Qur'an (Fr. Koran). Both "reading" or "recital," the Koran (or "Qur'an") represents for Muslim people the sacred text which conveys the sacred words of God as they were revealed to the prophet Muhammad between the years 612 and 632, first in Mecca and later in Medina. Structured in 114 surahs (or chapters) varying in length from 3 to 286 verses, the Koranic text is constructed around the prophet's recollections, mostly preserved by his companions and his wives.

Rabelais, François, b. France 1494, d. 1553. Renowned Renaissance French author of such satirical works as *Gargantua and Pantagruel.*

réel imaginaire. Oxymoron meaning literally "imaginary realism or reality." The term designates Maillet's (q.v.) deliberate attempt in her works to create a confusion or to blur the lines between history and storytelling whereby the boundary between the two, which normally is well defined, is unclear.

Régent, Catherine, b. New Caledonia 1951. European settler descendant who writes historical novels dealing with colonial settlement—*Valesdir* (1993), *Justine* (1995). A teacher, she has also adapted New Caledonian legends in the form of children's stories.

régime de l'indigénat. Colonial disposition regulating indigenous life in New Caledonia between 1887 and 1946, characterized by organization of "tribes," their relocation on reservations, restriction of movement, forced labor, etc., and general deprivation of the civic rights of the indigenous population.

Renard, Jules, b. France 1864, d. 1910. French writer whose works are obsessed with his childhood years which he detested and missed at the same time, all the while refusing to live in the present by either dwelling on the past or looking toward the future.

resistance. See strategy and De Certeau.

reverse mimicry. A reversal of Homi Bhabha's concept of mimicry, whereby colonials imitate subjects.

Roumain, Jacques, b. Haiti 1907, d. 1944. Born and raised in Haiti, Roumain received a classic education, studying both in Haiti and in Europe. He was one of the pioneers of the journal,

Revue indigène, headed by Dr. Price-Mars, which militated against the American occupation and rekindled national pride in popular culture. He was arrested several times and spent three years in prison for subversive activities, most notably, the creation of the Communist party. It was also during this time that he started to write short stories and novels, all of them addressing class exploitation. Given an early release, Roumain went into exile in France, where he worked at the Musée de l'Homme, then lived in New York until 1941. Once home, he created the Bureau d'ethnologie and pursued his writings. He finished his most significant novel, *Gouverneurs de la rosée*, shortly before his death in 1944. Acclaimed by many as a Haitian masterpiece, *Gouverneurs de la rosée* has been translated in many languages and adapted to theatre and the screen. The love story between Manuel and Elisa is filtered through a Haitian worldview where Creole, vodou, dance and rituals richly texture the plight of poor people in need of hope and betterment of their living conditions. The novel gives ample treatment to the notion of community and collective effort such as *combite* (cooperative work group), to the importance of memory and to a new ethic which can lead to social transformation.

RPCR, *Rassemblement pour la Calédonie dans la République*. Anti-independence, "loyalist" political party formed in 1978 to counter rising calls for independence by Kanaks. Its founder and current leader is Jacques Lafleur, one of the two New Caledonian *députés* in the French Parliament.

Schwarz-Bart, Simone, b. Guadeloupe 1938. She studied in Pointe-à-Pitre, Paris and Dakar. Wrote a first novel *Un Plat de porc aux bananes vertes* with her husband André Schwarz-Bart, who obtained the Prix Goncourt for *Le Dernier des justes*. She resides in Switzerland and Guadeloupe. Her later novels *Ti-Jean l'Horizon* and *Pluie et vent sur Télumée-Miracle* as well as her play *Ton Beau Capitaine* have received critical acclaim. *Pluie et vent* is often featured on syllabi for courses on Caribbean literature as an excellent example of magical realism.

seasonal workers. They are accorded a permit which enables them to work in Switzerland for nine months a year, mainly in areas such as construction, agriculture and hotels. Their status has long been controversial, given that they are required to leave Switzeland for three months every year and are not legally allowed to bring their families with them.

self-consolidating other. Phrase used by Gayatri Spivak to refer to "the other" as produced and represented in the cultural production of dominant systems, and that occludes absolute alterity.

Sembène, Ousmane, b. Senegal 1923. Novelist and filmmaker. A Marxist and autodidact, and the father of African film, Sembène was a *tirailleur sénégalais* during the Second World War, and a laborer and docker in Marseille before studying filmmaking in Moscow (1961–63). His novels and films range from the satirical to the historical and are as critical of European colonialism and its legacy as of the conduct of the ruling elites of post-independence Africa. In all Sembène's work, the emancipation of women is seen as key in the liberation of Africa.

sender (Fr. destinateur). In Greimas's actantial model, the actant who imparts values to the subject, motivates him/her, and sends him/her on a quest for a desired object.

Senegal, Republic of. West African state bordered by Mauritania, Mali, Guinea, Guinea-Bissau, Gambia and the Atlantic Ocean. A French possession by treaty with Holland and Britain from 1814, and the administrative base for France's expansion into West Africa from 1857 onwards. Free Senegalese officially had French citizenship and elected a deputy to the French *Assemblée nationale* from 1848. Gained independence from France in 1960; its first president was the renowned poet and statesman Léopold Sédar Senghor.

Senegalese wrestling. National sport of Senegal. Dating back to the days of the Mali kingdom in the eleventh century, this sport was once reserved for those of royal lineage. It is not only a show of physical strength, but a show of elegance and beauty, through the wrestling techniques themselves, and especially through the accompanying poetry, songs and dance. In

Aminata Sow Fall's novel, *L'Appel des arènes* (1982), the call of the wrestling arena symbolizes the call of tradition.

Sénès, Jacqueline, b. France 1930. Journalist and radio reporter turned writer. For thirty years she had a weekly radio program in New Caledonia, in which she interviewed people, particularly folklore "characters," from all over the island. Fascinated by the essence of daily life of the Territory, she wrote a study *La Vie quotidienne en Nouvelle-Calédonie de 1850 à nos jours* (1985), before turning to the form of the historical novel in *Terre Violente* (1987).

signifying. A term borrowed from the African-American tradition and folklore by African-American cultural studies and literary studies to designate a rhetorical figure of speech which imitates and deconstructs the discourse of power (cf. Henry Louis Gates, Jr. *The Signifying Monkey*).

Sow Fall, Aminata, b. Senegal 1941. First woman writer in Francophone Black Africa to publish a non-autobiographical novel, *Le Revenant* (1976). Her second novel, *La Grève des bàttu* (1979) received Le Grand Prix littéraire d'Afrique Noire in 1980, and was short-listed for the Prix Goncourt, as was *L'appel des arènes* in 1982. Both novels are being made into movies. Aminata Sow Fall has published three more novels since: *L'Ex-père de la nation* (1987), *Le Jujubier du patriarche* (1997) and *Douceurs du bercail* (1998). She has been very active defending human rights and promoting cultural exchanges, through a center she founded in 1987, le Centre Africain d'Animation et d'Echanges Culturels (CAEC), through her involvement in the Ministry of Culture of Senegal, and through her numerous speaking engagements around the world. With her keen sense of observation, Aminata Sow Fall strives to expose in her novels the problems of modern-day African society. She calls herself a realist but also an optimist, who believes that Africans can and must "become what they are."

Spivak, Gayatri. Has been described by one critic as "a thinker whom everybody knows and nobody reads" (Asha Varadharajan). Her essay "Can the subaltern speak?" was influential in the development of post-colonial studies in the U.S. academy, even though she also provides a critique of "post-colonialism." In a series of essays, she develops the notion of intervention and discusses several examples of literature that she qualifies as "interventionist." The notion of intervention, and her work in general, have contributed a constant critique of the fetishist notions of identity in American literary-critical discourse.

standard French. This corresponds to the variety of the language whose norms are found in reference books such as dictionaries and grammars and which is associated with a dominant social group. It is used in official documents, education and the mass media. The variety of French found in educated layers of Paris is often referred to as Standard French although regional or national norms have developed in recent years.

station. New Caledonian term (reflecting the historical influence of Australia on the local vocabulary and customs) for cattle station/ranch, particularly on the *Caldoche* West Coast.

strategy. For De Certeau, *strategies* imply the existence of well-defined boundaries, a self-contained place from which a subject can isolate him/herself from a certain power-structure and *resist* it. *Tactics*, on the other hand, are a type of action that take place when no such boundaries exist, that only take place on the territory of the other—"La tactique n'a pour lieu que celui de l'autre." In such situation, one can neither count on a proper space of one's own, nor on a well-defined boundary that makes the other a visible totality. In such a situation, resistance becomes impossible, and the subject can only *oppose* the system. This conception of opposition implies a porosity that undoes the clear dichotomies on which the dualistic view of (post)colonial cultures rests. See also de Certeau.

subaltern. Term used by Spivak in her analysis of colonial and post-colonial texts. She uses the Marxist notion of class as a model of subalternity, and emphasizes that the subaltern is not a positive or concrete identity based on interest or desire but that it is a formation, on the model of a nation, rather than a family. It is crucial to remember that "identity" is always produced as a subject-effect in relation to other positions.

Sufism. The mystical dimension of Islam. Sufism is practiced at the popular as well as intellectual levels. In North Africa the presence of Sufism is visible in the veneration of holy men and women, rituals and membership in brotherhoods (tariqas). These institutions played an important role in the community and fostered popular religious belief and practice. They were manipulated by the French during the colonial period but with limited success. The intellectual strand of Sufism draws on philosophical and theological ideas from Islamic and other sources. Early influential figures include Jalal al-Din al-Rumi (d. 1273), Mansur al-Hallaj (d. 922); Muhyi al-Din Ibn Arabi (d. 1240) and more recently, the leader of the first Algerian rebellion against the French, the Amir Abd al-Qadir (1808–83).

Suisse romande. Denotes the six Francophone cantons of Switzerland—Fribourg, Genève, Jura, Neuchâtel, Valais and Vaud—two of which (Fribourg and Valais) are in part also Germanophone.

tactic. See strategy and De Certeau.

Territoire d'outre-mer. New Caledonia officially ceased being a *colonie* and became a *territoire d'outre-mer* in 1946, with the repeal of the *régime de l'indigénat*, and the granting of citizenship to Melanesians. Following the 1998 *Accord de Nouméa*, it became a *pays d'outre-mer* on 1 January 2000, a unique situation within the French Republic.

Tjibaou, Jean-Marie, b. New Caledonia 1936, d. 1989. Kanak former priest turned politician who became leader of the pro-independence front, the FLNKS, in 1984, when he declared himself leader of the provisional government of *Kanaky*. He was a signatory to the Accords de Matignon (q.v.) in 1988, whose aim was to bring an end to the years of social unrest and violence known as *les événements*. He was assassinated by a fellow Kanak, opposed to these Accords, in 1989.

Tonton Makout (also *Tontons Macoutes*) translates literally "uncles with sisal sacks" (in opposition to Tonton Nowèl). This paramilitary force, officially members of the Volontaires de la Sécurité Nationale, was established by Papa Doc, François Duvalier, to counterbalance the power of the Haitian army. Although dismantled in 1986 by the National Council of government, the term is generally used to describe someone associated with illegal state activity (arbitrary arrest, brutality, murder).

topos (Pl. *topoi*). From the Greek for place, the term *topos* denoted a stock theme or "common place" in ancient rhetoric. It is used to denote the same in modern literature, art and film criticism.

trace (une). A path generally found in the hilly forested areas. Several were made by marooning slaves.

transgression. The act of going beyond the bounds or limits of what is hegemonically deemed to be acceptable. To violate or infringe.

Treaty of Utrecht. Treaty in 1713 marking the end of the War of the Spanish Succession and the end of French claims to Acadia (q.v.), which was turned over to the British.

trickster figure. An empowering figure in the African-American folklore, the trickster, through rhetorical tricks, beats the master at his own game.

Tunisia. Located in North Africa, Tunisia was colonized by France from 1881 to 1956, which prepared the way for French to become the second language in the country. The official religion is Islam, although there are small Christian and Jewish communities. The capital of Tunisia since the thirteenth century is Tunis, a large metropolis located few miles south of ancient Carthage. Tunis is the country's most populous city and main cultural center. The French helped build the modern part of the city alongside the old Medina.

Umma. The term "Umma" (or "Ummah") can be loosely translated into English by "Muslim community." Mentioned sixty-four times in the Koran, the term represents a central concept in Islam, expressing the fundamental unity of Muslim people across specific national identities. Due to the development of secular nation-states throughout the Muslim world, the notion of Umma lost part of its religious meaning. Despite the increasing secularization of public life, the notion of Umma still remains a very meaningful concept to describe social and collective identity in most Muslim countries.

Union Calédonienne. Political party set up in the early 1950s with a transracial social project under the motto of "*deux couleurs, un peuple.*" As New Caledonian political life became radicalized and polarized through the 1970s and 1980s, the *Union Calédonienne* gradually lost the support of its *petits blancs* followers, and became a "Kanak" party, the main component of the pro-independence coalition, the FLNKS.

Université de Moncton. Located in Moncton, New Brunswick, Acadia's (q.v.) French-language university and Canada's only French-language university outside the Province of Quebec. It was the scene in the late 1960s of student protests where a group of Acadian writers broke the silence and emerged to (re)claim the political and linguistic rights denied to them and to recognize their turbulent yet glorious past.

valeur-refuge. Term used by Roger Toumson (see *Mythologie du métissage*) to describe *métissage* as an ideological alibi which posits cultural intermingling (especially in the Caribbean and the Americas) as a humanistic ideal for the future without acknowledging the persistent socioeconomic, structural and cultural barriers to struggles for racial equality.

Victor Hughes. Sent by the Convention, the French regime in power, in 1794 to ensure that Guadeloupean planters would not oppose the law granting freedom to slaves. Many planters left rather than face the guillotine, which Hughes frequently used.

Vienna Conference. Conference held in Vienna in 1815 led by Austria, England, Prussia and Russia ; its purpose was to reorganize Europe's political map after Napoleon's fall. One of the decisions was to unite present Holland and Belgium in the "kingdom of the Low Countries."

Vietnam. Vietnam has had a rich and varied history. It was largely influenced by Chinese culture after years of enduring and rebelling against Chinese imperial forces. France became involved in Vietnamese affairs from the mid-seventeenth century onwards.

vodou. According to Joan Dayan, voodoo "is a word used by the Fon tribe of southern Dahomey to mean 'spirit,' 'god,' or 'image'" (1995: 288). Derived from complex West African traditional religions, art and rituals, it is the belief system of the Haitian majority who serve spirits. Based on the veneration of *lwa* (spirits), it recognizes the existence of one supreme being and has absorbed many of the saints and the mysticism of apostolic Catholicism.

vouloir-pouvoir-faire (Eng. wanting/being able to do). A modality representing a simultaneous desire and ability to act in a given way in a given situation.

Walloon. Walloon belongs to the Romance languages family. It covers four varieties of dialects found in the south of Belgium: "liègeois," "namurois," "wallo-picard" and "wallo-lorrain." Dialectal substrates such as "picard," "champenois" and "gaumais" are also found in French-speaking Belgium, but the geographical extent of Walloon has given the name of Wallonie, under which the south of the country is known.

Weber, Max, b. 1864, d. 1920. Influential economist, historian and philosopher, nowadays considered (alongside with Durkheim) as the founding father of modern sociology as a distinct social science. Strongly influenced by the neo-Kantian school of philosophy and opposed to Marxism, Max Weber elaborated a general framework for sociology which is nowadays still valid and influential. The key contributions of Weber's comprehensive sociology are the analysis of the processes of bureaucratization and rationalization, the economic study of religion and the definition of an ideal-type methodology.

Wolof. West African language widely spoken in Senegal and Gambia. The native language of Ousmane Sembène.

world-upside-down. Carnivalesque *topos* and conception of the world popularized in François Rabelais' (q.v.) literary works and Pieter Bruegel's paintings whereby imagery and roles are reversed.

zombification. The process by which an individual becomes a soulless being (zombie).

Selected Bibliography

Abbott, Peter. "Autobiography, Autography, Fiction: Groundwork for a Taxonomy of Textual Categories." *New Literary History* 19, no. 3 (1988): 597–615.

Abou, Sélim. *Le Bilinguisme au Liban.* Paris: PUF, 1962.

Abu Bakr al-Kalabadhi. *The Doctrine of the Sufis.* Trans. A. J. Arberry. Cambridge: Cambridge University Press, 1977.

Accad, Evelyne, and Rose Ghurayyib, eds. *Contemporary Arab Women Writers and Poets.* Beirut: Institute for Women's Studies in the Arab World, 1985.

Accad, Evelyne. *Coquelicot du Massacre.* Paris: L'Harmattan, 1988.

——. *L'Excisée.* Paris: L'Harmattan, 1982.

——. "Feminist perspective on the war in Lebanon." *Woman's Studies International Forum* 12, no.1 (1989): 91–95.

——. "L'Ecriture (comme) éclatement des frontières." *L'Esprit-Créateur* 33, no. 2 (summer 1993): 119–28.

——. "La Longue marche des héroïnes des romans modernes du Mashreq et du Maghreb." *Présence Francophone* 12 (spring 1976): 3–11.

——. "The Prostitute in Arab and North African Fiction." In *The Image of the Prostitute in Modern Literature.* Ed. Pierre L. Horn and Mary Beth Pringle. New York: Frederick Ungar, 1984.

——. "The Theme of Sexual Oppression in the North African Novel." *Women in the Muslim World.* Ed. Lois Beck and Nikki Keddie. Cambridge, Mass.: Harvard University Press, 1978.

——. "Writing to Explore (W) Human Experience: The Language Question." *Research in African Literatures* 23, no. 1 (spring 1992): 179–86.

——. *Sexuality and War: Literary Masks of the Middle East.* New York: New York University Press, 1990.

——. *Veil of Shame: The Role of Women in Contemporary Fiction on North Africa and the Arab World.* Montreal: Naaman, 1978.

——. *Women and the War Story.* Berkeley: University of California Press, 1996.

Achour, Christiane. "Ancrage, identité et dérision: L'humour dans le récit beur." In *Humour d'expression française,* 202–8, Nice: Z'Editions, 1990.

Adelaide-Merlande, Jacques. *Histoire Générale des Antilles et des Guyanes.* Paris: Éditions Caribéennes & L'Harmattan, 1994.

Adnan, Etel. *Sitt Marie Rose.* Paris: Editions des Femmes, 1978.

——. *L'Apocalypse arabe.* Paris: Editions Papyrus, 1980.

——. *Five Senses for One Death.* New York: The Smith, 1971.

——. Jebu suivi de l'Express Beyrouth–Enfer. Paris: P. J. Oswald, 1973.

Ager, Dennis. *Francophonie in the 1990's: Problems and Opportunities*. Clevedon: Multilingual Matters, 1996.

Ahmed, Leila. "Women and the advent of Islam." *Signs: Journal of Women in Culture and Society* 11, no. 4 (1986).

———. "Arab Culture and Writing Women's Bodies." *Feminist Issues* (spring 1989): 41–55.

———. "Between the Worlds: The Formation of a Turn-of-a-Century Egyptian Feminist." In *Life/Lines: Theorizing Women's Autobiography*. Ed. Bella Brodski and Celeste Schenck. Ithaca, N.Y.: Cornell University Press, 1988.

———. "Feminism and Cross-Cultural Inquiry: The Term of the Discourse in Islam." In *Coming to Terms: Feminism, Theory, Politics*, 143–51. Ed. Elizabeth Weed. New York: Routledge, 1989.

Aït Sabbah, Fatna. *La Femme dans l'inconscient musulman*. Paris: Albin Michel, 1986.

Al-Ali, Nadje Sadig. *Gender Writing / Writing Gender*. Cairo: The American University in Cairo Press, 1994.

Alexakis, Vassilis. *Contrôle d'identité*. Paris: Editions du Seuil, 1985.

———. *La langue maternelle*. Paris: Fayard, 1995.

———. *Papa*. Paris: Fayard, 1997.

———. *Paris-Athènes*. Paris: Fayard, 1997.

Allain, Mathé. "Le temps sacré et le temps profane chez Antonine Maillet." *Québec Studies* 4 (1986): 320–25.

Allami, Noria. *Voilées, dévoilées: être femme dans le monde arabe*. Paris: Editions L'Harmattan, 1988.

Anderson, Benedict. *Imagined Communities: Reflections on the Origins and Spread of Nationalism*. London: Verso, 1983.

Andrès, Bernard. "La génération de la Conquête: un questionnement de l'archive." *Voix et images* 59 (1995): 270–93.

Andrey, Georges, et al. *Nouvelle Histoire de la Suisse et des Suisses*. Lausanne: Payot, 1983.

Antoine, Claude. *Marthe Filmer, moeurs néo-algériennes*. Paris: Plon et Nourrit, 1895.

Apter, Emily. *Continental Drift: From National Characters to Virtual Subjects*. Chicago: The University of Chicago Press, 1999.

Arberry, A. J. *Sufism: an account of the mystics of Islam*. London: George Allen and Unzin Ltd, 1950.

Aresu, Bernard. "Introduction." *Québec Studies* 4 (1986): 224–35.

———. "*Emmanuel à Joseph à Dâvit* et la subversion du rituel." *Québec Studies* 4 (1986): 298–310.

Arnaud, Jacqueline. *La litterature maghrebine de langue francaise: I) Origines et perspectives*. Paris: Publisud, 1986.

Aron, Raymond. *Étapes de la pensée sociologique*. Paris: Gallimard Collection TEL, 1967.

Ascha, Ghassan. *Du Statut inférieur de la femme en Islam*. Paris: L'Harmattan, 1989.

Ashcroft, Bill, Gareth Griffith, and Helen Tiffin. *The Empire Strikes Back: Theory and Practice in Post-colonial Literatures*. New York: Routledge, 1989.

Assouline, Florence. *Musulmanes: une chance pour l'Islam*. Paris: Flammarion, 1992.

Aubert de Gaspé (père), Philippe. *Les Anciens Canadiens*. Montreal: Bibliothèque Québécoise, 1994.

Audisio, Gabriel. *Musette. Cagayous*. Paris: Balland, 1972.

Augé, Marc. *Non-Lieux: introduction à une anthropologie de la surmodernité*. Paris: Éditions du Seuil, 1992.

Auque, Hubert. *L'étranger qui fait exister la Suisse. Contribution psychanalytique à l'étude sociologique de la place de l'étranger dans la société suisse*. Perpignan: [s.n.] 1981.

Avineri, Shlomo, ed. *Marx on Colonialism and Modernization*. New York: Doubleday & Co, Anchor Books, 1969.

Awlad Ahmad, Muhammad al-Saghayyir. *A Hymn to the Six Days*. Tunis: Dimitir, 1988.

B.S. "Réalisation du projet de fonder en Algérie une ville par chaque département français." *Revue algérienne et orientale* 3, no. 4 (1847): 146–48.

Bâ, Mariama. *Une si longue lettre*. Dakar-Abidjan-Lomé: Nouvelles Éditions Africaines, 1979.

Bachelard, Gaston. *La Poétique de l'espace*. Paris: Presses Universitaires de France, 1957.

Badawi, M. M. *A Short History of Modern Arabic Literature*. Oxford: Clarendon Press, 1993.

Balibar, Etienne. "The Nation Form: History and Ideology." In *Race, Nation, Class: Ambiguous Identities*, 86–106. Ed. Étienne Balibar and Immanuel Wallerstein. New York: Verso, 1991.

Bankier, Joanna, et al., eds. *The Other Voice.* New York: W.W. Norton and Company, 1976.

Banks, James A. *Multiethnic Education: Theory and Practice.* Boston: Allyn & Bacon, 1994.

Barbançon, Louis-José. *Le Pays du Non-Dit. Regards sur la Nouvelle Calédonie.* Nouméa: Private publication, 1992.

Baroli, Marc. *La Vie quoditienne des Français en Algérie 1830–1914.* Paris: Hachette, 1967.

Barthes, Roland. *L'empire des signes.* Ed. Albert Skira. Génève: Editions d'Art, 1970.

———. *The Eiffel Tower and Other Mythologies.* Trans. Richard Howard. New York: Hill and Wang, 1979.

Basfao, Kacem, ed. *Imaginaire de l'espace, espaces imaginaires.* Casablanca: E.P.R.I., 1988.

Baudoux, Georges. *Légendes canaques.* Paris: Nouvelles Editions Latines, 1952.

Becel, Pascale. "*Moi Tituba, Sorcière . . . Noire de Salem* as a Tale of Petite Marrone." *Callaloo* 18, 3 (Summer1995): 608–15.

Becheur, Ali. *Les Rendez-vous manqués.* Tunis: CERES, 1993.

———. *Jours d'adieu.* Tunis: CERES, 1996.

Beck, Lois, and Nikki Keddie, eds. *Women in the Muslim World.* Cambridge, Massachusetts and London: Harvard Universtiy Press, 1978.

Becker, Lucille Frackman. *Twentieth-Century French Women Novelists.* Boston: Twayne Publishers, 1989.

Bednarski, Betty, and Irene Oore. *Nouveaux regards sur le théâtre québécois.* Montréal and Halifax: XYZ Éditeur and Dalhousie French Studies, 1997.

Begag, Azouz. *Le Gone du Chaâba.* Paris: Seuil, 1986.

———. *Béni ou le paradis privé.* Paris: Seuil, 1989.

———. *Ecarts d'identité.* Paris: Seuil, 1990.

———. *Les Chiens aussi.* Paris: Seuil, 1995.

———. *Zenzela.* Paris: Seuil, 1997.

Begag, Azouz, and Abdellatif Chaouite. *Écarts d'identité.* Paris: Seuil, 1990.

Begag, Azouz, and Christian Delorme. *Quartiers sensibles.* Paris: Seuil, 1994.

Beji, Hele. *L'oeil du jour.* Paris: Maurice Nadeau, 1985.

———. *Itinéraire de Paris à Tunis.* Paris: Noel Blondin, 1992.

Bekri, Tahar. *Litteratures de Tunisie et du Maghreb: essais; suivi de Reflexions et propos sur la poesie et la litterature.* Paris: L'Harmattan, 1994.

———. *Poèmes bilingues.* Paris: Bernard Lafabrie, 1978.

———. *Exils.* Paris: Ecole Nationale des Beaux Arts, 1979.

———. *Les lignes sont des arbres.* Paris: Bernard Lafabrie, 1984.

———. De la littérature tunisienne et maghrébine, et autres textes. Paris: L'Harmattan, 1999.

Belghoul, Farida. *Georgette!* Paris: Bernard Barrault, 1986.

Bel Hadj Yahia, Amna. *Chronique frontalière.* Tunis: CERES, 1991.

———. *L'Étage invisible.* Tunis: CERES, 1996.

Bell, M., Butlin R., and M. Hefferman, eds. *Geography and Imperialism 1820–1940.* Manchester: Manchester University Press, 1995.

Belotti, Carla, and Claire Masnata-Rubattel. *L'Émigrée.* Genève: Éditions Grounauer, 1981.

Ben el Messaï, Ali. "Chez les Touareg." *La Revue algérienne illustrée* 19, no. 5 (1894): 161–66.

———. "Chez les Touareg." *La Revue algérienne illustrée* 19, no.10 (1894): 325–29.

———. "Chez les Touareg." *La Revue algérienne illustrée* 19, no.11 (1894): 355–57.

———. "Chez les Touareg." *La Revue algérienne illustrée* 20, no. 1 (1894): 24–28.

———. "Chez les Touareg." *La Revue algérienne illustrée* 20, no. 2 (1894): 60–62.

———. "Chez les Touareg." *La Revue algérienne illustrée* 20, no. 3 (1894): 90–93.

———. "Chez les Touareg." *La Revue algérienne illustrée* 20, no. 10 (1894): 307–10.

Ben Othman, Ahmed, and Darmon Jean-Pierre, eds. *Cent poemes pour la liberté.* Paris: St-Germain-des-Près, 1984.

Benaïssa, Aïcha, and Sophie Ponchelet. *Née en France: histoire d'une jeune beur.* Paris: Payot, 1990.

Benguigui, Yamina. *Mémoires d'immigrés: l'héritage maghrébin.* Canal +/Bandits/Docstar/ Canal+Video, 1998.

Bensa, Alban. *La Nouvelle-Calédonie, Un paradis dans la tourmente.* Paris: Gallimard, 1990.

Bérard, Sylvie. "Hiatus." *Lettres québécoises* 87 (1997): 37–38.

Berbrugger, Louis-Adrien. "Inauguration de la presse en Algérie." *Revue africaine* 1, no. 3 (1857): 215–16.

———. "Introduction." *Revue africaine* 1, no.1 (1856): 3–11.

Berezak, F. *Le regard aquarel 2: Quotidien pluriel suivi de l'envers des corps.* Paris: L'Harmattan, 1988.

Bernabé, Jean, Patrick Chamoiseau, Raphaël Confiant. *Éloge de la créolité.* Paris: Gallimard, 1989.

———. *Éloge de la créolité.* Bilingual edition. Trans. by M. B. Taleb-Khyar. Paris: Gallimard, 1993.

Bernay, T., and D. W. Cantor, eds. *The Psychology of Today's Woman: New Psychoanalytic Views.* Hillside, N.J.: The Analytic Press, 1986.

Bernstein, Llisa. "Ecrivaine, sorcière, nomade: La Conscience critique dans *Moi, Tituba, sorcière . . . noire de Salem* de Maryse Condé." *Etudes Francophones* 13, no. 1 (spring 1998): 119–35.

Bertrand, Louis. *L'Afrique latine.* Rome: Reale Accademia d'Italia, 1938.

———. *Sur les routes du Sud.* Paris: Fayard, 1938.

Berzoff, J. "From Separation to Connection: Shifts in Understanding Women's Development." *Affilia: Journal of Women and Social Work* 1 (spring 1989).

Besson, Sylvain. "Les demandeurs d'asile sont devenus la cible privilégiée de la xénophobie suisse." *Le Temps* 31, no. 5(1999): 8.

Bestman, Martin. *Sembène Ousmane et l'esthétique du roman négro-africain.* Sherbrooke: Naaman, 1981.

Bey, Maïssa. *Nouvelles d'Algérie.* Paris: Grasset, 1998.

Beyala, Calixthe. *Tu t'appelleras Tanga.* Paris: Éditions J'ai Lu, s.d. [first published Éditions Stock, 1988].

———. *Le petit prince de Belleville.* Paris: Éditions J'ai Lu, s.d. [first published Éditions Albin Michel, 1992].

———. *Maman a un amant.* Paris: Éditions J'ai Lu, s.d. [first published Éditions Albin Michel, 1993].

Bhabha, Homi K. *The Location of Culture.* London and New York: Routledge, 1994.

Bhabha, Homi K., ed. *Nation and Narration.* New York: Routledge, 1990.

Bimpage, Serge. *La seconde mort d'Ahmed Alesh Karagün.* Genève: Zoé, 1986.

Bird John, Curtis Barry, et al., eds. *Mapping the Futures—Local Cultures, Global Change.* London: Routledge, 1993.

Bishop, Michael. "L'Année poétique: de Bonnefoy et Du Bouchet à Zins et Khoury-Ghata, et au delà." *The French Review* 66, no. 6 (May 1993): 86–87.

Bjornson, Richard. *The African Quest for Freedom and Identity: Cameroonian Writing and the National Experience.* Bloomington: Indiana University Press, 1991.

Black, Jeremy. *Maps and History: Constructing Images of the Past.* New Haven, Conn.: Yale University Press, 1997.

———. *Maps and Politics.* London: Reaktion Books, 1997.

Blair, Dorothy S. *Senegalese Literature: A Critical History.* Boston: Twayne, 1984.

Blampain, Daniel, et al. *Le Français en Belgique.* Louvain-la-Neuve: Duculot / Communauté française de Belgique, 1997.

Bloc, Paul. *Le Colon Broussard.* Nouméa: Société d'Études Historiques, 1996.

Block de Behar, Lisa, ed. *A Rhetoric of Silence and Other Selected Writings.* Berlin: Gruyter and Co.,1995.

Bloul, Rachel. "Veiled Objects of (Post)-Colonial Desire: Forbidden Women Disrupt the Republican Fraternal Sphere." In *Women's Difference: Sexuality and Maternity in Colonial and Post colonial Discourses.* Special issue of *The Australian Journal of Anthropology* 5, 1–2 (1994): 113–23.

Blunt, Alison, and Gillian Rose. *Writing Women and Space: Colonial and Postcolonial Geographies.* New York and London: The Guilford Press, 1994.

Bogliolo, François. *Paroles et ecritures. Anthologie de la littérature néo-calédonienne.* Nouméa: Éditions du Cagou, 1994.

Boly, Joseph. *La Wallonie dans le monde français.* Couillet: Institut Jules Destrée, 1971.

Bolzmann, Claudio, and Italo Musillo, eds. *Suisses migrateurs. Mythes, contes et réalités de la migration de retour.* Genève: Hospice général, 1996.

Bongie, Chris. *Islands and Exiles: The Creole Identities of Post-Colonial Literature.* Stanford: Stanford University Press, 1998.

Bonn, Charles, and Kachoukh Feriel. *Bibliographie de la littérature maghrebine 1980–1990.* Paris: EDICEF, 1992.

Bonn, Charles. *Bibliographie de la critique sur les littératures maghrebines.* Paris: L'Harmattan, 1996.

———. *Problématiques spatiales du roman algérien.* Alger: Entreprise Nationale du Livre, 1986.

———. *Repertoire international des theses sur les littératures maghrebines.* Paris: L'Harmattan, 1996.

Bonn, Charles, ed. Anthologie de la littérature algerienne (1950–1987). Paris: Livre de Poche, 1990.

Bouchard, Michel Marc. *La Contre-nature de Chrysippe Tanguay, écologiste.* Montréal: Leméac Éditeur, 1984.

———. Les Feluettes ou la répétition d'un drame romantique. Montréal: Leméac Éditeur, 1987.

Bouchrara Zannad, Traki. "Espaces humides féminins dans la ville." In *Espaces Maghrébins; pratiques et enjeux, Actes du colloque de Taghit, 23–26 Novembre 1987.* Ed. Marouf Nadir. Oran: URASC/ENAG Éditions, 1989.

Boudarel, Georges, and Nguyên Van Ky. *Hanoi 1936–1996: du drapeau rouge au billet vert.* Paris: Éditions Autrement, 1997.

Boudghedir, Férid. *Caméra Afrique.* Tunisia/France, 1983.

Boudjedra, Rachid. *Le démantèlement.* Paris: Denoël, 1982.

Bouhdiba, Abdel Wahab. *La Sexualité en Islam.* Paris: Presses Universitaires de France, 1975.

Bouhouche, Ammar. "The French in Algeria: The Politics of Expropriation and Assimilation." *Revue d'histoire maghrebine* 12 (1978): 238–60.

Boukhedenna, Sakinna. Journal. "*Nationalité: immigré(e).*" Paris: L'Harmattan, 1987.

Bouraoui, Hedi. *Musoktail.* Tower, 1966.

———. *Echosmos.* Toronto: Mosaic, 1986.

———. *Reflets pluriels.* Bordeaux: Éditions Universitaires, 1986.

———. "Culture et littérature au Maghreb." In *Cultures Maghrébine: Lectures croisées.* Ed. Abderrahman Tenkoul. Casablanca: Afrique Orient, 1991.

Bourdieu, Pierre, and Loïc Wacquant. *Réponses: pour une anthropologie réflexive.* Paris: Seuil, 1992.

Bourdieu, Pierre. "The economics of linguistic exchanges." *Social Science Information* 16, no. 6 (1997): 645–68

———. *Ce que parler veut dire: L'économie des échanges linguistiques.* Paris: Fayard,1982.

———. *La Distinction: critique sociale du jugement.* Paris: éditions de minuit, 1979.

Bourque, Denis. "Le rire carnavalesque dans *Les Crasseux* d'Antonine Maillet." *Études francophones* 12, no. 1 (1997): 21–36.

Bourque, Paul-André. "Entrevue avec Antonine Maillet." *Nord* 4, no. 5 (1972–73): 111–28.

Bousquet, Gisèle. *Behind the Bamboo Hedge: The Impact of Homeland Politics in the Parisian Vietnamese Community.* Ann Arbor: University of Michigan Press, 1991.

Bou-Yabès. *Récits et légendes de la grande Kabylie.* Ed. Ouahmi Ould-Braham. Paris: Edisud/La Boîte à Documents, 1993.

Bouyer, Frédéric. "Le brigand D'Chimbo, dit le Rongou. Ses crimes, son arrestation, sa mort." In *La Guyane Française. Notes et souvenirs d'un voyage effectué en 1862–1863*, 15–133. Cayenne: Guy Delabergerie, 1990.

———. "*L'Amour d'un Monstre: Scènes de la vie créole.*" *L'Événement*, 18 juillet-14 août 1866.

Box, Laura. "A Body of Words in Exile: North African women's theatre and performance." *International Journal of Francophone Studies* 1, no. 2 (1998).

Boyd, C. J. "Mothers and Daughters: A Discussion of Theory and Research." *Journal of Marriage and the Family* 51 (1989): 291–301.

Brahimi, Denise. *Maghrébines: portraits littéraires.* Paris: Awal / Editions L'Harmattan, 1995.

Brandt, Joan. *Geopoetics: The Politics of Mimesis in Poststructuralist French Poetry and Theory.* Stanford: Stanford University Press, 1997.

Brathwaite, Edward. "Timehri." In *Is Massa Day Dead? Black Moods in the Caribbean*, 29–44. Ed. Orde Coombs. New York: Anchor Books, 1974.

Breen, Jennifer. *In Her Own Write: Twentieth-Century Women's Fiction*. London: MacMillan, 1990.

Bretegnier, Aude. "L'insécurité linguistique: Objet insécurisé? Essai de synthèse et perspectives." In *Le français dans l'espace francophone, Tome II*, 903–923. Ed. Didier de Robillard & Michel Beniamino. Paris: Honoré Champion, 1996.

Bridel, Yves. "Y a-t-il une littérature romande aujourd'hui?" In *Vous avez dit "Suisse romande?"* 125–37. Ed. René Knusel and Daniel Seiler. Lausanne: Institut de Science politique, 1984.

Brière, Éloïse A. "L'inquiétude généalogique: tourment du Nouveau Monde." *Présence Francophone* 36 (1990): 57–72.

———. "Maillet and the Construction of Acadian Identity." In *Postcolonial Subjects*, 3, no. 21. Ed. Mary Jean Green et al. Minneapolis: University of Minnesota Press, 1996.

Brinker-Gabler, Gisela, and Sidonie Smith, eds. *Writing new identities—Gender, Nation and Immigration in Contemporary Europe*. Minneapolis: University of Minnesota Press, 1997.

Brocheux, Pierre, and Daniel Hémery. *Indochine: la colonisation ambiguë, 1858–1954*. Paris: Éditions de la Découverte, 1995.

Brooks, Peter. *Reading for the Plot: Design and Intention in Narrative*. New York: Knopf, 1984.

Brown, Anne. "Maillet." *Canadian Literature* 135 (1992): 192–94.

Brown-Guillory, Elizabeth, ed. *Women of Color: Mother-Daughter Relationships in the 20th-Century Literature*. Austin: University of Texas Press, 1996.

Brown, Peter. "A Singular Plurality of Voices: Tradition and Modernity in Déwé Gorodé (New Caledonia)." In *Francophone Voices*, 125–140. Ed. Kamal Salhi. Exeter: Elm Bank Publications, 1999.

———. "A l'écoute de Nicolas Kurtovitch (Nouvelle-Calédonie)." *Les Mots Pluriels* 10 (May 1999).

Buckhardt, Titus. *An Introduction to Sufi Doctrine*. Trans. D. M. Matheson. Lahore: sh. Muhammad Ashraf, 1968.

Bugul, Ken. *Le Baobab fou*. Dakar: Les Nouvelles Éditions Africaines, 1982.

Burniaux, Robert, and Robert Frickx. *La littérature belge d'expression française*. Paris: Presses Universitaires de France.

Busekist, Astrid von. *La Belgique: Politique des langues et construction de l'État (de 1780 à nos jours)*. Paris: Duculot, 1998.

Butt, Gerald. *The Arabs: Myth and Reality*. London: I. B. Tauris, 1997.

Cagnon, Maurice. "Passages: Renewal and Survival in *Pointe-aux-Coques* and *On a mangé la dune*." *Québec Studies* 4 (1986): 241–51.

Calame, Christophe. *Sept cents ans de littérature en Suisse romande*. Paris: Éditions de la Différence, 1991.

Calmes, Alain. *Le Roman colonial en Algérie avant 1914*. Paris: L'Harmattan, 1984.

Caloz-Tschopp, Marie-Claire. *Le tamis helvétique. Des réfugiés politiques aux "nouveaux réfugiés."* Lausanne: Éditions d'En bas, 1982.

Candau, Joël. *Anthropologie de la mémoire*. Paris: Presses Universitaires de France, 1996.

Case, Frederick Ivor. "Esthétique et discours idéologique dans l'œuvre d'Ousmane Sembène et d'Assia Djebar." In *Littérature et cinéma en Afrique francophone*, 35–48. Ed. Sada Niang. Paris: L'Harmattan, 1996.

Cassidy, Madeline. "Love Is a Supreme Violence." In *Violence, Silence, and Anger: Women's Writing As Transgression*. Ed. Deirdre Lashgari. Charlottseville: University Press of Virginia, 1995.

Castelnuovo-Frigessi, Delia. *La condition immigrée. Les ouvriers italiens en Suisse*. Lausanne: Éditions d'En bas, 1978.

Cazenave, Odile. "Gender, Age and Reeducation: A Changing Emphasis in Recent African Novels in French, as exemplified in *L'Appel des arènes* by Aminata Sow Fall." *Africa Today* (3rd Quarter, 1991).

Célestin, Roger. "Interview with Serge Doubrovsky." *Sites* 1, no. 2 (1997): 397–405.

Centlivres, Pierre, ed. *Devenir Suisse. Adhésion et diversité culturelle des étrangers en Suisse*. Genève: Georg, 1990.

Certeau, Michel de. *L'Invention du quotidien, 1. Arts de faire*. Paris: Gallimard, 1990.

Césaire, Aimé. *Cahier d'un retour au pays natal*. Paris: Présence Africaine, 1983.

———. *Letter to Maurice Thorez*. Paris: Présence Africaine, 1957.

————. The Collected Poetry. Trans. with an introduction and notes by Clayton Eshleman and Annette Smith. Berkeley: University of California Press, 1983.

Césaire, Suzanne. "Misère d'une poésie." *Tropiques* 4 (janvier 1942): 48–50. Reprint. Paris: Jean-Michel Place, 1978.

Chafiq, Chahla, and Farhad Khosrokhavar. *Femmes sous le voile: face à la loi islamique.* Paris: Éditions du Félin, 1995.

Chailley, Baudoin. *Nouméa, ville ouverte.* Paris: Stock, 1989.

Chambordon, Gabrielle. *La Suisse des autres.* Genève: Zoé, 1981 and 1988.

————. *Les enfants c'est comme les éléphants.* Genève: Zoé, 1982 and 1988.

————. *Les mots disent plus rien.* Genève: Zoé, 1985 and 1988.

Chammas, Leyla. *Leyla.* Genève: Zoé, 1997.

Chamoiseau, P., R. Confiant, J. Bernarbé. *Éloge de la créolité.* Paris: Gallimard, 1993.

Chamoiseau, Patrick. *Chemin d'école.* Paris: Gallimard, 1994.

————. *Solibo Magnifique.* Paris: Gallimard, 1988.

————. *Texaco.* Paris: Gallimard, 1992.

Chamoiseau, Patrick, and Rodolphe Hammadi. *Guyane. Traces-mémoires du bagne.* Paris: Caisse Nationale des Monuments Historiques et des Sites, 1994.

Chamoiseau, Patrick, and Raphaël Confiant. *Lettres créoles: tracées antillaises et continentales de la littérature.* Paris: Hatier, 1991.

Charef, Mehdi. *Le Thé au harem d'Archi Ahmed.* Paris: Mercure de France, 1983.

Charlier, Gustave, and Hanse Joseph. *Histoire illustrée des lettres françaises de Belgique.* Bruxelles: Renaissance du Livre, 1958.

Charnley, Joy. "Four Literary Depictions of Foreigners and Outsiders in French-speaking Switzerland." In *Occasional Papers in Swiss Studies* 1, 9–28. Ed. Joy Charnley and Malcolm Pender. Bern: Lang, 1998.

————. "'J'aime bien ma Suisse': some Italian reactions to the Schwarzenbach Initiative 1970." In *Occasional Papers in Swiss Studies* 3. Ed. Joy Charnley and Malcolm Pender. Bern: Lang, 2000.

Chaseray, Stephen. "Djezaïra." *La Revue algérienne illustrée* 28, no. 9 (1897): 274–78.

————. "Lettre du Père Robin." *La Revue algérienne illustrée* 15, no. 8 (1893): 226–30.

Chatelain, Yves. *La vie littéraire et intellectuelles en Tunisie de 1900–1937.* Paris: Geuthner, 1937.

Chatterjee, Partha. "Whose Imagined Community?" In *Mapping the Nation.* Ed. Batakrishna, Gopal. London: Verso, 1996.

Chaudenson, R. *La Francophonie: representations, realites, perspectives.* Paris: Institut d'Études Creoles et Francophones, 1991.

Chaurette, Normand. *Le passage de l'Indiana.* Montréal and Arles: Leméac and Actes Sud, 1996.

————. *Provincetown Playhouse, juillet 1919, j'avais 19 ans.* Montréal: Leméac, 1981.

Chebbi, Lahbib. *La Fêlure: mémoires d'un cheikh.* Tunis: Éditions Salammbô, 1985.

Chebel, Malek. *Le Corps dans la tradition au Maghreb.* Paris: Presses Universitaires de Farnce, 1984.

Chedid, Andree. *Ceremonial de la violence.* Paris: Flammarion, 1976.

Chikhi, Beïda. *Les Romans d'Assia Djebar.* Alger: Office des Publications Universitaires, 1987.

Chodorow, Nancy, and S. Contratto. "The Fantasy of the Perfect Mother." In *Rethinking the Family: Some Feminist Questions.* Ed. B. Thorne and M. Yalom. New York: Longman, 1982.

Chodorow, Nancy. *The Reproduction of Mothering.* Berkeley: University of California Press, 1978.

Christnacht, Alain. *La Nouvelle-Calédonie.* Paris: La Documentation Française, 1987.

Cissé, Souleymane. *Den Muso*, Mali, 1974. Color and b/w, 95 mins., Bambara.

————. *Baara*, Mali. 1978. Color, 90 mins., Bambara.

————. *Finye*, Mali, 1982. Color, 100 mins., Bambara.

————. *Yeelen*, Mali, 1987. Color, 105 mins., Bambara and French.

————. *Waati*, Mali/France, 1995. Color, 143 mins., English, French, Bambara.

Cixous, Hélène, Madeleine Gagnon, and Annie Leclerc. *La Venue à l'écriture.* Paris: Union Générale d'Éditions, 1977.

Cixous, Hélène. "Sorties." *La Jeune née.* Paris: Union Générale d'Éditions, 1975.

Clerc, Jeanne-Marie. *Assia Djebar: écrire, transgresser, résister.* Paris et Montréal: Éditions L'Harmattan, 1997.

Cliche, Anne Élaine. "Un romancier de carnaval?" *Études françaises* 23 (1988): 43–54.

Clifford, James. *Routes: Travel and Translation in the Late Twentieth Century.* Cambridge, London: Harvard University Press, 1997.

Collin, Françoise. "Antonine Maillet: Interview." *Cahiers du GRIF* 12, no. 13 (1976): 41–48.

Collins, Patricia Hill. "Shifting the Center: Race, Class, and Feminist Theorizing about Motherhood." In *Representations of Motherhood.* Ed. Donna Bassin Margaret Honey and Meryle Mahrer Kaplan. New Haven, Conn.: Yale University Press, 1994.

Comité de rédaction. "La Société des Beaux-Arts et *la Revue algérienne.*" *Revue algérienne* 1 (1877): 1–3.

Condé, Maryse. *Moi, Tituba sorcière . . . Noire de Salem.* Paris: Mercure de France, 1988.

———. *La Parole des femmes.* Paris: Éditions l'Harmattan, 1993.

———. "Order, Disorder, Freedom, and the West Indian Writer." *Yale French Studies* 83 (1993): 121–35.

———. *Traversée de la Mangrove.* Paris: Laffont, 1989.

Cooke, Miriam. "Telling Their Lives: A Hundred Years of Arab Women's Writings." *World Literature Today* 60 (spring 1986): 212–16.

———. *War's Other Voices: Women Writers on the Lebanese Civil War.* Cambridge: Cambridge University Press, 1988.

———. *Women and the War Story.* Berkeley: University of California Press, 1996.

———. *Arms and the Woman: War, Gender, and Literary Representation.* Ed. Cooper, Helen, Adrienne Munich, and Susan Squier. Chapel Hill: University of North Carolina Press, 1989.

Coquet, J.-C. "L'Ecole de Paris." In *Sémiotique: L'Ecole de Paris*, 3–14. Ed. J.-C. Coquet. Paris: Hachette. 1982,.

Cornwell, Stephen, and Hartmann Douglas. *Ethnicity and Race.* Thousand Oaks, Calif.: Pine Forge Press, 1998.

Corvin, Michel. "Otez toute chose que j'y voie." Vue cavalière sur l'écriture théâtrale contemporaine. "In *Théâtre contemporain en Allemagne et en France*, 3–14. Ed. Wilfried Floeck. Tubingen: Francke, 1989.

Corzani, Jack. *La littérature des Antilles-Guyane françaises.* Fort-de-France: Désormeaux, 1978.

Costa-Lascoux, Jacqueline, and Live Yu-Sion. *Paris-XIIIe, lumières d'Asie.* Paris: Les Éditions Autrement, 1995.

Coulson, Anthony, ed. "Introduction." In *Exiles and Migrants: Crossing Thresholds in European Culture and Society*, 1–19. 1998.

Cowan, Doris. "Interview." *Books in Canada* 11 (1982): 24–26.

Crecelius, Kathryn J. "L'histoire et son double dans *Pélagie-la-Charrette.*" *Studies in Canadian Literature* 6 (1981): 211–20.

Crevoisier, Benoîte. *Le Miroir aux alouettes.* Vevey: Aire, 1994.

Crosta, Suzanne. "Les Structures spatiales dans *L'Appel des arènes* d'Aminata Sow Fall." *Revue francophone de Louisiane* 3, no.1 (1988).

Culler, J. *On Deconstruction: Theory and Criticism after Structuralism.* London: Routledge and Kegan Paul, 1982.

Cuneo, Anne. *Âme de bronze.* Yvonand: Campiche, 1998.

———. *D'Or et d'oublis.* Orbe: Campiche, 1999.

———. *Objets de splendeur. Mr Shakespeare amoureux.* Yvonand: Campiche, 1996.

———. *Les portes du jour.* Vevey: Galland, 1980.

———. *Le temps des loups blancs.* Vevey: Galland, 1982.

Dahlem, Henri-Charles. *Sur les pas d'un lecteur heureux. Guide littéraire de la Suisse.* Lausanne: Aire, 1991.

Daly, Mary. *Beyond God the Father: Toward a Philosophy of Women's Liberation.* Boston: Beacon Press, 1973.

Danis, Daniel. *Cendres de cailloux.* Montréal and Arles: Leméac Éditeur and Actes Sud, 1992.

———. *Celle-là.* Montréal: Leméac Éditeur, 1993.

Darot, Mireille. *La Nouvelle-Calédonie: un exemple de situation du français en Francophonie.* Nouméa: CTRDP, 1993.

Dash, J. Michael. "Introduction." In *The Ripening*, 1–17. Ed. Edouard Glissant. Portsmouth: Heinemann, 1985.

Davies, Carole Boyce, and Elaine Savory Fido. "Introduction: Women and Literature in the Caribbean: An Overview." In *Out of the Kumbla. Caribbean Women and Literature*, 1–22. Ed. Carole Boyce Davies and Elaine Savory Fido. Trenton, N.J.: Africa World Press, 1990.

Davies, Miranda. *Third World—Second Sex: Women's Struggles and National Liberation, Third World Women Speak Out*. Ed. Miranda Davies. London: Zed, 1983.

Dawood, N. J., trans. *The Koran*. London: Penguin, 1994.

de Beauvoir, Simone. *Le Deuxieme Sexe II: L'experience vecue*. Paris: Gallimard, 1949.

de Bruijn, J. T. P. *Persian Sufi Poetry: an introduction to the mystical use of classical poems*. Richmond: Curzon Press, 1977.

de Certeau, Michel. *The Practice of Everyday Life*. Berkeley: University of California Press, 1984.

de Finney, James. "Antonine Maillet: un exemple de réception littéraire régionale." *Revue d'histoire littéraire du Québec et du Canada français* 12 (1986): 17–33.

———. "Maariaagélas [*sic*], ou l'épopée impossible." *Revue de l'Université de Moncton* 8 (1975): 37–46.

de Roulet, Daniel. *Double*. Saint-Imier/Frasne: Canevas, 1998.

———. "Eloge de mes grands-parents." *Ecriture* 51 (printemps, 1998): 211–16.

de Rudder, V., I. Taboada-Léonetti, and F. Vourch. *Stratégies d'insertion et migration*, study conducted under the Direction régionale de l'équipement de l'Ile-de-France. Paris: IRESCO, 1990.

Deena, Seodial. "The Caribbean: Colonial and Postcolonial Representations of the Land and the People's Relationships to Their Environment." In *Literature of Nature: An International Sourcebook*, 366–73. Ed. Patrick D. Murphy. Chicago: Fitzroy Dearborn Publishers, 1998.

Déjeux, Jean. *Assia Djebar*. Sherbrooke, Canada: Éditions Naaman, 1984.

———. *Dictionnaire des auteurs maghrebins de langue française: Algerie . . . (1880–1982), Maroc . . . (1920–1982), Tunisie . . . (1900–1982)*. Paris: Karthala, 1984.

———. *La littérature féminine de langue française au Maghreb*. Paris: Karthala, 1994.

———. *La littérature maghrebine d'expression française*. Paris: Presses Universitaires de France, 1992.

———. *Maghreb littératures de langue française*. Paris: Arcantere, 1993.

———. *Situation de la littérature maghrebine de langue française*. Alger: Office de Presses Universitaires, 1982.

Delcroix, Catherine. *Espoirs et réalités de la femme arabe: Algérie-Egypte*. Paris: Éditions L'Harmattan. Collection Histoire et perspectives méditerranéennes, 1986.

Deleuze, G., and Guattari F. *Mille plateaux*. Paris: Éditions de Minuit, 1980.

Delvaux, Martine. "L'ironie du sort: Le tiers espace dans la littérature beure." *French Review* 68, no. 4 (1995): 93–681.

Demers, Jeanne. "Don l'Orignal." *Livres et auteurs québécois* (1972): 34–38.

Deniau, Xavier. *La Francophonie*. Paris: Presses Universitaires Françaises, *Que sais'je?*, 1983.

Dentith, Simon. *Bakhtinian thought: an introductory reader*. London: Routledge, 1995.

Derrida, Jacques. *De la grammatologie*. Paris: Minuit, 1967.

———. *D'un ton apocalyptique adopté naguère en philosophie*. Paris: Galilée, 1983.

———. *Le Monolinguisme de l'autre ou la prothèse d'origine*. Paris: Éditions Galilée, 1996

———. *L'écriture et la différence*. Paris: Éditions de Seuil, 1967.

———. *Marges de la philosophie*. Paris: Éditions de Seuil, 1972.

Desalvo, Jean-Luc. "L'écriture mailletienne ou le carnaval réussi." In *Les littératures d'expression française d'Amérique du Nord et le carnavalesque*, 75–89. Ed. Denis Bourque and Anne Brown. Moncton, N.B.: Éditions d'Acadie, 1998.

———. "Entretien avec Antonine Maillet." *Études francophones* 13, no. 1 (1998): 5–18.

———. *Le Topos du mundus inversus dans l'œuvre d'Antonine Maillet*. Bethesda: International Scholars Publications, 1999.

———. "La Vision globaliste d'Antonine Maillet: Entretien avec Jean-Luc Desalvo." *Women in French Studies* 6 (1998): 102–13.

Descartes, René. "Meditations on First Philosophy." In *Descartes: Selected Philosophical Writings*. Ed. Cottingham Stroothoff Murdoch. Cambridge: Cambridge University Press, 1988.

Devésa, Jean-Michel. *Sony Labou Tansi: Écrivain de la honte et des rives magiques du Kongo*. Paris: L'Harmattan, 1996.

Diallo, Bakary. *Force Bonté*. Paris: Rieder, 1926.

Diallo, Nafissatou. *De Tilène au plateau: une enfance dakaroise*. Dakar-Abidjan: Nouvelles Éditions Africaines, 1976.

Dine, Philip. *Images of the Algerian War: French Fiction and Film, 1954–1992*. Oxford: Clarendon Press, 1994.

Diop, Birago. *Les Contes d'Amadou Koumba*. Paris: Fasquelle, 1947.

Djebar, Assia. *Femmes d'Alger dans leur appartement*. Paris: Des femmes, 1980.

———. *Le blanc de l'Algérie*. Paris: Éditions Albin, 1995.

———. *L'amour, la fantasia*. Paris: Albin Michel, 1995. 1st published Lattès, 1985.

———. *Ombres Sultanes*. Paris: Lattès, 1987.

———. *Fantasia. An Algerian Cavalcade*. Trans. Dorothy S. Blair: Heinemann, 1993, 1985.

———. "Ecrire dans la langue de l'autre: pour une quête d'identité." In *Identité, culture et changement social*, 23–29. Ed. M. Lavallée F. Ouellet F. Larose. Paris: L'Harmattan, 1991.

———. "Territoires des Langues." In *L'écrivain à la croisée des langues, Entretiens avec Lise Gauvin*, 17–34. Ed. Lise Gauvin. Paris: Karthala, 1997.

———. "La langue dans l'espace ou l'espace dans la langue." In *Mise en scènes d'écrivains*. Grenoble: Presses Universitaires de Grenoble, 1993.

Djura. *Le Voile du silence*. Paris: Lafon, 1990.

Dolar, Mladen. "I Shall Be with You on Your Wedding Night: Lacan and the Uncanny." *October 58* (1991).

Donadey, Anne. "Assia Djebar's Poetics of Subversion." *L'Esprit Créateur* 23, no. 2 (summer 1993): 107–16.

———. *Polyphonic and Palimpsestic Discourse in the Works of Assia Djebar and Leïla Sebbar*. Evanston, Ill. Northwestern University, 1993.

Donald, James. "The Citizen and the Man about Town." In *Questions of Cultural Identity*, 170–90. Ed. Stuart Hall and Paul du Gay. London: Sage, 1996.

Drolet, Bruno. *Entre dune et aboiteaux . . . un peuple*. Montréal: Pleins Bords, 1975.

Dubois, René-Daniel. *26 bis, impasse du Colonel Foisy*. Montréal: Leméac Éditeur, 1983.

Dubuis, Catherine. "Chronique des livres." *Ecriture* 46 (automne 1995): 261–71.

———. *Ecriture* 37 (printemps 1991).

Ducrocq-Poirier, Madeleine. "La 'Québécité' d'Antoine Maillet. *Itinéraires* 1 (1982): 131–38.

Duffey, Carolyn. "Tituba and Hester in the Intertextual Jail Cell: New World Feminisms in Maryse Condé's *Moi, Tituba, sorcière . . . noire de Salem*." *Women in French Studies* 4 (fall 1996): 100–10.

Dufresnois, Huguette, and Christian Miquel. *La philosophie de l'exil*. Paris: L'Harmattan, 1996.

Dugas, Guy. *Bibliographie critique de la littérature judéo-maghrébine d'expression française (1896–1990)*. Paris: L'Harmattan, 1992.

Dukats, Mara L. "The Hybrid Terrain of Literary Imagination: Maryse *Condé's Black Witch of Salem*, Nathaniel Hawthorne's *Hester Prynne*, and Aimé *Cesaire's Heroic Poetic Voice*." In *Race-ing RepresentationL Voice, History, and Sexuality*. Ed. Kostas Myrsiades and Linda Myrsiades. Lanham: Rowman & Littlefield, 1998.

———. "A Narrative of Violated Maternity: *Moi, Tituba, sorcière . . . Noire de Salem. World Literature Today* 67, no. 4 (fall 1993): 745–50.

Dumont, Georges-Henri. *La Belgique*, Paris: Presses Universitaires de France, *Que sais-je?* 1993.

Dundes, Allan. "Slurs International: Folk Comparisons of Ethnicity and National Character." *Southern Folklore Quarterly* 39 (1975): 15–38.

Eckstein, Barbara. *The Language of Fiction in a World of Pain: Reading Politics as Paradox*. Philadelphia: University of Pennsylvania Press, 1990.

Edouard, Glissant. *Le Discours antillais*. Paris: Seuil, 1981.

Edwards, John. *Multilingualism*. London: Penguin, 1995.

Eichenbaum, L., and S. Orbach. *Understanding Women*. Harmondsworth: Penguin, 1985.

Eisenstein, H. *Contemporary Feminist Thought.* Boston: G. K. Hall, 1983.

El Bah't (L. J.). "Le Canon des Beni Iffen." *La Revue algérienne illustrée* 35, no. 18 (1898): 566–67.

El Djezaïry. "Postface à la *Femme incendiée.*" *La Revue algérienne illustrée* 40, no. 4 (1900): 123–24

El Khayat—Bennaï, Ghita. *Le Monde arabe au féminin.* Paris: L'Harmattan, 1985.

Eliade, Mircea. *Mythes, rêves et mystères.* Paris: Gallimard, 1957.

Ellis, Rod. *Second Language Acquisition.* Oxford: Oxford University Press, 1997.

Elshtain, Jean Bethke. *Women and War.* New York: Basis Books, 1987.

Evans, Martha Noel. *Masks of Tradition: Women and the Politics of Writing in Twentieth-Century France.* Ithaca: Cornell University Press, 1987.

Fahrni, Dieter. *An Outline History of Switzerland. From the Origins to the Present Day.* Zurich: Pro Helvetia, 1992.

Falconnier, Isabelle. "L'enfance dans un cri." *L'Hebdo* 25, no. 3 (1999): 89.

———. "Histoire de femmes à l'italienne." *L'Hebdo* 47 nos. 11–19 (1998): 107–9.

Fall, Aminata Sow. *La Grève des Bàttu.* Dakar-Abidjan-Lomé: Nouvelles Éditions Africaines, 1979.

Fanon, Frantz. *Les damnés de la terre.* Paris: Gallimard, 1991.

Fanon, Frantz. *Peau noire, masques blancs.* Paris: Éditions de Seuil, 1952/1995.

Fauquenoy, Marguerite, ed. *Atipa revisité ou les itinéraires de Parépou.* Paris: L'Harmattan, 1989.

Feraoun, Mouloud, *Le Fils du pauvre.* Paris: Éditions du Seuil. 1954.

Fernea, Elizabeth. "Ways of Seeing Middle Eastern Women." in *Women: A Cultural Review* 6, no.1.

———. "The Case of *Sitt Marie Rose*: an Ethnographic Novel from the Modern Middle East." In *Literature and Anthropology*, edited by Philip Dennis and Wendell Aycock. Lubbock, Texas: Texas Tech University Press, 1989.

———. ed. *Women and the Family in the Middle East: New Voices of Change.* Austin: University of Texas Press, 1985.

Fiala, Pierre, and Marianne Ebel. *Langages xénophobes et consensus national en Suisse 1960–80.* Lausanne: Cedips, 1983.

Fitzpatrick, Marjorie A. "Antonine Maillet and the Epic Heroine." In *Traditionalism, Nationalism, and Feminism: Women Writers of Quebec*, 141–55. Ed. Paula Gilbert Lewis. Wesport, Conn.: Greenwood, 1985.

———. "Antonine Maillet: The Search for a Narrative Voice." *Journal of Popular Culture* 15 (1981): 4–13.

Flood, John, Ed. *Modern Swiss Literature. Unity and Diversity.* London: Wolff, 1985.

Fontaine, J. *Études de littérature tunisienne.* Tunis: Éditions Dar Annawras, 1989.

———. *Aspects de la littérature tunisienne (1975–83).* Tunis: Rasm, 1985?

———. *al-'Adab al-Tunisi al-Mu`asir* (Contemporary Tunisian Literature). Tunis: al-Dar al-Tunisiyya li al-Nashr, 1989.

———. *Études de la littérature tunisienne* (Studies in Tunisian Literature). Tunis: Dar al-Nawras, 1989.

———. *Regards sur la littérature tunisienne* (Views on Tunisian Literature). Tunis: Ceres, 1991.

———. *Bibliography of Modern Tunisian Arabic literature (1954–1996).* Tunis: IBLA, 1997. (in Arabic)

Fornerod, Françoise. "Enseigner la littérature romande?" *Études de Lettres* 1 (1988): 35–40.

Fortier, France, and Mercier Andrée. "Le récit littéraire des années quatre-vingt et quatre-vingt-dix." *Voix et Images* 69 (1998): 437–525.

Foster, Thomas. "Circles of Oppression, Circles of Repression: Etel Adnan's *Sitt Marie Rose.*" *PMLA* 110, no. 1 (January 1995): 59–74.

Foucault, Michel. "The History of Sexuality" in *Power/Knowledge: Selected Interviews and Other Writings.* Ed. Colin Gordon. New York: Pantheon Books, 1980.

———. "Des Espaces Autres" in *Dits et écrits—tome 4.* Paris: Gallimard, 1994.

———. *L'archéologie du savoir.* Paris: Gallimard, 1969.

———. *Madness and Civilisation: A History of Insanity in the Age of Reason.* London: Tavistock Publications, 1977.

———. *Surveiller et punir: naissance de la prison.* Paris: Gallimard, 1975.

Francard, Michel. "Entre Romania et Germania: la Belgique francophone." In *Le français dans l'espace francophone, Tome II*, 317–36. Ed. Didier de Robillard and Michel Beniamino. Paris: Honoré Champion, 1996.

————. "Trop proches pour ne pas être différents: profils de l'insécurité linguistique dans la Communauté française de Belgique." In *L'insécurité linguistique dans les communautés francophones périphériques.* Ed. Michel Francard. Louvain-la-Neuve: Cahiers de L'Institut de Linguistique de Louvain, 1993.

Franchini, Philippe, ed. *Tonkin 1873–1954: colonie et nation: le delta des mythes.* Paris: Éditions Autrement, 1994.

————. ed. *Saigon 1925–1945: De la "belle colonie" à l'éclosion révolutionnaire ou la fin des dieux blancs.* Paris: Éditions Autrement, 1994.

————. *Métis.* Paris: Éditions Jacques Bertoin, 1993.

Francillon, Roger, Claire Jacquier, and Adrien Pasquali. *Filiations et filatures. Littérature et critique en Suisse romande.* Genève: Zoé, 1991.

Francoeur. "Billet de la semaine." *La Revue algérienne illustrée* 15, no. 8 (1893).

Françoise, Pfaff. *Entretiens avec Maryse Condé.* Paris: Karthala, 1993.

Freud, A., ed. *Psychoanalytic Study of the Child.* New York: International University Press, 1967.

Friedman, Susan Stanford. *Mappings: Feminism and the Cultural Geographies of Encounter.* Princeton: Princeton University Press, 1998.

Froidevaux, Gérard. *Ecrivains de Suisse romande.* Zug: Klett und Balmer, 1990.

Gadant, Monique, ed. *Women of the Mediterranean.* London: Zed, 1986.

Galland, Bertil. *La littérature de la Suisse romande expliquée en un quart d'heure.* Genève: Zoé, 1986.

Gallant, Melvin. "Épopée, fantaisie et symbole dans *Don l'Orignal.*" *Québec Studies* 4 (1986): 286–97.

Gallet, Dominique. *Espace Francophone: le magazine du monde d'expression française.* Paris: ICAF, 1982.

Gallop, Jane. *Thinking Through the Body.* New York: Columbia University Press, 1988.

Gardies, André. *Cinéma d'Afrique Noire Francophone: l'espace miroir.* Paris: L'Harmattan, 1989.

Garmadi, Salah. *Avec ou sans.* Tunis: CERES, 1970.

————. *Mes ancêtres les Bédouins.* Paris: Oswald, 1975.

Garnier, Jules. *La Nouvelle Calédonie, côte orientale* (1871). Nouméa: Éditions du Cagou, 1978.

Gaspard, Françoise. *A Small City in France.* trans. Arthur Goldhammer, Cambridge, Mass.: Harvard University Press, 1995.

Gasser, Bermard. "New Caledonian literature in French." *New Literatures* Review 22 (1991): 27–28.

————. *Georges Baudoux. La quête de la vérité.* Nouméa: Grain de Sable, 1994.

Gates, Henry Louis, Jr. *The Signifying Monkey: Theory of African-American Literary Criticism.* New York and Oxford: Oxford University Press, 1988.

Gates, Henry Louis, Jr., ed. *Black Literature and Literary Theory.* London: Routledge, 1990.

Gebrane, May. "La Situation conflictuelle de la femme libanaise." Ph.D. dissertation. University of Paris VII, 1984.

Gelfand, Elissa, ed. *French Feminism Criticism: Women, Language, and Literature—An Annotated Bibliography.* New York: Garland Publications, 1985.

George, Rosemary Marangoly. *The Politics of Home-Post-Colonial Relocations and Twentieth Century Fiction.* Cambridge: Cambridge University Press, 1996.

Gérin, Pierre, and Pierre M. Gérin. *Marichette: Lettres acadiennes, 1895–1898.* Sherbrooke, P.Q.: Naaman, 1982.

Gérin, Pierre. "Marichette ou le carnaval manqué," *Dalhousie French Studies* 15 (1988): 3–25.

Gilligan, C. *In a Different Voice: Psychological Theory and Women's Development.* London: Harvard Press, 1982.

Girard, René. *La Violence et le sacré.* Paris: Grasset, 1972.

Glissant, Edouard. *La Lézarde.* Paris: Gallimard, 1997.

————. *Le discours antillais.*

————. *Poetics of Relation.* Ann Arbor: University of Michigan Press, 1997.

————. *Caribbean Discourse: Selected Essays.* Trans. J. Michael Dash. Charlottesville: University Press of Virginia, 1989.

————. *Introduction à une poétique du divers.* Paris: Gallimard, 1996.

———. *Poétique de la relation*. Paris: Gallimard, 1990.

Glover, Janet R. *The Story of Scotland*. London: Faber and Faber, 1960.

Gobin, Pierre. "*Le Huitième Jour*." *Dalhousie French Studies* 15 (1988): 26–47.

———. "Space and Time in the Plays of Antonine Maillet." *Modern Drama* 25 (1982): 46–59.

Godard, Barbara Thompson. "Maillet's *Don l'Orignal*." *Atlantis* 5 (1979): 51–69.

Godin, Jean-Cléo, and Lafon Dominique. *Dramaturgies québécoises des années quatre-vingt*. Montréal: Leméac Éditeur, 1999.

Goinard, Pierre. *Algérie, l'oeuvre française*. Paris: Robert Laffont, 1984.

Gope, Pierre. *Où est le droit?/Okorenetit?*. Nouméa: Grain de Sable, 1997.

Gorodé, Déwé. *Sous les cendres des conques*. Nouméa: Edipop, 1985.

———. *Utê Mûrûnû, petite fleur de cocotier*. Nouméa: Grain de Sable/Edipop, 1994.

———. *L'Agenda*. Nouméa: Grain de Sable, 1996.

———. *Dire le vrai* (avec Nicolas Kurtovitch). Nouméa: Grain de Sable, 1998.

Gracki, Katherine. "Writing Violence and the Violence of Writing in Assia Djebar's Algerian Quartet." *World Literature Today* 70 no. 4 (fall 1995): 835–43.

Green, M.J., et al., eds. *Postcolonial Subjects: Francophone Women Writers*. Minneapolis: University of Minnesota Press, 1996.

Green, Mary Jean, Karen Gould, et al., ed. *Postcolonial Subjects-Francophone Women Writers*. Minneapolis: University of Minnesota Press, 1996.

Greenburg, Joel. "Combining 2 Identities: Arab in Israel Parliament." *New York Times*, 20 July 1999.

Gregory, Derek. *Geographical Imaginations*. Cambridge and Oxford: Blackwell Publishers, 1994.

Greimas, A. J. *Du sens II: essais sémiotiques*. Paris: Seuil, 1983.

Grenaud, Pierre. *La Littérature au soleil du Maghreb; de l'antiquité à nos jours*. Paris: L'Harmattan, 1993.

Grévoz, Daniel. *Sahara 1830–1881; les mirages français et la tragédie Flatters*. Paris: L'Harmattan, 1989.

Grewal, Inderpal, and Caren Kaplan, eds. *Scattered Hegemonies: Postmodernity and Transnational Feminist Practices*. Minneapolis: University of Minnesota Press, 1994.

———. *Home and harem: Nation, Gender, Empire, and the cultures of travel*. London: Leicester University Press, 1996.

Grosz, E. A. *Sexual Subversions: Three French Feminists*. Sydney: Allen & Unwin, 1989.

Grutman, Rainier. *Des langues qui résonnent*. Montreal: Fides, 1996.

Gsteiger, Manfred. *La nouvelle littérature romande*. Vevey: Galland, 1978.

Guellouz, Souad. *Les jardins du nord*. Tunis: Éditions Salammbô, 1982.

———. *La Vie simple*. Tunis: MTE, 1975.

Guelpa, Béatrice, and Alain Maillard. "Le dossier asile." *L'Hebdo* 24, (11 June 1998).

Gueunier, Nicole, Genouvrier Emile, and Khomi Abdelhamid. *Les Français devant la norme*. Paris: Champion, 1978.

Guiart, Jean. *Contes et légendes de la Grande Terre*. Nouméa: Éditions des Études Mélanésiennes, 1955.

Guidicelli, Jean-Claude. *De père en fils* (1991).

Guilhaune, Jean-François. *Les Mythes fondateurs de l'Algérie française*. Paris: L'Harmattan, 1992.

Haddour, Azzedine. "Algeria and Its History: Colonial Myths and the Forging and Deconstructing of Identity in Pied-Noir Literature." In *French and Algerian Identities from Colonial Times to the Present; A Century of Interaction*, 77–94. Ed. Alec G. Hargreaves and Michel J. Heffernan. Lewiston: The Edwin Mellon Press, 1993.

Hafez, Sabry. "Women's Narrative in Modern Arabic Literature: A Typology." In *Love and Sexuality in Modern Arabic Literature*. Ed. Roger Allen Hilary Kilpatrick and Ed de Moor. London: Saki Books, 1995.

Hagmann, Hermann-Michel. *Les travailleurs étrangers, chance et tourment de la Suisse. Problème économique, social, politique, phénomène sociologique*. Lausanne: Payot, 1966.

Hajjar, Jacqueline A. "Death, Gangrene of the Soul in *Sitt Marie Rose* by Etel Adnan." *Revue Celfan* 7, no. 3 (May 1988): 27–33.

Hall, Stuart, ed. *Representation: Cultural Representations and Signifying Practices*. London: Sage, 1997.

———. "Who needs Identity." In *Questions of Cultural Identity*, 1–17. Ed. Stuart Hall and Paul du Gay. London: Sage, 1996.

Harding, Sandra. "The Instability of the Analytical Categories of Feminist Theory." *Signs: Journal of Women in Culture and Society* 11, no. 4.

Hare, John. "Journal du voyage de M. Saint-Luc de la Corne, écuyer, dans le navire l'Auguste, en l'an 1761. Crit. ed." *Revue d'histoire littéraire du Québec et du Canada français* 2 (1980–1981): 136–61.

Hargreaves, Alec G. *The Colonial Experience in French Fiction; A Study of Pierre Loti, Ernest Psichari and Pierre Mille*. London: Macmillian, 1981.

———. *Immigration, "Race" and Ethnicity in Contemporary France*. London: Routledge, 1995.

———. *Voices from the North African Immigrant Community in France: Immigration and Identity in Beur Fiction*. Providence, R.I.: Berg, 1991.

———. "Resistance at the Margins: Writers of Maghrebi Immigrant Origin in France." In *Post-Colonial Cultures in France*, 226–29. Ed. Alec Hargreaves and Mark McKinney. London: Routledge, 1997.

———. *Voices From the North African Community in France: Immigration and Identity in Beur Fiction*. New York: Berg, 1991.

———. *La Littérature beur: un guide autobiographique*, 1992.

———. *Immigration and Identity in Beur Fiction: Voices from the North African Immigrant Community in France*. Berg: 1991–1997.

Hargreaves, Alec G., and McKinney Mark, eds. *Postcolonial Cultures and Literatures in France*. London and New York: Routledge, 1997.

Harlow, Barbara. *After Lives: Legacies of Revolutionary Writing*. London and New York: Verso, 1996.

———. *Barred: Women, Writing, and Political Detention*. Hanover, N.H.: University Press of New England, 1992.

———. "The Middle East." In *Longman Anthology of World Literature by Women*. Ed. Marian Arkin and Barbara Shollar. New York: Londman, 1989.

———. *Resistance Literature*. New York: Methuen, 1987.

Harlow, Barbara, and Carter Mia, eds. *Imperialism and Orientalism, a Documentary Sourcebook*. Malden, Mass.: Blackwell, 1999.

Harrow, Kenneth W. "*Camp de Thioraye*: Who's Hiding in Those Tanks and How Come We Can't See Their Faces?" *Iris* 18 (1995): 147–52

Harvey, David. *The Condition of Postmodernity*. Cambridge: Blackwell, 1990.

———. *The Condition of Postmodernity: An Enquiry into the Origins of Cultural Change*. Cambridge and Oxford: Blackwell Publishers, 1989.

Hathorn, Ramon. "*Pélagie-la-Charrette*: éléments rabelaisiens, éléments acadiens." In *Canadiana*, 88–99. Ed. Jørn Carlsen and Knud Larsen. Aarhus: Conférence d'Études Canadiennes, 1984.

Hawthorne, Nathaniel. *The Scarlet Letter*. New York: New American Library, 1959.

Hayes, Jarrod. "Rachid O. and the Return of the Homopast." *Sites* 1, no. 2 (1997): 502.

Hébert, Anne. *La Cage, suivi de L'île de la Demoiselle*. Paris/Montreal: Seuil/Boréal, 1990.

Hekman, Susan. *Gender and Knowledge: Elements of a Postmodern Feminism*. Boston: Northeastern University Press, 1990.

Henningham, Stephen. *France and the South Pacific. A Contemporary History*. Sydney: Allen and Unwin, 1992.

Hermann, Claudine. *The Tongue Snatchers*. Trans. Nancy Kline. Lincoln and London: University of Nebraska Press, 1989.

Herz, Micheline. "A Québécois and an Acadian Novel Compared: The Use of Myth in Jovette Marchessault's" *Comme une enfant de la terre* and Antonine Maillet's *Pélagie-la-Charrette*." In *Traditionalism, Nationalism, and Feminism: Women Writers of Quebec*, 173–183. Ed. Paula Gilbert Lewis. Wesport, Conn.: Greenwood, 1985.

Hesse, Barnor. "Black to Front and Black Again." In *Place and the Politics of Identity*, 82–162. Ed. Michael Keith and Steve Pile. London: Routledge, 1993.

Hexter, Ralph. "Sidonian Dido." In *Innovations of Antiquity*. Ed. Ralph Hexter and Daniel Selden. London: Routledge, 1992.

Hirsch, Charles, and Marie Madeleine Davy. *L'arbre, les symboles*. Paris: Éditions du Félin, 1997.

Hirsch, Marianne. *The Mother/Daughter Plot*. Bloomington and Indianapolis: Indiana University Press, 1989.

Hitchcock, Peter. *Dialogics of the Oppressed*. Minneapolis: University of Minnesota Press, 1993.

Hobsbawm, Eric. *Age of Extremes: The Short Twentieth Century, 1914–1991*. London: Abacus, 1995.

Hodier, Catherine, and Pierre Michel. *L'Exposition coloniale*. Paris: Éditions Complexe, 1991.

Holmes, Diana. *French Women's Writing 1848–1994*. London: Athlone, 1996.

Hooks, Bell. "Postmodern Blackness." In *Contemporary Literary Criticism: Literary and Cultural Studies*. Ed. Robert Con Davis and Ronald Schleifer. New York: Longman, 1998.

———. "Representing Whiteness in the Black Imagination." In *Displacing Whiteness: Essays in Social and Cultural Criticism*. Ed. Ruth Frankenberg. Durham: Duke University Press,1997.

Hottell, Ruth A. "A Poetics of Pain: Evelyne Accad's Critical and Fictional World." *World Literature Today* 71, no. 3 (summer 1997): 511–16.

Houari, Leïla. *Zeida de nulle part*. Paris: L'Harmattan, 1985.

Humbert, Jean-Charles. *La Découverte du Sahara en 1900*. Paris: L'Harmattan, 1996.

Huston, Nancy. "The Matrix of War: Mothers and Heroes." In *The Female Body in Western Culture: Contemporary Perspectives*, 119–36. Ed. Susan Rubin Suleiman. Cambridge, Mass.: Harvard University Press, 1986.

Hutcheon, Linda. *The Politics of Postmodernism*. London: Routledge, 1989.

Ijere, M. I. "La Condition féminine dans Xala de Sembène Ousmane." *L'Afrique littéraire* 85 (1989): 25–34.

Iliffe, John. *Africans, The History of a Continent*. Cambridge: Cambridge University Press, 1995.

Imache, Tassadit. *Une Fille sans Histoire*. Paris: Calmann-Levy, 1989.

Imsand, Christiane. "La loi sur l'asile se heurte au drame du Kosovo." *La Tribune de Genève*, 28 mai 1999.

Irele, Abiola. *The African Experience in Literature and Ideology*. London: Heinemann Educational Books Ltd., 1981.

Israel Nico. *Outlandish-Writing between Exile and Diaspora*. Stanford: Stanford University Press, 2000.

Jabbra, N.W. "Sex Roles and Language in Lebanon." *Ethnology* 19, no. 4 (1980): 459–74.

Jack, Belinda. *Francophone Literatures: An introductory survey*. Oxford New York: Oxford University Press, 1996.

Jacobus, M., ed. *Women Writing and Writing about Women*. London: Crook Helm, 1979.

Jacques, Claudine. *Nos silences sont si fragiles*. Nouméa: Les Éditions du Cagou, 1996.

———. *Les Cœurs barbelés*. Nouméa: Éditions du Niaouli, 1998.

Jacquot, Martine L. "'Je suis la charnière': Entretien avec Antonine Maillet." *Studies in Canadian Literature* 13 (1988): 250–63.

———. "Last Story-Teller." *Waves* 14 (1986): 93–95.

Jacubus, Mary. *Reading Woman: Essays in Feminist Criticism*. New York: Columbia University Press, 1986.

Jakubec, Doris. *Femmes écrivains suisses de langue française. Solitude surpeuplée*. Second edition. Lausanne: Éditions d'En bas, 1997.

James, Louis. *Caribbean Literature in English*. London and New York: Longman, 1999.

Jameson, Fredric. *Postmodernism, or the Cultural Logic of Late Capitalism*. Durham: Duke University Press, 1991.

Jamieson, Neil L. *Understanding Vietnam*. Berkeley: University of California Press, 1993.

JanMohamed, Abdul R., and David Lloyd, eds. *The Nature and Context of Minority Discourse*. New York and Oxford: Oxford University Press, 1991.

Jaubert, Jacques. "Antonine Maillet s'explique." *Lire* 50 (1979): 24–38.

Johnson, Barbara. *A World of Difference*. Baltimore: The Johns Hopkins University Press, 1987.

Joubert, J.-L., Lecarme J., Tabone E., and Vercier B., eds. *Les littératures francophones depuis 1945*. Paris: Bordas, 1986.

Julien, Eileen, et al. *African Literature in Its Social and Political Dimensions*. Washington, D.C.: Three Continents Press, 1986.

Junod, Roger-Louis. "La critique de la société dans les lettres romandes du XXe siècle." In *La Licorne. La Suisse romande et sa littérature*, 439–52. Ed. Peter André Bloch. Poitiers: UFR de Langues et Littératures, 1989.

Kane, Cheik Hamidou. *L'aventure ambigüe*. Paris: 10/18 s.d. [first published Juillard, 1962].

Kane, Cheikh Hamidou. *L'Aventure ambiguë*. Paris: René Julliard, 1961.

Kane, Mohamadou. *Roman africain et traditions*. Dakar: Les Nouvelles Éditions Africaines, 1982.

Kanneh, Kadiatu. "Feminism and the Colonial Body." In *The Post-Colonial Studies Reader*. London: Routledge, 1995.

Kaplan, Alice. *French Lessons*. Chicago: University of Chicago Press, 1993.

Kaplan, Caren. *Questions of Travel: Post-modern Discourse of Displacement*. London, Durham: Duke University Press, 1991.

Karamcheti, Indira. "Aimé Césaire's Subjective Geographies: Translating Place and the Difference it Makes." In *Between Languages and Cultures: Translation and Cross-Cultural Texts*. Ed. Dingwaney Anuradha and Carol Maier. Pittsburgh: University of Pittsburgh Press, 1994.

Karnow, Stanley. *Vietnam: A History*. New York: Penguin, 1991.

Kaspi, André, and Jean-Claude Ruano-Borbalan, eds. "Identité, identités: l'individu, le groupe, et la société." In *Sciences humaines* (15 décembre 1996—janvier 1997): 4–49.

Kathleen, M. Balutansky. "Créolité in question: Caliban in Maryse Condé's *Traversée de la Mangrove*." In *Penser la créolité*, 101–320. Ed. Maryse Condé and Madeleine Cottenet-Hage. Karthala, 1995.

Kauffman, Linda S. *Discourses of Desire: Gender, Genre, and Epistolary Fictions*. Ithaca, N.Y.: Cornell University Press, 1986.

Kaye, Jacqueline, ed. *Maghreb: New Writing from North Africa*. York: Talus Editions/University of York, 1992.

Kechichian, Patrick. "La Voix des démons." *Le Monde des livres* (18 September 1998): 3.

Keith, Michael, and Steve Pile. *Places and the Politics of Identity*. London: Routledge, 1993.

Kerbrat-Orecchioni, Catherine. *L'Implicité*. Paris: Armand Colin, 1986.

Kesteloot, Lilyan. *Les écrivains noirs de langue française: naissance d'une littérature*. Bruxelles: Éditions de l'Université de Bruxelles, 1977.

Khadar, H., ed. *Anthologie de la poesie tunisienne de langue française*. Paris: L'Harmattan, 1985.

Khalaf, Saher. *Littérature libanaise de langue française*. Ottawa: Naaman, 1974.

Khatibi, Abdelkebir. *Maghreb Pluriel*. Paris: Denoel, 1983.

———. *Le roman maghrébin*. Paris: Maspéro, 1968.

Kieser, Rolf, and Kurt R. Spillmann, eds. *The New Switzerland. Problems and Policies*. Palo Alto, Calif.: Society for the Promotion of Science and Scholarship, 1995.

Kirby, Kathleen. *Indifferent Boundaries: Spatial Concepts of Human Subjectivity*. New York and London: Guilford Press, 1996.

Klein, Juan-Luis, and Pena Orlando. *Compagnies multinationales et espaces géographiques. Noranda Mines, une étude de cas*. Rouyn: Collège d'Abitibi-Témiscamingue, 1984.

Klinkenberg, Jean-Marie. "Insécurité linguistique et production littéraire: le problème de la langue d'écriture dans les lettres francophones." In *L'insécurité linguistique dans les communautés francophones périphériques*. Ed. Michel Francard. Louvain-la-Neuve: Cahiers de L'Institut de Linguistique de Louvain, 1993.

———. "Le problème de la langue d'écriture dans la littérature francophone de Belgique. De Verhaegen à Verheggen." In L'identité dans les littératures francophones, 65–79. Ed. A. Vigh. ACCT: Presses de l'Université de Pécs, 1987.

———. "Les arts de la langue." In *Le français en Belgique*, 401–13. Ed. Daniel Blampain et al. Louvain-la-Neuve: Duculot, 1997.

Knight, M. M. "French Colonial Policy—The Decline of Association." *Journal of Modern History* 4 (1933): 208–24.

Koos, Leonard R. "Between Two Worlds: Constructing Colonialist Culture in Turn-of-the-Century Algeria." *French Literature Series* 26 (1999): 97–107.

Koppelman, Susan, ed. *Between Mothers and Daughters: Stories across a Generation*. New York: The Feminist Press, 1985.

Kristeva, Julia. *Etrangers à nous-mêmes.* Paris: Fayard, 1988.

Kröller, Eva-Marie. "Landscape, History and the Child: *On a mangé la dune.*" *Québec Studies* 4 (1986): 252–60.

Kurtovitch, Nicolas. *Souffles de la nuit.* Paris: Éditions St-Germain-des-Prés (Collection *Chemins profonds*), 1985.

———. *L'arme qui me fera vaincre.* Nouméa: Éditions Vents du Sud, 1988.

———. *Forêt, terre et tabac.* Nouméa: Éditions du Niaouli, 1993.

———. *Assis dans la barque.* Nouméa: Grain de Sable, 1994.

———. *Totem.* Nouméa: Grain de Sable, 1997.

———. *Le Sentier, Kaa wegna.* Nouméa: Grain de Sable, 1998.

———. *Dire le vrai* (avec Déwé Gorodé). Nouméa: Grain de Sable, 1998.

Kuttel, Mireille. *La Malvivante.* Lausanne: l'Âge d'Homme, 1978.

———. *La Maraude.* Lausanne: l'Âge d'Homme, 1986.

———. *La Pérégrine.* Lausanne: l'Âge d'Homme, 1983.

Kwame, Anthony Appiah. *In My Father's House: Africa in the Philosophy of Culture.* New York: Oxford University Press

L'Hérault, Pierre. "Passages." *Spirale* 153 (1997): 23.

———. "*Les Crasseux* ou le Mythe du retour aux origines." *Revue de l'Université de Moncton* 7 (1974): 47–56.

La Billiardière, Jacques. *Relation du voyage à la recherche de La Pérouse.* Paris: Jansen, 1800.

Laabi, Abdellatif. "Preface" In *Metamorphose de l'ile et de la vague*, 3–4. Ed. Amina Said. Paris: Arcantere, 1985.

Labeau, Emmanuelle. "Du wallon au français: le multilinguisme d'Arthur Masson." *Francophonie vivante* 1 (March 1997): 3–10.

Labou Tansi, Sony. *Les Commencement des douleurs.* Paris: Éditions de Seuil, 1995.

———. *La vie et demie.* Paris: Seuil Points s.d. [first published Éditions du Seuil, 1979].

———. *Les sept solitudes de Lorsa Lopez.* Paris: Seuil Points s.d. [first published Éditions du Seuil,1985].

Lacan, Jacques. *Écrits vol. ii.* Paris: Seuil, 1971.

Lacombe, Michèle. "Breaking the Silence of Centuries." *Canadian Theater Review* 46 (1986): 58–64.

Lacoste-Dujardin, Camille. *Des mères contre des femmes: maternité et patriarcat au Maghreb.* Paris: La Découverte, 1996.

———. *Yasmina et les autres de Nanterre et d'ailleurs: filles de parents maghrébins en France.* Paris: La Découverte, 1992.

Lafond, Jean, and Augustin Redondo. *L'Image du monde renversé et ses représentations littéraires et paralittéraires de la fin du XVIe siècle au milieu du XVIIe.* Paris: Vrin, 1979.

Lafontaine, Dominique. "Les mots et les Belges." *Français et Société* 2, Communauté française de Belgique. (March 1991): 36.

Lahontan, Louis-Armand de Lom d'Arce, baron de. "*Dialogues.*" In *Œuvres complètes*, 801–85. Ed. Réal Ouellet and Alain Beaulieu. "Bibliothèque du Nouveau Monde". Montreal: Presses de l'Université de Montréal, 1990.

Landry, Donna, and Gerald MacLean, eds. *The Spivak Reader: Selected Works by Gayatri Chakravorty Spivak.* New York: Routledge, 1996

Lanken, Dane. "L'Acadienne." *Quest* (December 1982):34–42.

Lapierre, Jean-William, and Roy Muriel. *Les Acadiens.* Paris: Presses Universitaires de France, 1983.

Lashgari, Deirdre, ed. *Violence, Silence, and Anger: Women's Writings As Transgression.* Charlottesville: University Press of Virginia, 1995.

Laubreaux, Alin. *Le Rocher à la voile.* Paris: Albin Michel, 1930.

Laye, Camara. *L'enfant noir.* Paris: Presses Pocket s.d.[first published Plon, 1953].

Le Blanc, René. "L'Oralité du style dans les romans d'Antonine Maillet." *Revue d'histoire littéraire du Québec et du Canada français* 12 (1986):35–49.

Le Clézio, J. M. G. *Le Chercheur d'or.* Paris: Gallimard, 1985.

———. *Étoile érrante.* Paris: Gallimard, 1992.

———. *Onitsha.* Paris: Gallimard, 1991.

———. *Pawana.* Paris: Gallimard, 1992.

———. *Poisson d'or.* Paris: Gallimard, 1997.

———. *La Quarantaine.* Paris: Gallimard, 1995.

Le Clezio, Marguerite, and Assia Djebar. "Assia Djebar: Écrire dans la langue adverse." *Contemporary French Civilization* 9, no. 2 (spring–summer 1985): 230–43.

Le Goupils. *Comment on cesse d'être colon.* Paris: Grasset, 1910.

Le Huu, Khoa, ed. *La Part d'Exil.* Aix en Provence: Université de Provence, 1995.

———. *Les Vietnamiens en France: insertion et identité. Le processus d'immigration depuis la colonisation jusqu'à l'implantation des réfugiés.* Paris: l'Harmattan, 1985.

———. *L'Immigration confucéenne en France.* Paris: l'Harmattan, 1996.

Lê, Linda. *Les Dits d'un idiot.* Paris: Christian Bourgois Éditeur, 1995.

———. *Les Évangiles du crime.* Paris: Julliard, 1992.

———. *Lettre morte.* Paris: Christian Bourjois, 1999.

———. *Fuir: roman.* Paris: La Table ronde, 1988.

———. *Un si tendre vampire.* Paris: Éditions de la table Ronde, 1987.

———. *Les Trois parques.* Paris: Christian Bourgois Editeur, 1997.

———. "Les Pieds nus." In *La Part d'Exil,* 57–58. Ed. Le Huu Khoa. Aix-en-Provence: Université de Provence, 1995.

———. *Voix: une crise.* Paris: Christian Bourjois, 1998.

LeBlanc, Emery. *Les Acadiens.* Ottawa: Éditions de l'homme, 1963.

LeBlanc-Rainville, Simone. "Entretien avec Antonine Maillet." *Revue de l'Université de Moncton* 7 (1974): 13–24.

———. "Notes sur la Sagouine et nous." *Revue de l'Université de Moncton* 7 (1974): 35–37.

LeBlanc, Raymond. "Lire Antonine Maillet de *Pointe-aux-Coques* à *La Sagouine*." *Revue de l'Université de Moncton* 7 (1974): 57–68.

Leenhardt, Maurice. *Do Kamo, la personne et le mythe dans le monde mélanésien.* Paris: Gallimard, 1985.

Lefebvre, Henri. *The Production of Space.* Trans. Donald Nicholson-Smith. Oxford: Blackwell, 1991.

———. *La Pensée marxiste et la ville.* Paris: Éditions Casterman, 1972.

———. *La Production de l'espace.* Paris: Éditions Anthropos, 1974.

Lefebvre, Paul. "La dramaturgie québécoise depuis 1980." *Théâtre/Public* 117 (1994): 46–48.

Lejeune, Philippe. *Le Pacte autobiographique.* Paris: Éditions du Seuil, 1975.

Lemaire, Jacques. *Le français et les Belges.* Bruxelles: Éditions de l'Université de Bruxelles,1989.

Lemire, Maurice, ed. *Dictionnaire des œuvres littéraires du Québec.* Montréal: Fides, 1978–1987.

Lempen, Blaise. *Un modèle en crise: la Suisse.* Lausanne: Payot, 1985.

Leprun, Sylviane. *Le Théâtre des colonies.* Paris: L'Harmattan, 1986.

Leroux, Laurence. *Une saison folle.* Paris: Gallimard, 1986.

LeRoy Ladurie, Emmanuel. *Le carnaval de Romans.* Paris: Gallimard, 1979.

Lespérance, Pierre. "La Fortune littéraire du Journal de voyage de Saint-Luc de la Corne." *Voix et images* 59 (1995): 329–346.

Levy-Beaulieu, Victor. *Ma Corriveau, suivi de La Sorcellerie en finale sexuée, théâtre.* Montreal: V.L.B., 1976.

Lewis, Martin Deming. "One Hundred Million Frenchmen: The Assimilation Theory in French Colonial Policy." *Comparative Studies in Society and History* 4, no. 2 (1962): 129–53.

Liking, Werewere. *Elle sera de jaspe et de corail.* Paris: L'Harmattan, 1983.

———. Orphée Dafric. Paris: L'Harmattan, 1981.

Lindholm, C. *The Islamic Middle East: An Historical Anthropology.* Oxford: Blackwell, 1996.

Linfors, Bernth. "Penetrating *Xala.*" *The International Fiction Review* 24 (1997): 65–69.

Lings, Martin. *What is Sufism?* London: George Allen and Unwin Ltd, 1975.

Lionnet, Françoise. *Autobiographical Voices–Race Gender, Self-portraiture.* Ithaca, N.Y.: Cornell University Press, 1989.

——. *Postcolonial Representations.* Ithaca NY: Cornell University Press, 1995.

Lobet, Marcel. *Arthur Masson ou la richesse du coeur.* Bruxelles: Vanderlinden, 1971.

——. *Toine Culot obèse ardennais.* Bruxelles: Racine, 1996.

——. *Toine maïeur de Trignolles.* Bruxelles: Racine, 1995.

——. *Toine dans la tourmente.* Bruxelles: Racine, 1995.

——. *Toine chef de tribu.* Bruxelles: Racine, 1995.

——. *Toine retraité.* Bruxelles: Racine, 1995.

Lowe, L. "Literary Nomadics in Francophone Allegories of Post Colonialism: Pham Van Ky, and Tahar Ben Jelloun." *Yale French Studies* 82 (1992): 43–61.

Lydie, Moudileno. "Ecrire l'écrivain: créolité et spécularité." In *Penser la créolité*, 191–320. Ed. Maryse Condé and Madeleine Cottenet-Hage. Karthala, 1995.

——. "Portrait of the Artist as Dreamer: Maryse Condé's *Traversée de la Mangrove* and *Les Derniers rois mages.*" in *Callalloo* 18, no. 3 (summer 1995): 626–40.

M, Pennée. *The Canadians of Old. An Historical Romance.* Trans. Georgina. Quebec: Desbarats, 1865.

M'henni, Mansour. "Fawzi Mellah." In *La littérature maghrébine de langue française.* Ed. Charles Bonn Naget Khadda and Abdallah Mdarhri-Alaoui. Paris: EDICEF-AUPELG, 1996.

Maazaoui, A. "Eroticism and the Sacred: The Novels of Tahar Ben Jalloun, Assia Djebbar and Fawzi Mellah." *Romance Notes* 38, no. 2 (1998): 149–56.

Madubuike, Ihechukwu. *The Senegalese Novel: A Sociological Study of the Impact of the Politics of Assimilation.* Washington, D.C.: Three Continents Press, 1983.

Magnier, Bernard. *"Ken Bugul ou l'Ecriture thérapeutique."* Notre Librairie 81 (octobre–décembre 1985).

Maillet, Antonine. *L'Acadie pour quasiment rien.* Montréal: Leméac, 1973.

——. *Le Bourgeois gentleman.* Montréal: Leméac, 1978.

——. *Cent ans dans les bois.* Montréal: Leméac, 1981.

——. *Le Chemin Saint-Jacques.* Montréal: Leméac, 1996.

——. *Christophe Cartier de la Noisette dit Nounours.* Montréal: Hachette/Leméac, 1981.

——. *Chronique d'une sorcière de vent.* Montréal: Leméac, 1999.

——. *Les Confessions de Jeanne de Valois.* Montréal: Leméac, 1992.

——. *La Contrebandière.* Montréal: Leméac, 1981.

——. *Les Cordes-de-Bois.* Montréal: Leméac, 1977.

——. *Crache à Pic.* Paris: Grasset, 1984.

——. *Les Crasseux.* Montréal: Holt, Rinehart and Winston, 1968.

——. *Les Crasseux.* Intro. Jacques Ferron and Rita Scalabrini. Montréal: Leméac, 1973.

——. *Les Crasseux.* Intro. Rita Scalabrini. Montréal: Leméac, 1974.

——. *Don l'Orignal.* Montréal: Leméac, 1977.

——. *Les Drôlatiques, Horrifiques et Épouvantables Aventures de Panurge, ami de Pantagruel.* Montréal: Leméac, 1983.

——. *Emmanuel à Joseph à Dâvit.* Montréal: Leméac, 1975.

——. *Évangéline Deusse.* Montréal: Leméac, 1975.

——. *"Expériences d'écriture: Mon pays, c'est un conte."* Études françaises 12 (1976): 79–83.

——. *La Foire de la Saint-Barthélemy.* Montréal: Leméac, 1994.

——. *Gapi.* Montréal: Leméac, 1976.

——. *Gapi et Sullivan.* Montréal: Leméac, 1973.

——. *Garrochés en paradis.* Montréal: Leméac, 1986.

——. *La Gribouille.* Paris: Grasset, 1982.

——. *Le Huitième Jour.* Montréal: Leméac, 1986.

——. *L'Île-aux-Puces.* Montréal: Leméac, 1996.

——. *Margot la Folle.* Montréal: Leméac, 1987.

——. *Mariaagélas.* Montréal: Leméac, 1973.

——. *La Nuit des rois.* Montréal: Leméac, 1993.

——. *On a mangé la dune.* Montréal: Leméac, 1977.

———. *L'Oursiade.* Paris: Grasset, 1991.

———. *Par derrière chez mon père.* Montréal: Leméac, 1972.

———. *Pélagie-la-Charrette.* Paris: Grasset, 1979.

———. *Pointe-aux-Coques.* Montréal: Fides, 1977.

———. *Rabelais et les traditions populaires en Acadie.* Québec: Presses Universitaires Laval, 1971.

———. *Richard III.* Montréal: Leméac, 1989.

———. *La Sagouine.* Montréal: Leméac, 1971.

———. "La Sainte," *Québec Studies* 4 (1986): 236–40.

———. *La Veuve enragée.* Montréal: Leméac, 1977.

———. *William S.* Montréal: Leméac, 1991.

Maillet, Antonine, and Liano Petroni. "Histoire, fiction et vie; langue, forme, mémoire: un entretien sur *Pélagie-la-Charrette.*" *Francofonia* 2 (1982): 3–17.

Maillet, Marguerite, and Judith Hamel. *Réception des œuvres d'Antonine Maillet.* Moncton, N.B.: Chaire d'études acadiennes, 1989.

Maillet, Marguerite, et al., eds. *Anthologie de textes littéraires acadiens, 1606–1975.* Moncton, N.B.: Éditions d'Acadie, 1979.

Majiri, Jamila. *Diwan al-Nisa (Women's Divan).* Tunis: SOTEPA, 1997.

Major, André. "Entretien avec Antonine Maillet." *Écrits du Canada Français* 36 (1973): 11–38.

Makward, Christiane P. "Cherchez la Franco-femme." *Postcolonial Subjects: Francophone Women Writers.* Ed. Mary Jean Green et al. Minneapolis: University of Minnesota Press, 1996.

Makward, Edris. "Women, Tradition, and Religion in Sembène Ousmane's Work.", In *Faces of Islam in African Literature,* 187–200. Ed. K. Harrow. Portsmouth: Heinemann; London: James Currey, 1991.

Mallebay, Ernest. "Bou-Yabès." *La Revue algérienne illustrée* 28, no. 15 (1897): 458.

———. *Cinquante ans de journalisme.* 2 vols. Algiers: Fontana, 1937.

Malti-Douglas, Fedwa. *Men, Women, and God(s): Nawal el-Saadawi and Arab Feminist Poetics.* Berkeley: University of California Press, 1995.

———. *Women's Body, Woman's Word: Gender and Discourse in Arabo-Islamic Writing.* Princeton, N.J.: Princeton University Press, 1991.

Mam Lam Fouck, Serge. *D'Chimbo du criminel au héros. Une incursion dans l'imaginaire guyanais.* Cayenne: Ibis Rouge Editions, 1997.

———. *L'Esclavage en Guyane. Entre l'occultation et la revendication.* Cayenne: Ibis Rouge Éditions, 1998.

Mangaro, Elise Salem. "Bearing Witness: Recent Literature from Lebanon." *The Literary Review* 37, no. 3 (spring 1994): 373–82.

Manzor Coats, Lillian. "Of Witches and Other Things: Maryse Condé's Challenges to Feminist Discourse." *World Literature Today* 67, no. 4 (fall 1993): 737–44.

Maran, René. *Batouala: véritable roman nègre.* (1921) Paris: Albin-Michel, 1938.

Marc, Edmond. *Identité et communication.* Paris: Presses Universitaires de France, 1992.

Mariotti, Jean. *Œuvres complètes.* Nouméa: Grain de Sable, 1996–2000.

———. *A bord de l'incertaine.* Nouméa: Grain de Sable, 1996.

Marks, Elaine, and Isabelle de Courtivron, eds. *New French Feminisms.* Amherst: University of Massachusetts Press, 1980.

Marshall, Catherine. *Militarism Versus Feminism: Writings on Women and War.* London: Virago, 1987.

Martel, Reginald. "Livres d'artistes ou non," *La Presse,* 3 Mai 1980.

Marx-Scouras, Danielle. "Muffled Screams/ Stifled Voices." *Yale French Studies* 82 (1993): 172–82.

Maryse, Condé. *Traversée de la Mangrove.* Paris: Mercure de France (Folio), 1992.

Massard, Janine. *Ce qui reste de Katharina.* Vevey: Aire, 1997.

———. *Christine au dévaloir.* Genève: Éditions Eliane Vernay, 1981.

———. *Trois mariages.* Vevey: Aire, 1992.

Masson, Arthur, *Toine Culot obèse ardennais.* Bruxelles: Racine. 1996.

———. *Toine maïeur de Trignolles.* Bruxelles : Racine. 1995.

——. *Toine dans la tourmente.* Bruxelles : Racine. 1995.

——. *Toine chef de tribu.* Bruxelles: Racine, 1995.

——. *Toine retraité.* Bruxelles: Racine, 1995.

Mathieu, Jean-Luc. *Histoire des DOM-TOM.* Paris: Presses Universitaires de France, 1993.

——. *Les DOM-TOM.* Paris: Presses Universitaires de France, 1988.

Maupassant, Guy de. *Lettres d'Afrique (Algérie—Tunisie).* Ed, Michèle Salinas. Paris: La Boîte à Documents, 1997.

Mauss, Marcel. "Essai sur le don." In *Sociologie et société,* 1923–1924. Paris: Quadrige/Presses Universitaires de France, 1950.

Maximin, Daniel. *Lone Sun.* Charlottesville: University Press of Virginia, 1989.

McAdams, Dan R. *The Person.* 2nd ed.: Harcourt Brace, 1994.

McClintock, Anne. "The Angel of Progress: Pitfalls of the Term 'Post-Colonialism.'" *Social Text* 31, no. 2 (1992): 84–98.

McCormick, Robert H. jr. "From Africa to Barbados via Salem: Maryse Condé's Cultural Confrontations." *Caribana* 5 (1996): 151–57.

McCumber, John. "Dialectical Identity in a 'Post-Critical' Era: A Hegelian Reading." *The South Atlantic Quarterly* 94 (fall 1995):1144–59.

McDowell, Linda, and Joanne P. Sharp, eds. *Space, Gender, Knowledge: Feminist Readings.* London: Arnold, 1997.

Mckay, Donald Vernon. "Colonialism in the French Geographical Movement, 1871–1881." *The Geographical Review* 33 (April 1934): 214–32.

Meddeb, Abdelwahab. *Talismano.* Paris: Christian Bourgeois, 1979.

——. *Phantasia.* Paris: Sindbad, 1986.

——. *Tombeau d'Ibn Arabi.* Paris: Noel Blondin, 1987.

——. *L'Enfant et la gazelle.* Paris: Actes Sud, 1992.

Mellah, Fawzi. *Néron ou les oiseaux de passage.* Paris: P. J. Oswald, 1974.

——. *Le palais du non-retour.* Paris: P. J. Oswald, 1976.

——. *De l'Unité arabe.* Paris: L'Harmattan, 1985.

——. *Elissa, la reine vagabonde.* Paris: Seuil, 1988.

——. *Elissa,* Trans. Howards Curtis. London: Quartet Books, 1990.

——. *Le Conclave des pleureuses.* Paris: Seuil, 1987.

Memmi, Albert. *La statut de sel.* Paris: Buchet Chastel, 1953.

——. *Agar.* Paris: Buchet Chastel, 1953.

——. *Le Desert, ou la vie et les aventures de Jubair Ouali-el-Mammi.* Paris: Gallimard, 1977.

Mendel, Gérard. "La violence est un langage." *Violences et non-violences: Raison Présente.* Ed. Duvignaud Jean. Paris: Nouvelles Éditions Rationalistes, 1980.

Menke, Anne, M. "'Boy!': The Hinge of Colonial Double Talk." *Studies in Twentieth Century Literature* 15, no.1 (1991): 11–28.

Mercier, Andrée. "Poétique du récit contemporain: négation du genre ou émergence d'un sous-genre?" *Voix et Images* 69 (1998): 461–80.

Merle, Isabelle. *Expériences coloniales. Nouvelle-Calédonie (1853–1920).* Paris: Belin, 1995.

Mernissi, Fatima. *Le Harem politique: le prophète et les femmes.* Paris: Éditions Albin Michel, 1987.

——. *Beyond the Veil: Male-Female Dynamics in Modern Muslim Society.* Bloomington and Indianapolis: Indiana University Press, 1987.

——. *Dreams of Trespass: Tales of a Harem Girlhood.* Reading: Perseus Books, 1994.

——. *Sexe, idéologie et Islam.* Paris: Éditions Tierce, 1983.

——. *Le Harem politique; le prophète et les femmes.* Paris: Albin Michel. 1987

Mertens, Pierre, and Jacques Franck. "La littérature française de Belgique et le français." In *Le français et les Belges,* 87–97. Ed. Jacques Lemaire. Bruxelles: Éditions de l'Université de Bruxelles, 1989.

Michael, Lucey. "Voices Accounting for the Past: Maryse Condé's *Traversée de la Mangrove.*" In *L'Héritage de Caliban,* 123–32. Ed. Marsye Condé. Pointe-à-Pitre: Éditions Jasor, 1992.

Michaud, Ginette. "La Version acadienne d'une double expropriation." *Le Devoir*, 22 novembre 1980.

Michel, Louise. *Aux amis d'Europe. Légendes et chants de gestes canaques.* (1875–1885) Nouméa: Grain de Sable, 1996.

Miller, Christopher L. "Senegalese Women Writers, Silence, and Letters: Before the Canon's Roar." In *Theories of Africans. Francophone Literature and Anthropology in Africa*, 246–293. Chicago and London: Chicago University Press, 1990.

——. *Theories of Africans: Francophone Literature and Anthropology in Africa.* Chicago and London: Chicago University Press, 1990.

——. *Nationalisms and Nomads: Essays on Francophone African Literature and Culture.* Chicago: University of Chicago Press, 1998.

Miller, Nancy, ed. *The Poetics of Gender.* New York: Columbia University Press, 1986.

Mimouna. *Ni le Voile, ni l'oubli.* Paris: Édition no.1, 1995.

Minces, Juliette. *La Femme dans le monde arabe.* Paris: Éditions Mazarine, 1980.

——. *La Femme voilée: l'Islam au féminin.* Paris: Calmann-Lév, 1990.

Minh-ha, Trinh T. *When the Moon Waxes Red: Representation, Gender and Politics.* New York and London: Routledge, 1991.

——. *Woman, Native, Other: Writing Postcoloniality and Feminism.* Bloomington: Indiana University Press, 1989.

Miomandre, Francis de. *Figures d'hier et d'aujourd'hui.* Paris: Dorbon-Aîné, 1911.

Miquel, Christian. *La quête de l'exil. Pratique de l'exil.* Paris: L'Harmattan, 1996.

Mireille, Rosello. *Littérature et identité créole aux Antilles.* Paris: Karthala, 1992.

Mitchell, W. J. T. "Imperial Landscape." In *Landscape and Power*, 5–34. Ed. W. J. T. Mitchell. Chicago: University of Chicago Press, 1994.

Mitscherlich, Margarete. *La Femme pacifique.* Trans. Sylvie Ponsard. Paris: Des Femmes, 1988.

Mohanty, Chandra Talpade. "Cartographies of Struggle: Third World Women and the Politics of Feminism." In *Third World Women and the Politics of Feminism*, 1–47. Ed. Chandra Talpade Mohanty. Bloomington: Indiana University Press, 1997.

——. "Feminist Encounters: Locating the Politics of Experience." *Copyright* 1 (1987): 30–44.

Moi, Toril. *Sexual/Textual Politics: Feminist Literary Theory.* London and New York: Routledge,1988.

Monnier, Jean-Pierre. *Écrire en Suisse romande entre le ciel et la nuit.* Vevey: Galland, 1979.

Montefiore, J. *Feminism and Poetry.* London: Pandora, 1987.

Mortimer, Mildred. "Entretien avec Assia Djebar, écrivain algérienne." *Research in African Literature* 19, no. 2 (summer 1988): 197–205.

——. *Journeys through the French African Novel.* Portsmouth, N.H.: James Currey, 1990.

Mouillaud-Fraisse, Geneviève. *Les Fous cartographes: littérature et appartenance.* Paris: Éditions L'Harmattan, 1995.

Moumouni, Abdou. *Education in Africa.* New York: Praeger, 1968.

Mountain, Anthony. "Eden, a Modern Myth." *The Dalhousie Review* 52, no. 2 (1972).

Moura, Jean-Marc. *Littératures francophones et théorie postcoloniale.* Paris: Presses Universitaires de France, 1999.

Mouralis, Bernard. *Littérature et développement.* Paris: Éditions Silex, 1984.

Mudimbe-Boyi, Elisabeth. "The Poetics of Exile and Errancy: Ken Bugul's *Le Baobab fou* and Simone Schwarz-Bart's *Ti Jean L'Horizon*." *Yale French Studies* 83, no. 2 (1993).

——. "Giving a Voice to Tituba: The Death of the Author?" *World Literature Today* 67, no. 4 (fall 1993): 751–56.

Muller, Jean-Marie. "Signification de la non-violence." In *Violences et non-violences: Raison Présente.* Ed. Duvignard Jean. Paris: Nouvelles Éditions Rationalistes, 1980.

Mulvey, Laura. *Visual and Other Pleasures.* Bloomington: Indiana University Press, 1983.

Naaman, Abdallah. *Le Français au Liban, essai socio-linguistique.* Jounieh, Lebanon: Naaman, 1979.

Naccache, Gilbert. *Cristal.* Tunis: Éditions Salammbô, 1982.

Ndagano, Biringanine, and Blérard-Ndagano Monique. *Introduction à la littérature Guyanaise.* Cayenne: Centre Départmental de Documentation Pédagogique de la Guyane (CDDP Guyane), 1996.

Ndagano, Biringanine. *La Guyane entre maux et mots. Une lecture de l'oeuvre d'Elie Stephenson.* Paris: L'Harmattan, 1994.

New, Mitya. *Switzerland Unwrapped. Exposing the Myths.* London: Tauris, 1997.

Nguyen, N. *Between East and West: A Study of selected works by Vietnamese Francophone Writers from 1930 to 1990.* Unpublished doctoral thesis, University of Oxford, 1993.

Nice, Vivien E. *Mothers and Daughters: Distortion of a Relationship.* New York: St. Martin's Press, 1992.

Nickrosz, John. "Les origines populaires de la littérature acadienne contemporaine en prose." *Présence Francophone* 13 (1976): 83–91.

Nicollier, Alain, and Henri-Charles Dahlem. *Dictionnaire des écrivains suisses d'expression française.* 2 vols. Genève: Éditions GVA, 1994.

Nini, Soraya. *Ils disent que je suis une beurette.* Paris: Fixot, 1993.

Nisbet, Anne-Marie. *Littérature Néo-Calédonienne.* Sherbrooke: Naaman, 1985.

Noiriel, Gérard. "Immigration Amnesia and Memory." *French Historical Studies* 19, no. 2 (fall 1995): 367–80.

———. *The French Melting Pot—Immigration, Citizenship and National Identity.* Trans. Geoffroy de Laforcade. Minneapolis: University of Minnesota Press, 1996.

Nora, Pierre. "Between Memory and History: Les Lieux de Mémoire." In *Memory and Counter Memory,* 7–25. Ed. Natalie Zemon Davis and Randolph Starn. Special issue of *Representations* 26 (spring 1989).

Norindr, Panivong. *Phantasmatic Indochina: French Colonial Ideology in Architecture, Film and Literature.* Durham and London: Duke University Press, 1996.

O'Dwyer, Michael. "Julien Green—Expatrié et Sudiste." In *Exiles and Migrants: Crossing Thresholds in European Culture and Society,* 185–92. Ed. Anthony Coulson. Brighton: Sussex Academic Press, 1997.

Obinaju, Nwabueze Joe. "'Quête' et 'initiation' dans *Une vie de boy.*" *Neohelicon* 22, no. 2 (1986): 97–120.

Ogunsanwo, Olatubosun. "The Narrative Voice in Two Novels of Ferdinand Oyono." *English Studies in Africa* 29, no. 2 (1986): 97–120.

Ojo, S. Ade. "Le 'Xala' dans *Xala* de Sembène Ousmane." *Éthiopiques* 5, nos. 1–2 (1988): 185–204.

Okolie, Maxwell. "Le regard et le drame de Toundi dans *Une vie de boy.*" *Éthiopiques* 5, nos. 1–2 (1988): 205–12.

Okri, Ben. *Infinite Riches.* London: Orion, 1998.

Olaniyan, Tejumola. *Scars of Conquest/Masks of Resistance.* New York: Oxford University Press, 1995.

Onimus, Jean. *Pour lire Le Clézio.* Paris: Presses Universitaires de France, 1994.

Ouellet, Lise. "Mythe, intertextualité et fonctionnement de la parole chez la vieille femme dans *La Sagouine et Évangéline Deusse* d'Antonine Maillet." *Dalhousie French Studies* 15 (1988): 48–68.

Oyono, Ferdinand. *Une vie de boy.* Paris: Julliard, 1956.

Paget, Elsie. "La Sagouine d'Antonine Maillet: une œuvre brechtienne?" M.A. thèse. McMaster University, 1984.

Pallister, Janis L. "Antonine Maillet: Spiritual Granddaughter of François Rabelais." *Québec Studies* 4 (1986): 261–85.

Parfitt, Derek. "Personal Identity." *The Philosophical Review* 80 (January 1971): 3–27

Parisette. "El Bah't." *La Revue algérienne illustrée* 40, no. 24 (1901): 752.

Pasquali, Adrien. *Le pain de silence.* Genève: Zoé, 1999.

Patient, Serge. *Guyane pour tout dire,* suivi de *Le mal du pays.* Paris: Éditions Caribéennes, 1980.

———. *Le Nègre du gouverneur.* Honfleur: Pierre Jean Oswald, 1972.

Pauleau, Christine. *Le français de Nouvelle-Calédonie. Contribution à un inventaire des particularités lexicales.* Vanves: EDICEF, 1995.

Peirce, Bonny. "Social identity, investment and language learning." in *TESOL Quarterly* 29 (1995): 9–31.

Pellegrin, Arthur. *La Littérature nord-africaine.* Tunis: Bibliothèque Nord-Africaine, 1920.

Pepin, Ernst. "La Femme Antillaise et son corps." *Presence Africaine* 141 (1987): 181–93.

Perrin, Liliane. *Un Marié sans importance.* Genève: Metropolis, 1994.

Peteet, Julie. "Icons and Militants: Mothering in the Danger Zone." *Signs* 23, no. 1 (fall 1997): 103–29.

Peters, Emrys. "The Status of Women in Four Middle Eastern Communities." *Women in the Muslim World*. Cambridge, Mass.: Harvard University Press, 1978.

Peterson, Carla. "Le Surnaturel dans *Moi, Tituba sorcière . . . Noire de Salem* de Maryse Condé et *Beloved* de Toni Morrison." In *L'Oeuvre de Maryse Condé: A propos d'une écrivaine politiquement incorrecte*. Araujo-Nara. Paris: l'Harmattan, 1996.

Pfaff, Françoise. *The Cinema of Ousmane Sembène, a Pioneer of African Film*. Westport, Conn.: Greenwood Press,1984.

Pham, Dan Binh. "Écrivains Vietnamiens d'expression française. Création et Créativité." in *Cahiers d'Études Vietnamiennes* 11 (1994): 95.

Pinter, Frances, ed. *Social Science Research and Women in the Arab World*. Paris: Unesco, 1984.

Pisier, Marie-France. *Le Bal du gouverneur*. Paris: Grasset, 1984.

Pohl, Jacques. *Les variétés régionales du français: études belges (1945–1977)*. Bruxelles: Éditions de l'Université de Bruxelles, 1979.

Pratt, Mary Louise. "Scratches on the Face of the Country, or what Mr. Barrow saw in the land of the Bushmen" in *"Race," Writing and Difference*. Ed. Henry Gates Jr. Chicago: University of Chicago Press, 1985.

Prevost-Paradol, Lucien-Anatole. *La Nouvelle France*. Paris: Michel Lévy, 1868.

Prince, Gerald Prince. *A Dictionary of Narratology*. Lincoln: University of Nebraska Press, 1987.

Prince, Gerald. *Dictionary of Narratology*. Lincoln and London: University of Nebraska Press, 1987.

Prochaska, Daniel. *Making Algeria French: Colonialism in Bône 1870–1920*. Cambridge: Cambridge University Press, 1990.

Proulx, Patrice J. "Inscriptions of Female Community and Liberation in Maryse *Condé's Moi, Tituba sorcière*." *Europe Plurilingue* (*mars* 1997): 148–61.

Quaghebeur, Marc. *Balises pour l'histoire des lettres belges*. Bruxelles: Labor, 1998.

———. "Belgique: la première des littératures francophones non françaises." In *La Belgique francophone: lettres et arts*, 5–36. Ed. R. Pop. Studia Universitatis Babes-Bolyai ("philologie 1–2"): Cluj-Napoca, 1991.

Quaghebeur, Marc, Verheggen Jean-Pierre, and Jago-Antoine. V. *Un pays d'irréguliers*. Bruxelles: Labor (Archives du futur), 1990.

Randau, Robert. *Les Algérianistes*. Paris: Sansot, 1911.

———. "Le Mouvement littéraire dans l'Afrique du nord." *Les Belles lettres* 2 (1920): 350–66.

Rastier, François. *Essais de sémiotique discursive*. Tours: Mame, 1973.

Régent, Catherine. *Valesdir*. Nouméa: Éditions du Cagou, 1993.

———. *Justine ou un amour chapeau de paille*. Nouméa: Éditions du Belvédère, 1995.

Renard, Pierrette. "Le miroir d'Elissa ou les lectures contemporaines de Carthage." *Recherches et travaux* 54 (1998): 249–59.

Revill, George. "Reading *Rosehill*: Community, Identity and Inner-city Derby." In *Place and the Politics of Identity*, 117–40. Ed. Michael Keith and Steve Pile. London: Routledge, 1993.

Reynaert, François. « Y a-t-il une culture beur?" *Le Nouvel Observateur*, 2–8 December 1993.

Rich, Adrienne. *"Notes toward a Politics of Location."* In *Blood, Bread, and Poetry: Selected Prose, 1979–1985*, 210–31. Ed. New York: Norton, 1986.

———. *Of Woman Born*. London: Virago, 1977.

Richard, Marcel-François. Reported in *Le Moniteur Acadien*, Shediac, 28 août 1884.

Ricœur, Paul. *Temps et récit. Le temps raconté* (t.III). Paris: Seuil, 1985.

———. "Le Soi et l'identité." In *Soi-même comme un autre*, 167–98. Paris: Seuil, 1990.

———. *Oneself as another*. Trans. Kathleen Blamey. Chicago: Chicago University Press, 1992.

———. *The Conflict of Interpretations: Essays in Hermeneutics*. Ed. Don Ihde. Evanston, Ill.: Northwestern University Press, 1974.

Ripault, Ghislain. "Sleeve note" in *Gisements de lumiere*. Ed. Amina Said. Paris: La Difference, 1998.

Rivaz, Alice. *Traces de vie*. Vevey: Aire, 1998. First edition. Vevey: Galland, 1983.

Rivkin, Julie, and Michael Ryan. *Literary Theory: An Anthology*. Oxford: Blackwell, 1998.

Robbe-Grillet, Alain. *Le miroir qui revient*. Paris: Minuit, 1985.

———. *Angélique ou l'enchantement*. Paris: Minuit, 1988.

———. *Pour un nouveau roman*. Paris: Minuit, 1963.

Robertson, George, Mash Melinda, et al., ed. *Travellers' Tales: Narratives of Home and Displacement*. London, New York: Routledge, 1994.

Roche, Sylviane, and Marie-Rose De Donno. *L'Italienne*. Orbe: Campiche, 1998.

Rochefort, Henri. *L'Évadé. Roman canaque* (1880). Paris: Éditions Viviane Hamy, 1993.

Roderick, Rick. *Habermas and the Foundations of Critical Theory*. London: Macmillan, 1986.

Rosello, Mireille. "North African Women and the Ideology of Modernization: From Bidonvilles to Cités de Transit and HLM." In *Post-Colonial Cultures in France*, 240–54. Ed. Alec Hargreaves and Mark Mckinney. London: Routledge, 1997.

———. "'Beur Nation': toward a Theory of 'Départenance.'" *Research in African Literatures* 24, no. 3 (fall 1993): 13–24.

———. *Declining the Stereotype: Ethnicity and Representation in French Cultures*. Hanover, N.H.: University Press of New England Press, 1997.

———. *Littérature et identité créole aux Antilles*. Paris: Karthala, 1992.

———. *Declining the Stereotype*. Hanover and London: University Press of New England, 1998.

Rossillon, Philippe, ed. *Atlas de la langue française*. Paris: Bordas, 1995.

Rousseau, Jean-Jacques. *Essai sur l'origine des langues*. Ed. Jean Starobinski, Paris: Gallimard Folio, 1990.

Runte, Hans R. "'Projet de pays': la hantise du spatio-temporel dans l'œuvre acadienne d'Antonine Maillet." *Présence Francophone* 11 (1975): 111–18.

———. *Writing Acadia*. Amsterdam: Rodopi, 1997.

Saïd, Amina. *Métamorphose de l'île et de la vague*. Paris: Arcantère, 1985.

———. *Sables funambules*. Paris: Aracantère, 1988.

———. "Feu d'oiseaux." *Sud* 84 (1989).

———. *Demi-coq et compagnie: fables de Tunisie*. Paris: L'Harmattan, 1997.

———. *Gisements de lumiere*. Paris: La Différence, 1998.

———. *Le Secret et autres histoires*. Paris: Criterion, 1994.

———. *Marcher sur la terre*. Paris: La Différence, 1994.

———. *Paysages, nuit friable*. Paris: Barbare, 1980.

Said, Edward. "The Politics of Knowledge." in *Falling into Theory. Conflicting Views on Reading Literature*. London: Bedford Books, 1994.

———. *Orientalism*. New York: Pantheon Books, 1978.

———. *The Pen and the Sword: Conversations with David Barsamian*. Monroe, Me.: Common Courage Press, 1994.

———. *The World, the Text, and the Critic*. London: Faber, 1984.

———. *Orientalism*. New York: Vinatage Books, 1979.

———. "Yeats and Decolonization." In *Nationalism, Colonialism, and Literature*, 69–95. Minneapolis: University of Minnesota Press, 1990.

———. *Orientalism*. New York: Pantheon Books, 1978.

Saint-Gemme. "Choses de la littérature." *La Revue algérienne illustrée* 39, no. 9 (1900): 282–83.

Sala-Molins, Louis. *Le Code Noir ou le calvaire de Canaan*. Paris: Presses Universitaires de France, 1987.

Salhi, Kamal, ed. *Francophone Voices*. Exeter: Elm Bank Publications, 1999.

Salinas, Michèle. *Voyages et voyageurs en Algérie 1830–1930*. Toulouse: Privat, 1989.

Sarrazac, Jean-Pierre. *Théâtres intimes*. Arles: Actes Sud, 1989.

Sarrazin, Jean. "Entrevue avec Antonine Maillet." *Forces* 44 (1978): 28–35.

Sarvan, C. P. "French Colonialism in Africa: The Early Novels of Ferdinand Oyono." *World Literature Today* 59, no. 3 (1985): 333–37.

Savigneau, Josyane. "Linda Lê, au nom du père." *Le Monde des livres*, 7 mai 1999.

Savoie, Donald J., and Maurice Beaudin. *La Lutte pour le développement.* Sillery, Québec: Presses de l'Université de Québec, 1988.

Savoie, Jacques. *Raconte-moi Massabielle.* Moncton, N.B.: Les Éditions d'Acadie, 1979.

———. *Massabielle.* Office National du Film du Canada, 1983.

Scarry, Elaine. *The Body in Pain: The Making and Unmaking of the World.* New York: Oxford University Press, 1985.

———. *Resisting Representation.* New York: Oxford University Press, 1994.

Scharfman, Ronnie. "Fonction romanesque féminine: rencontre de la culture et de la structure dans *Les Bouts de bois de Dieu.*" *Ethiopiques* 1, nos. 3–4 (1983): 134–44.

Schipper, Mineke, ed. *Unheard Words: Women and Literature in Africa, the Arab World, Asia, the Caribbean and Latin America.* London: Allison and Busby, 1984.

Schlocker, Georges. "La parole affolée. La propension au monologue du théâtre français contemporain." *Jeu* 72 (1994): 104–8.

Schor, Naomi. *Breaking the Chain: Women, Theory and French Realist Fiction.* New York: Columbia University Press, 1985.

Scott, Joan Wallach. *Gender and the Politics of History.* New York: Columbia University Press, 1989.

Scott, Joanna C. *Indochina's Refugees: Oral Histories from Laos, Cambodia and Vietnam.* Jefferson, N.C.: McFarland & Company, 1989.

Sebbar, L., ed. *Une enfance algérienne.* Paris: gallimard, 1997.

Segarra, Marta. *Leur Pesant de poudre: romancières francophone du Maghreb.* Paris: Editions L'Harmattan, 1997.

Seghers, Pierre. *Dialogue.* Paris: Seghers, 1965.

———. *Piranese.* Neuchatel: Ides et calendes, 1960.

———. *Racines.* Paris: Intercontinentale du Livre, 1956.

Sellers, Susan. *Language and Sexual Difference: Feminist Writings in France.* London: Macmillan Education, 1991.

Sellin, Eric. "Fortune de la littérature maghrébine en Amerique du Nord." *Revue du Monde musulman et de la mediterrannée* 59, no. 60 (1991): 253–58.

Sembène, Ousmane. *Borom Sarret,* Senegal, 1963. b/w, 18 mins., French.

———. *La Noire de . . . ,* Senegal/France, 1966. b/w, 65 mins., French.

———. *Emitai,* Senegal, 1971. Color, 103 mins., French.

———. *Xala,* Senegal, 1975. Color, 119 mins., Wolof and French.

———. *Ceddo,* Senegal, 1977. Color, 120 mins., Wolof and French.

———. *Guelwaar,* France/Germany/Senegal, 1992. Color, 125 mins., Wolof and French.

———. *Le Docker noir.* Paris: Nouvelles Éditions Debresse, 1956.

———. *O Pays, mon beau peuple!* Paris: Amiot-Dumont, 1957.

———. *Les Bouts de bois de Dieu: Banty mam Yall.* Paris: Le Livre contemporain, 1960.

———. *Voltaïques.* Paris: Présence Africaine, 1962.

———. *Véhi-Ciosane ou Blanche Genèse suivi du Mandat.* Paris: Présence Africaine, 1965.

———. *Xala.* Paris: Présence Africaine, 1973.

———. *Le Dernier de l'empire: roman sénégalais.* 2 vols. Paris: L'Harmattan, 1981.

———. *Niiwam suivi de Taaw.* Paris: Présence Africaine, 1987.

———. *Guelwaar.* Paris: Présence Africaine, 1996.

Sembène, Ousmane, and Faty Sow Thierno. *Camp de Thiaroye,* Algeria/Senegal/Tunisia, 1987. Color, 150 mins., Wolof and French.

Sénès, Jacqueline. *Terre violente.* Paris: Hachette, 1987.

Serres, Michel. "Apprentissage, voyage, métissage." *Hommes et Migrations* 1161, janvier 1993.

Sezirahiga, Jadot. "*Waati,* une œuvre politique et culturelle." *Ecrans d'Afrique/Screen Africa* 11 (1st quarter 1995): 46–47.

Shah, Idries, ed. *The World of the Sufi: An Anthology of Writing about Sufis and Their work.* London: The Octagon Press, 1979.

Sharabi, Hisham. *Neopatriarchy: A Theory of Distorted Change in Arab Society.* New York: Oxford University Press, 1988.

Sharif, Muhammad al-Hadi. *Tarikh Tunis (A History of Tunisia)*. Tunis: CERES, 1985.

Shek, Ben Z. "Antonine Maillet and the Prix Goncourt." *Canadian Modern Language Review* 36 (1980): 392–96.

Shorrock, William I. *French Imperialism in the Middle East: the Failure of Policy in Syria and Lebanon.* Madison: University of Wisconsin Press, 1976.

Smart, B. *Michel Foucault*. London and New York: Tavistock Publications, 1985.

Smith Sidonie, and Julia Watson, ed. *Women, Autobiography and Theory—A Reader*. Wisconsin: University of Wisconsin Press, 1998.

Smith, Donald. "L'Acadie, pays de la ruse et du conte: Entrevue avec Antonine Maillet." *Lettres québécoises* 19 (1980): 45–53.

Smith, Michelle. "Reading in Circles: Sexuality and /as History in *I Tituba, Black Witch of Salem.*" *Callaloo* 18, no. 3 (summer 1995): 602–7.

Snitgen, Jeanne. "History, Identity, and the Constitution of the Female Subject: Maryse Condé's Tituba." *Matatu* 3, no. 6 (1989): 55–73.

Socé, Ousmane. *Karim, roman sénégalais*. Paris: Impr. M. Puyfourcat, 1935.

Socken, Paul G. "The Bible and Myth in Antonine Maillet's *Pélagie-la-Charrette.*" *Studies in Canadian Literature* 12 (1987): 187–98.

Soja, Edward, and Barbara Hooper. "The Spaces that Difference Makes." In *Place and the Politics of Identity*, 183–205. Ed. Michael Keith and Steve Pile. London: Routledge, 1993.

Soja, Edward. *Postmodern Geographies: The Reassertion of Space in Critical Social Theory*. London and New York: Verso, 1989.

Soren, Doran, et al. *Carthage*. New York: Simon and Schuster, 1990.

Sorrell, Martin. *Elles*. Exeter: University of Exeter Press, 1995.

Souriau, Christiane. *Femmes et politique autour de la Méditerranée*. Paris: L'Harmattan, 1980.

Sow Fall, Aminata. *L'Appel des arènes*. Dakar: Les Nouvelles Éditions Africaines, 1982.

———. *Douceurs du bercail*. Abidjan: Nouvelles Éditions Ivoiriennes, 1998.

Spivak, Gayatri Chakravorty. "A Response to 'The Difference Within: Feminism and Critical Theory.'" In *The Difference Within: Feminism and Critical Theory*. Ed. Elizabeth Meese and Alice Parker. Amsterdam and Philadelphia: John Benjamins Publishing Company, 1989.

Spivak, Gayatri, and Elizabeth Grosz. "Criticism, Feminism, and the Institution." In *The Post-Colonial Critic*. Ed. Sarah Harasym. New York and London: Routledge, 1990.

Spivak, Gyatri. "Can the Subaltern Speak?" In *Colonial Dicourse and Post-Colonial Theory: A Reader*, 66–111. Ed. Patrick Williams and Laura Chrisman. Hemel Hempstead: Harvester Wheatsheaf, 1993.

———. "A Literary Representation of the Subaltern: A Woman's Text From the Third World." In *Other Worlds*, 242–68. New York and London: Routledge, 1987.

———. "Subaltern Studies: Deconstructing Historiography." In *Selected Subaltern Studies*, 3–32. Ed. R. Guha and G. C. Spivak. New York and Oxford: Oxford University Press, 1988.

———. "Acting Bits/ Identity Talk." *Critical Inquiry* 18, no. 4 (summer 1992): 770–803.

———. "Echo." *New Literary History* 24, no. 1 (winter 1993): 17–43.

———. "Ghostwriting." *Diacritics* 25, no. 2 (summer 1995): 65–84.

———. "Teaching for the Times." In *Dangerous Liaisons. Gender, Nation, and Postcolonial Perspectives*, 468–90. Ed. Anne McClintock Aamir Mufti and Ella Shohat. London and Minneapolis: University of Minnesota Press, 1997.

Spurr, David. *The Rhetoric of Empire: Colonial Discourse in Journalism, Travel Writing and Imperial Administration*. 3rd. ed. Durham and London: Duke University Press, 1996.

Sraieb, Noureddine. *Le Collège Sadiki de Tunis (1875–1956): enseignement et nationalisme*. Paris: Éditions de la méditerranée, 1995.

Steinberg, Jonathan. *Why Switzerland?* 2nd ed. Cambridge University Press, 1996.

Stephan, Wafa. "Women and War in Lebanon." *Al-Raïda* 30 (1984).

———. *La nouvelle légende de D'Chimbo* suivi de *Massak*. Cayenne: Ibis Rouge Éditions, 1996.

Stephenson, Elie. *Une flèche pour le pays à l'encan*. Paris: Éditions J. P Oswald, 1975.

———. *Catacombes de Soleil.* Paris: Éditions Caribéennes, 1979.

———. *Terres mêlées.* Paris: Akpagnon, 1984.

———. *Comme des.gouttes de sang.* Paris: Présence Africaine,1988.

———. *O Mayouri* (Bilingual edition co-edited with Marguerite Fauquenoy). Paris: L'Harmattan, 1988.

Still, Judith, and Martin Worton. *Textuality and Sexuality.* Manchester: Manchester University Press, 1993.

Stora, Benjamin. "France and the Algerian War: Memory Regained?" *Journal of Maghrebi Studies* 1, no. 2 (fall 1993): 95–102.

———. *La gangrène et l'oubli. La mémoire de la guerre d'Algérie.* Paris: La Découverte, 1991.

Stringer, Susan. *The Senegalese Novel by Women.* New York: Peter Lang Publishing, 1996.

———. "Innovation in Ken Bugul's *Le Baobab fou.*" *Cincinnati Romance Review* 10 (1991).

———. "Cultural Conflict in the Novels of Two African Writers, Mariama Bâ and Aminata Sow Fall." *Sage: A Scholarly Journal on Black Women, Student Supplement 1988.*

Sturrock, John. *The Language of Autobiography.* Cambridge: Cambridge University Press, 1993.

Suleiman, S. *Subversive Intent: gender, politics and the avant garde.* Cambridge, Mass.: Harvard University Press, 1990.

Suleiman, Susan Rubin. *Authoritarian Fictions: The Ideological Novel as a Literary Genre.* New York: Columbia University Press, 1983.

Swamy, Vinay. "Should Paradise be Private? Cultural and Fictive Constructs of National Identity in Two Novels by Azouz Begag." In *Die Kinder der Immigration.* Ed. Ernstpeter Ruhe. Volume 4 of series "Studien zur Literatur und Geschichte des Maghreb." Würzburg: Königshausen & Neumann, 1999.

Swensen, Alice L. "Voice in Search of Itself: Evelyne Accad's *L'Excisée.*" *Journal of Modern Literature* 20, no.1 (summer 1996): 115–20.

Swiggers, Pierre. "L'insécurité linguistique: du complexe (problématique) à la complexité du problème." In *L'insécurité linguistique dans les communautés francophones périphériques,* 19–29. Ed. Michel Francard. Louvain-la-Neuve: Cahiers de L'Institut de Linguistique de Louvain, 1993.

Swindells, Julia. Introduction to *The Uses of Autobiography.* London: Taylor and Francis, 1995.

Tabone, Eliane. "Tunisie." In *Les litteratures francophones depuis 1945,* 219–37. Ed. J. L. Joubert, J. Lecarme, E. Tabone, B. Vercier. Paris: Bordas, 1986.

Tai, Hue-Tam Ho. *Radicalism and the Origins of the Vietnamese Revolution.* Cambridge, Mass. and London, England: Harvard University press, 1992.

Tap, Pierre. *La Socialisation de l'enfance à l'adolescence.* Paris: Presses Universitaires de France, 1991.

———. *La Société Pygmalion, Intégration sociale et réalisation de la personne.* Paris: Dunod, 1988.

———. *Marginalités et troubles de la socialisation.* Paris: Presses Universitaires de France, 1993.

Taylor, Charles. *Sources of the Self.* Cambridge: Cambridge University Press, 1989.

Telkamp, Ross, et al., eds. *Colonial Cities: Essays on Urbanism in a Colonial Context.* Dordrecht: Martinus Nyhoof Publishers, 1985.

Tenkoul, A. *Écritures maghrebines: lectures croisees.* Casablanca: Afrique Orient, 1991.

Thériault, Joseph Yvon. *L'Identité à l'épreuve de la modernité.* Moncton: Éditions d'Acadie, 1995.

Thibault, André, and Pierre Knecht. *Dictionnaire suisse romand.* Genève: Zoé, 1997.

Thibault, Bruno. "*Le Livre des fuites* de J. M. G. Le Clézio et le problème du roman exotique moderne." *The French Review* 65, no. 3 (1992): 425–33.

Thomas, Nicholas. *Colonialism's Culture: Anthropology, Travel and Government.* Cambridge: Polity Press, 1994.

Thompson, William. "Voyage and Immobility in J.M.G. Le Clézio's *Désert and La quarantaine.*" *World Literature Today* 71, no. 4 (1997): 709–16.

Thurler, Anne-Lise. *Le crocodile ne dévore pas le pangolin.* Genève: Zoé, 1996.

Tiffin, Helen. "Post-colonial Literatures and Counter-discourse." In *The Post-Colonial Studies Reader.* Ed. Ashcroft Griffiths Tiffin. London: Routledge, 1995.

Tillion, Germaine. *Le harem et les cousins.* Paris: Editions du Seuil, 1966.

Tine, Alioune. "La Diglossie linguistique et la disglossie littéraire et leurs effets dans la pratique esthétique d'Ousmane Sembène." In *Littérature et cinéma en Afrique francophone*, 82–109. Ed. Sada Niang. Paris: L'Harmattan, 1996.

Tjibaou, Jean-Marie. *La Présence Kanak* (édition établie et présentée par Alban Bensa et Eric Wittersheim). Paris: Éditions Odile Jacob, 1996.

Tlili, Mustapha. *La rage au tripes*. Paris: Gallimard, 1975.

———. *Le bruit dort*. Paris: Gallimard, 1978.

———. *Gloire des sables*. Paris: Pauvet, 1982.

Tobing Rony, Fatima. *The Third Eye: Race, Cinema and Ethnographic Spectacle*. Durham and London: Duke University Press, 1996.

Todd, Emmanuel. *Le destin des immigrés. Assimilation et ségrégation dans les démocraties occidentales*. Paris: Seuil, 1994.

Todorov, Tzvetan. *Nous et les autres; la réflexion française sur la diversité humaine*. Paris: Éditions du Seuil, 1989.

———. *Théories du symbole*. Paris: Seuil, 1977.

———. "La Synecdoque." In *Sémantique de la poésie*, 7–26. Paris: Éditions du Seuil, 1979.

Toumson, Roger. *Mythologie du métissage*. Paris: Presses Universitaires de France, 1998.

Tremblay, Michel. *Messe solennelle pour une pleine lune d'été*. Montréal: Leméac Éditeur, 1996.

———. *Albertine, en cinq temps*. Montréal: Leméac Éditeur, 1984.

———. *Le vrai monde?* Montréal: Leméac Éditeur, 1987.

Tucker, Judith E., ed. *Arab Women: Old Boundaries, New Frontiers*. Bloomington: Indiana University Press, 1993.

Turin, Yvonne. *Affrontements culturels dans l'Algérie coloniale; écoles, médecines, religion, 1830–1880*. Paris: Maspero, 1971.

Usmiani, Renate. "Recycling an Archetype: the Anti-Evangelines." *Canadian Theatre Review* 46 (1986): 65–71.

Van Renterghem, Marian. "Le sabbat de Lady Lê." *Le Monde des livres*, 31 Octobre 1997.

———. *Belgique, côté francophone*. Supplément à Le Monde du 15 septembre 1998.

Vast, and Malterre's. *Atlas historique. Formation des états européens*. Paris: 1900.

Vergil. *Aeneid*. New York: Dover, 1995.

Vernex, Jean-Claude. *Les Acadiens*. Paris: Entente, 1979.

Vidal de la Blache, Paul. *Tableau Géographique de la France*. Paris: La Table Ronde, 1994.

Vietnam, Ashcroft B., G. Griffiths, and H. Tiffin. *The Postcolonial Reader*. London: Routledge, 1998.

Vuilleumier, Marc. *Immigrés et réfugiés en Suisse*. Zurich: Pro Helvetia, 1989.

Walcott, Derek. "The Muse of History." In *Is Massa Day Dead? Black Moods in the Caribbean*, 1–27. Ed. Orde Coombs. New York: Anchor Books, 1974.

Walter, Henriette. *Le français dans tous les sens*. Paris: Robert Laffont, 1988.

Walzer, Pierre-Olivier. *Dictionnaire des littératures de Suisse romande*. Lausanne: Aire, 1991.

Warner, Michael. "New English Sodom." *American Literature* 64, no. 1 (1992): 19–47.

Waterson, Karolyn. "L'envergure des revendications de *La Sagouine*." *Présence Francophone* 13 (1976): 121–28.

———. "The Mythical Dimension of *Pélagie-la-Charrette*." *Francophone Literatures of the New World* 2 (1982): 43–69.

Weber, Max. *The Theory of Social and Economic Organization*. New York: The Free Press, 1964.

Wélépane, Wanir. *Aux vents des îles*. Nouméa: ADCK, 1993.

Wieviorka, Michel. *La Démocratie à l'épreuve: Nationalisme, populisme, ethnicité*. Paris: La Découverte, 1993.

Wilcox, Helen, et al., eds. *The Body and the Text: Hélène Cixous, Reading and Teaching*. New York and London: Harvester and Wheatsheaf, 1990.

Windisch, Uli, with Jean-Marc Jaeggi, and Gérard de Rham. *Xénophobie? Logique de la pensée populaire*. Lausanne: L'Âge d'Homme, 1978.

Woodhill, W. "Rereading *Nedjma*: Feminist Scholarship and North African Women." *SubStance* 69 (1992).

Wyczynski, Paul, et al., eds. *Le Théâtre canadien-français*. Montréal: Fides, 1976.

Yacono, Xavier. *Histoire de la colonisation francaise*. Paris. Presses Universitaires de France, 1988.

———. *Les Etapes de la decolonisation francaise*. Paris. Presses Universitaires de France, 1991.

Yasmina. "Flocons de neige." *La Revue algérienne illustrée* 41, no. 9 (1901): 274–76.

———. "Pauvre Mingôh (souvenir d'enfance)." *La Revue algérienne illustrée* 36, no. 4 (1898): 107–11.

Yeager, Jack. "Culture, citizenship, nation: the narrative texts of Linda Lê." In *Post-Colonial Cultures in France*, 255–67. Ed. Alec G. Hargreaves and Mark McKinney. London: Routledge, 1997.

———. "Kim Lefèvre's *Retour à la saison des pluies*: Rediscovering the Landscapes of Childhood." *L'Esprit créateur* 33 (1992): 45–57.

———. "La politique "intimiste": la production romanesque des écrivains vietnamiennes d'expression française." *Présence Francophone* 43 (1993): 131–47.

———. *The Vietnamese Novel in French: A Literary Response to Colonialism*. Hanover and London: University Press of New England, 1987.

Yetiv, Isaac. "Le rire, arme de combat contre le colonialisme dans les romans de Ferdinand Oyono." *Griot* 4, nos. 1–2 (1985): 8–17.

Young, Robert J. C. *Colonial Desire: Hybridity in Theory, Culture and Race*. London and New York: Routledge, 1995.

Zahn, Elizabeth. *Literature and Cruelty*. New York: Columbia University Press, 1996.

Zakka, Najib, ed. *Littératures et cultures d'exil: terre perdue, langue sauvée*. Lille III: Université Charles-de-Gaulle, 1993.

Zimra, Clarisse. "'When the Past Answers Our Present': Assia Djebar Talks about *Loin de Médine*." *Callaloo* 16, no. 1 (1993): 116–31.

———. "Sounding Off the Absent Body: Intertextual Resonances in 'La femme qui pleure' and 'La femme en morceaux.'" *Research in African Literature* 30, no. 3 (1999): 108–24.

Index

About the Contributors

Jacques Allard is professor of literature in the *Département d'études littéraires* of the University of Quebec, Montreal. He taught at the Universities of Montreal, Toronto, Kingston, Vancouver (UBC), Paris VIII, Bordeaux III, Bologne and Porto Alegre. He has published three hundred articles on the *roman québécois*. He is also literary director at Québec Amérique. In addition to his book, T*raversée de la critique littéraire au Québec* (Boréal, 1991), a selection of hundred chronicles from his writings between 1992 and 1996 on the *livre Québécois* in the daily *Le Devoir* appeared as *Roman mauve: microlectures de la fiction récente au Québec* (Éditions Québec Amérique, 1997). His has recently authored *Le Roman du Québec* (Québec Amérique, 2000) and edited *Récits de la fête* (Québec Amérique, 2000).

Philippe Barbé is assistant professor in the Department of French and Italian at the University of California, Irvine. He has expertise in the field of postmodern writers, and his current research interests focus on the question of space and time in twentieth-century French literature.

Peter Brown is senior lecturer in French at the Australian National University, Canberra. His research interests are in French literature and *la francophonie*, particularly concerning the Pacific. For the past decade he has been the Australian correspondent for *L'Année Francophone Internationale* and is currently a member of the *Asia-Pacific Observatoire du Français*, a project of the *Agence Universitaire de la Francophonie*.

Micheline Cambron is professor and director of the Center for Quebec Studies (CETUQ) at the University of Montreal. As a specialist in nineteenth- and twentieth-century Quebec literature, she has published several articles and chapters, authored a book, *Une société, un récit, Discours culturel au Québec 1967–1976* (l'Hexagone: 1989) and edited *Le Journal Le Canadien. Littérature, espace public et utopie* (Fides: 1999), and *Les Soirées du Château de Ramezay de l'école littéraire de Montréal* (Fides: 1999).

Jonathan Carr-West teaches French literature and literary theory in the Department of French at the University College London. He is developing expertise in post-colonial literature and theory and the representation of cultural identity in Francophone African fiction.

Joy Charnley is lecturer in the Department of Modern Languages and in charge of the Centre for Swiss Cultural Studies at the University of Strathclyde. Her specialty is in women writers in Suisse Romande, Pierre Bayle and seventeenth/eighteenth-century travel writing. She the author of *25 Years Emancipation: Women in Switzerland 1971–1996* (Lang, 1996) and *Pierre Bayle, Reader of Travel Literature* (Lang, 1998).

Suzanne Costa is professor in the Department of French at McMaster University.

Pascale De Souza is professor and head of the French programme at the Graduate School of Advanced International Studies of the Johns Hopkins University. She has an extensive record of publications in epistolary novels, gendering of historical and environmental issues in French Caribbean literature. She has recently focused on comparative Caribbean literature.

Jean-Luc Desalvo is associate professor of French at the State University of San Jose. His areas of interest are nineteenth/twentieth-century French literature and culture. He has developed expertise in Francophone (African, Caribbean, Canadian and Vietnamese) literature and culture. His publications include "La vision globaliste d'Antonine Maillet" (in *Women in French Studies* 6, 1998), "Antonine Maillet: Iconoclaste et briseuse de statue" (in *Études francophones* 15.1, 2000) and "Le 'je(u)' acadien dans l'œuvre d'Antonine Maillet" (in *Cincinnati Romance Review* 19, 2000). He is the author of *Le topos du mundus inversus dans l'œuvre d'Antonine Maillet* (International Scholars Publications, 1999).

Peter Hawkins is senior lecturer in the Department of French at the University of Bristol, where he teaches courses on Francophone Literature. He is currently vice-president of the Association for the Study of Caribbean and African Literature in French. His research work focuses on the literatures and cultures of the francophone Indian Ocean, on which he has published widely.

Leonard R. Koos is an associate professor of French and Cinema Studies at Mary Washington College. He has published extensively on nineteenth- and twentieth-century French literature and culture and, most recently, is the co-editor of the volume *Dead Ringers: The Remake in Theory and Practice* (State University of New York Press, 2002). He is currently writing a book on French colonial culture in North Africa.

Emmanuelle Labeau teaches in the School of Languages and European Studies at Aston University. She worked extensively on French linguistics, theoretical description and language acquisition with a focus on French in Belgium. Her publications include "Le français de Belgique filerait-il à l'anglaise?" (in *Current Issues in Language and Society* 6.3/4, 1999). She is the editor of *France-Belgique: des frères ennemis de la langue de chez nous* (University of Laval, 2000).

Rachael Langford is lecturer in French in the School of European Studies at the University of Wales Cardiff. Her discipline is French Studies with specialties in the literature and culture of early Third Republic France, the culture and history of French colonialism and contemporary Francophone African literature and film. She is particularly interested in the relationship between discourses of time, space, and the self as mediated through French colonial ideology and the reconfiguration of these areas in post-independence Francophone African literature and film. Her publications include *Jules Vallès and the Narration of History: Contesting the French Third Republic in the Jacques Vingtras Trilogy* (Peter Lang, Bern, 1999), "Writing and Resistance:

Jules Valles and the Language of Education" (in Michael Grenfell and Michael Kelly, eds., *Pierre Bourdieu: Language, Culture and Education. Theory into Practice,* Peter Lang: 1999), and "Black and White in Black and White: Identity and Cinematography in Ousmane Sembene's *La Noire de.../Black Girl.* (in *Studies in French Cinema* 1:1, 2001). Rachel Langford is the co-editor of *Marginal Voices, Marginal Forms: Diaries in European Literature and History* (Rodopi: 1999).

Marie-Christine Lesage is *Professeure adjointe* in the Department of French Studies at the University of Montreal. Her research interests are theatre studies, contemporary theatre, arts and poetics. Her publications include "La dynamique de la mémoire: fragmentation et pensée analogique" (in *Le bref et l'instantané. À la rencontre de la littérature québécoise du XXIe siècle,* Éditions David, 2000), "Le théâtre et les autres arts" (in *Archives des lettres canadiennes,* Tome X, Fides, 2001), "Installations scéniques. Le cas du Théâtre UBU et du collectif Recto Verso" (in *L'Annuaire théâtral* 26, 1999), "Du particulier à l'universel: réception critique de Joie, de Pol Pelletier, au Théâtre du Soleil, à Paris," *L'Annuaire théâtral* 27, 2000) and "De l'emprunt à l'empreinte: le plagiat dans *Le passage de l'Indiana*" (in *Voix et Images* 75, 2000).

Dominique Licops is a doctoral researcher in the Department of French and Italian at the Northwestern University, developing expertise in Francophone, post-colonial and gender studies. Her publications include "Expériences diasporiques et migratoires des villes dans *La vie scélérate et Desirada* de Maryse Condé" (*Nottingham French Studies,* 39:1, 2000) and "Origination and Narration: identity as épanouissement in Gisèle Pineau's *Exil selon Julia*" (*MaComère,* 2, 1999).

Margaret Majumdar is professor of French and Francophone Studies and head of Postgraduate Programmes, Humanities and Social Sciences at the University of Glamorgan. As a specialist in French political philosophy, Francophone studies, particularly Franco-Maghrebian issues, she has published widely. She is the author of *Althusser and the End of Leninism?* (Pluto Press: 1995) and the editor of *The Francophone Studies: The Essential Glossary* (Edward Arnold, 2002).

Florence Martin is Associate Professor of French at Goucher College, Baltimore. Her specialist areas are Francophone literature and cinema, French cinema and the literature and culture of the African diaspora. Her publications include "Enchantements ex-centriques: les 'voix' des romancières francophones d'Afrique de l'Ouest" (in *Études Francophones* XIII. 1, 1998), "Echos et grains de voix dans Le Jujubier du patriarche d'Aminata Sow Fall" (in *French Review* 74.2, 2000), "Going Down South: le detour des Africaines-Américaines" (in *Cahiers de Recherches de CORHUM* 8, 1994). She is the author of *Bessie Smith* (Limon: 1994; Parentheses: 1996).

Robert Alvin Miller lectures in the Department of French, Hispanic and Italian Studies at the University of British Columbia. His areas of specialism are twentieth-century French literature, hermeneutics and literary theory, African and Caribbean literatures. His publications include *Hermès et Aminadab: essai d'herméneutique littéraire* (Paratexte, 1999) and "Schleiermacher et l'interprétation du discours romanesque" (*Revue de littérature comparée* 3,1995). He is the co-editor of *Theoretical Perspectives on African and Caribbean Literatures* (University of Toronto: 1987)

Michael F. O'Riley is professor at the Colorado College. He is a specialist in post-colonial, cultural and ethnic studies. His has published widely on Assia Djebar, Sylvie Germain, Tahar Ben Jelloun and Patrick Modiano in *The French Review, Dalhousie French Studies, Purdue Romance Languages Annual* and *Romance Notes.* He is the co-editor of the anthology, *The*

Fractured Mirror: Representations of the Occupation in Post-World War II France (Harvard University Press: 2001).

Mohamed-Salah Omri is lecturer in the Institute of Arab and Islamic Studies at the University of Exeter. He areas of interest are the literature and culture of North Africa, pre-modern Arabic prose, comparative literature and literary theory. His Francophone publications include "Memory and representation in the novels of Fawzi Mellah" (in *International Journal of Francophone Studies* 3.1, 2000), " 'Gulf laughter break': cartoons in Tunisia during the Gulf Conflict" (in *Political Cartoons in the Middle East,* Princeton, 1998) and " 'There is a Jahiz for every age': narrative construction and intertextuality in al-Hamadhani's Maqamat" (in *Arabic and Middle Eastern Literatures* 1, 1998)

Gloria Nne Onyeoziri is associate professor in the Department of French, Hispanic and Italian Studies at the University of British Columbia. She is a specialist in African and Caribbean literatures, semantics and African women writers. Her publications include *La Parole poétique d'Aimé Césaire: Essai de sémantique littéraire* (L'Harmattan; 1992), "Le Toussaint d'Aimé Césaire: Réflexions sur le statut d'un texte" (*L'Esprit créateur* 32.1, 1992) and "Moi, laminaire . . . d'Aimé Césaire: de la réception à l'interprétation" (*Oeuvres et critiques* 20.2, 1995). She is the co-editor of *Theoretical Perspectives on African and Caribbean Literatures,* (University of Toronto: 1987).

Eric Luis Prieto is Assistant Professor of French in the Department of French and Italian at the University of California, Santa Barbara. His research interests are in the areas of twentieth-century French and Francophone literature, Caribbean literature, narrative theory, aesthetics, music and literature. His publications include "La musique et la mimesis du moi" (in *Poétique* 104, 1995), "Recherches pour un roman musical," (*Poétique* 94,1993), "The Poetics of Place, the Rhetoric of Authenticity, and Aimé Césaire's *Cahier d'un retour au pays natal*" (in *Dalhousie French Studies,* 2001).

Emily Vaughan Roberts is a research associate at the University of the West of England. She works on Vietnamese Francophone literature, and researches into the French colonialist and post-colonialist literature that emanated from the colonial encounter. Her publications include "Close Encounters: French women of Vietnamese origin and the homeland in Kim Lefèvre's *Retour à la saison des pluies* and Linda Lê's *Les Trois Parques*" (in *Women, Immigration and Identities in France,* Berg, 2000). She is the co-editor of *Group Identities on French and British Television* (Berghahn, 2001).

Kamal Salhi is director of the Centre for Francophone Studies in the Department of French at the University of Leeds and member of the Advisory Committee of the Leeds Centre for African Studies. His area of specialty is Francophone studies with particular interest in the colonial and post-colonial cultural production and language/cultural policy of North and Sub-Saharan Africa. He is the author of *The Politics and Aesthetics of Kateb Yacine: from Francophone literature to popular theatre* (Mellen,1999) and the editor of *African Theatre for Development: An art for self-determination* (Intellect, 1998), *Francophone Voices* (Elm Bank, 1999), *Francophone Studies; discourse and identity* (Elm Bank, 2000) and *French in and out of France: Language Policies, Intercultural Antagonisms and Dialogue* (Peter Lang, 2002). He is the founder and editor of the *International Journal of Francophone Studies.*

Tony Simons is lecturer in the Department of French Studies at the University of Reading and specializes in Francophone literaure and cinema. His publications include "The Problem of Narrative Dialogue: Translation and reception of *Le Journal d'une femme de chambre*" (in *Rodopi Perspectives on Modern Literature*, 1996), "The fin de siècle: reception and understanding of *Cyrano de Bergerac* and *Ubu roi*" (in *New Perspectives on the Fin de Siècle in Nineteenth- and Twentieth-Century France*, Edwin Mellen Press, 2000) and "Le Jeu des espaces dans *Jésus de Montréal* de Denys Arcand" (*Globe* 2.2, 1999).

Susan Stuart is Lecturer in French and Head of Languages Division at the University of Paisley. She research focus is on migrant autobiography and cross-cultural issues in language teaching.

Kristin Swenson Musselman is teaching assistant of French language and literature in the Department of French and Italian at Northwestern University. Her main research interests are francophone post-colonial fiction and autobiography.

Chantal P. Thompson is a teaching professor of French at Brigham Young University, where she has received numerous teaching awards. She is the author of three major textbooks: *Ensuite, Cours intermédiaire de français* (McGraw-Hill, 1989, 1993, 1998); *Moments littéraires: Anthologie pour Cours intermédiaires* (D. C. Heath, 1992) and *Mais oui!* (First-year French text, Houghton-Mifflin, 1996, 2000). As a consultant for the American Council on the Teaching of Foreign Languages (ACTFL), she conducts workshops on the teaching and assessment of foreign language proficiency, and has been a keynote speaker at national and international conferences. In 1995, she received a grant from the French government to study African literature in Dakar, Senegal, and in 2000, pioneered a Study Abroad program in Senegal, in collaboration with Senegalese writer Aminata Sow Fall. Chantal Thompson currently directs the African Studies Program at Brigham Young University.

Holly Woodson Waddell is Associate Professor at Northwestern University. She is developing expertise in French literature and is assistant editor of the journal *Eighteenth Century Studies*.

Mary-Angela Willis is Lecturer in the Department of Modern and Classical Languages and Literatures at the University of Rhode Island. She is developing expertise in the Francophone literature of the Middle East and North Africa, the literature in exile / immigrant literature and Gender Studies.